# Tolley Corporation Tax Self-Assessment 2000–01

by

Janek Matthews MA(Cantab), FCA,
Barrister of Pump Court Tax Chambers

Nigel Eastaway
of WJB Chiltern

with

Richard Vallat BA (Oxon) Barrister

Tolley Publishing

Published by Tolley
2, Addiscombe Road
Croydon CR9 5AF England
020 8686 9141

Typeset by
YHT Ltd, Ealing, London

Printed by
Hobbs the Printers Ltd, Totton, Hampshire

© Reed Elsevier (UK) Ltd 2000
ISBN 0 75451 026 3

# Preface

The Inland Revenue, with the introduction of corporation tax self-assessment, took the sensible decision to keep the changes from the previous pay and file regime to the minimum. This is both helpful to practitioners dealing with the completion of returns and the production of accounts and computations, but is also a potential danger in that the apparent familiarity may disguise the fundamental change of responsibility which arises from self-assessment.

No longer is it necessary merely to disclose how transactions have been dealt with in the accounts and computations, knowing that there might be an argument with the Revenue if the treatment adopted is challenged. Under self-assessment it is necessary to take a view on matters such as transfer pricing and the application of controlled foreign company rules instead of waiting for a Revenue direction, in the knowledge that a failure to show that such matters had been carefully considered, supported by the appropriate documentation, could give rise not only to tax and interest but also penalties.

Companies outside the small company rules are required to make in-year payments on account, based on reasoned projections made in accordance with the best available information, with penalties for negligent failure. Unlike income tax self-assessment there are no provisions for calculating payments on account by reference to the preceding years' results, nor are there provisions for electronic lodgement of returns or for requiring the Revenue to calculate the tax payable.

While some of the new legislation has been drafted using the tax law rewrite 'new speak' principles, much of the secondary legislation, in particular that relating to shadow ACT, is bordering on the incomprehensible. It is hoped however that tax managers and their advisers will find this work useful and we would like to thank the Revenue team on the Corporation Tax Self-Assessment sub-committee, for helping us unscramble some of the more obscure points and listening to many of the representations made to them. We are fully convinced that genuine consultation improves both the comprehensibility and the workability of complex tax legislation.

We would like to thank our colleagues in Pump Court Tax Chambers and WJB Chiltern for their help and advice, and in particular to our secretaries Elaine Bauchop and Elizabeth Lisle for typing and amending our manuscript and to those who toiled through the drafts and proofs to try and ensure both the accuracy and comprehensibility of the text.

*Preface*

The Crown Copyright material is reproduced by permission of the Controller of Her Majesty's Stationery Office.

The law and practice is stated as at 1 August 2000.

Jan Matthews, Nigel Eastaway and Richard Vallat

Pump Court Tax Chambers  
16 Bedford Row  
LONDON  
WC1R 4EB

WJB Chiltern  
Sceptre House  
169–173 Regent Street  
LONDON  
W1R 7FB

# Contents

|  | *Page* |
|---|---|
| *Table of cases* | xvii |
| *Table of statutes* | xxxiii |
|  | Section |

## 1. Introduction

| | |
|---|---|
| Background and timing | 1.1 |
| Comparison with pay and file | 1.3 |
| Tax return and self-assessment | 1.5 |
| Revenue determinations and assessments | 1.7 |
| Payment of corporation tax | 1.8 |
| Record keeping | 1.9 |
| Schedule A income | 1.10 |
| Revenue powers of enquiry and discovery | 1.11 |
| Controlled foreign companies | 1.13 |
| Transfer pricing | 1.14 |
| Appeals | 1.15 |
| References | 1.16 |

## 2. Notices and Returns

| | |
|---|---|
| Legislative background | 2.1 |
| Notification of chargeability | 2.3 |
| Notice to deliver a return and period covered | 2.5 |
| Filing date | 2.7 |
| Form of return | 2.9 |
| CT600 | 2.12 |
|    Supplementary pages | 2.24 |
|    Calculation of tax payable | 2.33 |
|    Accounts, other documents and information | 2.34 |
|    Estimates | 2.40 |
|    Valuations | 2.42 |
|    Rulings and clearances | 2.46 |
|    Companies in liquidation | 2.53 |

## 3 Assessments and Determinations

| | |
|---|---|
| Introduction | 3.1 |
| Self-assessment | 3.2 |
| Loans to participators and controlled foreign companies | 3.5 |
| Losses and other negative amounts | 3.7 |
| Amendments and corrections | 3.8 |
| Revenue determination where no return filed | 3.12 |
| Revenue determination superseded by actual self-assessment | 3.16 |
| Amendments to assessments pursuant to Revenue enquiry | 3.17 |
| Discovery assessment or determination | 3.18 |
| Time limits for Revenue assessment or determination | 3.19 |

## Contents

|  |  |
|---|---|
| Assessment to recover overpayment of tax | 3.20 |
| Excessive assessments or repayments | 3.22 |
|    Relief for double assessments | 3.22 |
|    Relief in case of mistake in return | 3.23 |
|    Recovery of excessive repayments | 3.25 |

### 4. Claims, Elections and Revisions

|  |  |
|---|---|
| Background | 4.1 |
| General position | 4.4 |
|    Outline of provisions: claims usually to be part of return | 4.4 |
|    Giving effect to claims | 4.7 |
|    Claims or elections affecting single accounting period | 4.9 |
|    Claims or elections involving more than one accounting period | 4.10 |
|    Estimates | 4.11 |
| Claims and elections not in tax return | 4.12 |
|    Outline procedure | 4.12 |
|    Record keeping | 4.15 |
|    Amendments to claims/corrections | 4.16 |
|    Revenue powers of enquiry | 4.18 |
| Group relief claims | 4.20 |
|    General | 4.20 |
|    Claims for more or less than amount available for surrender | 4.23 |
|    Notice of consent | 4.25 |
|    Time limits | 4.27 |
|    Reduction in the amount available for surrender | 4.28 |
|    Assessments to recover excessive group relief | 4.29 |
|    Regulations for special arrangements | 4.30 |
| Capital allowances claims | 4.32 |
| Relief for double assessments, errors or mistakes | 4.34 |
| Consequential amendments in cases where Revenue previously had a discretion | 4.36 |
| Consequential claims following Revenue enquiry, etc. | 4.40 |
| Crown option | 4.44 |

### 5. Payment/Repayment

|  |  |
|---|---|
| Introduction | 5.1 |
| Small and medium companies | 5.3 |
|    Date for payment | 5.3 |
|    Repayment before establishment of tax liability | 5.5 |
| Large companies | 5.8 |
|    How to determine whether a company is a large company | 5.8 |
|    Companies becoming large | 5.12 |
|    Companies with associated companies becoming large | 5.13 |
|    Due dates for instalments | 5.14 |
|    Calculation of amount of each instalment | 5.16 |

|   |   |
|---|---|
| The transitional period | 5.20 |
| Revision of estimates – claims for repayment | 5.22 |
| Intra-group surrender of excessive instalment payments | 5.26 |
| Group payment arrangements | 5.27 |
|     Outline | 5.27 |
|     Eligibility | 5.29 |
|     Entering into the arrangement | 5.31 |
|     Removal of companies from an arrangement and termination | 5.32 |
|     The undertaking in the arrangement | 5.34 |
| Practical issues regarding instalment payments | 5.37 |
| Estimates and quarterly instalment payments | 5.40 |
| The Board's information powers | 5.41 |
| Anti-avoidance | 5.42 |
| Insurance companies and friendly societies | 5.46 |
| Double assessment | 5.47 |
| Mistake | 5.48 |
| Excessive repayments | 5.50 |
|     Time limits | 5.52 |
| Payment methods – effective date of payment | 5.53 |
|     Payment by cheque | 5.53 |
|     Payment by electronic funds transfer | 5.54 |
|     Payment by Bank Giro | 5.55 |
|     Payment by Girobank | 5.56 |
| Special cases |  |
|     Sub-contractors in the construction industry | 5.57 |
|     Personal service companies | 5.59 |
|     Worker treated as receiving Schedule E income | 5.62 |
|     Calculation of deemed Schedule E payments | 5.63 |
|     Treatment of payments made under construction industry scheme | 5.64 |
|     Application of PAYE | 5.65 |
|     Company taxation consequences | 5.66 |

## 6. Advance Corporation Tax

|   |   |
|---|---|
| Introduction | 6.1 |
| Distributions | 6.5 |
|     Non-distributions | 6.12 |
| Rate of ACT | 6.13 |
| Non-payable tax credits | 6.15 |
| Payable tax credits | 6.17 |
| ACT returns and FII | 6.22 |
| Set off of ACT against corporation tax | 6.25 |
| Carry back of surplus ACT | 6.27 |
| Surrender of ACT | 6.29 |
| New procedure of ACT surrender claims under *TA 1988 13A Sch* | 6.33 |
|     General | 6.34 |
|     Withdrawal of claims and amendments | 6.36 |

## Contents

|   |   |
|---|---|
| Claims made after set off of ACT against mainstream corporation tax – further self-assessments by the surrendering company | 6.38 |
| Excess relief on surrender – further self-assessments by subsidiary | 6.40 |
| Miscellaneous | 6.41 |
| Foreign income dividends | 6.43 |
| Change of ownership | 6.47 |
| Legislative changes | 6.49 |
| Shadow ACT | 6.52 |
|    Anti-avoidance regulations | 6.57 |
|    Computation of shadow ACT | 6.60 |
|    Utilisation of shadow ACT | 6.64 |
|    Intra-group allocation of surplus shadow ACT | 6.66 |
|    Set off of unrelieved surplus ACT against liability to corporation tax | 6.68 |
|    Restrictions on set off | 6.69 |
|    Change of ownership | 6.70 |
|    Miscellaneous provisions | 6.71 |

### 7. Computation of Profits

|   |   |
|---|---|
| Introduction | 7.1 |
| Trading profits Schedule D Case 1 | 7.7 |
|    Generally accepted accounting principles | 7.7 |
|    Expenses not allowed | 7.15 |
|    Expenses allowed | 7.25 |
|    Capital allowances | 7.33 |
| Investment companies | 7.66 |
| Income from land in the UK: Schedule A | 7.69 |
|    Introduction | 7.69 |
|    Scope of charge and single business | 7.72 |
|    Non-resident companies | 7.73 |
|    Recipients charged | 7.74 |
|    Lease premiums, assignments, sales with right to reconveyance | 7.76 |
|    Exclusions from Schedule A charge | 7.79 |
|    Schedule A business | 7.80 |
|    Computation of profit | 7.81 |
|    Interest | 7.88 |
|    Capital expenditure and allowances | 7.91 |
|    Furnished lettings – wear and tear allowances | 7.95 |
|    Transitional provisions | 7.96 |
|    Property investment companies | 7.98 |
|    Property development companies | 7.101 |
|    Partnerships | 7.103 |
|    Joint ownership | 7.104 |
|    Land managed as one estate | 7.105 |
|    Maintenance funds for historic buildings | 7.108 |
|    Chargeable gains and reliefs | 7.110 |

# Contents

## 8. Capital Gains
| | |
|---|---:|
| Introduction | 8.1 |
| Former discretionary powers of Revenue | 8.2 |
| Payment of tax by instalments | 8.5 |
| Business assets roll-over relief | 8.6 |
| Roll-over relief on compulsory acquisition of land | 8.13 |
| Allowable losses | 8.15 |
| Premiums for leases | 8.18 |
| Scheme of reconstruction: transfer to investment trust | 8.20 |
| Valuations for Capital Gains | 8.21 |

## 9. Losses
| | |
|---|---:|
| General | 9.1 |
| Company reconstructions | 9.9 |
|     Charge in ownership restrictions | 9.15 |
| Farming and market gardening | 9.22 |
| Leasing trades | 9.24 |
| Schedule A losses | 9.26 |
| Miscellaneous | 9.30 |

## 10. Loan Relationships and Foreign Exchange Rules
| | |
|---|---:|
| Loan relationship debits and credits | 10.1 |
|     General rules | 10.1 |
|     Anti-avoidance | 10.9 |
|     Disclosure | 10.12 |
|     Normal accounting treatment | 10.17 |
| Foreign exchange gains and losses | 10.30 |
|     Matched liabilities | 10.39 |
|     Anti-avoidance | 10.40 |
|     Deferral of unrealised gains | 10.45 |
| Interest rates and currency contracts | 10.54 |

## 11. Groups and Consortia
| | |
|---|---:|
| Group relief | 11.1 |
| Consortia | 11.11 |
| Claims | 11.16 |
| Simplified arrangements for group relief | 11.19 |
| Chargeable gains: intra-group transfers | 11.28 |
|     Deemed intra-group transfers | 11.31 |
|     Pre-entry losses and gains | 11.37 |
|     Company leaving a group | 11.39 |
|     Recovery from group members | 11.42 |

## 12. Partnerships and Joint Ventures
| | |
|---|---:|
| Introduction | 12.1 |
| Corporate partners | 12.2 |
|     Deemed company | 12.5 |
| Partnership and joint venture | 12.6 |
|     Relevance of sharing profits and losses | 12.7 |
|     Partners as notional sole traders | 12.9 |

## Contents

| | |
|---|---|
| No separate taxable entity | 12.10 |
| Partnership as deemed company | 12.11 |
| Allocation of profits | 12.15 |
| Investment income | 12.17 |
| Non-trading businesses | 12.20 |
| Joint investments | 12.21 |
| Overseas aspects | 12.22 |
| Overseas income of a UK partnership | 12.22 |
| Foreign trades and professions | 12.24 |
| Income from let property overseas | 12.25 |
| UK resident company in foreign partnership | 12.26 |
| Non-resident company in UK partnership | 12.28 |
| Foreign partnerships with UK trade activities | 12.29 |
| UK investment income of non-resident partners | 12.30 |
| Income from land in the UK | 12.31 |
| UK representative | 12.32 |
| Chargeable gains | 12.34 |
| Partnership changes | 12.35 |
| Loan relationships, foreign exchange and financial instruments | 12.40 |
| Foreign exchange legislation | 12.41 |

### 13. Controlled Foreign Companies

| | |
|---|---|
| Introduction | 13.1 |
| Outline of charge and exemptions | 13.4 |
| Determining whether a company is a CFC | 13.7 |
| What is a company? | 13.7 |
| Residence | 13.8 |
| Control by UK residents | 13.14 |
| Lower level of taxation | 13.17 |
| 'Designer rate' tax provisions | 13.19 |
| Calculation of CFC charge | 13.20 |
| Outline | 13.20 |
| The accounting period | 13.21 |
| Persons interested | 13.24 |
| Chargeable profits | 13.26 |
| Creditable tax | 13.29 |
| Apportionment | 13.30 |
| Exemptions | 13.34 |
| Interest of less than 25 per cent | 13.34 |
| Acceptable distribution policy | 13.35 |
| Exempt activities | 13.38 |
| Public quotation | 13.41 |
| Profits de minimis | 13.43 |
| Excluded Countries List | 13.44 |
| Motive exemption | 13.47 |
| CTSA provisions | 13.48 |
| Company self-assessment of CFC charge | 13.48 |
| The return | 13.49 |

|  |  |
|---|---|
| Clearances | 13.54 |
| Intention to pursue an ADP | 13.57 |
| Enquiries | 13.58 |
| Records | 13.59 |
| Penalties | 13.61 |
| Appeals | 13.62 |
| Reliefs | 13.63 |
| Special recovery provisions | 13.67 |
| Transitional provisions | 13.68 |
| Miscellaneous | 13.69 |
| Interaction with TA 1988 s 739 | 13.69 |
| Insurance companies | 13.70 |

## 14. Transfer Pricing

|  |  |
|---|---|
| Introduction | 14.1 |
| Outline of charge: basic rule | 14.5 |
| Meanings of terms used in the basic rule | 14.8 |
| Establishing the arm's length provision | 14.19 |
| Traditional methods | 14.20 |
| Transactional profit methods | 14.24 |
| Exception for UK transactions | 14.27 |
| Charities | 14.28 |
| Claims for relief from double counting | 14.29 |
| Capital allowances and capital gains | 14.33 |
| Application of the Schedule in particular circumstances | 14.34 |
| Financial arrangements | 14.34 |
| Goods and services | 14.40 |
| Intellectual property and know-how | 14.42 |
| Oil and gas | 14.44 |
| Self-assessment | 14.45 |
| The CT return | 14.45 |
| Record keeping | 14.46 |
| Penalties | 14.51 |
| Advance Pricing Agreements | 14.55 |
| Outline of basic statutory provisions | 14.55 |
| Impact on non-parties | 14.59 |
| Impact on APA of double tax arrangements | 14.60 |
| Revocation of APA | 14.61 |
| Revenue practice | 14.62 |
| Enquiries | 14.69 |
| Determinations | 14.72 |
| Appeals | 14.74 |
| International agreement procedures for relieving double taxation | 14.75 |
| Mutual Agreement Procedure | 14.76 |
| The Arbitration Convention | 14.80 |

## Contents

### 15. Other Overseas Aspects

| | |
|---|---|
| Non-resident companies | 15.1 |
| UK representatives of non-residents | 15.10 |
|    Non-resident partners | 15.14 |
|    Obligations imposed upon UK representatives | 15.15 |
|    Independent agents | 15.16 |
|    Criminal offences | 15.18 |
| Persons not treated as UK representatives – investment managers and brokers | 15.19 |
|    General | 15.19 |
|    Persons not regular agents of non-residents | 15.24 |
|    Brokers | 15.25 |
|    Investment managers | 15.28 |
|    Participating investment managers – the 20 per cent rule | 15.35 |
|    Collective investment schemes | 15.39 |
|    Non-resident members of Lloyd's | 15.41 |
|    Certain overseas funds in existence at 29 November 1994 | 15.42 |
| Schedule D, Case VI | 15.43 |
| Income from land in the UK: Schedule A | 15.44 |
|    Background | 15.44 |
|    Non-resident landlords | 15.47 |
|    Knowledge of landlord's status by letting agents and tenants | 15.48 |
|    Landlord's ability to apply for rent to be paid gross | 15.49 |
|    Deduction at source | 15.56 |
|    Letting agents | 15.57 |
|    Chains of letting agents | 15.60 |
|    Branches of letting agents | 15.61 |
|    Notices from FICO to operate the scheme | 15.65 |
|    Tenant finders | 15.66 |
|    Registration | 15.68 |
|    Calculation of payment of tax by letting agents | 15.69 |
|    Tenants of non-resident landlords | 15.80 |
|    Rental income | 15.93 |
|    Deductible expenses | 15.98 |
|    Record keeping and audit | 15.105 |
|    Practical implication of transfer pricing legislation | 15.107 |
| Investment income | 15.108 |
| Intellectual property | 15.111 |
| E-commerce | 15.114 |
| Double taxation relief | 15.122 |
|    Unilateral relief | 15.122 |
|    Treaty relief | 15.125 |
|    Underlying tax | 15.141 |

*Contents*

## 16. Record Keeping
| | |
|---|---|
| Introduction | 16.1 |
| A guide to keeping records for the self-employed | 16.7 |
| Record keeping for companies | 16.11 |
|     Transfer pricing records | 16.14 |
|     Period for retention of records | 16.16 |

## 17. Finality and Certainty, Powers of Enquiry and Discovery
| | |
|---|---|
| Finality and certainty | 17.1 |
| Revenue enquiry/audit | 17.3 |
|     Revenue powers of enquiry: introduction and time limits for notice of enquiry | 17.3 |
|     Outline of enquiry procedure | 17.8 |
|     Code of practice | 17.11 |
|     Aspect enquiries | 17.13 |
|     District enquiries | 17.15 |
|     Preventing an enquiry starting | 17.19 |
|     Special Compliance Office enquiries | 17.23 |
|     Production of documents | 17.28 |
|     Right of appeal against notice to produce documents | 17.32 |
|     Jeopardy amendment of assessment by Revenue after opening of enquiry | 17.34 |
|     Amendment of return by company during enquiry | 17.36 |
|     Conclusion of enquiry and amendment of return | 17.38 |
|     Direction to complete enquiry | 17.41 |
| Revenue enquiry into claims | 17.43 |
|     General position | 17.43 |
|     Conclusion of enquiry and amendment of claim | 17.46 |
| Discovery | 17.49 |
|     Previous position and background | 17.49 |
|     Discovery under self-assessment | 17.53 |
|     Practical aspects | 17.61 |
|     Discretionary and judgemental issues | 17.69 |
|     Valuations | 17.70 |
|     Error and prevailing practice | 17.72 |
|     Time limit for discovery assessment | 17.73 |

## 18. Interest and Penalties
| | |
|---|---|
| Interest | 18.1 |
|     Summary of basic provisions | 18.1 |
|     Interest chargeable on tax paid late ('late payment interest') | 18.3 |
|     Interest payable on tax repaid ('repayment interest') | 18.9 |
|     Revenue practice regarding computer treatment of losses and deficits carried back (and of relief to which *s 419(4A)* applies) | 18.13 |
|     Interest on late and inadequate instalment payments ('debit interest') | 18.15 |
|     Interest on early paid tax and overpaid instalments ('credit interest') | 18.16 |

## Contents

|  |  |
|---|---|
| Handling debit and credit interest: Revenue practice | 18.18 |
| Interest rate-setting arrangements and formulae | 18.19 |
| ACT and income tax deducted from payments by a company | 18.21 |
| Penalties | 18.22 |
| Introduction | 18.22 |
| Failure to notify Revenue of chargeability | 18.23 |
| Late filing of or failure to make return | 18.25 |
| Late filing penalties: practical issues | 18.27 |
| Incorrect or uncorrected return etc. | 18.29 |
| Failure to produce documents during enquiry | 18.32 |
| Failure to retain and preserve records | 18.35 |
| Penalty for unpaid tax instalments by larger companies | 18.37 |
| Failure to provide information regarding instalment payments | 18.38 |
| Reasonable excuse for failure | 18.39 |
| Time limit for tax-related penalties | 18.40 |
| Interest on penalties | 18.41 |

### 19. Appeals: Collection and Recovery

|  |  |
|---|---|
| Appeals under self-assessment | 19.1 |
| General position | 19.1 |
| Appeals on substantive grounds in relation to Revenue enquiries | 19.2 |
| Appeals in relation to group relief and capital allowances | 19.4 |
| Appeals in relation to discovery assessments and determinations | 19.6 |
| Appeals against penalties | 19.7 |
| Supervisory powers over Revenue investigations | 19.8 |
| Whether appeal heard by General or Special Commissioners | 19.11 |
| Questions to be determined by Special Commissioners | 19.14 |
| Jurisdiction of Special Commissioners over certain claims included in returns | 19.16 |
| Questions to be determined by Lands Tribunal | 19.17 |
| Rules for assigning proceedings to General Commissioners | 19.18 |
| Procedure on appeal | 19.20 |
| Postponement of tax pending appeal | 19.21 |
| Collection and recovery | 19.22 |

### Appendices                                                                 Page

1  Inland Revenue Bulletins                                                   309
   Issue 12–Matrix Securities: Guidance to Taxpayers
   Issue 17–Intra-Group Interest and Similar Sums Treated as Distributions

Issue 18–Non-Residents Trading in the UK: The Arm's
     Length Principle
Issue 20–Self-Assessment: Assessment of Schedule A
     Income arising to a Partnership
Issue 32–Relationship Between Accountancy and Taxable
     Profits
Issue 37–The New Transfer Pricing Legislation
     Records to be Kept under Self-Assessment
     Self-Assessment: Incomplete returns and the Use
          of Provisional Figures in Returns
Issue 38–Penalties and the New Transfer Pricing Legislation
Issue 39–Relationship between Accountancy and Taxable
     Profits: Current Points of Interest
Issue 40–Interaction of Tax Law and Accountancy Practice:
     Recent Developments
     A Modern System for Corporation Tax Payments:
          Quarterly Instalment Payments and Group
          Payment Arrangements

2  A Modern System for Corporation Tax
     Payments: Group Payment Arrangements                409

3  Statutory Instruments                                 430
   1998 No. 3081 The Controlled Foreign Companies (Excluded
        Countries) Regulations 1998
   1998 No. 3175 The Corporation Tax (Instalment Payments)
        Regulations 1998
   1998 No. 3176 The Taxes (Interest Rate) (Amendment No. 2)
        Regulations 1998
   1999 No. 358 The Corporation Tax (Treatment of Unrelieved
        Surplus Advance Corporation Tax) Regulations 1999
   1999 No. 1929 The Corporation Tax (Instalment Payments)
        (Amendment) Regulations 1999
   1999 No. 2975 The Corporation Tax (Simplified Arrangements for
        Group Relief) Regulations 1999

4  Statement of Practice 4/98: Application of loan relationships,
     foreign exchange and financial instruments legislation to
     partnerships which include companies                473

5  Statement of Practice 3/99: Advance Pricing Agreements  481

6  Inland Revenue Press Releases                          498

7  Code of Practice 14: Enquiries into Company Tax Returns  538

8  Company Tax Returns and Guidance Notes                 550

9  Codes of Practice 10: Information and Advice           594

Index                                                     608

# Table of Cases

**A**

Abbott Laboratories Ltd v Carmody (Inspector of Taxes) [1968] 2 All ER 879, 44 TC 569, 47 ATC 88, [1968] TR 75, L (TC) 2270     7.41

Absalom v Talbot (Inspector of Taxes) [1944] AC 204, [1944] 1 All ER 642, 26 TC 166, 113 LJ Ch 369, 88 Sol Jo 203, 171 LT 53, 60 TLR 434, HL     7.22

Alexander v Wallington General Comrs and IRC [1992] STC 314n, 65 TC 777; affd [1993] STC 585, 65 TC 777, CA     App 1

Alianza Co Ltd v Bell (Surveyor of Taxes) [1905] 1 KB 184, 5 TC 60, 74 LJKB 219, 53 WR 257, 92 LT 184, 21 TLR 134, CA; on appeal [1906] AC 18, 5 TC 172, 75 LJKB 44, 54 WR 413, 50 Sol Jo 74, 93 LT 705, 22 TLR 94, HL     7.21

Anderton and Halstead Ltd v Birrell (Inspector of Taxes) [1932] 1 KB 271, 16 TC 200, 101 LJKB 219, [1931] All ER Rep 796, 146 LT 139     7.22

Applicant v Inspector of Taxes [1999] STC (SCD) 128     App 1

Aproline Ltd v Littlejohn [1995] STC (SCD) 201     6.25

Aramayo Francke Mines Ltd v Eccott (Inspector of Taxes) [1925] AC 634, 9 TC 445, 94 LJKB 688, 69 Sol Jo 825, 133 LT 561, 41 TLR 542, HL     15.5

Atherton (Inspector of Taxes) v British Insulated and Helsby Cables Ltd [1925] 1 KB 421, 10 TC 155, 94 LJKB 319, 69 Sol Jo 103, 132 LT 288, 41 TLR 55, CA; affd sub nom British Insulated and Helsby Cables Ltd v Atherton (Inspector of Taxes) [1926] AC 205, 10 TC 155, 4 ATC 47, 95 LJKB 336, [1925] All ER Rep 623, 134 LT 289, 42 TLR 187, HL     7.21

Attwood (Inspector of Taxes) v Anduff Car Wash Ltd [1997] STC 1167, sub nom Anduff Carwash Ltd v Attwood (Inspector of Taxes) 69 TC 575, CA     7.47

Ayrshire Pullman Motor Services and D M Ritchie v IRC (1929) 14 TC 754     12.6

**B**

BSC Footwear Ltd (formerly Freeman, Hardy and Willis Ltd) v Ridgway (Inspector of Taxes) [1972] AC 544, [1971] 2 All ER 534, [1971] 2 WLR 1313, 47 TC 495, 50 ATC 153, [1971] TR 121, 115 Sol Jo 408, L (TC) 2403, HL     7.14

Bank Line Ltd v IRC [1974] STC 342, 49 TC 307, 53 ATC 114, [1974] TR 115, L (TC) 2519, 1974 SLT 306     7.67, 9.4

Barclays Mercantile Industrial Finance Ltd v Melluish (Inspector of Taxes) [1990] STC 314, [1990] 12 LS Gaz R 42     7.56

Barlow v IRC (1937) 21 TC 354     10.27

Belfour v Mace (Inspector of Taxes) (1928) 13 TC 539, 138 LT 338, CA     15.8

*Table of Cases*

| | |
|---|---|
| Bennet (Inspector of Taxes) v Underground Electric Rlys Co of London Ltd [1923] 2 KB 535, 8 TC 475, 92 LJKB 909, 67 Sol Jo 769, 129 LT 701, 39 TLR 560 | 7.67 |
| Ben-Odeco Ltd v Powlson (Inspector of Taxes) [1978] 2 All ER 1111, [1978] 1 WLR 1093, [1978] STC 460, 52 TC 459, 470, [1978] TR 359, 122 Sol Jo 573, L (TC) 2704, HL | 7.47 |
| Benson (Inspector of Taxes) v Yard Arm Club Ltd [1979] 2 All ER 336, [1979] 1 WLR 347, [1979] STC 266, 53 TC 67, [1979] TR 1, 123 Sol Jo 98, CA | 7.47 |
| Bentleys, Stokes and Lowless v Beeson (Inspector of Taxes) [1952] 2 All ER 82, 33 TC 491, 31 ATC 229, 45 R & IT 461, [1952] TR 239, 96 Sol Jo 345, [1952] TLR 1529, CA | 7.16 |
| Berry (L G) Investments Ltd v Attwooll (Inspector of Taxes) [1964] 2 All ER 126, [1964] 1 WLR 693, 41 TC 547, 43 ATC 61, [1964] TR 67, 108 Sol Jo 318 | 7.67 |
| Bestway (Holdings) Ltd v Luff (Inspector of Taxes) [1998] STC 357, 70 TC 512, 142 Sol Jo LB 87 | 7.41 |
| Bidwell v Gardiner (1960) 39 TC 31, 39 ATC 83, 53 R & IT 158, [1960] TR 13 | 7.18 |
| Bispham (Inspector of Taxes) v Eardiston Farming Co (1919) Ltd [1962] 2 All ER 376, [1962] 1 WLR 616, 40 TC 322, 41 ATC 74, [1962] TR 73, 106 Sol Jo 309 | 9.4 |
| Blackpool Marton Rotary Club v Martin (Inspector of Taxes) [1988] STC 823; affd [1990] STC 1, CA | 2.11 |
| Bolam (Inspector of Taxes) v Regent Oil Co Ltd (1956) 37 TC 56, 35 ATC 499, 50 R & IT 79, [1956] TR 403, L (TC) 1806 | 7.21 |
| Bolton (Inspector of Taxes) v International Drilling Co Ltd [1983] STC 70, 56 TC 449 | 7.46 |
| Bourne (Inspector of Taxes) v Norwich Crematorium Ltd [1967] 2 All ER 576, [1967] 1 WLR 691, 44 TC 164, 46 ATC 43, [1967] TR 49, 111 Sol Jo 256 | 7.41 |
| Bowater Paper Corpn v Murgatroyd (Inspector of Taxes) [1969] 1 Ch 78, [1968] 1 All ER 868, [1968] 2 WLR 834, 46 TC 37, 46 ATC 413, [1967] TR 397, 112 Sol Jo 73; on appeal [1969] 1 Ch 78, [1968] 2 All ER 936, [1968] 3 WLR 471, 46 TC 37, 47 ATC 180, [1968] TR 157, 112 Sol Jo 423, CA; affd [1970] AC 266, [1969] 3 All ER 111, [1969] 3 WLR 412, 46 TC 37, 48 ATC 250, [1969] TR 251, 113 Sol Jo 657, HL | 15.141 |
| Bowden (Inspector of Taxes) v Russell and Russell [1965] 2 All ER 258, [1965] 1 WLR 711, 42 TC 301, 44 ATC 74, [1965] TR 89, 109 Sol Jo 254 | 7.16 |
| Bradley (Inspector of Taxes) v London Electricity plc [1996] STC 1054, 70 TC 155, 140 Sol Jo LB 210 | 7.47 |
| Bricom Holdings Ltd v IRC [1997] STC 1179, 70 TC 272, CA | 15.125 |
| Bridge House (Reigate Hill) Ltd v Hinder (Inspector of Taxes) (1971) 47 TC 182, 50 ATC 44, [1971] TR 173, CA | 7.34 |

*Table of Cases*

Bristow (Inspector of Taxes) v William Dickinson & Co Ltd [1946] KB 321, 27 TC 157, 174 LT 310, 62 TLR 252, sub nom Dickinson (William) & Co Ltd v Bristow (Inspector of Taxes) [1946] 1 All ER 448, 25 ATC 43, 115 LJKB 296, CA ... 7.22

Briton Ferry Steel Co Ltd v Barry (Inspector of Taxes) [1940] 1 KB 463, [1939] 4 All ER 541, 23 TC 414, 109 LJKB 250, 84 Sol Jo 59, 162 LT 202, 56 TLR 248, CA ... 9.11

Brown (Inspector of Taxes) v Burnley Football and Athletic Co Ltd [1980] 3 All ER 244, [1980] STC 424, 53 TC 357, [1980] TR 77, 124 Sol Jo 278 ... 7.19, 7.47

Brown v Tapscott (1840) 9 LJ Ex 139, 6 M & W 119 ... 12.7

Buckingham (Inspector of Taxes) v Securitas Properties Ltd [1980] 1 WLR 380, [1980] STC 166, 53 TC 292, [1979] TR 415, 124 Sol Jo 17 ... 7.41

Bulloch (Alexander) & Co v IRC [1976] STC 514, 51 TC 563, [1976] TR 201 ... 12.6

Bullock (Inspector of Taxes) v Unit Construction Co Ltd [1959] Ch 147, [1958] 3 All ER 186, [1958] 3 WLR 504, 38 TC 712, 37 ATC 292, 51 R & IT 625, [1958] TR 277, 102 Sol Jo 654; on appeal [1959] Ch 315, [1959] 1 All ER 591, [1959] 2 WLR 437, 38 ATC 36, 52 R & IT 194, [1959] TR 37, 103 Sol Jo 238, CA; revsd sub nom Unit Construction Co Ltd v Bullock (Inspector of Taxes) [1960] AC 351, [1959] 3 All ER 831, [1959] 3 WLR 1022, 38 TC 712, 38 ATC 351, 52 R & IT 828, [1959] TR 345, 103 Sol Jo 1027, HL ... 15.4

**C**

Caillebotte (Inspector of Taxes) v Quinn [1975] 2 All ER 412, [1975] 1 WLR 731, [1975] STC 265, 50 TC 222, 54 ATC 61, [1975] TR 55, 119 Sol Jo 356 ... 7.16

Cairns v MacDiarmid (Inspector of Taxes) [1983] STC 178, 56 TC 556, 127 Sol Jo 89, CA ... 10.27

Calcutta Jute Mills Co Ltd v Nicholson (Surveyor of Taxes) (1876) 1 Ex D 428, 1 TC 83, 88, 45 LJQB 821, 25 WR 71, [1874-80] All ER Rep 1102, 35 LT 275 ... 15.4

Calder v Allanson (1935) 19 TC 293 ... 12.6

Calders Ltd v IRC (1944) 26 TC 213, 1944 SC 433, 1945 SLT 125 ... 7.22

Caledonian Rly Co v Banks (Surveyor of Taxes) (1880) 1 TC 487, 8 R 89 ... 7.45

Capital and National Trust Ltd v Golder (Inspector of Taxes) [1949] 2 All ER 956, 31 TC 265, 28 ATC 326, 42 R & IT 576, [1949] TR 395, 93 Sol Jo 755, 65 TLR 772, L (TC) 1503, CA ... 7.67

Carr (Inspector of Taxes) v Armpledge Ltd [1998] STC 999 ... 6.27

Carr (Inspector of Taxes) v Fielden & Ashworth Ltd [2000] STC 410, CA ... 6.27

Carr (Inspector of Taxes) v Sayer [1992] STC 396, 65 TC 15 ... 7.41, 7.47

Cattermole (Inspector of Taxes) v Borax and Chemicals Ltd (1949) 31 TC 202, [1949] TR 195 ... 7.20

## Table of Cases

Cenlon Finance Co Ltd v Ellwood (Inspector of Taxes) [1962] AC 782, [1962] 1 All ER 854, [1962] 2 WLR 871, 40 TC 176, 41 ATC 11, [1962] TR 1, 106 Sol Jo 280, HL   17.50

Chancery Lane Safe Deposit and Offices Co Ltd v IRC (1964) 43 TC 83, 43 ATC 111, [1964] TR 123, 190 Estates Gazette 19, L (TC) 2098; on appeal [1965] 1 All ER 335, [1965] 1 WLR 239, 43 TC 83, 43 ATC 321, [1964] TR 347, 108 Sol Jo 1029, 192 Estates Gazette 901, L (TC) 2119, CA; affd [1966] AC 85, [1966] 1 All ER 1, [1966] 2 WLR 251, 43 TC 83, 44 ATC 450, [1965] TR 433, 110 Sol Jo 35, 197 Estates Gazette 13, L (TC) 2172, HL   7.14

Chapman (A W) Ltd v Hennessey (Inspector of Taxes) [1982] STC 214, 55 TC 516, [1981] TR 513, 125 Sol Jo 864   11.5

Clerical, Medical and General Life Assurance Society v Carter (Surveyor of Taxes) (1889) 22 QBD 444, 2 TC 437, 53 JP 276, 58 LJQB 224, 37 WR 346, 5 TLR 291, CA   4.44

Cole Bros Ltd v Phillips (Inspector of Taxes) [1982] 2 All ER 247, [1982] 1 WLR 1450, [1982] STC 307, 55 TC 188, 126 Sol Jo 709, HL   7.46

Collins (Edward) & Sons Ltd v IRC (1925) 12 TC 773, 4 ATC 179, 1925 SC 151, 1925 SLT 51   7.10

Colquhoun v Brooks (1889) 14 App Cas 493, 2 TC 490, 54 JP 277, 59 LJQB 53, 38 WR 289, [1886-90] All ER Rep 1063, 61 LT 518, 5 TLR 728, HL   12.22, App 1

Commercial Union Assurance Co plc v Shaw (Inspector of Taxes) [1998] STC 386; affd [1999] STC 109, CA   9.3, 15.137

Conn v Robins Bros Ltd (1966) 43 TC 266, 45 ATC 59, [1966] TR 61   7.19

Conservative and Unionist Central Office v Burrell (Inspector of Taxes) [1982] 2 All ER 1, [1982] 1 WLR 522, [1982] STC 317, 55 TC 671, [1981] TR 543, 126 Sol Jo 50, CA   2.11

Cooke (Inspector of Taxes) v Beach Station Caravans Ltd [1974] 3 All ER 159, [1974] 1 WLR 1398, [1974] STC 402, 49 TC 514, 53 ATC 216, [1975] RA 360, [1974] TR 213, 118 Sol Jo 777, L (TC) 2524   7.46

Cooper, Re [1911] 2 KB 550, 80 LJKB 990, 18 Mans 211, 105 LT 273, sub nom Boulter, Re, ex p Manchester and Liverpool District Banking Co 55 Sol Jo 554, CA   10.27

Copeman (Inspector of Taxes) v William Flood & Sons Ltd [1941] 1 KB 202, 24 TC 53, 19 ATC 521, 110 LJKB 215   7.31

Copol Clothing Co Ltd v Hindmarch (Inspector of Taxes) [1984] 1 WLR 411, [1984] STC 33, 57 TC 575, 128 Sol Jo 65, [1984] LS Gaz R 124, CA   7.41

Corinthian Securities Ltd v Cato [1970] 1 QB 377, [1969] 3 All ER 1168, [1969] 3 WLR 693, 46 TC 93, 48 ATC 416, [1969] TR 401, 113 Sol Jo 811, CA   10.27

Cricket plc v Inspector of Taxes [1998] STC (SCD) 101   6.30

## Table of Cases

| | |
|---|---|
| Crusabridge Investments Ltd v Casings International Ltd (1979) 54 TC 246 | 7.41 |
| Customs and Excise Comrs v Lord Fisher [1981] 2 All ER 147, [1981] STC 238, [1981] TR 59 | 12.21 |
| Cyril Lord Carpets Ltd v Schofield (1966) 42 TC 637, 45 ATC 16, [1966] TR 17, CA | 7.34 |

**D**

| | |
|---|---|
| Dale (Inspector of Taxes) v Johnson Bros (1951) 32 TC 487 | 7.41 |
| Davies v Braithwaite (1933) 18 TC 198, 77 Sol Jo 572 | 12.22 |
| De Beers Consolidated Mines Ltd v Howe (Surveyor of Taxes) [1905] 2 KB 612, 5 TC 198, 74 LJKB 934, 54 WR 9, 93 LT 63, 21 TLR 578, CA; affd [1906] AC 455, 5 TC 198, 75 LJKB 858, 13 Mans 394, 50 Sol Jo 666, 95 LT 221, 22 TLR 756, HL | 15.4 |
| Denver Hotel Co Ltd v Andrews (Surveyor of Taxes) (1895) 3 TC 356, 43 WR 339, 11 TLR 238, CA | 12.22, 15.5 |
| Dickenson v Gross (Inspector of Taxes) (1927) 11 TC 614, 137 LT 351 | 12.6 |
| Dixon (Inspector of Taxes) v Fitch's Garage Ltd [1975] 3 All ER 455, [1976] 1 WLR 215, [1975] STC 480, 50 TC 509, 54 ATC 151, [1975] TR 123, 119 Sol Jo 628, L (TC) 2569 | 7.47 |
| Dunk v Havant General Comrs [1976] STC 460n, [1976] TR 213 | 2.40, App 1 |

**E**

| | |
|---|---|
| ECC Quarries Ltd v Watkis (Inspector of Taxes) [1975] 3 All ER 843, [1975] STC 578, 54 ATC 221, [1975] TR 185 | 7.33 |
| Earlspring Properties Ltd v Guest (Inspector of Taxes) [1995] STC 479, 67 TC 259, CA | 2.3 |
| Edwards (Inspector of Taxes) v Warmsley Henshall & Co [1968] 1 All ER 1089, 44 TC 431, 46 ATC 431, [1967] TR 409 | 7.16 |
| Elliss (Inspector of Taxes) v BP Oil Northern Ireland Refinery Ltd [1987] STC 52, 59 TC 474, 131 Sol Jo 411, [1987] LS Gaz R 577, CA | 7.35 |
| Erichsen v Last (1881) 1 TC 351; affd 8 QBD 414, 4 TC 422, 46 JP 357, 51 LJQB 86, 30 WR 301, 45 LT 703, CA | 15.6, App 1 |
| Executive Network (Consultants) Ltd v O'Connor (Inspector of Taxes) [1996] STC (SCD) 29 | 7.16 |

**F**

| | |
|---|---|
| Fairrie v Hall (Inspector of Taxes) [1947] 2 All ER 141, 28 TC 200, 26 ATC 102, 40 R & IT 382, 177 LT 600, L (TC) 1425 | 7.20 |
| Falmer Jeans Ltd v Rodin (Inspector of Taxes) [1990] STC 270 | 9.11 |
| Family Golf Centres Ltd v Thorne (Inspector of Taxes) [1998] STC (SCD) 106 | 7.47 |
| Farrell (Surveyor of Taxes) v Sunderland Steamship Co Ltd (1903) 4 TC 605, 67 JP 209, 9 Asp MLC 416, 88 LT 741 | 12.7 |
| Fenston v Johnstone (1940) 23 TC 29, 84 Sol Jo 305 | 12.6 |
| Ferguson's Trustees v Donovan [1929] IR 489, 1 ITC 214, SC | 12.22 |

*Table of Cases*

Firestone Tyre and Rubber Co Ltd v Llewellin (Inspector of
   Taxes) [1956] 1 All ER 693, [1956] 1 WLR 352, 37 TC 111,
   35 ATC 17, 49 R & IT 218, [1956] TR 17, 100 Sol Jo 262,
   L (TC) 1761, CA; affd [1957] 1 All ER 561, [1957]
   1 WLR 464, 37 TC 111, 50 R & IT 172, 101 Sol Jo 228,
   HL                                              15.6, App 1
Fitton v Gilders and Heaton (Inspector of Taxes) (1955) 36 TC
   233, 34 ATC 215, 48 R & IT 516, [1955] TR 197, L (TC)
   1737                                                   7.34
Fragmap Developments Ltd v Cooper (Inspector of Taxes)
   (1967) 44 TC 366, 46 ATC 185, [1967] TR 169             7.67
**G**
Gallagher v Jones (Inspector of Taxes) [1994] Ch 107, [1994] 2
   WLR 160, [1993] STC 537, 66 TC 77, [1993] 32 LS Gaz R
   40, CA                                                  7.7
Gardner (John) & Bowring, Hardy & Co Ltd v IRC (1930) 15
   TC 602                                           12.6, 12.7
Garston Overseers v Carlisle (Surveyor of Taxes) [1915] 3 KB
   381, 13 LGR 969, 6 TC 659, 84 LJKB 2016, 113 LT 879   10.27
Getty Oil Co v Steele (Inspector of Taxes) [1990] STC 434, 63
   TC 376                                                15.129
Girobank plc v Clarke (Inspector of Taxes) [1998] 4 All ER
   312, [1998] 1 WLR 942, [1998] STC 182, 70 TC 387, [1998]
   06 LS Gaz R 25, 142 Sol Jo LB 43, CA                   7.41
Golder (Inspector of Taxes) v Great Boulder Proprietary Gold
   Mines Ltd [1952] 1 All ER 360, 33 TC 75, 31 ATC 61, 45
   R & IT 96, [1952] TR 25, 96 Sol Jo 73, [1952] 1 TLR 306  7.20
Gordon & Blair Ltd v IRC (1962) 40 TC 358, 41 ATC 111,
   [1962] TR 161, 1962 SC 267, 1962 SLT 373                 9.5
Goslings and Sharpe v Blake (Surveyor of Taxes) (1889) 23
   QBD 324, 2 TC 450, 58 LJQB 446, 37 WR 774, 61 LT 311,
   5 TLR 605, CA                                          10.27
Government of India, Ministry of Finance (Revenue Division)
   v Taylor [1955] AC 491, [1955] 1 All ER 292, [1955] 2
   WLR 303, 34 ATC 10, 48 R & IT 98, [1955] TR 9, 99 Sol
   Jo 94, HL                                              12.32
Grainger & Son v Gough (Surveyor of Taxes) [1896] AC 325,
   3 TC 462, 60 JP 692, 65 LJQB 410, 44 WR 561, 74 LT 435,
   12 TLR 364, HL                                    15.8, App 1
Gray (Inspector of Taxes) v Seymours Garden Centre
   (Horticulture) (a firm) [1995] STC 706, [1995] 30 LS Gaz
   R 35, CA                                                7.47
Greenwood (Surveyor of Taxes) v F L Smidth & Co [1922] 1
   AC 417, 8 TC 193, 91 LJKB 349, 66 Sol Jo 349, 127 LT 68,
   38 TLR 421, HL                                          15.8
Gresham Life Assurance Society v A-G [1916] 1 Ch 228, 7 TC
   36, 85 LJ Ch 201, 114 LT 399, 32 TLR 264                4.44
Grove v Elliots and Parkinson (1896) 3 TC 481        12.22, 15.5

## H

| | |
|---|---|
| Hall (George) & Sons v Platt (Inspector of Taxes) (1954) 35 TC 440, 33 ATC 340, 47 R & IT 713, [1954] TR 331, 164 Estates Gazette 497, L (TC) 1711 | 12.7 |
| Hammond Engineering Co Ltd v IRC [1975] STC 334, 54 ATC 92, [1975] TR 89 | 7.20 |
| Hampton (Inspector of Taxes) v Fortes Autogrill Ltd [1980] STC 80, 53 TC 691, [1979] TR 377 | 7.47 |
| Harrods (Buenos Aires) Ltd v Taylor-Gooby (Inspector of Taxes) (1964) 41 TC 450, 108 Sol Jo 117, sub nom Taylor-Gooby v Harrods (Buenos Aires) Ltd 43 ATC 6, [1964] TR 9, CA | 15.143 |
| Hawker v Compton (1922) 8 TC 306 | 12.6 |
| Heather (Inspector of Taxes) v P-E Consulting Group Ltd [1973] Ch 189, [1972] 2 All ER 107, [1972] 2 WLR 918, 48 TC 293, 50 ATC 461, [1971] TR 465, 116 Sol Jo 125, L (TC) 2436; affd [1973] Ch 189, [1973] 1 All ER 8, [1972] 3 WLR 833, 48 TC 293, 51 ATC 255, [1972] TR 237, 116 Sol Jo 824, L (TC) 2466, CA | 7.30 |
| Highland Rly Co v Baldeston (Surveyor of Taxes) (1889) 2 TC 485, 1889 26 SLR 657 | 7.18 |
| Hinton (Inspector of Taxes) v Maden and Ireland Ltd [1959] 3 All ER 356, [1959] 1 WLR 875, 38 TC 391, 38 ATC 231, 52 R & IT 688, [1959] TR 233, 103 Sol Jo 812, L (TC) 1913, HL | 7.46 |
| Hodgins v Plunder & Pollak (Ireland) Ltd [1957] IR 58, 3 ITC 135 | 7.19 |
| Hoechst Finance Ltd v Gumbrell (Inspector of Taxes) [1983] STC 150, 56 TC 594, CA | 7.67 |
| Holly v Inspector of Taxes [2000] STC (SCD) 50 | 17.4 |
| Humphries & Co v Cook (Inspector of Taxes) (1934) 19 TC 121 | 12.36 |

## I

| | |
|---|---|
| ICI plc v Colmer (Inspector of Taxes) [2000] 1 All ER 129, [1999] 1 WLR 2035, [2000] 1 CMLR 142, [1999] STC 1089, 72 TC 1, [1999] 46 LS Gaz R 40, 144 Sol Jo LB 7, HL | 11.3 |
| IRC v Alexander von Glehn & Co Ltd [1920] 2 KB 553, 12 TC 232, 89 LJKB 590, 123 LT 338, 36 TLR 463, CA | 7.20 |
| IRC v Barclay Curle & Co Ltd [1969] 1 All ER 732, [1969] 1 WLR 675, [1969] 1 Lloyd's Rep 169, 45 TC 221, 48 ATC 17, [1969] TR 21, 113 Sol Jo 244, [1969] RVR 102, 1969 SC (HL) 30, 1969 SLT 122 | 7.46 |
| IRC v Dowdall O'Mahoney & Co Ltd [1952] AC 401, [1952] 1 All ER 531, 33 TC 259, 31 ATC 126, 45 R & IT 204, [1952] TR 85, 96 Sol Jo 148, [1952] 1 TLR 560, HL | 15.143 |
| IRC v Hay (1924) 8 TC 636, 61 SLR 375, 1924 SC 521, 1924 SLT 470 | 10.27 |
| IRC v Lambhill Ironworks Ltd (1950) 31 TC 393, 29 ATC 240, 43 R & IT 677, [1950] TR 145, L (TC) 1516, 1950 SC 331, 1950 SLT 251 | 7.41 |

*Table of Cases*

IRC v National Coal Board. *See* National Coal Board v IRC
IRC v Olive Mill Spinners Ltd [1963] 2 All ER 130, [1963] 1
  WLR 712, 41 TC 77, 42 ATC 74, [1963] TR 59, 107 Sol Jo
  476                                                                       9.13, 11.3
IRC v Rossminster Ltd [1980] AC 952, [1980] 1 All ER 80,
  [1980] 2 WLR 1, 70 Cr App Rep 157, [1980] STC 42, 52
  TC 160, 191, [1979] TR 309, 124 Sol Jo 18, L (TC) 2753,
  HL                                          17.16
IRC v Saxone Lilley and Skinner (Holdings) Ltd [1967] 1 All
  ER 756, [1967] 1 WLR 501, 46 ATC 14, [1967] TR 17, 111
  Sol Jo 177, 1967 SC (HL) 1, 1967 SLT 81, sub nom Saxone
  Lilley and Skinner (Holdings) Ltd v IRC 44 TC 122     7.41
IRC v Scottish and Newcastle Breweries Ltd [1982] 2 All ER
  230, [1982] 1 WLR 322, [1982] STC 296, 55 TC 252, 126
  Sol Jo 189, 1982 SLT 407, HL                        7.46
IRC v Warnes & Co Ltd [1919] 2 KB 444, 12 TC 227, 89 LJKB
  6, 121 LT 125, 35 TLR 436                              7.20
IRC v Williamson (1928) 14 TC 335                       12.6
Innocent (Inspector of Taxes) v Whaddon Estates Ltd [1982]
  STC 115, 55 TC 476, [1981] TR 379                   11.28
Irving (Inspector of Taxes) v Tesco Stores (Holdings) Ltd
  [1982] STC 881, 58 TC 1                                 11.5

**J**

Jackson (Inspector of Taxes) v Laskers Home Furnishers Ltd
  [1956] 3 All ER 891, [1957] 1 WLR 69, 37 TC 69, 35 ATC
  469, 50 R & IT 48, [1956] TR 391, 101 Sol Jo 44, 168
  Estates Gazette 584, L (TC) 1805                      7.18
Jarrold (Inspector of Taxes) v John Good & Sons Ltd [1962] 2
  All ER 971, [1962] 1 WLR 1101, 40 TC 681, 41 ATC 170,
  [1962] RA 273, 9 RRC 188, [1962] TR 181, 106 Sol Jo 688,
  [1962] RVR 653; affd [1963] 1 All ER 141, [1963] 1 WLR
  214, 40 TC 681, 41 ATC 335, [1962] RA 681, 9 RRC 270,
  [1962] TR 371, 107 Sol Jo 153, [1963] RVR 25, CA      7.46
Jenners Princes Street Edinburgh Ltd v IRC [1998] STC
  (SCD) 196                                    App 1, App 6
Johnston (Inspector of Taxes) v Britannia Airways Ltd [1994]
  STC 763, 67 TC 99                              7.7, App 1
Joint (Inspector of Taxes) v Bracken Developments Ltd [1994]
  STC 300, 66 TC 560                                  2.3
Jones (Samuel) & Co (Devonvale) Ltd v IRC (1951) 32 TC
  513, 30 ATC 412, [1951] TR 411, L (TC) 1569, 1952 SC 94,
  1952 SLT 144                                        7.19

**K**

Kilmarnock Equitable Co-operative Society Ltd v IRC (1966)
  42 TC 675, 45 ATC 205, [1966] TR 185, 1966 SLT 224   7.41
Knight (Inspector of Taxes) v Parry [1973] STC 56, 48 TC 580,
  51 ATC 283, [1972] TR 267, 116 Sol Jo 885, L (TC) 2470    7.20

## L

Law Shipping Co Ltd v IRC (1923) 12 TC 621, 3 ATC 110,
    1924 SC 74                                                    7.18, 7.85
Lawrie v IRC (1952) 34 TC 20, 31 ATC 327, 45 R & IT 603,
    [1952] TR 305, L (TC) 1618, 1952 SC 394, 1952 SLT 413         7.18
Lawson (Inspector of Taxes) v Johnson Matthey plc [1992] 2
    AC 324, [1992] 2 All ER 647, [1992] 2 WLR 826, [1992]
    STC 466, 65 TC 39, [1992] 26 LS Gaz R 32, 136 Sol Jo LB
    164, HL                                                       7.21
Laycock (Inspector of Taxes) v Freeman, Hardy and Willis Ltd
    (1938) 22 TC 288; on appeal [1939] 2 KB 1, [1938] 4 All
    ER 609, 22 TC 288, 17 ATC 450, 108 LJKB 270, 83 Sol Jo
    53, 160 LT 41, 55 TLR 218, CA                                 9.11
Leeds Pemanent Building Society v Procter (Inspector of
    Taxes) [1982] 3 All ER 925, [1982] STC 821, 56 TC 293         7.46
Liverpool and London and Globe Insurance Co v Bennett
    [1913] AC 610, 6 TC 327, 82 LJKB 1221, 20 Mans 295, 57
    Sol Jo 739, 109 LT 483, 29 TLR 757, HL                        4.44
Lock v Jones (Inspector of Taxes) (1941) 23 TC 749, 85 Sol Jo
    322                                                           7.22
London Bank of Mexico and South America v Apthorpe
    (Surveyor of Taxes) [1891] 2 QB 378, 3 TC 143, 56 JP 86,
    60 LJQB 653, 39 WR 564, 65 LT 601, 7 TLR 567, CA              12.22
London County Freehold and Leasehold Properties Ltd v
    Sweet (Inspector of Taxes) [1942] 2 All ER 212, 24 TC
    412, 86 Sol Jo 312, 167 LT 175, 58 TLR 281                    7.67
Lothian Chemical Co Ltd v Rogers (Inspector of Taxes)
    (1926) 11 TC 508                                              7.18
Lurcott v Wakely and Wheeler [1911] 1 KB 905, 80 LJKB 713,
    [1911-13] All ER Rep 41, 55 Sol Jo 290, 104 LT 290, CA        7.19

## M

McKie v Luck (1925) 9 TC 511                                      12.7, 12.21
McKinney (Inspector of Taxes) v Hagans Caravans
    (Manufacturing) Ltd [1997] STC 1023, 69 TC 526, CA            7.34
McKnight (Inspector of Taxes) v Sheppard [1996] STC 627,
    140 Sol Jo LB 140; revsd [1997] STC 846, 141 Sol Jo LB
    115, CA; affd [1999] 1 WLR 1333, [1999] STC 669, [1999]
    NLJR 966, HL                                                  7.20
McLaren v Mumford (Inspector of Taxes) [1996] STC 1134, 69
    TC 173, [1996] 38 LS Gaz R 42                                 7.16
Macpherson & Co v Moore (Surveyor of Taxes) (1912) 6 TC
    107, 1912 SC 1315                                             15.8
Mallalieu v Drummond (Inspector of Taxes) [1983] 2 AC 861,
    [1983] 2 All ER 1095, [1983] 3 WLR 409, [1983] STC 665,
    57 TC 330, 127 Sol Jo 538, HL                                 7.16
Margrett (Inspector of Taxes) v Lowestoft Water and Gas Co
    (1935) 19 TC 481                                              7.19
Marshall Hus & Partners Ltd v Bolton (Inspector of Taxes)
    [1981] STC 18, 55 TC 539, [1980] TR 371, L (TC) 2804          9.20, 11.8

*Table of Cases*

Mason v Tyson (Inspector of Taxes) [1980] STC 284, 53 TC 333, [1980] TR 23, 124 Sol Jo 206 — 7.17, 7.47

Matrix-Securities Ltd v IRC [1994] 1 All ER 769, [1994] STC 272, sub nom R v IRC, ex p Matrix-Securities Ltd [1994] 1 WLR 334, 66 TC 587, HL — 2.49

Mawsley Machinery Ltd v Robinson (Inspector of Taxes) [1998] STC (SCD) 236 — 7.30

Meat Traders Ltd v Cushing (Inspector of Taxes) [1997] STC (SCD) 245 — 7.11, App 1

Memec plc v IRC [1998] STC 754, 71 TC 77, CA — 15.124

Minsham Properties Ltd v Price (Inspector of Taxes) [1990] STC 718 — 10.27

Morden Rigg & Co and R B Eskrigge & Co v Monks (Inspector of Taxes) (1923) 8 TC 450, CA — 12.7

Morse v Stedeford (Inspector of Taxes) (1934) 18 TC 457 — 7.33

Munby v Furlong (Inspector of Taxes) [1977] Ch 359, [1977] 2 All ER 953, [1977] 3 WLR 270, [1977] STC 232, 50 TC 491, [1977] TR 121, 141 JP 518, 121 Sol Jo 87, L (TC) 2643, CA — 7.46

Murgatroyd (Inspector of Taxes) v Evans-Jackson [1967] 1 All ER 881, [1967] 1 WLR 423, 43 TC 581, 45 ATC 419, [1966] TR 341, 110 Sol Jo 926 — 7.16

Murphy (Inspector of Taxes) v Australian Machinery and Investment Co Ltd (1948) 30 TC 244, 27 ATC 8, 41 R & IT 332, [1948] TR 1, L (TC) 1446, CA — 15.8

**N**

National Coal Board v IRC [1958] AC 104, [1957] 2 All ER 461, [1957] 3 WLR 61, 36 ATC 115, 50 R & IT 415, [1957] TR 119, 101 Sol Jo 502, sub nom IRC v National Coal Board 37 TC 264, HL — 7.41

New Zealand Shipping Co Ltd v Stephens (1907) 5 TC 553, 52 Sol Jo 113, 24 TLR 172, CA — 15.4

Norman v Golder (Inspector of Taxes) [1945] 1 All ER 352, 26 TC 293, 114 LJKB 108, 171 LT 369, CA — 7.16

Nuclear Electric plc v Bradley (Inspector of Taxes) [1996] 1 WLR 529, [1996] STC 405, 68 TC 670, [1996] 17 LS Gaz R 29, 140 Sol Jo LB 100, HL — 9.4

**O**

Odeon Associated Theatres Ltd v Jones (Inspector of Taxes) [1971] 2 All ER 407, [1971] 1 WLR 442, 48 TC 257, 49 ATC 315, [1970] TR 299, 115 Sol Jo 224, 218 Estates Gazette 1005; affd [1973] Ch 288, [1972] 1 All ER 681, [1972] 2 WLR 331, 48 TC 257, 50 ATC 398, [1971] TR 373, 115 Sol Jo 850, 221 Estates Gazette 1270, CA — 7.14, 7.19, 7.85

Ogilvie v Kitton (Surveyor of Taxes) (1908) 5 TC 338, 1908 SC 1003 — 12.22, 15.5

O'Grady (Inspector of Taxes) v Bullcroft Main Collieries Ltd (1932) 17 TC 93 — 7.18

Ostime (Inspector of Taxes) v Australian Mutual Provident Society [1959] Ch 427, [1958] 2 All ER 665, [1958] 3 WLR

| | |
|---|---|
| 354, 38 TC 492, 37 ATC 151, 51 R & IT 593, [1958] TR 185, 102 Sol Jo 599, CA; affd [1960] AC 459, [1959] 3 All ER 245, [1959] 3 WLR 410, 38 TC 492, 38 ATC 219, 52 R & IT 673, [1959] TR 211, 103 Sol Jo 811, HL | 15.125 |
| Ounsworth (Surveyor of Taxes) v Vickers Ltd [1915] 3 KB 267, 6 TC 671, 84 LJKB 2036, 113 LT 865, 31 TLR 530 | 7.18 |

**P**

| | |
|---|---|
| Padmore v IRC [1989] STC 493, 62 TC 352, [1989] 28 LS Gaz R 42, CA | 12.26, 15.125 |
| Parway Estates Ltd v IRC (1958) 45 TC 142, 37 ATC 164, [1958] TR 193, 171 Estates Gazette 833, CA | 9.13 |
| Patrick (Inspector of Taxes) v Broadstone Mills Ltd [1954] 1 All ER 163, [1954] 1 WLR 158, 35 TC 44, 32 ATC 464, 47 R & IT 41, [1953] TR 441, 98 Sol Jo 43, L (TC) 1675, CA | 7.14 |
| Pearce (Inspector of Taxes) v Woodall-Duckham Ltd [1978] 2 All ER 793, [1978] 1 WLR 822, [1978] STC 372, 51 TC 271, [1978] TR 87, 122 Sol Jo 299, L (TC) 2681, CA | 7.13 |
| Pobjoy Mint Ltd v Lane (Inspector of Taxes) [1985] STC 314, 58 TC 421, CA | 9.16 |
| Pommery and Greno v Apthorpe (Surveyor of Taxes) (1886) 2 TC 182, 56 LJQB 155, 35 WR 307, 56 LT 24, 3 TLR 242 | 15.7, App 1 |
| Pratt v Strick (Inspector of Taxes) (1932) 17 TC 459 | 12.7 |
| Prince v Mapp (Inspector of Taxes) [1970] 1 All ER 519, [1970] 2 WLR 260, 46 TC 169, 48 ATC 449, [1969] TR 443, 114 Sol Jo 110 | 7.16 |
| Procter & Gamble Ltd v Taylerson (Inspector of Taxes) [1990] STC 624, 63 TC 481, CA | 6.28 |
| Purchase (Inspector of Taxes) v Tesco Stores Ltd [1984] STC 304, 58 TC 46, [1984] LS Gaz R 1052 | 9.16 |

**R**

| | |
|---|---|
| R v Board of Inland Revenue, ex p MFK Underwriting Agencies Ltd [1990] 1 All ER 91, sub nom R v IRC, ex p MFK Underwriting Agents Ltd [1990] 1 WLR 1545, [1989] STC 873, 62 TC 607 | 2.47 |
| R v Hunt (1994) 16 Cr App Rep (S) 87, [1994] STC 819, 68 TC 132, [1994] Crim LR 747, CA | 17.16 |
| R v IRC, ex p Commerzbank AG: C-330/91 [1994] QB 219, [1993] 4 All ER 37, [1994] 2 WLR 128, [1993] ECR I-4017, [1993] 3 CMLR 457, [1993] STC 605, ECJ; affd 68 TC 252 | 15.130 |
| R v IRC, ex p MFK Underwriting Agencies Ltd. See R v Board of Inland Revenue, ex p MFK Underwriting Agencies Ltd | |
| RTZ Oil and Gas Ltd v Elliss (Inspector of Taxes) [1987] 1 WLR 1442, [1987] STC 512, 61 TC 132, 131 Sol Jo 1188, [1987] LS Gaz R 2196 | 7.21 |

*Table of Cases*

Ramsay (W T) Ltd v IRC [1982] AC 300, [1981] 1 All ER 865, [1981] 2 WLR 449, [1981] STC 174, 54 TC 101, [1982] TR 123, 125 Sol Jo 220, HL  11.30, 15.139

Regal (Hastings) Ltd v Gulliver (1944) 24 ATC 297  10.27

Reid's Brewery Co v Male (Surveyor of Taxes) [1891] 2 QB 1, 3 TC 279, 55 JP 216, 60 LJQB 340, 39 WR 459, 64 LT 294, 7 TLR 278  7.22

Revell (Surveyor of Taxes) v Edinburgh Life Insurance Co (1906) 5 TC 221  4.44

Rhodesia Rlys Ltd v Bechuanaland Protectorate Income Tax Collector [1933] AC 368, 102 LJPC 72, 77 Sol Jo 235, 149 LT 3, 49 TLR 376, [1933] All ER Rep Ext 1036, PC  7.19

Robroyston Brickworks Ltd v IRC [1976] STC 329, 51 TC 230, [1976] TR 151  9.5

Rolls-Royce Motors Ltd v Bamford (Inspector of Taxes) [1976] STC 162, 51 TC 319, [1976] TR 21  9.5, 9.11

Rose & Co (Wallpaper and Paints) Ltd v Campbell (Inspector of Taxes) [1968] 1 All ER 405, [1968] 1 WLR 346, 44 TC 500, 46 ATC 281, [1967] TR 259, 112 Sol Jo 174  7.47

**S**

Sainsbury (J) plc v O'Connor (Inspector of Taxes) [1991] 1 WLR 963, [1991] STC 318, 64 TC 208, 135 Sol Jo LB 46, CA  11.3, 11.4

St John's School v Ward (Inspector of Taxes) (1975) 49 TC 524, 53 ATC 279, [1975] RA 481, [1974] TR 273, L (TC) 2531, [1975] STC 7n, CA  7.34, 7.47

Salt v Chamberlain (Inspector of Taxes) [1979] STC 750, 53 TC 143, [1979] TR 203, 123 Sol Jo 490  15.22

San Paulo (Brazilian) Rly Co Ltd v Carter (Surveyor of Taxes) (1895) 3 TC 344, CA; affd [1896] AC 31, 3 TC 407, 60 JP 84, 452, 65 LJQB 161, 44 WR 336, 73 LT 538, 12 TLR 107, [1895-9] All ER Rep Ext 2078, HL  12.22, 15.5, App 1

Sargent (Inspector of Taxes) v Barnes [1978] 2 All ER 737, [1978] 1 WLR 823, [1978] STC 322, 52 TC 335, [1978] TR 93, 122 Sol Jo 299, L (TC) 2683  7.16

Savacentre Ltd v IRC [1995] STC 867, CA  6.28

Scammell (G) & Nephew Ltd v Rowles (Inspector of Taxes) [1939] 1 All ER 337, 22 TC 479, 83 Sol Jo 212, CA  7.20

Schofield (Inspector of Taxes) v R & H Hall Ltd [1975] STC 353, 49 TC 538, L (TC) 2536, CA  7.46

Scorer (Inspector of Taxes) v Olin Energy Systems Ltd [1985] AC 645, [1985] 2 All ER 375, [1985] 2 WLR 668, [1985] STC 218, 58 TC 592, 129 Sol Jo 248, [1985] LS Gaz R 1943, HL  17.50

Scottish and Universal Newspapers Ltd v Fisher (Inspector of Taxes) [1996] STC (SCD) 311  11.5

Self-assessed v Inspector of Taxes [1999] STC (SCD) 253  18.32, 17.28

Shepherd (Inspector of Taxes) v Law Land plc [1990] STC 795, 63 TC 692  11.5

*Table of Cases*

Shepherd (Inspector of Taxes) v Lyntress Ltd [1989] STC 617, 62 TC 495     11.37
Smidth (F L) & Co v Greenwood (Surveyor of Taxes) [1921] 3 KB 583, 8 TC 193, 37 TLR 949, CA; affd sub nom Greenwood (Surveyor of Taxes) v F L Smidth & Co [1922] 1 AC 417, 8 TC 193, 91 LJKB 349, 66 Sol Jo 349, 127 LT 68, 38 TLR 421, HL     App 1
Smith (Herbert) (a firm) v Honour (Inspector of Taxes) [1999] STC 173, [1999] 11 LS Gaz R 70, [1999] NLJR 250, [1999] EGCS 23, 143 Sol Jo LB 72     7.10, App 1, App 6
Southern (Inspector of Taxes) v Borax Consolidated Ltd [1941] 1 KB 111, [1940] 4 All ER 412, 23 TC 597, 19 ATC 435, 110 LJKB 705, 85 Sol Jo 94     7.33
Southern Rly of Peru Ltd v Owen (Inspector of Taxes) [1957] AC 334, [1956] 2 All ER 728, [1956] 3 WLR 389, 36 TC 602, 32 ATC 147, 49 R & IT 468, [1956] TR 197, 100 Sol Jo 527, L (TC) 1778, HL     7.11
Spiers v Mackinnon (Inspector of Taxes) (1929) 14 TC 386, 8 ATC 197     12.22, 15.5
Steeden v Carver (Inspector of Taxes) [1999] STC (SCD) 283   18.39, 2.8
Stekel v Ellice [1973] 1 All ER 465, [1973] 1 WLR 191, 117 Sol Jo 126     12.8
Stokes (Inspector of Taxes) v Costain Property Investments Ltd [1983] 2 All ER 681, [1983] 1 WLR 907, [1983] STC 405, 57 TC 688, 127 Sol Jo 446; affd [1984] 1 All ER 849, [1984] 1 WLR 763, [1984] STC 204, 57 TC 688, 128 Sol Jo 190, CA     7.34
Stone & Temple Ltd v Waters (Inspector of Taxes) [1995] STC 1n, 67 TC 145     7.21
Strick (Inspector of Taxes) v Regent Oil Co Ltd [1964] 3 All ER 23, [1964] 1 WLR 1166, 43 TC 1, 43 ATC 198, [1964] TR 207, 108 Sol Jo 500, CA; affd sub nom Regent Oil Co Ltd v Strick (Inspector of Taxes) [1966] AC 295, [1965] 3 All ER 174, [1965] 3 WLR 636, 43 TC 1, 44 ATC 264, [1965] TR 277, 109 Sol Jo 633, HL     7.21
Strong & Co of Romsey Ltd v Woodifield (Surveyor of Taxes) [1906] AC 448, 5 TC 215, 75 LJKB 864, [1904-7] All ER Rep 953, 50 Sol Jo 666, 95 LT 241, 22 TLR 754, HL     7.20
Sulley v A-G (1860) 2 TC 149, 24 JP 676, 5 H & N 711, 29 LJ Ex 464, 6 Jur NS 1018, 8 WR 472, 2 LT 439     15.8
Swedish Central Rly Co Ltd v Thompson (Inspector of Taxes) [1924] 2 KB 255, 9 TC 342, 93 LJKB 739, [1924] All ER Rep 710, 68 Sol Jo 575, 131 LT 516, CA; affd [1925] AC 495, 9 TC 342, 4 ATC 163, 94 LJKB 527, [1924] All ER Rep 710, 133 LT 97, 41 TLR 385, HL     15.4

**T**

Taylor v Chalklin (1945) 26 TC 463     12.6

*Table of Cases*

Texas Land and Mortgage Co Ltd v Holtham (Surveyor of
  Taxes) (1894) 3 TC 255, 63 LJQB 496, 1 Mans 429, 10 R
  398, 10 TLR 337, DC                                          7.33
Thomas v Ingram (Inspector of Taxes) [1979] STC 1, 52 TC
  428, [1978] TR 217                                           7.17
Thomas (Inspector of Taxes) v Reynolds [1987] STC 135, 59
  TC 502, [1987] LS Gaz R 742                                  7.47
Thomson and Balfour v Le Page (Inspector of Taxes) (1924) 8
  TC 541, 61 SLR 35, 1924 SC 27                                9.11
Threlfall v Jones (Inspector of Taxes) [1944] Ch 107, [1994] 2
  WLR 160, [1993] STC 537, 66 TC 77, [1993] 32 LS Gaz R
  40, CA                                                       7.7, App 1
Tilcon Ltd v Holland (Inspector of Taxes) [1981] STC 365, 54
  TC 464, [1981] TR 39, L (TC) 2821                            11.3
Tischler & Co v Apthorpe (Surveyor of Taxes) (1885) 2 TC 89,
  49 JP 372, 33 WR 548, 52 LT 814, 1 TLR 344                   15.7
Tod (Inspector of Taxes) v South Essex Motors (Basildon) Ltd
  [1988] STC 392, 60 TC 598                                    8.16
Todd (Inspector of Taxes) v Egyptian Delta Land and
  Investment Co Ltd [1928] 1 KB 152, 14 TC 119, 6 ATC 33,
  96 LJKB 554, 136 LT 786, 43 TLR 275, CA; revsd sub
  nom Egyptian Delta Land and Investment Co Ltd v Todd
  (Inspector of Taxes) [1929] AC 1, 14 TC 119, 7 ATC 355,
  98 LJKB 1, 72 Sol Jo 545, 140 LT 50, 44 TLR 747, HL          15.4
Turner (Thomas) (Leicester) Ltd v Rickman (Surveyor of
  Taxes) (1898) 4 TC 25                                        15.8

**U**

Union Corpn Ltd v IRC [1951] WN 448, 34 TC 207, 44 R & IT
  560, [1951] TR 271, 95 Sol Jo 484, [1951] 2 TLR 582; on
  appeal [1952] 1 All ER 646, 34 TC 207, 31 ATC 99, 45 R
  & IT 189, [1952] TR 69, 96 Sol Jo 150, [1952] 1 TLR 651,
  CA; affd [1953] AC 482, [1953] 1 All ER 729, [1953] 2
  WLR 615, 34 TC 207, 32 ATC 73, 46 R & IT 190, [1953]
  TR 61, 97 Sol Jo 206, HL                                     15.4
Union Texas International Corpn v Critchley (Inspector of Taxes)
  [1990] STC 305, 63 TC 244, [1990] 16 LS Gaz R 43, CA         15.129
Untelrab Ltd v McGregor (Inspector of Taxes) [1996] STC
  (SCD) 1                                                      15.4

**V**

Vale v Martin Mahony & Bros Ltd [1947] IR 30, 2 ITC 331         7.19
Vibroplant Ltd v Holland (Inspector of Taxes) [1982] 1 All ER
  792, [1982] STC 164, 54 TC 658, [1981] TR 485, 126 Sol Jo
  82, CA                                                       7.41

**W**

Waddington v O'Callaghan (Surveyor of Taxes) (1931) 16 TC
  187                                                          12.6
Wadsworth Morton Ltd v Jenkinson (Inspector of Taxes)
  [1966] 3 All ER 702, [1967] 1 WLR 79, 43 TC 479, 45
  ATC 347, [1966] TR 289                                       9.11

*Table of Cases*

Walker (Inspector of Taxes) v Centaur Clothes Group Ltd [1998] STC 814, [1998] 34 LS Gaz R 31, CA  6.25

Watson (Surveyor of Taxes) v Sandie and Hull [1898] 1 QB 326, 3 TC 611, 67 LJQB 319, 46 WR 202, 42 Sol Jo 151, 77 LT 528, 14 TLR 124  15.8

Werle & Co v Colquhoun (1888) 20 QBD 753, 2 TC 402, 52 JP 644, 57 LJQB 323, 36 WR 613, 58 LT 756, 4 TLR 396, CA  15.7, App 1

Westmoreland Investments Ltd v Macniven (Inspector of Taxes) [1998] STC 1131, sub nom McNiven (Inspector of Taxes) v Westmoreland Investments Ltd [1998] LS Gaz R 35, 142 Sol Jo LB 262, CA  10.29

Wilcock (Inspector of Taxes) v Pinto & Co [1924] 1 KB 304, 9 TC 111, 93 LJKB 149, 129 LT 534; affd [1925] 1 KB 30, 9 TC 111, 94 LJKB 101, 69 Sol Jo 178, 132 LT 74, CA  15.8, 15.27

Wild (Inspector of Taxes) v Madame Tussauds (1926) Ltd (1932) 17 TC 127  9.11

Wildbore v Luker (Inspector of Taxes) (1951) 33 TC 46, 30 ATC 269, 44 R & IT 591, [1951] TR 277, L (TC) 1578  7.17

Willingale (Inspector of Taxes) v International Commercial Bank Ltd [1978] AC 834, [1978] 1 All ER 754, [1978] 2 WLR 452, [1978] STC 75, 52 TC 242, [1978] TR 5, 122 Sol Jo 129, L (TC) 2672, HL  7.14

Willis (Inspector of Taxes) v Peeters Picture Frames Ltd [1983] STC 453, 56 TC 436, [1982] 12 NIJB, (N.I. CA)  9.16

Wilson (Thomas) (Keighley) Ltd v Emmerson (Inspector of Taxes) (1960) 39 TC 360, 39 ATC 318, 52 R & IT 740, [1960] TR 273, 176 Estates Gazette 1239  7.18

Wimpey (George) International Ltd v Rolfe (Inspector of Taxes) [1989] STC 609, 62 TC 597  15.122

Wimpy International Ltd v Warland (Inspector of Taxes) [1989] STC 273, 61 TC 51, CA  7.47

Wing Hung Lai v Bale (Inspector of Taxes) [1999] STC (SCD) 238  17.4

Wingate (James) & Co v Webber (Surveyor of Taxes) (1897) 3 TC 569, 34 SLR 699  15.8

Wisdom v Chamberlain (Inspector of Taxes) [1968] 2 All ER 714, [1968] 1 WLR 1230, 45 TC 92, 47 ATC 60, [1968] TR 49, 112 Sol Jo 314, L (TC) 2267; revsd [1969] 1 All ER 332, [1969] 1 WLR 275, 45 TC 92, 112 Sol Jo 946, L (TC) 2292, sub nom Chamberlain (Inspector of Taxes) v Wisdom 47 ATC 358, [1968] TR 345, CA  15.22

Wood (t/a A Wood & Co) v Provan (Inspector of Taxes) (1968) 44 TC 701, 47 ATC 166, [1968] TR 141, CA  7.34

Woods v R M Mallen (Engineering) Ltd (1969) 45 TC 619, 48 ATC 232, [1969] TR 233  7.43

Worthing Rugby Football Club Trustees v IRC [1987] 1 WLR 1057, [1987] STC 273, 60 TC 482, 131 Sol Jo 976, [1987] LS Gaz R 1415, CA  2.11

*Table of Cases*

Wynne-Jones (Inspector of Taxes) v Bedale Auction Ltd
    [1977] STC 50, 51 TC 426, [1976] TR 293, 120 Sol Jo 859,
    242 Estates Gazette 627, L (TC) 2619                    7.18

**Y**

Yarmouth v France (1887) 19 QBD 647, 57 LJQB 7, 36 WR
    281, 4 TLR 1                                                  7.46

Yates (Inspector of Taxes) v GCA International Ltd [1991]
    STC 157                                            15.122, 15.135

# Table of Statutes

**1890 Partnership Act**
s 1                                  12.6, 12.21

**1907 Limited Partnership Act**
                                        12.38
s 6                                          12.8

**1948 Income Tax Act**
s 11(2)                         *App. 3*

**1951 Finance Act**          14.3

**1967 Income Tax Act**
s 54A                            *App. 3*

**1970 Taxes Management Act**
                     1.16; 2.1; 14.46; 15.44;
                     *App. 1, App. 2, App. 4*
s 7(2)                                  5.4
8                                          16.1
  (1)                              *App. 1*
8A                                     16.1
10                                   2.3, 2.4
11                                       6.35
  (1)                                    2.9
  (1A)                               2.9
  (2)                                    2.6
  (3)                             2.9; 5.4
  (4), (5)                        2.8
  (8)                                    2.9
12AA                                 16.1
12AB                                 2.35
12B                16.1, 16.3, 16.11;
                                  *App. 1*
  (1)(b)                            16.1
  (3), (6)                      16.2
  (5)                         16.6; *App. 1*
  (5B)                                 16.5
19A                      4.44; *App. 1*
20                                     17.30
20A                              *App. 1*
20B, 20C, 20CC      17.16; *App. 1*
28(5)                            *App. 1*
28A(7A)(d)                   4.44

**1970 Taxes Management Act —** *contd*
s 28B(6A)(d)                  4.44
29                       9.21; 17.13
  (3)                 17.49, 17.62
30B                          14.73
33                             *App. 1*
41A                            9.8
42                               8.16
42A                12.31; 15.46
  (3)(b)                        15.85
43                     8.16; 14.77
43A                           4.42
44(2)                          19.19
46(2)                          17.49
46B                            19.14
46C                            19.16
46D                          19.17
50(1), (3), (4)               19.20
54                      17.49, 17.51
55                                5.7
  (1)                              19.21
  (3), (4)                      *App. 3*
59DA         5.25; 17.33; *App. 3*
  (1)                                 5.5
  (2)                            5.5, 5.6
  (4)                                 5.7
  (5)                            5.6, 5.7
  (6)                                 5.7
  (7)                            5.6, 5.7
59E(4)                        *App. 6*
60                                19.22
65(3)                          19.22
66, 69                          19.22
70(2)                          19.23
70A                            5.53
78                               15.11
  (2)                  15.28, 15.42
  (3)–(5)                       15.42
79–81                          15.11
82                               15.11
  (1)                 15.26, 15.42
83–85                          15.26
87                             *App. 6*
87A                     18.3; *App. 3*

*Table of Statutes*

| 1970 Taxes Management Act — contd | |
|---|---|
| s 87A(6), (7) | 18.6 |
| 90 | 18.4 |
| 91(1A), (1B) | 18.5 |
| 93(1)(b) | App. 1 |
| (2) | App. 1 |
| 95 | App. 1 |
| 95A | App. 1 |
| 98 | 18.38; App. 5 |
| 100 | 18.22, 18.32; 19.7 |
| (1) | 14.51; App. 1 |
| 100B | 18.22; 19.7 |
| (1) | App. 6 |
| 103(1) | 18.40 |
| 103A | 18.41 |
| 108 | 2.30 |
| (1) | 11.23; App. 3 |
| 118(1) | 15.13, 15.23 |
| (2) | 2.8; 18.39 |
| 246N | 5.4 |
| 246Q | 5.4 |
| Sch 1A | 4.09, 4.10, 4.12 |
| para 2(2) | 4.14 |
| (4) | 4.7, 4.13 |
| (5) | 4.13 |
| (6) | 4.14 |
| 2A | 4.15 |
| 5(1)–(3) | 17.43 |
| 6 | 17.44 |
| (2) | 17.46 |
| (3) | 17.46 |
| (3A) | 19.14 |
| (4) | 16.20; 17.46 |
| (5) | 17.47 |
| (9) | 19.3 |
| 6A | 17.44 |
| 7(2), (4) | 17.46 |
| (5) | 17.48 |
| 8(1) | 17.47 |
| 9(3) | 19.14 |
| para 2(1), (3) | 4.13 |
| para 3(1)(a) | 4.16 |
| (b) | 4.17 |
| (2) | 4.17 |
| (3) | 19.19 |
| (4) | 19.18 |
| (5), (6) | 19.19 |
| Sch 5, 6 | 4.18 |

| 1972 Finance Act | |
|---|---|
| s 127 | 14.71 |

| 1973 Income Tax Act | App. 3 |
|---|---|
| s 15(1) | App. 3 |

| 1973 Merchant Shipping Act | |
|---|---|
| s 86 | App. 3 |

| 1978 Industrial Incentive Act | |
|---|---|
| s 2(o) | App. 3 |

| 1979 Inland Revenue Act | App. 3 |
|---|---|

| 1982 Industrial Development Act | |
|---|---|
|  | 7.27 |

| 1982 Insurance Companies Act | |
|---|---|
| s 1 | App. 3 |

| 1984 Finance Act | 13.1 |
|---|---|

| 1985 Companies Act | 2.34 |
|---|---|
| s 14 | 10.10 |
| 221 | 16.13; App. 1 |
| 222 | 16.13 |
| 224(2) | App. 3 |
| 226 | 7.12 |
| 425 | 7.22 |

| 1986 Financial Service Act | 15.39 |
|---|---|

| 1986 Insolvency Act | 7.22; 10.10 |
|---|---|
| Pt I (ss 1–7) | App. 3 |
| s 411 | 16.13 |

| 1988 Companies Act | |
|---|---|
| s 246 | 2.34 |

| 1988 Finance Act | |
|---|---|
| s 36 | 5.27, 5.336 |
| 73(2) | 7.82 |
| 130 | 15.9; App. 1 |
| 131–132 | 15.9 |
| Sch 7 | 15.2 |
| Sch 18 | 2.33, 2.34, 2.35, 2.36; 3.2, 3.3 |
| para 8 | 5.4 |
| 34 | 6.41 |

## Table of Statutes

**1988 Income and Corporation Taxes Act**

| | |
|---|---|
| | 1.16; 4.39; App. 1, App. 3 |
| s 1A | 6.17 |
| 1B(1) | 6.17 |
| 6(1) | 7.2 |
| (2) | 4.5 |
| (a) | 7.2 |
| (b) | 7.2 |
| (4)(a) | 7.2 |
| 7(2) | 2.33; 3.3; 13.16, 13.29 |
| 8(1) | 2.2 |
| (2) | 2.2; 7.5; App. 4 |
| (3) | 2.2; 7.6 |
| 9 | 7.5, 7.12 |
| 11 | 7.2 |
| (1), (2) | 15.1 |
| (3) | 2.34; 3.3; 15.1 |
| (4) | 15.1 |
| 12 | 3.2; 9.20 |
| (2) | 2.7 |
| (3) | 2.7 |
| (c) | 5.43; 5.45; 7.21 |
| (d), (e) | 5.43 |
| (4) | 2.10 |
| 13 | 2.17; 5.8, 5.13; 7.5, 7.6 |
| (1)(a) | 7.66 |
| (2) | 2.33; App. 7 |
| (3) | 5.10 |
| (b) | 5.10 |
| (4) | 5.10 |
| (6) | 5.11 |
| (7) | App. 8 |
| 13A | 7.66 |
| 13AA | 7.6 |
| 14 | 6.1 |
| (2) | 6.5 |
| 15 | 7.72, 7.75, 7.80 |
| 15A | 7.88 |
| (1A) | 7.73 |
| 18(1) | App. 1 |
| (3) | App. 1 |
| (3A) | 10.26 |
| 19AC | 15.12 |
| 21(6), (7) | 7.103 |
| 21A | 7.82 |
| (1) | 7.81 |
| 21B | 7.82 |
| 25(3) | 7.83, 7.97 |

**1988 Income and Corporation Taxes Act — contd**

| | |
|---|---|
| s 25(4)–(8) | 7.83 |
| 26 | 7.105 |
| 27 | 7.108 |
| 29 | 7.75 |
| 30(4) | 18.37 |
| 31(3) | 7.97 |
| 34 | 7.26; 9.25 |
| (3) | 7.75 |
| (7A) | 7.76 |
| 35 | 7.26, 7.78; 9.25; App. 9 |
| 36 | 7.78; 9.25; 11.17 |
| 37 | 7.77 |
| 40(4) | 6.42 |
| 43A–43G | 7.71 |
| 53, 55 | 7.79 |
| 56 | 9.30; 15.109 |
| 59D(1) | 5.3 |
| (2) | 5.4 |
| (4) | 5.4 |
| 60 | 7.10 |
| 62(2)(b) | 12.19 |
| 63A | 12.19 |
| 65(3) | 12.24, 12.25 |
| 66 | 15.2 |
| 70(2) | 7.2 |
| 72 | 7.82 |
| Pt IV (ss 74–99) | 7.82 |
| s 74 | 10.4 |
| (1) | 7.81 |
| (a) | 7.15 |
| (d) | 7.18; App. 1, App. 6 |
| (e) | 7.20 |
| (f) | 7.21 |
| (h), (i) | 7.22 |
| (k) | 7.23 |
| (m), (o), (p) | 7.24 |
| (2) | 7.22 |
| 74A | 5.2 |
| 75 | 2.19; 7.67, 7.100; App. 7 |
| (1) | 13.62 |
| (3) | 14.16 |
| (4), (5) | 13.20 |
| 76 | 7.68 |
| 77 | 7.25 |
| (1), (4), (7) | 14.58 |
| 82A | 7.61 |
| 83 | 7.25 |

## Table of Statutes

**1988 Income and Corporation Taxes Act** — *contd*

| | |
|---|---|
| s 84A | 7.25 |
| 85 | 7.25 |
| 85A | 7.25 |
| 86 | 7.25 |
| 86A | 7.25 |
| 87 | 7.26; 18.21 |
| 87A | 18.15 |
| 88 | 7.26 |
| 89 | 7.22 |
| 90 | 7.26, 7.32 |
| 91 | 7.27 |
| 91A, 91B, 91C | 7.27 |
| 92, 93 | 7.27 |
| 94 | 7.22 |
| 96, 97 | 7.28 |
| 98 | 7.37, 7.79 |
| 99 | 7.37 |
| 103–106, 108 | 7.82 |
| 109A | 7.82 |
| 110(2) | 12.19 |
| 111 | 12.6, 12.33; 15.14; App. 1 App. 4 |
| (1) | 12.10 |
| (3) | 12.15 |
| (7) | 12.18 |
| (8) | 12.18, 12.32 |
| (9) | 12.19 |
| (10), (11) | 12.20 |
| (13) | 12.19 |
| 112 | 15.14 |
| 4 | 12.26 |
| 5 | 12.26, 12.27 |
| 113 | 15.14 |
| 114 | 12.17, 12.33, 12.40, 12.42; 15.14; App. 4 |
| (1) | 12.11, 12.14, 12.20 |
| (a), (b) | 12.12 |
| (c) | 12.14 |
| (2) | 12.12, 12.13 |
| 115 | 15.14 |
| (4) | 12.28, 12.30 |
| 116 | 9.30; 12.37 |
| (2) | 6.68 |
| 117 | 12.38 |
| 118 | 12.8 |
| 118A–118K | 10.26 |
| 119, 120 | 7.79 |

**1988 Income and Corporation Taxes Act** — *contd*

| | |
|---|---|
| s 121 | 19.16 |
| 130 | 7.66 |
| 137(2) | 6.24 |
| 150 | 15.109 |
| 154 | 6.11 |
| 170 | 11.28 |
| 172(4) | 12.40 |
| 198 | App. 1 |
| 208 | 6.5; 7.5 |
| 209 | 6.6; 10.9; 11.42; App. 1 |
| (1) | 6.12 |
| (2) | App. 1 |
| (c) | 6.5, 6.6 |
| (d) | 14.35 |
| (da) | 6.6; 14.35; App. 1 |
| (e) | 6.8 |
| (f) | 6.9, 6.10 |
| (4), (5), (7) | 6.9 |
| 210 | 6.5, 6.10 |
| (2), (3) | 6.10 |
| 211 | 6.6, 6.10 |
| 215 | 2.51 |
| (1)–(3) | App. 9 |
| 219 | 6.12 |
| 225 | App. 9 |
| 229 | 6.12 |
| 230 | 6.12 |
| 231 | 6.1 |
| 231A | 6.15, 6.17 |
| 234 | 16.3 |
| (1) | 18.35 |
| (5)–(9) | 6.5 |
| 238(1) | 6.13, 6.20 |
| 239 | 6.52 |
| (1) | 6.26 |
| (2) | 6.26; App. 4, App. 8 |
| (3) | 6.26, 6.27, 6.43 |
| (4) | 6.27; App. 8 |
| (6) | 6.27 |
| 240 | 6.47; App. 8 |
| (1) | 6.31, 6.34 |
| (1A) | 6.32, 6.34 |
| (1B) | 6.32 |
| (5) | 6.30 |
| (5A)–(5C) | 6.32 |
| (5D), (5E) | 6.31 |
| (6) | 6.29 |

## Table of Statutes

**1988 Income and Corporation Taxes Act** — *contd*

| | |
|---|---:|
| s 239(10) | 6.29, 6.30 |
| (11) | 6.30 |
| (7) | 6.42 |
| (8) | 6.42, 6.12 |
| 241(1), (2) | 6.20 |
| 242, 244 | 6.15 |
| 245 | 9.17 |
| (3A) | 6.47 |
| (6) | 6.47 |
| 245A | 6.70 |
| 245B | 6.48, 6.70; 9.19 |
| 246 | 6.22 |
| 246A | 6.43 |
| 246N, 246Q | 2.33; 3.42 |
| 246S, 246T | 6.45 |
| 247 | 2.19; 13.27 |
| (1) | 6.1 |
| (4) | 4.12; *App. 8* |
| 249(4)–(6) | 6.12 |
| 252 | 6.26 |
| 254 | 6.6, 6.10; *App. 1* |
| 255 | 6.14 |
| 338 | 6.12 |
| (1) | 13.62 |
| 339 | 6.12; 7.32 |
| (6), (8) | 6.12 |
| 342(5) | 2.53 |
| 343 | 9.10, 9.13, 9.24; 12.14, 13.27 |
| (1) | 9.9 |
| (2) | 9.9; 11.28 |
| (4A) | 9.10 |
| (5) | 9.13 |
| (7)–(10) | 9.10 |
| 344(1)–(4) | 9.12 |
| (5), (6) | 9.10 |
| 347A(2)(a) | 7.32 |
| 348 | 15.113 |
| 349 | 15.113 |
| (1)(a) | 7.23 |
| (b) | 7.23, 7.24; 15.111 |
| (2) | *App. 1* |
| (a) | 10.26 |
| (b) | 12.46; *App. 4* |
| (c) | *App. 1* |
| (3)(a)–(c) | 10.26 |
| 350 | 10.27; 15.113 |

**1988 Income and Corporation Taxes Act** — *contd*

| | |
|---|---:|
| s 352 | 10.27; 16.4 |
| 369 | 7.24 |
| 379A | 7.71, 7.107, 7.109 |
| Pt X (ss 380–413) | 14.16; 18.22 |
| s 392A | 9.26 |
| (1) | 13.62 |
| (3) | 7.100; 9.27 |
| (5) | 9.27 |
| (6)(a) | 9.29 |
| (7) | 9.29 |
| 392B | 9.28 |
| 393 | 9.18 |
| (1) | 4.10, 4.26; 9.2, 9.7, 9.24; 18.6 |
| (7) | 9.1 |
| (9) | 9.7 |
| 393A | 9.18, *App. 8* |
| (1) | 9.24; 13.62 |
| (b) | 9.6 |
| (1A) | 9.2 |
| (3), (4) | 9.2 |
| (7) | 9.7 |
| (8) | 9.7 |
| (9) | 9.3 |
| (a), (b) | 9.1 |
| (10) | 4.4; 9.2 |
| (2A), (2B) | 9.7 |
| 395(1), (3), (4) | 9.24 |
| 396 | 9.25 |
| 397 | 9.3 |
| (3) | 9.23 |
| (4) | 9.22 |
| 398 | 9.30 |
| 399, 400 | 9.30 |
| 401 | 7.31, 7.82; 9.31 |
| 402 | 6.12 |
| (1) | 11.2; *App. 3* |
| (2) | 11.2 |
| (3)–(5) | 11.11 |
| (6) | 11.10, 11.12 |
| 403(1)(a) | 11.6 |
| (b) | 9.26; 11.6 |
| (2), (3) | 11.6 |
| (4) | 11.6 |
| 403A(3)–(10) | 11.8 |
| 403B(1) | 11.8 |

*Table of Statutes*

## 1988 Income and Corporation Taxes Act — *contd*

| | |
|---|---|
| s 403c | 11.13 |
| 403za | 11.6 |
| 403zb | 11.6, 11.7 |
| 403zc | 11.6 |
| 403ze | 11.7 |
| 404 | 11.6 |
| 405 | 11.14 |
| 406(1)–(4) | 11.14 |
| (5)–(8) | 11.15 |
| 407 | 11.9 |
| 410(1) | 11.5 |
| 411a | 11.5 |
| 413 | *App. 1* |
| (2a) | 11.8 |
| (3)(a) | 11.3 |
| (4), (5) | 11.3 |
| (7) | 11.4, 11.12 |
| (8)–(10) | 11.12 |
| 414 | 7.66; *App. 8* |
| 415 | 7.66 |
| 416 | 5.43; 7.66; 13.14, 13.24 |
| (1) | 13.34 |
| 417 | 7.66; 12.45; *App. 4* |
| (1) | *App. 8* |
| (3)(a), (b) | *App. 8* |
| 418 | 6.6; 7.66 |
| (3) | 6.11 |
| (4) | 6.11 |
| (5) | 6.11, 6.12 |
| (6) | 6.11, 6.12 |
| (7), (8) | 6.11 |
| 419 | 2.12, 2.19, 2.24, 2.27; 3.2, 3.5; 5.2, 5.9; 6.11, 6.50; 7.66; 19.18; *App. 1, App. 6, App. 8* |
| (1) | 2.2, 2.33; 5.49; 18.23; |
| (2)(a) | *App. 8* |
| (4) | 18.7, 18.12, 18.24 |
| (4a) | 2.26; 18.12, 18.14, 18.24, 18.29; *App. 8* |
| (4b) | 2.26; *App. 8* |
| 419a | 18.26 |
| 420 | 7.66; 19.18 |
| (1), (2) | *App. 8* |
| 421, 422 | 7.66 |
| 431 | 14.27 |
| 432a | *App. 8* |

## 1988 Income and Corporation Taxes Act — *contd*

| | |
|---|---|
| s 434(3a), (3b) | 5.10 |
| 441b(2a) | *App. 8* |
| 459 | 19.16 |
| 467 | 19.16 |
| 468(1) | 6.12; 7.4 |
| 468l | 14.16; *App. 8* |
| (7) | 2.19 |
| 468q | 6.50 |
| 477a(3b) | 6.12 |
| 486(1), (10)–(12) | 6.12 |
| 492 | 14.44 |
| (1) | 14.56 |
| (8) | 11.2, 11.6 |
| 494a | 11.6 |
| 503 | 7.71; 12.20 |
| 504 | 7.71 |
| 505(1)(e) | *App. 8* |
| (3) | *App. 8* |
| 506 | *App. 8* |
| 520 | 4.43 |
| (4)(a)(ii) | 7.37 |
| 530(2)(a)(ii) | 7.37 |
| 536, 537 | 15.111 |
| 538 | 4.43 |
| 559 | 5.4, 5.6, 5.7, 5.9, 5.57, 5.64 |
| 560–565 | 5.57 |
| 566 | 5.57; 16.4 |
| 562–572 | 5.57 |
| 573–576 | 9.32 |
| 577 | 7.28, 7.29, 7.82 |
| 577a | 7.29, 7.82 |
| 578 | 7.29 |
| 579 | 7.29, 7.32, 7.82 |
| 589a, 589b | 7.29, 7.82 |
| 590, 591 | *App. 9* |
| 592(4) | *App. 1* |
| 617 | 15.108 |
| 686 | *App. 1* |
| 703 | 2.51; 6.51; 7.3; *App. 1, App. 9* |
| 704 | 6.10, 6.51, 6.72; *App. 1* |
| 704d, 704e | 6.51 |
| 705 | 6.51; *App. 1* |
| 706 | *App. 1* |
| 707 | 2.51; 6.51; *App. 1, App. 9* |
| 708–709 | *App. 1* |

## Table of Statutes

**1988 Income and Corporation Taxes Act** — *contd*

| | |
|---|---|
| s 739 | 13.69 |
| 747 | 2.12, 2.19, 2.28; 5.9; 13.12, 13.16, 13.51, 13.58; 15.116; *App. 1*, *App. 6*, *App. 7* |
| (1) | 2.3; 13.4, 13.5 |
| (4)(a) | 2.2, 2.33; 3.2, 5.49; 13.48, 13.66; 15.125; 18.23; 19.15 |
| (b) | 13.69 |
| (6) | 13.26 |
| 748(1), (a) | 13.5, 13.35 |
| (b) | 13.5, 13.38 |
| (c) | 13.5, 13.41 |
| (d) | 13.5, 13.43 |
| (e) | 13.5, 13.45; *App. 3* |
| (3) | 13.47 |
| 749 | 2.28; 3.6; 13.8, 13.51 |
| (1) | 13.9 |
| (5) | 13.9 |
| 749A | 13.11, 13.13 |
| 749B(1), (2) | 13.24 |
| (5)–(8) | 13.25 |
| 750(1) | 13.17 |
| (2), (3) | 13.16 |
| 751 | 13.18, 13.25 |
| (1) | 13.21 |
| (2)–(5) | 13.22 |
| (6) | 13.29 |
| (7) | 13.22 |
| 752(2)–(4) | 13.32 |
| 752A | 13.31 |
| 752B | 13.33 |
| 754 | 13.60 |
| (1) | 13.48 |
| (3A), (3B) | 13.62 |
| (5) | 13.63, 13.64, 13.65, 13.66 |
| 754A | 13.57 |
| (6)–(8) | 13.67 |
| 754B | 13.58 |
| 755A | 13.70 |
| 755B, 755C | 13.70 |
| 755D | 13.15, 13.16 |
| 756(3) | 13.14 |
| 765, 765A | *App. 1* |
| 767A | *App. 1*, *App. 2* |

**1988 Income and Corporation Taxes Act** — *contd*

| | |
|---|---|
| s 767AA | 5.33; *App. 1*, *App. 2* |
| 768(1)(a), (b) | 9.15 |
| (4) | 9.16 |
| (9) | 9.21 |
| 768A | 6.47 |
| (1) | 9.18 |
| 768B | 6.47, 9.18, 9.19 |
| 768C | 9.18 |
| 769 | 9.17 |
| 770 | 2.45; 14.3, 14.4, 14.39, 14.44; *App. 1* |
| 770A | *App. 4*, *App. 5*, *App. 6* |
| 774(4)(a) | 7.3 |
| 775 | 7.3 |
| 776 | 7.3; 11.30; *App. 9* |
| (11) | 2.51 |
| 777(13) | 7.4 |
| 788 | 2.33; 12.23; 15.125; 16.4 |
| (3), (c), (ii) | *App. 1* |
| 790 | 2.33; 12.23; 15.128, 15.134 |
| (1) | 15.122 |
| (2) | 7.3; 15.122 |
| (3) | 15.122 |
| (4) | 15.122, 15.124 |
| (5) | 15.131 |
| (a), (b) | 15.122 |
| (c)(i)–(iii) | 15.123 |
| (6) | 15.123 |
| (7) | 15.123, 15.131 |
| (8)–(10) | 15.123 |
| 792(2) | 15.123 |
| 793A | 15.128 |
| 794 | 15.134 |
| 795A | 15.128 |
| 797 | 15.135, 15.137 |
| (4) | 15.138 |
| 797A | 15.140 |
| 798 | 15.134 |
| 798A, 798B | 15.134 |
| 799(1)–(4) | 15.141 |
| (6) | 15.142 |
| 800 | 15.142 |
| 801 | 15.142 |
| 801A | 15.139, 15.142 |
| 801B | 15.142 |
| 802 | 15.123 |

*Table of Statutes*

**1988 Income and Corporation Taxes Act** — *contd*

| | |
|---|---|
| s 803 | 15.134 |
| 804A | 15.134 |
| 805 | 15.143 |
| 806(1)(b) | 15.144 |
| (2)–(6) | 15.144 |
| 806A, 806B | 15.145 |
| 807 | *App. 1* |
| 807A | 15.146 |
| 808A | 15.146 |
| 808 | 9.32 |
| 810 | 15.147 |
| 811 | 14.32; 15.143, 15.152 |
| (1) | 14.27 |
| 812 | 15.148 |
| 813–815 | 15.148 |
| 815A | 15.149 |
| 816 | 15.150 |
| 824 | 5.53 |
| 825 | 5.51; 18.9 |
| (4A) | 6.28 |
| 826 | 5.53; *App. 2, App. 3* |
| (4) | 18.12 |
| (8A) | 3.25; 5.51, 5.50 |
| 826A | *App. 3* |
| 830 | 19.15 |
| 832 | 2.12; 11.28; *App. 4* |
| (1) | 7.3, 7.37; 11.12; 13.7 |
| (2) | 7.4; 13.7 |
| 834(4) | 11.9 |
| 837 | 7.106 |
| 837A, 837B | 7.34, 7.61 |
| 838 | 6.56; 11.12 |
| (1) | 6.9, 6.30 |
| (a) | 5.44; *App. 3* |
| (b) | 11.28, 11.3 |
| (2)–(10) | 11.3 |
| 839 | 13.34, 15.23 |
| (8) | 7.4 |
| 840 | 14.11 |
| 842 | |
| (1) | *App. 8* |
| Sch 3 | 15.12 |
| para 41, 42 | 6.23 |
| Sch 5 | |
| para 10 | 7.75 |
| Sch 9 | *App. 9* |
| Sch 13 | |
| para 1 | 6.22, 6.24 |

**1988 Income and Corporation Taxes Act** — *contd*

| | |
|---|---|
| Sch 13, para 2, 3 | 6.22 |
| 4 | 6.23 |
| Sch 13A | 6.23, 6.31, 6.32, 6.34 |
| para 1, 2 | 6.34 |
| 3, 4 | 6.35 |
| 5, 6 | 6.35 |
| 7 | 6.33, 6.36 |
| 8 | 6.36 |
| 9(5) | 6.37 |
| 10 | 6.34, 6.37 |
| 11 | 6.38 |
| 12 | 6.39 |
| 13 | 6.40 |
| 14 | 6.41 |
| 15 | 6.41 |
| Sch 15 | 7.79; *App. 9* |
| para 1(a), (b) | 7.75 |
| 4(a), (b) | 7.75 |
| Sch 16 | 10.27 |
| Sch 18 | 11.4; *App. 8* |
| Sch 19 | |
| para 5, 6 | 4.45 |
| 23 | 6.24 |
| 23A | |
| Sch 19AB | 2.31; 5.46; *App. 3, App. 6, App. 8* |
| para 2(2) | 6.61 |
| Sch 20 | 13.61; *App. 8* |
| Sch 24 | 13.18, 13.26, 13.27, 13.28, *App. 1* |
| Sch 25 | 13.36, 13.38, 13.39, 13.41, 13.42; *App. 1* |
| Sch 26 | 13.63, 13.64; *App. 1* |
| Sch 28A | 9.19 |
| Sch 28AA | 13.27; 14.5, 14.6, 14.7, 14.10, 14.12, 14.15, 14.18, 14.30, 14.32, 14.33, 14.38, 14.44, 14.45, 14.52, 14.56, 14.59, 14.68, 14.72; *App. 1, App. 4, App. 5, App. 6* |

**1988 Malta International Business Activities Act** *App. 3*

**1989 Finance Act**

| | |
|---|---|
| s 42 | 7.82 |
| 43 | 7.31, 7.82; *App. 1, App. 6* |

## Table of Statutes

**1989 Finance Act** — *contd*
| | |
|---|---|
| s 44 | 7.31 |
| 46(1), (2) | 7.82 |
| 67(2) | 7.30 |
| 76 | 7.82 |
| 86 | 14.27 |
| 88 | 14.27 |
| (4) | 5.10; *App. 3* |
| 88A | 14.27 |
| 102 | 5.26; 11.17; *App. 3, App. 8* |
| (2) | 5.4 |
| s 112, 113 | 7.82 |
| 115 | 15.129 |
| 178 | *App. 3, App. 6* |

**1989 International Banking Centre Regulatory Act**
| | |
|---|---|
| s 25 | *App. 3* |

**1989 Malta Freeports Act**
| | |
|---|---|
| s 18 | *App. 3* |

**1990 Capital Allowance Act**
| | |
|---|---|
| | 2.1; **4.39**, 7.63; 14.33 |
| s 1 | 7.40 |
| 3 | 7.42 |
| 4 | 7.43 |
| 4A | 7.43 |
| 5 | 7.43 |
| 6 | 7.40 |
| 7 | 7.42 |
| 8 | 7.43 |
| 9 | 7.43 |
| (1), (2) | 7.92 |
| 10 | 7.43 |
| 10A, 10B | 7.43 |
| 11–13 | 7.43 |
| 15ZA | 7.92 |
| 17A | 7.40 |
| 18 | 7.41 |
| 19 | 7.42 |
| 20 | 7.43 |
| 22 | 7.37, 7.45 |
| 22A | 7.37 |
| 24 | 7.44 |
| 25 | 7.45 |
| 26 | 7.48 |
| (3) | 7.38 |

**1990 Capital Allowance Act** — *contd*
| | |
|---|---|
| s 28 | 7.6 |
| 28A | 7.48 |
| 29 | 7.6, 7.48, 7.91, 7.94 |
| 30 | 7.49 |
| 33 | 7.49 |
| 33F | 7.49 |
| 34–36 | 7.50 |
| 37, 38 | 7.51 |
| 38A, 38B | 7.52 |
| 38D, 38E | 7.52 |
| 38F, 38G | 7.52 |
| 39, 40 | 7.53 |
| 41 | 7.53 |
| 42 | 7.12 |
| 42A | 2.5 |
| 44 | 7.13 |
| 51–59 | 7.53 |
| 59C | 7.53 |
| 60 | 7.54 |
| 60A | 7.54 |
| (2A) | 7.54 |
| 61 | 7.54, 7.94 |
| 67 | 7.54 |
| 64 | 7.43 |
| 75, 76 | 7.38 |
| 76A | 7.39 |
| 76B | 7.39 |
| 79, 79A | 7.37 |
| 80 | 7.34 |
| 82A | 7.39 |
| 92 | 7.91 |
| 144 | 7.33 |
| 145 | 7.35; 9.1; *App. 8* |
| 147, 149 | 7.35 |
| 150 | 7.34 |
| 152 | 7.36 |
| 152B | 7.36; 9.10 |
| 153 | 7.34 |
| 157, 158 | 7.36 |
| 159A | 7.36 |
| 67A | 7.54 |
| 68 | 7.55 |
| 69 | 7.54 |
| 70 | 7.54 |
| 84, 85 | 7.45, 7.57 |
| 86, 97 | 7.57 |
| 98–121 | 7.58 |

## Table of Statutes

**1990 Capital Allowance Act —** *contd*

| | |
|---|---|
| s 122–130 | 7.59 |
| 131 | 7.59 |
| 134, 135 | 7.60 |
| 136, 137, 139 | 7.61 |
| Sch A1 | 7.65 |
| Sch AA1 | 7.62 |

**1990 Finance Act**

| | |
|---|---|
| Sch 5 | 6.12 |

**1990 Offshore Companies Act (Island of Labaun)** App. 3

**1992 Taxation of Chargeable Gains Act** 4.39; 10.23; 14.33; 19.15

| | |
|---|---|
| s 2(1) | 12.34 |
| 10 | 7.2; 12.34; 15.12 |
| 16 | 8.15 |
| (2A) | 8.16 |
| 19 | 3.7 |
| 25 | 11.36 |
| 35 | 11.30 |
| 41 | 11.33 |
| 49 | 8.3 |
| 59 | App. 4 |
| 99(1) | 7.4 |
| 100, 101 | 8.20 |
| 101A | 8.20 |
| 114 | 12.2, 12.4 |
| 115 | 10.3; 12.2, 12.4 |
| 121 | 2.36 |
| 135 | 2.51; 11.28 |
| 136 | 2.51 |
| 137, 138 | 2.51; App. 9 |
| 139 | 8.20; 11.36; App. 9 |
| 140A, 140B | 9.10; App. 9 |
| 140D | App. 9 |
| 152 | 7.110; 8.6 |
| (3) | 8.12 |
| 153A | 8.6, 8.7 |
| (3)–(5) | 8.8 |
| 161 | 11.33 |
| 170 | 11.40, 11.43 |
| 171 | 9.18; 11.28, 11.38; 15.136 |
| 171A | 11.31 |

**1992 Taxation of Chargeable Gains Act —** *contd*

| | |
|---|---|
| s 172 | 11.32 |
| 173 | 11.33 |
| 175 | 11.34 |
| 176 | 11.35 |
| 179 | 11.39, 11.40 |
| 181 | 11.41 |
| 185–187 | 15.9 |
| 189–190 | 11.42 |
| 241(3) | 7.110 |
| 246(1) | 8.14 |
| 247A(1), (2) | 8.13 |
| 263 | 2.36 |
| 276 | 19.15 |
| 277 | 15.124 |
| 278 | 15.143, 15.151 |
| 280 | 8.5 |
| 283 | 5.53 |
| 288(1) | 7.4 |
| Sch 7A | App. 8 |
| para 3 | 11.37 |
| 6–12 | 11.37 |
| Sch 7AA | |
| para 2–4 | 11.38 |
| 5–7 | 11.38 |
| Sch 8 | 7.111 |
| para 3(4) | 8.18 |
| (5) | 8.19 |

**1993 Finance Act** 4.39; App. 1, App. 4, App.8

| | |
|---|---|
| s 30–32 | 12.47 |
| Pt II (ss 45–47) | 7.88 |
| s 92 | 10.48 |
| 93, 94 | 10.48, 10.53 |
| 95 | 10.48 |
| (5) | 10.53 |
| 125 | 10.9, 10.30, 10.51; 14.17 |
| (1)–(3) | 10.34 |
| (4)(b) | 10.34 |
| 126 | 10.9, 10.30, 10.36, 10.51; 14.17 |
| (1) | App. 3 |
| 127 | 10.9, 10.30, 10.42, 10.51; 14.18 |
| 128 | 10.9, 10.31; 14.18; App. 4 |
| (10A), (10B) | 10.31 |

*Table of Statutes*

**1993 Finance Act** — *contd*
| | |
|---|---|
| s 129 | 10.9, 10.30, 10.32; 14.18; *App. 4* |
| (7) | 10.4 |
| 130 | 10.9, 10.30; 14.18; *App. 4* |
| 134 | 10.9, 10.30, 10.38; 14.18 |
| 135 | 10.9, 10.30, 10.40; 12.47; 14.18; *App. 4* |
| 136 | 10.9, 10.30; 12.47; 14.18; *App. 4* |
| (1), (4)–(10) | 10.41 |
| (11)–(15) | 10.42 |
| 136A | 10.42 |
| 137 | 10.9, 10.30, 10.43; 12.47; 14.18; *App. 4* |
| 138 | 10.9, 10.30; 12.47; 14.18; *App. 4* |
| 139 | 10.9, 10.30, 10.45; 12.47; 14.18 |
| 140 | 10.9, 10.30, 10.45; 14.18; *App. 4* |
| 141 | 10.9, 10.30, 10.45, 10.46; 14.18; *App. 4* |
| 143 | 10.9, 10.30, 10.45, 10.49; 14.18; *App. 4* |
| 144, 145 | 10.9, 10.30, 10.45, 10.49; 14.18 |
| 146–148 | 10.9, 10.30. 10.45, 10.50; 14.18 |
| 149 | 10.9, 10.30, 10.45; 14.18 |
| (4), (5) | 10.51 |
| 150, 151 | 10.52; 14.18 |
| 152 | 10.9, 10.30 |
| (2A) | 10.30 |
| (3), (4) | 10.30 |
| 153 | 10.9, 10.30; 12.41 |
| (1)(a) | 10.46 |
| (2)(a) | 10.46 |
| (4) | 10.33 |
| 154–157 | 10.9, 10.30 |
| 158 | 10.9, 10.30, 10.37 |
| 159 | 10.9, 10.30; *App. 4* |
| 160 | 10.9, 10.30, 10.40; *App. 4* |
| 161 | 10.9, 10.30, 10.40 |
| 162–164 | 10.9, 10.30 |
| 165 | 10.9, 10.30 |

**1993 Finance Act** — *contd*
| | |
|---|---|
| s 166 | 10.9, 10.30, 10.44 |
| 167–170 | 10.9, 10.30 |
| 171–174 | 15.41 |
| Sch 15 | |
| para 3 | 10.38 |
| 4 | 10.39 |

**1994 Finance Act**    1.2, 1.16; 4.39; *App.1*, *App. 4*
| | |
|---|---|
| Pt IV (ss 75–230) | 7.88 |
| s 139 | 15.109 |
| 147 | 10.4, 10.54; *App. 3* |
| 148–150 | 10.4, 10.54; *App. 8* |
| 150A | 10.4 |
| 151–164 | 10.4, 10.54 |
| 165–168 | 10.4, 10.54; 12.47; *App. 4* |
| 169–171 | 10.4, 10.54 |
| 172 | *App. 4* |
| 173–177 | 10.4, 10.54 |
| 199 | *App. 3* |
| (3) | 2.1; 6.41; 16.4 |
| 215(2) | 12.4 |
| 219–230 | 15.41 |
| 249 | 13.9; 15.3 |

**1995 Finance Act**    1.10; *App. 1*
| | |
|---|---|
| s 12 | 12.35 |
| 39(2) | 7.103 |
| (4)–(6) | 7.108 |
| 40 | 12.31; 15.46; *App. 1* |
| (1) | 15.17 |
| 87 | 6.7; 7.108 |
| 113(2) | 8.16 |
| 117(2) | *App. 1* |
| 124, 125 | *App. 1* |
| 126 | 15.11, 15.112; *App. 1* |
| (1) | 12.34 |
| (2) | 15.12 |
| (3), (4) | 15.13 |
| (5), (6) | 12.32; 15.14 |
| (7) | 12.1, 12.32; 15.14 |
| (8) | 15.13 |
| 127 | 15.11, 15.109; *App. 1* |
| (1)(a) | 15.24 |
| (b) | 15.25 |
| (c) | 15.29 |
| (d) | 15.41 |

*Table of Statutes*

| 1995 Finance Act — *contd* | |
|---|---|
| s 127(2) | 15.25 |
| (3) | 15.29, 15.31 |
| (4), (5) | 15.36 |
| (6) | 15.38 |
| (8) | 15.37 |
| (9) | 15.39 |
| (12), (13) | 15.30, 15.39 |
| (14) | 15.26, 15.38, 15.39 |
| (15) | 15.23, 15.39 |
| (16) | 15.41 |
| (17) | 15.23, 15.39 |
| (18) | 15.16, 15.31 |
| (19) | 15.23 |
| 128 | 15.11; *App. 1* |
| (1)–(3) | 15.109 |
| (4) | 15.110 |
| 129 | 15.11, 15.109; *App. 1* |
| Sch 6 | |
| para 1 | 7.75 |
| 5 | 7.107 |
| 36 | 7.110 |
| 37 | 7.111 |
| Sch 23 | 15.16, 15.17, 15.112; *App. 1* |
| para 1, 2 | 15.15 |
| 4(3) | 15.17 |

| 1996 Finance Act | 7.88; 8.1, 8.2, 8.3, 8.5; 12.42, 12.43; *App. 1, App.3* |
|---|---|
| s 80 | 10.1; 12.47 |
| 81 | 12.47 |
| (1)–(4) | 10.2 |
| 82 | 10.1, 10.33; 12.47 |
| (1)–(7) | 10.4 |
| 83 | 7.89; 10.1, 10.33; 12.47, 14.16 |
| (2) | 10.5; *App. 4* |
| (b) | 11.6 |
| (3)–(8) | 10.5 |
| 84 | 10.8; 12.47 |
| (1)(a), (b) | 10.8 |
| (2)(a), (b) | 10.8 |
| (3), (4) | 10.8 |
| (5) | 10.12 |
| (6) | 10.8 |
| (7) | 10.9 |
| 85 | 10.10; 12.47 |

| 1996 Finance Act — *contd* | |
|---|---|
| s 83(1)(a) | 10.17 |
| (b) | 10.18 |
| (2) | 10.17 |
| (3) | 10.17 |
| (c) | 10.10 |
| (4)–(6) | 10.18 |
| 86 | 10.1; 12.47 |
| (1)–(4) | 10.18 |
| (5), (6) | 10.19 |
| 87 | 10.1; 12.47 |
| (3) | 12.45 |
| (a)–(c) | 10.20 |
| (5)–(8) | 10.20 |
| 88 | 10.1, 10.20; 12.47 |
| 89 | 10.1, 10.21; 12.47 |
| 90 | 10.1, 10.21; 12.47 |
| 91 | 10.1, 10.22; 12.47; *App. 4* |
| 92 | 10.1, 10.33; 12.47 |
| (1)–(3) | 10.23 |
| 93–95 | 10.1, 10.23; 12.47 |
| 96 | 10.3; 12.47 |
| 97 | 10.1; 12.47 |
| 98, 99 | 10.24; 12.47 |
| 100 | 10.24, 10.25; 12.47 |
| (2), (4) | *App. 1* |
| 101–105 | 10.24; 12.47 |
| 106–109 | 10.24 |
| 125(4) | 10.33 |
| 130 | 10.32 |
| 134 | 4.36; 17.69 |
| 140 | 8.20 |
| 141 | 8.6 |
| (3) | 8.12 |
| (4) | 8.14 |
| (6) | 8.13 |
| 142(4) | 8.18 |
| (5) | 8.19 |
| 153 | 10.33 |
| Sch 8 | 10.6 |
| para 3, 4 | 10.6 |
| 15 | 10.1 |
| Sch 9 | 10.10 |
| para 1 | 10.9 |
| 5 | *App. 4* |
| 10 | 10.11; *App. 4* |
| 12 | 10.14; *App. 4* |
| 14–16 | 10.15 |
| Sch 11 | 10.12 |

## Table of Statutes

**1996 Finance Act** — *contd*
Sch 13
   para (1)–(5)     10.13
        (9)     *App. 1*
Sch 19
   para 4, 5     4.44
Sch 20     4.36, 4.39; 17.69
   para 65     8.5
Sch 25
   para 1     6.31
       (3)     6.32
      2, 4     6.31

**1997 Finance Act**
Sch 12     7.31; *App.1*

**1997 Finance (No 2) Act**     6.46
s 19     6.15
20     6.15
21–23     6.15
24–29     6.15
30     6.16
   (4)     6.18
32, 33     6.19
34     6.21
35     6.18
36     6.43
47     *App. 1*
Sch 4     6.21
     6     6.43
   para 22     6.45

**1997 Taxes Consolidated Act**
    *App. 3*

**1998 Finance Act**     8.1; 13.2; 14.3; *App. 1*
s 1, 6, 11     2.5
22A     7.45
30     *App. 3*
31     6.3; 7.49
   (3)     6.20
32     6.3, 6.52; 7.49; *App. 3*
36     *App. 1*
   (4)     11.17; *App. 2*
38(1)     7.70, 7.72
   (2)     7.71, 7.72
   (3)     7.70, 7.72

**1998 Finance Act** — *contd*
s 39     7.105
42     12.15
   (1)     12.25
44     12.15; *App. 1*
66–75     11.16
76     6.16; 11.16
77     11.16
107     *App. 1*
108     14.5
110     14.73
   (4)     14.72
111     14.73
117(1), (5)     2.1
122     17.28
134     17.66
419(4a)     2.4
Sch 3     2.4
    7     6.49
    12     6.26, 6.27
    (4)     6.33, 6.51
    14     6.20
    15, 17     6.48
    19     6.50
    21     6.26
    23     6.14
    24     6.50
    27     6.50
    (1)–(3)     17.27
    31     17.16
    32     6.51
    42     6.33; 7.71
    43     6.51
    44     6.51
    (4)     6.33
Sch 4     7.81
Sch 5     7.70, 7.71, 7.73, 7.88
   para 4     7.82
      6     7.84
      7     7.105
     15(5)     7.76
     16     7.78
     18     7.77
     33–46     7.112
     47     7.92, 7.112
     48–50     7.92, 7.112
     51–61     7.94, 7.112
     66     7.96
     68     7.97

## Table of Statutes

**1998 Finance Act** — *contd*

| Sch 5, para 73 | 7.96, 7.97 |
| 75 | 7.97 |
| Sch 6 | |
| para 2 | 7.13 |
| 3 | 12.15 |
| 6 | 12.15 |
| (3) | 12.16 |
| Sch 8 | App. 6 |
| Sch 12 | |
| para 3 | App. 3 |
| Sch 17 | 7.78; 13.68 |
| Sch 18 | 1.2; 2.1, 2.2, 2.3, 2.4, 2.5, 2.6, 2.7, 2.8, 2.9, 2.10, 2.38, 2.39; 7.63; 11.21, 11.25; 16.2, 16.3, 16.6, 16.16; 18.22, 18.26; App.2, App. 3 |
| para 2(2), (3) | 18.23 |
| 7 | 3.2 |
| 8 | 3.3 |
| 9, 10 | 4.5 |
| 15 | 3.8 |
| 16 | 3.11 |
| 17 | 18.25 |
| 20 | 14.51 |
| 21 | 16.11; 18.35; App. 1 |
| (1)(a) | 16.12 |
| (3)–(5) | 16.16 |
| 22 | App. 1 |
| 23 | 14.51; 16.11; 19.7; App. 1 |
| (1) | 18.35 |
| 24 | 17.3 |
| 25 | 17.3, 17.5; App. 1 |
| 26 | 17.3 |
| 27 | 17.3; App. 1 |
| (1), (3) | 17.29 |
| (5) | 17.31 |
| 28 | 17.3; 19.10 |
| (1)–(6) | 17.32 |
| 29 | 17.3; 18.32 |
| (2)(a), (b) | 18.32 |
| 30 | 3.17; 17.3; 19.2, 19.14, 19.16 |
| (1), (2) | 17.34, 17.36 |
| (3) | 17.36 |
| 31 | 17.3, 17.37; 19.14 |

**1998 Finance Act** — *contd*

| Sch 18, para 32 | 17.3, 17.38; 19.14 |
| 33 | 17.3, 17.41; 19.9, 19.14 |
| 34 | 3.17; 17.3, 17.36, 17.39; 19.3 |
| (2) | 19.14, 19.16 |
| 35 | 17.3, 17.35 |
| 36 | 3.13 |
| 37 | 3.14 |
| 39 | 3.15 |
| 40 | 3.16 |
| 41 | 3.18; 17.55 |
| 42 | 17.55 |
| 43 | 17.56 |
| 44 | 17.57 |
| (1) | 17.64 |
| (2) | 17.62 |
| 45 | 17.72 |
| 46 | 17.73 |
| (1) | 3.19 |
| 48 | 3.18; 19.5, 19.6 |
| 49 | 19.6 |
| 50 | 3.22; 4.34 |
| (1)–(3) | 5.47, 5.48 |
| 51(1)–(3) | 3.23; 4.35 |
| (4) | 3.24 |
| (5)–(6) | 3.24; 5.49 |
| 52 | 3.20, 3.25 |
| (4)–(6) | 5.50 |
| 53 | 3.21, 3.25; 5.52 |
| 54, 55 | 4.4 |
| 56 | 4.8; 5.48 |
| 57 | 4.09; 17.43 |
| 58 | 4.10; 17.43 |
| 59 | 17.43 |
| 61 | 4.41 |
| (1) | 4.40 |
| 62 | 4.41 |
| 63 | 4.42 |
| 65 | 4.41 |
| 66, 67 | 4.22 |
| 69 | 4.24 |
| 70 | 4.22 |
| 71 | 4.25 |

*Table of Statutes*

| 1998 Finance Act — *contd* | | 2000 Finance Act — *contd* | |
|---|---|---|---|
| Sch 18, para 72 | 4.26 | s 40, 41 | 6.12 |
| 73 | 4.22 | 59 | 5.59 |
| 74 | 4.27 | 62 | 7.32 |
| 75 | 4.28 | 85 | 6.8 |
| (8) | 19.5 | 96 | 11.3 |
| 76 | 4.29 | 101 | 11.43 |
| 77 | 4.30, 4.31 | 104, 105 | 10.48 |
| 78–82 | 4.32 | Sch 8 | 7.25 |
| 82(1), (2) | 7.64 | Sch 12 | |
| 83 | 4.33; 19.5 | para 1 | 5.61 |
| (1)–(6) | 7.65 | 2-6 | 5.62 |
| 89 | 18.30 | 7 | 5.63 |
| 93, 94 | 19.13 | 8 | 5.64 |
| Sch 19 | 1.2 | 11 | 5.65 |
| Sch 21 | 14.46 | 13 | 5.66 |
| Sch 22 | 16.3 | 17 | 5.67 |
| **1988 Late Payment of Commercial Debts (Interest) Act** | 10.27 | Sch 15, 16 | 7.32 |
| | | Sch 20 | 7.25 |
| | | Sch 21 | 7.25 |
| | | Sch 27 | 11.3 |
| **1999 Finance Act** | 1.16; 2.50; 13.31; *App. 4* | Sch 29 | |
| | | para 3 | 11.36 |
| s 76(1)(c) | 14.57 | 4 | 11.40 |
| (2) | 14.55 | 6 | 11.36 |
| (5) | 14.58 | 8 | 11.38 |
| (7) | 14.56 | 9 | 11.42 |
| (8) | 14.58 | 11 | 11.33 |
| 77(2) | 14.62 | 46 | 11.43 |
| (3) | 14.60 | Sch 30 | |
| (5), (8) | 14.61 | para 8 | 15.141 |
| 78 | 14.59 | 9 | 15.142 |
| 80 | 18.38 | 10 | 15.139 |
| 85, 86 | *App. 5, App. 6* | 18 | 15.147 |
| 87 | *App. 1, App. 5* | 19 | 15.143 |
| 88 | 13.36 | 21 | 15.152 |
| | | Sch 31 | |
| **2000 Finance Act** | 13.2, 13.14, 15.134 | para 2, 4 | 13.16 |

xlvii

*Chapter 1*

# Introduction

## Background and timing

**1.1** Following the introduction of Pay and File for companies with effect from October 1993, the priority under self-assessment was to put in place a workable system for individuals and trustees. The complexity of doing this meant that self-assessment had to be deferred for corporation tax. But with the passing of the first full year for individuals and trustees (1996/97) and the final 31 January 1998 filing date, the Revenue felt confident to proceed with the implementation of self-assessment for companies (CTSA).

**1.2** Certain parts of the original provisions introduced by *FA 1994* were in fact applicable to companies as well as individuals. However, the corporate provisions were reviewed and to a large extent superseded by specific legislation for companies contained in *FA 1998 18* and *19 Sch*. The new provisions took effect for companies with accounting periods ending on or after 1 July 1999. Accordingly, with the most usual accounting date for companies being 31 December, the commencement date for such companies was 1 January 1999. CTSA has general application to all companies chargeable to corporation tax, whether or not UK resident. Non-resident companies chargeable to income tax (e.g. those in receipt of non-trading UK source income) are subject to the income tax self-assessment rules.

## Comparison with pay and file

**1.3** Many aspects of Pay and File are retained, notably the filing date for returns and the payment date (nine months after the end of the corporation tax period), other than for larger companies. The penalty provisions are likewise not substantially altered.

**1.4** The fundamental change is the obligation imposed on a company to make its own self-assessment of its corporation tax liability as part of its tax return. This extends to any liability under the controlled foreign companies or transfer pricing legislation, where previously a tax liability only arose if a Revenue direction was made. It also includes any liability under the loans to participators provisions. A related major

**1.5** *Introduction*

change is the unfettered ability of the Revenue to enquire into any tax return within twelve months of the filing date, and to obtain access to all company records.

## Tax return and self-assessment

**1.5** There is a redesigned corporation tax return, form CT600, the details of which are considered in Chapter 2. There is a summary which needs to be completed by all companies, and alternative short or long form calculations of the tax at Sections 3 and 4. Claims for relief generally have to be included in the return itself, with specific sections in the return allocated to capital allowances, losses and overpayment and repayment claims. Whereas under the old system the Revenue generally had to be satisfied as to the validity of such claims, this has largely disappeared under self-assessment with the discretion transferred to the company.

**1.6** There are then a series of supplementary pages to be completed where relevant, notably relating to loans by close companies to participators, group and consortium relief and controlled foreign companies. The filing of the return and the making of the self-assessment will create the actual charge to tax. After the return has been filed a company may amend it within twelve months from the filing date if mistakes have been made.

## Revenue determinations and assessments

**1.7** Whilst compulsory self-assessment is fundamental to the system, provision is made for the Revenue to impose a tax liability when a company either fails to make a self-assessment or is otherwise in default. A Revenue determination can be made where no return has been filed which takes effect as a self-assessment for collection purposes, but which is to be superseded by an actual self-assessment by the company. The Revenue may also make certain determinations and assessments in relation to enquiries or their powers of discovery. In such cases the company generally has a right of appeal.

## Payment of corporation tax

**1.8** For small and medium companies the payment provisions have not been changed, corporation tax being payable nine months after the end of the accounting period. However, companies which are categorised as large (generally with profits over £1.5 m), have to make payments by quarterly instalments. This may in part be regarded as linked to the termination after 5 April 1999 of the obligation to account for ACT on the payment of dividends.

## Record keeping

**1.9** Companies are required to establish and keep detailed records relating to transactions carried out to support the self-assessment for at least six years after the end of the accounting period.

## Schedule A income

**1.10** The new Schedule A rules introduced by *FA 1995* for individuals and trustees did not initially apply to companies, but these rules have now been introduced for companies with effect from 1 April 1998.

## Revenue powers of enquiry and discovery

**1.11** The transfer of the responsibility to a company to make its own self-assessment is matched by extensive powers of enquiry given to the Revenue, with unlimited access to company information and records. There is generally a twelve month time limit from the filing date for an enquiry to be opened. If the Revenue consider there has been a loss of tax, then on conclusion of the enquiry the company is to amend its tax return accordingly. If the company fails to do so the Revenue can make the amendment with the company having a right of appeal to the Commissioners.

**1.12** Once the twelve month enquiry period has elapsed, the tax liability for the period in question becomes final, save that in the event of fraud or neglect, or where the Revenue 'discover' an error or mistake, the tax liability for that period may be re-opened.

## Controlled foreign companies

**1.13** The controlled foreign companies ('CFCs') legislation, introduced in 1984, was designed to prevent UK tax avoidance by channelling income to subsidiaries resident in countries with low tax rates. This legislation has been reviewed for CTSA, with all CFCs having to be listed in the corporation tax return and any profits chargeable under the CFC rules having to be self self-assessed, rather than by a direction from the Revenue.

## Transfer pricing

**1.14** The objective of the transfer pricing legislation is to ensure that transactions between companies under common control are taxed on an arm's length basis, particularly in respect of multi-nationals engaged in cross-border transactions. Previously the legislation only applied to a transaction if the Board made a direction. Under CTSA, in cases where

**1.15** *Introduction*

the provisions are in point, a company is obliged to apply relevant arm's length principles in making its tax return and self-assessing, with the obligation to retain the appropriate records to support the treatment adopted in the return.

## Appeals

**1.15** The existing procedure for appeals to the General or Special Commissioners is preserved for cases where assessments are made by the Revenue, or where the Revenue seek to amend the company's self-assessment.

## References

**1.16** The *Finance Acts 1994–2000* make numerous amendments to the existing legislation, particularly in the *Taxes Management Act 1970* and the *Taxes Act 1988*. References are to the legislation as amended unless otherwise specified. Where it would be helpful for clarity, reference is made to 'amended' or 'substituted' sections, meaning as amended or substituted by the provisions of the *Finance Acts 1994–2000* or to 'original enactment' referring to the legislation prior to those Finance Acts.

*Chapter 2*

# Notices and Returns

## Legislative background

**2.1** The administrative framework for CTSA has conveniently been brought together in *FA 1998 18 Sch*, which replaces the provisions in *TMA 1970*, parts II and IV, relating to returns, assessment and claims so far as they relate to corporation tax, and part X relating to penalties; *TA 1988 17A Sch* relating to group relief claims and *CAA 1990 A1 Sch* covering claims for corporation tax capital allowances. [*FA 1998 s 117(1)*]. The provisions are treated by *FA 1998 s 117(2)* as if they were part of *TMA 1970* and are supplemented by various minor amendments to that Act, in *FA 1998 19 Sch*; *FA 1998 s 117(2)* and *(3)*. These new provisions are written in the style adopted for the Tax Law rewrite, generally known as 'new speak'. They apply from the CTSA appointed day under *FA 1994 s 199(3)*, which is for accounting periods ending on or after 1 July 1999. [*FA 1998 s 117(4)* and *(5)* and *SI 1998 No. 3173, Finance Act 1994, Section 199, (Appointed Day) Order 1998*].

**2.2** CTSA applies to corporation tax within *TA 1988 s 8*, which charges corporation tax on all the profits of a company, wherever arising, including profits accruing for its benefit under any trust or arising under any partnership. [*TA 1988 s 8(1)* and *(2)*]. Corporation tax is chargeable by reference to accounting periods, which are apportioned where necessary between the financial years in which the accounting period falls. [*TA 1988 s 8(3)*]. CTSA extends to any amount assessable or chargeable as if it were corporation tax, i.e. a loan or advance made to a participator by a close company under *TA 1988 s 419(1)* and profits of a controlled foreign company (CFC) taxable under *TA 1988 s 747(4)(a)*; *FA 1998 18 Sch 1*.

## Notification of chargeability

**2.3** Where a company is chargeable to tax for an accounting period, and has not received a notice requiring a company tax return, it must give notice to the Revenue that it is chargeable to tax within twelve months from the end of the accounting period. [*FA 1998 18 Sch 2(1)* and *(2)*]. It is understood that, as most companies are professionally represented and submit substitute corporation tax returns under Pay and File, the Revenue will only issue full corporation tax returns to new companies or those that have previously submitted Revenue Pay and File returns, with other

## 2.4 Notices and Returns

companies being sent a notice requiring a CTSA return. Chargeability for this purpose includes chargeability to tax on loans to close company participators, which were previously notifiable under *TMA 1970 s 10*. [*Earlspring Properties Ltd v Guest (1995) 67 TC 259, Joint v Bracken Developments Ltd [1994] STC 300*]. However CFCs are brought into the disclosure net for the first time, as previously the CFC provisions only applied where the Board of Inland Revenue made a direction under *TA 1988 s 747(1)*.

**2.4** The penalty for failure to give notice of chargeability will not exceed the tax payable for the accounting period which remains unpaid twelve months after the end of the period [*FA 1998 18 Sch 2(3)*] excluding any relief due in respect of the repayment of an earlier close company loan to a participator, under *TA 1988 s 419(4A); FA 1998 18 Sch 2 (4)*. It is, in practice, unlikely that a company will have made a payment on account without notifying liability to the Revenue. These provisions replace *TMA 1970 s 10* for CTSA, the only change of substance being the extension to CFCs.

## Notice to deliver a return and period covered

**2.5** The Inland Revenue will normally issue a notice, on form CT603, requiring a company to deliver a company tax return [*FA 1998 18 Sch 3 (1)*], which must specify the period to which the notice relates. [*FA 1998 18 Sch 5 (1)*]. A return is required for each accounting period of the company ending in the specified period. [*FA 1998 18 Sch 5(2)*]. Where an accounting period began during the specified period, for example because a dormant company has begun to trade or acquires a source of income, a return is required for the specified period up to the date the new accounting period began. The income from the new source would be included in the next return covering the new accounting period. [*FA 1998 18 Sch 5 (3)*]. A company outside the charge to corporation tax for the whole of the period may be required to complete a company tax return for that period. This would apply to a non-resident company not carrying on a trade in the UK through a branch or agency within *TA 1998 s 11*. Such a company is liable to income tax under *TA 1988 ss 1* and *6*, for example on income from property in the UK taxable under *TA 1988 s 42A*, under the *Taxation of Income From Land (Non Residents) Regulations, SI 1995 No. 2902; FA 1998 18 Sch 5(4)*.

**2.6** If none of these provisions apply, for example because the specified period is less than twelve months so that there is no accounting period beginning or ending in the period, it may be ignored. [*FA 1998 18 Sch 5(5)*]. These provisions effectively re-enact *TMA 170 s 11(2)* for CTSA. If the notice relates to a period beginning before 1 July 1999, where an accounting period ends before that date, then the return is not under CTSA but Pay and File. [*FA 1998 18 Sch 6*].

*Notices and Returns* **2.7**

*Example 1*

A Ltd was incorporated on 1 October 2000 and began trading on 1 April 2001. It planned to prepare its first accounts to 31 March 2002. It is likely that a notice to deliver a return would be issued by the Revenue for the year to 30 September 2001. As no accounting period ends in the year to 30 September 2001 but one commenced on 1 April 2001, A Ltd would have to render a nil return for that part of the specified period to 31 March 2001. The new accounting period commencing 1 April 2001 would then be the subject of a return required by the next notice issued.

## Filing date

**2.7** The deadline for filing a company tax return is the latest of the following dates:

(a) Twelve months from the end of the period for which the return is made, which will normally be the first anniversary of the end of the accounting period. [*FA 1998 18 Sch 14 (1A)*]. Provided that the company's relevant period of account is not longer than 18 months, the return is required twelve months from the end of that period, even though two returns are required, one for 12 months from the previous accounting date and the second for the short period to the new accounting date. [*FA 1998 18 Sch 14 (1)(d)*].

An accounting period begins for the purposes of corporation tax when the company first comes within the charge to corporation tax, for example by becoming resident in the UK or acquiring a source of income. An accounting period ends for corporation tax on the first occurrence of any of the following:

  (i) The expiration of twelve months from the beginning of the accounting period;

  (ii) An accounting date of the company, or the end of a period for which it does not make up accounts;

  (iii) The company beginning or ceasing to trade where all trades carried on by it cease;

  (iv) The company beginning or ceasing to be resident in the UK; or

  (v) The company ceasing to be within the charge to corporation tax. [*TA 1988 s 12 (2) and (3)*].

(b) If the company's relevant period of account is longer than 18 months, the filing date is 30 months from the beginning of the period.

## 2.8 Notices and Returns

*Example 2*

B Ltd prepares accounts for a 27 month period ending on 31 March 2002. It will have to prepare returns for three accounting periods, the calendar years 2000 and 2001 and the three months to 31 March 2002, all of which would be due for filing on 30 June 2002. [*FA 1998 18 Sch 14 (1)(c)*].

(c)   In other cases, the return must be filed within three months from the date of the notice. [*FA 1998 18 Sch 14 (1) (d)*].

*Example 3*

For an accounting period ended 31 December 2002 the return would be required by 31 December 2003, provided that the notice to deliver the return was served by 1 October 2003. If the notice was served after that date the return would have to be submitted within three months.

**2.8**   The references to period of account means the period for which the company makes up accounts. [*FA 1998 18 Sch 14(2)*]. These provisions effectively re-enact for CTSA, *TMA 1970 s 11(4)* and *(5)*. There are penalties for late filing (see 18.25–18.28) which in the income tax context were considered in *Steeden v Carver (1999) STC (SCD) 283*. The concept of reasonable excuse for corporation tax arises from *TMA 1970 s 118(2)*, see 18.39.

## Form of return

**2.9**   *FA 1998 18 Sch 3(1)* enables the Revenue to prescribe in the notice requiring a company to deliver a tax return, such information, accounts, statements and reports, relevant to its tax liability, or otherwise relevant to the application of the Corporation Tax Acts to the company, as may reasonably be required. Different information may be required from different types of company. The return must be delivered to the Revenue by the filing date, and include a declaration by the person making the return that it is, to the best of his knowledge, correct and complete. [*FA 1998 18 Sch 3 (2) to (4)*]. These provisions merely re-enact for CTSA, *TMA 1970 s 11(1), (1A), (3)* and *(8)*. The company tax return is only validly delivered if it contains all the information, accounts, statements and reports required. [*FA 1998 18 Sch 4*]. CTSA, unlike income tax self-assessment, requires the company to submit its accounts and computations. As a consequence, the electronic lodgement system is not available for company tax returns, as it cannot handle information, such as accounts, in a non-standard format.

**2.10**   A company tax return has to include a self-assessment of the tax payable by the company for the period, on the basis of the information contained in the return, taking into account any reliefs or allowances claimed either in the return or required to be given in relation to the accounting period. [*FA 1998 18 Sch 7(1)*]. The self-assessment therefore includes tax payable on close company loans to participators and CFC liabilities, if any. A company tax return is regarded as a return of an accounting period of up to twelve months, even though it may in fact not be an accounting period as defined by *TA 1988 s 12*. This could apply for example, where a company started to trade part way through the accounting period which would be the commencement of a new accounting period, under *TA 1988 s 12(4)*. [*FA 1998 18 Sch 7(2)*].

**2.11** The company tax return also applies to members' clubs and voluntary organisations and other associations chargeable to corporation tax whether or not incorporated. This arises from the definition of company in *TA 1988 s 832, Conservative and Unionist Central Office v Burrell [1982] STC 317, Blackpool Marton Rotary Club v Martin [1988] STC 823, Worthing Rugby Football Club Trustees v IRC [1987] STC 273*. A general guide to corporation tax self-assessment is due to be published by the Revenue in the autumn of 2000.

## CT600

**2.12** The basic company tax return consists of a core return form CT600 and one or more supplementary pages; CT600A, loans to participators by close companies, covering liabilities under *TA 1988 s 419*; CT600B, CFCs, required where there is a charge to tax under *TA 1988 s 747*; CT600C, group and consortium, where group or consortium relief is being claimed; CT600D, for insurance companies, corporate members of Lloyd's and Friendly Societies carrying on long-term insurance business; CT600E for charities; CT600F tonnage tax for shipping companies; and CT600G for companies participating in the corporate venturing scheme (Appendix 8), Tax Bulletin, Issue 42, August 1999, p 682 (Appendix 1), Inland Revenue Press Release, 30 June 1999 (Appendix 6).

**2.13** The core return, in broad terms follows, so far as practical, the format of the Pay and File return CT200, although there are many differences in detail. Section 1, the company information summary and declaration, asks for the company name, company registration number, tax reference, as shown on the notice requesting the return, CT603, the address if different from the notice, and the period covered by the return. There is a request for confirmation if the return contains a repayment claim for the period or contains estimated provisional figures, or if more than one return is being filed at the same time. Confirmation is also required that accounts are attached for the period to which the return relates or for a different period, or reasons why accounts are not attached if appropriate. As section 1 is a summary, it requests details of the relevant pages of form CT600 enclosed and the supplementary pages, if any. There is then a warning against giving false information and a declaration that the form is correct and complete, signed by the company Secretary or Treasurer.

## 2.14 Notices and Returns

**2.14** The return must be submitted, together with company accounts and, where prepared, directors' and auditors' reports. The return also requests payment of any outstanding tax, due nine months after the end of the accounting period (see Chapter 5), whereas the return is not normally due until twelve months after the end of the period. In many cases therefore, payment will already have been made before the return is submitted. The return contains a reminder that interest will be charged on tax paid late and penalties may be due if it is late or incorrect, see Chapter 18.

**2.15** Section 1 of the core return describes the supplementary pages and gives the order line telephone number, which is 0845 300 6555, and fax number, 0845 300 6777. There is no helpline for corporation tax. The tax changes introduced by *FA 2000* with effect from 1 April 2000 mean that a new form CT600(2000) will be required, which will be available from September 2000 (CT600 Budget Insert, April 2000). The changes take account of gift aid donations being paid gross and with no minimum limit, and shares gifted to charities, which are treated as charges on income paid for return purposes. Other changes reflect research and development expenditure and first year allowances for small and medium-sized enterprises, the corporate venturing scheme, tonnage tax for shipping companies and starting rate as well as small companies' rate and their corresponding marginal reliefs. Section 2 requires the total turnover from a trade or profession, except in the case of banks, building societies, insurance companies, unit trusts and other financial concerns. Turnover is regarded as the best single indicator of the size of the company, and is required for audit purposes rather than being directly relevant to the tax calculations.

**2.16** Section 3 is a short calculation which may be used in simpler cases where, for example, the company has no overseas income or intra-group income and is not an investment company, and where any entry is less than £10 m. The Revenue emphasise that they do not want any entry in a box where there was no source applicable to that box, and 0s should be used where there is a source but no taxable income. For example, the first box in the section (box 3) asks for the trading and professional profits, from which may be deducted box 4 (trading losses brought forward), up to the amount of the profits in box 3, to arrive at the net trading and professional profits. This would be 0 where entirely covered by losses brought forward.

**2.17** Section 3 thereafter requests details of profits and gains from non-trading loan relationships, other annuities, annual payments and discounts paid gross, income received under deduction of tax, income from UK land and buildings and other annual profits and gains. It then requires details of chargeable gains less losses to give net chargeable gains, and a sub total of profits before other deductions and reliefs. From this may be deducted current trading losses or those brought back from a future period to give profits before charges. Charges are then deducted to give profits chargeable to corporation tax. If tax is chargeable at the small companies rate under *TA 1988 s 13*, details are required of franked investment income and foreign income dividends received in the return period, and the number of associated companies in each of the financial years covered by the return.

**2.18** This then enables the corporation tax chargeable to be calculated for each of the financial years to arrive at the corporation tax chargeable for the accounting period, before reliefs and deductions given in terms of tax. These could include marginal starting rate and small companies relief and ACT, or shadow ACT relief, to leave the tax chargeable, from which may be deducted a credit for income tax already suffered on income liable to corporation tax. This will either result in income tax repayable to the company, if this is in excess of the corporation tax liability, or corporation tax payable. Credit may also be claimed in respect of tax deducted under the construction industry scheme for sub-contractors, and for any tax already paid and not repaid, to arrive at the tax outstanding or overpaid. It is also necessary to indicate if it is believed that the company should have paid tax by instalments or if a group accounting arrangement applies for the period. [See Chapter 5].

**2.19** Section 4 is the detailed calculation which broadly follows the short calculation, but has additional provision for exchange fluctuations in the accounting period; overseas income within Sch D, case V; intra group income under an election to pay gross, under *TA 1988 s 247(4)*; tonnage tax profits; losses brought forward against certain investment income and non-trade losses on loan relationships, exchange fluctuations and certain financial instruments brought forward from previous years. It also provides for corporate venturing loss relief; losses on unquoted shares; management expenses under *TA 1988 s 75*; interest distributions under *TA 1988 s 468L(7)* in relation to distributions of authorised unit trusts, Schedule A losses; capital allowances for investment companies in management of the business; current non-trade losses for the accounting period from loan relationships, exchange fluctuations or certain financial instruments; and non-trade capital allowances and group relief. The boxes for corporation tax chargeable allow for different rates of tax for different types of income as well as different financial years. Provision is also made for the deduction of Corporate Venturing Scheme investment relief and double taxation relief. To the net corporation tax liability there must be added tax due on close company loans to participators under *TA 1988 s 419*, and in respect of CFCs under *TA 1988 s 747*. Credit may also be taken for ACT on foreign income dividends paid before 6 April 1999 when the FID arrangement ceased.

**2.20** Section 5 covers claims for Research and Development tax credit and deductions under the Construction Industry Scheme, capital allowances and details of Research and Development enhanced expenditure and balancing charges arising. The section requires totals of Research and Development expenditure and expenditure on which first year allowances are claimed, qualifying expenditure on long-life assets and

## 2.21 Notices and Returns

qualifying expenditure on other assets. This is as well as charges and allowances included in calculation of trading profits or losses, i.e. balancing charges and capital allowances in respect of cars, machinery and plant, long-life assets, other machinery and plant, industrial buildings and structures including hotels and enterprise zone allowances, and other charges and allowances such as agricultural building allowances, mineral extraction allowances, scientific research allowances and capital allowances on patents. Charges and allowances not included in the calculation of trading profit or loss, including balancing charges, must also be shown. As there is a requirement to enclose explanations and calculations of any figures which are estimated or not immediately recognisable from the companies accounts, it is apparent that detailed computations will still be required.

**2.21** Section 6 covers losses, surpluses and other amounts such as non-trade capital allowances, excess charges, excess management expenses and excess interest distributions of authorised unit trusts. The trading losses arising and the maximum available for surrender as group relief must be shown, as must Schedule D Case V losses, non-trade deficits on loan relationships, Schedule A and overseas property business losses, Sch D Case VI losses and capital losses.

**2.22** Section 7 deals with overpayments and repayment claims, and asks for the repayment of corporation tax, income tax, tax credits or advance corporation tax, and the bank details of the person to whom the repayment is to be made and how the repayment is to be dealt with. This section also includes repayment claims by clubs and unincorporated associations. An authorised signature is required to claim repayment.

**2.23** Section 8 is an optional section requesting details of directors' remuneration charged in the accounts supporting the return form. As it has no immediate relevance to the company's tax liability it is not a statutory requirement to complete, but it is intended to assist the Revenue and cut down unnecessary enquiries. The section asks for the company name, remuneration claimed as a deduction in the accounts in total, the period covered by the accounts and when the accounts were laid before the company in general meeting or approved by the directors. The analysis is by name of director, national insurance number, salary and bonus, and fees or commission, together with any reconciliation necessary, and names and national insurance numbers of directors commencing or ceasing in the period.

**Supplementary pages**

*Loans to participators by close companies*

**2.24** CT600A covers loans to participators by close companies falling within *TA 1988 s 419* and asks for the company's name, tax reference and period covered. Part 1 then requests details of such loans made during the return period and outstanding at the end of the period. A box must be ticked where the loan made during the period was released or written off in the period. Details are also required of the participator or his associate to whom a loan or advance has been made, together with the total of such loans, and the tax chargeable. This becomes a flat 25 per cent of the amount of the loan or advance in respect of a loan or advance made or written off on or after 6 April 1999, as a result of amendments to *TA 1988 s 419* by *FA 1998 3 Sch 24*.

**2.25** Part 2 requires details of loans made during the return period which have been repaid, released or written off after the end of the period, but within nine months of the end of the period. The information requested is the name of each participator or associate, the amount repaid, the amount released or written off and the relevant date together with the totals repaid, released or written off and the relief due, being 25 per cent of this amount. Part 2 may therefore include loans or advances already included in part 1, as being made in the year and outstanding at the year end, but repaid within nine months.

**2.26** Part 3 will not normally apply because it is only relevant where loans were made during the return period which have been repaid, released or written off more than nine months after the end of the period and relief is due at the time of submission of the return. As relief arising from the repayment of the loan or advance cannot be given until the due date of payment of the tax for the accounting period in which the return was made, *TA 1988 s 419(4A)* and *(4B)*, Section 3 would only be relevant if the return was filed late, in which case, interest and penalties would be due. In these exceptional circumstances the supplementary pages request details of the participator or associate, together with the amount repaid, released or written off and the appropriate date and the total for such payments and the relief calculated at 25 per cent of such total.

**2.27** Part 4 requests the total of loans outstanding at the end of the return period. Part 5 contains the box for the tax payable under *TA 1988 s 419*, being that in respect of loans made during the return period less relief for loans repaid, released or written off, for which relief is due at the time of the return. In most cases, where a loan is repaid more than nine months after the end of the accounting period in which it is made, it would be necessary for the company to make a separate claim for relief for the tax recoverable on repayments.

*Controlled foreign companies (CFCs)*

**2.28** The CFCs' supplementary pages, CT600B, require details of the company name, tax reference and accounting period and then a list of CFCs, the territory of residence of each under *TA 1988 s 749*, the exemption due, if any (for example under an acceptable distribution policy clearance letter), the percentage of apportionable profits and creditable tax, the chargeable profits, tax on the chargeable profits, creditable tax, any reliefs in terms of tax, any ACT and finally the tax

## 2.29 Notices and Returns

chargeable under *TA 1988 s 747*, the total of which is transferred to form CT600. For more details of CFCs under CTSA, see Chapter 13.

### Groups and consortia

**2.29** The group and consortium supplementary pages, CT600C, request the company name, tax reference and period of account. Part 1 is the claim for group relief, specifying the name of the surrendering company, the accounting period, together with the start and end dates of any period that is different from that covered by the return, the tax reference and the amount claimed, the total of which is carried to form CT600.

**2.30** In part 2, particulars are required of the amounts surrendered as group relief, and the name of the company surrendering relief, its tax reference and accounting period and the analysis of the amount surrendered as group relief, split between trading losses, excess non-trading capital allowances, non-trading deficits on loan relationships, excess charges, excess Schedule A losses and excess management expenses. Details of the recipients of the surrender are required with the name of the claimant company, the accounting period including the start and end dates where not the same as that covered by the return, and the tax reference of each company together with the amount surrendered. Part 2 amounts to a claim to surrender group relief and therefore must be signed by duly authorised signatories. *TMA 1970 s 108* provides that the proper officer of a company for doing things that have to be done under the Taxes Act, including signing returns, is the secretary unless the company is in liquidation, in which case it is the liquidator. Group relief claims may be signed by a person authorised by the company as an alternative to the company's secretary, ESC C20.

### Insurance companies

**2.31** The insurance supplementary pages, CT600D, identify the company, its tax reference and accounting period and then go through a number of steps in respect of pension business, payments on account of tax credits and deducted tax under *TA 1988 19 Sch AB*, to arrive at the amount due to the Revenue.

### Charities, Tonnage Tax and the Corporate Venturing Scheme

**2.32** The charities supplementary pages, CT600E, require a return by a charity claiming exemption or partial exemption from tax. The Tonnage Tax supplementary pages CT600F must be completed by all shipping companies making a tonnage tax election and require details of training allowances and the ships operated by the company. CT600F also asks for but does not require particulars of shipping profits replaced by tonnage tax. Companies claiming relief under the Corporate Venturing Scheme have to complete CT600G with details of the qualifying investments, disposals and deferral relief claimed.

## Calculation of tax payable

**2.33** The statutory authority for the computation in the tax return of the tax payable for an accounting period is in *FA 1988 18 Sch 8*, which, in accordance with new-speak policies, is divided into a number of steps:

(a) The first step is to calculate the corporation tax chargeable on the company's profits, by computing the amount of those profits for the period and applying the rate of corporation tax applicable to the company.

(b) The second step is to give any appropriate reduction for marginal or small companies' relief under *TA 1988 s 13(2)*, any double taxation relief under *TA 1988 s 788* or *790* and any relief for ACT under *TA 1988 s 239* or shadow ACT. [See chapter 6].

(c) The third step is to add any amount chargeable as if it were corporation tax in respect of loans or advances made by a close company to a participator, under *TA 1988 s 419(1)*, and in respect of profits of a CFC, chargeable under *TA 1988 s 747(4)(a)*.

(d) The fourth step is to deduct any amount that can be set against the company's overall tax liability, such as income tax deducted at source under *TA 1988 s 7(2)* or *11(3)* and ACT paid in respect of a foreign income dividend under *TA 1988 s 246N* or *246Q*.

This is the net amount that should be arrived at on completion of form CT600 (2000).

## Accounts, other documents and information

**2.34** *FA 1998 18 Sch 3, 4* give a wide meaning to the term 'company tax return', which includes not only the return itself but all the information, accounts, statements and reports required to comply with the notice to file. *FA 1998 18 Sch 11* provides that if the company is resident in the UK, and is required under the *Companies Act 1985* to prepare accounts for the period for which it is required to deliver a company tax return, the Companies Act accounts are sufficient to meet the requirements for accounts to be submitted with the company tax returns. These will be the full accounts which the company is required to prepare under the *Companies Act 1985*, not the abridged or modified accounts which they may be permitted to file as small or medium-sized companies under *CA 1988 s 246*.

**2.35** The statutory provisions relating to the production of information refer specifically to partnerships. *FA 1998 18 Sch 12* requires the company tax return to include the company's share, as shown in a relevant partnership statement made under *TMA 1970 s 12AB*. These provisions require a partnership of which a company is a member to compute its profits as if the partnership were a company and to prepare a partnership statement, allocating those profits in profit sharing ratio to the corporate partner or partners.

## 2.36 Notices and Returns

**2.36** So far as chargeable gains are concerned, *FA 1998 18 Sch 13* provides that a notice requiring a company tax return may require details of assets acquired by the company in the period specified in the notice, except for Government non-marketable securities under *TCGA 1992 s 121*, exempt passenger vehicles under *TCGA 1992 s 263*, and tangible, moveable property acquired for £6,000 or less, apart from commodities and currency. Assets acquired as trading stock are also exempt unless they are held for the purposes of long-term business carried on by an insurance company. The normal return form CT600 does not require these details, merely the chargeable gains and capital losses.

**2.37** There is no indication in the legislation of what is meant by statements and reports but the return does require explanations and calculations of figures which are not immediately recognisable from the company's accounts. These clearly encompass computations of adjusted profits and capital allowances, chargeable gains and other sources of income and reliefs, summarised on the return form CT600. Companies will therefore effectively continue to file accounts and computations as previously.

**2.38** Where there has been an enquiry into a company tax return and it is finally determined that the return was for the wrong period, and there is an outstanding period for which a return has not been made, the original notice requiring the return may be taken to require the company to deliver a return for the revised period, under *FA 1998 18 Sch 35*. Such return is due within 30 days of the correct period being finally determined, or the original filing date if later.

**2.39** The statutory requirements which, in practice, will indicate what additional information, statements and reports are required, are dealt with in Chapter 17. In particular *FA 1998 18 Sch 44* enables a Revenue officer to make a discovery if he could not have reasonably been expected, on the basis of the information made available to him, to have been aware that the return was incorrect, or tax under-collected, within *FA 1998 18 Sch 41(1)* or *(2)*. Information is regarded as made available to the Revenue if it is contained in documents accompanying the return or, in the case of a claim, documents accompanying the claim or documents provided on enquiry, or it is information the existence and relevance of which could reasonably have been inferred from the information available to them or notified to them in writing by the company. [*FA 1998 18 Sch 44(2)*]. If, therefore, information would be required by the Revenue for the proper consideration of the company's return, this would be information which should be made available to the Revenue under *FA 1998 18 Sch 3* and *4*, and if this information is contained in statements or reports, then these should accompany the return.

**Estimates**

**2.40** The return form CT600 requires explanations and calculations of any figures which have been estimated. In *Dunk v Havant General*

*Comrs [1976] STC 460n*, the taxpayer had lost some of his documents and argued that it was therefore impossible for him to prepare a tax return that was correct and complete. However, Goulding J stated: 'What the taxpayer has to declare is that the return is to the best of his knowledge correct and complete. If . . . a taxpayer finds particular circumstances that make the best of his knowledge more than usually unreliable it is open to him to put against his figure for a particular item of income such words as "estimated" (see accompanying memorandum) or something of that kind and explain the circumstances. If he has done his best, and of course he is under a duty to use all proper sources of knowledge, he will not in my view, be guilty of making a false statement, providing as I say, he puts in a genuine estimate and if necessary explains that it is not very reliable'.

**2.41** Such circumstances would no doubt require a report or statement from the taxpayer to accompany the tax return. However there are many cases where accounts include estimates, for example the allocation of overheads to stock and work in progress. Where these estimates are reasonably accurate and are not provisional figures likely to be supplanted at a later date when more information becomes available, it is not necessary to draw specific attention to them.

Where however, figures are provisional, a note to this effect should accompany the return and amended figures submitted to the Revenue as a correction of the return, as soon as these become available. It is, for example, sometimes difficult to obtain the details of minority interests in controlled foreign companies within the time required for submission of the return. (See IR Tax Bulletin, Issue 37, pp 593–596 on Incomplete Returns and the Use of Provisional Figures.)

**Valuations**

**2.42** Form CT600 also requests that where a valuation is included, the company should state where the valuation was obtained. Valuations will often be required for computations of company chargeable gains. Valuation of land and shares in unquoted companies and other intangibles is an art rather than a science and an area where there is room for difference of professional opinion, even among experts, as to the open market value of such assets in hypothetical circumstances.

**2.43** In the case of specialist valuations where the taxpayer is unlikely to have the required specialist knowledge, it may be necessary to obtain a professional valuation from a surveyor or valuer, in the case of land, or an accountant or share and business valuer in the case of unquoted shares or other intangibles, but the size of the transaction and the amount of tax at stake would also be relevant. It would not be reasonable for the Revenue to expect a taxpayer to obtain a professional valuation for items of trifling value. Provided that the company has taken proper care in the preparation of the return and obtained professional advice where appropriate, it would not be penalised for a valuation merely because a

**2.44** *Notices and Returns*

different figure is subsequently agreed by negotiation with the District Valuer or the Shares Valuation Division of the Inland Revenue. Tax would be payable by reference to the finally agreed figure and any interest adjustment made. If on the other hand, the valuation was little more than a wild guess, the Revenue could regard the return as being made negligently and seek penalties if the tax under-declared was material.

**2.44** There was originally no provision for companies, unlike that available to individual taxpayers and trustees, to have a valuation referred to the District Valuer or Shares Valuation Division as soon as the disposal had been made, under the CG 34 procedure. However, the scheme has been extended to companies from 10 January 2000. See Inland Revenue Press Release, 10 January 2000 (Appendix 6), Tax Bulletin, Issue 45, February 2000, p 728 (Appendix 1). For companies, valuations will be referred to the Specialist Valuation departments of the Revenue following submission of the return or CG 34. The provisions of SP1/99, regarding self-assessment enquiries being limited to valuation disputes after the end of the normal twelve month enquiry window, unless already under enquiry or on discovery, do not apply to companies.

**2.45** An area of valuation which will become increasingly important under CTSA is in respect of transfer pricing on the transfer of goods or services between connected parties in different jurisdictions, where a non-arm's length value could result in an adjustment for tax purposes under *TA 1988 s 770*, et seq. Where a transfer takes place at a deliberate under or over valuation, the tax consequences should be disclosed and tax paid on any adjustment required to bring the figure to market value for tax purposes. Failure to do so could, on enquiry, lead to allegations of negligence and penalties. The question of transfer pricing is dealt with in more detail in Chapter 14.

**Rulings and clearances**

*Pre-transaction rulings*

**2.46** There are currently no formal pre-transaction rulings available for UK tax purposes. The Revenue produced a consultation paper on pre-transaction rulings in November 1995 (Pre-transaction rulings – a Consultative document) but discussions with taxpayers and representative bodies did not convince them that the demand for a ruling system was such that it would be cost effective to introduce.

**2.47** Informal guidance as to the tax treatment of proposed transactions may, however, be available from the Revenue in appropriate circumstances (see Code of Practice 10 (Appendix 9)). These were published in Tax Bulletin 12, August 1994 (see Appendix 1) following the case of *R v IRC (ex p MFK Underwriting Agencies Ltd [1989] STC 873)* which held that the Revenue would not be bound by anything less than a clear, unambiguous and unqualified representation of the tax treatment of a particular transaction. The guidance in Tax Bulletin 12, from the Deputy Chairman, referred to his earlier letter of 18 October 1990, in which he confirmed that Head Office staff had been told that they should be prepared, when they can, to answer requests for guidance on the Revenue's interpretation of Tax Law, not only where they involve the interpretation of recent legislation, statements of practice and other published information, but also in cases where there is a major public interest in developments in an industry or in the financial sector, but where the operation of the law is uncertain. In addition, local inspectors of taxes will, of course, continue where practicable to inform practitioners of Tax Law as it applies to any case which falls within the responsibility of that office.

**2.48** It was made clear that a taxpayer who wished to rely on Revenue guidance must:

(a) put all his cards face upwards on the table;

(b) indicate the guidance sought;

(c) make it plain that it is fully considered guidance that is being sought; and

(d) indicate the use which it is intended to make of the guidance and in particular whether he proposes to tell others of it.

**2.49** In *Matrix Securities Ltd v IRC [1994] STC 272*, guidance given by the Revenue was not followed where the information submitted by the company had been inaccurate and misleading, and the Revenue were therefore entitled to withdraw the clearance.

*Advance pricing agreements*

**2.50** *FA 1999* includes provisions approving cross-border transfer pricing as advance pricing agreements. For details see Chapter 14.

*Pre-transaction clearances*

**2.51** Pre-transaction clearances are available by statute in connection with proposed transactions in securities, where an application may be made under *TA 1988 s 707* for clearance that the proposed transaction does not give rise to a tax advantage which would be cancelled under *TA 1988 s 703*. *TA 1988 ss 703* et seq are outside the Corporation Tax self-assessment requirements and are dealt with separately by the Section 703 Compliance Unit (see Tax Bulletin, Issue 46, April 2000, p 742). It is also possible to apply to the local inspector for statutory confirmation that the provisions relating to the taxation of capital gains as income, in connection with transactions in land, would not apply in particular circumstances, under *TA 1988 s 776(11)*. Such clearance applications are rarely made in practice as local inspectors seem loathe to provide the

## 2.52 Notices and Returns

requested confirmation. Paper for paper roll-over relief under *TCGA 1992 ss 135–136* on company reconstructions or take-overs is subject to a requirement in *TCGA 1992 s 137* that the transaction is effected for bona fide commercial reasons and does not form part of the scheme, the main purpose of which is the avoidance of liability to capital gains tax or corporation tax. Clearance may be applied for under *TCGA 1992 s 138* for confirmation that the anti-avoidance provisions in *TCGA 1992 s 137* would not be invoked in the transaction in point. The clearance only confirms that the particular anti-avoidance provisions would not be invoked, not that the paper for paper roll-over relief would be available. Advance clearance is also available, under *TA 1988 s 215*, that a demerger carried out for bona fide commercial reasons will not be treated as a distribution for tax purposes.

*Post transaction rulings*

**2.52** The Revenue, in Code of Practice 10 (Appendix 9), have confirmed that a taxpayer may request his own tax office to give a ruling on the application of Tax Law to a specific transaction. They will deal with such a request only after the transaction has been completed. The Revenue will usually consider themselves bound by a post transaction ruling that has been given to a particular person on a particular transaction unless the information provided proves to be incomplete or incorrect. A company could therefore confirm such points with the Revenue before completing the self-assessment return. The company is not bound to accept the Revenue's ruling, but it would probably be wise to disclose, specifically, if it decides to adopt a different view of the law, in order to provide full disclosure. If it had not asked for the ruling it would have been at liberty to adopt what it considered to be the correct taxation treatment without referring to it specifically, although it would only have protection against a subsequent Revenue discovery if sufficient information was disclosed to show the treatment of the transaction for tax purposes.

## Companies in liquidation

**2.53** The Revenue have confirmed that CTSA has not changed their approach to companies in liquidation. *TA 1988 s 342(5)* allows a liquidator to self-assess before the end of an accounting period. The Revenue will accept an information return, such as a letter, from liquidators wishing to finalise affairs before formal completion of winding-up, although if there is any income or are any gains, it may be more practical if the liquidator makes the return on form CT600. The Revenue will provide clearance, if appropriate, that they will not take the return up for enquiry (see Guide to CTSA, para 6.2.5).

**2.54** The liquidator can still ask for clearance under ESC C16 in connection with distributions during the winding-up (Revenue Manual CT 3222).

Chapter 3

# Assessments and Determinations

## Introduction

**3.1** The principal change for companies under CTSA is that for accounting periods ending on or after 1 July 1999 self-assessment is compulsory. This is unlike the position for individuals and trustees, where by filing before 30 September following the end of a year of assessment, the taxpayer can still leave it to the Revenue to calculate the tax and make the assessment. There are, however, default provisions as outlined in this chapter which can still give the Revenue power in some cases to raise an assessment or 'quasi assessment' (in fact a determination) on recalcitrant companies.

## Self-assessment

**3.2** Every corporation tax return for an accounting period ending on or after 1 July 1999 must include a self-assessment based on the information in the return and after taking into account any reliefs or allowances, specifying the amount of tax due for the period in question. This self-assessment then creates a charge to tax without any action by the Revenue. This extends to any tax payable under *TA 1988 s 419* (loans to participators) and *s 747(4)(a)* (profits of controlled foreign companies). A return is regarded as for an accounting period if it is treated as such in the return, and is not longer than twelve months, even though it may not be an accounting period as defined in *TA 1988 s 12*. [*FA 1998, 18 Sch 7*]. A self-assessment is required even though the tax may be nil or the company is entitled to a net repayment.

**3.3** The method of calculating the tax payable for a particular period is specifically set out by *FA 1998 18 Sch 8* in a series of steps as follows:

(a) calculate the corporation tax on the company's profits, taking the amount of the profits which are chargeable to corporation tax and applying the appropriate rate;

(b) give effect to any reliefs or set-offs available for marginal small companies relief, double tax relief and (whilst still available) ACT;

### 3.4 *Assessments and Determinations*

(c) add any amounts due in respect of loans to participators and the controlled foreign companies provisions;

(d) deduct income tax suffered on any excess of unfranked investment income over annual payments [*TA 1988 s 7(2)* or *11(3)*] and ACT on any excess of foreign income dividends paid over those received. [*TA 1988 ss 246N* or *246Q*].

**3.4** Further details of the information and calculations required are contained in Chapter 2 in relation to the corporation tax return. Once the return and the self-assessment have been submitted, the tax liability as so computed becomes final unless (a) the company amends it within twelve months; (b) the Revenue make a correction for any obvious errors and omissions or commence an enquiry; or (c) the Revenue make a 'discovery' assessment.

## Loans to participators and controlled foreign companies

**3.5** As indicated in 3.3 the self-assessment must include any amount due under the loans to participators provisions of *TA 1988 s 419*. The company return form contains a supplementary page specifically designed to cover such loans. Details are to be given about the making of such loans and the tax chargeable thereon. Further information is to be provided about loans which have been repaid, released or written off, together with any relief due for such loans.

**3.6** The self-assessment is likewise to include any tax chargeable under the controlled foreign companies provisions of *TA 1988 s 747(4)(a)*. There are also special supplementary pages to be completed for such companies, the issues being considered more fully in Chapter 13.

## Losses and other negative amounts

**3.7** Under CTSA all negative amounts (e.g. trading losses, amounts which can be surrendered as group relief, allowable losses under *TCGA 1992 s 19*) have to be included in the company tax return. Such negative amounts then become final in the same way as the self-assessment, unless subject to a Revenue enquiry or discovery. Thereafter the company has to use the same figure for the negative amount in any other return and self-assessment affected by it. The same applies if the negative amount is included in an amended return. Including the negative amount in a later return does not give the Revenue a further opportunity to enquire into it, although they are not prevented from making an enquiry into how the negative amount has been used in the later return. A negative figure brought forward from a pre-CTSA return period does not become final by being included in a CTSA return.

*Example 1*

Chalk Ltd files its return for the period ended 31 December 2001 on time, and this indicates a trading loss of £50,000. No enquiry is made into the return before the deadline of 31 December 2003. Chalk Ltd's return for the next period to 31 December 2002 which is also filed on time, indicates trading profits of £120,000 and a deduction of the brought forward losses of £50,000. The Revenue commence an enquiry into this return in August 2004. The Revenue cannot enquire into the £50,000 loss other than whether relief for it can properly be given against the 2002 trading profit.

## Amendments and corrections

**3.8** After a return has been filed, a company is permitted to amend it and the self-assessment by notifying the Revenue accordingly. An amendment has to be in such form, contain such information and be accompanied by such statements as the Revenue reasonably require. The Revenue have stated that for the time being they do not propose to prescribe any particular format or provide official forms. Instead, amendments can be made informally in correspondence. This has to be done within twelve months of the filing date, or, in the case of a return for the wrong period, what would have been the filing date if the period had in fact been an accounting period. [*FA 1998 18 Sch 15*]. Unless the return is under an enquiry (see Chapter 17), such an amendment to the return will be recorded by the Revenue and the self-assessment adjusted. An amendment made during the course of an enquiry will only be effective, so far as any change affecting the company's tax liability, once the enquiry is completed.

**3.9** Such corrections will cover cases, for example, where a company, having filed its return, subsequently realises that there has been a mistake in the computation, or where the self-assessment was initially based on an estimate, and a final figure has since become available. Where the company corrects its return in these circumstances, although interest will run on any additional tax which is payable, the Revenue will not generally seek to exact penalties.

**3.10** The Revenue may also correct a return for obvious errors or omissions (whether errors of principle, arithmetical mistakes or otherwise) by serving notice on the company within nine months of the filing of the return or an amended return. But the process of correction will not involve any judgement as to the accuracy of the figures in the return. This would be handled by an enquiry into the return. If the correction is necessitated by an amendment to a return made by the company, the nine months runs from the date the amendment was made.

### 3.11 *Assessments and Determinations*

**3.11** The Revenue consider that an 'obvious' error or mistake is one which is self-evident, such as the transposition of figures, arithmetical mistakes and other matters which are obvious in the everyday sense of the word. If the company wishes to reject such a correction it can do so, either by amending its return accordingly (provided that the twelve month period for making amendments has not expired) or by serving notice on the Revenue within three months of the issue of the notice of correction. Otherwise the correction will stand. [*FA 1998 18 Sch 16*].

## Revenue determination where no return filed

**3.12** There are provisions which give power to the Revenue to make a determination where a company has failed to file a tax return. This power (which lasts for five years) becomes exercisable at any time after the filing date has passed, when this can be ascertained. Otherwise, it is exercisable on the later of 18 months from the period specified in the notice requiring the return or three months from the date on which the notice was served.

**3.13** The Revenue are empowered to determine the tax liability for all accounting periods ending in the period specified in the notice. But if the Revenue cannot identify the accounting period, the determination can be for any period they specify. The determination is of no effect if the company can show that there is no accounting period ending in the period specified in the notice; or that it has already delivered a return for the accounting period concerned; or that no return is yet due for that period. [*FA 1998 18 Sch 36*].

**3.14** If the company has filed a return, but the Revenue consider that there is another period ending in a period specified in the notice, they can make a similar determination for that 'outstanding period'. The time limits are the same, except that the 18 month period is extended to 30 months. Also such a determination is ineffective if the company can show that the accounting period is not an accounting period or that it has already delivered a return. [*FA 1998 18 Sch 37*].

**3.15** A determination will cover much the same ground and will resemble an estimated assessment under the old system. Where such a determination is made, it will take effect as a self-assessment for the purposes of payment, collection and recovery, interest on tax and penalties. A determination is treated as being made for a period even if the Revenue have insufficient information to determine whether the period is in fact an accounting period. [*FA 1998 18 Sch 39*]. The Revenue have indicated that they will normally review cases for determination 18 months after the end of what they assume or believe is the company's accounting period. Where they believe that the filing date is later than that, they will wait until after the filing date before making a determination. In some cases (e.g. where the Revenue believe there may be a loss of tax if immediate action is not taken), the Revenue may review the need to make a determination before 18 months.

## Revenue determination superseded by actual self-assessment

**3.16** Unlike an estimated assessment, a determination is not subject to appeal. Instead, a determination is simply superseded if the company later files a tax return (including a self-assessment) for the accounting period concerned, provided that this is done within the later of twelve months from the date of determination or five years from the date on which the Revenue first had the power to make the determination. Where proceedings have been commenced by the Revenue to recover any tax charged by a determination, and a return is made before the proceedings have been concluded, these may be continued in respect of so much of the tax shown due under the self-assessment as has not been paid. [*FA 1998 18 Sch 40*].

## Amendments to assessments pursuant to Revenue enquiry

**3.17** As described in Chapter 17, the Revenue have extensive 'policing' powers which enable the Revenue to amend a company's self-assessment during an enquiry. This is tantamount to a Revenue own assessment, and there are wide powers of appeal against such amendments. [*FA 1998 18 Sch (30), (34)*].

## Discovery assessment or determination

**3.18** As also described in Chapter 17, outside the normal one year enquiry period the Revenue have discovery powers, which extend to the ability to make an assessment or determination on companies in certain circumstances. Again a company has the right of appeal against any such assessment or determination. [*FA 1998 18 Sch (41)–(48)*].

## Time limits for Revenue assessment or determination

**3.19** The time limit for the making of assessments by the Revenue (including discovery assessments and determinations) remains at six years after the end of the accounting period for corporation tax. [*FA 1998 18 Sch 46(1)*]. In the case of fraudulent or negligent conduct, the time limit becomes 21 years after the end of the accounting period for corporation tax.

**3.20** *Assessments and Determinations*

## Assessment to recover overpayment of tax

**3.20** In circumstances where tax has been repaid to a company and the Revenue consider that this ought not to have been done, they may raise an assessment on the company to recover the tax overpaid. [*FA 1998 18 Sch 52*]. The assessment and appeals procedure set out in Chapter 17, relating to discovery by the Revenue, is then to apply.

**3.21** The usual six year time limit for such an assessment is amended, permitting the Revenue to raise an assessment to recover the tax before the later of:

(a) the end of the accounting period following that in which the amount assessed was paid; and

(b) if there has been a Revenue enquiry into the company's return, three months from the end of the enquiry period. [*FA 1998 18 Sch 53*].

## Excessive assessments or repayments

### Relief for double assessments

**3.22** A company which believes that it has been assessed more than once for the same cause and for the same accounting period may claim relief by written notice to the Board. If the Board are satisfied as to the validity of the claim, they are to amend the assessments or give relief by discharge or repayment of tax so as to eliminate the double charge. The company has a right of appeal against the refusal of such a claim. [*FA 1998 18 Sch (50)*].

### Relief in case of mistake in return

**3.23** A company may make an 'error or mistake' claim for recovery of overpaid tax within six years after the end of the accounting period to which the claim relates. The Board are then to enquire into the matter and make such repayment as is 'reasonable and just'. However, relief is not to be given where the mistake was as to the basis on which the tax liability should have been computed when the return was made in accordance with the then prevailing practice. Furthermore, no claim for relief may be made for a mistake in a claim or election included in the return. Instead, a supplementary claim or election may be made within the time allowed for the original claim or election; see 4.8. [*FA 1998 18 Sch 51(1), (2), (3)*].

**3.24** In deciding the issue, the Board are to consider the company's liability for other accounting periods and whether the granting of relief would result in amounts being excluded from the charge to tax, e.g. where the mistake related to profits which should have been included in an earlier return which is no longer capable of being amended. There is a right of appeal to the Special Commissioners against the Board's decision. The only right of appeal against the Commissioners' decision is then on a point of law arising in connection with the computation of the company's profits, any amount assessable as a loan to a participator or any amount assessable under the controlled foreign company provisions. [*FA 1998 18 Sch (4), (5), (6)*].

**Recovery of excessive repayments**

**3.25** The Revenue may make an assessment to recover any excessive repayments, repayment supplement and interest on overpaid tax, where the amount is assessable under the discovery provisions or is overpaid interest and recoverable under *TA 1988 s 826(8A)*. Any such assessment is made under Sch D Case VI and is treated as an assessment for the accounting period concerned. The normal six year time limit does not apply. Such an assessment can be made before the end of the accounting period following that in which the amount assessed was paid or, if later, before the end of three months from the completion of an enquiry into a relevant tax return of the company. [*FA 1998 18 Sch (52), (53)*].

*Chapter 4*

# Claims, Elections and Revisions

## Background

**4.1** Under the old system, the Taxes Acts provided for a multitude of claims, elections and notices, with different sets of rules and varying time limits. Claims needed Revenue acceptance to be valid, whilst elections simply required unilateral action by the taxpayer, generally by the service of a written notice on the Inspector. For claims it was often necessary for the taxpayer to satisfy the Revenue that particular conditions had been complied with. This necessitated an investigation by the Inspector into the facts, and then the exercise of a judgment.

**4.2** It is an integral part of CTSA that a company can file its return and determine its corporation tax liability without reference to the Revenue. This has required a radical change in respect of claims. The essence of the new system is that the company alone needs to be satisfied that the conditions for relief have been met, and it will pay tax accordingly. The claim will then only be subject to review by the Revenue, if at all, under the enquiry procedure. The change has been implemented by a series of specific amendments to a number of charging sections in the legislation, as set out in 4.36 et seq.

**4.3** The matter is somewhat complicated by the time frame relating to claims. Most will relate to the income and gains of the particular period covered by the return, and can generally be dealt with simply by inclusion in the return. Effect will then be given to them by a reduction in the tax bill for that period. But some claims will relate to income and gains of future years, and these will be made in advance. Other claims allow a carry back to earlier years, for example in respect of trading losses, permitting a revision of the corporation tax paid.

## General position

### Outline of provisions: claims usually to be part of return

**4.4** The procedure for company claims and elections is contained in *FA 1998 18 Sch* and has effect for accounting periods ending on or after 1 July 1999. Where a claim affects a single accounting period it

*Claims, Elections and Revisions* **4.7**

usually has to be included in the corporation tax return itself, or in an amendment to it. Claims have to be quantified at the time they are made, i.e. expressed in figures, so that formula claims are not allowed. Generally they must be submitted within six years from the end of the accounting period to which they relate. [*FA 1998 18 Sch 54, 55*]. However, this will be overriden where specific shorter time limits apply, e.g. trading loss carry back claims under *TA 1988 s 393A(10)*, where there is a specific two year limit. There are also special rules for group relief and capital allowances claims.

**4.5** Claims for the repayment of income tax under *TA 1988 s 6(2)* or exemptions from income tax cannot be made before the company has delivered its return for the period to which the claim relates. Effectively therefore, such a claim has to be made by inclusion in the return. The same applies to:

(a) claims for payments of tax credits (except where the company is wholly exempt from corporation tax, or is exempt except for trading income, and the tax credit is not one for which a payment on account may be claimed by an insurance company carrying on pension business);

(b) group relief claims; and

(c) capital allowances claims. [*FA 1998 18 Sch 9, 10*].

**4.6** The form of the return reflects the fact that claims and elections are to be made with the return if at all possible. Certain reliefs will be claimed merely by a deduction of the relevant amount. Others will be claimed by adoption of a particular treatment, such as by set-off of trade losses. Others again will be in a formal claim either on the return or as a separate claim to be submitted with the return. Examples are claims for capital allowances, for which there is a separate section in the return, and claims for group relief, for which there are supplementary pages to the return. The procedure for such claims is considered in more detail below. In some circumstances it will be impossible or inappropriate for a claim to be made as part of a return or an amendment to it, and the procedure set out in 4.12 et seq. will then apply. This separation between the two procedures does not depend on the type of claim, but purely on whether a claim in the return is appropriate or possible.

**Giving effect to claims**

**4.7** Where a claim is made by being included in the return, effect will be given to the claim by the company itself making an appropriate reduction in the amount of corporation tax payable. Where the claim is made outside the return, the Revenue are required to give effect to the claim as soon as is practicable after the claim is made by way of a discharge or repayment of tax. [*TMA 1970 1A Sch 4*]. Where such a claim results in entitlement to a tax repayment, this will generally be made

### 4.8   Claims, Elections and Revisions

automatically subject only to certain security checks instituted by the Revenue. In cases where risk is perceived to be involved, the Revenue may verify the claim before any tax repayment is made. The Revenue also have the right to audit the claim, with essentially the same rights as under their normal enquiry procedures, as set out in 4.18.

**4.8**   Where a company discovers that there is a mistake in a claim or election it has made, it may make a supplementary claim or election within the time allowed for the original claim or election. [*FA 1998 18 Sch 56*].

### Claims or elections affecting single accounting period

**4.9**   In the case of a claim or election affecting only one accounting period, e.g. a claim to double tax relief, where the company has received a tax return the claim or election must be made in that return (or in an amendment to it) if it can be so made. This will be the case for most claims. If the claim cannot be made by inclusion in the return or an amendment to it (for example, where a return has not been received or after the time has passed for amending a return) then the provisions of *TMA 1970 1A Sch* are to apply. [See 4.12]. [*FA 1998 18 Sch 57*]. Claims have to be in such form, contain such information and be accompanied by such statements as the Revenue require. Where joint claims are required, a written claim signed by an authorised person need be delivered with only one of the claims. But the return of the other parties must reveal the existence of the claim and be prepared in accordance with it.

### Claims or elections involving more than one accounting period

**4.10**   The position may arise where a claim or election relates to an event or occasion occurring in one accounting period, but which affects another accounting period. If the company has already delivered a return for that other period, and the twelve month period for making amendments to the return has not passed, then the return must be duly amended. Otherwise the provisions of *TMA 1970 1A Sch* are to apply. [See 4.12]. [*FA 1998 18 Sch 58*].

---

*Example 1*

---

Magenta Ltd incurs a trading loss of £130,000 in its accounting period to 31 December 2002, but has other profits of £50,000 in the same accounting period. It had trading profits of £60,000 in the year to 31 December 2001. Magenta Ltd is entitled to loss relief against the profits of the two accounting periods.

The loss relief claim is made in Magenta Ltd's return for the accounting period ended 31 December 2002. Partial effect is given to the claim by set-off of £50,000 of the losses against other profits in the self-assessment for that period. If the time limit has not passed for amending the return for the period to 31 December 2001, effect is given to the carry back element of £60,000 by an amendment of the return and the self-assessment for that period. Otherwise the procedure in 4.12 will be in point and the Revenue will give effect to the claim by discharge or repayment. The balance of the loss of £20,000 is carried forward under *TA 1988 s 393(1)*.

Magenta Ltd indicates in the computations forming part of the return for the period to 31 December 2002, that the loss relief claim includes a carry back component. On page 1 of the return it shows a repayment due for the earlier period. In these circumstances the Revenue regard such actions as (a) making an amendment to the earlier return if the time limit has not expired, or (b) making a Schedule 1A claim if the time limit has expired.

### Estimates

**4.11** A provisional claim in an estimated amount may not be made. However, in cases where, for example, it is clear that a claim will be appropriate but the amount cannot precisely be determined, the Revenue will accept the taxpayer's best estimate, which will have to be revised to the final figure as soon as available. An example will be where a loss has been established but the exact amount cannot be finalised before the return is filed.

## Claims and elections not in tax return

### Outline of procedure

**4.12** As set out above, a claim normally has to be made by being included in the corporation tax return, or by an amendment to it. Only where the time limit has passed for amending the return is a 'stand alone' claim generally appropriate. In such a case a new *TMA 1970 1A Sch* sets out the procedure which is then to apply for the making of a claim. This 'sweep up' provision mainly applies to elections not related to a particular accounting period, but having effect, for example, to a particular sort of income until withdrawn, e.g. an election under *TA 1988 s 247(4)* that income tax should not be deducted from payments of interest between companies in the same group.

**4.13** A claim is to be made to a Revenue Officer, except where there is a specific provision requiring the claim to be made to the Board, and it has to be in the prescribed form. [*TMA 1970 1A Sch 2(1), (3)*]. There has to be a declaration to the effect that all the particulars given are correctly

**4.14** *Claims, Elections and Revisions*

stated to the best of the information and belief of the person making the claim. [*TMA 1980 1A Sch 2(4)*]. The form of claim may require:

(a) a statement of the tax which is to be discharged or repaid to give effect to the claim;

(b) such information as the Revenue may reasonably require to determine whether the claim is correct, and also the delivery of such accounts, statements and documents relating to information contained in the return as are reasonably required to substantiate the claim; and

(d) any particulars of assets acquired as may be required in a tax return containing information about chargeable gains. [*TMA 1970 1A Sch 2(5)*].

**4.14**  No claim requiring the repayment of tax is to be made unless the claimant has documentary proof of payment. [*TMA 1970 1A Sch 2(2)*]. In the case of a claim by or on behalf of a non-UK resident, or a person claiming to be not resident, not ordinarily resident, or not domiciled in the UK, a statement or declaration in support of the claim may be required by way of affidavit. [*TMA 1970 1A Sch 2(6)*].

**Record keeping**

**4.15**  A company is required to keep and preserve the records required to make such a claim, which must be kept until the later of the date on which a formal enquiry into the claim is completed, or the date on which it becomes impossible for any such enquiry to be opened. A penalty of up to £3,000 may be charged for failure to comply with the record keeping requirements. [*TMA 1970 1A Sch 2A*].

**Amendments to claims/corrections**

**4.16**  As with the 'corrections' procedure relating to a company's return and self-assessment outlined in Chapter 3, the Revenue may correct a claim submitted outside a return. They can do so at any time within nine months from the date on which the claim is made, correcting any obvious errors or mistakes, whether errors of principle, arithmetical mistakes or otherwise. [*TMA 1970 1A Sch 3(1)(a)*].

**4.17**  The taxpayer may likewise amend his claim within twelve months from the day on which the claim is made by the appropriate notice on a Revenue Officer. [*TMA 1970 1A Sch 3(1)(b)*]. However, where the Revenue initiate a formal enquiry into the claim, no amendment of the claim may be made thereafter until the enquiry is completed. [*TMA 1970 1A Sch 3(2)*]. This follows the similar prohibition on corrections to a return.

**Revenue powers of enquiry**

**4.18** The Revenue are given the same powers to enquire into claims made outside the tax return and call for documents as apply to enquiries into tax returns. The time limit for opening enquiries is the quarter day following the first anniversary of the day on which the claim or amendment was made, or twelve months after the end of the accounting period to which the claim relates. [*TMA 1970 1A Sch 5, 6*].

**4.19** The rules are essentially the same as for enquiries into a self-assessment or the return itself as described in Chapter 17, with the same procedure for completing the enquiry, the ability of the company to apply to the Commissioners for a notice that the enquiry is complete, for amendments to the claim by the Revenue, and for an appeal by the company to the Commissioners against any such amendment.

# Group relief claims

### General

**4.20** Under CTSA, the group relief claims regime is little changed from Pay and File, although there are changes to the Special Arrangement under which some groups can submit Joint Amended Returns. The general effect is to reduce the formal requirements for claiming and surrendering group relief. These changes are made by regulations. [See 4.30].

**4.21** Claims for group and consortium relief have to be made by inclusion in the claimant company's tax return (or in any amended return) for the accounting period in which the claim is made. Supplementary pages CT600C have been designed for this purpose. The claimant must specify the name of the surrendering company and the precise amount of relief claimed, being an amount quantified at the time the claim is made. [*FA 1998 18 Sch 68*]. In this regard, 'quantified' means that the claim must be expressed in figures, as opposed to a formula, e.g. 'A Ltd claims £35,705 group relief from B Ltd' is a valid claim. But 'A Ltd claims sufficient group relief from B Ltd to reduce its profits to £125,000' is invalid.

**4.22** Except where a company is a member of a special arrangement [see 4.30], written consent by the surrendering company or each member of the consortium concerned must be given to the Revenue at or before the time at which every claim is made, and a copy of that consent has to accompany the claim, otherwise the claim is ineffective. [*FA 1998 18 Sch 66, 67, 70*]. Once a claim has been made it cannot be amended, but it can be withdrawn and a fresh claim made. A withdrawal can only be made by the claimant company amending its return. [*FA 1998 18 Sch 73*].

**4.23** *Claims, Elections and Revisions*

**Claims for more or less than amount available for surrender**

**4.23** A claim can be for less than the amount available for surrender but it is ineffective if it is for more than the amount available for surrender at the time when the claim is made. The amount which is so available for relief is calculated as follows:

(a) work out the total amount available for surrender under *TA 1988 s 403* on the basis of the surrendering company's tax return, but excluding any amendments whose effect is deferred because an enquiry is taking place;

(b) deduct the total group relief for the same accounting period for which the company has already given notices of consent and which have not been withdrawn (hence earlier claims will take precedence where more than one claim is made).

**4.24** Where more than one claim is made on the same day, which in aggregate exceed the amount of relief available for surrender, the Revenue are to determine which of the claims is to be ineffective, but only so far as necessary to bring the total amount claimed within the level of available relief. Where claims are withdrawn on the same day as new claims are made, effect is to be given to the withdrawals first (so that new claims are not ineffective). [*FA 1988 18 Sch 69*].

**Notice of consent**

**4.25** Other than cases where special arrangements are in force, the consent notice by the surrendering company to be sent to the Revenue must state the name of that company, the name of the claimant company, the amount of relief being surrendered, the accounting period to which the surrender relates and the tax references of both companies. Otherwise the notice is ineffective. The supplementary return pages CT600C are designed to contain this information. A notice of consent cannot be amended but it can be withdrawn and replaced by another notice. Any withdrawal has to be accompanied by a notice from the claimant company specifying its consent to the withdrawal (except where a withdrawal is necessary because the amount available for surrender is less than the amounts claimed) and the claimant company has to submit an amended tax return if the time limit for amendments permits. [*FA 1988 18 Sch 71*].

**4.26** Where the surrendering company has filed its tax return before giving its consent, it must amend that return reflecting the consent. Where the notice of consent by the surrendering company relates to a loss in respect of which relief has been given under *TA 1988 s 393(1)* (carry forward of trading losses), the surrendering company has to amend its return for the periods in which it has obtained relief. For this purpose, *s 393(1)* relief is treated as given for earlier before later periods. The notice of consent is invalid if the requisite amendments had not been made, and the normal time limits for amending a return do not apply. [*FA 1998 18 Sch 72*].

**Time limits**

**4.27** The general time limits for amending a return do not apply. Instead a claim for group relief can be made or withdrawn up to whatever is the latest of the following dates under *FA 1998 18 Sch 74:*

(a) the first anniversary of the filing date of the claimant company's tax return for the period for which the claim is made (normally two years after the end of the accounting period);

(b) 30 days after any Revenue enquiry into the tax return is completed (except where the enquiry is limited in its scope under *18 Sch 25* to the amendment of a return, which is itself made to claim or withdraw relief);

(c) 30 days after any Revenue amendment to a tax return following an enquiry;

(d) 30 days after the determination of any appeal brought against such a Revenue amendment under (c);

(e) any later date which the Revenue allow. (A Statement of Practice is to be issued explaining how the Revenue will exercise its discretion regarding late claims. In the meantime SP11/93 will be applied.)

*Example 2*

White Ltd makes up its accounts to 31 December each year. On 21 January 2002, the Revenue issue a Notice to file specifying the period 1 January to 31 December 2001. White Ltd submits its tax return in November 2002. The Revenue do not enquire into the return.

White Ltd may make and withdraw group relief claims at any time up to 31 December 2003, the first anniversary of its filing date.

*Example 3*

Black Ltd makes up accounts for the same accounting period as White Ltd in the previous example and submits its return for the year to 31 December 2001 before the filing date, 31 December 2002. But the Revenue enquire into this return, issuing a closure notice on 15 March 2004.

Black Ltd has until 14 April 2004, 30 days following the completion of the enquiry, to make and withdraw group relief claims.

*Example 4*

The Revenue enquire into Green Ltd's return for the accounting period ended 31 July 2001, issuing a closure notice on 15 October 2003. Green Ltd fails to amend its return in accordance with the conclusions stated in the closure notice, and the Revenue therefore amend the return on 21 November 2003.

Green Ltd may make and withdraw group relief claims at any time up to 21 December 2003, 30 days after notice of the amendment was issued.

*Example 5*

Blue Ltd's return for its accounting period ended 31 December 2003 gives rise to a serious dispute which goes to appeal. A final decision on Blue Ltd's appeal against the Revenue's amendment to its return is given by the Court of Appeal on 19 April 2010.

Blue Limited has until 19 May 2010 to make and withdraw claims to group relief, 30 days after the date on which its appeal was finally determined.

There is no overriding six year and three month limit on making and withdrawing group relief claims, as there was under Pay and File.

**Reduction in the amount available for surrender**

**4.28** In the event that, after any consent notices have been given, the amount available for surrender is reduced to less than the amounts in such notices, the surrendering company is required within 30 days to withdraw sufficient consent notices to bring the total amount surrendered within the reduced amount available for surrender. The company may also give new consent notices as appropriate. These must be in writing and sent both to the Revenue and the claimant companies. Should the surrendering company fail to comply, the Revenue may issue directions to specify which consent notices are ineffective or are to be for a reduced amount, although the surrendering company has a right of appeal. The claimant companies are then required to amend their returns accordingly, if time limits permit. [*FA 1988 18 Sch 75*].

**Assessments to recover excessive group relief**

**4.29** The Revenue are empowered to make an assessment to recover any group relief which they discover to have been excessive, this power being without prejudice to their general discovery assessment power. [*FA 1998 18 Sch 76*]. Again the company has a right of appeal.

**Regulations for special arrangements**

**4.30** Under the previous Pay and File regime SP10/93 set out special arrangements for group relief claims, the purpose being to simplify the procedure for making and revising claims to group relief and giving and revising notices of consent to surrender relief. Groups of companies could submit a single 'joint amended return' showing the group relief claims and surrenders for all the companies in the group. These arrangements are replaced for accounting periods on or after 1 July 1999 by new arrangements made under regulations.

**4.31** *FA 1998 18 Sch 77* provides enabling powers allowing the Revenue to make regulations regarding amendments to returns relating to group relief. The regulations are the *Corporation Tax (Simplified Arrangements for Group Relief) Regulations (SI 1992 No. 2975)* (see Appendix 3). The details are discussed in Chapter 11. Under these regulations a single group company can be authorised to act on behalf of all group companies. Aimed at reducing the compliance burden on larger groups and simplifying the procedures, the additional benefits of arrangements under these regulations, compared with the previous SP10/93 practice, include:

(a) provision for the authorised company to amend group relief claims and surrenders on behalf of all group companies by providing only one copy of the statement containing details of the charges;

(b) inclusion of group companies whose accounting periods do not coincide exactly with those of the group as a whole; and

(c) inclusion of consortium companies which can claim group relief from, or surrender group relief to, the group.

# Capital allowances claims

**4.32** Under Pay and File there was a comprehensive code for capital allowances claims at *CAA 1990 Schedule A1*. This is replaced with a new CTSA code, albeit similar to the old code. A claim by a company for capital allowances has to be made by inclusion in the return for the accounting period for which the claim is made, or by an amendment to the return. The claim has to quantify the amount claimed. 'Quantified' in this context means that the claim must be expressed in figures. Section 5 of the return form CT600 contains the relevant boxes for the claims. Once a claim has been made it can only be amended or withdrawn by amending the return. [*FA 1998 18 Sch 78–81*]. As with claims for group relief, the general time limits for amending a return do not apply. Instead a claim can be made, amended or withdrawn up to the latest of the dates set out in 4.27. [*FA 1998 18 Sch 82*].

## 4.33 Claims, Elections and Revisions

**4.33** Where the effect of a claim reduces the amount available for capital allowances for another accounting period for which a return has already been filed, the company must amend the return for the other period within 30 days. If it fails to do so the Revenue may amend the return accordingly by notifying the company. The normal time limits for amending returns do not preclude such a Revenue amendment. An appeal may be made against such a Revenue amendment. [*FA 1998 18 Sch 83*].

## Relief for double assessments, errors or mistakes

**4.34** If a company believes that it has been assessed to tax more than once for the same cause and for the same accounting period, it may make a written claim for relief to the Board. If the Board are satisfied as to the validity of the claim, they are to amend the assessment or assessments, or give relief by discharge or repayment of tax as appropriate. If a claim is rejected, an appeal may be made to the Commissioners. [*FA 1998 18 Sch 50*].

**4.35** A company which believes that it has overpaid tax, under an assessment which was excessive by reason of an error or mistake, may make a repayment claim. The time limit is six years after the end of the accounting period to which the return relates. [*FA 1998 18 Sch 51(1)*]. On receiving the claim the Board are to enquire into the matter, and give by way of repayment such relief as is reasonable and just. However, there is no relief where the return was made on the basis of or in accordance with the practice generally prevailing at the time when it was made, or where the error or mistake was in a claim which was included in the return. [*FA 1998 18 Sch 51(2), (3)*].

## Consequential amendments in cases where Revenue previously had a discretion

**4.36** As set out in 4.1, under the old system the Inspector generally had to be satisfied as to the validity of a claim before it was allowed. Essentially this disappears under the 'process now – check later' format of self-assessment. The removal of the former discretionary powers of the Revenue has been implemented in the great majority of cases by specific amendments to a number of the charging sections of the Taxes Acts, these being contained in *FA 1996 20 Sch*. The changes take place for corporation tax purposes for accounting periods ending on or after 1 July 1999. [*FA 1996 s 134*].

**4.37** Previously there were four main categories of claim which required a decision from the Revenue:

(a) where the claimant had to *show* or *prove* that a condition existed;

(b) where the Revenue had to be *satisfied* that a condition existed;

## Claims, Elections and Revisions  4.39

(c) where the Revenue had to make a *judgment* whether a condition existed;

(d) where the Revenue needed to *direct* that a particular treatment applied.

**4.38** Under CTSA a company is simply required to self-assess on the basis that the particular condition for any relief or treatment exists, and it will only be called upon to prove it if the Revenue make an investigation under their enquiry powers. The position will be essentially the same in the context of judgmental issues. Here the company will have to be satisfied that on an objective appraisal of all the facts the relief is available. It is in such judgmental areas that inevitably problems are likely to arise, whether on an enquiry by the Revenue or on a later discovery. In doubtful cases it will be advisable for the company to draw to the Revenue's attention any questionable matters on the corporation tax return.

**4.39** The following sets out in summary form the principal sections relevant to companies which are amended by *FA 1996 20 Sch* to reflect the above changes.

*Taxes Act 1988*

(1) *Section 24(2):* lease premiums, presumption that any sums paid are by way of premium unless the contrary can be shown.

(2) *Section 38(4):* in ascertaining the duration of a lease the assumptions as to any benefits conferred apply unless it can be shown that the benefits were not conferred for the purposes of securing a tax advantage.

(3) *Section 74(1)(j):* no longer necessary to prove a debt to be bad in order to claim relief.

(4) *Section 393A:* corporation tax losses can be carried back to an earlier accounting period without having to show in advance that the trade was carried on on a commercial basis with a view to the realisation of gain.

(5) *Section 582(2)(b):* the Board no longer has to be satisfied to give relief for cases where retention of funding bonds is impracticable.

(6) *Section 584:* the provisions giving relief for unremittable overseas income are recast to bring in an objective test of when income is unremittable.

(7) *Section 769:* under the rules for ascertaining the change of ownership of a company leading to the disallowance of trading losses, it is no longer necessary to show in advance that a gift is unsolicited.

(8) *Section 812:* the provisions relating to the withdrawal of tax credit for certain non-resident companies connected with the unitary

**4.39** *Claims, Elections and Revisions*

states is recast to make the various tests objective, rather than having to prove them to the satisfaction of the Board. *Section 812* only comes into effect if a Treasury order to this effect has been approved by a resolution of the House of Commons, which has not yet happened.

(9) *Section 815A:* the provisions on the transfer of a non-UK trade within the mergers directive is recast to avoid the necessity of producing an appropriate certificate.

*Capital Allowances Act 1990*

(1) *Section 29(3):* capital allowances are available where a letting relates partly to holiday accommodation in appropriate circumstances without having to appear just and reasonable.

*Taxation of Chargeable Gains Act 1992*

(1) *Section 30(4):* the value shifting anti-avoidance provisions do not apply where there is no tax avoidance purpose for the obtaining of benefits without it having to be shown to that effect.

(2) *Section 30(5), (6), 32(4)(b) and 33(7), (8):* the just and reasonable adjustments required in the value shifting benefit provisions apply on an objective basis.

(3) *Section 48:* the reduction for consideration proving to be irrecoverable is amended from a subjective to an objective basis.

(4) *Section 49:* if a contingent liability becomes enforceable a consequential adjustment may be made on an appropriate claim.

(5) *Section 52(4):* the just and reasonable apportionment required in computations, where necessary, is put on an objective footing.

(6) *Section 116(13):* in the case of reorganisations, conversions and reconstructions within *s 116* any cash element is chargeable unless it may be ignored as being small. This is now arrived at on an objective basis. Although there is no statutory definition of small, in June 1965 the CCAB published a press release confirming that the Revenue will normally regard one amount as small in comparison with another if the first amount does not exceed 5 per cent of the second. The Revenue manual at paragraph CG 53857 confirms that in the Revenue's view small means 5 per cent or less of the market value of the old assets.

(7) *Section 122*: a capital distribution treated as a part disposal is deducted from the cost of the shares, if small. This is now put on an objective basis. Again there is no statutory definition of small, but the Revenue manual at paragraph CG 57801 confirms that small means 5 per cent or less of the value of the shares.

(8) *Section 133*: a small premium on the conversion of securities may be

deducted from cost rather than treated as a part disposal on an objective basis. The Revenue manual paragraph CG 55031 confirms that in the Revenue's view small means 5 per cent or less of the market value of the converted securities before the conversion. Also see CG 57836.

(9) *Section 176(4), (6):* the disallowance of losses arising out of depreciatory transactions within a group are to be calculated on an objective, just and reasonable basis.

(10) *Section 181(1)(b):* relief for a bona fide merger is given on an objective basis.

(11) *Section 241(7):* the apportionment provisions in relation to accommodation only partly let as holiday accommodation are put on an objective basis.

(12) *Section 279:* the requirements for relief for delayed remittance of foreign gains are put on an objective basis.

(13) *Section 280:* where consideration is payable by instalments it will now be possible for the taxpayer to elect to pay the tax by instalments without having to show hardship. The instalments will be such as the Board may allow over a period not exceeding eight years. The Revenue manual at CG 14912 states that the tax instalments should be limited to 50 per cent of each instalment of future consideration as it becomes receivable. The total period for paying the tax should not exceed eight years, the period for paying the tax should not end later than the date on which the last instalment of consideration is receivable, and where practicable the agreed instalment should be payable at not less than six monthly intervals. CG 14920 states 'for the purposes of charging interest on late paid tax the collector uses a series of reckonable dates determined by reference to the date on which the agreed instalments of tax become payable'.

(14) *8 Sch 10(2):* in the curved line depreciation provisions for leases of less than 50 years as wasting assets, the presumption of sums being paid by way of premium is excluded where other sufficient consideration for the payment can be shown to have been given.

*Finance Act 1993*

(1) *Section 144:* the irrecoverable debt provisions for exchange gains and losses are put on an objective basis.

(2) *Section 145:* similarly, the requirement for the Inspector's satisfaction or opinion is removed from the decision as to the recoverability of the outstanding amount of an exchange debt.

(3) *15 Sch 3(4):* for the purpose of the alternative calculations for exchange gains and losses the meaning of unremittable income is put on an objective basis.

**4.40**   *Claims, Elections and Revisions*

*Finance Act 1994*

(1)   *Section 163:* the definition of an irrecoverable payment, for interest rate and currency contracts, is recast on an objective basis.

## Consequential claims following Revenue enquiry, etc.

**4.40**   As set out in Chapter 17, following the conclusion of a Revenue enquiry into a corporation tax return, the Revenue may make an amendment to another return of the company, increasing the tax payable. The Revenue also have powers to make discovery assessments or to recover excess group relief. In such cases the company is given the opportunity to make claims or elections varying those already made. [*FA 1998 18 Sch 61(1)*].

**4.41**   In the absence of fraud or neglect, where a Revenue amendment or assessment has increased a company's tax liability for an accounting period, the company may (within twelve months of the end of the accounting period in which the enquiry was concluded), make a claim or election, or amend one previously made unless it was irrevocable. The claim or election is to relate to the accounting period concerned or be made by reference to an event occurring in that period. It can reduce the increased tax arising from the Revenue amendment or assessment, or reduce any other tax liability of the company for the accounting period concerned or any subsequent accounting period ending within a year thereof. In the case of fraud or neglect, a claim can only be made for the relief that would have been available for the accounting period in question if it had been made within the time allowed by the Taxes Acts. So claims for subsequent accounting periods are not allowed. [*FA 1998 18 Sch 61, 62, 65*].

**4.42**   All necessary adjustments to the company's tax liability are then to be made, whether by discharge of tax or repayment, etc. The company has a right of appeal against a refusal by the Revenue to accept the amended claim. In the event that the making or varying of such a claim would be to alter the tax liability of another person, that person's prior consent (or that of his personal representatives) must be obtained. Where such consent is given, those other persons may not make claims under *para 62* if companies, or *TMA 1970 s 43A* if individuals or trustees. [*FA 1998 18 Sch 63*].

**4.43**   In a case where the reduction in tax liability arising from such a claim or election would exceed any consequent increase in liability, the excess is not available to reduce any tax liability (i.e. in such a case it is not possible to obtain a repayment). Should this limitation apply to different periods or different persons, it is to be apportioned as the parties specify, or by the Revenue if there is no such specification. [*FA 1998 18 Sch 64*].

## Crown option

**4.44** The Inland Revenue has power to determine, in the case of a financial trader, whether the investment income should be assessed under Schedule D Cases III, IV or V or under Cases I or II. Similarly in the case of a life insurance company, the Revenue may determine whether
the company's profits should be assessed under Schedule D, Case 1 or on the basis of the income less management expenses (normally known as the I–E basis). This right to determination which the Revenue have is normally known as the Crown option, and arises from case law such as *Clerical, Medical and General Life Assurance Society v Carter (1889) 2 TC 437*, *Revell v Edinburgh Life Insurance Co (1906) 5 TC 221*, *Liverpool and London and Globe Insurance Co v Bennett (1913) 6 TC 327* and *Gresham Life Assurance Society v A-G (1916) 7 TC 36*. The existence of the Crown option is confirmed by *TMA 1970 s 28A(7A)(d)* and *TMA 1970 s 28B(6A)(d)* is introduced by *FA 1996 19 Sch 4* and *5*. To enable the Revenue to determine which of the alternative bases should be applied, the power to call for documents provisions in *TMA 1970 s 19A* are extended to enable the Revenue to call for these documents which would enable them to apply the Crown option correctly.

**4.45** The Crown option, which in practice is rarely used, is generally to discourage taxpayers from switching accounting bases to produce the lowest tax bill each year. Where it is used, the alternative chosen by the Revenue must be applied for the purposes of CTSA and any enquiries and amendments relating thereto. The provisions enabling a partnership statement to be amended are duly modified to provide for the application of the Crown option. [*FA 1996, 19 Sch 5*]. There is no right of appeal against the exercise of the Crown option, as the choice is entirely at the discretion of the Revenue. [*FA 1996 19 Sch 6*].

*Chapter 5*

# Payment/Repayment

## Introduction

**5.1** Under CTSA, for small and medium-sized companies, tax is still payable nine months after the end of the accounting period. For large companies, there is a radical change with tax becoming payable by quarterly instalments partly within and partly without the company's accounting period. This effectively coincides with the abolition of ACT from 6 April 1999. The provisions which determine whether a company is large and which then require instalment payments are considered later in this chapter. The Revenue has published 'A Guide to Quarterly Instalment Payments', available on the Internet at www.inlandrevenue.gov.uk and further guidance in Tax Bulletin, Issue 45, February 2000 at pp 723–726.

**5.2** 'Tax' includes not just corporation tax, but also any liability under *TA 1988 s 419* (loans to participators) and *TA 1988 s 74A* (controlled foreign companies). The three components of the tax liability are not distinguished in the Revenue's payment applications. Such payment applications and reconciliations will continue to relate to a single accounting period as under Pay and File. As described in Chapter 18, interest is chargeable in respect of tax paid late, and 'credit interest' is due in certain cases on tax paid early.

## Small and medium companies

### Date for payment

**5.3** For companies that are not large, corporation tax for an accounting period continues to be payable on the day following the expiry of nine months (being calendar months) from the end of the period ('the normal due date'). [*TMA 1970 s 59D(1)*]. Assuming that an accounting period ends on the last day of the calendar month, the normal due date is the first day of the tenth following month; i.e. for a 31 December 2000 year end it is 1 October 2001. If the accounting date ends on another day the normal due date will be the day after the correspondingly numbered day in the ninth following month; i.e. for a 1 July 1999 year end it will be 2 April 2000. When there is no corresponding day, the normal due date is the first day of the tenth following month; i.e. for year ends of 29, 30 or 31 May 2000 it will be 1 March 2001.

**5.4** If the tax payable on the due date is less than relevant amounts previously paid, the difference is to be repaid [*TMA 1970 s 59D (2)*] or the right to a refund may be surrendered to another company within the same group under *FA 1989 s 102*. Relevant amounts are:

(a) excess corporation tax previously paid by the company and not repaid;

(b) a corporation tax refund surrendered to a company by another group company;

(c) any excess of the amounts available for set off under step 4 of the tax liability calculation in *FA 1998 18 Sch (8)*, namely:

   (i) any tax borne by deduction under *TA 1988 s 7(2)* or *11(3)*; or

   (ii) any amount to be set off as a deduction under *TA 1988 ss 246N* or *246Q* as ACT paid in respect of a FID;

(d) any amount treated as corporation tax paid in respect of profits of the company as a payment to a sub-contractor under *TA 1988 s 559*. [*TMA 1970 s 59D(4)*].

*Example 1*

Cat Ltd would in principle be liable for corporation tax in respect of its accounting period ending 31 January 2002 in the amount of £40,000 due for payment on 1 November 2002. However in May 2002 an appeal relating to Cat Ltd's and its sister company Dog Ltd's liability for the year to 31 January 2000 was determined in their favour, with the result that £30,000 fell to be repaid to each. In June 2002 Cat Ltd and Dog Ltd gave notice to the Board under *FA 1989 s 102(2)* that the whole of the repayment was to be treated as tax paid by Cat Ltd. Accordingly, a repayment of £20,000 (being £60,000–£40,000) is due by the Revenue to Cat Ltd rather than tax being due on 1 November by Cat Ltd.

**Repayment before establishment of tax liability**

**5.5** A company may claim a repayment of tax where it has made a payment of tax for an accounting period but its circumstances have changed so it has grounds for believing that this payment was excessive before its tax liability has been finally established. [*TMA 1970 s 59DA(1), (2)*]. This might be because the company had not yet made a return or because its return was under enquiry, or possibly because the Inspector had made a discovery assessment that was under appeal. If the liability had been finally established the mechanics for recovery would be an amendment of the return or a claim for mistake relief.

## 5.6 Payment/Repayment

**5.6** The claim is made by giving notice to the Inspector stating (a) the amount the company considers should be repaid; and (b) its grounds for believing the amounts paid exceed its expected liability. [*TMA 1970 s 59DA(2), (3)*]. A claim cannot be made before the normal due date. [*TMA 1970 s 59DA(2)*]. If a company has not delivered its tax return for the period when it makes such a claim, deductions under *TA 1988 s 559* for payments to sub-contractors are to be disregarded in determining whether any repayment is due. [*TMA 1970 s 59DA(7)*]. Such a claim is heard in the same way as an appeal. [*TMA 1970 s 59DA(5)*].

**5.7** An application for repayment may be made while an appeal against an amendment or assessment relating to the tax liability in question is pending. In this case, the claim is made to the Commissioners dealing with the appeal and may be combined with an application to postpone payment of tax under *TMA 1970 s 55*. The application is heard in the same way as an appeal. [*TMA 1970 s 59DA(4), (5), (6)*]. The decision as to whether any repayment is due is subject to the same proviso as above if the tax return has not been delivered, namely that sub-contractor deductions under *TA 1988 s 559* are disregarded. [*TMA 1970 s 59DA(7)*].

## Large companies

### How to determine whether a company is a large company

*Basic provisions*

**5.8** The requirement for large companies to pay tax in quarterly instalments is contained in *The Corporation Tax (Instalment Payments) Regulations (SI 1998 No. 3175)* ('*the Regulations*') (see Appendix 3). A large company for the purposes of determining whether the instalment regime applies is one whose total liability exceeds £10,000 (this de minimis limit is £5,000 for accounting periods ending before 1 July 2000) *and* whose profits for an accounting period exceed the 'upper relevant maximum amount' as found in *TA 1988 s 13* [*Regulation 3(1), (2)*] as amended by the *Corporation Tax (Instalment Payment) (Amendments) Regulations (SI 2000 No. 892)*. That upper relevant maximum amount is currently £1.5 m. *Section 13* determines qualification for small companies relief; companies that do not qualify even for marginal relief will generally also be liable to pay in instalments.

**5.9** The 'total liability' of a company is the company's aggregate tax liability for a period, i.e. corporation tax plus any amounts due under *TA 1988 s 419* and any sums chargeable under *TA s 747* but reduced by the amount of any deductions from payments made to sub-contractors under *TA 1988 s 559*. [*Regulation 2(3)*]. Profits are defined as the aggregate of the amount of profits on which tax will be assessed and the amount of franked investment income received otherwise than from within its

## Payment/Repayment  5.10

group. [*Regulation 2(2)*]. Profits under *Regulation 3* also include certain sums which are left out of account in determining qualification for small companies relief [*Regulation 3(4)*], namely:

(a) investment income in respect of investments held in connection with a company's life assurance business [*TA 1988 s 434(3A), (3B)*];

(b) where a company carries on a life assurance business, the policy holders' share of profits [*FA 1989 s 88(4)*].

*Associated companies*

**5.10**   Where a company has associated companies the upper relevant maximum amount is reduced by reference to the number of its associated companies during that accounting period. [*TA 1988 s 13(3)–(6)* applied by *Regulation 3(4)*]. Two companies are associated if one has control of the other or both are under the control of the same person or persons. [*TA 1988 s 13(4)* applied by *Regulation 3(4)*]. The relevant upper maximum amount for a company becomes £1.5 m divided by one plus the number of its associated companies. [*TA 1988 s 13(3)(b)* applied by *Regulation 3(4)*]. Any associated company which has not carried on any trade or business during the accounting period is ignored for these purposes. [*TA 1988 s 13(4)*]. Even if a company has associated companies, however, it will not be a large company unless its own tax liability exceeds £5,000.

*Example 2*

White Ltd is associated with five other companies. Its profits for the year to 31 December 2000 are £220,000 and its tax liability is £6,500. It is not a large company for this period since its profits are under the upper relevant maximum amount, being £1.5 m ÷ 6 = £250,000.

*Example 3*

Black Ltd is likewise associated with five other companies. Its profits for the year to 31 December 2000 are £270,000 but its tax (because of available reliefs) is only £4,000. It is also not a large company for this period since its tax liability is under £10,000, notwithstanding that its profits exceed the upper relevant maximum amount.

*Example 4*

Yellow Ltd and Mauve Ltd are associated, both having the same accounting period to 31 July. In the year to 31 July 2001 Yellow Ltd makes profits

## 5.11 Payment/Repayment

of £2 m on a turnover of £3 m; tax payable £580,000. Mauve Ltd only makes profits of £10,000 on a similar turnover, with tax payable £3,000. Yellow Ltd must pay tax by instalments, its profits exceeding £1.5 m ÷ 2 = £750,000. However, Mauve Ltd does not, because its own tax liability is under £10,000.

*Short accounting periods*

**5.11** If a company's accounting period is less than twelve months, the upper relevant maximum and the £10,000 threshold are proportionately reduced. [*TA 1988 s 13(6); Regulation 3(2)*].

*Example 5*

In June 2005, Mr Argyll purchases Blue Ltd, which has an accounting period ending 31 October. He owns two other companies, Red Ltd and Green Ltd, which have periods ending 31 July. Accordingly he decides that Blue Ltd should have a short period to 31 July 2005, of nine months, so that its year end coincides with its associated companies. In that period, Blue Ltd has profits of £450,000 but an expected tax liability of only £3,000. Blue Ltd now has two associated companies so the upper relevant maximum amount would be £500,000 for a full year. This is reduced by 3/12, to £375,000, because Blue Ltd has a short accounting period. The tax liability threshold is also reduced by 3/12, to £7,500. Accordingly, in these circumstances, despite its profits exceeding the upper relevant maximum amount as reduced, Blue Ltd would not have to pay its tax by instalments because of its low expected tax liability.

**Companies becoming large**

**5.12** There are provisions to ease a company's transition from being a small or medium company to being a large company. The instalment regime does not apply to a company in the first year it becomes large unless its profits for that period exceed £10 m. [*Regulations 3(3), (6)*]. This provision also applies in the first year of a company's existence.

**Companies with associated companies becoming large**

**5.13** The £10 m threshold for the 'growing companies' relief is also reduced where a company has associated companies. In such cases, the threshold is £10 m divided by the number of associated companies at the end of the immediately preceding accounting period plus one. If there was no immediately preceding accounting period, or if the immediately preceding accounting period did not end on the day before the account-

*Payment/Repayment* **5.15**

ing period for which the relief is sought began, the number of associated companies at the beginning of that period is used. [*Regulation 3(5)*].

*Example 6*

(Continuing Example 5). Red Ltd had profits of only £200,000 in the period ending 31 July 2005. Business improves remarkably in the year following the acquisition of Blue Ltd, and in the period ending 31 July 2006 Red Ltd expects profits of £4 m and to pay £600,000 in corporation tax, sufficient to make Red Ltd a large company within *TA 1988 s 13*. Since Red Ltd had two associated companies at the end of the previous accounting period, the threshold for the growing companies relief is £10 m ÷ 3 = £3$\frac{1}{3}$ m and Red Ltd does not qualify. Had Blue Ltd been acquired in August 2005 rather than June 2005, Red Ltd would only have had one associated company at the end of the accounting period before that in which it became large so the threshold would have been £10 m ÷ 2 = £5 m and Red Ltd would have qualified for the relief.

**Due dates for instalments**

**5.14** Under the CTSA regime (i.e. accounting periods ending on and after 1 July 1999), tax is payable by large companies in four equal instalments. For twelve monthly accounting periods the first instalment is payable six months and thirteen days after the start of the accounting period. The second instalment is payable three months after the first, and the third instalment is payable three months after the second. The last is payable three months and 14 days after the end of the accounting period. Where the first or second instalment is due on the last day of the calendar month the second or third instalment, as the case may be, will be due on the last day of the third following month. Where the first or second instalment is due on some other day, the second or third instalment will be due on the correspondingly numbered day in the third following month. Where there is no correspondingly numbered day in the third following month, the second or third instalment will be due on the last day of the third following month.

**5.15** If the accounting period is less than twelve months, the last payment will still be made three months and fourteen days after the end of the period. As many other payments on the standard pattern are to be made before that as can be fitted in, the first being made six months and thirteen days after the start of the period. [*Regulation 5(3)*]. Thus, if the accounting period is three months or less, only the final instalment is required. If it is between three months one day and six months, the first and final instalments will be required. If between six months one day and nine months, the first, second and final instalments will be required. If the accounting period is over nine months, four instalments will be required.

## 5.15 Payment/Repayment

*Examples of 12 month accounting periods*

### Example 7

Accounting period ends 1 July 1999

| | |
|---|---|
| First instalment | 15 January 1999 |
| Second instalment | 15 April 1999 |
| Third instalment | 15 July 1999 |
| Final instalment | 15 October 1999 |

### Example 8

Accounting period ends 17 July 2000

| | |
|---|---|
| First instalment | 31 January 2000 |
| Second instalment | 30 April 2000 |
| Third instalment | 31 July 2000 |
| Final instalment | 31 October 2000 |

### Example 9

Accounting period ends 31 December 2001

| | |
|---|---|
| First instalment | 14 July 2001 |
| Second instalment | 14 October 2001 |
| Third instalment | 14 January 2002 |
| Final instalment | 14 April 2002 |

*Examples of accounting periods less than 12 months*

### Example 10

Accounting period 15 October 2000 to 19 July 2001

| | | |
|---|---|---|
| First instalment | 28 April 2001 | (6 months and 13 days after 15 October 2000) |
| Second instalment | 28 July 2001 | (3 months after 1st instalment) |
| Third instalment | 28 October 2001 | (3 months after 2nd instalment) |
| Final instalment | 2 November 2001 | (3 months and 14 days after 19 July 2001) |

*Example 11*

Accounting period 1 January 1999 to 31 July 1999

| | |
|---|---|
| First instalment | 14 July 1999 |
| Second instalment | 14 October 1999 |
| Third instalment | not due |
| Final instalment | 14 November 1999 |

*Example of a change of accounting period*

*Example 12*

Albion Ltd has a twelve month accounting period ending on 31 July. For its year to 31 July 2004, it estimates that its corporation tax liability will be £500,000. It makes payments on 14 February 2004, 14 May, 14 August and 14 November, each of £125,000, being £500,000 × 3/12 (the number of months in its period). On 14 February 2005, it will make its first payment in respect of its estimated liability for the year to 31 July 2005.

In May 2005, Albion Ltd decides to change its accounting period so as to have its year end on a quarter day and chooses Lady Day, 25 March. This means it will have a shortened accounting period running from 1 August 2005 to 25 March 2006, being seven months and 24 days. The company expects to pay £390,000 corporation tax for the period. It will have to make payments on 14 February 2006, 14 May 2006 and a final payment on 9 July 2006. The first two payments will be of £390,000 × 3/7.80 = £150,000. The final payment will be for £90,000, the amount of corporation tax by that time outstanding.

**Calculation of amount of each instalment**

**5.16** As each instalment becomes due, the company will have to make an estimate of its total tax liability ('CT') for the accounting period in question. That estimate then has to be multiplied by three and divided by 'n', where n is the number of months in the accounting period. There is thus a formula for calculating the amount of each instalment, being:

$$3 \times \frac{CT}{n}.$$

### 5.17 Payment/Repayment

**5.17** Part months are calculated by reference to the number of spare days, divided by 30 and expressed as a decimal to two decimal places, rounded arithmetically. [*Regulations 5(4), (5), (6), (7)*]. Hence, where the accounting period goes from 1 January 2000 to 31 August 2000 n will be 8. An accounting period from 1 January 2000 to 28 July 2000 will consist of six complete months and 28 days. The part month will be calculated as

$$\frac{28}{30} \times 100 = 93.33 \text{ recurring: so take } 0.93.$$

Accordingly, n will be 6.93.

**5.18** For accounting periods of twelve months, the formula will result in a quarter of the liability being due at each instalment date. Where the accounting periods are less than twelve months, the amount payable on each instalment date will be the smaller of the formula amount and the amount of tax not allocated to earlier instalments.

**5.19** Because an estimate is required as each instalment payment becomes due, such estimates are likely to vary over time as the accounting period advances. With changing circumstances, earlier instalments may have become excessive, and there is then provision to make a repayment claim. [See 5.22].

**The transitional period**

**5.20** To ease the impact on companies' cash flow which a sudden change to instalment payments would entail, for the first three years after 1 July 1999 only a limited percentage of a company's liability will be payable by instalments, the balance being paid on the due and payable date nine months and one day after the end of the accounting period. After 1 July 2002, the full amount will be payable by instalments.

**5.21** The percentage payable in instalments increases during the three year period:

(a) for accounting periods ending between 1 July 1999 and 30 June 2000, 60 per cent is payable by instalments;

(b) for accounting periods ending between 1 July 2000 and 30 June 2001, 72 per cent is payable by instalments; and

(c) for accounting periods ending between 1 July 2001 and 30 June 2002, 88 per cent is payable by instalments.

This percentage applies to reduce not only the total amount payable, but also the amount payable in each instalment. [*Regulations 4, 5(2)*]. In each case the balance of any tax is payable on the normal due date.

*Payment/Repayment*  **5.21**

*Example 13*

Berwick Ltd has a 31 December year end and, with annual profits of £2 m and corporation tax liability of £600,000, is a large company. For the first four years of the new regime, it will have to make the following payments of tax:

(a) in respect of the year ending 31 December 1999, payments on 14 July 1999, 14 October 1999, 14 January 2000 and 14 April 2000 each of £90,000 (60 per cent of £150,000) and a final payment of £240,000 on 1 September 2000;

(b) in respect of the year ending 31 December 2000, payments on 14 July 2000, 14 October 2000, 14 January 2001 and 14 April 2001 each of £108,000 (72 per cent of £150,000) and a final payment of £168,000 on 1 September 2001;

(c) in respect of the year ending 31 December 2001, payments on 14 July 2001, 14 October 2001, 14 January 2002 and 14 April 2002 each of £132,000 (88 per cent of £150,000) and a final payment of £72,000 on 1 September 2000;

(d) in respect of the year ending 31 December 2002, payments on 14 July 2002, 14 October 2002, 14 January 2003 and 14 April 2003 each of £150,000.

*Example 14*

Tweed Ltd is a large company, with a seven month accounting period from 1 January to 31 July 2000, so n is 7. Its estimated tax liability is £70,000. 72 per cent is payable by instalments, being £50,400. Three instalments are due on 14 July, 14 October and 14 November 2000. Both the first and second instalments are:

$$\frac{3 \times 50{,}400}{7} = £21{,}600; \text{ i.e. a total of } £43{,}200.$$

The third instalment would likewise be £21,600, but the company's total instalment liability is £50,400. So the amount payable is limited to the unpaid balance of £7,200. The remaining 28 per cent of the total tax liability, amounting to £19,600, is payable on the normal due date of 1 May 2001.

## 5.22 Payment/Repayment

**Revision of estimates – claims for repayment**

**5.22** Since companies have to base their instalments on their estimated total tax liability for the year, which will depend on estimated profits, it may well happen that a company revises its estimated liability between payments and has grounds for believing that its total liability is likely to be lower than previously calculated. If this revision is the result of a change in the company's circumstances and the total amount paid by that stage exceeds the amount that would have been payable had the revised figure for total liability been used to calculate the amount of every instalment so far, the company may make a claim for repayment of the excess. [*Regulation 6(1), (2), (7)*]. Such a claim may be made at any time after an instalment payment has been made and before the liability has been finally established. Alternatively, the company could leave the excess with the Revenue and reduce the next instalment payment accordingly. Equally, if a company finds at any point that it has underestimated its liability it can make a top-up payment immediately or adjust the next instalment payment accordingly. Making an early payment will reduce the interest payable in due course.

**5.23** The Revenue accept that if an instalment payment is found to be excessive, the following payment or payments can be reduced so that the running total of payments made equals the right amount. This remedy, unlike a claim for repayment, may also be available where the original over-estimate was due to a miscalculation rather than a difference in circumstances. It does not require a specific claim to be made to the Revenue.

---

*Example 15*

---

Clyde Ltd, with a twelve month accounting period ending 31 May 2003 is due to make a first instalment payment on 14 December 2002. At that time the business is booming and it expects a tax liability for the year of £1 m and accordingly makes a first instalment payment of £250,000. By the time the next payment is due on 14 March, the profits forecast is less good and so the estimated tax liability has fallen to £900,000. If this had been the estimate three months earlier, instalments of only £225,000 would have been due. Accordingly, the company makes a second instalment payment of £200,000 so as to bring the total paid for the first two instalments up to £450,000.

In the spring the situation worsens, and the estimated tax liability falls again to £600,000. On this estimate each instalment would have had to be only £150,000, so that the first three instalments would total £450,000. Thus, when the next instalment is due on 14 June, the company makes no further payment, since the correct amount has already been paid on account. After the year end, it emerges that an insurance claim for loss of trading receipts following a factory fire has been rejected and accordingly the tax liability for the year will be only £300,000. At this point Clyde Ltd makes a claim for repayment of £150,000.

**5.24** A claim for repayment where excessive instalment payments have been paid is made by giving notice to an officer of the Board. This notice must specify the amount that the company believes should be repaid and the grounds for this belief. Appeal against a refusal of repayment lies to the General or Special Commissioners in the usual way. [*Regulation 6(2), (3)*].

**5.25** If a company has appealed against an assessment or an amendment in respect of its total liability for the period concerned and that appeal has not been finally determined, it may apply to the Commissioners dealing with the appeal for a determination of an amount to be repaid pending the outcome of the appeal. Such an application may be combined with an application to postpone payment of tax under *TMA 1970 s 55* and is heard and determined in the same way as an appeal. These provisions take the place of the substantially identical provisions in *TMA 1970 s 59DA* for companies not paying by instalments (see para 5.7 above). [*Regulation 6(4), (5), (6), (8)*].

### Intra-group surrender of excessive instalment payments

**5.26** Excesses of tax paid by instalments over the actual liability can be surrendered between members of a group rather than actually claimed back by the overpaying company. In this case there is no need to make a claim, but the surrendering company is treated for all tax purposes as having received a repayment and the recipient company as having paid an equivalent amount of tax. [*Regulation 9* amending *FA 1989 s 102*]. For these purposes two companies are members of the same group only if they qualify to be treated as such for group relief purposes. When coupled with the need for an amount to be repayable, this makes such a surrender less flexible than a Group Payment Arrangement as next considered.

# Group payment arrangements

### Outline

**5.27** Under *FA 1998 s 36*, the Revenue is able to enter into arrangements with groups of companies under which instalment payments are made by a single company on the basis of group profit forecasts. The purpose is to assist groups with large companies to manage uncertainties over the amount of the individual companies' tax liabilities prior to the filing date. They obviate the need for separate forecasts for each individual company and dividing up payments between the group companies.

### 5.28 Payment/Repayment

They also mitigate the effect of differential interest rates on overpaid and unpaid tax. A group for these purposes is a parent company, its 51 per cent subsidiaries, the subsidiaries' own 51 per cent subsidiaries and so on.

**5.28** An arrangement simply takes the form of a non-negotiable contract between the Revenue and the members of the group. A copy of the standard form document is in Appendix 2. Arrangements may be entered into for accounting periods ending on or after 31 December 1999. Group payment arrangements are set up and administered by the Group Payment Teams of the Revenue Accounts offices. The effect of the arrangements is described in *[1999] SWTI 308–312*.

**Eligibility**

**5.29** The companies that are eligible to enter into an arrangement are members of a group defined as above, where there are reasonable grounds to believe that at least one of the companies is a large company. However, not all the companies need to be liable themselves to pay in instalments, nor resident in the UK. All the companies must have filed tax returns and paid the tax due for the last but one accounting period. One of the participating companies is nominated to pay the instalments ('the nominated company') which must be UK resident and the arrangement will relate to periods of account of this company. It need not be a large company which would be liable in any event to pay by instalments. If at a later date, the group wishes a different company to be the nominated company, this can be done by written agreement between the Revenue and all the participating companies.

**5.30** The companies covered by an arrangement must have the same accounting period, but provision can be made for companies which join the group and align their accounting periods with that of the nominated company. Such a company cannot be within the arrangement in respect of an accounting period beginning before the period covered by the arrangement. The arrangement need not cover every company in a group, and a group might choose to set up several arrangements each covering a sub-group.

---

*Example 16*

---

The Jamboree Group have a group payment arrangement for the period of account ending on 31 December 2002. Banjo Ltd joins the group on 1 April 2002, and it had previously prepared accounts to 31 August each year. It draws up accounts to 31 March 2002, and then aligns its accounting date within the group, preparing its next accounts for the period 1 April 2002 to 31 December 2002. Although Banjo Ltd cannot join the group payment arrangement for its period 1 September 2001 to 31 March

2002, it can do so in respect of its period 1 April 2002 to 31 December 2002. This requires the Jamboree Group to notify the Revenue before 14 July 2002, the due date of the first instalment under the arrangement.

### Entering into the arrangement

**5.31** In order to enter into an arrangement, a group must first contact the group payment team at the Revenue office to which it normally makes its payments. That office will then send further information, and the group must return its signed contract for the arrangements at least two months before the first payment is due. Thus a group with an accounting period ending on 31 March 2000 would have to pay its first instalment on 14 October 1999 and would have to return its signed contract by 14 August 1999. Once the arrangement is in place, it will roll forward automatically to cover subsequent accounting periods. The Revenue will have to be notified of additional companies to be brought in and of any to be left out of the arrangement for the next period of account. Such notification must be made before the due date of the first payment for the new period.

### Removal of companies from an arrangement and termination

**5.32** The nominated company may remove from the arrangement a participating company which ceases to be a group member before the 'closing date' (the date when all the companies within the arrangement have either filed their returns or had their corporation tax determined by the Revenue). The nominated company must do so if the company ceases to be a group member during the period of account to which the arrangement relates or turns out not to have an accounting period ending on the last day of the period to which the arrangement relates. The nominated company may then apportion payments to the departing company and it will not have any liability for the departing company after it has left the arrangement. The nominated company can also terminate any arrangement for any period provided it notifies the Revenue before the first payment is due for that period.

**5.33** The Revenue may remove from the arrangement a company which ceases to be a group member or does not make up its accounts to the same date as the nominated company. The Revenue also have the right to terminate the arrangement if the nominated company breaks any of the terms of the arrangement or if it appears to the Revenue that any of the companies may become liable under the anti-avoidance legislation concerned with changes in control of a company. [*TA 1988 ss 767A, 767AA*].

## 5.34 Payment/Repayment

**The undertaking in the arrangement**

**5.34** Under the arrangement the nominated company is to account for all the corporation tax payable by the companies covered by the arrangement, making instalment payments on the most recent forecasts of group profits but otherwise on the same basis as an individual company would make payments (and so on the basis of cumulative rather than quarterly profit forecasts). Payments are to be adjusted if the forecasts change, with those payments increased or reduced, and topped up, as appropriate. These payments must be made by electronic funds transfer (including 'Bank Giro Credit'). Any adjustments to the amount due resulting from a change in a company's return after the 'closing date' will be dealt with on an individual company, not group, basis.

**5.35** After the closing date, the nominated company will be issued with a notice by the Revenue showing what it has paid on behalf of the group and its liability at closing. If there is a shortfall, the nominated company may either make it good and apportion payments to companies within the group or, if it has reason to believe the shortfall is likely to decrease after the closing date, allocate it. Similarly, a surplus may either be reclaimed or allocated.

**5.36** The Revenue will not seek to recover tax from individual companies covered by the arrangements until their closing date. The group payment arrangement only deals with liability to pay tax, not actual liability to tax, and after the closing date, an individual company may be pursued for the tax by the Revenue in the usual way. The Revenue also has the power to override any allocation of shortfall if payment cannot be secured from the company to which the allocation was made.

---

*Example 17*

---

Apples Ltd owns 75 per cent of the shares in Bramley Ltd, which in turn owns 70 per cent of the shares in Cox Ltd and 60 per cent of the shares in Delicious Ltd. Apples Ltd makes annual profits of £2 m and is a large company liable to make instalment payments. A large part of these profits are derived from providing services to the other companies within the group which are not invoiced until the end of the group accounting period on 30 April. The other companies have much smaller profits of around £100,000 each. All the companies, bar Delicious Ltd, are UK resident and all are liable to UK corporation tax.

The companies are a group within *FA 1998 s 36* and are eligible to enter a Group Payment Arrangement. Apples' first instalment for the period ending 30 April 2001 would be due on 14 November 2000, so the contract has to be returned signed by 14 September 2000 to have the arrangement in place for the period. The companies enter the arrangement, with Bramley as the nominated company. When the first payment is made in

November, the group expects its profits to be stable and its overall CT liability for the year to be £650,000. Accordingly Bramley makes a payment of £117,000 on 14 November 2000 and another on 14 February 2001 (i.e. ¼ of the 72 per cent of tax liable to be paid by instalments under the transitional provisions: 5.21 above).

In March it becomes clear that the UK profits of Delicious will be far better than expected, up to £300,000 after payments to Apples. This will result in an additional liability of £60,000 so the payment on 14 May 2001 is £117,000 + £32,400 = £149,400. The final instalment of £127,800 is paid on 14 August 2001 and the balance of £198,800 is paid on 1 February 2002, so that the group has paid £710,000 CT for the period to 30 April 2001.

Delicious had underestimated the increase in its profits by £50,000 (resulting in tax of £15,000), but that this further increase had come at the expense of Bramley's profits. In the normal course of events, Delicious would be liable to interest at 7.5 per cent (rate applicable from 6 March 1999 on unpaid tax) and Bramley would be able to claim a refund with interest at only 4 per cent. Under the arrangement, however, Bramley's overpaid tax can be apportioned to Delicious so that it need pay no interest.

## Practical issues regarding instalment payments

**5.37** The onus is on companies themselves to ascertain whether they need to make quarterly instalment payments and to take the initiative to make the payments. However, the Revenue run a computer check of the most recent return received and alert companies that seem likely to need to review their position. The Revenue issue payslips to such companies between one and two months before the likely due date for an instalment payment that the company might need to make.

**5.38** Companies which consider that they are or may be liable to make quarterly instalment payments should review the position before each instalment due date. If the current estimate of total liability indicates that too little tax has been paid at previous instalment due dates, the company should make a top-up payment. If a company considers that it has paid too much, it may deduct the excess from the current payment. If the cumulative payments exceed the cumulative liability, the company may claim repayment under *Regulation 6*. A top-up payment (or a repayment claim) may be made at any time.

**5.39** Companies may make quarterly instalment payments using any means available for the payment of tax, including electronic transfers. Where companies pay by cheque, it is helpful to the Revenue if they use a Revenue payslip for the accounting period concerned.

## Estimates and quarterly instalment payments

**5.40** Because the instalment payments system proceeds on the basis of estimates of the company's likely tax liability, there will be occasions on which companies make payments that they later judge (or discover) to have been excessive or unnecessary. Also there will be occasions on which companies judge (or discover) that they should have made payments that they have not made, or should have made larger payments. Such judgements and discoveries are an inescapable part of the regime and the Revenue have stated that they will not lead to the imposition of a penalty under *Regulation 13* unless the company has deliberately or recklessly failed to make an instalment payment or has made a fraudulent or negligent repayment claim under *Paragraph 6*.

## The Board's information powers

**5.41** Under the Regulations, the Board have very wide powers to demand information; so wide in fact that it has been questioned whether they are appropriate to have been granted by secondary legislation. The Board may require, by giving notice, any company to furnish it with such information as it may reasonably require for verifying that the correct instalments have been paid. This power extends to inspection of any relevant books, documents or other records of the company. It can be exercised against any company, seemingly whether or not it is the relevant taxpayer, and without any prior issue of a notice of enquiry or similar. There is no requirement that the Board explains its reasons to the company and no mechanism in place for appealing against the issue of the notice as there would be if a notice is issued after an enquiry has been commenced into the final tax liability of a taxpayer. [*Regulations 10–12*]. To resist inspection a company would have to apply for judicial review. The Revenue has published guidance on use of the information and penalty powers in Tax Bulletin, Issue 42, August 1999, pp 683–4 (Appendix 1) (cf IR Press Release, 8 June 1999, *[1999] STI 1021*). Under the guidance, the Revenue will only use the information powers 'where there are indicators that a company may have deliberately or recklessly failed to comply with its payment obligations under the regulations, or fraudulently or negligently made a claim for repayment'.

## Anti-avoidance

**5.42** The Revenue were concerned that companies might seek to defer payment of instalments by manipulating their accounting periods or shifting profits into group companies with different accounting periods. Anti-avoidance provisions have consequently been introduced covering the period from 25 November 1997 to 30 June 2002, i.e. the period from the announcement of the new system to the end of the transition period. The intention of the provisions is to tax companies performing manipulations as if they had not done so.

**5.43** Companies are potentially caught if they change the dates of any 'relevant accounting periods' before 1 July 2002 except in specified circumstances [*Regulation 14(1)(a)(i)*], namely:

(a) if the change derives from a decision taken before 25 November 1997;

(b) if the change occurs as a result of the company beginning or ceasing to trade, beginning or ceasing to be resident in the United Kingdom or ceasing to be within the charge to corporation tax [*TA 1988 s 12(3)(c), (d), (e)*]; or

(c) if the change of period is caused by a change in the ultimate control of the company and an alignment of the company's period with its new ultimate parent. Control is, broadly, ability to exercise practical control of the company's affairs [*TA 1988 s 416*], and a change in ultimate control means either a change in control of the top company in the group or a change in control of the company concerned. [*Regulation 14(6), 11(a), (d)*].

A relevant accounting period for these purposes is one which:

(i) would have ended between 25 November 1997 and 30 June 2002 inclusive; and

(ii) would have been of twelve months duration and followed immediately after the previous accounting period. [*Regulation 14(5)*].

**5.44** Companies are also potentially caught if they enter into arrangements or transactions (except in certain circumstances) the effect of which is to transfer profits to another group company (except for certain companies) and this defers the payment of corporation tax. [*Regulation 14(1)(a)(ii)*]. A group for these purposes is a 51 per cent group as in *TA 1988 s 838(1)(a)*. [*Regulation 14(11)(b)*]. The circumstances in which a company may make such a transfer are:

(a) the two companies have the same accounting period and the transferor has not effected a change of period that would be caught by the other limb of the anti-avoidance provision (see 5.43 above); or

(b) as a result of the transfer, the transferor's profits are reduced by less than £5 m (or a proportion thereof if the transferor has an accounting period of less than twelve months). [*Regulation 14(7)*].

The excluded transferee companies are those which:

(i) are resident outside the United Kingdom; and

(ii) either:

(1) are not trading in the UK through any branch or agency; or

**5.45** *Payment/Repayment*

(2) if so trading, are not companies for which the profits transferred form part of the taxable profits of such a branch or agency. [*Regulation 14(8)*].

**5.45** If a company makes such a change in its accounting period or makes such a transfer of profits, the Regulations impose an interest charge if, as a result, any amount of corporation tax in respect of the profits for an accounting period is due and payable later than it would have been but for the change or transfer. [*Regulation 14(1)(b)*]. This comparison involves considering a hypothetical position, that in which no action had been taken, and the Regulations specify certain assumptions to be made when calculating how and when profits would have been taxable in that case:

(a) any reliefs available to the company or group would have been so allocated as to result in tax being payable later rather than sooner;

(b) any profits actually covered by reliefs would have been covered, and any profits not so covered would not have been covered;

(c) not more than twelve months' profits would have been allocated to any of the years covered by the transitional provisions (from 1 July to 30 June each year from 1999 to 2002), with profits for actual accounting periods being allocated first. [*Regulation 14(9)*].

There are further provisions for deciding the 'hypothetical dates' on which amounts of corporation tax would have been payable:

(i) where necessary, profits are attributed between accounting periods (including but not limited to relevant accounting periods) on a time basis, or, if that would be unjust and unreasonable, on a just and reasonable basis; and

(ii) those dates are determined as if the taxable profits concerned (i.e. those hypothetically reallocated) were the only taxable profits for an accounting period. [*Regulation 14(10)*].

---

*Example 18*

---

Jade Ltd has an accounting period to 31 December 1998. For no 'legitimate' reason it then has a four month accounting period to 30 April 1999 and an eight month accounting period to 31 December 1999. Jade Ltd's profits for these two periods are £300,000 (tax payable £100,000) and £2 m (tax payable £600,000) respectively. Had Jade Ltd not changed its accounting period, the hypothetical due dates for instalments for the year to 31 December 1999 would have been 14 July 1999, 14 October 1999, 14 January 2000 and 14 April 2000. With the transitional relief the tax payable by instalments would have been 60 per cent, and the balance of 40 per cent would have been due on 1 October 2000. The hypothetical

## Payment/Repayment 5.45

and actual due dates will need to be compared for the two periods separately in order to ascertain the interest charge.

For the four month period the total liability is £100,000, which is actually payable on 1 February 2000. On a hypothetical basis, 60 per cent would have been payable by instalments and 40 per cent as the balance on 1 October 2000.

| Hypothetical due date | Actual due date | Hypothetical tax due | | Tax paid | Interest chargeable | Interest allowable |
|---|---|---|---|---|---|---|
| | | Amount | Cumulative | | | |
| 14/07/99 | | 15 | 15 | | Yes | |
| 14/10/99 | | 15 | 30 | | Yes | |
| 14/01/00 | | 15 | 45 | | Yes | |
| | 01/02/00 | | | 100 | — | — |
| 14/04/00 | | 15 | 60 | | — | Yes |
| 01/10/00 | | 40 | 100 | | — | Yes |

For the eight month period the total liability is £600,000 of which £360,000 (60 per cent) is payable by instalments and the balance of £240,000 is payable on 1 October 2000.

| Hypothetical due date | Actual due date | Hypothetical tax due | | Tax paid | | Interest chargeable | Interest allowable |
|---|---|---|---|---|---|---|---|
| | | Amount | Cumulative | Amount | Cumulative | | |
| 14/07/99 | | 90 | 90 | — | | Yes | — |
| 14/10/99 | | 90 | 180 | — | | Yes | — |
| | 14/11/99 | — | | 135 | 135 | Yes | — |
| 14/01/00 | | 90 | 270 | — | | Yes | — |
| | 14/02/00 | — | | 135 | 270 | — | — |
| 14/04/00 | 14/04/00 | 90 | 360 | 90 | 360 | — | — |
| 01/10/00 | | 240 | 600 | 240 | 600 | — | — |

The results for the two accounting periods cannot be netted off. Thus a credit position on the earlier period cannot be netted off against an interest charge arising for the later period. Moreover, a net credit cannot be repaid, this being prohibited by *Regulation 14(3)(b)*. However, if the company pays tax on what would have been the due date had there been no change in accounting period, the Revenue have stated that they regard payment as being accelerated within *Regulation 14(3)*. Hence an interest charge will not arise unless the amounts paid are less than the amounts due.

### 5.45 *Payment/Repayment*

*Example 19*

Egg Ltd, whose business is the owning and operating a chain of dry cleaning shops, has its year end on 31 July each year. For the year to 31 July 2000 it expects profits of £8 m and a corporation tax liability of £2.4 m, of which it would be due to pay 72 per cent (£1,728,000) in equal instalments (£432,000) on 14 February, 14 May, 14 August and 14 November 2000 and 28 per cent (£672,000) on 1 May 2001. If it moved its year end forward to 30 June 2000, it might expect profits of £7.3 m and a tax liability of £1,440,000, of which it would then be due to pay only 60 per cent (£864,000) in equal instalments (£216,000) on 14 January, 14 April, 14 July and 14 October 2000 with a balancing payment of 40 per cent (£576,000) on 1 April 2001. Some tax would be payable later than if the change of accounting period had not been made within *Regulation 14(1)(a)(i)* and *(b)* and Egg Ltd would be liable to a charge under the anti-avoidance provisions.

Rather than move its year end therefore, Egg Ltd incorporates a subsidiary Yolk Ltd to operate the shops and becomes, instead, a holding company. Transfer of the shops is complete by 30 April 2000, at which time Egg Ltd's accounting period is treated as ending by virtue of *TA 1988 s 12(3)(c)* since it ceases to trade. It has already paid one instalment of corporation tax on 14 February 2000 of £432,000 because at that time it expected 72 per cent of its tax to be payable by instalments on the basis of an accounting period running from 1 August 1999 to 30 July 2000. It now has to recalculate its liability on the basis of a short period from 1 August 1999 to 30 April 2000 (i.e. nine months) with expected profits of £5.6 m and tax of £1.8 m of which only 60 per cent is payable in instalments. The instalments are now due on 14 February, 14 May and 14 August 2000 and each payment should be of £360,000 (i.e. (60 per cent of £1,800,000) × 3/9), with the balance of £720,000 payable on 1 February 2001. The amount actually payable on 14 May is £288,000 (i.e. £720,000 (£360,000 × 2) – £432,000) and on 14 August £360,000. Although this has resulted in a delayed payment of corporation tax, Egg Ltd is not caught by the anti-avoidance provision because the earlier year end was the result of the operation of *TA 1988 s 12(3)(c)*, as allowed by *Regulation 14(6)(b)* and because the transfer of taxable profits was less than £5 m as allowed by *Regulation 14(7)(b)*. Yolk Ltd does not have to pay any corporation tax by instalments for its first accounting period because its profits for the period will not exceed £10 m and it was not a large company in the twelve months preceding that period (see *Regulation 3(3)*).

## Insurance companies and friendly societies

**5.46** The Regulations allow companies entitled to provisional repayments under *TA 1988 19AB Sch* to set those payments off against instalment payments. These provisional repayments are made to pension businesses who receive dividends on which tax has been borne by deduction. Claims can be made for every three month period starting at the beginning of the company accounting period (unless the company has a short accounting period or ceases to carry on the pensions business) and the repayment claimed may be set off against the instalment that will be payable 14 days after the end of each of those three month periods. For the purposes of calculating any interest due on either the provisional repayment or the instalment payment, the set off is treated as both a repayment and an instalment paid on the date when the instalment payment became due and payable (i.e. 14 days after the end of the three month period). [*Regulation 15*].

## Double assessment

**5.47** If a company believes it has been assessed to tax more than once in respect of the same cause and the same accounting period, it may claim relief. Such a claim is made by giving the Board notice of the overassessment in writing. If the Board is satisfied that the company has been assessed more than once, it may amend the assessment or assessments in question, or order a repayment or discharge of tax, or give such other relief as is appropriate, so as to eliminate the reduplication of charge. [*FA 1998 18 Sch 50(1), (2)*]. If the company disagrees with the Board's decision on such a claim for relief, an appeal lies to the Commissioners who would have jurisdiction to hear an appeal against the later of the assessments to which the claim relates. [*FA 1998 18 Sch 50(3)*].

## Mistake

**5.48** A company may also claim relief if it believes it has paid excessive tax because of a mistake in a tax return. Such a claim is made by giving the Board notice in writing within six years of the end of the accounting period to which the mistaken return relates. On receiving the claim, the Board enquires into the matter and directs such repayment as is reasonable and just, except that no relief may be given:

(a) if the mistake alleged is the computation of liability in accordance with the practice generally prevailing at the time; or

(b) in respect of a mistake in a claim or election included in the return (in which case an amended claim may be made within the time allowed for the original claim). [*FA 1998 18 Sch 56*].

The Board is required to take into account all relevant circumstances and

### 5.49 Payment/Repayment

in particular whether the granting of relief would result in amounts being excluded from charge to tax. For these purposes it may consider the liability of the claimant company for periods other than that to which the claim relates. [*FA 1998 18 Sch 51(1), (2), (3), (4)*].

**5.49** Any appeal against the Board's decision on such a claim is heard by the Special Commissioners in accordance with the principles applicable to the Board's original consideration of the matter. Further appeal from the Special Commissioners' decision is limited to points of law arising in connection with the computation of:

(a) profits for the purposes of corporation tax;

(b) tax on loans or advances by close company to a *participator (TA 1988 s 419(1))*; or

(c) tax on profits of controlled foreign companies (*TA 1988 s 747(4)(a)*). [*FA 1998 18 Sch 51(5), (6)*].

## Excessive repayments

**5.50** If too much tax is repaid (see below), the Revenue may raise an assessment under Sch D Case VI for recovery of the excess unless that excess is overpaid interest recoverable under *TA 1988 s 826(8A)*. The raising of such an assessment is governed by the rules for discovery assessments (see Chapter 17) and the assessment once raised is treated as an assessment to tax for the accounting period in relation to which the overpayment was made. The sum assessed carries interest from the date of the excessive repayment by the Revenue until payment by the company. [*FA 1998 18 Sch 52(1), (4), (5), (6)*].

**5.51** The repayments to which this procedure applies are:

(a) repayment of corporation tax or income tax paid by the company;

(b) payment of a tax credit;

(c) repayment supplement under *TA 1988 s 825*; and

(d) interest paid under *TA 1988 s 826* and not recoverable under *s 826(8A)*.

For these purposes an amount is treated as paid if it is allowed as a set-off and treated as repaid if is intended as a repayment but exceeds the amount paid by the company.

### Time Limits

**5.52** The time limit for an assessment of this sort is six years from the end of the accounting period to which it relates, as for discovery assessments, but extended so that an assessment is not out of time if made:

*Payment/Repayment* **5.55**

(a) before the end of accounting period following that in which the excessive repayment was made; or

(b) if later, before the end of the period of three months beginning with the day on which the Revenue completes an enquiry into a relevant tax return by the company concerned.

The time limit is further extended, up to 21 years, in cases of fraud or negligence. [*FA 1998 18 Sch 53*].

## Payment methods – effective date of payment

### Payment by cheque

**5.53** *TMA 1970 s 70A* and a Revenue press release of 1 April 1996, clarify the date on which a payment made by cheque is treated as received. For the purposes of the *TMA* and the repayment supplement provisions (*ICTA 1988 ss 824–826* and *TCGA 1992 s 283*), a payment by cheque is made when the cheque is received by the Revenue, so long as that cheque is subsequently honoured on first presentation. Otherwise the payment is made when the funds are actually received by the Revenue. If the cheque is handed in at, or posted to a Revenue office, payment is made when the cheque is received by the Revenue. If a cheque is received by post following a day when the office has been closed for any reason, including a weekend, the date of receipt is the date the office was first closed. Thus if a cheque arrives on a Tuesday after a bank holiday, payment is treated as having been made on the previous Saturday. If the cheque is post-dated, the payment date will be the date of the cheque.

### Payment by electronic funds transfer

**5.54** Electronic funds transfers may be made by BACS (Bankers' Automated Clearing System) and CHAPS (Clearing House Automated Payment System). BACS is a system through which Bank-sponsored organisations make payments into accounts at any bank branch in the UK. CHAPS provides same-day settlement for high value inter-bank payments and is used by the twelve settlement banks and the Bank of England. The Revenue practice, set out in the 1 April 1996 press release, is to treat payments using any form of electronic funds transfer as made one working day before the value is received. A working day is a Bank of England working day.

### Payment by Bank Giro

**5.55** Under this system money can be paid into any bank to the credit of an account holder recognised for acceptance of payment by Bank Giro. The 1 April 1996 press release confirms that payment will be

**5.56** *Payment/Repayment*

treated as received three working days prior to processing by the Revenue.

**Payment by Girobank**

**5.56** This is a similar system to Bank Giro except payments are made through Girobank. Taxpayers with a Girobank account can pay by Girobank Transfer by notifying payment details to Girobank direct. Payments at a post office counter by cash or cheque (Transcash) are also dealt with by Girobank. The Revenue will also treat such payments as received three days before processing.

# Special cases

**Sub-contractors in the construction industry**

**5.57** Special provisions apply to sub-contractors in the construction industry under *TA 1988 ss 559–572* inclusive, and the *Income Tax (Sub-contractors in the Construction Industry) Regulations (SI 1993 No. 743)*. The sub-contractors rules have been modified a number of times since their original introduction and the scheme is again substantially recast from 1 August 1999, although the scheme is once again under review, following the announcement of a joint working group in the Budget 2000 (Inland Revenue Press Release, REV 11, 21 March 2000).

**5.58** Basically, a contractor carrying on construction operations which makes a payment to a sub-contractor in the UK, must deduct tax from the labour-only element of the sub-contractor's invoice at 18 per cent from 6 April 2000 (*SI 2000 Nos. 921* and *922*) and pay it over to the Inland Revenue. The sub-contractor must hold a valid registration card, which in the case of a corporate sub-contractor is issued to a director or secretary of the company. Large sub-contractors, with a turnover in excess of £3 m, may qualify for a certificate CIS 5, which allows the contractor to pay them gross. Companies which do not qualify for a CIS 5 may, as with individuals or partners, apply for a form CIS 6, provided that they have a satisfactory record of past and prospective tax compliance in respect of taxation and National Insurance and any Companies Act obligations. In order to qualify, a company must have a turnover of construction contract receipts of £200,000 or a minimum of net construction industry receipts of £30,000 per employee engaged in construction operations. It is anticipated, therefore, that there may be a substantial number of corporate sub-contractors who do not qualify for sub-contractors' tax certificates and will therefore be subject to deduction of tax at source at 18 per cent. In such cases they will receive a certificate of deduction of tax on Form CIS 25 from the contractor which may be used to frank the employer's liability to PAYE on salary payments to employees, or against its own corporation tax liability. An over-deduction can be recovered as an overpayment of corporation tax and the problems arising

*Payment/Repayment* **5.62**

for an uncertificated corporate sub-contractor are those of cashflow and bureaucracy. See Tax Bulletin, Issue 41, June 1999, p 667, Appendix 1. If, however, the corporate sub-contractor is also a personal service company (see below) further problems may arise.

**Personal service companies**

**5.59** In his 1999 Budget the Chancellor of the Exchequer announced his intention to put a stop to what he saw as tax and National Insurance avoidance through the use of intermediary companies and partnerships providing the services of individuals to client companies in cases where, had there not been an intermediary, the worker would be a direct employee of the client. The provisions remain highly controversial, and are often known as the IR35 provisions after the number of the 1999 Budget Press Release of 9 March 1999. As so often happens with anti-avoidance legislation the provisions are widely drawn and could apply to a number of cases outside the original target area. The legislation is contained in *FA 2000 s 60, 12 Sch.*

**5.60** From 6 April 2000 a person working for a personal service company, 'the worker', who provides services for clients through his company, 'the intermediary', has to pay the same amount of tax and National Insurance as if he were a direct employee, subject to a minor exemption for costs, if in the absence of the company, the arrangements with the client would have amounted to an employment rather than a self-employed individual providing freelance services.

**5.61** The tax provisions are supplemented by the *Social Security Contributions (Intermediaries) Regulations 2000 (SI 2000 No. 727)*, and the *Social Security Contributions (Intermediaries) (Northern Ireland) Regulations 2000 (SI 2000 No. 728)*, dealing with the National Insurance charge. The rules apply where the worker personally provides his services to a business client, not as a direct employee of the client but through the intermediary, in such circumstances that if there was a direct contract between the worker and the client for the provision of those services it would amount to a contract of employment. Although the third party would normally be a personal services company it could be a partnership or an unincorporated body. The arrangements must take account of the contractual terms, and the fact that the worker may be an officer of the client is ignored. [*FA 2000 12 Sch 1*, Tax Bulletin Issue 47 (June 2000) pp 751–757, Appendix 1].

**Worker treated as receiving Schedule E income**

**5.62** Where there is such a relevant engagement the intermediary is deemed to have paid to the worker a payment chargeable to tax under Schedule E, if the intermediary meets the required criteria and the worker, or an associate, receives a payment or other benefit from the

## 5.63 Payment/Repayment

intermediary, not subject to tax under Schedule E, such as a dividend, or has similar rights. The 'deemed Schedule E payment' is normally treated as made on 5 April in each tax year, with the tax due on 19 April, and there is only one such deemed payment irrespective of the number of engagements during the year. [FA 2000 12 Sch 2–6].

**Calculation of deemed Schedule E payments**

**5.63** There is a mullet-step calculation of the deemed Sch E payment as follows:

*Step 1* is the total amount received – on a cash basis, by the intermediary during the fiscal year from all relevant engagements, including any benefits in kind provided to the intermediary. The calculation is made on a fiscal year basis irrespective of the accounting date of the intermediary. The total amount received is reduced by 5 per cent as a notional allowance for the running costs of the intermediary. There are provisions to exclude receipts relating to pre 6 April 2000 and to include receipts in advance received before that date for work to be done later.

*Step 2* includes any payments or benefits in kind received by the worker in respect of any relevant engagements from anyone other than the intermediary, which are not otherwise within Schedule E, but which would have been if the worker had been employed by the client.

*Step 3* allows a deduction for any expenses which would have been allowed if the worker had paid for them and had been an employee of the client.

*Step 4* also allows as a deduction any capital allowances that would have been claimable had the worker been an employee of the client.

*Step 5* allows as a deduction any contributions paid by the intermediary to an approved pension scheme for the benefit of the worker.

*Step 6* deducts any employer's NIC paid by the intermediary in respect of salary or benefits in kind provided to the worker during the year as employee of the intermediary.

*Step 7* deducts the salary and benefits in kind provided to the worker by the intermediary during the year which have already been taxed under Schedule E and subjected to NIC. If, after Step 7, the total is a nil or a negative figure there is no 'Schedule E payment' under these provisions.

*Step 8* allows a deduction for the employer's NIC on the deemed Schedule E payment, which results in the final amount chargeable in Step 9, i.e. Step 7 shows the amount available to tax as the 'Schedule E payment' together with the NIC on that payment. [FA 2000 12 Sch 7].

## Treatment of payments made under construction industry scheme

**5.64** If the worker is subject to the construction industry scheme (5.57), under *TA 1988 s 559* it is the gross receipt which is brought into account at Step 1. It appears, however, that the amount withheld under the construction industry scheme cannot be set against the amount due on the deemed Schedule E payment, and therefore will have to be recovered at the end of the intermediary's tax year as an overpayment. This would appear to present the worker with considerable cashflow problems. [*FA 2000 12 Sch 8*].

## Application of PAYE

**5.65** The ordinary Schedule E rules and PAYE provisions apply to deemed Schedule E payments in the same way as ordinary payments of salary or benefit, as if the worker was employed by the intermediary and engagements were carried out as part of his employment with the intermediary, rather than as if he were employed direct by the client. Where the deemed Schedule E payment cannot be calculated accurately by 19 April a provisional calculation and payment would normally be accepted, but interest on any subsequent underpayment would run from 19 April. [*FA 2000 12 Sch 11*, Tax Bulletin, Issue 47, June 2000, pp 751–757, Appendix 1].

## Company taxation consequences

**5.66** To prevent double taxation, where the intermediary is a company which is treated as making a Schedule E payment in the tax year, and has already paid a dividend during that or any other subsequent year, the intermediary may submit a claim in writing to the Revenue, who, if satisfied with the claim, will make any amendment, discharge or repayment of tax to avoid a double charge to tax, by whatever method appears relevant to the Revenue. Relief is given by reducing the tax liability on the distribution or the deemed Schedule E payment. Relief is given against earlier distributions first. Relief is not available in calculating the deemed Schedule E payment for subsequent bonuses accrued and paid within nine months of the year end. [*FA 2000 12 Sch 13*].

**5.67** A deemed Schedule E payment is deductible as a trading expense of the business carried on by the intermediary for the period of account in which it is treated as made, as is the employer's NIC on the deemed Schedule E payments [*FA 2000 12 Sch 17*], i.e. if the company has a 31 March year end, a deemed Schedule E payment at 5 April 2000 is relieved in the year ended 31 March 2001 even though it relates largely to receipts included in the company's accounts to 31 March 2000. If the company's expenses exceed the notional 5 per cent allowance it may end up with an unrelievable corporation tax loss and be unable to pay the employee the full amount on which tax has been paid.

*Chapter 6*

# Advance Corporation Tax

## Introduction

**6.1** Under the system of Advance Corporation Tax (ACT) a company, on paying a dividend or making a qualifying distribution prior to 6 April 1999, became liable to ACT under *TA 1988 s 14* in respect of the distribution. The amount payable could be reduced by franked investment income received, under *TA 1988 s 231*. Intra-group dividends could be paid without incurring a liability to ACT by making a joint election by the paying and receiving companies, under *TA 1988 s 247(1)*. The company could treat the ACT paid in respect of its distribution as a payment on account of its corporation tax liability for the year, known as its mainstream liability. It was therefore, in effect, a payment on account as far as many companies were concerned.

**6.2** The great disadvantage of the ACT system was that a multinational company, which generated a lot of its profits overseas, would be paying dividends back to the parent company in the UK from the overseas subsidiaries out of taxed income. This would carry with it sufficient double taxation relief credits to eliminate or reduce to a small amount any additional UK corporation tax on the dividend received. When the UK parent company made a distribution, however, it would be liable to pay ACT of an amount in excess of the final corporation tax liability, after foreign tax credit relief. This meant the ACT ceased to be a payment on account of the mainstream corporation tax liability and became an additional cost.

**6.3** ACT which could not be set against the mainstream liability was known as surplus ACT and could be carried back or forward to be set against the mainstream liability in past or future years or surrendered to other companies in the group. For a multi-national, neither of these possibilities was particularly helpful because each year it would have dividends paid out of the UK parent company and additional surplus ACT arising which could not be utilised. It was estimated that the total surplus ACT of UK companies had accumulated to several billion pounds by April 1998 and a number of multi-nationals were considering whether to run the parent company from outside the UK. The Government therefore decided to introduce a system of payments on account for large companies in place of ACT, which was abolished from 6 April 1999

## Advance Corporation Tax  6.8

by *FA 1998 s 31*. Companies with pools of surplus ACT at 6 April 1999 are allowed to continue the old system on a notional basis and utilise the surplus built up against the mainstream corporation tax liability, broadly, as if the old system had continued, under *FA 1998 s 32* and the *Corporation Tax (Treatment of Unrelieved Surplus ACT) Regulations 1998 (SI 1999 No. 358)* (see Appendix 3).

**6.4** The ACT system, therefore, has to be considered because, for many companies, it will continue in force during part of the first accounting period under CTSA and because of the shadow system of ACT which continues into the future for those companies with an unrelieved surplus at 6 April 1999.

## Distributions

**6.5** As stated in 6.1, ACT was payable on qualifying distributions made before 6 April 1999. Non-qualifying distributions are bonus redeemable share capital and securities within *TA 1988 s 209(2)(c)* which are not distributions within *TA 1988 s 210*. All other distributions are qualifying distributions. [*TA 1988 s 14(2)*]. Returns of non-qualifying distributions are required by *TA 1988 s 234(5)* to *(9)*. The effect of treating a payment or transfer as a distribution is to disallow it for tax purposes in the paying company and exclude it from the income chargeable to corporation tax of the recipient company. [*TA 1988 s 208*].

**6.6** A distribution for tax purposes is defined by *TA 1988 ss 209–211* and *418* as including: dividends, including capital dividends [*TA 1988 s 209(2)(a)*]; any other distribution out of assets of the company in respect of shares in the company, except for a repayment of share capital or in respect of which new consideration is received [*TA 1988 ss 209(2)(b) and 254*]; the issue of redeemable share capital in respect of shares or securities of the company except to the extent that it is referable to new consideration [*TA 1988 s 209(2)(c)*]; interest or other distributions in respect of securities, to the extent that it exceeds a reasonable commercial return [*TA 1988 s 209(2)(d)*]; and any interest or other distribution in respect of securities issued to a connected company, i.e. by a 75 per cent subsidiary to its holding company or to a fellow 75 per cent subsidiary where the whole or any part of the distribution would not have been made, apart from the relationship. [*TA 1988 s 209(2)(da)*].

**6.7** These last provisions were inserted by *FA 1995 s 87* as part of the attack on thin capitalisation and to override treaty protection which might otherwise have been available. The operation of these provisions is explained in Tax Bulletin 17, June 1995, pp 218–220 (Appendix 1).

**6.8** The definition of distribution also includes any interest or other distribution in respect of securities, except so far as it relates to the principal secured where the securities are:

## 6.9 Advance Corporation Tax

(a) bonus securities;

(b) unquoted convertible securities, unless issued on terms reasonably comparable with those of listed securities;

(c) securities carrying rights to scrip dividends;

(d) securities where the interest varies with the results of the company's business or any part of it, except that under *FA 2000 s 86* payments of interest from 21 March 2000 on 'ratchet loans' will no longer be treated as a distribution solely by virtue of the fact that under the terms of the loan the rate of interest is inversely linked to the business results. Interest will therefore be allowable under the normal loan relationship rules in *FA 1996 ss 80–105, Schs 8–15*, see Chapter 10; or

(e) securities carrying rights connected with other shares in the company, which makes it advantageous to treat the holdings jointly, as in a staple stock and equity notes held by a company associated with the issuing company or funded by the issuing company. [*TA 1988 s 209(e)*].

**6.9** A transfer of assets between a company and its members is a distribution to the extent that the market value of any benefit received by the members exceeds the new consideration received by the company. [*TA 1988 s 209(2)(f) and (4)*]. This does not apply to intra-group transfers between companies in a UK group. [*TA 1988 s 209(4), (5)*]. For these purposes, a group is a UK parent company and its 51 per cent UK subsidiaries, ignoring shares held as trading stock or by non-resident companies. [*TA 1988 s 209(7)*]. Otherwise the definition of 51 per cent or 75 per cent subsidiary is that within *TA 1988 s 838(1)* measured by reference to the ordinary share capital. Transfers of assets other than cash or of liabilities between unconnected UK companies, neither of which are 51 per cent subsidiaries of a non-resident company, are also excluded from the definition of distributions by *TA 1988 s 209(7)*.

**6.10** Repayment of share capital followed by a bonus issue causes the amount paid up on the bonus shares to be treated as a distribution under *TA 1988 ss 209(f) and 210*, unless the bonus issue takes place more than ten years after the repayment and does not consist of redeemable shares, and provided that the company is not under the control of five persons under the transaction in securities definition of *TA 1988 s 704 para D, TA 1988 s 210(3)*. There are exemptions for redemption of fully paid preference shares held at 6 April 1995 or issued subsequently for new consideration. [*TA 1988 s 210(2)*]. Distributions in respect of bonus shares are not treated as a repayment of share capital. [*TA 1988 s 211*]. *TA 1988 s 254* defines terms such as new consideration, shares and security.

**6.11** Benefits given by a close company to participators, or their associates, are treated as distributions under *TA 1988 s 418* unless

## Advance Corporation Tax  6.14

already taxed under Schedule E as benefits in kind. [*TA 1988 s 418(3)*]. This also extends to reciprocal arrangements to participators in holding companies. [*TA 1988 s 418(7)* and *(8)*]. Under Schedule E the amount of the benefit is the cash equivalent or expense to the company under *TA 1988 s 154* et seq, *TA 1988 s 418(4)*.

**Non-distributions**

**6.12**  Stock dividends treated as income which has been subject to tax at the lower rate by the recipient under *TA 1988 s 249(4)–(6)*, are nonetheless excluded from the definition of distribution by *TA 1988 s 230*. Liquidation distributions are returns on capital not treated as distributions for ACT purposes. [*TA 1988 s 209(1)*]. Other specific exemptions include payments for group relief up to the amount surrendered [*TA 1988 ss 240(8), 402(6)*], and dividends, interest or bonuses in respect of deposits with registered industrial and provident societies or mutual companies under *TA 1988 s 486(10)–(12)* or building societies under *TA 1988 s 477A, (3B)* and *FA 1990 5 Sch 4* and co-operative associations under *TA 1988 s 486(1), (8)* and *(9)*. Covenanted donations to charities were previously excluded from being distributions by *TA 1988 s 339(6), (8)*, as are small distributions on the dissolution of an unincorporated association, by extra-statutory concession C15. Charitable payments from 1 April 2000 are qualifying payments dealt with under gift aid as annual payments paid gross under *TA 1988 ss 338* and *339* as amended by *FA 2000 ss 40, 41* and relieved as charges on income. Monies paid to trustees of a corporate profit-sharing scheme are not treated as distributions. [CCAB Memorandum TR308 June 1978]. Certain purchases by a company of its own shares under *TA 1988 ss 219–229* are not treated as distributions. Interest is not a distribution unless specifically caught under these provisions. Distributions within a UK 51 per cent group are ignored. [*TA 1988 s 418(5)* and *(6)*].

## Rate of ACT

**6.13**  The rate of ACT in respect of qualifying distributions made between 6 April 1994 and 5 April 1999 is 25 per cent of the amount or value of the distribution. The ACT added to the dividend is available as a credit to a UK resident recipient, the total of the dividend and credit being franked investment income (FII). [*TA 1988 s 238(1)*].

**6.14**  The rate of ACT has normally been fixed at a level equal to the basic rate of tax applicable to savings income, on the distribution and tax combined. Thus a dividend of £80 would have a credit of 25 per cent, £20, being the tax due at 20 per cent of the total of £100 at the rate of basic income tax applicable to savings. In the case of preference shares issued before 6 April 1973, the rate of dividend was reduced to 70 per cent of its former gross rate by what is now *TA 1988 s 255*, but will revert to the

## 6.15  Advance Corporation Tax

previous gross rate after 6 April 1999, as a result of the repeal of that section by *FA 1998 3 Sch 23*.

## Non-payable tax credits

**6.15**  The ACT credit element of dividends received used to be a payable tax credit, but for distributions made on and after 2 July 1997, *F(No2)A 1997 s 19* inserted *TA 1988 s 231A* (which prevents pension funds from reclaiming tax credits on qualifying distributions received) and *F(No2)A 1997 s 20* provided that companies could no longer recover ACT credits by setting off losses under *TA 1988 ss 242–244* for accounting periods commencing on or after 2 July 1997. Payable tax credits were also withdrawn from 2 July 1997 from beneficiaries of estates in administration, Lloyd's underwriters, insurance companies, pension funds and friendly societies by *F(No2)A 1997 ss 21–23*. There are additional anti-avoidance provisions in *F(No 2)A 1997 ss 24–29*.

**6.16**  From 6 April 1999, tax credits will cease to be payable in most other circumstances, under *F(No2)A 1997 s 30*, except on investments held through individual savings acccounts or personal equity plans up to 6 April 2004. [*FA 1998 s 76*].

## Payable tax credits

**6.17**  Where available, the credit fraction is reduced to 1/9 of the dividend received, *TA 1988 s 231(1)A*. This is equivalent to 10 per cent of the sum of the distribution and credit. UK resident recipients of dividends will, however, only be taxed under the Schedule F ordinary rate under *TA 1988 s 1A*, unless liable for tax at the higher rate when the Schedule F upper rate will apply under *TA 1988 s 1B(1)*. The Schedule F rates from 6 April 1999 are initially 10 per cent for the ordinary rate and 32.5 per cent for the upper rate. [*TA 1988 s 1B(2)*]. The net effect is to leave an individual recipient of dividends with the same net amount after tax in 1999/00 as he would have had on the same cash dividend in 1998/99.

---

*Example 1*

---

A UK company pays dividends of £800 on 1 September 1998 and 1 September 1999 to a higher rate taxpayer. His liability will be:

*Advance Corporation Tax* **6.22**

|  |  | 1998–99 |  | 1999–2000 |
|---|---|---|---|---|
|  |  | £ |  | £ |
| Dividend |  | 800 |  | 800 |
| Tax credit | 1/4 | 200 | 1/9 | 88.89 |
|  |  | 1,000 |  | 888.89 |
| Tax charge | 40% | 400 | 32.5% | 288.89 |
| Less tax credit |  | 200 |  | 88.89 |
| Tax payable |  | 200 |  | 200.00 |

**6.18** Companies in receipt of qualifying distributions after 6 April 1999 will cease to be entitled to any tax credit under *F(No2)A 1997 s 30(4)* other than charitable companies entitled to a reducing credit under *F(No2)A 1997 s 35*. This reducing credit is also available to unincorporated charities.

**6.19** Beneficiaries of discretionary trusts, in receipt of qualifying distributions which are distributed to them, will suffer a fall in income from 6 April 1999 as a result of *F(No2)A 1997 s 32*, and beneficiaries of estates of deceased persons in administration will receive a non-payable credit for the Schedule F ordinary rate tax paid by the estate. [*F(No2)A 1997 s 33*].

**6.20** A company in receipt of FII before 6 April 1999 may reduce its liability to ACT on its qualifying distributions (franked payments). The ACT payable is reduced to 20 per cent of the excess of franked payments over FII, *TA 1988 s 241(1), (2), FA 1998 s 31(3)* and *3 Sch 14*. FII and franked payments are defined by *TA 1988 s 238(1)*. Prior to 6 April 1999, if a company had an excess of FII over its franked payments, the excess was treated as surplus FII and could be carried forward to cover franked payments made in subsequent periods.

**6.21** Consequential amendments on the withdrawal of payable credits from 6 April 1999 are included in *F(No2)A 1997 s 34* and *4 Sch*.

## ACT returns and FII

**6.22** Return periods for ACT payments ended on 31 March, 30 June, 30 September, 31 December and at the end of the company's accounting period. [*TA 1988 s 246* and *13 Sch 1*]. There is also an ACT return period for distributions made between 1 and 5 April 1999 after which the system ceases to apply, except for shadow ACT, but this is not treated as a short period so that ACT on distributions in this period was normally due on 14 July 1999. A return of distributions was required on form CT61 (Z) and any ACT payable was required to be paid within 14 days of the end of a return period. The FII deductible was that received in the return period together with surplus FII brought forward from an earlier accounting

## 6.23 Advance Corporation Tax

period which remained unused, and FII carried forward from an earlier return period in the same accounting period. [*TA 1988 13 Sch 2 and 3*].

**6.23** FII received in a later return period cannot be carried back, but a separate repayment claim may be made for that period. The claim is limited to the tax credit on the FII subsequently received or the tax paid in the accounting period on the excess of the franked payments over FII received in earlier return periods within the same accounting period. [*TA 1988 13 Sch 4*]. The ACT election procedures in *TA 1988 13 Sch* are abolished from 6 April 1999 by *FA 1998 3 Sch 41*, as is *TA 1988 13A Sch* relating to surrenders of ACT, under *FA 1998 3 Sch 42*.

**6.24** The ACT collection procedures under *TA 1988 13 Sch 1* were modified for self-assessment by *FA 1996 23 Sch* for periods ending on or after 1 July 1999 by *FA 1996 s 137(2)*, and are therefore repealed without ever having come into effect.

## Set off of ACT against corporation tax

**6.25** Where a company pays ACT, the amount paid (unless already repaid on a claim arising from the receipt of further FII within the accounting period or in a later return period) can be set against the mainstream corporation tax liability of the company on its profits for the accounting period. A dividend paid after cessation of trade is not in an accounting period where there is no source of income (*Walker v Centaur Clothes Group Ltd [1998] STC 814* and *Aproline Ltd v Littlejohn [1995] STC (SCD) 201*).

**6.26** The maximum ACT that can be set off against the mainstream liability is 20 per cent of the chargeable profits. The first year for CTSA is the accounting period ending on or after 1 July 1999 and if that period began before 6 April 1999 there is a deemed end of the account period for the purposes of the ACT set off, at 5 April 1999. Therefore only the pro rata proportion of the chargeable profits for the year ending on or after 1 July 1999 which falls before 6 April 1999 is available for any ACT remaining unutilised as surplus ACT at 6 April 1999. [*TA 1988 s 239(1) to (3) and (6), FA 1998 3 Sch 12*]. Excessive credits of ACT may be recovered by assessment under *TA 1988 s 252* and *FA 1998 3 Sch 21*.

---

*Example 2*

---

VVA Ltd, which has no associated companies, has the following profits for the year ended 30 September 1999:

|  |  |  | £ |
|---|---|---|---|
| Trading profits |  |  | 1,750,000 |
| Rents |  |  | 50,000 |
|  |  |  | 1,800,000 |
| Bank interest |  |  | 20,000 |
|  |  |  | 1,820,000 |
| Chargeable gains |  |  | 80,000 |
|  |  |  | 1,900,000 |
| Annual charges (gross) |  |  | (100,000) |
| Chargeable profits |  |  | 1,800,000 |

Corporation tax payable:

| FY 1998 | £900,000 @ 31% |  | 279,000 |
|---|---|---|---|
| FY 1999 | £900,000 @ 30% |  | 270,000 |
|  | £1,800,000 |  | 549,000 |
| Dividend paid 31.3.99 |  | 1,200,000 |  |
| ACT thereon @ 25% |  | 300,000 |  |
| Restricted to 20% × 1,800,000 × $\frac{187}{365}$ = |  | 184,438 | 184,438 |
| Surplus ACT at 6.4.99 |  | 115,562 |  |
| Mainstream corporation tax liability |  |  | £364,562 |

## Carry back of surplus ACT

**6.27** A claim to carry back surplus ACT to earlier accounting periods beginning in the six years preceding the accounting period in which the surplus arose may be made within two years of the end of that accounting period, under *TA 1988 s 239(3), FA 1998 3 Sch 12*. Surplus ACT may normally be relieved in the order in which the claims were made (*Carr v Armpledge Ltd; Carr v Fielder & Ashworth Ltd [2000] STC 410*) but only until 6 April 1999. [*TA 1988 s 239(4), FA 1998 3 Sch 12*]. Any surplus remaining at that date, which cannot otherwise be used, can only be dealt with under the shadow ACT provisions dealt with below.

**6.28** Losses carried back from subsequent accounting periods can displace an ACT credit set against the original mainstream liability and create additional surplus ACT. In *Procter & Gamble Ltd v Taylerson [1990] STC 624*, the revised claim was rejected as out of time, being way beyond the two year time limit. Carry back claims were accepted in *Savacentre Ltd v IRC [1995] STC 867*, but repayment supplements denied under *TA 1988 s 825(4A)*.

## Surrender of ACT

**6.29** A UK resident company may surrender the benefit of ACT paid by it, and not repaid, to any 51 per cent UK resident subsidiary. This also applies to other distributions arising from the redemption, repayment or purchase by a company of its own shares, but not in respect of other qualifying distributions which are not dividends. Surrenders may be made to any number of 51 per cent subsidiaries which qualified as such throughout the accounting period in which the dividend was paid. [*TA 1988 s 240(10)*]. A claim to surrender ACT must be made within six years of the end of the accounting period and requires the written consent of the subsidiary. [*TA 1988 s 240(6)*].

**6.30** Surplus ACT carried forward as the result of a surrender was lost if at a later date the group relationship was broken, unless both companies remained subsidiaries of a third company. [*TA 1988 s 240(5)*]. A 51 per cent subsidiary for this purpose is one in which more than 50 per cent of the ordinary share capital is held [*TA 1988 s 838(1)*], ignoring shares held as trading stock, or held by a non-resident. [*TA 1988 s 240(10)*]. A company can also be disqualified where an arrangement exists whereby other persons could obtain control of the subsidiary company, but not the parent, and where the parent is not beneficially entitled to more than 50 per cent of the profits available for distribution to equity shareholders, and 50 per cent of the assets available for distribution to equity shareholders on a winding up. [*TA 1988 s 240(11), Cricket plc v Inspector of Taxes [1998] STC (SCD) 101*].

**6.31** The essence is to allow a subsidiary to take credit for the amount surrendered as soon as the claim is made, a surrender then taking effect in accordance with *TA 1988 13A Sch*. A claim to surrender more than the amount available will be of no effect. [*TA 1988 s 240(1), (1A), (1B)* substituted by *FA 1996 25 Sch 1(1), (2)* and *(4)*]. The amount of ACT available for surrender is the amount paid on dividends in the accounting period, less: (a) any amount repaid to the surrendering company; (b) any surplus ACT brought forward from an earlier period; and (c) any amount already surrendered under a claim which has not been withdrawn. [*TA 1988 s 240(5D)* and *(5E)* substituted by *FA 1996 25 Sch 193*].

**6.32** A claim for surrender may be withdrawn by the surrendering company, with the consent of the company to whom the ACT is surrendered; in which case the former status quo is restored with any necessary alterations. The withdrawal of a claim does not prevent the surrendering company from making a further claim for that accounting period or a surrender to the same company or different subsidiaries. [*TA 1988 s 240(5A), (5B), (5C)* substituted by *FA 1996 25 Sch 1(3)*].

# New procedure for ACT surrender claims under *TA 1988 13A Sch*

**6.33** The self-assessment amendments to the surrender of ACT, in *TA 1988 13A Sch* described below, only apply to the pre 6 April 1999 proportion of an accounting period ending on or after 1 July 1999, and therefore within CTSA, but beginning prior to 6 April 1999 when the ability to surrender ceases and the shadow ACT rules come into play. [*FA 1998 3 Sch 12(4), 42* and *44(4)*]. The effect of *TA 1988 13A Sch (7)* is primarily to allow surrender claims to be withdrawn with the consent of the subsidiary, instead of amending existing claims.

**General**

**6.34** For the purposes of the new provisions contained in *TA 1988 13A Sch*, a 'claim' is a claim falling within *TA 1988 s 240(1A)*, whilst 'relevant accounting period' is the accounting period referred to in *s 240(1)*, namely the period for which the claim is made. Surrenders to different subsidiaries or to the same subsidiary at different times are to be treated as separate claims. Where more than one claim is made at the same time, the claims are to be treated as made in the order in which the surrendering company elects or, in default of such an election, by a Revenue determination. [*TA 1988, 13A Sch 1* and *2*]. Given that the procedure only permits withdrawals, and not variations [*TA 1988 13A Sch 10*], and that earlier claims will go to exhaust available ACT, claims will be dealt with in the order they are made. Hence if a number of claims are submitted in the wrong order, it seems that they will have to be withdrawn and resubmitted as appropriate.

**6.35** A claim must specify the subsidiary to whom the surrender is made and the amount thereof and it must be made within six years of the end of the relevant accounting period of the surrendering company. [*TA 1988 13A Sch 3* and *4*]. As the claim must actually be quantified, 'formula' claims will seemingly not be permitted. The claim must be made in a corporation tax return or amendment to such a return under *TMA 1970 s 11* wherever possible. A claim outside a return must be made in such form as the Revenue may determine, be accompanied by such supporting documentation as the Revenue may require and include a declaration to the effect that all the particulars are correct to the best belief of the claimant. [*TA 1988 13A Sch 5* and *6*].

**Withdrawal of claims and amendments**

**6.36** Withdrawal of a claim under CTSA must be made by notice to the Revenue in the required form specifying the surrendering company, the amount surrendered, the subsidiary to whom the surrender was made and the relevant accounting period of the surrendering company. It must

## 6.37 *Advance Corporation Tax*

be accompanied by the consent of the subsidiary. Wherever possible the withdrawal must be made by an amendment to the return. [*TA 1988 13A Sch 7*]. Where a claim is withdrawn and another substituted, the withdrawal is treated as taking place before the subsequent claim. [*TA 1988 13A Sch 8*].

**6.37** A claim cannot be withdrawn after the earlier of (i) six years after the end of the relevant accounting period of the surrendering company, and (ii) the date on which an assessment for the accounting period of the company to whom the surrender is made becomes final. In this regard, in the absence of a Revenue enquiry and the making of a discovery assessment, the latter time limit will generally be that under the normal CTSA rule, being twelve months after the filing date. However a claim may be withdrawn at any time within the first six-year period so long as (a) none of the ACT in the claim has been finally dealt with to the subsidiary's advantage, (b) the claim was made after the date on which an assessment for a relevant accounting period of the subsidiary had become final, and (c) a further assessment has been made by the Revenue (i.e. where there has been a discovery assessment). For this purpose ACT has been finally dealt with if it has been set against any liability of the subsidiary to corporation tax which has become final or any of it has been repaid to the subsidiary. [*TA 1988 13A Sch para 9(5)*]. A claim to surrender cannot be amended; it can only be withdrawn and replaced by a new claim. [*TA 1988 13A Sch 10*].

**Claims made after set off of ACT against mainstream corporation tax – further self-assessments by the surrendering company**

**6.38** Where the claim under CTSA is made to surrender ACT after it has already been set against the mainstream corporation tax liability of the surrendering company, that company must make a further self-assessment and pay the additional corporation tax due as a result of the claim. The tax is treated as due nine months and one day after the end of the accounting period. Such additional self-assessment may be enquired into by the Revenue in the normal way. [*TA 1988 13A Sch 11*].

---

*Example 3*

---

Bark Ltd has a 100 per cent subsidiary, Bite Ltd, with accounts drawn up to 31 December. Bark Ltd pays a dividend on 1 April 1999 on which the ACT is £20,000. It sets the whole of this ACT against its own mainstream corporation tax liability. Bite Ltd submits a self-assessment for the year to 31 December 1999 showing a nil corporation tax liability. Following a Revenue enquiry Bite's corporation tax liability is finally determined at £80,000. Bark then decides to surrender to Bite the whole of the ACT paid on 1 April 1999 and does so before the time limit of 31 December 2005. Bark will be obliged to submit a revised self-assessment for the year

## Advance Corporation Tax  6.42

to 31 December 1999, and pay the additional tax. Interest will run from the normal due date of 1 October 2000. Bite may claim a repayment of the tax arising from the ACT set off, with repayment interest.

---

**6.39** Similar provisions apply where the surrendering company has set ACT against the mainstream corporation tax liability of a subsequent accounting period and then makes a claim to surrender. An additional self-assessment is required and the tax is due nine months and one day after the end of the later accounting period, i.e. as if the claim to set off the brought forward ACT had not been made. Enquiries into such additional self-assessments may be made in the normal way. [*TA 1988 13A Sch 12*].

**Excess relief on surrender – further self-assessments by subsidiary**

**6.40** Where ACT has been set off against a subsidiary's liability which is in excess of the amount that should have been so deducted (i.e. where the parent purported to surrender more ACT than was available), whether in respect of surrendered ACT for the accounting period or brought forward, the subsidiary must, within three months of becoming aware of the true facts, submit a self-assessment of the amount of corporation tax which would have been due on the basis of the true facts. Tax is due on the day following nine months after the end of the accounting period as if it had been calculated correctly. The Revenue may enquire into such additional self-assessment in the normal way. ACT correctly treated is set against the subsidiary's liability before any ACT incorrectly dealt with. [*TA 1988 13A Sch 13*].

**Miscellaneous**

**6.41** The normal enquiry provisions apply to additional self-assessments to recover ACT which apply to any other self-assessments under *FA 1988 18 Sch 34*. [*TA 1988 13A Sch 14*]. If, as a result of a withdrawal of a claim to surrender, the surrendering company has overpaid, it is entitled by notice to claim repayment. Similarly, a subsidiary company which has overpaid tax as a result of a claim made after the corporation tax for that accounting period has been paid, may reclaim tax overpaid. [*TA 1988 13A Sch 15*]. The ACT changes take effect from accounting periods ending after the appointed day, under *FA 1994 s 199(3)*, 1 July 1999.

**6.42** ACT set against earlier years' liabilities cannot also be surrendered and surrendered ACT is not available to set against earlier years' liabilities or carried forward as surplus ACT. [*TA 1988 s 240(7)*]. Where ACT is surrendered to a subsidiary, it is treated as having paid the ACT surrendered as if it had made a distribution on the same date as the dividend giving rise to the surrender was paid by the surrendering

**6.43** *Advance Corporation Tax*

company. It can be set against the subsidiary's mainstream corporation tax liability for the accounting period in which the dividend is deemed to have been paid, or carried forward to a subsequent accounting period. It cannot be carried back [*TA 1988 s 239(3)*], but is to be set against the subsidiary's mainstream liability before any ACT on the subsidiary's own dividends. [*TA 1988 s 240(4)*]. A company is permitted to make a payment for surrendered ACT up to the amount of the ACT surrendered. [*TA 1988 s 240(8)*].

## Foreign income dividends

**6.43** Under the foreign income dividend (FID) scheme *TA 1988 ss 246A–246Y*, it was possible for a UK resident company to pay a dividend in cash and elect for that dividend to be a FID provided that it met the requirements of a highly complex piece of legislation. The scheme was abolished with effect from 6 April 1999 by *F(No2)A 1997 s 36* and *6 Sch* and is therefore only of marginal interest for CTSA.

**6.44** Where a dividend qualified as a FID, ACT was payable when the FID was paid. If it was paid out of foreign source profits any surplus ACT in respect of the FID would be repayable by the Revenue. There were complex matching rules for the identification of foreign source profits out of which the FID could be paid. Shareholders receiving a FID were treated as receiving the actual dividend grossed up at 20 per cent but lower and basic rate taxpayers had no further tax liability. The notional credit, however, was not payable. Higher rate taxpayers had a liability of 20 per cent on the total of the FID and notional credit.

**6.45** An international headquarters company, as defined by *TA 1988 s 246S*, could avoid the initial payment of ACT in respect of the FID under *TA 1988 s 246T*. The working of the FID system was explained in some detail in Tax Bulletin, Issue 12, pp 141–145. Transitional provisions apply on the abolition of the FID scheme where there is a transitional period beginning before 6 April 1999 but ending after that date, which allow a company which has paid a FID prior to 6 April 1999 to match it against a distributable foreign profit in the immediately following transitional period. [*F(No2)A 1997 6 Sch 22*].

**6.46** Where a foreign income dividend is paid by a company before 6 April 1999 but received by a corporate recipient after that date, it is treated by the recipient as if it had received a qualifying distribution of 9/10 of the actual amount of the FID. [*F(No2)A 1997 6 Sch 23*].

## Change of ownership

**6.47** Where there is a change in ownership of a company occurring before 6 April 1999 which is accompanied by a major change in the nature or conduct of a trade or business within three years before or after

## Advance Corporation Tax  6.51

the change, a new accounting period is deemed to commence when the change in ownership occurs. [*TA 1988 s 245*]. The deemed new accounting period applies for the purposes of calculating relief for FII available against the ACT payable as well as bringing to an end a return period and the setting off of ACT against the company's mainstream corporation tax liability. The company's income or profit is apportioned between the two deemed accounting periods on a time basis. Surplus ACT up to the date of change in ownership is lost and cannot be carried forward to future accounting periods. Conversely, ACT in respect of distributions made after the change cannot be carried back and set against profits prior to the change of ownership. [*TA 1988 s 245(3)* and *3(A)*]. A major change in the nature or conduct of a trade is explained in SP10/91 and similar provisions apply to losses under *TA 1988 s 768A* and *s 768B*. The restriction applies to corporation tax surrendered to a company under *TA 1988 s 240* by *TA 1988 s 245(6)*. It also applies to the surrendering company which has a change in ownership and within three years a major change in the nature or conduct of the trade. [*TA 1988 s 245A*].

**6.48**   *TA 1988 s 245(B)* prevents ACT being used against a capital gain on an intra-group transfer immediately before the change in ownership which would crystallise the chargeable gain, although these provisions no longer apply to a change of ownership on or after 6 April 1999. [*FA 1998 3 Sch 15–17*]. The major change in the nature or conduct of the trade could take place any time up to three years after the change in ownership, which could be after 6 April 1999.

## Legislative changes

**6.49**   The abolition of ACT requires the deletion of references to it in numerous places throughout the Taxes Acts and these references cease to have effect in relation to accounting periods on or after 6 April 1999 by *FA 1998 3 Sch*. *FA 1998 3 Sch 7* amends the small companies' rate provisions by excluding from FII not only dividends but other distributions received from group or consortium companies.

**6.50**   *FA 1998 3 Sch 19* and the intra-group dividend provisions in *paras 1, 2* and *3* are deleted as they are no longer required for distributions after 6 April 1999, and therefore, the provisions relating to intra-group interest are amended to preserve the definition of group. *FA 1998 3 Sch 24*, in respect of close company loans to participators under *TA 1988 s 419*, removes the reference to an amount equal to ACT and substitutes a flat rate of 25 per cent of the amount of the loan or other advance. *TA 1988 s 468Q* (dividend distribution to corporate unit-holder) is amended by *FA 1998 3 Sch 27* consequent on the abolition of ACT.

**6.51**   The transactions in securities provisions in *TA 1988 ss 703–705* are amended by *FA 1998 3 Sch 32*, in particular to limit the income tax assessable on a person deemed to be in receipt of a distribution under *TA*

**6.52**  *Advance Corporation Tax*

*1988 s 704D* or *704E*, to limit the amount to the tax payable as if he had received a qualifying distribution from the company equal to the valuation of the consideration received. The controlled foreign company provisions are amended to take into account the abolition of surplus ACT from 6 April 1999, by *FA 1998 3 Sch 43* and *44*, by splitting the straddling period or ACT at 6 April 1999 and apportioning the profits of the company to the notional periods on a time basis under *FA 1998 3 Sch 12(4)*.

## Shadow ACT

**6.52** *FA 1998 s 32* introduces a system of shadow ACT which can be applied by companies with surplus ACT at 6 April 1999. Companies which do not opt out of the system continue to compute ACT on distributions on or after 6 April 1999 although no tax will actually be payable in respect of such distributions. They then apply the ACT offset rules, as if *TA 1988 s 239* had continued to apply, and to the extent that any further ACT offset would have been available, this becomes 'eligible surplus ACT' and may be used to reduce the corporation tax otherwise payable by the company. The actual regulations are contained in the *Corporation Tax (Treatment of Unrelieved Surplus ACT) Regulations SI 1999 No. 358*. Regulation 3 defines various terms, in particular a straddling accounting period being an accounting period, beginning before and ending on or after 6 April 1999, which by *Regulation 3(4)* is divided into two accounting periods, one ending on 5 April 1999 and the other beginning on 6 April 1999, to which the profits of the accounting period are apportioned on a time basis.

**6.53** The shadow ACT scheme does not allow unrelieved surplus ACT to be carried forward into accounting periods beyond the final accounting period, as defined for scheme purposes. This has got nothing to do with ceasing to trade, and is defined by *Regulation 4*. For a company which is not part of a group, the final accounting period is the accounting period beginning in the period of twelve months following the end of the relevant accounting period, which is the first accounting period after which no unrelieved surplus ACT is available to set against the corporation tax liability, in other words after the unrelieved surplus has been fully utilised.

**6.54** A company can, however, withdraw from the scheme, in which case the final accounting period will be that in which the company notifies the Revenue that it will cease to seek to recover any unrelieved surplus ACT in respect of that and any future accounting period. [*Regulation 4(4) and (5)*]. For a company which is a member of a group the relevant accounting period is the first such period after which no amount of surplus ACT belonging to the company or any other company in the group is available to set against any liability to corporation tax, i.e. all the surplus ACT in the group has been utilised. [*Regulation 5*].

**6.55** *Regulation 5(5)* and *(6)* provides that the parent company can make a notification to the Revenue that it will not seek to recover any amounts of unrelieved surplus ACT for the accounting period in which the notification is made (which becomes the final accounting period), or in any subsequent accounting period for all the group members. This is binding on each company in the group except, under *Regulation 5(10)*, where a company joins a group.

**6.56** 'Group', for shadow ACT purposes, is defined by *Regulation 6* as the parent company and its 51 per cent UK resident subsidiaries, as defined by *TA 1988 s 838*, but ignoring shares held as trading stock or in a non-resident company. Where company members enjoy extraordinary rights or power under the company's statutes, the 51 per cent subsidiary definition may be inappropriate and all classes of share capital may be included, or any particular category of share capital instead of ordinary share capital, in order to determine the effective commercial 51 per cent group. A subsidiary can be disqualified if arrangements exist whereby some other person could obtain control, for example through an option over the shares, or if the parent company is not entitled to more than 50 per cent of any profits available for distribution to equity holders, or on a liquidation to 50 per cent of the assets available for distribution to equity holders. Arrangements are widely defined.

**Anti-avoidance regulations**

**6.57** *Regulation 7* is an anti-avoidance provision to prevent interest that would otherwise have been received from being converted into a distribution to reduce the amount of shadow ACT. It is not, therefore, treated as franked investment income for the purpose of the shadow ACT regulations.

**6.58** Another anti-avoidance provision is introduced by *Regulation 8*, whereby arrangements to pass on the value of FII to another party disentitle it from being treated as FII, unless already caught under some other provision of the Taxes Acts. The disapplication of treatment as FII only applies where arrangements are entered into for an unallowable purpose, which is defined by *Regulation 8(6)*, if the arrangements include the purpose of reducing the amount of shadow ACT treated as paid on relevant distributions made by the paying company or another company

**6.59** *Advance Corporation Tax*

in the same group. Arrangements are widely defined by *Regulation 8(8)*. Dealers in shares where the income is treated as trading income cannot treat the distributions received as franked investment income under *Regulation 9*.

**6.59** Intra-group distributions may not be treated as FII, under *Regulation 10*. This applies where a company making the distribution thereafter becomes a member of the group, or was a former group member.

**Computation of shadow ACT**

**6.60** The basic computation of shadow ACT under *Regulation 11* applies where a company makes a distribution on or after 6 April 1999. Shadow ACT is calculated in respect of the dividend, which is treated as if it were ACT payable purely for the purpose of computing the surplus Act brought forward that is available to set against the company's liability to corporation tax for the accounting period.

---

*Example 4*

---

Delaero Ltd has surplus ACT of £800,000 at 5 April 1999. In the year ended 31 March 2000 it pays a dividend of £400,000 on which shadow ACT at 25 per cent would be £100,000. It has taxable profits of £2 m on which corporation tax at 30 per cent is £600,000. The maximum amount of surplus ACT that could be set off is 20 per cent of £2 m or £400,000. This however has to be reduced by the shadow ACT of £100,000 leaving £300,000 of the surplus ACT to be set off against the corporation tax payable. The surplus ACT carried forward is now £800,000 less £300,000, i.e. £500,000, and the corporation tax payable is £600,000 less surplus ACT used of £300,000, leaving £300,000 payable.

---

**6.61** The anti-avoidance provisions deemed necessary to prevent the manipulation of the shadow and surplus ACT rules are highly complex, and *Regulation 11 para 2* disapplies the shadow ACT treatment for manufactured dividends within *TA 1988 23A Sch 2(2)*, and intra-group dividends, unless the company making the distribution has received, in the accounting period in which the distribution is made, FII which would have reduced the shadow ACT. In addition the company making the distribution must have elected in its tax return for the accounting period, for 9/8ths of the FII to be included in computing its shadow ACT for the

## Advance Corporation Tax 6.64

period, and must have informed the recipient of the election. The election must be made within two years of the end of the accounting period in which the distribution is made and it is irrevocable. [*Regulation 11(3)* and *(4)*]. There are also provisions to deal with cases where a distribution does not fall within an accounting period where a company ceases to be a member of a group, or where there is a change of ownership of a company otherwise than as a result of its ceasing to be a member of the group. [*Regulation 11 paras 5–8*].

**6.62** Shadow ACT is treated as having been paid at the rate of 25 per cent of the amount or value of the relevant distribution under *Regulation 11(9)*. There are also restrictions in respect of life assurance companies receiving franked investment income in *Regulation 22*. Where a company is in receipt of surplus FII in any accounting period, the surplus must be carried forward to the next accounting period and treated as FII received in that period. [*Regulation 11(12)*]. A surplus of FII is calculated as equal to 9/8ths of the distributions received in the period, plus the surplus FII brought forward from the previous period, less the franked distributions made in the period. [*Regulation 11(13)*]. FII is calculated as equal to 9/8ths of the distribution received because the credit is equivalent to 1/9th of the distribution.

**6.63** In the straddling accounting period, surplus FII is ascertained for the period deemed to end on 5 April 1999 and for the remainder of the accounting period deemed to begin on 6 April 1999, under *Regulation 3(4)*.

**Utilisation of shadow ACT**

**6.64** Shadow ACT has to be set against the company's corporation tax liability for the accounting period as if it were ACT, but because it is purely notional, it does not reduce the corporation tax payable. [*Regulation 12(1)*]. Shadow ACT has to be utilised in priority to unrelieved surplus ACT. [*Regulation 12 para 2*]. The shadow ACT offset, as with ACT, is restricted to 20 per cent of the profits charged to corporation tax by *Regulation 12(3)(a)*.

---

*Example 5*

---

Continuing the facts in Example 2 (6.26) VVA Ltd had similar profits in the year ended 30 September 2000 and again paid a dividend of £1,200,000.

## 6.65 Advance Corporation Tax

|  |  | £ |
|---|---|---|
| Trading profits |  | 1,750,000 |
| Rents |  | 50,000 |
| Bank interest |  | 20,000 |
|  |  | 1,820,000 |
| Chargeable gains |  | 80,000 |
|  |  | 1,900,000 |
| Annual charges (gross) |  | (100,000) |
| Chargeable profits |  | 1,800,000 |

| Corporation tax payable | £ |  |
|---|---|---|
| FY 1999 | 900,000 @ 30% | 270,000 |
| FY 2000 | 900,000 @ 30% | 270,000 |
|  | 1,800,000 | 540,000 |
| Dividend paid 31/3/00 | 1,200,000 |  |
| Shadow ACT thereon @ 25% | 300,000 |  |
| *Maximum ACT set off* |  |  |
| 20% × £1,800,000 = | 360,000 |  |
| Reduce by shadow ACT | (300,000) |  |
| Actual maximum ACT set off | 60,000 | (60,000) |
| Surplus ACT bt/fwd @ 6/4/99 | 115,562 |  |
| Surplus ACT c/fwd | 55,562 |  |
| Corporation tax payable |  | 480,000 |

**6.65** Where double taxation relief is available, the income subject to foreign tax is excluded from the profits for the purpose of determining the maximum ACT credit, and the foreign tax credit is deducted from the corporation tax liability under *Regulation 12(4)*. A proportion of the shadow ACT may be set against the foreign income or gain, limited to the maximum ACT credit that would have applied had the foreign income or gain been the only income or gain for the accounting period, or, if lower, the corporation tax payable as reduced by the foreign tax credit, *Regulation 124(c) and (5)*. Surplus shadow ACT can be notionally carried back to the six preceding years and set against the latest profits first, but it only displaces unrelieved surplus ACT in the two years before the end of the principal period. [*Regulation 12(7)*]. Surplus shadow ACT not carried back may be carried forward under *Regulation 12(9)* and treated as having been paid in the next accounting period.

Advance Corporation Tax **6.69**

**Intra-group allocation of surplus shadow ACT**

**6.66** Provisions in the regulations deal with the notional surrender of surplus shadow ACT, the allocation being by the parent company to other companies in the group. The recipient company's shadow ACT has to be brought into account before any surplus shadow ACT surrendered to it. [*Regulation 13(2)*]. The parent company may allocate the surplus shadow ACT among the group, except where it exceeds the amount which could be utilised by all the potential recipients, in which case it is allocated to them in accordance with their capacity to absorb surplus ACT. [*Regulation 13(5)*]. There are provisions for allocating surplus shadow ACT to the parent company at the time a company ceases to be a member of a group, except on a group reorganisation or transfer to a connected person. [*Regulation 13(6)*]. Surplus shadow ACT may be reallocated, although not normally more than twelve months after the company's filing date for its tax return. [*Regulation 13(7)*].

**6.67** Surplus shadow ACT is allocated to the accounting period coterminus with the surrendering company's accounting period and thereafter to an accounting period beginning before, but ending in, the surrendering company's accounting period and thereafter to an accounting period beginning in, but ending after, the end of the surrendering company's accounting period and thereafter to a period beginning 24 months or less, prior to the end of the surrendering company's accounting period. [*Regulation 13(8)*]. There are also provisions to deal with the unusual cases where a company is a member of more than one group and is allocated surplus ACT by the parent companies of more than one group. The Revenue may allocate surplus shadow ACT. [*Regulation 13(15)*].

**Set off of unrelieved surplus ACT against liability to corporation tax**

**6.68** Unrelieved surplus ACT can normally be set against a company's liability to corporation tax on any profits chargeable for an accounting period beginning on or after 6 April 1999, unless it has already been relieved, and the corporation tax payable is reduced accordingly. [*Regulation 14(1) and (2)*]. Unrelieved surplus ACT cannot be set against the corporation tax liability on partnership profits where the anti-avoidance provisions preventing arrangements for transferring relief in *TA 1988 s 116(2)* apply. The unrelieved surplus ACT to be used up is not to exceed 20 per cent of the profits charged to corporation tax, less any shadow ACT attributed to that period. [*Regulation 14(4)*].

**Restrictions on set off**

**6.69** *Regulation 15* applies a restriction on setting off a company's unrelieved surplus ACT against a subsidiary company's liability to corporation tax, where the recipient company was not a subsidiary of the

**6.70** *Advance Corporation Tax*

surrendering company, unless both were subsidiaries of a third company for the entire period.

**Change of ownership**

**6.70** As for actual ACT, a change in ownership of a company coupled with a major change in the nature or conduct of a trade or business carried on by the company, within three years of the change in ownership, restricts relievability of surplus ACT through the change in ownership, broadly re-enacting the provisions of *TA 1988 s 245A* and *245B*, *Regulations 16* and *17* and SP 10/91. Restrictions also apply on an intra-group transfer of assets which are disposed of within three years of a change in ownership. [*Regulation 18*].

**Miscellaneous provisions**

**6.71** Penalties for late or non-submission of a corporation tax return are to be calculated without regard to any reduction of the corporation tax liability by any unrelieved surplus ACT set off under *Regulation 14*, *Regulation 19*. Excessive set off of unrelieved surplus ACT may be countered by an appropriate assessment recovering the underpaid tax. [*Regulation 19*]. Unrelieved surplus ACT may be set off against the corporation tax liability on controlled foreign company income under *Regulation 20*. Where unrelieved surplus ACT is subsequently displaced, the additional tax payable may be recovered from other members of the group if not paid by the principal company within six months. [*Regulation 21*].

**6.72** Life assurance companies are dealt with by *Regulation 22* which excludes from credit under these provisions, the policyholders' share of FII received. The transactions of securities anti-avoidance provisions in *TA 1988 s 704* are extended to include as a tax advantage the application of FII under the shadow ACT regulations.

Chapter 7

# Computation of Profits

## Introduction

**7.1** There is nothing in the legislation or regulations on CTSA that has any direct bearing on the computation of profits for corporation tax purposes. However, it is necessary to reconsider the general approach to the preparation of tax computations as a result of the change in responsibility arising from CTSA. Thus it is no longer possible simply to take an optimistic view of the tax consequences of any transaction and wait for a Revenue challenge. Under CTSA any such view will not be reviewed by the Inspector but accepted, unless there is an enquiry or discovery. It will then be necessary to justify the optimistic treatment, otherwise there will be additional tax, interest and penalties.

**7.2** A company is subject to corporation tax under *TA 1988 s 6(1)* if it is resident in the UK [*TA 1988 s 6(2)(a)*], or is carrying on a trade through a branch or agency in the UK [*TA 1988 s 6(2)(b)* and *11(2)*], and on chargeable gains on assets used in such a trade. [*TCGA 1992 s 10*]. A company is not liable to capital gains tax or to income tax unless it is a non-resident company with non-trading income in the UK. [*TA 1988 s 6(2)(a)* and *(11)*]. A company is therefore normally chargeable to corporation tax on its profits which includes income and chargeable gains. [*TA 1988 s 6(4)(a)*]. A UK resident company is subject to corporation tax on its world-wide income computed under the rules of Schedule D Cases I to VI. [*TA 1988 s 70*]. A company with an overseas trade chargeable under Schedule D Case V, computes its profits in accordance with Schedule D Case I principles. [*TA 1988 s 70(2)*].

**7.3** 'Company' is defined by *TA 1988 s 832(1)* as any body corporate or unincorporated association that does not include a partnership, a local authority or a local authority association. This is subject to qualification in *TA 1988 s 832(2)* where 'company' is defined as including any body corporate but not an unincorporated association for the purposes of transactions in securities under *TA 1988 ss 703–709* [*TA 1988 s 709(2)*], for transactions between dealing companies and associated companies under *TA 1988 s 774* [*TA 1988 s 774(4)(a)*], for the sale by an individual of income derived from his personal activities under *TA 1988 s 775* and capital gains from transactions in land taxed as income under *TA 1988 s 776*. [*TA 1988 s 777(13)*].

## 7.4 Computation of Profits

**7.4** For the purposes of the connected persons rules in *TA 1988 s 839*, the normal meaning of company is extended to include a unit trust scheme by *TA 1988 s 839(8)*. Authorised unit trusts are also treated as if they were a company resident in the UK and the rights of the unit holders are treated as shares in the company by *TA 1988 s 468(1)*. For capital gains tax purposes, *TCGA 1992 s 288(1)* defines a company as including any body corporate or unincorporated association but not including a partnership. Unit trusts are also treated as companies for this purpose under *TCGA 1992 s 99(1)*. *TA 1988 s 832(2)* also disapplies the ordinary definition of company where the context otherwise requires because some other definition of company applies. For the purposes of this book, any reference to company has the wider meaning as defined above.

**7.5** A company is chargeable to corporation tax on its share of the profits of any partnership, or as a beneficiary of a trust, or on profits arising during the course of winding up. It is not chargeable however, on profits received in a purely fiduciary capacity, for example as trustee, except on its entitlement to any of that income, for example as trustee fees. [*TA 1988 s 8(2)*]. Profits do not include distributions from other UK companies. [*TA 1988 s 208*]. Income is computed for corporation tax in the same way as for income tax with similar exemptions unless specifically provided otherwise. [*TA 1988 s 9*]. Corporation tax is charged by reference to the accounting period, which then has to be apportioned between the financial years ended on 31 March. The rate of corporation tax for the financial years 1997 and 1998 (ending on 31 March 1998 and 31 March 1999 respectively) was 31 per cent for the main rate, 21 per cent for the small companies rate, under *TA 1988 s 13*, with the lower maximum profit level of £300,000 and the upper maximum profit level of £1,500,000, for a stand alone company. The marginal income fraction is 1/40th giving an effective marginal rate of 33.5 per cent.

**7.6** For the financial years 1999 and 2000 (ending on 31 March 2000 and 2001), the main rate of corporation tax is 30 per cent, the small companies rate 20 per cent with the upper and lower maximum band and marginal relief fraction remaining the same, giving an effective marginal rate of 32.5 per cent. [*TA 1988 ss 8(3)* and *13*, *FA 1998 ss 28* and *29* and *FA 1999 s 27*]. *TA 1988 s 13AA* introduces a 10 per cent starting rate for corporation tax for the year ended 31 March 2001, for the first £10,000 of profits with marginal relief up to £50,000 at 1/40th giving an effective marginal rate of 22.5 per cent. [*FA 1999 ss 28* and *29*]. For the financial year 2001 (ending on 31 March 2002) the main rate of corporation tax is 30 per cent. The small companies and starting rates will be fixed by *FA 2001*.

# Trading profits: Schedule D Case I

### Generally accepted accounting principles

**7.7** The starting point for computing the taxable profits of a trade are accounts prepared on generally accepted accounting principles.

[*Threlfall v Jones, Gallagher v Jones [1993] STC 537, Johnston v Britannia Airways Ltd [1994] STC 763*]. This topic is dealt with in Tax Bulletin Issue 32 (December 1997) p 485, Issue 39 (February 1999) p 623 and Issue 44 (December 1999) p 707 (see Appendix 1). A point to note is that generally accepted accounting principles are subject to continuing development and for example, the Accounting Standards Board's Financial Reporting Standard 12 (FRS 12), which applies to accounting periods ending on or after 23 March 1999 (para 98), prohibits the recognition of provisions for future operating losses (para 68).

**7.8** This means that the provision for future overhaul costs of aircraft engines allowed in *Johnston v Britannia Airways Ltd*, in accordance with then generally accepted accounting principles, would no longer be an allowable provision; not as a result of a change in tax law but due to a change in the generally accepted accounting practice. In such circumstances there would be a change of accounting policy requiring to be dealt with as a prior year adjustment, FRS 12 para 101, FRS 3 paras 7, 29 and 62. This means that the provision previously made in accordance with the then generally accepted practices would have to be recredited to the accounts, which in the Revenue view would be a receipt of taxable income.

**7.9** When the expenditure on the repairs was incurred, FRS 12 example 11A suggests that the actual expenditure should be capitalised and depreciated over its economic life of, say, five years. Notwithstanding the fact that depreciation is normally disallowed for tax purposes, the amount capitalised would not be capital expenditure in the tax sense of the word, it would be a major repair to an existing asset. The amount written off as depreciation would then actually be allowable for tax purposes as deferred revenue expenditure. [Tax Bulletin, Issue 39, February 1999, p 623 and Issue 40, April 1999, p 639, see Appendix 1]. Unfortunately there could be a timing problem in such circumstances as the write-back of previously written off expenditure would be a receipt for the year in which it was written back and the deferred revenue expenditure would be given over the life of the refurbishment.

**7.10** The Revenue do not accept, however, that accounting principles apply in all cases, for example the computation of a chargeable gain follows the statutory provisions irrespective of the accounting treatment. Where a future loss was anticipated in the accounts (under the requirements in SSAP 2 or FRS 12 to make a provision for a present obligation as a result of a past event) the Revenue argued that this amounted to anticipating a loss. This was considered by the High Court in *Herbert Smith (a firm) v Honour [1999] STC 173* which related to obligations of the law firm Herbert Smith under a lease of premises which it had vacated. The Revenue had succeeded before the Special Commissioners. However in the High Court, Lloyd J overturned the decision and held that there was no general prohibition against anticipating losses to be inferred from *TA 1988 s 60*, where it would be required in accordance

**7.11** *Computation of Profits*

with generally accepted accounting principles. Before the Special Commissioners the Revenue had relied in particular on *Edward Collins and Sons Ltd v IRC (1924) 12 TC 773* but Lloyd J pointed out that in that case, the provision was not justified by reference to generally accepted principles of commercial accounting. The Revenue decided not to appeal the High Court decision, Inland Revenue Press Release 20, July 1999 (Appendix 6).

**7.11** In *Meat Traders Ltd v Cushing [1997] STC (SCD) 245*, a specific provision for a possible bad debt, where trading with the customer was continuing on an ongoing basis, was disallowed. In *Southern Rly of Peru Ltd v Owen (1956) 36 TC 602* a provision was disallowed as not being sufficiently accurately quantified.

**7.12** *FA 1998 s 42* imposed a statutory requirement that for the purposes of Cases I or II of Schedule D, the profits of a trade, profession or vocation must be computed on an accounting basis which gives a true and fair view, subject to any adjustment required or authorised in law in computing profits for those purposes. Companies already had a requirement to produce accounts on a true and fair basis under the *Companies Act 1985 s 226*, but unincorporated associations liable to corporation tax carrying on a trade now have to comply with these provisions as *TA 1988 s 9* applies income tax principles for corporation tax purposes.

**7.13** Where there is a change of accounting basis, *FA 1998 s 44* and *6 Sch* apply to a company carrying on a trade, profession or vocation as they do for an individual or partnership from 6 April 1999. *FA 1998 6 Sch 2* provides that any adjustment is chargeable to tax under Schedule D Case VI but is treated for the purposes of loss relief to be set against it as if it were profits of the trade, profession or vocation for the chargeable period for which it is charged to tax. [*FA 1998 6 Sch 2(2)(b)* and *(d)*]. A negative adjustment is allowable as a deduction in computing profits [*FA 1998 6 Sch 2(1)(b)*], even though the adjustment is treated as a prior year adjustment in the company's accounts in accordance with FRS 12 para 101. These provisions overrule similar adjustments that would have been required under *Pearce v Woodall-Duckham Ltd [1978] STC 372*.

**7.14** Further authority for normal accounting practice is contained in *Odeon Associated Theatres Ltd v Jones (1971) 48 TC 257* and *Chancery Lane Safe Deposit and Offices Co Ltd v IRC (1965) 43 TC 83*. The Court will, however, always have the last word in connection with accounting principles and refused to accept the 'base stock' method of stock valuation in *Patrick v Broadstone Mills Ltd (1953) 35 TC 44* or the 'last in, first out' method in *BSC Footwear Ltd v Ridgway (1972) 47 TC 495* and refused to follow the accounting treatment of discounts in *Willingale v International Commercial Bank Ltd [1978] STC 75*.

## Expenses not allowed

**7.15** Although the commercial profit, computed on generally accepted accounting principles in accordance with statements of standard accounting practice, forms the starting point for the computation of taxable profits of a trade, this is subject to specific statutory provisions disallowing certain expenses for tax purposes. The most important of these is *TA 1988 s 74* which specifically disallows various expenses for Schedule D Cases I and II, notably under *TA 1988 s 74(1)(a)*, expenses not wholly and exclusively incurred for the purposes of the trade as part of the expenditure incurred to earn profits.

**7.16** It is this provision which gives rise to arguments over duality of purpose, where the entire expense is disallowed if the motive for incurring the expenditure is partly business and partly not, such as sponsorship of a controlling shareholder's wife's riding school (*Executive Network (Consultants) Ltd v O'Connor [1996] STC (SCD) 29*), travelling expenses partly for a holiday (*Bowden v Russell and Russell (1965) 42 TC 301*), travelling partly for private purposes between home and work (*Sargent v Barnes [1978] STC 322 (52 TC 335)*), excess cost of meals while working (*Caillebotte v Quinn [1975] STC 265*) and an operation partly for personal and partly for business reasons (*Prince v Mapp (1969) 46 TC 169, Murgatroyd v Evans-Jackson (1966) 43 TC 581*). Such cases are to be distinguished from those where part of an overall expense is incurred for the purpose of the trade, such as the use of a room at home wholly for the purpose of the business or the running costs of a car used for private and business purposes. The overall expense can be apportioned on a reasonable basis (*McLaren v Mumford [1996] STC 1134*). Where the expenditure is incurred wholly for business purposes, any private benefit is ignored (*Bentleys, Stokes & Lowless v Beeson (1952) 33 TC 491, Edwards v Warmsley Henshall & Co (1967) 44 TC 431*). Expenses on food, clothing and medical treatment are likely to be incurred, at least in part, for the benefit of the taxpayer as a human being and therefore disallowed on duality grounds (*Norman v Golder (1944) 26 TC 293, Mallalieu v Drummond [1983] STC 665*).

**7.17** *TA 1988 s 74(1)(b)* and *(c)* disallows expenses for personal purposes or domestic or private purposes as opposed to purposes of the trade. In several of the duality of purpose cases it is the private element disallowed under these provisions which leads to the duality, which then disqualifies, for example, rent for a dwelling house, except any part used for the purpose of the trade. [*Mason v Tyson [1980] STC 284, Wildbore v Luker (1951) 33 TC 46, Thomas v Ingram [1979] STC 1*].

**7.18** Expenditure on repairs to premises or plant in excess of the amount required purely for repair, in other words the improvement element of such expenditure, is disallowed under *TA 1988 s 74(1)(d)*. Such improvements were disallowed in *Highland Rly Co v Balderston (1889) 2 TC 485, Ounsworth v Vickers Ltd (1915) 6 TC 671, Law Shipping*

### 7.19 Computation of Profits

*Co Ltd v IRC (1923) 12 TC 621, Jackson v Laskers Home Furnishers Ltd (1956) 37 TC 69, Bidwell v Gardiner (1960) 39 TC 31, Lothian Chemical Co Ltd v Rogers (1926) 11 TC 508, O'Grady v Bullcroft Main Collieries Ltd (1932) 17 TC 93, William P Lawrie v IRC (1952) 34 TC 20, Thomas Wilson Keighley Ltd v Emmerson (1960) 39 TC 360, Wynne Jones v Bedale Auction Ltd [1977] STC 50.*

**7.19** The distinction between repairs and improvement or renewal, (which is capital), was explored in *Margarett v Lowestoft Water & Gas Co (1935) 19 TC 481*, in which reference was made to Buckley LJ's comment in *Lurcott v Wakeley and Wheeler [1911] 1 KB 905* that 'repair is restoration by renewal or replacement of subsidiary parts of a whole. Renewal as distinguished from repair is reconstruction of the entirety, meaning by the entirety, not necessarily the whole but substantially the whole subject matter under discussion' and see *Vale v Martin Mahony & Bros Ltd (1946) 2 ITC 331, Brown v Burnley Football & Athletic Co Ltd [1980] STC 424*. Cases where expenditure has been held to be genuine repair expenditure include *Samuel Jones & Co (Devonvale) Ltd v IRC (1951) 32 TC 513, Hodgkins v Plunder & Pollak (Ireland) Ltd (1955) 3 ITC 135, Conn v Robins Bros Ltd (1966) 43 TC 266, Odeon Associated Theatres Ltd v Jones (1971) 48 TC 257, Rhodesia Rlys Ltd v Bechuanaland Protectorate Income Tax Collector (1933) 12 ATC 223.*

**7.20** Losses not connected with or arising out of the trade are disallowed by *TA 1988 s 74(1)(e)*. Damages paid to a guest at an inn when the chimney fell in were disallowed under these provisions, as the expenditure was not for the purpose of earning profits. [*Strong & Co of Romsey Ltd v Woodifield (1906) 5 TC 215*]. Damages, fines and penalties fall under this heading. [*IRC v Warnes & Co Ltd (1919) 12 TC 227, IRC v Alexander von Glehn & Co Ltd (1920) 12 TC 232, McKnight v Sheppard [1996] STC 627, Cattermole v Borax & Chemicals Ltd (1949) 31 TC 202, Fairrie v Hall (1947) 28 TC 200, Knight v Parry [1973] STC 56*]. Although damages are disallowed under these provisions, compromise payments to settle actions may well be for the purpose of the trade. [*G Scammell & Nephew Ltd v Rowles (1939) 22 TC 479, Golder v Great Boulder Proprietary Gold Mines Ltd (1952) 33 TC 75, Hammond Engineering Co Ltd v IRC [1975] STC 334*].

**7.21** Capital expenditure is disallowed under *TA 1988 s 74(f)*. The leading case of *Atherton v British Insulated & Helsby Cables Ltd (1925) 10 TC 155* contained Viscount Cave's famous judgment that expenditure is normally capital if 'made not only once and for all but with a view to bringing into existence an asset or an advantage for the enduring benefit of the trade'. Other cases on the division between capital and revenue expenditure include *Strick v Regent Oil Co Ltd (1965) 43 TC 1, Bolam v Regent Oil Co Ltd (1956) 37 TC 56, Alianza Co Ltd v Bell (1905) 5 TC 60 and 172, RTZ Oil and Gas Ltd v Elliss [1987] STC 512, Lawson v Johnson Matthey plc [1992] STC 466* and *Stone & Temple Ltd v Waters [1995] STC 1n.*

**7.22** The capital element of improvements is specifically disallowed under *s 74(g)*. A deduction for notional interest on capital invested in the business is specifically disallowed by *s 74(1)(h)*. A deduction for a bad debt is permitted by *TA 1988 s 74(j)* where the debt either has become bad or has been released as part of a relevant arrangement or compromise under *TA 1988 s 74(2)* or is a specific provision for bad debts. The relief for bad debts after discontinuance is available under *TA 1988 s 89*. Bad debts recovered would normally be included as trading receipts under normal accounting practice. A bad debt that is formally released other than as part of a relevant arrangement or compromise under the *Insolvency Act 1986* or *CA 1985 s 425* or its Northern Ireland equivalent, is treated as a trading receipt of the company which previously wrote it off under *TA 1988 s 94*. Specific provisions for losses on trading debts are allowed following *Anderton & Halstead Ltd v Birrell (1931) 16 TC 200, Calders Ltd v IRC (1944) 26 TC 213, Reids Brewery Co Ltd v Male (1891) 3 TC 279*. Bad debt recoveries are taxed when recovered. [*Bristow v William Dickinson & Co Ltd (1946) 27 TC 157, Lock v Jones (1941) 23 TC 749, Absolom v Talbot (1944) 26 TC 166*].

**7.23** Losses are only allowed to the extent not covered by insurance under *TA 1988 s 74(1)(k)*. Insurance receipts or indemnity recoveries are taxable under *TA 1988 s 74(l)*. Annuities or annual payments other than interest are disallowed as a trading expense [*TA 1988 s 74*] but may be deductible under *TA 1988 s 349(1)(a)* or in the case of a patent royalty under *TA 1988 s 349(1)(b)*.

**7.24** Interest paid to a non-UK resident in excess of a reasonable commercial rate is disallowed by *TA 1988 s 74(m)*. *TA 1988 s 74(o)* disallows mortgage interest paid under deduction of tax [*TA 1988* s 369], which would not normally apply to a company. *TA 1988 s 74(p)* disallows a royalty in respect of the user of a patent, such royalties being deducted as a charge on income. [*TA 1988 s 349(1)(b)*].

**Expenses allowed**

**7.25** Expenses specifically allowable include incidental costs of obtaining loan finance [*TA 1988 s 77*], research and development costs [*TA 1988 ss 82A, 82B*], patent fees and expenses [*TA 1988 s 83*], gifts to educational establishments [*TA 1988 s 88*], costs of establishing a share option or profit sharing scheme [*TA 1988 s 84A*], payments to trustees of approved profit sharing schemes [*TA 1988 s 85*], which is being 'phased out', costs of establishing employee share ownership trusts [*TA 1988 s 85A*], and all employee share ownership plans [*FA 2000 8 Sch 111, 112*], and the costs of employees seconded to charities and educational establishments [*TA 1988 s 86*], including contributions to agents expenses. [*TA 1988 s 86A*]. Revenue expenditure on research and development may qualify for enhanced tax relief under *FA 2000 20, 21 Schs*.

**7.26** In respect of a premium on a lease on land that has been taxed as income on the recipient under *TA 1988 ss 34 or 35*, the proportion of the

### 7.27 Computation of Profits

expenditure so taxed is allowed as a trading expense apportioned equally over the period of the lease under *TA 1988 s 87*. Payments to the Export Credit Guarantee Department are deductible under *TA 1988 s 88*. Redundancy payments which would have been deductible but for the discontinuance of a trade continue to qualify for relief under *TA 1988 s 90*.

**7.27** *TA 1988 s 91* gives amortisation relief for cemeteries as the land is used up. Proportionate amortisation is allowed in respect of preparation expenditure for waste disposal under *TA 1988 s 91B* and waste disposal restoration payments are allowed under *TA 1988 ss 91A, 91BA*. Expenditure on mineral exploration and access is allowed under *TA 1988 s 91C*. Regional development grants are made tax free under *TA 1988 s 92* but other grants, under the *Industrial Development Act 1982* etc., are taxable as income under *TA 1988 s 93*.

**7.28** Dealers in land are excluded from taxation in respect of woodland under *TA 1988 s 99*. Expenses in connection with tied premises owned by brewers etc. are allowed under Schedule D Case I instead of Schedule A under *TA 1988 s 98*. *TA 1988 s 96* allows farm profit averaging and the herd basis is available for farming companies under *TA 1988 s 97* and *Schedule 5*. Losses arising from a subscription of shares by an investment company in an unquoted trading company can be deductible as a management expense under *TA 1988 s 577*.

**7.29** Business entertaining expenses are specifically disallowed by *TA 1988 s 577* and expenditure involving crime is disallowed by *TA 1988 s 577A*. Housing grants are exempt from tax under *TA 1988 s 578* and statutory redundancy payments are deductible under *TA 1988 ss 579* and *580*. Tax on unremittable overseas income may be deferred under *TA 1988 s 584*, training courses for employees are deductible under *TA 1988 ss 588* and *589* and counselling services for employees are deductible under *TA 1988 ss 589A* and *589B*.

**7.30** Tax relief is given for contributions to employee share ownership trusts under *FA 1989 s 67(2)*. Contributions to employee benefit trusts may be deductible on normal accounting principles following *Heather v P-E Consulting Group Ltd (1972) 48 TC 293* but not where part of the purpose is to benefit the shareholders, which failed the revenue or capital and the duality of purpose tests in *Mawsley Machinery Ltd v Robinson [1998] STC (SCD) 236*.

**7.31** Excessive directors' remuneration could be disallowed following *Copeman v William Flood & Sons Ltd (1940) 24 TC 53*. In the case of trading companies however, it would be most unusual for the Revenue to challenge remuneration of full time working directors up to the profits earned. Directors' remuneration and other emoluments of employees must be paid within nine months of the accounting period to be deductible as a provision. [*FA 1989 ss 43* and *44*]. Otherwise there is only a

Computation of Profits  **7.35**

deduction when the remuneration is actually paid. Capital receipts in respect of finance leasing arrangements may be taxed under the anti-avoidance provisions in *FA 1997 12 Sch*. Relief for pre-trading expenditure is given by *TA 1988 s 401* as amended.

**7.32** Statutory redundancy payments are relieved under *TA 1988 s 579* with additional payments which do not exceed three times the statutory payment being given under *TA 1988 s 90* as explained in Statement of Practice 11/81. Donations are deductible if they are for small amounts to local organisations or if they are covenanted donations to charity under *TA 1988 s 347A(2)(a)* or gift aid payments under *TA 1988 s 339*. The corporate venturing scheme under *FA 2000 s 63, 15, 16 Schs* allows loss relief for investment in unlisted trading companies as a corporate equivalent to the Enterprise Investment Scheme.

**Capital allowances**

**7.33** The prohibition of a deduction for capital expenditure requires depreciation and amortisation of capital assets to be added back. This also means that legal expenses relating to the acquisition of capital assets are also disallowed [*Texas Land & Mortgage Co v Holtham (1894) 3 TC 255, Morse v Stedeford (1934) 18 TC 457, ECC Quarries Ltd v Watkis [1975] STC 578*], which is to be contrasted with legal expenses relating to defending title to a company's existing assets, which are deductible. [*Southern v Borax Consolidated Ltd (1940) 23 TC 597*]. However, capital allowances are then given in respect of certain types of capital assets, but by no means all. Where capital allowances are available they are deductible as a trading expense. [*CAA 1990 s 144*].

**7.34** Industrial buildings qualify but commercial buildings normally do not. Patent rights and research and development [*TA 1988 ss 837A, 837B*] qualify but purchases of trade marks and copyright do not. Expenditure which qualifies for capital allowances is the net cost after any Government or Local Authority grant. [*CAA 1990 s 80*]. [*Stokes v Costain Property Investments Ltd [1983] STC 405, McKinney v Hagans Caravans (Manufacturing) Ltd [1997] STC 1023, Cyril Lord Carpets Ltd v Schofield (1966) 42 TC 637, CAA 1990 s 153*]. Where a building is acquired containing plant and machinery a just apportionment is necessary under *CAA 1990 s 150, St Johns School v Ward [1975] STC 7n*. Where there is a composite transaction it may require apportionment under *CAA 1990 s 151, Fitten v Gilders and Heaton (1965) 36 TC 233, A Wood & Co v Provan (1968) 44 TC 701*. Contributions to another's capital expenditure may qualify for capital allowances under *CAA 1990 s 154* and *155* but this does not include the cost of connection to main drainage. [*Bridge House (Reigate Hill) v Hinder (1971) 47 TC 182*].

**7.35** Capital allowances have to be claimed and it is not necessary to claim all the possible allowances. [*Elliss v BP Oil Northern Ireland*

**7.36** *Computation of Profits*

*Refinery Ltd [1987] STC 52]*. Some allowances are given by way of discharge or repayment if the asset is not used for a trade and are given primarily against income of the appropriate class, under *CAA 1990 s 145*. Allowances are available to non-resident companies in respect of assets and income arising in the UK under *CAA 1990 s 149* but double allowances are not unnaturally excluded by *CAA 1990 s 147*.

**7.36** Where a company commences to trade, or ceases to be within the charge to corporation tax there is a deemed disposal and reacquisition at market value for capital allowances purposes under *CAA 1990 s 152*. Market value may also be substituted for the sales price where assets other than know-how eligible for capital allowances are sold between persons under common control. [*CAA 1990 s 157*.] This does not apply to plant and machinery which is covered by *CAA 1990 ss 75–78* or to a transfer of trade within the EU if *CAA 1990 s 152B* applies. The tax written-down value may be substituted for the market value under *CAA 1990 s 158* for certain sales within common control. If additional VAT becomes payable as a result of the capital goods scheme, adjustments under *CAA 1990 s 159A* will be treated as additional or reduced consideration for capital allowances purposes.

**7.37** Capital allowances are given by reference to chargeable periods i.e. the accounting periods of companies, under *TA 1988 s 832(1)*. If the accounting period is less than twelve months, writing-down allowances are proportionately reduced, as they are when the proportion of qualifying use changes. [*CCA 1990 ss 79, 79A*]. Where a trade starts part way through an accounting period, capital allowances may also be proportionately restricted including patents (*TA 1988 s 520(4)(a)(ii)*), know-how (*TA 1988 s 530(2)(a)(ii)*), plant and machinery (*CAA 1990 s 24(2)(a)(ii)*), and mineral extraction allowances (*CAA 1990 s 98(6)*). First year allowances are given at 100 per cent on expenditure on information and communications technology incurred by small enterprises and at 40 per cent on plant and machinery acquired by small and medium-sized entities. [*CAA 1990 ss 22, 22A*].

**7.38** In respect of plant, purchases from connected parties qualifying for capital allowances are limited to the disposal value brought into account by the seller, or if there is no such disposal value, to the smallest of: the purchaser's capital expenditure, the capital expenditure incurred by the seller or person connected with him, and the open market value when acquired by the purchaser. [*CAA 1990 ss 26(3), 75 and 76*].

**7.39** There are special provisions for finance leases under *CAA 1990 s 76A* which provide that the capital allowances available to the purchaser in respect of machinery and plant which is sold and leased back under a finance lease, are restricted to the notional written down value of the seller. These reliefs are now extended by *CAA 1990 s 76B*, on making a joint election, to apply to sale and lease-back immediately after delivery of new equipment, which is a common commercial practice to remove from the lessor the risk of problems with delivery of the equipment. But allowances are not available where there is a sale and lease-back to the lessor under a finance lease, if the lessor has substantially divested himself of the risk of the lessee failing to meet his obligations under the lease, to prevent arrangements amounting in substance to the sale of allowances. These provisions apply to a sale and lease-back on or after 2 July 1997, unless made under an earlier contract. Finance lease is defined by *CAA 1990 s 82A* as a lease which would be treated as a finance lease or loan under Statement of Standards Accounting Practice (SSAP) 21 in the accounts of the lessor or the consolidated group accounts of the lessor's group.

*Industrial building allowances*

**7.40** Capital allowances are available for buildings and structures in enterprise zones at 100 per cent of the expenditure, under *CAA 1990 s 1*. This applies to industrial buildings, qualifying hotels and commercial buildings but not dwelling houses. Expenditure, other than on land, qualifies if it is contracted for while the building site is in an enterprise zone and the expenditure is incurred within ten years of expiry of the zone status, under *CAA 1990 s 17A*. Where the 100 per cent allowance is not claimed in full, writing-down allowances at 25 per cent per annum, straight line, are available under *CAA 1990 s 6*. All other industrial buildings not in an enterprise zone qualify for a straight line writing-down allowance of 4 per cent per annum.

**7.41** Industrial buildings are defined by *CAA 1990 s 18* as those in use for the purpose of a trade carried on in a mill, factory or similar premises, which does not include a plant hire depot. [*Vibroplant Ltd v Holland [1982] STC 164*]. It also includes a warehouse for the storage of raw materials or goods awaiting processing or finished goods or imported goods. [*Dale v Johnson Bros (1951) 32 TC 487, IRC v Saxone Lilley & Skinner (Holding) Ltd (1967) 44 TC 122, Bestway (Holdings) Ltd v Luff [1998] STC 357*]. It does not include a drawing office (*IRC v Lambhill Iron Works Ltd (1950) 31 TC 393*), a house occupied by an employee (*IRC v National Coal Board (1957) 37 TC 264*), a crematorium (*Bourne v Norwich Crematorium Ltd (1967) 44 TC 164*), a security area for wage packaging (*Buckingham v Securitas Properties Ltd [1980] STC 166*), an inland warehouse (*Copol Clothing Ltd v Hindmarch [1984] STC 33*), nor kennels (*Carr v Sayer [1992] STC 396*). Subjecting goods to a process was considered for industrial buildings allowances in *Kilmarnock Equitable Co-operative Society Ltd v IRC (1966) 42 TC 675* and *Crusabridge Investments Ltd v Casing International Ltd (1979) 54 TC 246*. A data-processing centre is neither an industrial building nor an office. [*Girobank plc v Clarke [1998] STC 182*]. If the non-qualifying part of an industrial building does not exceed 25 per cent of the total cost, the whole building still qualifies. [*Abbott Laboratories Ltd v Carmody (1968) 44 TC 569*]. Expenditure on roads on an industrial estate qualifies for IBAs.

## 7.42 Computation of Profits

**7.42** A qualifying hotel as defined by *CAA 1990 s 19* qualifies for industrial buildings allowances under *CAA 1990 s 7*. The basic industrial buildings allowance is on the costs of building, excluding the cost of land. [*CAA 1990 s 3*].

**7.43** On a disposal within 25 years of acquisition, or 50 years for pre 6 November 1962 expenditure, there is a balancing allowance or charge on the difference between the residue of expenditure and the sale proceeds under *CAA 1990 s 4*. Where a lease is granted within seven years of incurring construction expenditure in an enterprise zone, there is a deemed disposal for balancing charge purposes under *CAA 1990 s 4A*. Intra-group sales cannot be used to accelerate allowances in view of *CAA 1990 s 5*. Residue of expenditure is calculated in accordance with *CAA 1990 s 8* and is the equivalent of written-down value for plant and machinery under *CAA 1990 s 9*. The allowances, where a building is purchased before use, are claimed by the purchaser, not the vendor, under *CAA 1990 s 10* and are subject to anti-avoidance provisions in respect of enterprise zones etc. under *CAA 1990 ss 10A–10B*. The grant of a long lease of more than 50 years may be treated as a disposal of the vendor's relevant interest on a joint election under *CAA 1990 s 11*. The allowances extend to improvements to industrial buildings treated as capital under *CAA 1990 s 12*. Site preparation for machinery and plant is included by *CAA 1990 s 13*, although alterations incidental to the installation of machinery or plant are treated as expenditure qualifying for machinery and plant allowances under *CAA 1990 s 64*. Relevant interest in an industrial building is defined by *CAA 1990 s 20*. [*Woods v R M Mallen Engineering Ltd (1969) 45 TC 619*].

*Machinery and plant*

**7.44** Machinery and plant normally qualifies for writing-down allowances under *CAA 1990 s 24* at 25 per cent per annum on the reducing balance basis. Capital allowances on machinery and plant are given by reference to the value of the equipment in a pool of expenditure. This is the value brought forward from the previous accounting period plus the qualifying additions (the qualifying expenditure), less the disposal value of any sales, normally the sale proceeds. If the disposal value exceeds the proceeds there is a balancing charge. If, on a cessation of trade, there is an excess of qualifying expenditure over the disposal value, it is given as a balancing allowance.

**7.45** In some cases expenditure qualifies for a first year allowance, which was 50 per cent (or 12 per cent for long-life assets) for expenditure incurred by a small or medium-sized enterprise between 2 July 1997 and 1 July 1998 under *CAA 1990 s 22*. This was reduced to 40 per cent (or 6 per cent) by *FA 1998 s 84* and *s 85* for later expenditure. Initial allowances are only available on certain assets. A small or medium-sized enterprise is defined by *FA 1990 s 22A*. Qualifying expenditure is defined by *CAA 1990 s 25*. If plant is bought after 1 July 1997 for leasing under a

## Computation of Profits 7.47

finance lease, only a proportion of the expenditure can be added to the pool for capital allowances purposes so that if, for example, in a calendar year accounting period, expenditure was incurred on 1 September, only 1/3 of it would qualify for capital allowances in the year of acquisition. In some cases, allowances for plant and machinery are dealt with on a renewals basis whereby the initial expenditure is not claimed but any replacements are written off as a trading expense. [*Caledonian Rly Co v Banks (1880) 1 TC 487*]. ESC B1 allows a change from the renewals to the capital allowance basis.

**7.46** Plant has been held to include:

- law books (*Munby v Furlong [1977] STC 232*);
- movable office partitioning (*Jarrold v John Good & Sons Ltd (1962) 40 TC 681*);
- a dry dock (*IRC v Barclay, Curle & Co Ltd (1969) 45 TC 221*);
- a swimming pool (*Cooke v Beach Station Caravans Ltd [1974] STC 402*);
- grain silos (*Schofield v R & H Hall Ltd [1975] STC 353*);
- loose tools, knives and lasts (*Hinton v Maden & Ireland Ltd (1959) 38 TC 391*);
- a horse (*Yarmouth v France (1887) 19 QBD 647*);
- certain electrical installations, but not all (*Cole Bros Ltd v Phillips [1982] STC 307*);
- light fittings and murals in a hotel (*IRC v Scottish & Newcastle Breweries Ltd [1982] STC 296*);
- decorative panels (*Leeds Permanent Building Society v Procter [1982] STC 821*);
- option cancellation payments (*Bolton v International Drilling Co Ltd [1983] STC 70*);

**7.47** Plant has been held not to include:

- prefabricated buildings (*St John's School v Ward [1975] STC 7n* – plant in the buildings did not qualify because there were no records apportioning the cost between plant and buildings);
- a garage canopy (*Dixon v Fitch's Garage Ltd [1975] STC 486*);
- a ship used as a floating restaurant (*Benson v Yard Arm Club Ltd [1979] STC 266*);
- restaurant improvements to the premises and light fittings for general illumination (not specific to the trade), (*Wimpy International v Warland [1989] STC 273*);
- finance charges for an oil rig (*Ben-Odeco Ltd v Powlson [1978] STC 460*);

**7.48** *Computation of Profits*

- wallpaper pattern books (*Rose & Co (Wallpapers & Paints) Ltd v Campbell (1967) 44 TC 500*);
- a football spectators' stand (*Brown v Burnley Football & Athletic Club Ltd [1980] STC 424*);
- suspended ceilings (*Hampton v Fortes Autogrill Ltd [1980] STC 80*);
- an inflatable tennis court cover (*Thomas v Reynolds [1987] STC 135*);
- kennels (*Carr v Sayer [1992] STC 396*);
- glasshouses (*Gray v Seymour's Garden Centre (Horticulture) [1995] STC 706*, see also IR Tax Bulletin, Issue 5, November 1992, p 46);
- a car wash site (*Attwood v Anduff Car Wash Ltd [1997] STC 1167*);
- the structure of an underground electricity substation to contain plant (*Bradley v London Electricity plc [1996] STC 1054*);
- newly constructed putting greens on a golf course (*Family Golf Centres Ltd v Thorne [1998] STC (SCD) 106*).
- furniture for a flat (*Mason v Tyson [1980] STC 284*).

**7.48** Disposal value is defined by *CAA 1990 s 26*. Plant used by investment companies, Schedule A businesses and various holiday lettings are treated as if they were trades for capital allowance purposes under *CAA 1990 ss 28–28A and 29*.

*Special classes of assets*

**7.49** Ships qualify for free depreciation and deferred balancing charges under *CAA 1990 ss 30–33F*.

**7.50** 'Expensive' motor cars, where the car costs in excess of £12,000, have a limited writing-down allowance which cannot exceed £3,000 a year and are treated as individual assets not pooled, so that there is a balancing charge or allowance as each car is sold. Although the writing down allowance is restricted, the balancing allowance on disposal is not, and therefore the whole cost of the car is allowed. [*CAA 1990 ss 34 and 36*]. Hired cars costing more than £12,000 have the rental restricted by the proportion of the hire rental which £12,000 plus half the difference between £12,000 and the retail value of the car, bears to the retail value. For example, if the car cost £30,000 when new, the proportion of hire rental that may be claimed as a trading expense is

$$£12,000 + (\tfrac{1}{2} \times £18,000) = \frac{£21,000}{£30,000} \text{ i.e. } \frac{21}{30} \times \text{rental},$$

[*CAA 1990 s 35*].

**7.51** Short-life assets, being machinery or plant other than those excluded by *CAA 1990 s 38*, such as ships, cars and certain leased equipment, may qualify for an election under *CAA 1990 s 37*. They may then be treated individually rather than as part of the pool, so that there is a balancing allowance or charge on disposal. If a short-life asset is not disposed of before the fourth anniversary or period, the written-down value is brought into the general pool. A disposal to a connected party is taken over at written-down value and the original date of acquisition is used for short-life asset treatment.

**7.52** Long-life assets are those having an expected useful economic life of at least 25 years from first being brought into use until ceasing to be used as a fixed asset in a business. Excluded from such assets are: fixtures in dwelling houses, retail shops, showrooms, hotels or offices, motor cars, hire cars, sea-going ships until 2011 and railway assets until the same date. [*CAA 1990 ss 38A* and *38B*]. There is a de minimis figure for companies' assets which are not treated as long-life assets if the total expenditure within a group of companies is no more than £100,000 in the year. [*CAA 1990 s 38D*]. Long-life assets go into a separate pool [*CAA 1990 s 38E*], which qualifies for capital allowances at 6 per cent per annum instead of the normal 25 per cent, on the reducing balance under *CAA 1990 s 38F*. Artificial disposals are deemed to be disposed of at written-down value under *CAA 1990 s 38G*. Expenditure on long-life assets prior to 31 December 2000 which was contracted prior to 26 November 1996 can be kept outside the long-life asset pool.

**7.53** Cars costing £12,000 or less and certain leased assets no longer have to be kept together in a separate pool under *CAA 1990 s 41*, from 1 April 2000. Assets leased outside the United Kingdom are either ineligible for writing-down allowances or are kept in a separate pool qualifying for writing-down allowances at 10 per cent per annum. [*CAA 1990, s 42*]. Various terms are defined by *CAA 1990 ss 39* and *40* for these purposes and expenditure incurred by the holder of an interest in land or an equipment lessor may qualify for capital allowances as machinery and plant under *CAA 1990 ss 51–59C*.

**7.54** Machinery and plant being acquired on hire-purchase is treated as if it had been bought outright by the hirer under *CAA 1990 ss 60, 60A*. Capital allowances for plant leased under an agreement without an option to purchase are due to the lessor and not to the hirer. Where a plant lessor is not carrying on a trade as such, its lease is treated as a deemed separate trade. [*CAA 1990 s 61*]. Where the equipment acquired on hire-purchase is to be used for a finance leasing trade, the purchaser is only entitled to allowances on the expenditure as it is incurred, not on the date the agreement commences in view of *CAA 1990 s 60(2A)*. Capital allowances on plant are available for expenditure on thermal insulation under *CAA 1990 s 67*, computer software under *CAA 1990 s 67A*, expenditure on fire safety under *CAA 1990 s 69*, and safety at sports grounds under *CAA 1990 s 70*.

**7.55** *Computation of Profits*

**7.55** Capital expenditure incurred in the production or acquisition of original master film, tape or disks may be written off on the basis of allocating the expenditure over the anticipated income stream of the asset under *CAA 1990 s 68*.

**7.56** In the case of plant acquired from connected parties or sold and leased back, where the sole or main benefit is likely to be additional capital allowances, the allowances are limited to the proceeds of sale by the vendor under *CAA 1990 ss 75* and *76*. [*Barclays Mercantile Industrial Finance Ltd v Melluish [1990] STC 314*].

**7.57** Expenditure on dwelling houses let on assured tenancies prior to 1 April 1992 qualified for capital allowances in broadly the same way as industrial building allowances under *CAA 1990 ss 84–97*.

**7.58** Mineral extraction allowances are given at 10 per cent of the expenditure incurred under *CAA 1990 ss 98–121* excluding the undeveloped market value of an interest in land. [*CAA 1990 s 110*].

**7.59** Agricultural buildings allowances are given at 4 per cent per annum on a straight line basis in the same way as industrial buildings allowances under *CAA 1990 ss 122–130*. No allowances are now available in respect of forestry as the income is not taxable. [*CAA 1990 ss 131*].

**7.60** Allowances for expenditure on dredging qualify for allowances under *CAA 1990 ss 134–135*.

**7.61** Research and development allowances are given at 100 per cent of the qualifying expenditure under *CAA 1990 s 137*. Revenue expenditure, including payments to researchers, associations, universities etc. qualifies as a trading expense under *TA 1988 s 82A*. The definition of research and development includes any activities in the field of natural or applied science for the extension of knowledge. [*TA 1988 ss 837A, 837B*]. This was rather a restricted definition and the Government consulted on ways of encouraging expenditure on innovation and research and development including the taxation reliefs available, and the taxation of intellectual property arising from such research. The definition has therefore been widened by *FA 2000 19 Sch*.

**7.62** *CAA 1990 Schedule AA1* specifically excludes expenditure on a building from qualifying as plant, by including, as part of the cost of the building, walls, floors, ceilings, doors, gates, shutters, windows and stairs, mains services and systems of water, electricity and gas, waste disposal systems, sewerage and drainage systems, shafts and other structures in which lifts, hoists, escalators and moving walkways are installed and fire safety systems. Similarly, structures such as tunnels, bridges, cuttings, standings such as roads, railways, car parks, airstrips, canals, dams, reservoirs, docks, piers, marinas, jetties, dykes, sea walls, weirs, drainage ditches and other structures do not count as plant.

*Making claims for capital allowances*

**7.63** For CTSA purposes the capital allowances provisions in *FA 1998 18 Sch* are deemed to be part of the *CAA 1990*, *FA 1998 18 Sch 78*. Claims for capital allowances must be included in the company tax return or any amendment thereof, *FA 1998 18 Sch 79*. Such a claim must specify the amount claimed, which has to be quantified at the time the claim is made [*18 Sch 80*], but may be amended or withdrawn by amending the company tax return. [*FA 1998 18 Sch 81*].

**7.64** A capital allowances claim may be made, amended or withdrawn up to the latest of the following dates:

(a) first anniversary of the company tax return filing date;

(b) 30 days after any enquiry into the return is completed;

(c) 30 days after an Inland Revenue notice to amend the return following an enquiry; or

(d) in the case of an appeal, 30 days after the appeal is finally determined. [*FA 1998 18 Sch 82(1)*].

The Revenue do have discretion to accept a late claim amendment or withdrawal. [*FA 1998 18 Sch 82(2)*].

References to an enquiry into a company's tax return do not include an enquiry restricted to a previous amendment relating to a claim for capital allowances. [*FA 1998 18 Sch 82(4)*].

**7.65** Where a capital allowances claim affects a claim for another accounting period for which a company tax return has been delivered, any consequential amendments to the previous return must be made within 30 days. [*FA 1998 18 Sch 83(1) and (2)*]. If the company does not do so, the Revenue may give a written notice amending the return even if otherwise out of time. [*FA 1998 18 Sch 83(3) and (4)*]. The company however may appeal against such an amendment notice in writing within 30 days. [*FA 1998 18 Sch 83(5) and (6)*]. The Pay and File rules for the making of capital allowances claims included in *CAA 1990 Sch A1*, are displaced by the CTSA rules explained above.

## Investment companies

**7.66** An investment company is defined by *TA 1988 s 130* as any company whose business consists of wholly or mainly in the making of investments and the principal part of whose income is derived therefrom. A close investment holding company does not qualify for the small companies rate of corporation tax under *TA 1988 s 13(1)(a)*, as defined by *TA 1988 s 13A*, if it is not carrying on a trade on a commercial basis or making investments in land let to unconnected persons, or as a holding company of such companies. A close company is one which is under the

**7.67** *Computation of Profits*

control of five or fewer participators or participators who are directors, under *TA 1988 ss 414–417*. Close company expenses can be subject to disallowance as distributions, under *TA 1988 s 418*, and taxable as loans to participators, under *TA 1988 ss 419–422*.

**7.67** An investment company is entitled to a deduction for management expenses under *TA 1988 s 75*. Management expenses have been held not to include commission to guarantee loan stock (*Hoechst Finance Ltd v Gumbrell [1983] STC 150*), exchange losses (*Bennet v Underground Rlys Co of London Ltd (1923) 8 TC 475*), the costs of a debenture issue (*London Country Freehold and Leasehold Properties Ltd v Sweet (1942) 24 TC 412*), brokerage and stamp duty (*Capital & National Trust Ltd v Golder (1949) 31 TC 265*), and service charges that cannot be justified for the services rendered to the extent that they are excessive (*Fragmap Developments Ltd v Cooper (1967) 44 TC 366*). The definition of investment company was considered in *Bank Line Ltd v IRC (1974) 49 TC 307*. Excessive directors' remuneration was disallowed in *L G Berry Investments Ltd v Attwoll (1964) 41 TC 547*.

**7.68** Management expenses of insurance companies are dealt with by *TA 1988 s 76* but this is a specialist area outside the scope of this book.

## Income from land in the UK: Schedule A

### Introduction

**7.69** The Schedule A income tax provisions were changed with effect from 1995/96 as part of a rationalisation process to update the previous outmoded and complicated rules. At that time the corporation tax provisions largely remained unchanged because, the Revenue argued, a change would have resulted in the loss of certain flexibilities which property companies enjoyed in relation to management expenses and their ability to offset interest against non-property income.

**7.70** Following many representations about the unsatisfactory state of separate rules for income tax and corporation tax, the Revenue reviewed the position, and the corporation tax provisions have generally been aligned with those for income tax with effect from 1 April 1998, independent of the move to CTSA. Companies now have a separate deemed Schedule A trade. [*FA 1998 s 38(1)(3), 5 Sch*]. Some differences remain; in particular there is an exclusion for interest, foreign exchange gains and losses, and profits and losses on financial instruments in the corporation tax computation, as these are dealt with under the separate loan relationship and foreign exchange provisions covered in Chapter 10. The provisions relating to the utilisation of losses also differ.

*Computation of Profits* **7.72**

**7.71** The timing and essential features of the system for companies are as follows:

(a) the rules came into force on 1 April 1998 (*FA 1998 s 38(2), (3)*);

(b) for periods straddling 1 April 1998 there are transitional rules contained in *FA 1998 5 Sch Part IV*;

(c) Schedule D, Case I computation rules apply, notably the true and fair accruals basis for income and expenditure (*FA 1998 s 42*);

(d) all income and expenditure is pooled, with no differentiation for different kinds of property or different leases;

(e) Furnished lettings and furnished holiday lettings under *TA 1988 ss 503* and *504* are included;

(f) capital allowances are treated as an allowable expense. The renewals basis, or wear and tear allowances, for furnished lettings, is maintained;

(g) a loss can be set against total profits for the same period under *TA 1988 s 379A*. Unrelieved losses can be carried forward into subsequent periods and set off against total profits. Losses may also be surrendered under the group relief provisions, but subject to certain restrictions;

(h) taxable income from property situated outside the UK is determined as for income from UK property but is treated as a separate business chargeable under Schedule D, Case V.

(i) the sale of a right to future rents (rent factoring) is a capital transaction and would normally be subject to corporation tax on chargeable gains, even though, if the rents themselves had been received, they would have been taxed as income under Schedule A. From 21 March 2000 rent factoring transactions of this nature will be charged to tax as income under Schedule A. The method of attack is to identify the correct accounting treatment which would have applied, either on a company or group basis, on the footing that all the companies were UK resident, with provisions to ensure that there is no double taxation. [*TA 1988 ss 43A–43G*].

**Scope of charge and single business**

**7.72** A substituted *TA 1988 s 15* is applied for corporation tax from 1 April 1998, by *FA 1998 s 38(1)–(3)* and *5 Sch*. Tax under Schedule A is charged on the annual profits arising from a business carried on for the exploitation, as a source of rents or other receipts, of any estate, interest or rights in or over any land in the UK. Any and all businesses and transactions entered into to this end are generally deemed to have been entered into in the course of such a single business. [*TA 1988 s 15 Sch A (1)–(3)*].

**7.73** *Computation of Profits*

**Non-resident companies**

**7.73** Non-resident companies carrying on a Schedule A business via a branch or agency are subject to corporation tax. Non-resident companies with no UK trading activities but UK source rental income are subject to income tax. Businesses which are chargeable to corporation tax, namely those carried on through a branch or agency, are treated as separate from those which are chargeable to income tax. This will be relevant in the context of a company beginning or ceasing to carry on a trade through a branch or agency. [*TA 1988 s 15(1A)* inserted by *FA 1998 5 Sch 2*].

**Receipts charged**

**7.74** The restructuring of Schedule A does not exclude any categories of receipt that were previously chargeable. Rather, Schedule A is extended to include furnished lettings and rents from caravans and houseboats, previously within Schedule D, Case VI. Items of a capital nature generally remain excluded by the continued use of the words 'annual profits'.

**7.75** Taxable receipts within Schedule A include the following:

(a) payments in respect of a licence to occupy or otherwise use land, or the exercise of any other right over land substituted [*TA 1988 s 15 Sch A (1)(4)(a)*];

(b) rent charges, ground annuals, fee duties and other annual payments reserved in respect of, or charges on or issuing out of, land substituted [*TA 1988 s 15 Sch A (1)(4)(b)*];

(c) income from furnished lettings, including furnished holiday lettings. Hence any money which a tenant pays for the use of furniture is within Schedule A, the former right to elect for a split of rent between the property itself and the furniture being abolished. [*FA 1995 6 Sch 1*]. If unusually the furniture rental forms part of a trade, it remains chargeable under Schedule D, Case I, substituted [*TA 1988 s 15 Sch A (4)(1)–(3)*];

(d) any income from caravans or houseboats (including any amounts for the use of any furniture) where the use is confined to use at one location in the UK. The definitions of caravans and houseboats respectively are such that they are essentially used as a place of human habitation [*TA 1988 s 15 Sch A paras 3(1)(2) and 4(4)*]; and

(e) all sporting rights' income and expenses; the sporting rights rules of *TA 1988 s 29* being disapplied for corporation tax by *FA 1988 5 Sch 10*.

**Lease premiums, assignments, sales with right to reconveyance**

**7.76** The lease premium provisions of *TA 1988 s 34*, which bring into charge premiums paid on the grant of leases under 50 years, less a deduction of 2 per cent for every year for the term of the lease other than the first, are retained with appropriate modifications to tie in with the concept of a Schedule A business. The notional rent is hence a receipt of Schedule A business and it is brought into the Schedule A computation for the period in which it is received. [*TA 1998 s 34(7A)* inserted by *FA 1998 5 Sch 15(5)*]. Premiums which are received by a person other than the landlord are likewise treated as Schedule A income (previously Schedule D, Case VI). But any deemed premium for work done by the tenant which would have been deductible as an expense of a Schedule A business carried on by the landlord, if incurred by him, is excluded from the definition of lease premium. [*TA 1988 s 34(3)*]. Reverse premiums are taxed under *FA 1998 s 40*.

**7.77** An intermediate landlord who has paid a premium to a head landlord on the grant of a lease may deduct the chargeable amount of such premium over the period of the lease as if it were an expense of the property. [*TA 1988 s 37; FA 1998 5 Sch 18*]. A double allowance for the same expenditure is prevented by *TA 1988 s 87(6)* which would have given relief to the lessee on the payment of the premium over the life of the lease as a result of Schedule A income being computed under Schedule D, Case I rules.

**7.78** The charge imposed by *TA 1988 s 35* on certain assignments of leases for less than 50 years granted at an undervalue, where the grantor could have charged a premium, is also included in the profit of a Schedule A business. [*FA 1998 5 Sch 16*]. Likewise the charge under *TA 1988 s 36* where land is sold on terms that it be reconveyed to the vendor or a connected person at a later date is retained. [*FA 1998 17 Sch*].

**Exclusions from Schedule A charge**

**7.79** There are a number of specific exclusions from the Schedule A charge as follows [substituted *TA 1988 s 15 Sch A(2)*]:

(a) farming and market gardening profits within *TA 1988 s 53*; profits charged under *TA 1988 s 55*, being:

    (i) mines and quarries;

    (ii) ironworks, gasworks, salt springs, alum mines and waterworks;

    (iii) canals, inland navigation, docks, drains or levels;

    (iv) fishing rights;

    (v) rights of market and fairs, tolls, bridges and ferries;

    (vi) railways;

    (vii) other concerns of a like nature;

**7.80** *Computation of Profits*

(b) lettings of tied premises by traders falling within *TA 1988 s 98*;

(c) rents related thereto, under *TA 1988 s 119*, and electric line wayleaves, under *TA 1988 s 120*.

**Schedule A business**

**7.80** Although there is no definition of a Schedule A business, paragraph 1(2) in substituted *TA 1988 s 15* brings within the ambit of a Schedule A business any transaction to generate income from land, i.e. a single transaction. The Revenue consider that the Schedule A charge extends to one-off or casual lettings that may not have the degree of organisation normally associated with a business; see SAT1(1995) para 9.19. Accordingly any receipt of an income nature relating to land will fall to be regarded as a receipt of a Schedule A business.

**Computation of profit**

*General rule: Schedule D, Case I principles apply*

**7.81** Profits are to be computed as if the Schedule A business were a trade carried on under Schedule D, Case I unless the contrary is expressly provided. Substituted [*TA 1988 s 21A(1)*]. Accordingly, Schedule D, Case I principles are to be applied, in particular the accruals concept. In determining taxable profits, the following general rules apply:

(a) Rents in arrears are to be included; rents paid in advance excluded. The Revenue have said that deposits paid by tenants or licensees will ordinarily be receipts of the business. Deposits should be recognised in accordance with generally accepted accounting practice, normally by being deferred and matched with the costs of providing the services or carrying out repairs. To the extent that a deposit taken from a tenant or licensee exceeds any relevant costs and is refunded, the Revenue accept that it should be excluded from the receipts of the business: Tax Bulletin, October 1996, p 349.

(b) Expenses accrued but not paid are likewise to be included; prepaid expenses are excluded.

(c) Any business expense is deductible unless precluded by the general Case I rules of *TA 1988 s 74(1)*, i.e. where it is capital in nature or not 'wholly and exclusively' incurred for the business. This replaces the former 'prescriptive' approach whereby an expense was only deductible if expressly allowed by statute. Hence the former Schedule A and Schedule D, Case VI deduction rules are disapplied. [*FA 1995 6 Sch 4*].

(d) The Case I bad debt rules apply in determining whether a deduction can be made for unpaid rent. So relief may be available either for a normal bad debt write off or by creating a specific reserve.

## Computation of Profits 7.83

(e) The commercial profits will be adjusted by applying any relevant tax rules.

*Specific statutory provisions*

**7.82** The following statutory provisions are specifically applicable [*TA 1988 s 21A* and *21B* inserted by *FA 1998 5 Sch 4*]:

(a) *TA 1988 s 72* (apportionment of profits to be made where necessary);

(b) the rules set out in *TA 1988 Part IV Chap V (ss 74–99)* except *ss 82* (interest paid to non-residents), *87* (treatment of premiums taxed as rent), *96* (farming and market garden; averaging relief for fluctuating profits) and *98* (tied premises; receipts and expenses treated as those of trade);

(c) *TA 1988 s 577* (business entertainment);

(d) *TA 1988 s 577A* (expenditure involving crime);

(e) *TA 1988 ss 579, 580* (redundancy payments);

(f) *TA 1988 ss 588, 589* (training courses for employees);

(g) *TA 1988 ss 589A, 589B* (counselling services);

(h) *FA 1988 s 73(2)* (consideration for restrictive undertakings);

(i) *FA 1989 s 43* (deductions in respect of certain emoluments);

(j) *FA 1989 s 76* (expenses in connection with non-approved retirement benefit schemes);

(k) *FA 1989 ss 112, 113* (security);

(l) *FA 1998 ss 42, 46(1), (2)* (computation of profits and losses);

(m) the post cessation receipts provision, including the ability to elect to carry back in *TA 1988 ss 103–106, 108*. Similarly, relief is available for post-cessation expenditure under *TA 1988 s 109A*.

(n) pre-trading expenditure under *TA 1988 s 401*.

*Pooling of income and expenses/repairs*

**7.83** Under the old rules contained in *TA 1988 s 25(3)–(8)*, let property was divided into three categories:

(a) properties let at full rents and not on tenants' repairing leases;

(b) properties let on tenants' repairing leases; and

(c) properties let at less than a full rent.

Income and expenses from properties within each category were ring-fenced, with restrictions on the availability of relief for losses arising from

## 7.84 Computation of Profits

the excess of expenditure over income on any particular category of property. Moreover, a deduction was precluded for expenditure on repairs incurred by reason of dilapidations attributable to a period before the owner acquired the property.

**7.84** These rules ceased to be applicable for companies from 1 April 1998. [*FA 1998 5 Sch 6*]. Thereafter all businesses and transactions chargeable under Schedule A are treated as entered into in the course of carrying on a single business. Accordingly, income and expenses from all types of property letting in the UK, whether residential, commercial or industrial etc., and whatever the repairing or other obligations under the terms of the lease and the levels of rent, are to be pooled. The effect is that any loss arising from one property will be relieved automatically from profits derived from another. It is to be noted, however, that a business carried on by a person in partnership with others is a different business from one carried on that person's own account.

**7.85** Moreover, there is no restriction on the cost of repairs incurred shortly after acquisition that fall within the principles of *Odeon Associated Theatres Ltd v Jones (1971) 48 TC 257* rather than *Law Shipping Co Ltd v IRC (1923) 12 TC 621*. The distinction is between property acquired in a state where it is fit for use, but in need of repair and redecorating and the purchase price is not materially reduced as a result of its condition, and property acquired in such a dilapidated condition that it was incapable of use as purchased and this was reflected in the acquisition price.

**7.86** However, such pooling will only apply to the total Schedule A income and expenditure of a particular person or partnership. It follows that a company partner in a Schedule A business is not able to aggregate its share of that income and expenditure with that of any separate business carried on alone, or in another partnership. In such a case the company is treated as having two distinct Schedule A businesses; one carried on by it alone, the other (effectively a share) carried on in partnership. Likewise, income treated in a representative capacity is charged separately.

*Travel expenses*

**7.87** Travel expenses may be deductible under the 'wholly and exclusively' rule for visits to the property to carry out or supervise repairs or collect rents. But if the company's base is located some distance from the property, the question may arise whether the expense is properly connected with the letting business. The issue may arise acutely in the context of furnished holiday lettings, especially for seaside properties where the base may be some distance away.

**Interest**

**7.88** As set out in para 7.69 above, one of the reasons for retaining initially the old Schedule A system for companies was the concern about the possible loss of a company's ability to offset interest against non-property income and gains. This issue has been addressed under the provisions of *FA 1998 5 Sch* by excluding interest from a company's Schedule A computation, and leaving credits or debits to be dealt with under the loan relationship provisions of *FA 1996*. Similarly excluded are foreign exchange gains or losses within *FA 1993 Part II Chap II* and qualifying payments under interest rate and currency contracts within *FA 1994 Part IV Chap II*, substituted *TA 1988 s 15A 3 Sch*.

**7.89** Interest incurred in a Schedule A business carried on by a company is accordingly dealt with under the non-trading loan relationships rules of *FA 1996 s 83*. In so far as there is an interest deficit this can be:

(a) set against current period profits of any description;

(b) used for group relief purposes in the current period;

(c) carried back against loan relationship profits in the previous year (but not against Schedule A profits of that year); or

(d) carried forward against non-trading profits for the next period (i.e. including Schedule A profits).

**7.90** It is understood that the Revenue accept that under (d) a deficit carried forward to the next year can augment the losses of that year and hence be carried forward to future periods to set against Schedule A income of those periods.

**Capital expenditure and allowances**

*New system*

**7.91** Allowances are available for certain capital expenditure. They are given by reference to the date when the expenditure was incurred, writing-down allowances being available in respect of the balance of expenditure at the end of the chargeable period for which the allowances are made, together with any balancing allowance or charge on disposals. Previously the allowances were given by way of discharge or repayment

## 7.92 Computation of Profits

of tax. Under the new rules the allowances are treated as an expense of the Schedule A business in determining the profit of that business. Likewise any balancing charges are treated as a Schedule A receipt. This treatment also applies to the letting of furnished holiday accommodation deemed to be a Schedule A business [*CAA 1990 s 29*] and dwelling houses let on assured tenancies. [*CAA 1990 s 92*].

### Industrial buildings

**7.92** Allowances or charges are to be given as an expense or receipt of the Schedule A business, with initial allowances being available before a building is let. [Amended *CAA 1990 s 9(1), (2)* inserted by *FA 1998 5 Sch 47*]. There are provisions for continued eligibility for allowances for buildings which are temporarily out of use. [Amended *CAA 1990 ss 15, 15ZA* inserted by *FA 1998 5 Sch 48–50*].

### Plant and machinery

**7.93** For corporation tax purposes, as for income tax, properties have been pooled from April 1997 for capital allowances purposes. The corporation tax provisions are then generally brought in line with those for income tax as from 1 April 1998.

**7.94** With regard to furnished holiday lettings (which qualify for allowances under *CAA 1990 s 29*) relief is given as a deduction in computing the profits from the letting as if the letting were a trade; and the activity is treated as a trade for the purposes of replacement asset relief, relief for loans to traders and retirement relief. [Amended *CAA 1990 ss 29, 61* inserted by *FA 1998 5 Sch 51, 61*]. Other consequential amendments are made by *FA 1998 5 Sch 52–60*. Capital allowances which generate a loss are relieved in the same way as management expenses as set out below. One effect is that it will no longer be possible to set excess allowances against total profits of the previous year.

### Furnished lettings – wear and tear allowances

**7.95** Although capital allowances are not available for expenditure incurred in connection with the furnished letting of a dwelling house, the Revenue will allow relief under the renewals basis, or alternatively a wear and tear allowance may be claimed under ESC B47. The latter is calculated at 10 per cent of the net rent for the year, namely the rent due less any amount included in the rent towards Council Tax, water rates or any services normally borne by the tenant.

*Example 1*

|  | Expenses Payable For Year £ | Income Receivable For Year £ |
|---|---:|---:|
| Dudakov Ltd Year ended 30 September 1999 Schedule A rental income and expenses |  |  |
| Rents receivable (furnished) |  | 26,970 |
| Less expenses: |  |  |
| Service charge and ground rent | 2,371 |  |
| Insurance | 179 |  |
| Repairs and maintenance | 366 |  |
| Wear and Tear allowance: |  |  |
| 10% × £26,970 − £2,371 | 2,460 |  |
| Advertising | 200 |  |
| Alarm rental and charges | 314 |  |
| Maintenance contracts | 68 |  |
| Inspections | 175 |  |
| Loan interest | 795 |  |
| Cleaning charges | 80 |  |
| Inventory check | 85 |  |
| Gas and electricity charges | 31 |  |
| Agency commission | 3,972 |  |
| Tenancy agreement legal charges | 500 |  |
| Sundries | 100 |  |
|  |  | 11,696 |
| Net income |  | 15,274 |

**Transitional provisions**

**7.96** The transitional provisions are contained in *FA 1998 5 Sch Part IV*, the new rules commencing on 1 April 1998. However, the old rules still apply to a source which ceases in the accounting period straddling that date, except where the company acquired the source in that period or in the preceding twelve months. [*FA 1998 5 Sch 73* and *75*]. The essence of the transitional provisions is that receipts and expenses are to be taxed/allowed once. So to the extent that they have been taken into account before commencement, they are thereafter to be excluded. If under the new rules receipts or expenses would have been accounted for

### 7.97 Computation of Profits

before 1 April, but they have not been, they are to be brought into account immediately thereafter. [*FA 1998 5 Sch 66* and *67*].

**7.97** Expenses incurred before commencement, but not then taken into account, are not to be carried back under *TA 1988 ss 25(3)* or *31(3)*. The transfer of interests in land to another person will not enable these provisions to be circumvented, as the new rules are then carried over. In the event that a deduction had been allowed for rent not received under the old rules, if it is subsequently received after 1 April 1998 it has to be brought into account. [*FA 1998 5 Sch 68* and *69*]. Any unrelieved Case VI loss from furnished lettings can be carried forward as a Schedule A loss. For group relief purposes, where the accounting period straddles 1 April 1998, amounts referable to the period before commencement are to be commuted separately from amounts referable to the subsequent period. [*FA 1998 5 Sch 73* and *75*].

*Example 2*

Valk Ltd received rents of £2,000 per quarter, in advance, on the quarter days. Its Schedule A computations for the calendar year 1998 are as follows:

|  | £ |
|---|---:|
| 3 months to 1 April 1998 | |
| Rent for period 26 March 1998 to 24 June 1998 | 2,000 |
| Less: expenses incurred in period | 500 |
| | 1,500 |
| Schedule A Income: | |
| 9 months to 31 December 1998 | |
| Rent for period 25 June 1998 to 31 December 1998 | |
| 190 days (£8,000 × $\frac{190}{365}$) | 4,164 |
| Less: expenses incurred after 31 March 1998 and accrued at 31 December 1998 and incurred before 1 April 1998 but not previously claimed | 1,625 |
| Schedule A income | £2,539 |

**Property investment companies**

**7.98** The management expenses regime will continue to apply to property investment companies. Accordingly if an expense is not deductible in computing the Schedule A profits (e.g. a general overhead of a property investment company) it may nevertheless qualify as a management expense and hence still be a deductible item eligible for separate relief under the management expenses rules. Accordingly it is academic whether a particular expense is relievable as a Schedule A deduction or a management expense.

**7.99** One question arises as to whether a deduction is available for certain Schedule A expenses such as insurance, business rates etc. which are capitalised in the cost of an investment property during the construction or redevelopment period. It is understood that the Revenue will accept that such expenditure under the new Schedule A regime ordinarily follows the treatment currently adopted for traders under Schedule D, Case I.

**7.100** Where an investment company ceases to carry on a Schedule A business, but continues as an investment company, unrelieved losses are treated as excess management expenses for the purposes of *TA 1988 s 75* and carried forward as such. [*TA 1988 s 392A(3)*].

**Property development companies**

**7.101** Certain property dealers and developers have been allowed to treat excess Schedule A expenses incurred in respect of land held as trading stock as a Schedule D, Case I deduction, rather than carried forward under Schedule A. It is understood that the Revenue's intention is that this will continue in the new regime. Indeed any excess expenditure will normally have been incurred under an obligation entered into for trading purposes, so it will be admissible as a Schedule D, Case I deduction on trading principles.

**7.102** It is also usual for rental income received during the course of a trading development to be credited against the work in progress. Under the previous regime this was taxed on an entitlement basis irrespective of the accounting treatment. The Revenue has confirmed that under the new regime, where rental income is so credited against the cost of work in progress in accordance with correct accountancy principles, it will not ordinarily be subject to tax under Schedule A until released to the profit and loss account through cost of sales.

**Partnerships**

**7.103** The current year basis rules applicable to partnerships are applied to a Schedule A business carried on by the firm. This means that each partner is assessed on his share of the Schedule A income. Where there is a corporate partner, this is computed on corporation tax principles, and there is no deemed cessation on a change of partner. It also means that the strict fiscal year basis is applied for a Schedule A trade coterminous with the Schedule D, Case I trade; substituted *TA 1988 s 21*. A partnership business is distinct from one which is separately carried on by a company on its own but each contributes to the total profits for the accounting period of the company. Profits from one can be set against

### 7.104 Computation of Profits

losses of the other because Schedule A losses are treated, largely, in the same way as management expenses. [See Chapter 9].

**Joint ownership**

**7.104** The mere joint ownership of property does not constitute a partnership and each joint owner has to self-assess on his/its share of the joint income of his/its own Schedule A business (Tax Bulletin No 20, December 1995, p 271). Where the joint ownership of property does not amount to a partnership and the Revenue wish to raise any enquiries, they will normally confine their initial enquiries to the managing co-owner. If it then appears that an amendment is required to the returns of the other co-owners, separate enquiry notices will be issued to those co-owners. If it is too late for an enquiry to start, any additional tax will normally be levied by a discovery assessment. [See Tax Bulletin, October 1996, p 350].

**Land managed as one estate**

**7.105** Provisions contained in *TA 1988 s 26* have allowed a 'one estate election', which effectively enables relief to be obtained for the cost of the owner occupied part, notably the upkeep of the estate manor, against total estate income. These provisions are temporarily continued under the new Schedule A, with the application of Schedule D, Case I principles potentially giving additional relief for specific provisions and accruals, and possibly relief for interest on a loan to improve or refurbish the principal house as an expense. However *FA 1998 s 39* abolishes *s 26* for corporation tax for accounting periods beginning on or after 6 April 2001. In the meanwhile it is to operate for corporation tax as for income tax. [*FA 1998 5 Sch 7*].

**7.106** Until the relief is so abolished the position is as follows. Where land has been managed as one estate continuously since 1962/63 and part of the estate is unlet or let at a rent below the annual value, the annual value is deemed to be the rent receivable in the Schedule A computation. The annual value is defined by *TA 1988 s 837* and Extra Statutory Concessions A56 and B30 as equivalent to the old gross rateable value, which is normally a very low figure compared with the market rent. The estate disbursements and expenses may be set against the deemed income and the actual income of the entire estate.

**7.107** This had the effect of relieving the excess expenditure relating to the unlet or reduced rent portion of the estate over the annual value. However, a deficit arising from excess maintenance expenditure on the unlet or reduced rent portion is effectively ring-fenced. It is not treated as a Schedule A loss, but may be carried forward against future income from the estate. But excess expenditure on the fully let portion of the estate may create a Schedule A loss deductible under *TA 1988 s 379A* against other Schedule A income. This may be particularly helpful in the case of interest relief relating to the fully let properties. [*FA 1995 6 Sch 5*].

**Maintenance funds for historic buildings**

**7.108** Under *TA 1988 s 27*, an estate owner who transfers a property on an estate subject to a one estate election into a maintenance fund for historic buildings has been allowed to continue to benefit from the one estate treatment of the settled property. The definition of income is widened to include all receipts of the estate. [*FA 1995 s 39(4)–(6) 6 Sch*]. As with the *s 26* one estate relief discussed above, *s 27* relief ends for accounting periods beginning on or after 6 April 2001 for corporation tax.

**7.109** Whilst the relief subsists the deduction for disbursements and expenses is brought into line with the Schedule D, Case I treatment of a Schedule A business. Excess maintenance expenditure of agricultural land may be deductible as a Schedule A loss under *TA 1988 s 379A*. Expenditure on maintaining any part of the estate within the maintenance fund can be deducted from income arising to the fund.

**Chargeable gains and reliefs**

**7.110** Although profits chargeable under Schedule A are taxed as a business, that business is nevertheless generally regarded as the holding of investments, rather than the carrying on of a trade, profession or vocation. Hence the CGT roll-over relief for disposals of business assets [*TCGA 1992 ss 152–153*] is not available. The exception is for gains attributable to property used for furnished holiday lettings, as this activity is assimilated to a trade. [*FA 1995 6 Sch 36; TCGA 1992 s 241(3)*].

**7.111** In determining the gain arising on the disposal of leases with less than 50 years unexpired, the curved-line depreciation rules in *TCGA 1992 8 Sch* exclude that proportion of the premium taxed under Schedule A as a receipt of a Schedule A business. There are similar provisions in respect of Schedule A charges on the sale of land with a right to reconveyance, the assignment of a lease granted at an undervalue and certain deemed premiums. [See *FA 1995 6 Sch 37*].

**7.112** *FA 1998 5 Sch 33–66* contain a number of miscellaneous amendments consequent upon the corporation tax treatment following the new income tax rules.

*Chapter 8*

# Capital Gains

## Introduction

**8.1**   No substantive changes relating to chargeable gains of companies have been implemented by CTSA. The main amendments, contained in *FA 1996*, relate to (a) statutory provisions which previously gave the Revenue a degree of discretion, notably in relation to certain claims for relief; and (b) the procedure for claiming reliefs in cases where investment decisions may be taken in subsequent years of assessment. Otherwise, indexation is retained for companies, unlike the position for individuals and trustees where, under *FA 1998*, it is replaced by taper relief.

## Former discretionary powers of Revenue

**8.2**   It is the essence of CTSA that a company should be able to file its tax return and self-assess without any reference to the Revenue. This has necessitated taking away from the Revenue many of their discretionary powers, a number of which related to capital gains. These issues, together with the particular capital gains provisions subject to the amendments in *FA 1996*, are further considered in 4.36. The potential for a discovery assessment, should the Revenue consider that the company's judgment is incorrect, is considered in Chapter 17.

**8.3**   Certain of these cases relate to liabilities of prior years. An instance in point is *TCGA 1992 s 49* which deals with contingent liabilities. In the first instance no account is to be taken, in determining the amount of the gain arising on the disposal of an asset, of any contingent liability assumed by the person making the disposal. Under the old rules a deduction was permitted if the Revenue were satisfied that a contingent liability had in fact crystallised. There is no longer any need so to satisfy the Revenue. The company may make a claim provided that the liability has become enforceable, and is being enforced, without reference to the Revenue. Should this be the case, the tax liability arising on the original disposal is recomputed, and any additional liability discharged. [Amended *TCGA 1992 s 49; FA 1996 20 Sch 49*].

**8.4** An example would be the giving of warranties on a sale of shares, where the vendor company was subsequently found to be in breach and, say, an appropriate adjustment was made to the sale price of the shares. The vendor company would accordingly be entitled to a corresponding discharge of its tax liability. Somewhat unfairly, in a case such as this, repayment supplement is not due to the company in respect of the overpaid tax, even though it may have an obligation to pay interest to the purchaser of the shares in respect of the excess consideration.

## Payment of tax by instalments

**8.5** There is provision for payment of tax by instalments where the consideration is payable by instalments: *TCGA 1992 s 280*. Under the old rules it was necessary for the company to be able to establish undue hardship. In practice the Revenue interpreted this requirement fairly leniently, so that in determining hardship the Revenue generally only looked at the instalments themselves, rather than the company's other available resources. But under the new rules there is no need for hardship. The ability to pay by instalments is solely at the company's option. [Amended *TCGA 1992 s 280; FA 1996 20 Sch 65*]. Interest will, however, be payable on unpaid instalments from the original due date.

## Business assets roll-over relief

**8.6** Under the provisions of *TCGA 1992 s 152*, gains arising on the disposal of certain qualifying business assets may be postponed if the consideration for the disposal is reinvested in replacement assets, either one year before or three years after the disposal. Under the previous system relief could not be obtained until the replacement asset had been acquired. However, in practice the Revenue accepted a postponement of the tax on the gain if the company could demonstrate an intention to acquire a qualifying asset shortly after the payment date for the tax and within the normal three year time limit. But in the absence of specific legislation the CTSA framework does not cater for such a possibility. The company might well not have made the reinvestment before it had to file its return and self-assess. This is resolved by a new *TCGA s 153A*, introduced by *FA 1996 s 141*, permitting roll-over relief to be obtained on a provisional basis in the first instance. The position is then finally determined at the end of the three year reinvestment period in the light of the events actually taking place.

**8.7** The company carrying on the trade may make a declaration in its return for the chargeable period in which the disposal takes place, that the whole or part of the sale consideration will be applied in the acquisition of a new qualifying asset within the relevant three year period, in which case, relief will be given provisionally. [*TCGA 1992 s 153A(1)(2)*]. The declaration should identify the assets disposed of and

## 8.8 Capital Gains

specify the amount of the consideration to be applied in acquiring the new assets which can be all or part of the consideration. Should the company wish to increase the specified amount, this has to be done by a subsequent amendment to the return.

**8.8** The declaration then ceases to have effect either if it is withdrawn by the 'relevant day' (being the fourth anniversary of the end of the accounting period in which the disposal took place), if the company no longer intends to make the reinvestment, or if it is superseded before then by a valid claim for relief. If the provisional claim has not been withdrawn or replaced by a valid claim, the Revenue will make the appropriate assessment. The due date for payment will be that on which the tax should have been paid if there had been no declaration. On the declaration ceasing to have effect, all necessary adjustments are to be made to the company's assessment, with any repayment or discharge of tax, as the case may be. [*TCGA 1992 s 153A(3), (4), (5)*].

**8.9** The Revenue have set out their practice in relation to roll-over relief claims in the Tax Bulletin of August 1996, pp 327–329. Where a provisional claim is followed by an actual claim, and the cost of acquisition of the new asset is the same or exceeds that in the provisional claim, the relief is confirmed and no further action is required by the company.

**8.10** If the cost of acquisition under the actual claim is less than that specified in the provisional claim the position is as follows. Should the company inform the Revenue that it no longer wishes to reinvest the full amount specified, and does so within the period in which amendments to its tax return are permitted (generally 12 months from the filing date), this is duly treated as an amendment to the return and the company's self-assessment. If the withdrawal of relief is made by the company during a Revenue enquiry into the return, the Revenue may amend the self-assessment. In either case the company should pay the additional tax to avoid interest accruing.

**8.11** After the periods in 8.10 have expired, and the company notifies the Revenue that it wishes to withdraw its claim for provisional relief, the Revenue will make an assessment to recover the relief. The precise amount of the assessment will depend on whether the company still intends to reinvest some of the consideration. If it does so, the position in relation to the amount it still proposes to reinvest will be held in abeyance until there is an actual claim to roll-over relief, a further withdrawal of the provisional claim by the company, or the period of availability of provisional relief ends.

**8.12** Although *TCGA s 152(3)* gives the Revenue a discretion to extend the three year period for reinvestment, there is no such discretion for extending the period within which a declaration is effective. So no tax postponement application will be allowed on the basis that reinvestment will take place shortly after. However, should the Board exercise its discretion in the company's favour when reinvestment has been made outside the three year period any tax will be repaid. Consequential amendments are made to the provisions regarding replacement of business assets by members of a group of companies, to permit the granting of provisional relief in cases where assets are only partly replaced. [*FA 1996 s 141(3)*].

## Roll-over relief on compulsory acquisition of land

**8.13** A form of roll-over relief is provided where land is compulsorily purchased. Parallel provisions for those outlined above in relation to business assets are also contained in *FA 1996 s 141*, permitting provisional claims for relief to be made. The company may make a similar declaration of intent to apply the whole or part of the sale proceeds of the compulsory disposal in the acquisition of a new qualifying asset within the time limits. The declaration continues to have effect until it is withdrawn, superseded, or expires on the relevant day. [*TCGA 1992 s 247A(1), (2)* inserted by *FA 1996 s 141(6)*].

**8.14** The time of disposal and acquisition of land acquired by a local authority under compulsory purchase powers in *TCGA 1992 s 246(1)* is amended so that the relevant date is the date on which the compensation is agreed, in all cases. [*FA 1996 s 141(4)*]. Under the previous rules the relevant date would have been the time on which the authority entered on the land, if earlier. This could have been problematical in that if agreement of the amount of compensation were delayed, there would have been no payment, and therefore the company would not have been in a position to reinvest.

## Allowable losses

**8.15** Under *TCGA 1992 s 16*, allowable losses can be carried forward indefinitely. Revenue practice in the past has been not to require details of such losses or to agree the allowable amount, other than where relief had actually been claimed, on the basis that until then there was no necessity to do so. This would have been inappropriate under CTSA, where the company needs to know the quantum of a loss in order to enable it to self-assess accurately.

**8.16** Under a new *TCGA s 16(2A)*, for a capital loss to be allowable, the particulars and the amount of the loss have to be notified to the Revenue as if it were a claim for relief under *TMA ss 42* and *43*. These sections require claims to be submitted within six years from the end of the accounting period. A loss claimed under these provisions for accounting periods beginning on or after 1 July 1998, is relieved before previous losses brought forward. [*FA 1995 s 113(2)*]. Consequently the Revenue only have to deal with losses quantified under the CTSA provisions,

**8.17** *Capital Gains*

unless it becomes necessary to quantify earlier losses in order to relieve them against gains. This is rather unsatisfactory in that the company will not know its capital loss availability for earlier years. [*Tod v South Essex Motors (Basildon) Ltd [1988] STC 392*].

**8.17** The new rules may have adverse ramifications in the case of past losses on disposals to connected persons. Where a loss arises on a disposal to a connected person, the loss cannot be set against all future capital gains, but only against gains arising on disposals to the same connected person. Given that CTSA losses have to be used up first, a company which realises a loss on one disposal and in the same year generates a gain on another disposal to a connected person, will have to utilise the general loss of the year against that gain. Thus it will not be able to benefit from any loss carried forward in respect of previous disposals to that connected person.

## Premiums for leases

**8.18** A capital sum paid by a tenant to obtain the variation, waiver or surrender of a lease, or the commutation of the rent payable under the lease, is treated as a taxable premium. [*TCGA 1992 8 Sch 3*]. Certain of these sums were treated under the original capital gains provisions as received when the lease was granted, which accordingly required a recomputation of the gain accruing on the grant of the lease. To avoid the reopening of earlier years under CTSA, these provisions have been modified. The position now is as follows for sums payable after 6 April 1996:

(a) Where the lease is surrendered, the property disposed of will be the landlord's leasehold interest, and the time of disposal will be when the premium is payable.

(b) Where the lease is varied, that will be treated as a part disposal of the landlord's freehold, or other interest out of which the lease was granted, and the time of disposal will again be when the premium is payable. Moreover, if the sum is payable in lieu of rent, it is treated as paid in respect of the period of the lease which the rent covers. [Substituted *TCGA 1992 8 Sch 3(4); FA 1996 s 142(4)*].

**8.19** There is a modification where the landlord is a lessee under a short lease of less than 50 years. The premium will be treated as paid in respect of the period to which the sublease relates. The sub-lessee is also treated as having incurred enhancement expenditure on any premium paid for the amendment of the terms of the sub-lease. [*TCGA 1992 8 Sch 3(5); FA 1996 s 142(5)*].

## Scheme of reconstruction: transfer to investment trust

**8.20** Under a scheme of reconstruction or amalgamation within *TCGA 1992 s 139*, any assets transferred to implement the scheme are treated as disposed of for no gain/no loss. Where the transferee company becomes an investment trust, what would have been the gain or loss otherwise arising on the reconstruction is crystallised, since a gain accruing to an investment trust is not taxable. [*TCGA 1992 ss 100, 101*]. Under the previous rules the gain was treated as taking place at the time of the reconstruction. To avoid reopening assessments for earlier years, the provisions have been changed so that the gain is treated as accruing in the accounting period immediately before the transferee company becomes an investment trust. The new provisions apply for accounting periods ending on or after 1 July 1998. [Inserted *TCGA 1992 s 101(1A); FA 1996 s 140*].

## Valuations for capital gains

**8.21** Originally there was no procedure for companies, unlike that available to individuals and trustees, to have valuations agreed with the Revenue post disposal, but prior to the filing of the self-assessment return. However, from 10 January 2000 the procedure has been extended to companies who may now send valuations used in computing capital gains to the Revenue for checking before they make their returns. [See IR Press Release, 10 January 2000 and Tax Bulletin, February 2000, p 728].

**8.22** The details of the service for companies are essentially the same as for individuals and trustees, the latter being set out in a Revenue Press Release of 4 February 1997, and also contained in an annex to Revenue Booklet CGT 14: Capital Gains Tax—An Introduction. Applications to use the service have to be made on form CG 34, with full information about the transactions concerned and relevant computations. The guidance notes on the form set out all the information and documents which need to be provided.

**8.23** If the Revenue do not agree the valuations submitted they will suggest alternatives. The Revenue expect that it will take a minimum of 56 days to agree a valuation or provide the taxpayer with an alternative. In complex cases the time may be much longer. In the event that the valuation has not been agreed by the filing date for the return, the return must nevertheless be submitted with a note as to the position. If the parties fail to reach agreement on the valuation, the company's right of appeal is preserved. Clearly this is a potentially very helpful service, but to ensure that wherever possible, agreement is reached before the filing date for the return, a company making a disposal will be advised to utilise this valuation agreement procedure as soon as possible thereafter.

*Chapter 9*

# Losses

## General

**9.1** There are no changes to the computation of losses under CTSA. However, what is imposed on the company is the onus of arriving at the correct figures to avoid any additional tax, interest and penalties on an enquiry or discovery, or loss of relief which might not be picked up by the Revenue in the absence of an enquiry and which would therefore become time barred. A trading loss is computed in the same way as a trading profit. [See Chapter 7, *TA 1988 s 393(7), 393A(9)(a)* and *(b)*]. A loss may be augmented by capital allowances given by way of discharge or repayment, as opposed to being treated as a trading expense, under *CAA 1990 s 145*.

**9.2** A trading loss may be set against other profits or gains of the same accounting period. [*TA 1988 s 393A(1A)*]. The claim must be made within two years after the end of the accounting period or such further time as the Revenue may allow. [*TA 1988 s 393A(10)*]. For further requirements of loss claims see Chapter 4. A loss can only be set against profits and gains in the accounting period, or carried back against income of the previous period, if the trade is carried on with a view to the realisation of profit on a commercial basis. [*TA 1988 s 393A(3), (4)*]. Otherwise losses can only be carried forward against profits of the same trade, under *TA 1988 s 393(1)*.

**9.3** Where a company carrying on a farming or market gardening trade, which is not part of a larger trade, makes a loss, ignoring capital allowances, in the accounting period and in each of the five consecutive years up to the beginning of that accounting period, it can only carry the loss forward against future profits. [*TA 1988 s 397*]. Where a company incurs charges for trading purposes in excess of its total income, the excess charges can be carried forward as additional trading losses against future profits from the same trade under *TA 1988 s 393(9)*, *Commercial Assurance Co plc v Shaw [1998] STC 386*.

**9.4** Trading income means the income from a trade assessed under Schedule D, Case I, except for banks and other financial institutions where interest and dividends may be included as trading income for loss relief purposes, if they would constitute trading income but for the fact

**9.9** *Losses*

## Company reconstructions

**9.9** Losses can be transferred where a trade ceases to be carried on by the predecessor company, and is transferred to a successor company where, on the cessation, or within two years thereafter, the trade is owned (as to at least 75 per cent) by the same persons as owned the predecessor within the year before the cessation, provided that throughout the period the trade is carried on by a company within the charge to corporation tax. [*TA 1988 s 343(1)*]. The trade transferred does not have to be isolated as a distinct trade but may be absorbed into a larger trade of the successor company. Capital allowances also can be transferred, but the successor company becomes liable for any balancing charge as if it had always carried on the trade. [*TA 1988 s 343(2)*].

**9.10** There is a restriction where the relevant liabilities of the trade exceed the relevant assets, the loss carried forward being reduced by the amount of the excess. [*TA 1988 s 344(5) and (6)*]. A dual resident investing company is not entitled to the relief in respect of capital allowances. [*TA 1988 s 343(2)*]. Where the Merger Directive 90/434/EEC applies to bona fide cross border mergers, capital gains tax relief is available under *TCGA 1992 ss 140A* and *140B*. The capital allowances provisions apply as if there had been no change under *CAA 1990 s 152B* and not under *TA 1988 s 343*. It is possible to make successive transfers within the ownership requirements. [*TA 1988 s 343(7)*]. Where any part of the trade is transferred, the losses may be carried forward as if it were a separate trade. [*TA 1988 s 343(8)–(10)*]. Non-trading losses are not covered by *TA 1988 s 343* and if the successor ceases to carry on the trade, any terminal loss cannot be carried back through the change. [*TA 1988 s 343(4)(A)*].

**9.11** Cases where only part of the trade is taken over include *Wadsworth Morton Ltd v Jenkinson (1966) 43 TC 479* and *Rolls-Royce Motors Ltd v Bamford [1976] STC 162*. Whether or not the trade has actually been continued by the successor company has been considered in a number of cases including *Laycock v Freeman Hardy & Willis Ltd (1938) 22 TC 288, Briton Ferry Steel Co Ltd v Barry (1939) 23 TC 414, Wilde v Madame Tussauds (1926) Ltd (1932) 17 TC 127, Thomson and Balfour v LePage (1923) 8 TC 541* and *Falmer Jeans Ltd v Rodin [1990] STC 270*.

**9.12** The continuity of ownership required for these provisions to apply is determined in accordance with *TA 1988 s 344(1)–(4)* by comparing the direct and indirect ownership of the company's ordinary share capital at any time within twelve months prior to the change and two years afterwards. The relief is available if, during that period, there is at least 75 per cent common ownership.

**9.13** In determining beneficial ownership it is important to remember that an agreement to transfer shares can pass beneficial ownership,

that they are otherwise taxed. [*Bank Line Ltd v IRC (1974) 49 TC 307, Nuclear Electric Plc v Bradley [1996] STC 405*]. Whether the same trade is continued will be a question of fact and degree, except in the case of a farming company where all farming and marketing gardening in the United Kingdom is treated as a single trade, under *TA 1988 s 53(1)*, *Bispham v Eardiston Farming Co (1919) Ltd (1962) 40 TC 322*.

**9.5** A cessation of manufacturing followed by recommencement elsewhere was held to be the same trade in *Robroyston Brickworks Ltd v IRC (1976) 51 TC 230*. However in *Gordon & Blair Ltd v IRC (1962) 40 TC 358*, a company which brewed and sold beer, ceased to manufacture but continued retailing and was held to have commenced a new trade. *Rolls Royce Motors Ltd v Bamford [1976] STC 162* concerned the hiving off of the trade of manufacturing cars from a combined trade which was mainly aircraft engine manufacture. It was held that the losses could not be carried forward from one composite trade to what was effectively a new trade consisting of a small part of the previous activity.

**9.6** Where a company, which incurs a trading loss and makes the appropriate claim to set the loss against income and chargeable gains for the accounting period, is left with any part of that loss unrelieved, it can claim to carry it back against the profits of the preceding accounting period, provided that the same trade was then being carried on, and set it against the total income and chargeable gains of the preceding year. From 1 July 1997 the period of carry back is reduced to twelve months prior to the accounting period of the loss. [*TA 1988 s 393A(1)(b)*]. Previously the carry back period was three years.

**9.7** Excess trade charges cannot normally be carried back, only forwards. [*TA 1988 s 393(1)* and *(9)*]. If a loss is carried back against the profits of the preceding period, non-trade charges in that period may become excess charges, which may then be unrelievable. Trade charges are not so displaced. [*TA 1988 s 393A(8)*]. When the carry back period of three years was reduced to one year, the terminal loss relief was effectively reinstated by *TA 1988 s 393A(2A)* and *(2B)*. In these circumstances the loss for the final twelve months of trading may be carried back for a three year period, apportioned on a time basis as necessary. Excess trade charges on a terminal loss claim may be included in the loss for the final twelve months, and carried back against total income of the three preceding years. [*TA 1988 s 393A(7)*]. Losses are set against the most recent profits first in a terminal loss carry back claim.

**9.8** Losses for accounting periods ending before 1 July 1999, and therefore within Pay and File, are subject to a formal determination of the loss [*TMA 1970 s 41A*], but for accounting periods ending on or after 1 July 1999, CTSA applies and there is no requirement for a Revenue determination, losses being self-assessed in the same way as profits under the normal return and claim procedures outlined in Chapters 2, 3 and 4.

*Losses* **9.17**

[*Parway Estates Ltd v IRC (1958) 45 TC 135*] but pledging the shares as security does not constitute a change of ownership. The appointment of a liquidator is a change in the beneficial ownership of the shares as the assets are thereafter held beneficially for the creditors and not the shareholders. [*IRC v Olive Mill Spinners Ltd (1963) 41 TC 77*]. Securities held as trading stock at the time of the change of ownership are deemed to be sold and reacquired at market value at that date. [*TA 1988 s 343(5)*].

**9.14** The provisions of *TA 1988 s 343* are often used in practice to transfer the whole or part of a trade into a new company prior to selling it. This however would normally result in a change in the ownership of the successor company and further loss restrictions may apply at that point.

**Change in ownership restrictions**

**9.15** Where there is a change in the ownership of a company, and within a period of three years prior to the change, or three years following the change, there is a major change in the nature or conduct of the trade, the losses cannot be carried forward in view of *TA 1988 s 768(1)(a)*. Carry forward is also denied where the scale of activities of the trade carried on by a company has become small or negligible, and there is then a change in ownership followed by a revival of the trade. [*TA 1988 s 768(1)(b)*].

**9.16** What constitutes a major change is considered in SP10/91 and in *Willis v Peeters Picture Frames Ltd [1983] STC 453*. In this case it was held on the facts that in spite of the company being taken over, having run into difficulties, there was not a major change in customers, outlets or markets within *TA 1988 s 768(4)*. In *Purchase v Tesco Stores Ltd [1984] STC 304* it was held that a major change in the business was something more than significant but less than fundamental. *Pobjoy Mint Ltd v Lane [1985] STC 314*, like *Purchase v Tesco Stores Ltd*, was a case on the similar provisions in relation to stock relief, which held that a change in purchasing by buying direct from wholesalers rather than its previous supplier, was, in the circumstances, a major change in the conduct of the company's trade.

**9.17** The circumstances which constitute a change in ownership of a company for these purposes is spelt out in *TA 1988 s 769*. The acquisition of more than half the ordinary share capital by a single individual or by persons holding more than 5 per cent of the shares would be such a change, connected persons being aggregated. There are anti-avoidance provisions but a change of ownership within a 75 per cent group is disregarded. These provisions are broadly similar to the restrictions on the carry forward of ACT under *TA 1988 s 245*.

## 9.18   Losses

**9.18**   *TA 1988 s 768* restricts the carry forward of losses under *TA 1988 s 393* through the change in ownership. *TA 1988 s 768A* restricts the carry back of losses under *TA 1988 s 393A* in similar circumstances. These apply where in the three years before or three years after the change in ownership there is a major change in the nature or conduct of the business, or the nature of its investments or its activities have become small or negligible before the change and are significantly revived after the change. [*TA 1988 s 768A(1)*]. *TA 1988 s 768B* applies to investment companies for the carry forward of management expenses. These anti-avoidance provisions are further extended by *TA 1988 s 768C* to cover the situation where a company with unutilised losses or management expenses etc. is acquired by another company and there is an intra-group transfer of an asset to that company within *TCGA 1992 s 171* on a no gain, no loss transfer within three years of the change of ownership and a chargeable gain arises on the subsequent disposal of the asset.

**9.19**   These provisions are similar to the ACT restrictions in *TA 1988 s 245B* referred to in Chapter 6. The circumstances in which the investment company restrictions apply are defined in *TA 1988 28A Sch*. Schedule A losses are similarly restricted by *TA 1988 s 768B*.

**9.20**   Under CTSA, company accounting periods are determined under *TA 1988 s 12* as explained in Chapter 2. However there are examples of accounts covering a longer period, even though there may be breaches of company law. The profits do not necessarily have to be apportioned to the accounting periods by reference to time where the actual profits and losses can be ascertained and allocated more precisely. [*Marshall Hus & Partners Ltd v Bolton [1981] STC 18*].

**9.21**   From a CTSA point of view it will obviously be important to identify cases where there is a change in ownership of the company within *TA 1988 ss 343* and *768* and then to consider whether there has been or is likely to be a major change in the nature or conduct of the trade which would disallow the losses. Although the Revenue have specific powers to require, by notice in writing, a shareholder to state whether he is the beneficial owner of the shares or securities under *TA 1988 s 768(9)*, in practice the company will have to identify cases where these provisions apply in order to prepare a complete and correct return. In cases of doubt as to whether a change in relation to the business is a material change, the facts should be brought to the notice of the Revenue, both to ensure a correct and complete return and to pre-empt any discovery at a later stage, under *TMA 1970 s 29*.

## Farming and market gardening

**9.22**   *TA 1988 s 397* restricts the ability to set off a loss arising from a trade of farming or market gardening against total income where a loss, ignoring capital allowances, has been incurred in the accounting period and in each of the five years up to the beginning of that accounting period. Losses in such circumstances can only be carried forward, unless the farming trade is part of, and ancillary to, a larger trading undertaking. [*TA 1988 s 397(4)*]. The restrictions also fail to bite where the farming activities are of such a nature as would have justified a reasonable expectation of the realisation of profits in the future (if they had been undertaken by a competent farmer) but they could not have reasonably expected to become profitable until after the period of loss. An obvious case would be building up a pedigree herd from scratch which could take 10–12 years before becoming profitable.

**9.23** From a CTSA point of view, if the provisions appear to bite to restrict the losses but for the competent farmer provisions in *TA 1988 s 397(3)*, it would be necessary to prepare a business plan and budget to show the reasonable expectation of profits. Such a business plan should be prepared as soon as a loss period arises, not at the end of the five years, because the requirement is to show that there was both a reasonable expectation of the realisation of profits in the future, but they could not reasonably have expected to arise in the five year period beginning with the first period of loss. It might not be sufficient to show that due to circumstances beyond the farmers' control, any competent farmer would have made a loss in the actual circumstances, as the legislation requires a planned development period, in which the loss is to be expected, leading up to a period of profitability. In practice the Revenue may accept a less stringent application of the competent farmer provisions, but under CTSA the taxpayer has to make the decision as to whether the case is sustainable, and to ensure that the Revenue have sufficient information to concur with this judgment, or challenge it if they see fit to do so.

## Leasing trades

**9.24** It used to be popular for companies to set up a separate trade of leasing in order to have the benefit of first year capital allowances, which could be set against other taxable profits. However such losses are now treated as constituting a separate trade under *TA 1988 s 395(3)* and *(4)* and relief for losses against total income, or carry back against total income under *TA 1988 s 393(1)* or *393(A)(1)*, are denied by *TA 1988 s 395(1)*, where arrangements are in existence to transfer the trade to a successor company under *TA 1988 s 343*.

**9.25** Schedule D, Case VI losses can be set against any other Case VI income in the accounting period, or any future accounting period, under *TA 1988 s 396*, except where the loss relates to a premium on a lease or a lease granted at an undervalue, where the income is taxed under Schedule A in accordance with *TA 1988 ss 34–36*.

## Schedule A losses

**9.26** *TA 1988 s 392A* allows a Schedule A loss for any accounting period to be set against the total profits for the period with any excess loss being carried forward against Schedule A profits in future. They are also eligible for group relief under *TA 1988 s 403(1)(b)*. [See Chapter 11].

**9.27** An investment company is allowed to treat excess Schedule A losses carried forward as excess management expenses, even if the company has then ceased to carry on the Schedule A business, so long as it remains an investment company. [*TA 1988 s 392A(3)*]. Schedule A loss relief is only allowed on this basis where the Schedule A business is carried on on a commercial basis or in the exercise of a statutory function. [*TA 198 s 392A(5–7)*].

**9.28** Where a loss arises in an overseas property business, the loss may be carried forward against profits of the overseas property business in the future. [*TA 1988 s 392B*].

**9.29** From a CTSA point of view, in order to claim tax relief for Schedule A losses it is necessary to show that the business was carried on so as to afford a reasonable expectation of profit. [*TA 1988 s 392A(6)(a)*].

## Miscellaneous

**9.30** Further loss restrictions that need to be considered are those applying to corporate partners where there are arrangements allowing the benefit of losses to be enjoyed by other parties, under *TA 1988 s 116*, and dealings in commodity partnerships, where the losses are likely to be disallowed under *TA 1988 s 399*, which was aimed against the commodity carry scheme. Transactions in deposits, whether certificated or not, give rise to profits taxable under Schedule D, Case VI under *TA 1988 s 56*, or losses allowable as Schedule D, Case VI losses, under *TA 1988 s 398*. Any write off of Government investment reduces losses under *TA 1988 s 400*.

**9.31** Pre-trading expenditure is treated as incurred on the first day of trading under *TA 1988 s 401*.

**9.32** Investment companies may claim relief against income for losses arising on the disposal of unquoted shares in qualifying trading companies, under *TA 1988 s 573, 575* and *576*. Interest or royalties, which have been excluded from taxation under a double taxation treaty, cannot create or increase a loss by leaving such income out of account in computing the trading results, in view of *TA 1988 s 808*.

Chapter 10

# Loan Relationships and Foreign Exchange Rules

## Loan relationship debits and credits

### General rules

**10.1** The loan relationship legislation, primarily in *FA 1996 ss 80–105* and *8–15 Sch*, applies for corporation tax purposes, and follows so far as possible, generally accepted accounting principles. Where a trading company is involved, receipts and surpluses from trading loan relationships are treated as trading receipts, while interest paid and premiums on redemption are treated as trading expenses. Profits from non-trading loan relationships, including non-trading exchange gains and losses, by a trading or non-trading company are taxed on the accruals basis under Schedule D, Case III with the expense side generating a loan relationship deficit. [*FA 1996 s 80*].

**10.2** A loan relationship is defined by *FA 1996 s 81* as arising where a company stands as a debtor, i.e. borrower, or a creditor, i.e. lender, for a money debt arising from a transaction for the lending of money. [*FA 1996 s 81(1)*]. Money debt is itself defined as a debt which falls to be settled by the payment of money, or the transfer of a right to settlement under a money debt. [*FA 1996 s 81(2)*]. Securities issued to protect the rights of a creditor of any money debt, amount to a transaction for the lending of money, except to the extent that the debt arises from rights arising from shares in the issuing company. [*FA 1996 s 81(3) and (4)*].

**10.3** A money debt may be in sterling or a foreign currency, and loan relationships include borrowings from banks or third parties, intra-group loans, amounts owed to the company, bank deposits and investments in gilt-edged securities or listed loan stock. *FA 1996 s 96* specifically excludes the capital profit or loss on 3.5 per cent Funding Stock 1999–2004 and 5.5 per cent Treasury Stock 2008–2012, provided that they are held for non-trading purposes. Interest on such gilts would nevertheless be brought into account for tax purposes on the normal accruals basis, and the capital profit or loss would be disregarded under *TCGA 1992 s 115*.

**10.4** Trading loan relationships are those where the loan relationship is incurred for the purpose of a trade and all credits, including interest,

## 10.5  Loan Relationships and Foreign Exchange Rules

are treated as trading receipts and all debits as trading expenses in computing the company's taxable profits. [*FA 1996 s 82(1) and (2)*]. Non-trading loan relationships give rise to non-trading credits and non-trading debits, and the excess of credits over debits is taxable under Schedule D, Case III and an excess of debits over credits is allowed as a non-trading deficit on loan relationships under *FA 1996 s 82 (3) to (6)*. These provisions overrule the ordinarily disallowable expenses rules in *TA 1988 s 74*. [*FA 1996 s 82(7)*]. Non-trading loan relationship credits and debits include those arising in respect of non-trading foreign exchange differences, under *FA 1993 s 129(7)*. The financial instruments legislation in *FA 1994 ss 147–177* is excluded for debt contracts and options where there is a loan relationship by *FA 1996 s 101 and 12 Sch* unless covered by *FA 1994 150A*. A loan to acquire an investment such as shares in a subsidiary would not be for the purposes of the trade and would therefore be a non-trading loan relationship.

**10.5**  A non-trading deficit on loan relationships, i.e. a net debit, can be relieved under *FA 1996 s 83(2)* by set off against total profits for the deficit period, carried back against profits for the preceding year, or carried forward against non-trading profits for the next year. Such treatment requires a claim within two years of the end of the deficit period. [*FA 1996 s 83(4)–(8)*]. In the absence of a claim the deficit is carried forward and treated as a non-trading deficit in the next period. [*FA 1996 s 83(3)*].

**10.6**  These provisions are expanded by *FA 1996 8 Sch*, which sets out the order of set off after relief for brought forward trading losses, but before any current or carried-back trading losses or Schedule A losses, and non-trade deficits carried back. [*FA 1996 8 Sch 1*]. A non-trading deficit for group relief purposes is calculated in the same way as a trading loss. [*FA 1996 8 Sch 2*]. A claim to carry back a non-trading deficit is restricted to the profits from loan relationships of the previous twelve months by *FA 1996 8 Sch 3*, and the carry-forward is limited to non-trading profits for the next accounting period by *FA 1996 8 Sch 4*. The surplus non-trading loan relationship deficit remaining after the above claims is then carried forward for set off against future non-trading profits. A claim for relief for non-trading deficits cannot be made by a company established for charitable purposes only. [*FA 1996 s 83(5)*].

**10.7**  From a CTSA point of view it is obviously important to ensure that appropriate claims are made for non-trading deficits on loan relationships in the most effective order of set off.

**10.8**  In computing debits or credits in connection with the loan relationship it is necessary to bring in not only all interest charges and allowable expenses [*FA 1996 s 84(1)(b)*], but also all profits, gains and losses including those of a capital nature [*FA 1996 s 84(1)(a)*], including those taken directly to, or transferred from reserves [*FA 1996 s 84(2)(b)*], but not including any amounts required to be transferred to the company's share premium account. [*FA 1996 s 84 (2)(a)*]. The charges and expenses included for the purpose of a loan relationship and related transactions are those incurred directly in bringing any such relationship into existence or giving effect to any related transaction, making any payment in respect of those relationships or transactions, and enforcing such arrangements. [*FA 1996 s 84(3)*]. Related transactions are a disposal or acquisition of rights or liabilities under the relationship. [*FA 1996 s 84(5)* and *(6)*]. Charges in respect of abortive attempts to enter into a loan relationship are allowed by *FA 1996 s 84(4)*.

**Anti-avoidance**

**10.9** *FA 1996 s 84(7)* and *9 Sch* contain a number of anti-avoidance provisions. Distributions, including interest treated as a distribution under *TA 1988 s 209*, are excluded from the loan relationship rules. [*FA 1996 9 Sch 1*]. Accrued interest on a loan from a connected person, as defined by [*FA 1996 s 87*], which remains unpaid more than twelve months after the end of the accounting period in which it is treated as accruing under the authorised accruals basis and which is not charged to corporation tax on the recipient (e.g. an overseas associate), is disallowed as a loan relationship debit until it is actually paid. [*FA 1996 9 Sch 2*]. In calculating accruals under the loan relationship rules, where any one party to the relationship has an option, it is assumed that the option will be dealt with in the most advantageous manner to the other party to the relationship, ignoring taxation. [*FA 1996 9 Sch 3*]. Loan relationship debits and credits exclude trading foreign exchange gains and losses brought into account under the Forex rules. [*FA 1996 9 Sch 4*]. However non-trading Forex gains and losses are taken into account under the loan relationship rules. [*FA 1993 ss 129–130*].

**10.10** The loan relationship accruals basis assumes that every amount due under the relationship will be paid in full as it becomes due. [*FA 1996 s 85(3)(c)*]. However, bad debts arising from a loan relationship may be provided for under *FA 1996 9 Sch 5*, except where the parties are connected. [*FA 1996 9 Sch 6*]. In the case of connected companies the debtor company does not have to bring into account the relevant credit on the release of the liability as the connected creditor has no relief for the bad debt. In other circumstances it is necessary to bring into credit a release, unless it is as a result of a relevant arrangement or compromise under the *Insolvency Act 1986* or *CA 1985 s 14*, or their Northern Ireland equivalents, or where the debt is a government investment written off. [*FA 1996 9 Sch paras 5(2)* and *7*].

**10.11** There are restrictions in relation to writing off overseas sovereign debt in *FA 1996 9 Sch 8, 9,* and to prevent a loss on a loan relationship being brought into the UK when it was incurred while the relationship was held outside the scope of UK tax. [*FA 1996 9 Sch 10*].

## 10.12 *Loan Relationships and Foreign Exchange Rules*

**Disclosure**

**10.12** A potential problem arises where there are debits or credits in respect of a loan relationship and a related transaction, e.g. an acquisition or disposal of rights or liabilities under a loan relationship, as defined by *FA 1996 s 84(5)*, where the transaction is not at arm's length. In such cases there has to be substituted the transaction which would have been entered into between independent persons, unless they are debits arising from the acquisition of the rights under a loan relationship at less than market value, or are intra-group transactions. [*FA 1996 9 Sch 11*]. In practice it may be a problem to determine the arrangements that parties at arm's length might have come to, and this may be a point that needs to be highlighted to the Revenue in order to avoid a subsequent discovery with interest and potential penalties under CTSA.

**10.13** A similar problem of recognising and calculating a potential disallowance arises under *FA 1996 9 Sch 13(1)* and *(2)* where, to the extent that a loan relationship debit is incurred for, or partially for (as apportioned on a just and reasonable basis), an unallowable purpose, i.e. one which is not amongst the business or other commercial purposes of the company, relief for the non-commercial debt is denied. Activities are not for commercial purposes where a main purpose of the arrangement is tax avoidance, i.e. it secures a tax advantage as defined for transactions in securities by *TA 1988 s 709(1)*. [*FA 1996 9 Sch 13(3) to (5)*]. The problem for the taxpayer company under CTSA is anticipating where the Revenue would regard the arrangements as being for an unallowable purpose, and then determining the just and reasonable disallowance. It may again be a problem of disclosure in order to avoid potential discovery, in cases of doubt, unless the company or its advisers are satisfied that the loan relationship debits do not relate to an unallowable purpose.

**10.14** Where a loan relationship is transferred intra-group, the transferee company normally stands in the shoes of the transferor company under *FA 1996 9 Sch 12*.

**10.15** Where loan relationship debits or credits are included in the value of a capital asset in accordance with normal accounting practice, they are brought into account for tax purposes as and when they are charged or released to profit and loss account in the company's accounts, in accordance with normal accountancy practice. [*FA 1996 9 Sch 14*]. Sale and repurchase arrangements (Repo transactions) and stock lending are excluded from loan relationships by *FA 1996 9 Sch 15*. Deemed interest brought into account on an arm's length basis under transfer pricing adjustments is deemed to have been paid or received under the loan relationship rules as if it were actual interest under *FA 1996 9 Sch 16*.

**10.16** There are provisions relating to securities which amount to relevant discounted securities, as defined by *FA 1996 13 Sch 3*, i.e. issued at a discount of 15 per cent or more (or where the redemption period is less than 30 years, the relevant percentage is half of the number of years in the period between the date of issue and the redemption date expressed as a percentage). Where such securities are issued by a close company for the benefit of another connected company, any debits relating to the discount on issue or premium on redemption are deferred until the security is redeemed, *FA 1996 10 Sch 17*. This also applies where a relevant discounted security is held by a participator. [*FA 1996 9 Sch 18*].

**Normal accounting treatment**

**10.17** Most non-financial companies use the accruals basis in calculating loan relationship debits and credits, as authorised by *FA 1996 s 85(1)(a), (2)* and *(3)*. The accruals basis effectively allocates debits and credits over the entire period of the loan on the assumption that all liabilities will be met and allocates them to the accounting periods on a time basis irrespective of actual dates of payment.

**10.18** Financial institutions such as banks and dealers in securities normally use the other authorised accounting method known as the 'mark to market' basis, under which loan relationships, which are quoted securities, are brought into their accounts at a fair value which would normally be the value as quoted on the relevant exchange. [*FA 1996 s 85(1)(b)* and *(4)–(6)*]. The mark to market basis can only be used where it is also used for accounting purposes in the company's statutory accounts [*FA 1996 s 86(1)* and *(3)*], although different methods may be used in respect of different loan relationships or for different accounting periods, or parts thereof. [*FA 1996 s 86(2)*]. The default basis is the accruals basis of accounting. [*FA 1996 s 86(4)*].

**10.19** The mark to market basis may be calculated on a basis which includes accrued interest, which is usually known as the 'dirty' basis, or on the 'clean' basis under which it is valued at the fair value excluding accrued interest. The accrued interest is then dealt with on the normal accruals basis. [*FA 1996 s 86(5) and (6)*].

**10.20** Where in a loan relationship the debtor and creditor are connected, only the accruals basis may be used. [*FA 1996 s 87(1) and (2)*]. For this purpose companies are connected if one company has control of the other or both are under the control of the same person, either in the accounting period or the two years prior to the beginning of that period. [*FA 1996 s 87(3)(a) and (b)*]. There is also a connection where the other party to the loan relationship was a participator in the accounting period, or in the previous two years. [*FA 1996 s 87(3)(c)*]. Normal close company definitions of control, participator and associate are applied and indirect debtors and creditors are included. [*FA 1996 s 87(5)–(7)*]. A participator who is only so included because he is a loan creditor is disregarded under *FA 1996 s 87(8)*. Connected party transactions do not include dealers in securities holding quoted or short-dated redeemable debt in the fellow group member. [*FA 1996 s 88*].

## 10.21 Loan Relationships and Foreign Exchange Rules

**10.21** Where there is a change in basis, a balancing debit or credit is relieved or taxed in the period of change, which is the difference between the debits or credits actually brought into account up to the end of the previous accounting period and those which would have been brought into account under the new basis. [*FA 1996 s 89*]. If the change, however, is from the accruals to a 'mark to market' basis, the loan relationship is deemed to cease at the date of change at the fair market value, so that any debits or credits up to that value are dealt with on the accruals basis, and thereafter the security is brought into account on a fair value basis under the normal 'mark to market' rules. [*FA 1996 s 90*].

**10.22** Where income tax is deducted from interest actually received, it may be set against the corporation tax liability for the accounting period into which it falls on the authorised accounting basis. A claim for the income tax credit must be made within two years of the end of the accounting period in which the interest is actually received, or if later, six years after the end of the accounting period in which the accrued interest fell. [*FA 1996 s 91(6)*].

**10.23** Convertible securities other than those held as trading stock are only within the loan relationship rules so far as interest is concerned, applying the accruals basis of accounting. [*FA 1996 s 92(1)–(3)*]. The capital profit or loss is dealt with under the chargeable gains rules in *TCGA 1992*. Convertible securities are distinguished from relevant discounted securities and are those where there is a more than negligible likelihood that the loan stock will be converted into share capital rather than repaid on redemption. [*FA 1996 s 92(1)*]. Similarly, loan relationships linked to the value of chargeable assets, such as equity loans, or an index of the value of chargeable assets, are only within the loan relationship rules so far as interest is concerned, which is dealt with on an accruals basis. [*FA 1996 s 93*]. The index linked element of index linked gilts is excluded from the loan relationship provisions by *FA 1996 s 94*, and special provisions to cater for gilt strips are contained in *FA 1996 s 95*. Manufactured interest arising on the transfer of loan relationships is included by *FA 1996*.

**10.24** The provisions relating to collective investment schemes and insurance companies in *FA 1996 s 98, 10 Sch* and *s 99 11 Sch* respectively are outside the scope of this book.

**10.25** Where interest is payable other than on a loan relationship, for example under a judgment debt, it is nonetheless dealt with under the loan relationship rules, on the accruals basis under *FA 1996 s 100*. This does not apply to discounts such as discounts for cash or prompt payment.

**10.26** Apart from the loan relationship arrangements, it is necessary to remember that in respect of annual interest paid by a company, income tax has to be deducted under *TA 1988 s 349(2)(a)*, unless it is paid by a bank in the ordinary course of its business or to a bank within the charge

## Loan Relationships and Foreign Exchange Rules 10.29

to corporation tax on the interest, *TA 1988 s 349(3)(a)* and *(b)*, or it is interest on a quoted Eurobond within *TA 1988 s 349(3)(c)*, or it is made by a paying and collecting agent under *TA 1988 ss 118A* to *118K*, up to 6 April 2001 when the scheme is abolished. From that date the definition of quoted Eurobond is widened to include any security issued by a quoted company which carries a right to interest [*FA 2000 s 111*]. Although *TA 1988 s 349(2)* refers to annual interest, chargeable under Schedule D, Case III when paid to a non-resident, it is actually charged under Schedule D, Case I if the recipient is within the charge to corporation tax, under the loan relationship rules in *TA 1988 s 18(3A)*. However, tax still has to be deducted at source in these circumstances. [Tax Bulletin, Issue 42, August 1999, p 685].

**10.27** Annual interest is interest other than short interest, where the loan is likely to be outstanding for less than twelve months. Short interest is paid gross. The definition of annual interest has been considered in a number of cases including *IRC v Hay (1924) 8 TC 636*, *Barlow v IRC (1937) 21 TC 354*, *Goslings and Sharpe v Blake (1889) 2 TC 450*, *Garston Overseers for the Poor v Carlisle (1915) 6 TC 659*, *Re Cooper (1911) 105 LT 273*, *Regal (Hastings) Ltd v Gulliver (1944) 24 ATC 297*, *Corinthian Securities Ltd v Cato (1969) 46 TC 93*, *Cairns v MacDiarmid [1983] STC 178* and *Minsham Properties Ltd v Price [1990] STC 718*. Interest paid under the *Late Payment of Commercial Debts (Interest) Act 1998* is not annual interest. [Tax Bulletin, Issue 42, August 1999, p 686]. Income tax deducted from interest payable has to be accounted for to the Revenue in the same way as tax deducted from annual payments under the quarterly accounting provisions of *TA 1988 16 Sch*, by *TA 1988 s 350*, and a certificate of deduction of tax (form R185) must be given to the payee on request under *TA 1988 s 352*.

**10.28** Some double taxation treaties allow interest to be paid gross with appropriate clearance from the Inland Revenue Financial Intermediaries and Claims Office (FICO). It is important under CTSA to ensure that such authorisation is in place. A provisional treaty relief scheme (PTR) was introduced from 1 September 1999 for 'one to one' company loans where there is no shareholding relationship or common ownership between the parties involved, or syndicated loans where there is a syndicate manager. Under this scheme the borrower can seek FICO's provisional authority for payment of interest gross. [Tax Bulletin, Issue 41, June 1999, p 669]. There is no similar requirement to withhold income tax from any part of the redemption payments on loans issued at a discount or redeemed at a premium.

**10.29** Relief for interest may be restricted where arrangements have been made such that the sole or main benefit that might be expected to accrue is a reduction in the tax liability. This particular provision was specifically aimed at artificial avoidance schemes involving payments of interest in advance, under the pre 1996 provisions, but it is still in force

**10.30** *Loan Relationships and Foreign Exchange Rules*

and is widely drawn. [See *Westmoreland Investments Ltd v Macniven [1998] STC 1131, TA 1988 s 787*].

## Foreign exchange gains and losses

**10.30** The foreign exchange gains and losses rules in *FA 1993 ss 125–170* and *15–18 Sch*, apply to companies, except for authorised unit trusts, investment trusts and open ended investment companies. [*FA 1993 s 152(2A) (SI 1997 No. 1154)* and *152(3)* and *(4)*]. Individuals, partnerships, trusts and non-qualifying companies are still dealt with under the original Case Law, as explained in some detail in SP 1/87. For the purposes of this book, the CTSA rules are considered in relation to qualifying companies. The legislation is supplemented by the *Exchange Gains and Losses (Transitional Provisions) Regulations 1994 (SI 1994 No. 3226)*, the *Exchange Gains and Losses (Alternative Method of Calculation of Gain or Loss) Regulations 1994 (SI 1994 No. 3227)*, the *Exchange Gains and Losses (Deferral of Gains and Losses) Regulations 1994 (SI 1994 No. 3228)*, the *Exchange Gains and Losses (Excess Gains and Losses) Regulations 1994 (SI 1994 No. 3229)*, the *Local Currency Elections Regulations 1994 (SI 1994 No. 3230)* and the *Exchange Gains and Losses (Insurance Companies) Regulations 1994 (SI 1994 No. 3231)*. The provisions apply in respect of accounting periods which began on or after 23 March 1995. [*FA 1993 s 165* and *SI 1994 No. 3224*].

**10.31** Trading gains and losses arise, under *FA 1993 s 128*, where an asset or currency contract gain or loss arises, or a liability was incurred, for the purpose of a trade. In such cases the exchange gain will be treated as a trading receipt, and the exchange loss will be deductible as a trading expense. It is no longer necessary to differentiate between whether the asset or liability was acquired on capital account or revenue account. Gains or losses are, however, ignored for Schedule D, Case I purposes as a trading receipt or expense if they are dealt with as a charge on income. [*FA 1993 s 128 (10A), (10B)*].

**10.32** Where the exchange gain or exchange loss does not arise entirely from trading activities, it is treated as a non-trading gain or loss under *FA 1993 s 129*. An exchange gain is brought within the loan relationship provisions as a non-trading loan credit taxable under Schedule D, Case III, in accordance with *FA 1996 s 82*, and an exchange loss is correspondingly treated as a non-trading deficit in accordance with *FA 1996 s 83*, under *FA 1993 s 130*.

**10.33** The initial exchange gain or loss is calculated for an accounting period, under *FA 1993 s 125(4)*, on qualifying assets and liabilities as defined by *FA 1993 s 153*. Qualifying assets are monetary assets including debts, currency and shares held as trading stock, other than convertible securities as defined for loan relationships by *FA 1996 s 92*, and loans linked to the value of chargeable assets as defined for loan relationships by *FA 1996 s 93, FA 1993 s 153(4)*. A qualifying liability is defined as a qualifying debt, a contingent liability for which provision has been made in the accounts, or an obligation to transfer securities or shares including bare sales.

**10.34** There is a comparison between the beginning and end of the accounting period by reference to the local currency equivalent, which is normally the sterling equivalent, of the asset or liability. [*FA 1993 s 125(1)*]. There is an initial exchange gain if there is an increase in the sterling value of the asset and an initial exchange loss if there is a decrease. [*FA 1993 s 125(2)*]. Conversely in the case of a qualifying liability, a decrease in the sterling equivalent of the liability of the accounting period amounts to an initial exchange gain, and an increase in the liability as an initial exchange loss. [*FA 1993 s 125(3) and (4)*].

---

*Example 1*

| | £ |
|---|---:|
| *Qualifying asset* | |
| Sterling value of loan of $1,500,000, made by a company on 1 April 2000 at $1.60 to £1 | 937,500 |
| Sterling value of same loan on 31 March 2001 at $1.50 to £1 | 1,000,000 |
| Difference in sterling terms | 63,000 |

Since this is an increase in assets over the accounting period, this is treated as an initial exchange gain. [*FA 1993 s 125(2)(a)*].

| | £ |
|---|---:|
| *Qualifying liability* | |
| Sterling value of amount borrowed of $1,000,000 on April 2000 at $1.60 to £1 | 625,000 |
| Sterling value of same borrowing on 31 March 2001 at $1.50 to £1 | 666,667 |
| Difference in sterling terms | 41,667 |

Since there is an increase in liabilities over the accounting period, this is treated as an initial exchange loss. [*FA 1993 s 125(4)(b)*].

| Net exchange gain | £21,333 |
|---|---:|

---

**10.35** If sterling strengthens during the accounting period, foreign currency liabilities will cost less to settle and there is an exchange gain, whereas foreign currency assets will realise less in sterling terms and there is an exchange loss. Conversely if sterling weakens during the period, foreign currency liabilities will cost more to repay and there is an exchange loss, whereas foreign currency assets will be worth more in sterling terms and there is an exchange gain.

## 10.36 Loan Relationships and Foreign Exchange Rules

**10.36** It is common practice to hedge foreign currency exposures through forward currency contracts or currency swaps. These are dealt with by *FA 1993 s 126*. At the end of each accounting period, and on completion of the contract, it is necessary to compare the local currency equivalent, i.e. normally the sterling equivalent of the foreign currency to be received or paid under the contract. This will take into account any net payments representing differences between the two currencies paid in settlement. If sterling strengthens compared with the currency receivable under the contract, less sterling will be received for the foreign currency and there will be an initial exchange loss. If sterling weakens a greater amount of sterling will be received and there will be an initial exchange gain. Conversely if sterling strengthens in relation to the overseas currency payable, a lesser amount of sterling will be needed to meet the liability and there will be an initial exchange gain. But if sterling weakens, a greater amount will be needed to meet the foreign currency payment and there will be an initial exchange loss. This will also apply to contracts where only the difference is payable. Where the amount of the loan or debt varies during the accounting period, the average sterling equivalent has to be computed by reference to each movement on the account compared with the nominal amount of the loan or debt at the year end.

**10.37** If the asset or liability has not existed for the entire accounting period, the gain or loss has to be computed for the accruals period, which is determined in accordance with translation times. There is a translation time at the acquisition of the asset or liability, at its disposal and at the end of each intervening accounting period. [*FA 1993 s 158*].

**10.38** There is an alternative calculation introduced by *FA 1993 s 134* and *15 Sch* and in the *Exchange Gains and Losses (Alternative Method of Calculation of Gain or Loss) Regulations 1994 (SI 1994 No. 3227)*. This disapplies the foreign exchange rules for any asset or liability held in exempt circumstances, i.e. for long-term insurance, mutual insurance and the occupation of commercial woodlands, by a housing association or by a self-build society. [*FA 1993 15 Sch 2*]. Relief is available for unremittable income. [*FA 1993 15(3) Sch*].

### Matched Liabilities

**10.39** A company may elect to match certain non-monetary assets with associated foreign currency borrowings used to finance their acquisition, provided that the assets are shares in an overseas subsidiary or a net investment in an overseas branch, ships or aircraft. The foreign currency loan must have been taken out to eliminate the economic risk of holding assets which would have arisen had sterling been borrowed, and exchange differences are carried to reserves for accounting purposes on translation in accordance with SSAP 20, *FA 1993 15 Sch 4*.

## Loan Relationships and Foreign Exchange Rules 10.44

**Anti-avoidance**

**10.40** There is an anti-avoidance provision in *FA 1993 s 135* whereby the exchange loss is disallowed if one of the main benefits of the nominal currency chosen is the exchange loss which might be expected to arise. The nominal currency is defined by *FA 1993 s 160* as the settlement currency which in turn is defined by *FA 1993 s 161*. Under CTSA, the taxpayer company has to make a judgement as to whether or not this provision might apply to disallow an exchange loss.

**10.41** If transactions are entered into other than at arm's length, any exchange loss is disregarded except for carry-forward against subsequent exchange gains on the same asset or liability under *FA 1993 s 136(1)*. This again requires a judgement as to whether or not the transactions would have been entered into had the parties been entirely independent. Where the only difference would have been that the amount borrowed would have been less, the exchange loss can be reduced pro rata to the amount of the arm's length loan, which would then qualify as an ordinary exchange loss. [*FA 1993 s 136(4)* to *(6)*]. This requires judgement as to what would have actually been lent in an arm's length transaction. Similarly where the amount of interest charged on a currency loan is not at an arm's length rate, the profit or loss for tax purposes has to be computed as if there had been an arm's length rate of interest charged. [*FA 1993 s 136(7)* to *(10)*]. If these provisions apply it will be necessary to decide on a market rate of interest.

**10.42** These provisions do not apply to intra-group transactions where there is no overall advantage to the group, and is not an aspect of a variable debt within *FA 1993 s 127*. [*FA 1993 s 136(11)* to *(15)*]. The ring-fencing of exchange losses on debts of varying amounts are broadly similar, under *FA 1993 s 136A*, with amendments to provide for variations in the amount of debt outstanding.

**10.43** Currency contracts entered into on non-arm's length terms can also give rise to a ring-fenced exchange loss, which can only be set against future exchange gains on the same contract under *FA 1993 s 137*. The problem for CTSA is again determining whether the contract would have been entered into, or if the terms would have been different if the parties had been at arm's length. The problems are in many ways similar to those in relation to transfer pricing considered in Chapter 14.

**10.44** If a company changes its accounting date in order to take advantage of favourable exchange rates, the Inspector or, on appeal, the Commissioners, may ignore the change for the purpose of arriving at the exchange gains or losses and make any just and reasonable adjustment to the company's corporation tax liability as a result. [*FA 1993 s 166*]. This is one anti-avoidance provision where it is still the Revenue which make the adjustment. The other anti-avoidance provisions have been changed so that the company, on making its self-assessment, must identify where

## 10.45 Loan Relationships and Foreign Exchange Rules

the provisions apply and incorporate the appropriate adjustments into its tax return and computations.

**Deferral of unrealised gains**

**10.45** A company may claim to defer certain unrealised gains arising in an accounting period on long-term foreign currency borrowings where the original term is in excess of twelve months. The claim must specify the amount of the gain to be deferred, and the assets or liabilities concerned. The claim would normally be made in the return or within two years of the end of the accounting period. [*FA 1993 s 139*]. The mechanism of deferral is to treat the gain as if it were not made in the first accrual period and carry it forward to the next, and on a claim for the next period again the gain would be carried forward so long as the asset existed. When the asset is disposed of, the gain crystallises as a trading or non-trading gain as appropriate. [*FA 1993 s 140*].

**10.46** The amount deferred on each occasion is the lower of $B-A$ or $C-A$ where B is the total unrealised exchange gains in the accounting period, less the corresponding losses on long-term capital assets and long-term capital liabilities; C is the total of exchange gains, less losses on relevant items, being a right to settlement under a qualifying debt on a duty to settle under a qualifying debt, etc. as defined by *FA 1993 s 153(1)(a)* and *153(2)(a)*. A is 10 per cent of the company's profits for the accounting period liable to corporation tax, excluding any claim for deferral of unrealised gains and group relief. [*FA 1993 s 141*].

**10.47** Where the claimant is a member of a UK group these provisions are supplemented by the *Exchange Gains and Losses (Deferral of Gains and Losses) Regulations 1994, SI 1994 No. 3228*, paragraph 4 of which effectively adds together the deferral limit criteria for all the companies in a group. Paragraph 2 allows a long-term capital debt to be repaid and replaced by a similar debt within 30 days before or after the repayment without necessarily crystallising the exchange gain or loss, as that amount is treated as an unrealised gain falling within the deferral rules. Paragraph 3 excludes from the company's profits, overseas income or chargeable gains to the extent that the tax thereon has been covered by foreign tax.

**10.48** Where gains or losses taken into account are expressed in currencies other than sterling they need to be converted in accordance with the rules in *FA 1993 ss 92–95* and where applicable the *Local Currency Elections Regulations 1994, SI 1994 No. 3230*, as modified by *FA 2000 ss 105, 106* for most accounting periods beginning on or after 1 January 2000, following which the Regulations cease to apply. The general rule for corporation tax is that profits and losses of all businesses carried on by a company should be computed in sterling, except in the circumstances authorised by substituted *FA 1993 s 93*. This also applies to management expenses, capital allowances and balancing charges. A

## Loan Relationships and Foreign Exchange Rules  **10.49**

company is allowed to use a currency other than sterling for tax purposes where it prepares its accounts in such a currency and in the case of a non-UK resident company it makes branch returns in the same non-sterling currency or some other non-sterling currency. Non-sterling currency is also permitted where the accounts of a company as a whole are prepared in sterling but business accounts or part of them are prepared in another currency. The conversion of the business results to sterling is after deduction of management expenses, losses and non-trading loan relationship deficits brought forward in the foreign currency. These rules do not apply to chargeable gains and allowable capital losses where the conversion into sterling is normally required to be made at the time of acquisition and disposal. Any monetary elements in *CAA 1990* are converted into the foreign currency. Separate parts of the business, which will usually be separate branches, may keep the results in different currencies or using different authorised conversion conventions. The appropriate accounts are those computed under the *Companies Act* where appropriate, or in accordance with the law of the state of incorporation or the most closely corresponding accounts. 'Branch' and 'return of accounts' are also defined, as are other terms. The rules for currency translation for corporation tax return purposes do not apply to exchange gains and losses on qualifying assets and liabilities (the FOREX legislation) in *FA 1993 ss 125–170*. In the case of accounts prepared in sterling the accounting translation rules in SSAP 20 are normally followed with conversion being at the arm's-length rate for the relevant date, or an average rate for the period. In other cases, the London closing rate for the day of the transaction must be used. The company using the company rate/net investment method must use the London closing rate or an average rate for the last day of the accounting period. The use of an average rate requires an appropriate election by the company concerned; the election is revocable but a fresh election cannot be made for another three years. These provisos do not override the controlled foreign company legislation or the Forex rules. The amounts that have been conclusively translated for one year may nonetheless be retranslated for the next year. When the new rules are first applied any unused management expenses, loan relationship deficits or losses must be translated at the London closing rate for the last day of the previous accounting period, as must any balance of expenditure for capital allowances. The advantage of using foreign currency accounts for tax purposes is that, by definition, there are no exchange gains or losses on translation and it greatly simplifies the reporting requirement, by allowing translation at the year end exchange rate.

**10.49** Where part of a debt has been repaid by the end of the accounting period an appropriate part of any deferred unrealised gain is treated as realised, making such apportionments as are just and reasonable. [*FA 1993 s 143*]. If a debt has become irrecoverable it is treated as having been disposed of immediately before the end of the accounting period, under *FA 1993 s 144*, but is resurrected as a new debt of a nominal amount,

**10.50**   *Loan Relationships and Foreign Exchange Rules*

equal to the recoverable amount if it subsequently becomes recoverable under *FA 1993 s 145*.

**10.50**   There are provisions dealing with the early termination of currency contracts which would crystallise a gain or loss when the contract is terminated. Where a forward contract is closed out by entering into a second contract on reciprocal terms, the first contract is treated as if it had been terminated and the second one is ignored. [*FA 1993 ss 146* and *147*]. Non-exchange gains or losses that are otherwise not charged to tax or relieved may come within the provisions of *FA 1993 s 148* and the *Exchange Gains and Losses (Excess Gains and Losses) Regulations 1994 (SI 1994 No. 3229)* paragraph 2, but any relief given is cancelled if the loss is later recovered, under paragraph 3.

**10.51**   *FA 1993 s 149* provides that the local currency referred to in *FA 1993 ss 125–127* is sterling except where the asset or contract was held, or the liability was owed, by the company solely for business purposes, treating assets in different currencies separately. [*FA 1993 s 149(4)* and *(5)*]. This use of foreign currency is disallowed by *FA 1993 s 135A* where the main benefit to be expected from using the foreign currency is that no exchange gain would accrue.

**10.52**   The exchange rate to be used for translation purposes is the London spot rate. [*FA 1993 ss 150* and *151*]. Other provisions in *FA 1993* deal with the interpretation of the legislation.

**10.53**   For CTSA purposes the company not only has to decide whether or not it is in breach of any of the anti-avoidance provisions in relation to foreign exchange transactions, but also whether a claim should be made to use a currency other than sterling, where the primary economic environment of the trade is overseas, under *FA 1993 ss 93–95* and the *Local Currency Election Regulations 1994, SI 1994 No. 3230*. For these purposes the ecu shall be regarded as a currency other than sterling. [*FA 1993 s 95(5)*].

## Interest rates and currency contracts

**10.54**   The provisions in *FA 1994 ss 147–177* and *18 Sch* do not appear to have any particular self-assessment implications except that there are anti-avoidance provisions in *FA 1994 ss 165* and *166* where transfers of value have arisen as a result of such contracts. There is no longer any requirement in respect of transactions not at arm's length for the Board of Inland Revenue to direct that non-arm's length transactions provisions in *FA 1994 s 167* should apply. The company therefore has to decide whether any transactions have been entered into on different terms than those which would have been entered into had all the transactions been at arm's length, in the same way as for transfer pricing. These provisions are extended to some qualifying contracts with non-residents by *FA 1994 s 168*.

Chapter 11

# Groups and Consortia

## Group relief

**11.1** Group relief enables a UK resident company or branch of a non-resident company, within a 75 per cent group, to surrender a loss incurred in an accounting period to another such company or branch in the group which has taxable profits for the same period. The procedure for group relief claims is explained in Chapter 4 and this chapter therefore deals with whether any group relief claim is available to ensure that the self-assessment return including group relief surrenders is correct and the right amount of tax is paid at the right time. There are no changes to the group or consortium relief calculations merely as a result of CTSA.

**11.2** The starting point for any group relief claim is to ensure that the companies constitute a group, and that both the surrendering company and the claimant company are members of the same group. [*TA 1988 s 402(1) and (2)*]. Oil extraction activities are ring-fenced for tax purposes and a claimant company cannot set group relief surrendered to it against its ring-fenced profits, except to the extent that the losses incurred by the surrendering company arose from oil extraction activities or oil rights. [*TA 1988 s 492(8)*].

**11.3** A group of companies for group relief purposes exists if one of the companies is a 75 per cent subsidiary of the other, or both are 75 per cent subsidiaries of the third company [*TA 1988 s 413(3)(a)*] with a 75 per cent subsidiary being defined in accordance with *TA 1988 s 838, TA 1988 s 413(4)*. *TA 1988 s 838(1)(b)* defines a 75 per cent subsidiary as one where not less than 75 per cent of its ordinary share capital is owned directly or indirectly, which includes ownership which is partly direct and partly indirect, through a chain of companies. [*TA 1988 s 838(2)*]. Ownership refers to beneficial ownership [*TA 1988 s 838(3)*], and therefore a company leaves a group for this purpose if it is put into liquidation. [*IRC v Olive Mill Spinners Ltd (1963) 41 TC 77*]. The meaning of beneficial ownership in this context was considered in *J Sainsbury plc v O'Connor [1991] STC 318*. A chain of holdings is defined by *TA 1988 s 838(4)* to (*10*). Ordinary share capital is defined by *TA 1988 s 832*. *Tilcon Ltd v Holland [1981] STC 365* confirmed that fixed rate preference shares are not ordinary share capital. The definition of group is amended by *FA 2000 s 97* and *27 Sch* in relation to accounting periods ending on or after

## 11.4 Groups and Consortia

1 April 2000, to include UK resident branches of non-resident companies and to allow the group relationship to be traced through non-UK resident companies. For earlier periods a group is confined to companies resident in the UK and excludes holdings by or through a non-resident company. [*TA 1988 s 413(5)*], except for certain structures within the European Union, *ICI plc v Colmer [1999] STC 1089*.

**11.4** There have been many attempts over the years to create artificial groups to obtain group relief and therefore the definition of a 75 per cent subsidiary is extended by *TA 1988 s 413(7)* to require the parent company to be beneficially entitled to not less than 75 per cent of any profits available for distribution to equity holders, and not less than 75 per cent of any assets of the subsidiary company available for distribution to its equity holders in a winding up. This is also expanded by *TA 1988 18 Sch* which defines equity shareholders and profits available for distribution to include, for example, a loan creditor in respect of a 'non-commercial' loan and which, in para 5B, overrules the decision in *J Sainsbury plc v O'Connor [1991] STC 318*. These provisions are further amended by *FA 2000 27 Sch* to take account of the extended definition of groups and consortia, and the extension of group relief to UK branches of non-resident companies. *TA 1988 18 Sch 5F* restricts the relief available where equity shareholders' interests are directly related to the results of the UK trade, so that the interest is measured by reference to the interest in the UK trade if that is less than the interest in the results of the company as a whole. Provisions relating to options are explained in SP3/93 and at ESC C10.

**11.5** The group relationship is also broken where there are arrangements in existence which could result in one of the companies leaving the group and becoming a member of another group, or under the control of another company, or the trade is taken over by a successor company. [*TA 1988 s 410(1)*, SP3/93 and ESC C10]. The disentitlement to group relief operates only while the arrangements exist [*Shepherd v Law Land plc [1990] STC 795*], but conditional arrangements are ignored. [*Scottish and Universal Newspapers Ltd v Fisher [1996] STC (SCD) 311*]. Arrangements were held to exist in *Pilkington Bros and Irving v Tesco Stores (Holdings) Ltd [1982] STC 881*. Where the necessary group relationship does exist relief may be claimed in substitution of loss relief carried forward. [*TA 1988 s 411A*]. A claim for group relief can be made after the company has left the group. [*A W Chapman Ltd v Hennessey [1982] STC 214*].

**11.6** The losses which can be surrendered by way of group relief are trading losses, excess capital allowances and non-trading deficits on loan relationships, which may be surrendered even if the surrendering company has other profits of the surrender period against which they could be set. [*TA 1988 s 403(1)(a) and (2)*]. Also available for surrender are charges on income, Schedule A losses and management expenses, to the extent that they exceed the aggregate of the surrendering companies' profits for the surrender period. [*TA 1988 s 403(1)(b)* and *(3)*]. Losses available for surrender by a UK branch of a non-resident company are restricted to cases where, if there was a profit it would be subject to corporation tax, and not exempt under a double taxation agreement, and relief is not available against non-UK profits for foreign tax purposes, to prevent double dipping. Total profits of non-resident companies exclude the profits relating to activities which are outside the UK charge under any double taxation arrangements, which limits the profits available against which losses can be surrendered to those in the UK. Non-UK profits are those charged to foreign tax which are not liable to UK corporation tax. Amounts are not treated as relievable against foreign tax where, as in the Netherlands, overseas branch profits are not brought into charge to tax. [*TA 1988 s 403D*]. From 1 April 2000 overseas branch losses will no longer be deductible against UK profits if they are relievable against non-UK profits of any other person under the foreign equivalent of overseas group relief or consolidated return procedure. This does not, however, apply to life assurance business losses. The revised group relief rules, except for qualification as a group, apply from 1 April 2000 so that any parts of any accounting period falling before that date are excluded, with apportionment on a time basis, as necessary, for an accounting period which straddles 1 April 2000. Relief is not available where the surrendering company is a dual resident investing company within *TA 1988 s 404* or for ring-fenced oil extraction activities within *TA 1988 ss 492(8)* and *494A, TA 1988 s 403(4)*. Other losses ineligible for surrender are losses of a foreign trade chargeable under Schedule D, Case VI or losses of trades not carried on on a commercial basis with a view to profit. [*TA 1988 s 403ZA*]. Capital allowances which are usually given by way of discharge or repayment of tax against a specified class of income, are only eligible for surrender to the extent that they exceed such relevant income. [*TA 1988 s 403ZB*]. Non-trading deficits on loan relationships are as defined by *FA 1996 s 83* in respect of which a claim for group relief has been made under *FA 1996 s 83(2)(b)*. [*TA 1988 s 403ZC*].

**11.7** Charges on income are those paid by the surrendering company in the surrender period, and those incurred in the surrender period, excluding losses carried forward from an earlier period and uncommercial losses. Management expenses are those disbursed by the surrendering company excluding amounts carried forward from earlier periods. [*TA 1988 s 403ZB*]. Charges on income, Schedule A losses and management expenses are only surrenderable to the extent that they exceed the surrendering company's gross profits of the surrender period. Gross profits are those prior to any such deduction or loan relationship deficits and excluding losses or excess management expenses brought forward. [*TA 1988 s 403ZE*].

**11.8** Group relief is limited to the smaller of the unused part of the surrendering company's available losses for the corresponding accounting period and the amount of the claimant company's total profits less

## 11.9 Groups and Consortia

any previous surrenders or group relief claims for that period. The corresponding accounting period is that which falls wholly or partly within an accounting period of the surrendering company. [*TA 1988 s 413(2A)*]. The surrenderable amount for the corresponding accounting period and the claimant company's total profits for the period, are for the entire period where the periods coincide or as apportioned on a time basis. [*TA 1988 ss 403A(3)–(10) 403B(1)* and *834(4)*]. The time basis may be replaced by some other basis which is just and reasonable. [*Marshall Hus & Partners Ltd v Bolton (1981) STC 18*].

**11.9** Group relief is allowed as a deduction from total profits, before any losses carried back from a subsequent accounting period but after relief for non-trading loan relationship deficits and charges on the assumption that all possible claims are made to set trading losses and capital allowances for the current period and brought forward, against total profits for the period. [*TA 1988 s 407*].

**11.10** A payment made by the claimant company to the surrendering company, under an agreement relating to the surrender of group relief, up to the amount of the relief surrendered, is ignored for corporation tax purposes by both the surrendering and claimant company. [*TA 1988 s 402(6)*].

## Consortia

**11.11** Consortium relief is available for a trading company which is owned by, or is a 90 per cent subsidiary of a holding company, which is owned by the consortium and is not a 75 per cent subsidiary of any company other than the holding company. [*TA 1988 s 402(3)*]. Linked companies are dealt with in *TA 1988 s 406*, see below. A consortium claim cannot be made if the consortium members' interest in the surrendering company is nil, in the period, or if the shares in that company are held as trading stock. [*TA 1988 s 402(4)*]. Two or more claimant companies may make claims relating to the surrendering companies' accounting period for their share of the consortium relief. [*TA 1988 s 402(5)*].

**11.12** A company is owned by a consortium if 75 per cent or more of the ordinary share capital is beneficially owned by companies in the consortium, none of which own less than 5 per cent of the ordinary share capital. [*TA 1988 s 413(6)*]. The definition of ordinary share capital, and 75 per cent and 90 per cent subsidiaries follow the group relief provisions using the definitions in *TA 1988 s 838* relating to ordinary share capital, which is defined by *TA 1988 s 832(1)*, and subject to the anti-avoidance requirement to own the appropriate proportion of distributable profits and assets available for distribution in a winding up which are applied to consortia by *TA 1988 s 413(7)–(10)* and *18 Sch*.

**11.13** Consortium relief is given in the same way as group relief except that it must be proportionate to the claimant company's interest in the consortium company. [*TA 1988 s 403C*]. Where one of the members of the consortium held its interest for only part of the period for which relief was claimed, the claim is limited to the relevant fraction of the amount available for surrender for the overlapping period. The fraction is the lowest of the percentage of the surrendering company's ordinary share capital beneficially owned by the claimant company, the percentage of distributable profits of the surrendering company to which the claimant company is beneficially entitled, and the percentage of the net assets of the surrendering company on a winding up. Where there has been a change in the percentages in the overlapping period, i.e. the period which is common to the accounting periods of the claimant company and of the surrendering company, where the qualifying conditions for group relief are satisfied, relief is apportioned. There are similar apportionment rules for the surrender by a consortium member of losses claimed by the consortium company, with appropriate amendments where there is a consortium holding company.

**11.14** Where the consortium company has subsidiaries, any group relief has to be dealt with in priority to consortium relief claims by members of the consortium. [*TA 1988 s 405*]. Where the company holding the interest in the consortium is a member of a group of companies, its share of the consortium company loss may be claimed by another company in the group, provided that the other company has been a member of the group for the whole of the accounting period concerned. In such circumstances the company owning the interest in the consortium is known as a link company. This relief is useful because the company owning the interest in the consortium may have no other activities and could not therefore itself use the consortium relief. [*TA 1988 s 406(1)–(4)*].

**11.15** Conversely a loss in the group holding the interest in the consortium can be surrendered via the link company to the consortium company, which can set the relief against its profits. [*TA 1988 s 406(5)–(8)*].

## Claims

**11.16** The form of group and consortium relief claims under CTSA is set out in *FA 1998 18 Schs 66–77*. [See Chapter 4].

**11.17** The problem with group relief and the interim payments regime of CTSA is not only estimating the corporation tax payable, but also the arrangements whereby some or all of the members of a group of companies arrange for one company to discharge the corporation tax liability on behalf of the others under a group accounting contract. [*TA 1998 s 36*]. This might include payments in relation to interest and penalties, and amounts treated as corporation tax under, for example, the controlled foreign company rules. Group for this purpose is a 51 per cent group. [*FA 1998 s 36(4)*]. [See Chapter 5]. It is also possible to surrender a tax

**11.18** *Groups and Consortia*

refund due to one company within a UK group as defined prior to 1 April 2000 (see 11.3) [*FA 1989 s 102*] which can sometimes be useful in mitigating interest charges within a group. [See Chapter 5].

**11.18** Group demergers under *TA 1988 ss 213–218* are not changed by self-assessment and are therefore outside the scope of this book. For group capital gains see 11.28 et seq.

## Simplified arrangements for group relief

**11.19** The *Corporation Tax (Simplified Arrangements for Group Relief) Regulations 1999 (SI 1999 No. 2975)* (see Appendix 3) provide for arrangements under which corporation tax group relief may be claimed or surrendered by an authorised company, acting on behalf of the companies in the group covered by the arrangement in relation to accounting periods ending on or after 1 July 1999, Inland Revenue Press Release, 2 November 1999 (Appendix 6). The regulations replace SP10/93, and introduce broadly similar arrangements in a statutory form, as is necessary under self-assessment.

**11.20** Various terms are defined, and *Regulation 4* provides that a company may be authorised by other companies in the same group to act on behalf of those companies in relation to the simplified arrangements. *Regulation 5* provides that an applicant company must be part of a group of companies or a consortium company, and is either the authorised company itself or an authorising company listed in the application made under *Regulation 6* and not challenged by the Revenue under *Regulation 7* within three months or is accepted under *Regulation 7(2)*, or is treated as a later addition to the application and duly accepted. The Revenue has power, under Regulation 7(3) or (4), to exclude certain companies from the arrangements if it has grounds to believe that the company in question has failed to comply with its obligations under the Taxes Acts in relation to any accounting period. Eligible companies can also be excluded from the arrangements by the authorised company.

**11.21** The application under *Regulation 6* is made by the authorised company on behalf of all the participant companies, in writing, and must specify the name and tax office reference of all the companies involved and details of the relationship within the group or consortium. The participating companies must agree to be bound by the arrangements and the application must be accompanied by a specimen copy of the written statement required by the Revenue containing the information necessary to deal with the group relief claims under *FA 1998 18 Sch Part VIII (paras 66–77)* except for the requirement for the consent of the surrendering companies, as appropriate, where claims are made or adjusted. In particular, the application must specify the quantified amount of the relief claimed up to the amounts available for surrender and the name of the surrendering company.

**11.22** The statement must be in a form approved by the Inland Revenue which presumably will follow the format of CT600C, Group and Consortium supplementary pages. Similar arrangements are required in connection with consortium companies.

**11.23** The application must be signed on behalf of the authorised company by a duly authorised officer of the company under *TMA 1970 s 108(1)*. This would normally be the company secretary or tax manager. It must be sent to the tax district dealing with the authorised company. Where there are changes in members of a consortium, a revised application is required under *Regulation 8*.

**11.24** The Revenue may refuse an application, under *Regulation 7(4)* on the grounds that one or more of the companies is not a participating company or has failed to comply with its corporation tax obligations, or substantially all of the companies in the group or consortium do not make their returns to the same tax office (which is obviously much more likely to apply in the case of a consortium rather than a group) or the specimen statement is inadequate.

**11.25** Under the arrangements, the authorised company can act on behalf of itself and all the participating companies in the group or consortium under *Regulation 10(1) and (2)*. The participating companies may claim and surrender group relief without the involvement but under the authority of the authorised company and without the requirement to have a formal claim and surrender, provided that all the other provisions in *FA 1998 18 Sch Part VIII* are complied with, in particular the requirement in *FA 1998 Sch 70(4)* that a claim for group relief made at the time of submission of form CT600 would need to be accompanied by a formal notice of consent to surrender. Where a nominated company has a period of account in excess of 12 months it is divided like a 12 month accounting period and a short accounting period on giving the appropriate undertaking (Appendix 8).

**11.26** The Revenue have confirmed that a CT600 without a group relief claim could be followed immediately by an amended return with a claim or matrix of claims under the Regulations without formal claims for surrender. This peculiar situation results from a change of mind in the structure of the Regulations which is inhibited by *FA 1998 18 Sch 70(4)*, which is amended by increasing the Regulation-making powers in *FA 1998 18 Sch 77* by *FA 2000 s 99* which will be followed by Corporation Tax (Simplified Arrangements for Group Relief) (Amendment) Regulations in due course, which should remove the problem.

**11.27** *Groups and Consortia*

**11.27** Either the Revenue or the authorised company may give notice terminating the arrangements, with effect from the date of the notice, under *Regulation 11*.

## Chargeable gains: intra-group transfers

**11.28** Transfers of assets within a group of companies are deemed to take place at such a price as gives no gain and no loss to the transferor company. [*TCGA 1992 s 171, Innocent v Whaddon Estates Ltd [1982] STC 115*]. A group for chargeable gains purposes consists of the principal company and all 75 per cent subsidiaries, measured according to ordinary share capital as defined by *TA 1988 ss 832* and *838(1)(b)*. In addition, each subsidiary must be, in effect, a 51 per cent subsidiary of the principal company, measured according to beneficial entitlement to profits and assets available on a winding up. Where a subsidiary does not qualify as a member of one group it may itself be the principal company of another group if it itself has subsidiaries. A company cannot be a member of more than one capital gains group. Prior to 1 April 2000 non-resident companies were excluded from the definition, and if a non-resident parent had a number of UK subsidiaries it was normally desirable to interpose a UK holding company which could result in a UK sub-group. [*TA 1988 s 170*]. The intra-group transfer provisions do not apply to transfers in satisfaction of a debt or redemption of shares, or where the transfer involves an investment trust company or a dual resident investment company. [*TA 1988 s 343(2)*]. Nor do they apply where the transfer is in exchange for shares by another group company, which should be treated as a reorganisation under *TCGA 1992 s 135*. A dual resident company may be treated as a non-resident company under *FA 1994 s 249*, where, under the tie-breaker clause in a treaty, it is regarded as non-resident for treaty purposes by reason of its management and control being outside the UK.

**11.29** From 1 April 2000 an intra-group transfer is tax neutral where a company disposes of an asset to another company, if both are resident in the UK, or if the asset is a chargeable asset, for example by being used by a UK branch, notwithstanding that one or both of the companies is non-resident. A chargeable asset is one which would give rise to a chargeable gain on disposal.

**11.30** Where the transferor company held the asset on 31 March 1982 the transferee company can benefit from rebasing on a subsequent disposal, under *TCGA 1992 s 35*. Prior to 1 April 2000 it used to be important to ensure that one company in the group was used to make disposals outside the group for assets showing a chargeable gain or allowable loss. Assets were transferred to such a company and resold, so that all losses and profits of a capital nature were made by the same company and could be offset. The Revenue did not, in normal circumstances, argue that such transactions were carried out purely for tax avoidance purposes under the doctrine in *WT Ramsay v IRC [1981] STC 174* or, in the case of land, were caught by *TA 1988 s 776* as an acquisition with the intention of realising a profit on resale.

**Deemed intra-group transfers**

**11.31** In respect of disposals outside the group on or after 1 April 2000 however, two members of a group may elect within two years of the end of the accounting period in which such a disposal takes place to compute the chargeable gains for corporation tax purposes as if the asset had been transferred intra-group on a no gain, no loss basis, without actually having to make a transfer. [*TCGA 1992 s 171A*]. This will be a considerable administrative advantage and could avoid stamp duty complications which may have resulted from actual intra-group transfers.

**11.32** *TCGA 1992 s 172* provided for a no gain, no loss transfer when a non-resident company incorporated a UK branch, but this relief is repealed as no longer necessary for disposals on or after 1 April 2000, because the transfer of a UK branch of a non-resident company to a UK company within the same group would be an intra-group transfer under the revised group definitions. [*FA 2000 29 Sch 3*].

**11.33** If a company acquires a capital asset as trading stock from a member of the world-wide group, it is deemed to have acquired it as a capital asset and appropriated it to trading stock within *TCGA 1992 s 161*. Where the company disposes of trading stock to a company that acquires it as a capital asset, it is treated as having appropriated the asset immediately before disposal for purposes other than trading stock, thus crystallising a trading disposal. From 1 April 2000 the trades covered are those carried on by a UK resident company, or UK branch of a non-resident company. [*TCGA 1992 s 173* as amended by *FA 2000 29 Sch 11*]. Where an asset is transferred around a group within these intra-group provisions and then disposed of, any capital allowances restriction under *TCGA 1992 s 41* applies as if capital allowances given to any company within the world-wide group, while in group ownership, had been given in respect of the assets sold by the vendor. Where the asset is eligible for capital allowances these provisions would normally eliminate any capital loss.

**11.34** Roll-over relief for capital gains is available to roll over or hold over a chargeable gain on the disposal of a business asset by any member of the world-wide group under *TCGA 1992 ss 152–160*, provided that the asset into which the gain is rolled remains within the UK tax net, in respect of disposals on or after 1 April 2000. [*TCGA 1992 s 175* as amended by *FA*

## 11.35 Groups and Consortia

*2000 29 Sch 10*]. All trades carried on by group members are treated as one trade for the purposes of this relief. [*TCGA 1992 s 175(1)*].

**11.35** A disposal of assets within a group at below market value may be a depreciatory transaction which could result in the value of the transferor company being reduced. If the shares are then sold, any loss arising on the disposal of the shares and attributable to the depreciatory transaction would be disallowed, under *TCGA 1992 s 176*. A depreciatory transaction does not give rise to a chargeable gain but merely restricts the allowability of the loss. Although non-payment for group losses or ACT surrendered could be a depreciatory transaction, the normal practice is not to seek an adjustment. [Inland Revenue Press Release, 3 February 1981]. A dividend paid from accumulated profits as an intra-group dividend could be treated as giving rise to a depreciatory transaction under *TCGA 1992 s 176*.

**11.36** The deemed disposal charge under *TCGA 1992 s 25* where a non-resident company transfers assets does not apply to intra-group transfers within *TCGA 1992 s 171* or where there is a reconstruction or amalgamation within *TCGA 1992 s 139*. [*FA 2000 29 Sch 6*]. Where a business is transferred within *TCGA 1992 s 139* as a result of a reconstruction or amalgamation, the transfer is regarded as tax free intra-group provided that, from 1 April 2000, the participant companies are part of a world-wide group and the asset transferred remains within the UK tax net.

**Pre-entry losses and gains**

**11.37** The restriction of set off of pre-entry losses, under *TCGA 1992 Sch 7A* is recast for accounting periods ending on or after 21 March 2000 by reference to the new definition of group for capital gains purposes, and it also applies where a non-resident company becomes resident, or transfers assets to bring them within the UK tax net. [*TCGA 1992 7A Sch as amended by FA 2000 29 Sch 7*]. The purpose of these provisions is to prevent the acquisition of companies with realised or latent capital losses by a group of companies to shelter chargeable gains elsewhere in the group, which was at one stage possible under *Shepherd v Lyntress Ltd [1989] STC 617*. The pre-entry loss disallowed is the appropriate portion of the loss accruing on the pre-entry asset which relates to the period before it came into the group, with special provisions for pooled assets to prevent them being treated as post-entry losses. [*TCGA 1992 7A Schs 3, 4*]. The taxpayer may elect to have the asset revalued to market value at the date it came into the group's tax net. Pre-entry losses are ring-fenced and may only be set against gains which accrue to the company on assets which it held before joining the group, with further anti-avoidance provisions where there is a major change in the nature or conduct of the trade or assets are appropriated to stock. [*TCGA 1992 7A Schs 6–12*].

**11.38** The converse of a company acquiring a company with losses to shelter group gains is for a group to acquire a company with latent gains against which it may set group losses. Such transactions are caught by *TCGA 1992 7AA Sch* and applies where a company becomes a member of the group in an accounting period in which it has realised chargeable gains, and applies to the world-wide group for assets within the UK tax net as a result of modification to *TCGA 1992 7AA Sch* by *FA 2000 29 Sch 8*. Pre-entry gains are ring-fenced and may only be reduced by qualifying losses which arose before the gain, or before it joined the group or which arose in respect of disposals of assets held when it joined the group or came into the UK tax net. [*TCGA 1992 7AA Schs 2–4*]. There are anti-avoidance rules relating to pooled assets, etc. [*TCGA 1992 7AA Schs 5–7*].

**Company leaving a group**

**11.39** Where a company which leaves a group holds assets which have been acquired from another group company within the previous six years, those assets are deemed to have been sold and immediately reacquired at their market value at the time of the original intra-group transfer, under *TCGA 1992 s 179*. A similar rule applies where the company holds an asset against which a gain has been rolled over under *TCGA 1992 ss 152–160*, in respect of the disposal of an asset which was previously acquired intra-group within the previous six years.

**11.40** Although the chargeable gain or loss on the deemed transfer is calculated by reference to the market value at the date of the intra-group transfer, the gain or loss is deemed to arise at the beginning of the accounting period in which, or at the end of which, the company leaves the group or, if later, when it actually acquired the asset. A company ceases to be a member of a group by ceasing to be a 75 per cent subsidiary, or an effective subsidiary under *TCGA 1992 s 170*, or the asset was within the UK tax net within the world-wide group, and ceases to be so as a result of the company leaving the group. [*TCGA 1992 s 179* as amended by *FA 2000 29 Sch 4*].

**11.41** There is an exception for a company leaving a group by reason of another member of the group ceasing to exist, for example on the final act of liquidation. If a merger is carried out for bona fide commercial reasons, without the avoidance of tax being a main object, the deemed disposal and reacquisition at market value may be avoided under *TCGA 1992 s 181*.

## 11.42  Groups and Consortia

**Recovery from group members**

**11.42**  Where a company has a chargeable gain and all or part of the corporation tax remains unpaid six months after it became payable, the Revenue may serve a notice on another company in the group or a controlling director of the company originally assessed, or another company in the group, where the company which made the disposal was resident in the UK when the gain arose, or it is taxable as a disposal by a UK trading branch of a non-resident company. The Revenue notice must be issued within three years of the final determination of liability and is treated as if it were an assessment for the purposes of interest, collection of tax and appeals. The person to whom the notice is issued has a right of recovery against the company liable. These provisions apply in respect of gains accruing after 1 April 2000. [*TCGA 1992 s 190*]. The earlier provisions in this section and *section 191* were replaced by *FA 2000 29 Sch 9*. In the unusual case where there is a capital distribution of a chargeable gain, the tax could be recovered from the shareholders under *TCGA 1992 s 189*. Distributions are usually taxable as income under *TA 1988 s 209*.

**11.43**  Although the new group definition under *TCGA 1992 s 170* introduced by *FA 2000 s 102* and *29 Sch* may result in a change in the constituents of a group for capital gains tax purposes, it is nonetheless treated as the same group, and an existing member of the group will continue to be treated as part of the new group as long as it remains a 51 per cent subsidiary of the principal company of the old group. [*FA 2000 29 Sch 46*].

*Chapter 12*

# Partnerships and Joint Ventures

## Introduction

**12.1** There are fundamental changes to partnership taxation generally under self-assessment. Under the previous rules partnerships were assessed to tax as a single unit and the partnership profits allocated among the partners in accordance with their profit sharing ratios in the year of assessment, not in accordance with the ratios in which they actually shared the profits in the accounting period forming the basis period for that assessment. Moreover the tax payable by the partnership was calculated as a joint and several liability of the partners. Under self-assessment each partner is responsible for his own taxation in connection with his share of the partnership profit and there is no joint liability, except for non-resident partners under *FA 1995 s 126(7)*.

## Corporate partners

**12.2** Where one of the partners in a partnership was a company, *TA 1988 ss 114* and *115* provided that the profits of the whole partnership were computed in accordance with corporation tax rules and the company's share of profits was subject to corporation tax in the accounting period, as if it were a separate Schedule D, Case I source of income. If the accounting period of the company differed from that of the partnership, the company's share of the partnership profits was apportioned on a time basis to the company's accounting period.

**12.3** Partners who were individuals in a corporate partnership were assessed on their share of the profits in the normal manner as though they carried on a separate trade district from the corporate partner(s). Capital allowances, balancing charges and charges on income were all computed separately on corporation tax lines and allocated as between the corporate and non-corporate partners. Capital allowances and balancing charges for individual partners were time apportioned to the tax years covered by the partnership's accounting period.

**12.4** Where a corporate partner is involved, under CTSA the provisions relating to partnerships in *TA 1988 ss 114* and *115* are amended by *FA 1994 s 215(2)* to apply to cases where the partnership is carrying on a

## 12.5 Partnerships and Joint Ventures

profession or business as well as a trade, but they continue to provide that in calculating the corporate partner's taxable profit it is necessary to compute the partnership results as if it were a corporation.

**Deemed company**

**12.5** Where there is a mixture of partners, therefore, it is necessary to compute the profits under corporation tax rules to arrive at the corporate partner's share and to recompute the same profits under income tax rules in order to arrive at the individual partners' shares, with separate partnership returns and partnership statements submitted for corporate and individual partners.

## Partnership and joint venture

**12.6** The existence or otherwise of a partnership is governed by the *Partnership Act 1890 s 1*, which defines a partnership as the relationship which subsists between persons carrying on business in common with a view to profits. The original version of *TA 1988 s 111* referred to a trade or profession carried on by two or more persons jointly, whereas the new version refers to a trade or profession carried on by persons in partnership. The original wording suggested that a joint venture, that is a business operation between two or more parties not constituting a full partnership, might be assessed for taxation purposes as a partnership. [*John Gardner and Bowring, Hardy & Co Ltd v IRC (1930) 15 TC 602*]. Whether or not a partnership exists for tax purposes is primarily a question of fact. [*IRC v Williamson (1928) 14 TC 335, Calder v Allanson (1935) 19 TC 293*]. The existence or otherwise of a partnership agreement is not itself conclusive. [*Hawker v Compton (1922) 8 TC 306, Dickinson v Gross (1927) 11 TC 614, Fenston v Johnstone (1940) 23 TC 29*]. A partnership agreement can confirm the existence of a partnership already in being, but cannot retrospectively create a partnership which did not exist at the time. [*Ayrshire Pullman Motor Services and Ritchie v IRC (1929) 14 TC 754, Waddington v O'Callaghan (1931) 16 TC 187, Taylor v Chalklin (1945) 26 TC 463*]. Although there is no age limit for partnership, minor children were not accepted as genuine partners in *Alexander Bulloch & Co v IRC [1976] STC 514*.

**Relevance of sharing profits and losses**

**12.7** Although an agreement to share profits implies a partnership [*Morden Rigg and R B Eskrigge & Co v Monks (1923) 8 TC 450; George Hall & Sons v Platt (1954) 35 TC 440; John Gardner and Bowring Hardy & Co Ltd v IRC (1930) 15 TC 602*)], it is not conclusive [*Pratt v Strick (1932) 17 TC 459*] and could merely indicate a joint venture. The sharing of losses however, is highly indicative of a partnership, although again not conclusive. [*Brown v Tapscott (1840) 6 M & W 119; Bond v Pittard*

*(1838) 3 M & W 357]*. The mere joint ownership of property is specifically excluded from being a partnership [*Partnership Act 1890 s 2(1)* as confirmed in *McKie v Luck (1925) 9 TC 511*], although where the property is used for a business the totality of the arrangement may amount to a partnership. [*Farrell v Sunderland Steamship Co Ltd (1903) 4 TC 605*]. This distinction is recognised in relation to a Schedule A business by Tax Bulletin Issue 20 p 271(Appendix 1).

**12.8** Salaried partners who do not have a proportional interest in the firm are normally assessed as employees under Schedule E or possibly as self-employed consultants under Schedule D, Case I or II, but not as partners although each case depends on the actual facts. [*Stekel v Ellice [1973] 1 All ER 465*]. A limited partner under the *Limited Partnerships Act 1907* is prohibited from taking part in the management of the firm by *LPA 1907 s 6*. However, a limited partner may well be, and indeed would normally be, a partner for tax purposes, although losses and charges could be restricted under *TA 1988 s 118*.

### Partners as notional sole traders

**12.9** Under the self-assessment rules a company which becomes a partner is treated as commencing a new trade or profession and its share of profits is taxed accordingly. Similarly, a corporate partner which leaves the firm is treated as ceasing to carry on that trade or profession.

### No separate taxable entity

**12.10** *TA 1988 s 111(1)* provides that a partnership is not treated for tax purposes as an entity separate and distinct from the partners who carry it on. This radical change means partnerships are not assessed in the partnership name under the new provisions; even where, as in Scotland, a partnership is a separate legal entity.

### Partnership as deemed company

**12.11** *TA 1988 s 114(1)* provides that where there is a corporate partner, a partnership is treated as a UK resident company for the purpose of computing the profits chargeable to corporation tax; so even though a partnership is not a separate entity for tax purposes, it is effectively treated as such for determining the amount of chargeable profits.

**12.12** However, *TA 1988 s 114(1)(a)* provides that the distribution provisions do not apply to the deemed company. Deductions or additions are made for charges on income, capital allowances and charges, or losses on prior trading expenditure. [*TA 1988 s 114(1)(b)*]. The corporate partner's share of the trading profit or loss is taken into its own accounts as a separate Schedule D source, and its share of charges, capital

### 12.13 Partnerships and Joint Ventures

allowances etc., excluded under *TA 1998 s 114(1)(b)*] above, are taken into account in its corporation tax computation for the corresponding accounting period. [*TA 1988 s 114(2)*].

**12.13** The corresponding accounting periods are the company's accounting periods which include the accounting period of the partnership, apportioned on a time basis. [*TA 1988 s 114(2)*]. For example, if the partnership accounting period is the calendar year and a corporate partner makes up its accounts to 31 March, it would take 3/12ths of the partnership results for 2000 into its accounts to 31 March 2000 and 9/12ths into its accounts to 31 March 2001.

**12.14** A change in corporate partners is treated as a transfer of a trade from the old deemed company to a new deemed company. [*TA 1988 s 114(1)(c)*]. If the old and new corporate partners were at least 75 per cent under the same ownership, the company reconstruction without change of ownership provisions in *TA 1988 s 343* may apply. Any change in the remaining parties is ignored in computing the corporate partner's profit share. [*TA 1988 s 114(1)*].

## Allocation of profits

**12.15** Substituted *TA 1988 s 111(3)* provides that each non-corporate partner is taxed as if he were carrying on a separate business, but the measure of profit is his share of the adjusted results of the partnership for the period. This means that usually the only difference between the accounting profit on which the partner's drawings are based and the taxable profit, is that arising from the normal adjustments for tax purposes; i.e. disallowing depreciation, entertaining etc., and allowing capital allowances and other statutory deductions. Where a partnership carrying on a profession changes its accounting basis to a true and fair accruals basis under *FA 1998 ss 42* and *44*, the transitional relief in *FA 1998 6 Sch 3* and *6* is calculated at partnership level and allocated among the partners in accordance with their profit-sharing ratio in the 12 month period to the first day of the new basis and subsequent anniversaries thereof. The relief is calculated separately as if the partnership were a company, if there are corporate partners. [*FA 1998 6 Sch 6(1)(b)*].

**12.16** This means that retiring partners cease to be liable for any of the adjustment instalments due after their retirement and that incoming partners are liable for their share for periods after they become partners. On cessation of the partnership any remaining instalments remain the personal liability of the partners in accordance with their profit-sharing ratio for the period from the anniversary of the first day to the date of cessation. Elections for accelerated payments must be made jointly by all partners in the relevant 12 month period to the election, or after cessation by the former partners individually. [*FA 1998, 6 Sch 6(3)9b, (4)(b)*; Revenue Press Release, 17 March 1998]. The spreading provisions do not apply to corporate partners, but the change in basis adjustments do. [*FA 1998 6 Sch (2) (2)*].

**Investment income**

**12.17** Each corporate partner's share of taxed investment income received by a partnership in any fiscal year is brought into self-assessment on the basis of the income arising in the partnership accounting period, apportioned on a time basis to each corporate partner's accounting periods. [*TA 1988 s 114*]. Each individual partner's share of taxed investment income received by a partnership in any fiscal year is brought into his individual self-assessment on the basis of the income arising in the fiscal year and apportioned to him under the partnership profit-sharing arrangements in force for the period in which the income actually arises, not by apportionment of the accounts in which the income is included over the fiscal years.

---

*Example 1*

---

A partnership with a 31 December year end receives a dividend payment of £1,000 on 1 September 2000, which would be shared amongst the partners in accordance with their profit sharing ratio for the accounts year in which the dividend payment falls. The income would therefore be taxed as income of the corporate partners, apportioned to their respective accounting periods, and as income of individual partners for the year ended 5 April 2001.

---

**12.18** Untaxed investment income is assessed by reference to the partnership accounting period, as applied for Schedule D, Case I or II purposes. The income remains assessable under Schedule A or Schedule D, Cases III, V or VI as appropriate, but is allocated to each partner, whether corporate or not, as if it were income arising from a second deemed trade, which is segregated from the actual trading income, and is deemed to continue so long as the partner remains in the partnership, or until the partnership ceases to have any untaxed investment income. This avoids any complications that would arise on the cessation of any particular source of income as a result, for example, of the sale of an investment property or closure of an overseas bank account. This treatment also brings into play, for individual but not corporate partners, the opening year, change of accounting date and cessation provisions applicable to trades which arise as a result of taxing the income by reference to the partnership accounting period ending in the current fiscal year, applying a strict fiscal year basis. [*TA 1988 s 111(7)(8)*].

**12.19** The post-cessation receipts provisions in *TA 1988 s 110(2)* are applied on the deemed cessation of a trade or deemed second trade and

**12.20** *Partnerships and Joint Ventures*

losses of the deemed second trade are calculated according to the partnership basis period as applied for the calculation of actual trading losses by *TA 1988 s 111(13)*. Overlap relief arising to individual partners from the deemed second trade as a result of a basis period exceeding twelve months under *TA 1988 s 62(2)(b)*, or on cessation under *TA 1988 s 63A*; may be set against total income under substituted *TA 1988 s 111(9)*. This applies to property income assessable under Schedule D, Case III income from overseas securities under Schedule D, Cases IV and V and even sundry income under Schedule D, Case VI but not to dividends under Schedule F and taxed income which are taxable on a fiscal year basis.

## Non-trading businesses

**12.20** If the partnership carries on a business, but not a trade, the same rules apply as if it were carrying on a trade. [*TA 1988 s 114(1)*]. This is presumably intended to cover income such as that from furnished holiday accommodation which is assessable under Schedule D, Case VI but under the rules of Schedule D, Case I, under *TA 1988 s 503*. It is understood that this does not presage any move by the Revenue to extend the meaning of trade, but to permit joint investment activities which are carried on as a business to be treated as a partnership for tax purposes (as indeed it may need to be for VAT purposes in order to obtain VAT registration where appropriate so that input tax can be recovered). It is unclear whether such a business has to use fiscal year accounting on the basis that the income is chargeable under Schedule D, Case VI, or whether as a partnership, it can have any accounting date ending in the year and prepare accounts and computations accordingly. [*TA 1988 s 111(10)(11)*]. The latter would be consistent with assimilating partnership businesses to trades, particularly where there are corporate partners.

## Joint investments

**12.21** The partnership provisions would not extend to mere investments which were jointly owned, where there was no business. [*McKee v Luck (1925) 9 TC 511*]. There is no statutory definition of a partnership for tax purposes and therefore the definition in the *Partnership Act 1890 s 1* of the 'relationship which subsists between persons carrying on business in common with a view to profits', applies. The meaning of business has been considered in the context of VAT and the relevant principles were summarised in the case of *Customs and Excise Comrs v Lord Fisher [1981] STC 238*. The following criteria were considered relevant in determining whether an activity constituted a business:

(a) whether the activity was a serious undertaking earnestly pursued;
(b) whether the activity was an occupation or function pursued with reasonable or recognisable continuity;

(c) whether the activity had a measure of substance;

(d) whether the activity was conducted in a regular manner and on sound and recognised business principles;

(e) whether the activity was predominantly concerned with making supplies for a consideration; and

(f) whether the supplies were of a kind commonly made by those who sought to profit by them.

## Overseas aspects

### Overseas income of a UK partnership

**12.22** Merely because a partnership has overseas activities does not mean that it has overseas income assessable as such under Schedule D, Case V, as the income may be assessable as part of the world-wide income of a UK based trade or profession taxable under Schedule D, Cases I or II. [*London Bank of Mexico v Apthorpe (1891) 3 TC 143* and *Davies v Braithwaite (1933) 18 TC 198*]. It really depends on where the control, the head and brain of the enterprise, is located. [*Ogilvie v Kitton (1908) 5 TC 338, Spiers v Mackinnon (1929) 14 TC 386, San Paulo (Brazilian) Rly Co Ltd v Carter (1895) 3 TC 344, Denver Hotel Co Ltd v Andrews (1895) 3 TC 356, Grove v Elliots and Parkinson (1896) 3 TC 481*]. Wherever there is no control of the trade from the UK, for example where a power of attorney is given to an overseas manager, or where the trade is under the control of non-resident partners, it would be regarded as overseas income assessable under Schedule D, Case V. [*Ferguson's Trustees v Donovan (1927) 1 ITC 214, Colquhoun v Brooks (1889) 2 TC 490*].

**12.23** Whether the income from the foreign activities of a UK partnership is assessed under Schedule D, Cases I or II as part of the world-wide income or under Schedule D, Case V as income from an overseas trade or profession, is not dependent on whether or not there is a taxable presence in the overseas country. There may well be a foreign tax liability as a result of there being an overseas branch or agency which may be chargeable to foreign tax either on the partnership or on the partners. This will depend on the overseas tax rules, and on the business profits and residence provisions of any double taxation agreement. If any foreign tax is payable by reference to the overseas profits, a credit should be available in the UK either as treaty relief under *TA 1988 s 788* or unilateral relief under *TA 1988 s 790*. The relief would be for the tax charged abroad on the partners or on the apportionment of the partnership liability where the partnership itself is assessed to foreign tax, which would be allocated through the partnership statement to the partners and claimed in their self-assessments, whether as individuals or companies.

## 12.24 Partnerships and Joint Ventures

**Foreign trades and professions**

**12.24** *TA 1988 s 65(3)* provides that the Schedule D, Case I and II rules apply to an overseas trade or profession assessed under Schedule D, Case V. In the partnership context however, the Schedule D, Case V income would be that of the partnership accounting period as income of a deemed second trade and allocated among the partners in accordance with the profit sharing ratio for the partnership accounting period.

**Income from let property overseas**

**12.25** In most cases the letting of foreign property by a UK partnership gives rise to income assessable under Schedule D, Case V. Nevertheless the accounts of the partnership would be prepared on the normal accounts basis in view of *FA 1998 s 42(1)* and *TA 1988 s 65(3)*.

**UK resident company in foreign partnership**

**12.26** A UK resident company may be a partner in a partnership controlled abroad, as defined by *TA 1988 s 112*, as a direct partner, as opposed to being entitled to the overseas income of a UK partnership as a result of its interest in a foreign branch, agency or partnership. The charging provisions are extended to corporate partners by *TA 1988 ss 112(5)* and *115(5)*. *TA 1988 s 112(4)* provides that any exemption from UK tax under a double taxation agreement is ignored in computing a UK resident partner's share of partnership profits, overruling *Padmore v IRC [1989] STC 493*.

**12.27** If the foreign partnership is in receipt of a qualifying distribution from a UK company, a UK resident company partner will qualify for its share of any tax credit which corresponds to its share of the distribution. [*TA 1988 s 112(5)*].

**Non-resident company in UK partnership**

**12.28** Where a non-resident company is a partner in a UK partnership, it is treated as if it had a share of the profits of a non-resident company carrying on a trade, profession or business through a branch or agency in the UK. [*TA 1988 s 115(4)*].

**Foreign partnerships with UK trade activities**

**12.29** The extent to which non-UK resident companies which are in a foreign partnership are liable to tax in the UK in relation to trading activities with a UK element is discussed in Chapter 15.

### UK investment income of non-resident partners

**12.30**  As the partnership is deemed to be a non-resident company under *TA 1988 s 114(1)* and *s 115(4)*, the deemed second trade rules apply to fix the basis period as the accounting period of the partnership as opposed to the fiscal year. The income is otherwise assessed as if each partner's share of that income were held by it as a non-resident company, subject to the comments set out below.

### Income from land in the UK

**12.31**  Tax is assessed under Schedule A on income from land in the UK as explained in Chapter 5. Under the self-assessment rules which came into operation on 6 April 1996, a non-resident may elect to self-assess in respect of Schedule A income rather than to suffer deduction of tax at source. *TMA 1970 s 42A* was inserted by *FA 1995 s 40* to set out the statutory framework. The flesh on the bones is provided by the *Taxation of Income from Land (Non-Residents) Regulations 1995* (*SI 1995 No. 2902*). See Chapter 15 for further details. Although the Schedule A provisions for non-residents are usually dealt with by the Financial Intermediaries and Claims Office (FICO), in the case of ancillary income of a foreign partnership trading in the UK, the partnership return and statement would be submitted to the normal district for where the partnership is based.

### UK representative

**12.32**  The partnership, as a deemed entity, is appointed a non-resident partner's UK representative under *FA 1995 s 126(5)(6)* for the assessment and collection of tax. Where there is a UK resident partner, the partnership is treated as the branch or agent of each non-resident partner in respect of his share of partnership profits. [*FA 1995 s 126(7)*]. This applies to the partnership's other income as well as to its trading profits under *TA 1988 s 111(8)* and has the effect of making any partners present or resident in the UK jointly liable for tax on the non-resident's share of partnership profits. This overcomes the difficulty of collecting tax from a non-resident partner under the general rule that a country cannot proceed against a resident of another country for the collection of tax. [*Government of India v Taylor (1955) 34 ATC 10*].

**12.33**  It also has the effect of retaining the previous joint and several liability of partners for the tax liabilities of non-resident partners, even though such liability will no longer apply under self-assessment for a UK resident partner in respect of the tax liability of other UK partners, as *TA 1988 ss 111* and *114* makes each partner liable for his or its own tax as if he were carrying on a notional sole trade. In the unusual case where the non-resident partnership trading in the UK was trading through a branch without any UK resident partners, the branch itself would be appointed the non-resident partners' UK representative.

## 12.34 Partnerships and Joint Ventures

**Chargeable gains**

**12.34** A non-resident is not normally liable for UK capital gains tax, as *TCGA 1992 s 2(1)* confines the charge to persons resident or ordinarily resident in the UK. However *TCGA 1992 s 10* brings into charge gains on assets used for the purposes of a trade, profession or vocation carried on in the UK, where the assets are situated in the UK, which means that broadly speaking, assets used in a UK partnership would be subject to capital gains tax on a non-resident and the appointment of the partnership as UK representative also applies for capital gains tax under *FA 1995 s 126(1)*. Payment of the tax would therefore be the responsibility of the UK partners. A UK resident but non-domiciled partner is liable to capital gains tax only in respect of gains on disposals of assets in the UK or on remittances of overseas gains, under *TCGA 1992 s 12*.

## Partnership changes

**12.35** Under the new rules, as each individual or corporate partner is taxed separately on his or its share of the partnership profits, and by reference to his or its joining and leaving the partnership, there is no requirement for the partnership itself to be deemed to cease on a change in partners, subject to any election for continuation. The partnership only remains relevant in the sense that there is a single partnership set of accounts and where there are both corporate and non-corporate partners, two computations and two partnership returns and statements allocating the profits to the partners, as if the firm were an individual and as if it were a company.

**12.36** A merger can give rise to a situation where one business ceases and the other business is simply enlarged. This gives rise to a cessation of one business and continuation of the other. Where the merger creates an entirely new business there is a cessation of both businesses and commencement of a new business. [*George Humphries & Co v Cook (1934) 19 TC 121*]. The third possibility is a continuation for tax purposes of both businesses. This may require the mixed basis period treatment where, for example, one part of the combined business is deemed to cease and the other to continue, or where one is on a preceding year and the other on a current year basis. As soon as practicable, the merged business will be assessed on a common basis.

**12.37** *TA 1988 s 116* is an anti-avoidance section aimed at preventing the exploitation of reliefs in a trading partnership where a limited company is one of the partners. It applies where the company partner's share in the profits or losses of the accounting period is enjoyed by other partners or the company receives any payment or other benefit other than a payment for group relief in respect of its share of the loss of the partnership. In such cases the company's share of any trading loss or charges on income is ring-fenced and can only be used against the company's share of the partnership profits. Therefore non-partnership trading losses and charges on income cannot be set against its share of the partnership profits. ACT and shadow ACT similarly cannot be set against the corporation tax liability on the company's share of partnership profits. Profits or gains charged under Schedule D, Case VI are treated for these purposes as if they were trading profits. For the purpose of these restrictions the company's share of profits is calculated after capital allowances have been deducted.

**12.38** Losses of limited partners are restricted in the case of individuals by *TA 1988 s 117* and in the case of companies by *TA 1988 s 118*. This applies not only to general partners but also to limited partners under the *Limited Partnership Act 1907* who are not entitled to take part in the management of the business and whose liabilities are capped and any excess borne by another party. It also applies to an overseas business where the partner is not entitled to take part in the management of the business and whose liability for debts is limited.

**12.39** Tax relief in respect of losses of limited partners within the definition is restricted to a limited partner's contribution to the partnership at the end of the tax year in which the loss arises. Only this limited amount of loss may be set against other income with any excess being ring-fenced and only available against partnership profits in future. A similar restriction applies to capital allowances and interest. Schedule A losses and company capital allowances and charges are similarly restricted.

# Loan relationships, foreign exchange and financial instruments

**12.40** SP4/98 (see Appendix 4) explains the application of the loan relationships, foreign exchange and financial instruments legislation to partnerships which include companies. *TA 1988 s 114* treats a partnership in which there is a corporate partner as if it were a separate company. For the purpose of the financial instruments legislation, *FA 1994 s 172* distinguishes between a qualifying company and a company other than an authorised unit trust or open-ended investment company. Where a partnership includes both a qualifying company and a non-qualifying company it is treated as two separate companies for the financial instruments legislation, under *FA 1994 s 172(4)*.

**Foreign exchange legislation**

**12.41** *FA 1993 s 153* recognises qualifying and non-qualifying companies for the foreign exchange legislation and as for financial instruments, where both are members of a partnership they are treated as two separate companies for corporation tax purposes. [SP4/98 para 8].

## 12.42 Partnerships and Joint Ventures

**12.42** Under the loan relationship provisions, authorised unit trusts and open-ended investment companies are treated as if they were subject to income tax rules by *FA 1996 10 Sch 8, 2(2)*. Also the *Open-Ended Investment Companies (Tax) Regulations 1997 (SI 1997 No. 1154)* provide that where such entities are corporate partners in a partnership they will not be treated as companies to whom credits and debits under the loan relationship legislation can be attributed. [SP4/98 para 9]. Where a partnership contains qualifying companies, the foreign exchange gains and losses, financial instruments and loan relationships legislation applies to the partnership as if it were a company under *TA 1988 s 114*. [SP4/98 para 10].

**12.43** Where the partnership contains an investment trust, an open-ended investment company or authorised unit trust, a separate computation has to be prepared under corporation tax rules, ignoring the foreign exchange and financial instrument legislation, except where an investment trust is a party to interest rate or debt contracts. In the case of an authorised unit trust or an open-ended investment company, only the income tax provisions relating to discounted securities legislation in *FA 1996 13 Sch* applies so far as loan relationships are concerned. [SP4/98 para 11].

**12.44** The intra-group loan relationship rules do not apply to a corporate partner. A change in partner profit-sharing ratios does not of itself give rise to a related transaction in a loan relationship. [SP4/98 para 13]. Each corporate partner will be assessed and charged to corporation tax on its share of any trading profit or losses, including loan relationship, foreign exchange and financial instrument trading profits and losses as if its share were profits of a separate trade carried on by it alone. [SP4/98 para 17]. However, non-trading loan relationship profits or non-trading deficits of the partnership are added to the corporate partner's own income or deficits and do not form a separate pot. [SP4/98 paras 18 and 19].

**12.45** The Statement of Practice also deals with the interaction with capital gains tax of non-corporate partners, and others not subject to corporation tax, and confirms that a partnership is not treated as a company for the purposes of the accounting methods for connected parties in *FA 1996 s 87(3)* and is neither a participator nor an associate of a participator within *TA 1988 s 417*. [SP4/98 paras 21–26].

**12.46** Yearly interest paid by a partnership with a corporate partner should be paid under deduction of tax under *TA 1988 s 349(2)(b)* unless it is paid to a bank etc. under *TA 1988 s 349(3)*. [SP4/98 para 27].

**12.47** A partnership involving a qualifying company may make a local currency election for Forex purposes [SP4/98 para 29], and may defer unrealised exchange gains under *FA 1993 ss 30–32* but the *Exchange Gains and Losses (Deferral of Gains and Losses) Regulations 1994.* (SI

1994 No. 3228) do not apply to partnerships involving companies. [SP4/98 para 32]. Such a partnership can, however, take advantage of the matching rules under the *Exchange Gains and Losses (Alternative Method of Calculation of Gain or Loss) Regulations 1994 (SI 1994 No. 3227)*. [SP4/98 paras 33 and 40]. The anti-avoidance rules relating to loan relationships in *FA 1996 ss 80–105*, foreign exchange in *FA 1993 ss 135–138*, and financial instruments in *FA 1994 ss 165–168* will apply to a partnership with a corporate partner as if it were a qualifying company, and also to the individual members of such a partnership. [SP4/98 para 41].

Chapter 13

# Controlled Foreign Companies

## Introduction

**13.1** In a system in which companies have considerable freedom where and when to earn their profits there is scope for manipulating and diverting profits so that they fall to be taxed by countries with lower tax rates than the UK. *FA 1984* introduced the Controlled Foreign Companies ('CFC') legislation in order to reduce the opportunities for tax planning of this sort. There are a number of exemptions from the provisions relating both to the foreign entities concerned and the jurisdictions covered, so that in practice the effect is largely confined to major UK-based multinationals.

**13.2** Under the old rules a liability only arose if the Revenue made a direction imposing a tax charge on shareholders in the CFC. There was no obligation on UK shareholder companies to notify the Revenue of potential chargeability, or indeed to report details of interests held, within their own returns. The fundamental change under CTSA has been to dispense with the role of the Board in making a formal direction, leaving any liability to be self-assessed. No substantial alteration in the charge itself was intended. The changes are implemented in *FA 1998* and the *Controlled Foreign Companies (Excluded Countries) Regulations 1998 (SI 1998 No. 3081)* (see Appendix 3). Various anti-avoidance amendments discussed below are contained in *FA 2000*.

**13.3** The regime described below is that which applies for accounting periods ending after 1 July 1999, although some of the old provisions may still be relevant because of mismatches between the accounting periods of the CFCs and the UK companies affected. The substantive law is covered in more detail in Tolley's Corporation Tax at Chapter 18. The Revenue's own 'Controlled Foreign Companies Self Assessment Guidance Notes' also cover the subject comprehensively.

## Outline of charge and exemptions

**13.4** A company is a CFC if it:
(a) is resident outside the UK (see 13.8–13.11);
(b) is controlled by persons resident in the UK (see 13.14–13.16); and

(c) pays tax in the territory in which it is resident, equivalent to less than 75 per cent of the tax it would pay in the UK (see 13.17–13.18 below). [*TA 1988 s 747(1)*].

The 'chargeable profits' and 'creditable tax' of a CFC (see 13.26–13.29 below) are apportioned among all persons (whether UK resident or not) with an interest in the company at the relevant time. Companies (but not individuals) to whom profits are thus apportioned are subject to a charge.

**13.5** There are several exemptions, namely where:

(a) the UK company's interest in the CFC is less than 25 per cent (see 13.34) [*TA 1988 s 747(5)*]; or

(b) the CFC pursues an acceptable distribution policy ('ADP') (see 13.35–13.37) [*TA 1988 s 748(1)(a)*]; or

(c) the CFC is engaged in exempt activities (see 13.38–13.39) [*TA 1988 s 748(1)(b)*]; or

(d) the CFC is a publicly quoted company (see 13.41–13.42) [*TA 1988 s 748(1)(c)*]; or

(e) the chargeable profits (from which capital gains are excluded by *TA 1988 s 747(6)(b)*) of the CFC do not exceed £50,000 (see 13.43) [*TA 1988 748(1)(d)*]; or

(f) the CFC is resident in a country which the Board has specified as excluded from the operation of the CFC provisions (and, if the exclusion is conditional, the CFC satisfies the conditions) (see 13.44–13.46) [*TA 1988 s 748(1)(e); Controlled Foreign Companies (Excluded Countries) Regulations 1998 (SI 1998 No. 3081)*]; or

(g) avoidance of UK tax was not one of the main reasons for operating the CFC ('the motive exemption') (see 13.47). [*TA 1988 s 748(3)*].

**13.6** As explained in 13.2, the crucial aspect is that charges under the CFC provisions are now subject to self-assessment (see 13.48 and following).

## Determining whether a company is a CFC

### What is a company?

**13.7** There is no definition of 'company' peculiar to the CFC provisions, so the normal definition in *TA 1988 s 832(1)* and *(2)* applies: a company is any body corporate or an unincorporated association, but not a partnership. Some foreign entities, such as the German silent partnership, do not fit easily within this definition, but the Revenue's International Division should provide guidance if required.

## 13.8 Controlled Foreign Companies

**Residence**

**13.8** The residence criteria for the purposes of establishing whether a company is a CFC are found at *TA 1988 s 749*. They are not the same as those applied when establishing whether a CFC is exempt because it satisfies the *Excluded Country Regulations* (found in the *1998 Regulations reg 2(2)*; see 13.44–13.46).

**13.9** If a company is not UK resident, it is regarded as resident in the territory in which it is liable to tax by reason of domicile, residence or place of management. [*TA 1988 s 749(1)*]. Companies are not UK resident for this purpose if they are resident in the UK and also in another country under a double taxation relief treaty. [*FA 1994 s 249*]. 'Territory' includes jurisdictions such as the Channel Islands with a separate taxation system but without full independence; it does not include individual states of a federal state (such as the USA). 'Tax' means a tax similar to UK income or corporation tax, not a flat rate levy (such as Council Tax) or a turnover tax (such as VAT).

**13.10** If a company is not resident in *any* jurisdiction under this test, it is conclusively presumed to be resident in a territory with a lower rate of taxation [*TA 1988 s 749(5)*]; it will be a CFC if controlled by UK resident persons.

**13.11** If a company is resident in two or more jurisdictions under the test, there are a number of tie-breakers, applied successively, to decide in which of the eligible territories it will be treated as resident for the purposes of the CFC provisions. These are, in order of application:

(a) if an election or designation (see below) has been made in relation to an accounting period, it continues to apply for subsequent accounting periods until the territories which are eligible change [*TA 1988 ss 749(2)(b), (4), 749A(1), (2)*];

(b) if throughout the accounting period the company's place of effective management has been in just one of the eligible territories, the company is resident in that territory [*TA 1988 s 749(3)(a)*];

(c) if the company's place of management is in two or more territories, then (choosing between territories in which the company is managed) it is resident in that territory in which the greater amount of its assets are present (assessed by reference to the market value of assets actually in the eligible territories) at the end of the accounting period [*TA 1988 s 749(3)(b), (6)*];

(d) failing this, the company is resident in whichever of all the eligible territories the greater amount of assets (assessed as above) are situated in at the end of the accounting period [*TA 1988 s 749(3)(c), (6)*];

(e) failing this, such person or persons as together have a majority assessable interest in the company may specify a country of residence by election within twelve months of the end of the CFC's accounting period [*TA 1988 s 749(3)(d), s 749A(3)*];

(f) if no election is made within time, the Revenue may justly and reasonably designate a territory of residence from among the eligible territories [*TA 1988 s 749(5)*].

**13.12** For the purposes of the election mentioned in 13.11(e) above, one or more person or persons together have a 'majority assessable interest' if they all have assessable interests and it is likely that, if an apportionment were to be made under *TA 1988 s 747(3)* (see 13.30–13.33) at least 50 per cent of the chargeable profits would be attributed to them. The election itself is made by giving notice to a Revenue officer within twelve months of the end of the accounting period of the company. It must state what proportion of chargeable profits (and creditable tax) would be likely to be apportioned to each member of the majority and be signed by each of them. An election once made is irrevocable. [*TA 1988 s 749A(3)*].

**13.13** If the Board makes a designation (13.11(f)) it must notify every UK resident company which appears to have an interest in the CFC at any time during the accounting period, specifying the date on which the designation was made, the CFC concerned, the accounting period concerned, and the territory designated. The designation is irrevocable. [*TA 1988 s 749A(5), (6), (7)*].

**Control by UK residents**

**13.14** Before *FA 2000* the test for control was simply the test in *TA 1988 s 416(2)* applicable for close companies, with appropriate modifications (i.e. replacement of references to 'five or fewer participators' by references to 'persons resident in the United Kingdom'). [*TA 1988 s 756(3)*]. A non-UK resident company was controlled by UK residents (including companies, individuals and trusts) if those residents together exercised or were able to acquire direct or indirect control over the company's affairs. This test was based on actual control, so the persons controlling the CFC might not be those with assessable interests in the company.

**13.15** *FA 2000 31 Sch 4* introduces a new control test for CFC purposes. Under new *section 755D* a person controls a company if he or she is able to ensure that the affairs of the company are conducted in accordance with his or her wishes by means of:

(a) holding shares or possessing voting power in the company concerned (or any other company); or

(b) powers conferred by that or any company's articles of association or similar.

There are also provisions for the attribution of various rights and powers

## 13.16 Controlled Foreign Companies

to persons potentially in control of the company. The attributed powers include:

(1) those that a person is entitled to acquire (or will become entitled to acquire);

(2) those of another person which have, or may have, to be exercised on behalf of, under the direction of or for the benefit of the potential controlling person; and

(3) those of connected UK resident persons.

**13.16** The test is also extended to include the case where two persons together control the company and only one of those persons is UK resident provided that they each satisfy a new '40 per cent' test (based on that applied for transfer pricing purposes (see 14.14 below). That test is satisfied by each of two persons if each has at least 40 per cent of the shareholdings, voting rights or other powers by virtue of which they control the company. There is an important exemption, however, if the non-resident person holds more that 55 per cent of those shareholdings, rights and powers. [*TA 1988 ss 747, 755D* amended and inserted by *FA 2000 31 Sch 2, 4*].

**Lower level of taxation**

**13.17** A company regarded as resident in a particular territory other than the UK is subject to a lower level of taxation for an accounting period if the tax paid in the territory of residence in respect of profits (excluding capital profits) ('local tax') is less than 75 per cent of the 'corresponding UK tax' on those profits. [*TA 1988 s 750(1)*].

**13.18** The corresponding UK tax is the UK corporation tax that would have been payable if:

(a) the 'chargeable profits' were calculated on the basis of certain assumptions set out in *TA 1988 Sch 24* (see 13.27);

(b) UK double taxation relief in respect of local tax were ignored;

(c) deductions from UK corporation tax were allowed for:

  (i) any amounts to be set off under *TA 1988 s 7(2)* (sums received under deduction of income tax); and

  (ii) any corporation tax actually paid on the chargeable profits [*TA 1988 s 750(2),(3)*];

(d) tax paid in third countries were relieved against UK tax and local tax as determined by the appropriate treaty arrangements.

*Example 1*

Blackwater plc is a UK tax resident multinational. It owns all the shares in Candida Corp which is resident in Mongoland. Candida has chargeable profits of £100,000 in its year to 31 March (year 1) and pays Mongoland tax on those profits of £20,000 (the local tax). Corresponding UK tax would have been (at 30 per cent) £30,000. Thus Candida is subject to a lower level of taxation and is a CFC.

In year 2, Candida opens a branch in the UK, and earns £50,000 through that branch. Its local tax becomes £30,000, but it also pays £15,000 UK corporation tax. The computation of its corresponding UK tax is now:

|      | £150,000 at 30%      | £45,000 |
|------|----------------------|---------|
| less | Corporation tax      | £15,000 |
|      | Corresponding UK tax | £30,000 |

The local tax is now more than 75 per cent of the corresponding UK tax, so the company is no longer subject to a lower level of taxation.

Through a locally resident nominee, Blackwater also owns all the shares in Verdi Inc, resident in the Cabaho islands. Verdi has chargeable profits of £50,000 in its year to 31 March (year 1) but earns all these profits through a branch in Mongoland. It is liable to normal Mongoland tax of £10,000 and a non-resident surcharge of £2,500. The computation of its corresponding UK tax is:

|      | £50,000 at 30%       | £15,000 |
|------|----------------------|---------|
| less | Mongoland tax        | £12,500 |
|      | Corresponding UK tax | £ 2,500 |

Since the comparison is made not with the non-UK tax paid but with the tax paid in the country of residence (none in this case), Verdi is subject to a lower level of taxation. In year 2, Verdi earns its £50,000 profits in the Cabaho islands instead and is subject to Cabaho islands tax at 25 per cent, amounting again to £12,500. Its corresponding UK tax is now £15,000 (being 30 per cent of £50,000 without any deductions) and it is no longer subject to a lower level of taxation.

## 'Designer rate' tax provisions

**13.19** *FA 2000 31 Sch 3* introduces an anti-avoidance clause (announced in October 1999, see *STI [1999] 1641*) to counter the use of 'designer rate' tax provisions, i.e. arrangements under which companies can choose to pay just enough tax to pass the 75 per cent test. New *section 750A TA 1988* sets aside the 75 per cent test where a non-UK resident company pays at least 75 per cent of the corresponding UK tax but does

### 13.20 Controlled Foreign Companies

so under 'designer rate tax provisions'. Such provisions are those 'which appear to the Board to be designed to enable companies to exercise significant control over the amount of tax which they pay' and which are specified in regulations. No regulations have yet been made, but according to the Press Release of 6 October 1999, the first provisions covered will be:

(a) Guernsey – bodies with international tax status;

(b) Jersey – international business companies;

(c) Isle of Man – international companies;

(d) Gibraltar – income tax qualifying companies;

(e) Ireland – companies taxed in accordance with the *Irish Taxes Consolidation Act 1997 s 448(7)*.

## Calculation of the CFC charge

### Outline

**13.20** To determine the amount charged on a company with an interest in a non-exempt CFC, one needs to ascertain for the accounting period concerned:

(a) the persons interested;

(b) the chargeable profits of the CFC; and

(c) the creditable tax of the CFC.

A just and reasonable apportionment of the chargeable profits and the creditable tax is then made among all persons interested. All companies (but not individuals) are then charged a sum equivalent to corporation tax on the chargeable profits apportioned to them.

### The accounting period

**13.21** The accounting period of a CFC begins whenever:

(a) the CFC comes under control of UK residents;

(b) the CFC commences business; or

(c) an accounting period of the CFC ends without the CFC ceasing to carry on business and/or have any source of income. [*TA 1988 s 751(1)*].

**13.22** The accounting period of a CFC ends if and when:

(a) the CFC ceases to be under the control of UK residents;

(b) the CFC becomes, or ceases to be, liable to tax in a territory (i.e. there is a change in the group of eligible territories);

(c) the company ceases to have any source of income whatsoever. [*TA 1988 s 751(2)*].

In addition, the CFC is governed by the normal corporation tax rules for determining accounting periods (but omitting references to the company's being or becoming within or without the charge to corporation tax). In particular this means that any CFC's accounting period will end twelve months after it began. [*TA 1988 s 751(3)* applying *s 12(3), (5), (7)*].

**13.23** If the Board considers that the beginning or end of an accounting period is uncertain, it may specify by notice such accounting period as seems appropriate, and may amend that notice if further facts come to light to suggest that another period is the true accounting period for the CFC. [*TA 1988 s 751(4), (5)*].

**Persons interested**

**13.24** The following persons are interested in a CFC:

(a) any person possessing or entitled to acquire share capital or voting rights in the company;

(b) any person possessing or entitled to acquire a right to receive or participate in distributions by the company;

(c) any person entitled to ensure that income or assets of the company are applied, directly or indirectly, for his benefit;

(d) any other person who, whether alone or together with others has control of the company, control having the *TA 1988 s 416* meaning described above (13.14). [*TA 1988 s 749B(1)*].

A loan creditor *per se* is not interested in the company. [*TA 1988 s 749B(2)*].

**13.25** In establishing interests in companies for these purposes, one looks through intermediaries, so that a person having an interest in a company with an interest in a CFC is treated as having an interest in the CFC. [*TA 1988 s 749B(5), (6), (7)*]. Persons jointly entitled to any interest are treated as entitled to that interest in equal shares, unless entitled in a fiduciary or representative capacity. [*TA 1988 s 749B(8)*].

**Chargeable profits**

**13.26** The chargeable profits of a CFC for an accounting period are those profits which would have been charged to corporation tax, on the assumptions set out in *TA 1988 24 Sch*. Profits in this context do not include chargeable gains. [*TA 1988 s 747(6)*]. Chargeable profits are computed and expressed in the currency used by the CFC for the accounting period concerned.

**13.27 Controlled Foreign Companies**

**13.27** The assumptions to be made are:

(a) that calculations of chargeable profits have been made for previous periods on the basis of the same assumptions [*TA 1988 24 Sch 2(2)*];

(b) that the CFC is UK resident [*TA 1988 24 Sch 2(1)*];

(c) that the CFC is not a close company [*TA 1988 24 Sch 3*];

(d) that the CFC has made such claims and elections as would have been necessary to give the maximum amount of relief, subject to the right of one or more UK companies together having a majority interest to give notice cancelling such claims or elections (see Chapter 4) [*TA 1988 24 Sch 4*];

(e) that the CFC is not a member of any group or consortium [*TA 1988 24 Sch 5*];

(f) that the conditions for a group income election under *TA 1988 s 247* were not fulfilled by the CFC [*TA 1988 24 Sch 6*];

(g) that no ACT was surrendered to the CFC [*TA 1988 24 Sch 7*];

(h) that the CFC is not the 'successor' to the trade of any other company within *TA 1988 s 343* (except in so far as the CFC is trading in the UK through a branch or agency) [*TA 1988 24 Sch 8*];

(i) where losses have been incurred at some time in the six years before an apportionment falls to be made, any one or more companies together having a majority interest may make a claim for the chargeable profits to be calculated as if they had also been calculated for earlier periods, so that losses may be carried forward [*TA 1988 24 Sch 9*];

(j) capital allowances (i.e. writing down allowances and balancing charges) are given or charged as if the plant or machinery was first used for the purposes of the trade in the first accounting period for which an apportionment has to be made [*TA 1988 24 Sch 10*];

(k) relief for unremittable overseas income covers income that cannot be remitted to the territory of residence as well as the UK, and notice that such relief is required is to be given by any one or more companies together having a majority interest [*TA 1988 24 Sch 12*];

(l) exchange gains and losses are computed by reference to the currency in which the accounts of the CFC are drawn up [*TA 1988 24 Sch 14–19*];

(m) transfer pricing adjustments under *TA 1988 28AA Sch* are to be made to the profits of both the CFC and an interested UK company where there has been a transfer between such companies, but not, subject to certain conditions, to the profits of two CFCs when there has been a transfer between them [*TA 1988 24 Sch 20*].

## Controlled Foreign Companies 13.31

**13.28** Where a notice has to be given by a 'majority interest', this means one or more companies to which would be apportioned more than half of those profits which are apportioned to UK companies and thereby give rise to a liability. [*TA 1988 24 Sch 4(2), (3)*]

**Creditable tax**

**13.29** The 'creditable tax' in a CFC's accounting period is the aggregate of:

(a) the amount of any double taxation treaty relief attributable to any income that is part of the 'chargeable profits' of the CFC;

(b) any amount that would (on the *TA 1988 24 Sch* assumptions) have been paid to the CFC subject to deduction of income tax and set off under *TA 1988 s 7(2)*; and

(c) the amount of any income or corporation tax actually paid in respect of the chargeable profits of the accounting period (less any tax that falls to be repaid, or would fall to be repaid on the making of a claim or otherwise). [*TA 1988 s 751(6)*].

**Apportionment**

**13.30** The chargeable profits and creditable tax are apportioned between persons with 'relevant interests' in the CFC. A UK resident company with a direct interest in a CFC has a relevant interest by virtue of that interest. A UK resident company with an indirect interest in a CFC has a relevant interest by virtue of that interest unless that indirect interest is derived from an interest in another UK resident company (the 'water's edge' principle by which only one UK resident company is to be charged under the provisions). A related person (i.e. someone who is not a UK resident company but is connected or associated with a UK resident company with a relevant interest) who has a direct or indirect interest in the CFC has a relevant interest except:

(a) if it has the interest by virtue of a direct or indirect interest in a UK resident company or another related person; and

(b) to the extent that a UK resident company has the same interest indirectly, by virtue of having directly or indirectly an interest in the relevant person, and thereby has a relevant interest in the CFC.

**13.31** A person with a direct interest in a CFC who does not have a relevant interest under the rules above nonetheless has a relevant interest except to the extent that another person has a relevant interest by

## 13.32 Controlled Foreign Companies

virtue of having the same interest indirectly under those rules. [*TA 1988 s 752A*].

**13.32** The chargeable profits and creditable tax will be apportioned between interested companies in direct proportion to the percentage of the issued ordinary share capital of the CFC that their relevant interest represents where:

(a) all the persons with relevant interests in the CFC at any time during its accounting period have those interests by virtue only of direct or indirect holdings of ordinary shares in the CFC;

(b) each of those persons is either UK resident throughout the accounting period or not UK resident at any time during the period; and

(c) no company with an intermediate interest in the CFC at any time has that interest otherwise than by virtue of directly or indirectly holding ordinary shares in the CFC.

Otherwise the apportionment will be on a 'just and reasonable basis' between persons with relevant interests in the CFC at any time during the accounting period. [*TA 1988 s 752(2), (3), (4)*].

**13.33** The percentage of the issued share capital which a relevant interest represents is determined under *TA 1988 s 752B*. Broadly, it is determined as follows:

(a) if the shares are held directly, it is simply the shareholding expressed as a percentage of issued shares;

(b) if shares are held indirectly (i.e. through a chain of companies), the percentage is the product of the interests held in the companies in the chain, so if A owns 90 per cent of B and B owns 90 per cent of C, A's relevant interest in C represents 81 per cent;

(c) if a person has several indirect shareholdings, the percentages are calculated for each as in (b) above and aggregated;

(d) if the size of a person's holding varies over the accounting period, an average is taken over that period.

---

*Example 2*

---

Another part of the Blackwater group is structured as follows:

## Controlled Foreign Companies 13.33

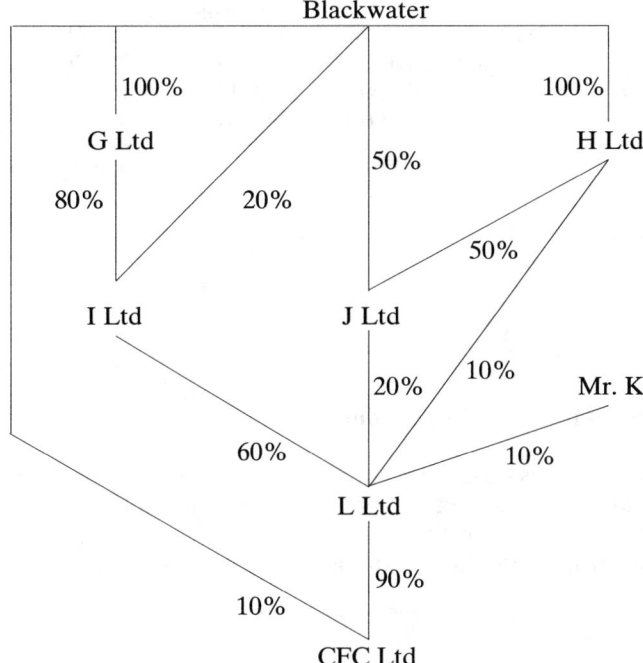

G Ltd, H Ltd and Blackwater itself are UK resident; the other companies, as well as Mr. K, are not.

Blackwater's relevant interest is the aggregate of its direct shareholding in the CFC and its indirect holdings via J Ltd and I Ltd. It does not have a relevant interest by virtue of its holdings in the other UK resident companies. The measure of this interest is 10% plus 9% (50% × 20% × 90%) plus 10.8% (20% × 60% × 90%) equals 29.8%.

G Ltd has a relevant interest by virtue of its shareholding in I Ltd. This interest is 43.2% (80% × 60% × 90%).

H Ltd has a relevant interest through its shareholdings in J Ltd and L Ltd. This interest is 18% ((50% × 20% × 90%) + (10% × 90%)).

I Ltd and J Ltd do not have relevant interests because their interests are held indirectly by UK resident companies.

L Ltd has an interest to the extent that its share capital is held by Mr. K. This interest is 9% (10% × 90%).

In year 1, CFC earns chargeable profits of £500,000 and pays £60,000 tax in its country of residence. The appropriate rate of tax is 30%. The apportionment is as follows:

**13.34** *Controlled Foreign Companies*

|  | Interest | Profits £ | Tax at Appropriate Tax rate | Creditable £ | Charge £ |
|---|---|---|---|---|---|
| Blackwater | 29.8% | 149,000 | 44,700 | 17,880 | 26,820 |
| G | 43.2% | 216,000 | 64,800 | 25,920 | 38,880 |
| H | 18% | 90,000 | 27,000 | 10,800 | 16,200 |
| L | 9% | 45,000 | 13,500 | 5,400 | 8,100 |
|  | 100% | 500,000 |  | 60,000 |  |

NB. But see *Example 3* below for exemptions.

## Exemptions

### Interest of less than 25 per cent

**13.34** There is no charge unless a UK resident company, together with associated or connected persons, is apportioned at least 25 per cent of the CFC's chargeable profits. 'Associated or connected persons' have the normal corporation tax meanings. [*TA 1988 s 416(1), s 839*].

*Example 3*

There would be no charge on H Ltd or L Ltd in *Example 2* above because their relevant interests are less than 25 per cent.

### Acceptable distribution policy

**13.35** No apportionment will be made and no charge arises if a CFC pursues an acceptable distribution policy ('ADP'). [*TA 1988 s 748(1)(a)*].

**13.36** A CFC pursues an ADP in respect of any accounting period for which dividends paid during and within 18 months of the end of the period, other than out of specified profits, total not less than 90 per cent of the CFC's 'net chargeable profits.' Broadly, net chargeable profits for a period are chargeable profits less any creditable profits which would arise were an apportionment to be made. Paying a dividend out of specified profits means paying it out of profits representing dividends received from other CFCs; these specified profits and the dividends paid are left out of account in making the comparison (see further Tolley's Corporation Tax 18.12) [*TA 1988 25 Sch Pt I*]. To close a loophole which previously existed, dividends will no longer be counted to the extent that they are paid out of UK dividends. [*FA 1999 s 88*].

**13.37** For cases where it is has not become clear whether an ADP is being pursued by the time an interested UK company has to make a return, see 13.49 and following.

**Exempt activities**

**13.38** The chargeable profits of a CFC are not apportioned if that CFC is, throughout the accounting period, engaged in exempt activities as defined in *TA 1988 25 Sch Pt II*. [*TA 1988 s 748(1)(b)*]. The purpose of the exempt activities test is to grant relief to companies genuinely set up to trade in their territory of residence and not merely to provide a token offshore residence for trading or services companies (including group service companies). However, the structure of the exemption is quite complicated.

**13.39** In order to be engaged in exempt activities the CFC must fulfil three conditions:

(a) it must have a 'business establishment' in the territory in which it is resident, meaning premises occupied and used with a reasonable degree of permanence from which the company's business in the territory is wholly or mainly carried on (such as an office, shop, factory, mine, oil or gas well, quarry, or building site for a project with a minimum twelve month duration) [*TA 1988 25 Sch Pt II 6(1)(a), 7*];

(b) it must manage its business affairs in the territory from the business establishment (as well as carrying on its business), and in order to do so it must have sufficient staff in the territory to deal with the work in the territory and not provide services for people outside the territory by performance in the UK [*TA 1988 25 Sch Pt II 6(1)(b), 8*];

(c) it must either be a holding company (of a certain sort: (see further *TA 1988 25 Sch Pt II 6(3)–(4A), 12*) or avoid the following:

   (i) having an investment business (including holding or dealing in securities or other property rights, see *TA 1988 25 Sch Pt II 9*);

   (ii) dealing in goods for delivery to or from the UK or connected or associated persons (unless goods are actually delivered to the territory of residence, see *TA 1988 25 Sch Pt II 10*);

   (iii) being mainly engaged in a wholesale, distributive, financial or service business in which more than half the gross trading receipts are derived directly or indirectly from a specified class of persons. The specified class consists of (a) connected or associated persons, (b) persons with a 25 per cent assessable interest in the company in the accounting period in question (see 13.24–13.25 for calculation of assessable interests), or (c) persons connected or associated with any persons

**13.40** *Controlled Foreign Companies*

satisfying the 40 per cent test in relation to the company (see 13.16 for the 40 per cent test). Special provisions apply for banking and insurance businesses. (See further *TA 1988 25 Sch Pt II 11*). [*TA 1988 25 Sch Pt II 6(2)* as amended by *FA 2000 3 Sch 5*].

**13.40** *FA 2000 31 Sch 6, 7* amend the requirements to be satisfied by holding companies.

### Public quotation

**13.41** No apportionment is made of the profits of a publicly quoted CFC. [*TA 1988 s 748(1)(c)*]. A CFC is publicly quoted if:

(a) shares carrying 35 per cent of the voting rights have been allotted unconditionally to, or acquired unconditionally by, and are held by, the public (i.e. anyone except 'principal members' of the CFC, or persons connected or associated with it);

(b) such shares are listed and dealt with on a recognised stock exchange in the territory of residence; and

(c) the principal members do not own 85 per cent of the voting power. [*TA 1988 25 Sch Pt III 13, 14*].

**13.42** The principal members are persons possessing a minimum 5 per cent holding each, but limited to the five persons with the largest holdings. If two or more people have the same size holding so that the five largest holdings cannot be identified, there may be more than five principal members. Thus, if A, B, C, D, E and F had holdings of 20 per cent, 15 per cent, 10 per cent, 5 per cent, 5 per cent, and 5 per cent respectively, they would all be principal members. [*TA 1988 25 Sch Pt III 15*].

### Profits de minimis

**13.43** The chargeable profits (defined above) of a CFC are regarded as de minimis, and no apportionment is made in respect of them if they are below £50,000 for an accounting period (or an appropriate proportion of £50,000 if the accounting period is less than twelve months). [*TA 1988 s 748(1)(d)*].

### Excluded Countries List

**13.44** A CFC is exempt if it is resident in one of the countries on the now statutory Excluded Countries List (an ECL country) and not more than the greater of £50,000 or 10 per cent of its commercially quantified net income is 'non-local source income' meaning a **gross** amount, broadly, the aggregate of:

(a) gross income from distributions of companies resident in other territories (except branch or agency income);

(b) gross income and gains received from loans to non-residents (except branch or agency income);

(c) gross income and gains received in respect of royalties payable by non-residents (except branch or agency income);

(d) gross income and gains received from premiums and rent payable in respect of property situated outside the territory of residence (except branch or agency income);

(e) income received from a branch in another ECL country net of tax paid in that other country;

(f) net income from non-resident agencies;

(g) gross income not treated by the laws of the territory of resident as arising in the territory (or, if there are no such laws, that would not be treated as arising in the territory if UK law applied).

**13.45** For calculating the non-local source income of a banking or insurance business, income under heads (a)–(e) is ignored if (i) it would form part of the income of a trade for UK corporation tax purposes (if the company were UK resident) and (ii) it is actually taxable in the territory if resident. [*TA 1988 s 748(1)(e); Controlled Foreign Companies (Excluded Countries) Regulations 1998 (SI 1998 No. 3081)*].

**13.46** The Excluded Countries List (see Appendix 3) has two groups. CFCs resident in countries in Group I are unconditionally exempt; CFCs resident in countries in Group II are exempt provided they do not benefit from certain designated tax breaks. The list has most recently been amended with effect for CFC accounting periods beginning on or after 9 July 1998 by the *Controlled Foreign Companies (Excluded Countries) Regulations 1998 (SI 1998 No. 3081)*.

**Motive Exemption**

**13.47** The motive test has two limbs, each of which must be satisfied:

(a) in so far as any transactions reflected in the profits of the period achieved a 'reduction in UK tax' (as defined in *TA 1988 25 Sch pt IV*) either the reduction was minimal or that reduction was not a main purpose of the CFC (or a person interested in the CFC) in carrying out the transactions; and

(b) the CFC was not set up to achieve a 'reduction in UK tax' by a 'diversion of profits' from the UK (also defined in *TA 1988 25 Sch pt IV*). [*TA 1988 s 748(3)*].

### 13.48 Controlled Foreign Companies

## CTSA provisions

### Compulsory self-assessment of CFC charge

**13.48** For accounting periods of UK resident companies ending on or after 1 July 1999 the CFC charge applies automatically where the conditions are met. The sum charged under s 747(4)(a) is due and payable in the same way as any other amount of corporation tax. [TA 1988 s 754(1)]. This is a fundamental change from the previous requirement that the Board issue a direction before a charge on a UK company was considered.

### The return

**13.49** Companies must include in supplementary pages to their returns information about any relevant interests in CFCs *unless*:

(a) the CFC satisfies the *Excluded Countries Regulations* (see 13.44–13.46); or

(b) the relevant interest, taken together with the relevant interests of any connected or associated persons, is less than 25 per cent (see 13.34).

**13.50** A company may also include information about its interests in companies which may or may not be relevant interests in CFCs. This might be because, for example, it is not clear whether the CFC is subject to a lower level of taxation, or because the CFC is an open-ended investment company and it is not clear whether it is controlled in the UK at any given time.

**13.51** The supplementary pages (form CT600B and see Chapter 2) require the following information:

(a) name of CFC and territory of residence (as determined under s 749, and specifying any elections that apply and when made: see 13.11 and following); and

(b) either:

  (i) the exemption that applies (together with any clearance obtained and when); or

  (ii) the information required to work out the charge (i.e. the measure of apportionment, the CFC's chargeable profits, tax on those profits and creditable tax, and any reliefs and any ACT available) and the s 747 charge itself.

**13.52** Companies need only indicate a single exemption, and need not apply the tests in any particular order. Thus if the motive exemption applies, there is no need for the UK resident company to go on to calculate the CFC's chargeable profits. Moreover, the fact that only one exemption is specified on a return and later shown not to apply does not bar the UK resident company from later relying on one of the other exemptions.

**13.53** The return itself must include a self-assessment of the amount of UK tax payable as a result of interests in CFCs. Such a charge is included in the return for the UK company's accounting period in which the CFCs' accounting period ends.

**Clearances**

**13.54** The Revenue is operating a comprehensive procedure for providing clearances in relation to CFCs. The objective is to answer enquiries within 28 days of receipt of all relevant information. Once obtained a clearance will normally apply as long as the underlying facts and legislation remain unchanged. Reasons will be given where a clearance is refused. Applications should be made to:

Inland Revenue (CFC Clearances)
International Division
Room 311, Melbourne House
Aldwych
London WC2B 4LL

**13.55** Any UK holder of a relevant interest may apply for a clearance on any aspect of the CFC legislation that is relevant to a given case. Because one question may affect several interest holders, the application may be made by one person on behalf of others.

**13.56** The Revenue has published (in the Draft Guidance notes) a list of the information it requires before considering an application:
(a) In respect of all applications:
  (i) name of CFC;
  (ii) UK company's interest in the CFC's share and loan capital;
  (iii) tax District and reference number of UK interest holders where known;
  (iv) territory or residence and details of branches including those in the UK;
  (v) place and, for new companies, date of incorporation;
  (vi) a copy of the most recent accounts.
(b) Additionally, in respect of applications under the exempt activities and motive tests:
  (i) actual or expected equity at beginning and end of accounting period;
  (ii) full description of business including all transactions with associates;

**13.56** *Controlled Foreign Companies*

- (iii) where there is more than one business, what is considered the main business and why;
- (iv) details of investments held and actual or projected income from these during the accounting period for which the clearance is sought;
- (v) details of projected tax payable for the accounting period for which the clearance is sought and how computed.

(c) Specifically, for the exempt activities test:
- (i) full details (including address) of business establishment, number of hours, days etc. occupied on company business, whether shared with other businesses, and rent etc. paid;
- (ii) full details of staff employed, place of employment and duties and salaries of each. Details of management companies employed and amounts paid. Details of services provided by the company for persons resident outside the territory or residence and where performed. Details of persons engaged wholly or mainly in the business of the company whose remuneration is paid by a person connected with and resident in the same territory as the CFC;
- (iii) reasons why it is considered the company satisfies the exempt activities test.

(d) Specifically, for the exempt activities test where the CFC is a holding company:
- (i) whether the CFC falls within the definition of a holding company or superior holding company at *para 12(1)* to *(6)* and *para 12A* of *25 Sch*;
- (ii) whether the CFC falls within the definition of a local holding company at *para 6(3)* of *25 Sch*;
- (iii) whether the CFC derives at least 90 per cent of its income directly or indirectly from controlled local holding companies or companies engaged in exempt activities. [*(Paras 6(4)* and *(4A)* of *25 Sch)*].

(e) In addition to the information at (a) above, applications under the motive test should contain:
- (i) details of any direct or indirect transactions between the United Kingdom and the CFC, including interest on loans (direct or indirect), royalties, payments for services, purchases or sales or goods etc.;
- (ii) the effect on UK tax (including the effect on losses or repayments) if such transactions had not taken place;
- (iii) the reasons for the transactions;
- (iv) the reasons, if any, why the business of the CFC could not be

carried on by a UK resident (which includes the overseas branch of a UK company, a non-UK incorporated company with its central management or control in the UK and a UK incorporated company);

(v) the tax effect, if any, if that business could have been carried on in the United Kingdom;

(vi) the reasons for the company's existence in the accounting period;

**Intention to pursue an ADP**

**13.57** Since an ADP may be followed even where distributions are not made until 18 months after the end of the accounting period, it may be that an interested UK resident company has to make a return before it is clear whether the exemption will apply or not. If the company considers it 'likely' that the CFC will make appropriate distributions, it may make its return on the basis that it will do so; otherwise, it must make its return on the basis that it will not. If in either case that initial judgement proves wrong, the UK company must amend its return within 30 days of the end of the period of establishing whether an ADP has been pursued, namely within 18 months of the end of the CFC's accounting period or such longer period as the Board may allow (and failure to amend in circumstances where tax became payable renders the UK company to a penalty not exceeding the amount of tax understated). If it has not been established by the time that such a policy has been pursued, it is assumed that the CFC's chargeable profits are not exempt on this basis. [*TA 1988 s 754A*].

**Enquiries**

**13.58** After a company has completed the CFC supplement to its self-assessment, the Revenue may make enquiries on the normal basis (see Chapter 17). However, special rules apply before a closure notice can be issued, or a discovery assessment made, in respect of the *s 747* charge. It is only the Board (and not an Inspector) that can authorise the conclusion that the amount payable under *s 747* should be amended, unless there is an agreement with the taxpayer in force covering the disputed figures. Any notice of closure or discovery assessment involving a determination that requires the Board's sanction and has not received it (or fails to record that it has received it) is treated as if that determination had not been taken into account. This requirement is intended to ensure that all companies are assessed on the same basis. [*TA 1988 s 754B*].

**Records**

**13.59** Under the general scheme of CTSA a company is required to keep certain records for the purposes of enabling it to make a complete

**13.60** Controlled Foreign Companies

and correct return, and the provisions apply to the CFC supplement as much as to any other aspect of the return (see Chapter 16). The Revenue may also require the company to produce such documents as are in its possession or power and to provide such information as it may reasonably require for the purposes of an enquiry, and the company may appeal against such a request in the normal way. The Revenue has indicated that it expects the records of any CFC (particularly if within the same group) to be within the power or possession of a UK company with a relevant interest. There is a right of appeal (see Chapter 19).

**13.60** The Revenue should not ask for more than the minimum information necessary to confirm what is said in a company's return regarding a CFC. If an exemption is claimed, only that exemption need be justified, by production of the CFC's records and possibly the UK company's records (particularly in relation to the motive test). The Inspector might reasonably require the accounts of the CFC to confirm the level of chargeable profits and records showing how the figures are derived. Although when a clearance application is made the information required is more comprehensive, the areas covered will be broadly the same (see 13.56).

**Penalties**

**13.61** The Revenue may also impose the usual tax-geared penalties under *18 Sch 20* where a company fraudulently or negligently submits an incorrect return or fails to remedy an error within a reasonable time of discovery. In particular, a penalty is imposed where a return was made on the basis that an ADP would be pursued and the return is not amended when such a policy is not actually pursued (see 13.57 above).

**Appeals**

**13.62** Any appeal against amendments or discovery determinations which involve questions about the application of the CFC provisions, including questions as to whether the basis of apportionment is 'just and reasonable,' are to be heard by the Special Commissioners. If the determination in relation to the CFC is likely to affect the tax liability of a person other than the appellant taxpayer, that person is entitled to appear before and be heard by the Special Commissioners, or make written representations. In such a case, the Commissioners determine the CFC question separately from the rest of the appeal, and that determination is treated as the determination of an appeal to which all the persons affected were party, including any person who chooses not to make any representations. [*TA 1988 s 754(3), (3A), (3B)*].

## Reliefs

**13.63** Where a company is liable in respect of CFC chargeable income apportioned to it, it may make a claim for a sum equal to the corporation tax on the following amounts to be set off against it:
(a) trading losses (under *TA 1988 s 392A(1), s 393A(1)*);
(b) charges on income (under *TA 1988 s 338(1)*);
(c) management expenses (under *TA 1988 s 75(1)*);
(d) excess capital allowances;
(e) any amounts available as group relief; and
(f) any non-trading deficit on loan relationships. [*TA 1988 s 754(5), 26 Sch (1)*].

**13.64** A company may also make a claim for surplus ACT to be set off against its liability in respect of apportioned CFC chargeable profits although this set off is capped at the amount of ACT for which the company would have had to account had it made a distribution such that the amount of the distribution plus the amount of ACT is equal to the amount of apportioned chargeable profits less any amounts set off under a claim under 13.63 above. [*TA 1988 s 754(5), 26 Sch (2)*].

**13.65** For the purposes of double taxation relief, the total liability of UK companies in respect of the chargeable profits of CFCs apportioned to them, is treated as underlying tax where the CFC pays a dividend in respect of the profits from which the gross profits are derived (see Chapter 15 for double taxation treaty relief). [*TA 1988 s 754(5), 26 Sch (4)*].

**13.66** Relief is also available where, after a CFC's profits have been apportioned, a UK company thereby liable to a *TA 1988 s 747(4)(a)* charge, disposes of its interest in the CFC (i.e. either shares in the CFC or shares that gave it an indirect interest). If the UK company makes a claim, its chargeable gain on the disposal of the interest is reduced by the 'appropriate fraction' of the liability. The appropriate fraction is the ratio between the average market value (in the relevant period) of the interest disposed of and the average market value (in the relevant period) of the interest in the CFC by virtue of holding which, the UK resident company became liable to the charge. The relief is reduced where the CFC pays a divided before the disposal which either reduces the value of the shares dividend of or gives rise to a claim for relief as discussed in 13.63 above. [*TA 1988 s 754(5), 26 Sch (3)*].

## Special recovery provisions

**13.67** Where the same interest in a CFC is held directly by one UK resident person and indirectly by another, income will first be apportioned to the direct holder (as indicated in 13.30 above). However, if the charge resulting from that apportionment is not paid by the date it becomes due and payable, the Board may serve a notice of liability on a company that holds the interest indirectly. The tax and interest both before and after the date when the amount first became payable is payable by the company served with the notice. If the charge is not paid within three months of the notice, the money may be recovered in the usual way from any of the companies involved (in proportion to their direct or indirect interests). [*TA 1988 s 754A(6)–(8)*].

**Transitional provisions**

**13.68** There are transitional provisions covering the case where, of the UK companies interested in a CFC, some have accounting periods covered by CTSA (and therefore the new CFC rules) and some do not. Broadly, two sets of determinations and computations are made, one on the assumption that all the companies are covered by the new rules and one on the assumption that they are covered by the old rules (for which see Tolley's Corporation Tax 1998–99 ch 18). [*FA 1998 17 Sch 37*].

## Miscellaneous

**Interaction with TA 1988 s 739**

**13.69** Where *TA 1988 s 739* would otherwise deem an amount of the income of a CFC that forms part of chargeable profits to be income of a UK resident, the amount of deemed income is reduced proportionately with the amount of chargeable profits apportioned to UK resident companies. Thus if a CFC has income of £100 as a result of a transfer of assets abroad, and chargeable profits of £200, of which £100 is apportioned to a UK company, only £50 of the CFC's income may be treated as that of the transferor under *s 739 TA 1988*. [*TA 1988 s 747(4)(b)*].

**Insurance companies**

**13.70** Where chargeable profits of a CFC are apportioned to a company carrying on a life assurance business as a result of shares held in the company's long term business fund, they are assessed to tax, broadly, as if they were a dividend paid to the company. [*TA 1988 s 755A*]. There are also provisions for extending the various periods and making regulations concerning the operation of the CFC provisions in the case of an insurance company with an interest in a CFC which does not make up its accounts on an annual basis. [*TA 1988 s 755B, s 755C*].

Chapter 14

# Transfer Pricing

## Introduction

**14.1** Multinational companies can often choose where their profits are recognised. One way of doing this, the use of corporate vehicles based in low tax jurisdictions, is countered by the CFC provisions discussed in the previous chapter. Another method is to arrange transactions between group members in ways other than those that would apply between independent parties.

**14.2** This is a subject of international concern and was covered by the Organisation for Economic Cooperation and Development (OECD) in its *Model Tax Convention on Income and on Capital* ('the OECD Model') which forms the basis for many bilateral tax treaties. After consultation, the OECD also published its *Transfer Pricing Guidelines for Multinational Enterprises and Tax Administrations* ('the OECD Guidelines') in 1995, the aim of which was to provide a framework for fair transfer pricing legislation that would prevent loss of revenue to the countries concerned and double taxation of the taxpayers. Broadly, the intention is for profits to be taxed where earned.

**14.3** The UK first introduced transfer pricing provisions in *FA 1951* which remained essentially unchanged for nearly 50 years, being contained in *TA 1988 s 770*. New provisions, which were introduced by *FA 1998*, were intended to bring the UK treatment into line with the OECD model and to cover the transition to CTSA. The Revenue have subsequently published guidance on how the new regime will operate. [See Tax Bulletins 37 and 38, Appendix 1].

**14.4** Under *s 770* the old provisions did not apply unless the Revenue made a direction on a company. The crucial change under CTSA is that where a company has been involved in non-arm's length transactions which have reduced its profits chargeable to tax, it will be required to self-assess its tax liability on the basis of arm's length pricing. To reduce the potential for disputes and give companies some certainty, a system of advance pricing agreements with the Revenue is introduced.

## 14.5 Transfer Pricing

### Outline of charge: basic rule

**14.5** The new provisions are contained in *TA 1988 28AA Sch* (inserted by *FA 1998 s 108 and 16 Sch*). Although they have been drafted in accordance with UK drafting conventions, they are to be construed in such a way as best ensures consistency with the OECD Model and Guidelines. [*TA 1988 28AA Sch 2*].

**14.6** The Schedule starts with the 'basic rule on transfer pricing.' It applies where 'provision' ('the actual provision') has been made or imposed between any two persons ('the affected persons') by means of a transaction or series of transactions, and at the time of the making or imposing of the actual provision either:

(a) one of the affected persons was directly or indirectly participating in the management, control or capital of the other; or

(b) the same person or persons was or were directly or indirectly participating in the management, control or capital of each of the affected persons. [*TA 1988 28AA Sch 1*].

**14.7** If in these circumstances (subject to certain exceptions), the actual provision differs from the provision ('the arm's length provision') which would have been made or imposed between independent enterprises (including the case where no such provision would have been made) and confers a potential 'advantage in relation to United Kingdom taxation' on one or both of them (whether or not the same advantage), the profits and losses of the potentially advantaged affected person (or of each of them) are computed for tax purposes as if the arm's length provision (or no provision) had been made or imposed instead of the actual provision. [*TA 1988 28AA Sch 1 (2), (3)*].

**Meanings of terms used in the basic rule**

*Provision*

**14.8** 'Provision' is not defined in the Schedule. The word was intended by Parliament to mean 'what the transaction provides' (see the Paymaster General in Hansard Standing Committee E, 9 June 1998, col 676), or in other words 'the sum of all the terms and conditions attaching to [the] transaction or series of transactions' (para 5.4 of the Revenue Consultative Document on the Reform of the Transfer Pricing Legislation 10/10/97). The OECD Model refers to 'conditions.'

**14.9** The arm's length provision, accordingly, does not mean merely the price that would have been paid, but can be different from the actual provision in a number of ways. It may be that the actual provision involves a lump sum payment for an intellectual property right, for example, whereas the arm's length provision would have been a licensing

*Transfer Pricing* **14.12**

agreement over many years. How one is to establish the arm's length provision is discussed below.

*Transaction or series of transactions*

**14.10** 'Transaction' includes arrangements, understandings and mutual practices whether or not intended to be legally enforceable and a 'series' of transactions includes a number of transactions each entered into (whether or not one after another) in pursuance of, or in relation to, the same arrangement (meaning scheme or arrangement of any kind whether or not intended to be legally enforceable). A series of transactions is not prevented from being a series of transactions by means of which provision has been made or imposed between two people merely because (i) there is no transaction to which both persons are parties; (ii) the parties to any arrangement in pursuance of which the transactions in the series are entered into do not include one or both of those persons; or (iii) there is one or more transactions in the series to which neither affected person is party. [*TA 1988 28AA Sch 3*].

*Participation in the management, control or capital of a person*

**14.11** A person is *directly participating* in the management, control or capital of another person at a particular time if, and only if, that other person is at that time a body corporate or partnership controlled by the first person. The test for control in this section is the narrow test in *TA 1988 s 840*:

(a) a person controls a body corporate if he has power to secure that the affairs of the body corporate are conducted in accordance with his wishes either by means of the holding of shares or the possession of voting power in or in relation to that or any other body corporate, or by virtue of any powers conferred by the articles of association or other document regulating that or any other body corporate, and

(b) a person controls a partnership if he has a right to a share of more than one-half of the assets, or of more than one-half of the income, of the partnership.

**14.12** A person ('the potential participant') is *indirectly participating* in the management, control or capital of another person at a particular time if and only if at that time either (i) he would be taken to be directly participating if certain rights and powers were attributed to him (see below); or (ii) if he is one of a number of 'major participants' in the other person's enterprise. The rights and powers to be attributed are:

(a) those which the potential participant is entitled to acquire at a future date or which he will, at a future date, become entitled to acquire;

**14.13** *Transfer Pricing*

(b) those of others which are required or may be required to be exercised on behalf of the potential participant, under his direction or for his benefit;

(c) those of any person with whom the potential participant is connected (see below); and

(d) those which would be attributed to a person with whom the potential participant is connected if that connected person were himself the potential participant.

**14.13** References to the rights and powers of a person other than the potential participator include such rights and powers as that person is entitled to acquire at a future date or will, at a future date, become entitled to acquire. References to the rights and powers of any person include rights or powers which are (or will be, once acquired) exercisable only jointly with one or more other persons. Two persons are connected with each other if:

(a) one of them is an individual and the other is his spouse, or a relative (meaning brother, sister, ancestor or lineal descendant) of his or his spouse, or the spouse of such a relative; or

(b) one of them is the trustee of a settlement and the other is a settlor of that settlement or a person connected with a settlor. [*TA 1988 28AA Sch 4*].

**14.14** A person (a 'potential major participant') is a major participant in another person's enterprise at any given time if (i) that other person is a body corporate or partnership; and (ii) the potential major participant is one of two people who between them control (as above) the body corporate and each of whom has interests, rights and holdings representing at least 40 per cent of the interests, rights and holdings that give that control. This is the '40 per cent test' and in considering whether a potential major participant is an actual major participant, the same rights and powers are attributed to him as when considering whether a person is otherwise indirectly participating in a body corporate or partnership.

*Advantage in relation to UK taxation*

**14.15** Having an 'advantage in relation to UK taxation' depends on profits and losses as computed for tax purposes rather than the amount of tax actually paid (in line with the OECD Model). Thus, the actual provision is taken to confer a potential advantage on a person in relation to UK taxation wherever (in the absence of the transfer pricing provisions themselves) the effect of making or imposing the actual provision instead of the arm's length provision, would be either that a smaller amount would be taken for tax purposes to be that person's chargeable profits for any chargeable period, or that a larger amount would be taken for tax purposes to be losses of that person for any chargeable period (including the conversion of profits into losses), or both. The comparison is to be made between the tax position in which the actual parties were following the actual provision and that in which the same actual parties would have been following the arm's length provision. [*TA 1988 28AA Sch 5*].

**14.16** 'Losses' does not cover only straightforward losses but also:

(a) excess management expenses under *TA 1988 s 75(3)*;

(b) allowances for interest distributions of a unit trust under *TA 1988 s 468L(5)*;

(c) loss relief and group relief under *TA 1988 Pt X*; and

(d) deficits on loan relationships under *FA 1996 s 83, 8 Sch* and *1 Sch 4*. [*TA 1988 28AA Sch 14*].

**14.17** Where the same parties are involved in several transactions they may be evaluated together to decide whether a UK tax advantage results. However, this is only true where the transactions form part of the same provision, and does not apply where, for example, three associates are involved in routing a loan through the UK. In that case, for the purposes of the Schedule, two provisions are involved and the question whether a tax advantage arises must be answered separately in relation to each. Thus there may still be a 'tax advantage' where the margin on such a loan is reasonable (i.e. consistent with the arm's length provision), but the interest rate applied each time is excessive. Normally this will not matter, since the middle party's profits will be adjusted upwards in light of one transaction and back down again in light of the other, but if there is intervention (see below) in relation to one transaction and not the other, it is the taxpayer who bears the cost not the exchequer. [See Tax Bulletin 37, Appendix 1].

**14.18** Gains and losses resulting from foreign exchange movements within *FA 1993 ss 125–170* and the various financial instruments covered by *FA 1994 ss 147–177*, continue to be assessed according to those provisions and are not taken into account when considering the question of a person's tax advantage. [*TA 1988 28AA Sch 8*; see Tax Bulletin Issue 37, Appendix 1].

## Establishing the arm's length provision

**14.19** Both the Schedule and the OECD Model and Guidelines require the arm's length price to be established. In some cases this may be easy to ascertain, for example where a company sells to independent enterprises for £1 and to associated companies for 10p. The Guidelines discuss two different types of methods for establishing the arm's length provision in more complex cases, 'traditional methods' and 'transactional profit methods'. None of these methods is sure to result in a transfer price with which every expert would agree.

### 14.20 Transfer Pricing

**Traditional methods**

**14.20** The three traditional methods are the comparable uncontrolled price method (the CUP method), the resale price method and the cost plus method. All of these methods rely on there being information available with which to make comparisons.

**14.21** The *CUP method* simply compares the price charged for property or services transferred in a controlled transaction to the price charged in a comparable uncontrolled transaction in comparable circumstances. Transactions are comparable if either none of the differences (between the products, the market conditions, the contracting parties) could materially affect the open market price or if reasonably accurate adjustments can be made to eliminate the material effects of such differences. Where comparable transactions are available, the CUP method is direct and reliable, and, in such circumstances, it is the OECD's preferred method. [*OECD Guidelines 2.6–2.13*].

**14.22** The *resale price method* (also called the *resale minus method*) begins with the price at which the product purchased otherwise than at arm's length is resold to an independent party. This price is then reduced by an appropriate gross margin representing the amount out of which the reseller would seek to cover its expenses and make an appropriate profit. The amount so reduced is treated as the arm's length price for the original transfer. This method also requires the availability of transactions for comparison. Where the method is used for marketing operations, for which the OECD recommends it, it is more important that the functions performed by the reseller (e.g. packaging, distributing, giving warranties and so on) and the rights he has (e.g. an exclusive licence) are comparable than the products concerned. [*OECD Guidelines 2.14–2.31*].

**14.23** The *cost plus method* starts from the costs incurred by the supplier of the property or services in a controlled transaction for the property transferred (or the services provided) in a transaction otherwise than at arm's length. One then adds an amount appropriate to allow a level of profit commensurate with the functions performed and market conditions. The total is the arm's length price. Ideally the comparison should be made using the mark-up earned by the same supplier in comparable uncontrolled transactions. The OECD recommends this method for semi-finished goods sold between related parties, for related parties with joint facility arrangements or long-term buy-and-supply arrangements, and for the provision of services. [*OECD Guidelines 2.32–2.48*].

**Transactional profit methods**

**14.24** Where insufficient information is available for the traditional methods to be used reliably, it may be necessary to use a method based on the expected profit on an arm's length transaction rather than the expected price. The two transactional profit methods considered by the OECD are the Profit Split method and the Transactional Net Margin method.

**14.25** The *profit split method* first identifies the profits realised from transactions in which associated parties are engaged together and then divides them along the lines two independent enterprises would have chosen had they entered a partnership together in similar circumstances. The profits thus divided might be the total profits or the residual profits after some of the profits have been accounted for using one of the traditional methods outlined above. Again an analysis of the functions performed by each party is central and the profit split should be compared with that achieved by independent enterprises carrying out comparable functions (for example by agreeing for each party to make the same return on capital invested). One advantage of this method, however, is that it does not rely so heavily on comparisons. It is also unlikely to lead to extreme results, since the positions of each party are considered at the same time. On the other hand, for these reasons and because independent enterprises simply do not tend to use partnerships to determine their transfer pricing, the method is harder than the traditional methods, to apply accurately. The method might be appropriate for long-term relationships (e.g. research and development) and cases in which economies of scale and other joint efficiencies are significant. [*OECD Guidelines 3.5–3.25*].

**14.26** The *transactional net margin method* is similar to the traditional resale price and cost plus methods: it starts with an appropriate base (e.g. costs, sales, or assets) and assumes a reasonable net profit margin. Again, it requires comparable data, ideally the net profit margin the taxpayer concerned earns from similar transactions with unconnected parties. Since this method focuses on net profits, it is less sensitive to differences between products and even types of function performed (a variation in operating costs may well not affect net profit in the way it would affect gross profit). It is also necessary to consider only one party to a transaction. On the other hand, the net profit margin is sensitive to a wide range of factors that do not affect price or gross margins, which makes it harder to compare transactions reliably. The one-sidedness of the method may also be a weakness. [*OECD Guidelines 3.26–3.48*].

## Exception for UK transactions

**14.27** The Schedule applies to all transactions whether or not one or both of the parties are in the UK. However, where the following conditions are met by both parties (essentially where there is no foreign element to the transaction and both parties are within a UK tax charge), there is taken not to be any potential advantage in relation to UK taxation:

**14.28** *Transfer Pricing*

(a) they are within the charge to income tax or corporation tax in respect of profits arising from relevant activities (i.e. those in relation to which the provision in question was made or imposed) and not exempt in respect of all or part of the income from those activities, and, if within the charge to income tax, resident in the United Kingdom in the chargeable periods in which they are within that charge;

(b) they neither have any entitlement to a foreign tax credit in any chargeable period in respect of profits from such activities nor would have such an entitlement if there were any such profits or if they exceeded a certain level;

(c) the amounts taken into account in computing the profits or losses arising to them from the relevant activities in any chargeable period in which they are within the charge, do not include any income from which a deduction for foreign tax is made under *TA 1988 s 811(1)* where no credit is allowed; and

(d) (in the case of insurance companies within *TA 1988 s 431*) the profits from relevant activities in respect of which the company is within the charge to corporation tax, do not include any profits wherein acquisition expenses have been brought into account under *FA 1989 s 86* (i.e. expenses of acquiring insurance business), or any profits in relation to which a lower rate of tax is applied by *FA 1989 ss 88* or *88A*. [*TA 1988 28AA Sch 5, 14*].

**Charities**

**14.28** Transactions between charities and affiliates otherwise than at arm's length are not within the exception because charities are not within the charge to UK income or corporation tax. A particular area in which this might cause difficulty is funding by charities of trading affiliates, which will tend not to involve commercially negotiated terms. However, charities are expected to follow the advice and guidance of the Charity Commission in this area, and the Revenue accept that if they do so there is no tax advantage to counter (in line with the OECD Guidelines' approach to government intervention discussed at 1.55). Understandably, this acceptance does not extend to cases where charities fail to follow the Commission's advice or indulge in deliberate tax avoidance. It is an area in which International Division is willing to offer 'up-front' advice. [See Tax Bulletin 37, Appendix 1].

# Claims for relief from double counting

**14.29** The basic charging provision outlined above can be described as a 'one-way street' in that the arm's length provision is, in the first instance, only applied where the actual provision would be to the Revenue's disadvantage. Without more, this might mean that the one party paid tax on the actual transaction (under which he received more profits than he would have done under the arm's length provision) while the other party paid tax on the arm's length provision (under which his costs were lower than otherwise).

**14.30** Relief is available where a profit adjustment is imposed by the Schedule on only one of the affected persons by the actual provision ('the advantaged person') and the other one is within the charge to income tax or corporation tax (leaving aside exemptions) and, if chargeable to income tax, resident in the UK in the chargeable periods in which he is within that charge ('the disadvantaged person'). On a claim, the disadvantaged person's profits and losses may also be computed for tax purposes as if the arm's length provision had been made and any adjustments necessary may be made notwithstanding any time limits otherwise imposed. Such a claim cannot be made unless a tax computation has been made for the advantaged person on the basis of the adjusted profits and must be consistent with that computation. It must be made within two years of the advantaged person submitting his self-assessment return (subject to the usual provisions for extension of time for claims). [*TA 1988 28AA Sch 6*].

**14.31** For the purposes of establishing entitlement to credit for foreign tax paid, after a claim has been made, it is to be assumed that the foreign tax does not include tax which would not be or have become payable had the arm's length provision been made or imposed, and that the profits from the relevant activities (as above) in respect of which the tax credit relief arises are reduced commensurately. Where application of the arm's length provision in such a case results in the reduction of income that also falls to be treated as reduced under *TA 1988 s 811* (i.e. deduction for foreign tax paid where no tax credit is available), the arm's length adjustment is made before the *s 811* adjustment and only so much foreign tax may be deducted as does not represent tax on income in respect of which the arm's length adjustment has been made.

**14.32** Any adjustments to double tax relief arising from a claim by a disadvantaged person may be made by setting the amount off against any relief or repayment to which he is entitled as a result of that claim, and may be made without regard to any time limits otherwise imposed. [*TA 1988 28AA Sch 7*].

## Capital allowances and capital gains

**14.33** The Schedule does not affect the computation of the amount of any capital allowance or balancing charge under the *Capital Allowances Act 1990* or of any chargeable gain or allowable loss under the *Taxation of Chargeable Gains Act 1992*, nor does it require any profits or losses of a person to be computed for tax purposes as capital profits and losses rather than revenue. [*TA 1988 28AA Sch 13*].

**14.34** *Transfer Pricing*

## Application of the Schedule in particular circumstances

**Financial arrangements**

**14.34** The Schedule is apt to cover any form of financial arrangement that might be put in place between two parties, including any interest, discount or other payment for the use of money. This is an area already covered by more specific anti-avoidance provisions. The Revenue have published their guidance on some of the possible traps and have promised to review the interaction between the Schedule and other parts of domestic legislation and international treaties which also deal with capitalisation of companies and payments of interest at uncommercial rates. There are also some specific exclusions from the Schedule and some other cases where application of the OECD approach results in there being no adjustment required. [See Tax Bulletin 37].

**14.35** Where a non-UK company invests in a UK company at a rate of interest that exceeds a reasonable commercial rate of return, the UK company's payments will continue to be reclassified as a distribution (with the corresponding (shadow) ACT consequences) under *TA s 209(2)(d)* rather than being caught by the new Schedule. Likewise, *TA s 209(2)(da)* will continue to reclassify as distributions, payments where excessive interest is charged or discounts etc. are allowed (otherwise than by providing for an excessive rate) and either the borrower is a 75 per cent subsidiary of the lender or both are 75 per cent subsidiaries of a third party.

**14.36** In other cases where non-arm's length interest is charged however, the Schedule may be in point. These are cases which involve partnerships and corporate structures within the control provisions of *para 4* (but which do not satisfy the 75 per cent test). How the Schedule applies may not be straightforward. The OECD Guidelines give the example of an investment in an associated enterprise structured as an interest-bearing debt which would, if made at arm's length and having regard to the circumstances of the borrower, have been in the form of an equity contribution (*OECD Guidelines 1.37*). In that case, it might be more appropriate to treat the investment as a subscription of capital than as a loan.

**14.37** Another situation in which the Revenue accept that the Schedule does not have any effect is where a company guarantees a bank loan to an associate, the only effect of which is to reduce the rate of interest. This is not seen as a tax advantage. On the other hand, where the borrower is so thinly capitalised that no loan would have been made by the bank without a guarantee (or back to back deposit) from an associated company, an adjustment might be required. A tax advantage in such a case would be the deductibility of interest paid from the borrower's profits.

**14.38** Where the lender and borrower are associated, there may also be tax consequences for the lender in respect of the UK source income. The relevant double tax treaty might not allow excessive interest to be paid without deduction of income tax at UK domestic rates. In this case the interest would be disallowed in the borrower's UK tax computation by *Schedule 28AA* and in the lender's non-UK computation would suffer deduction of tax at source without the benefit of any other reduced rate that might otherwise apply under the treaty. In the normal arm's length case, interest paid to an unconnected bank would avoid any such difficulties even where backed by a parental guarantee.

**14.39** Under the old *s 770* provisions, loans to overseas associates at nil or low-rate interest were caught and taxed as if a market rate had been imposed. However, where it was accepted by the Revenue that Competent Authority proceedings would result in the conclusion that the borrower could not have obtained an equivalent arm's length loan, then, in theory as a matter of discretion, the Board declined to impute any additional interest on the grounds that the loan was performing an equity function. This result however, depended on the existence of a double tax treaty between the two countries and the availability of a Mutual Agreement procedure (see below). Under the new regime the UK resident lender will have to consider whether the outward interest-free loan is tantamount to a equity contribution or not when making its self-assessment return (see the *OECD Guidelines 1.37* discussed above).

**Goods and services**

**14.40** The Revenue draw a distinction between organisations which are 'genuinely' involved in selling (which are entitled to a share in the overall profit) and organisations which are providing services peripheral to that genuine selling (which are entitled to remuneration on a cost plus profit basis). This approach accords with the OECD discussion of the various methods for establishing the 'arm's length provision'. The question of which side of the line any given company falls will depend very much on the facts.

**14.41** The examples given of genuine selling are employing sales staff, seeking out customers, and providing brochures, sales literature and after sales services. The examples of peripheral activities are compiling market analyses and collating and analysing sales figures. There will be a considerable overlap in practice since many companies will perform functions of both sorts. The Inspector's Manual at 4658 also suggests the circumstances in which an Inspector might investigate further. The OECD Guidelines deal with the problems raised by intra-group provision of services in chapters VII and VIII (the latter being specifically concerned with cost contribution arrangements).

**14.42** *Transfer Pricing*

**Intellectual property and know-how**

**14.42** Particular difficulties also arise when trying to establish the arm's length provision appropriate for intangibles, including know-how that is commercially valuable but not seen by the courts as property, as well as patents, copyrights and so on. Some of the difficulties result from the problems of valuing such rights. Others flow from the difficulty of simply identifying the rights that should be treated as valuable (particularly since they may not have any value attributed to them in the company's books). These problems are discussed in the OECD Guidelines chapter VI. The Inspector's Manual indicates the circumstances in which the Revenue will be inclined to investigate further at IM 4659.

**14.43** There are no particular statutory provisions relating to the transfer pricing of intangibles, but, in assessing whether there was a UK tax advantage and also the effects of any adjustments in profits required, the usual provisions relating to patent receipts and so on (*TA 1988 ss 520–538*), should be taken into account.

**Oil and gas**

**14.44** The special treatment of the oil and gas business under the old *s 770* regime is to some extent preserved under the new regime. In summary the special provisions are:

(a) the Schedule applies where a buyer purchases oil from a company that owns the extraction rights ('the producer'), and the buyer and its associates own more than 20 per cent of the producer's ordinary share capital (because consortia are common in the oil business) [*TA 1988 28AA Sch 9*];

(b) where a company is carrying on two trades, one of which is a ring-fence trade within *TA 1988 s 492*, the Schedule applies to 'transactions' between the two trades. [*TA 1988 28AA Sch 11*].

## Self assessment

**The CT return**

**14.45** Under the new regime, where transactions have been made otherwise than at arm's length, companies must make appropriate adjustments to take into account the *Schedule 28AA* charge. As set out in 2.45 any transfer pricing adjustments should be fully disclosed, as well as any doubts about the position. Otherwise on a Revenue enquiry further tax, interest and penalties could be due. For an advance clearance procedure see 14.55.

*Transfer Pricing* **14.49**

**Record keeping**

**14.46** Under *TMA 1970 s 12B* and *FA 1998 18 Sch 21*, companies are required to keep and preserve the records needed to make and deliver a correct and complete return for any chargeable period. This applies as much to transfer pricing records as to any other. Chapter V of the OECD Guidelines deals with the record keeping. The Revenue's understanding of this chapter is contained in Tax Bulletin 37 (see Appendix 1).

**14.47** The OECD Guidelines say 'The taxpayer's process of considering whether transfer pricing is appropriate for tax purposes should be determined in accordance with the same prudent business management principles that would govern the process of evaluating a business decision of a similar level of complexity and importance'. This is reflected in the Revenue's avowed desire to strike a balance between the costs of compliance and the taxpayer's ability to self-assess accurately and 'justify transfer prices together with the quantum of income, profits or losses returned for tax purposes'.

**14.48** The Tax Bulletin indicates that companies should keep such documentation as is reasonable and which identifies:

(a) commercial and financial relations falling within the scope of the new legislation;

(b) nature and terms (including prices) of relevant transactions (including transactions which form a series and any relevant off-setting transactions). Transactions which are clearly in one family (e.g. regular purchases made by a distributor throughout a return period of the same or similar products for sale) may be aggregated, provided any significant changes during the period in the nature or terms of the transactions are recorded;

(c) method or methods by which the nature and terms of relevant transactions were arrived at, including any study of comparables and any functional analysis undertaken;

(d) how that method has resulted in arm's length terms etc. or, where it has not, what computational adjustment is required and how it has been calculated. This will usually include an analysis of market data or other information on third party comparables;

(e) terms of relevant commercial arrangements with both third party and affiliated customers. These will include commercial agreements (e.g. service or distribution contracts, loan agreements), and any budgets, forecasts or other papers containing information relied on in arriving at arm's length terms etc. and/or in calculating any adjustment made in order to satisfy the requirements of the new transfer pricing legislation.

**14.49** The Revenue do not require new documentation to be prepared for ongoing arrangements that extend into the first CTSA period so long

**14.50** *Transfer Pricing*

as the taxpayer can make a complete and accurate return in using existing documentation. In the same way, there is no need for arrangements that continue from year to year to be freshly documented each year so long as the original documentation is sufficient to allow the taxpayer to make a proper return. If there are significant changes in the nature of terms of the transaction they should of course be recorded.

**14.50** The documentation should exist by the time the return is made, although it can be prepared after the transaction has been entered into, and should be preserved until the later of (i) six years from the end of the chargeable period to which they refer or for which there could be a related tax effect or (ii) completion of enquiries to which the documents are relevant. [*FA 1998 18 Sch 21*].

**Penalties**

**14.51** Bringing the transfer pricing legislation within CTSA also allows the Revenue to impose penalties on companies which fail to complete returns in accordance with the new schedule. As well as flat rate and capped penalties (e.g. for failing to keep proper records [*FA 1998 18 Sch 23*]), it is possible for a penalty to be imposed equal to the amount of tax understated. [*FA 1998 18 Sch 20*]. As set out in Chapter 18 a penalty can be imposed wherever a company (i) fraudulently or negligently delivers an incorrect return or (ii) discovers an error in a return and does not correct it without unreasonable delay. Once these criteria are fulfilled, the full penalty can be imposed since there is no statutory safeguard relating the level of penalty to the seriousness of the mistake. An officer of the Board does, however, have discretion to limit the amount of penalty actually imposed. [*TMA 1970 s 100(1)*].

**14.52** Given the acknowledged difficulty of establishing accurate transfer prices for the purposes of the new legislation, this provision could operate very harshly. Reacting to comments to this effect, the Revenue have published guidelines in Tax Bulletin 38 (see Appendix 1) indicating how they intend to operate the penalty power in relation to transfer pricing problems. Since the penalty provisions are not contained within *Schedule 28AA*, there is not a strict requirement that they be operated in line with the OECD Guidelines, which deal with penalties in chapter IV; in the Bulletin the Revenue nonetheless state that their approach will be consistent with that chapter. In levying penalties for negligence, the Revenue will have to show that the taxpayer has not made an honest and reasonable attempt to comply with the legislation. The Revenue say acting as a reasonable person involves:

(a) using commercial knowledge and judgement to make arrangements and set prices which conform to the arm's length standard (or to make computational adjustments in their returns where they do not);

(b) being able to show (for example, by means of good quality documentation) that they made an honest and reasonable attempt to comply with the arm's length standard and with the legislation; and

(c) seeking professional help where they know they need it.

**14.53** These obligations are tied in with the guidance on record keeping discussed above. However, it is clear that merely keeping good records is not enough if those records do not show good reasons for adopting the prices or adjustments actually chosen. The Revenue also give four examples based on intra-group service companies and using the cost plus method discussed above. The companies that are penalised are those which fail to undertake comparative studies (whether or not they assert that they have done so). The difference in these examples is between a 5 per cent mark-up chosen by the company and the 10 per cent–15 per cent regarded as reasonable by the Revenue. The companies that are not penalised are those which have run checks on available industry data and have documentary proof of having done so, but unfortunately misinterpret those data as supporting their prices. These companies chose mark-ups of 8 per cent, whilst the Revenue still regarded 10 per cent–15 per cent as acceptable. It remains to be seen what view the courts will take of the penalty regime and how it will operate in more complex cases than the relatively simple facts used for the examples.

**14.54** The Bulletin contains two further statements of intent. First, the Revenue should link a penalty to the 'size and gravity' of the default, taking into account:

(a) the absolute size of the adjustment;

(b) the size of the adjustment relative to the turnover and profitability of the business against which the adjustment is being made; and

(c) where possible, the size of the adjustment in relation to the volume and value of the related party transactions giving rise to the adjustment.

Second, all potential penalty cases are to be monitored by Revenue's International and Compliance Divisions working in conjunction.

## Advance pricing agreements

### Outline of basic statutory provisions

**14.55** *FA 1999 s 85* establishes a formal system for obtaining Advance Pricing Agreements ('APAs') which, once signed, are binding until revoked by the Revenue. APAs are designed to clarify the transfer pricing position in relation to any of the following matters:

(a) the attribution of income tax to a branch or agency through which

**14.56** *Transfer Pricing*

      the taxpayer has been carrying on a trade in the UK, or is proposing to do so;

(b) the attribution of income to any permanent establishment of the taxpayer (wherever situated) through which he has been carrying on, or is proposing to carry on, any business;

(c) the extent to which income which has arisen or may arise to the taxpayer is to be taken for any purpose to be income arising in a country or territory outside the UK;

(d) the treatment for tax purposes of any provision made or imposed (whether before or after the date of the APA) as between the taxpayer and any associates;

(e) the treatment for tax purposes of any provision made or imposed (whether before or after the date of the APA) as between a ring-fence trade carried on by the taxpayer and any other activities so carried on. [*FA 1999, s 85(2)*].

**14.56** For the purposes of the above, two persons are associates if (within 14.11 et seq.) (a) one is directly or indirectly participating, at the time of the making or imposition of the provision, in the management control or capital of the other; or (b) the same person or persons is or are, at that time, directly or indirectly participators in the management etc. of each of the two persons. In relation to the sale of oil two persons are treated as associates where *TA 28AA Sch 9(2)* would require them to be treated as falling within (b). [*FA 1999 s 85(6)*]. 'Ring-fence trade' in relation to the taxpayer means any activities which (a) are carried on by the taxpayer as, or as part of a trade; and (b) in accordance with *TA 1988 s 492(1)* (tax treatment of oil extraction activities), either (i) fall to be treated as a separate trade for tax purposes, distinct from all the taxpayer's other activities; or (ii) would so fall if the taxpayer did carry on any other activities as part of that trade. [*FA 1999 s 85(7)*].

**14.57** In order to obtain an APA the taxpayer has to initiate the process by an application to the Board. [*FA 1999 s 85(1)(c)*]. Such an application must set out:

(a) the taxpayer's understanding of what would, in his case, be the effect of the transfer pricing provisions in the absence of any APA;

(b) the respects in which it appears to the taxpayer that clarification is required; and

(c) how the taxpayer proposes that matters should be clarified in a manner consistent with his understanding of the position. [*FA 1999 s 85(5)*].

**14.58** Once an APA has been entered into, it has effect for any chargeable period ending on or after the enactment of *FA 1999*, provided the APA is made on or after that day and in relation to that period. [*FA*

*1999 s 85(8)*]. However, prior periods can be included. [*FA 1999 s 86(1)*]. Any party to the APA is duty bound to provide the Revenue from time to time with all reports and information which are required under the agreement or which are requested by the Revenue in accordance with the terms of the agreement. [*FA 1999 s 86(4)*]. Where an APA relates to a chargeable period before the agreement is made, and it provides for the manner in which adjustments can be made for tax purposes, the adjustments are duly to be made in that manner. [*FA 1999 s 86(7)*]. Under the terms of the APA, provision can be made for its modification or revocation to take effect as from such time as the Revenue determine.

**Impact on non-parties**

**14.59** It may happen that an APA operates to disapply certain of the *Schedule 28AA* rules which would otherwise be applicable, and this affects persons who are not party to the agreement. Where this is the case in relation to questions of whether (a) a potential UK tax advantage is conferred on the taxpayer by the actual provision and (b) what constitutes the arm's length provision in relation to the actual provision, the provisions of *28AA Sch 6* and *7* (relief from double counting in the case of disadvantaged persons) are to have effect in the other party's case on the assumption that those questions are to be determined by reference to the APA. This is subject to any APA between the Revenue and the other party. [*FA 1999 s 87*].

**Impact on APA of double tax arrangements**

**14.60** Where there is an APA and this is inconsistent with a mutual agreement made under and for the purposes of any double tax arrangements, the Revenue are obliged to make any appropriate modifications to the APA. [*FA 1999 s 86(3)*]. APAs will in fact either be unilateral (binding only the UK Revenue) or bilateral (binding also taxing authorities of other countries). Where possible a bilateral APA will be preferable since this reduces the risk of double taxation. If this is not possible so that either a Mutual Agreement Procedure or the Arbitration Convention has to be invoked to prevent such double taxation, the unilateral APA will not bind the Revenue in their negotiations. See 14.76 below for APAs under Mutual Agreement Procedures.

**Revocation of APA**

**14.61** An APA no longer has affect in relation to the determination of a question which relates to (a) a time after the agreement has been revoked by the Revenue in accordance with its terms or (b) a time after which a party to the APA has failed to comply with a provision on which the agreement is conditional. This is also the case where there has been a failure to satisfy a condition which has been made a prerequisite of the APA applying. [*FA 1999, s 86(2)*]. Furthermore an APA is deemed never

**14.62** *Transfer Pricing*

to have been made where false or misleading information was fraudulently or negligently provided to the Revenue before the agreement was entered into, and the Revenue have notified the taxpayer that the APA is nullified. [*FA 1999 s 86(5)*]. A penalty up to £10,000 can be imposed for the fraudulent or negligent making of any false or misleading statement to the Board or an officer. [*FA 1999 s 86(8)*].

**Revenue practice**

**14.62** The Revenue have published an extensive Statement of Practice on APAs, SP3/99 (see *STI [1999] 1467*) (Appendix 5). The Revenue have reserved the right to refuse to consider an APA in certain circumstances. The factors to be considered are:

(a) whether the issues are complex enough;

(b) whether the transactions are large enough (in relation to the size of the taxpayer or absolutely);

(c) whether enough information has been provided; and

(d) whether the transactions are hypothetical.

**14.63** The APA process will typically involve four stages:

(1) the expression of interest (which may be made anonymously);

(2) the application for clarification;

(3) evaluation by the Revenue; and

(4) agreement.

**14.64** When expressing interest, the taxpayer will be asked for the following information:

(a) the nature and value of the transactions, and the parties involved;

(b) the business activities of the parties, and how the transactions relate to these;

(c) a description of the transfer pricing method to be applied and an explanation of how it is said to accord with the arm's length standard;

(d) an indication of any ongoing transfer pricing enquiries in which the parties are involved; and

(e) confirmation where appropriate that a bilateral APA is required, or an explanation of the reasons why one is inappropriate.

The company should include four copies of the expression of interest. The Revenue will then consider the matter, possibly discuss it with the company, and should then notify the company whether or not the full application will be entertained.

**14.65** The next stage, providing the Revenue consent, is to make the formal 'application for clarification.' This should be made no later than six months before the start of the first chargeable period to be covered by the APA. The application must contain a proposal for clarifying the effects of the legislation and the most important part of the proposal will be a description of the method by which the arm's length transfer price will be established, and the explanation of how and why the method satisfies the OECD Guidelines.

**14.66** However, in addition to the information provided for the expression of interest (which must apparently be repeated) the application should also include:

(a) the names of the parties and historic financial data (anonymity is no longer possible);

(b) a description of the transfer pricing issues to be covered, an analysis of the functions to be performed and the risks to be borne by the parties, and projected financial data;

(c) a description of the world-wide group structure and the part to be played by the transactions covered by the APA;

(d) a description of the records to be maintained in order to support the method proposed;

(e) a description of any current tax disputes relating to the issues covered by the APA;

(f) the chargeable periods to be covered;

(g) the identification of which assumptions supporting the proposals are critical; and

(h) a request for a bilateral APA or reasons why one cannot be reached.

**14.67** The importance of the critical assumptions is that if they are proved false, the Revenue will reconsider the APA. Assumptions about the technology available to rivals in the same sector might be critical in this respect, for example. As when conducting an enquiry after the event, the Revenue will be keen for the consideration and agreement process to involve discussion with the company, and some negotiation. Lack of cooperation will result in the application being dismissed. If, despite cooperation, the Revenue cannot agree, they should issue a formal statement explaining why.

**14.68** If an APA is concluded, it is legally enforceable and *Schedule 28AA* applies on the basis of the APA for its duration. APAs are intended to last three to five years, and may be renewed at the end of that period if the circumstances have not changed materially. If a new method is proposed, a new application will have to be made, however. The APA may be revoked prematurely if its terms are breached. Among the terms

**14.69** *Transfer Pricing*

to be implied into all APAs are a commitment from the taxpayer to demonstrate adherence to the agreement and to continue to monitor the critical assumptions on which it is based. Each year a report should be provided confirming that the method agreed has been applied during the year and recording the financial results of its application. The report will also have to disclose the prices actually charged and an assessment of the continuing soundness of the critical assumptions.

## Enquiries

**14.69** The Revenue's Inspector's Manual (at 4657) contains a list of the circumstances when a further transfer pricing investigation might be undertaken. Because an enquiry notice must be issued if at all within twelve months of the filing of the return, it may be that the Revenue will tend to issue notices as a matter of course to companies (and particularly large companies) which are involved in transactions with overseas associates.

**14.70** Enquiries will probably be conducted in much the same way as present, with the District level Inspector taking day to day charge of the case and International Division providing specialist support and supervision. The first step will probably be to request the records mentioned above and review them and then decide whether there is a prima facie case that warrants further investigation. Thereafter, negotiations will commence, conducted by correspondence and also with meetings to cover the detailed points that transfer pricing issues inevitably involve. The tension between Government departments will continue: for example, Customs may want goods to be imported at a higher value (resulting in greater duty) whilst the Revenue argue for a lower value (resulting in higher UK profits).

**14.71** The Revenue have become increasingly reluctant to guarantee that information revealed during negotiations will not be passed on to other taxing authorities, although only in limited cases is such exchange actually required by treaty. Certain exchanges are governed by the 'Code of Good Conduct' agreed between France, Germany, the UK and the US; more extensive provision is made in the joint working arrangements agreed by the Revenue with the US Internal Revenue Service (see Revenue Press Release 2nd March 1978). Information may also be passed to Customs and Excise under *FA 1972 s 127*.

## Determinations

**14.72** Under the old regime, assessments under the transfer pricing regulations could only be made on the Board's direction (except in respect of certain oil transactions). This was intended to ensure uniformity of application of the provisions and an element of this protection has been preserved in the new provisions. Determinations of an amount falling to be brought into account under *Schedule 28AA* require the sanction of the Board [*FA 1998 s 110(4)*] except in certain cases where an agreement has been reached between the Board and the person concerned. [*FA 1998 s 110(5)–(7)*].

**14.73** Where such a determination is required and a closure notice, or notice under *TMA 1970 s 30B* amending a partnership return or notice of a discovery assessment, is given without the Board's approval of the determination (or without a copy of the Board's approval being served on the person concerned at the same time), the notice or assessment is treated as made or notified as if the determination had not been taken into account. The approval must specifically address the case in question and the amount determined, but otherwise may be given before or after the determination in any form the Board may determine. The Board's approval may only be questioned on appeal to the extent that the grounds for questioning it are grounds for questioning the determination itself. [*FA 1998 s 110*]. If a determination is made, the Revenue is also obliged to give notice to anyone who appears to be a disadvantaged person by reference to that determination. [*FA 1998 s 111*].

## Appeals

**14.74** An appeal against the amendment of a return, the refusal of a claim, or a discovery assessment or determination that involves questions about the application of the Schedule, must be heard by the Special Commissioners. If those questions relate to a provision between two persons who are subject to UK income or corporation tax (or would be but for exemptions) and are UK resident for such periods as they are subject to income tax, each of those people is entitled to appear or make written representations and the Commissioners must determine the questions separately from other questions in the appeal. That determination is treated as made in an appeal to which each of those persons was party. [*TA 1988 28AA Sch 12*].

## International agreement procedures for relieving double taxation

**14.75** There are two international procedures available in cases of double taxation:

(a) a Mutual Agreement Procedure (if provided for in the relevant Double Taxation Agreement); and

(b) the Arbitration Convention (if the countries concerned are signatories and have ratified the convention – the EU states, including new members, are signatories but not all have ratified).

**14.76** *Transfer Pricing*

**Mutual Agreement Procedure**

**14.76** This procedure is provided for in many of the UK's Double Tax Agreements and also under Article 25 of the OECD Model Tax Convention. The competent authorities (i.e. the taxing authorities) of the two countries are empowered to consult one another, where the taxpayer claims he is being taxed otherwise than in accordance with the treaty. The taxpayer has no right to participate, but in practice will often be involved. The OECD has published an annex to its Transfer Pricing Guidelines covering the conduct of advance pricing agreements under mutual agreement procedures.

**14.77** The taxpayer initiates the process by making a claim in writing to the competent authority of the country of residence or nationality, depending on the treaty. In the UK there is no form prescribed, but the claim should include:

(a) the years concerned;

(b) the nature of the action giving rise to the double charge; and

(c) the full names and addresses of the parties concerned, including the UK company's Tax District and reference number.

The claim should be sent to the Deputy Director (International Compliance), International Division, or, if related to the petroleum industry, to the Controller, Oil Taxation Office.

**14.78** *TMA 1970 s 43* imposes a six year time limit for claims, although the Revenue will accept protective claims. Other jurisdictions have different rules and operate different policies. There is no guarantee that the procedure will result in agreement and no remedy is provided where this happens. Moreover, where an issue relating to transfer pricing has been settled by the Special Commissioners or the courts, the order cannot be varied, but does not automatically mean that a corresponding adjustment will be made in other jurisdictions affected. The Revenue undertake to try and persuade the other competent authorities to accept the UK determination, but there is always a risk that they will not succeed.

**14.79** If an agreement is reached, relief will be granted either by allowing a deduction against UK profits or a tax credit. Other jurisdictions may allow or require secondary adjustments, intended to restore the financial situation of the associated companies which have entered into the transactions involved, to that which would have existed had the transaction's been at arm's length. The UK does not itself require such adjustments, but the Revenue consider the grant of relief where a secondary adjustment is required by another country. Another method adopted by some jurisdictions (but not the UK) is to require the repatriation of funds so as to remove the need for deemed secondary adjustments. The Revenue should not tax funds repatriated in accordance with such requirements unless the amounts exceed the transfer pricing adjustment imposed. [Tax Bulletin Issue 25, October 1996].

**The Arbitration Convention**

**14.80** The Arbitration Convention (the 'Convention on the elimination of double taxation in connection with the adjustment of profits of associated enterprises' 90/463/EEC) came into force with effect from 1 January 1995 for five years, and has subsequently been extended so as to apply for at least a further five years. Cases can be considered under the Arbitration Convention if validly presented while it is in force. The periods concerned might be before it came into force and the process might still be running after it has been terminated. Unlike the Mutual Agreement Procedure, the Arbitration Convention provides for independent resolution of disagreements between signatory states.

**14.81** Under the Convention there are three stages:

(a) the taxpayer who considers he is facing double taxation presents his case to the relevant competent authority; then,

(b) if the competent authority cannot solve the problem itself, it enters a Mutual Agreement Procedure (as above save that any agreement reached will be implemented notwithstanding any time limits otherwise imposed by the domestic law of either country concerned); and finally,

(c) the arbitration procedure itself.

**14.82** The taxpayer must first present his case 'within three years of the first notification of the action which results or is likely to result in double taxation' (*Art 6(1)*). There is no provision for extending this time limit, but what constitutes a 'first notification' is to be construed in the taxpayer's favour so far as possible. For UK purposes, it means the finalising of the transfer pricing enquiry, marked by the determination of the quantum of the additional profits which are to be taken into account in the assessment.

**14.83** If the competent authorities concerned cannot eliminate the double taxation by agreement within two years of the presentation, the case goes to an advisory commission. The two year limit is extended if an appeal is still in progress through domestic procedures, or alternatively (for the UK or France), the second stage cannot commence until the time limits for appealing have passed without any appeal. For practical purposes this may oblige taxpayers to choose between domestic remedies and the convention, although a factor also to be borne in mind is that domestic remedies will apply only to the UK tax position.

**14.84** The advisory commission must deliver within six months a decision that will eliminate the double taxation (*Arts 10(2), 11*). The

**14.84** *Transfer Pricing*

competent authorities must implement this decision, or another method of eliminating the double taxation, within a further six months (*Art 12*). Neither the Mutual Agreement Procedure nor the arbitration stage will start if any of the parties is liable to serious penalties. In the UK this means criminal sanctions or other penalties in respect of the fraudulent or negligent delivery of incorrect accounts, claims or returns for tax purposes. [*Art 8*]. [Tax Bulletin Issue 31, October 1997].

Chapter 15

# Other Overseas Aspects

## Non-resident companies

**15.1** A company which is not resident in the UK is not within the charge to corporation tax, unless it carries on a trade in the UK through a branch or agency, but if it does so, it is subject to corporation tax on the world-wide profits of its UK branch. [*TA 1988 s 11(1)*]. The profits liable to corporation tax are any trading income from the branch or agency, and any income from property or rights used or held by the branch or agency and chargeable gains on assets used by the branch for the purpose of its trade. [*TA 1988 s 11(2)*]. Any profits of the UK trade which have suffered income tax by deduction are subject to corporation tax, but with a credit for the income tax suffered against the corporation tax payable, except in the case of relevant loan interest on a mortgage under the MIRAS scheme. [*TA 1988 s 369* and *s 11(3)* and *(4)*]. A non-resident company not carrying on a trade through a branch or agency is chargeable to income tax on income arising in the UK, unless exempt under a double taxation agreement. [Inland Revenue Company Taxation Manual CT 3351].

**15.2** In determining whether a company is non-resident, *TA 1988 s 66* applies, which states that a company incorporated in the UK is treated as resident in the UK, subject to the transitional provisions in *FA 1988 7 Sch*. These provisions are explained in SP1/90.

**15.3** Where a double taxation treaty has a tie-breaker clause applicable to companies, the company may be regarded as resident in the other territory. [SP1/90 para 23]. In such circumstances the company is, under *FA 1994 s 249*, non-resident for the purposes of the Taxes Acts.

**15.4** A company incorporated outside the UK may be resident in the UK, if its central management and control is in the UK. [*Calcutta Jute Mills Co Ltd v Nicholson (1876) 1 TC 83, De Beers Consolidated Mines Ltd v Howe (1906) 5 TC 198, New Zealand Shipping Co Ltd v Stephens (1907) 5 TC 553, Todd v Egyptian Delta Land and Investment Co Ltd (1928) 14 TC 119, Bullock v Unit Construction Co Ltd (1959) 38 TC 712, Untelrab Ltd v McGregor [1996] STC (SCD) 1*]. A company can be dual resident. [*Swedish Central Rly Co Ltd v Thompson (1925) 9 TC 342, Union Corpn Ltd v IRC (1953) 34 TC 207*].

## 15.5 Other Overseas Aspects

**15.5** A UK resident company is normally liable to corporation tax on the profits of the trade carried on wholly or partly in the UK under Schedule D, Case 1. [*Ogilvie v Kitton (1908) 5 TC 338, Spiers v Mackinnon (1929) 14 TC 386*]. A UK resident company with a trade carried on wholly abroad is assessable under Schedule D, Case V. A company with branches in the UK and abroad may be carrying on a single trade assessable under Schedule D, Case 1. [*Aramayo Francke Mines Ltd v Eccott (1925) 9 TC 445, San Paulo (Brazilian) Rly Co Ltd v Carter (1895) 3 TC 344, Denver Hotel Co Ltd v Andrews (1895) 3 TC 356, Grove v Elliots & Parkinson (1896) 3 TC 481*].

**15.6** In deciding the scope of trading activities assessable under Schedule D, Case 1, the cases have drawn a distinction between trading in the UK, for example manufacture or sales taking place in the UK, and trading with the UK, for example sales made outside the UK to UK customers. Essentially a person is regarded as trading in the UK if the economic activities from which the profits are derived are carried on in the UK. See for example *Firestone Tyre & Rubber Ltd v Llewellin (1957) 37 TC 111*. The test propounded in that case was where the activities were carried on from which the profits in substance arose. [*Erichsen v Last (1881) 1 TC 351*].

**15.7** In cases where a non-resident carries on a trade partly in the UK and partly outside, the charge is imposed only on the profits from the part of the trade carried on in the UK. [*Pommery & Greno v Apthorpe (1886) 2 TC 182, Tischler & Co v Apthorpe (1885) 2 TC 89, Werle & Co v Colquhoun (1888) 2 TC 402*]. In order to arrive at the measure of taxable profits in such cases, the Revenue adopt the internationally accepted arm's length principle set out in *article 7(2) and (3)* of the OECD Model Double Tax Convention, which is in any event explicitly required wherever a double taxation agreement applies. *Article 7(2)* adopts a separate entity approach requiring the profits to be computed as if the activities carried on in the UK were carried on by a separate person dealing wholly independently and at arm's length with the non-residents. *Article 7(3)* allows actual expenditure incurred by the non-resident for the purposes of the UK business to be deducted plus an appropriate mark-up for expenditure on trading stock transferred to the UK business. The Revenue have set out their understanding of the relevant principles in relation to trading with or trading in the UK in Tax Bulletin Issue 18, August 1995, p 237 (see Appendix 1).

**15.8** There have been numerous cases of non-residents assessed to tax in the UK in the name of an agent including: *James Wingate & Co v Webber (1897) 3 TC 569, Murphy v Australian Machinery & Investment Co Ltd (1948) 30 TC 244, Watson v Sandie and Hull (1898) 3 TC 611, Thomas Turner (Leicester) v Rickman (1898) 4 TC 25, Macpherson & Co v Moore (1912) 6 TC 107, Wilcock v Pinto & Co (1924) 9 TC 111, Balfour v Mace (1928) 13 TC 539 and 582*. However, merely soliciting orders in the UK is not sufficient to amount to a branch or agency in the UK,

*Other Overseas Aspects* **15.12**

[*Grainger & Son v Gough (1896) 3 TC 311, Smith v Greenwood (1922) 8 TC 193*], nor does merely buying goods in the UK for sale abroad necessarily constitute trading here. [*Sulley v A-G (1860) 2 TC 149*].

**15.9** Where a company ceases to be resident in the UK, there will normally be a deemed disposal and reacquisition at market value for the purposes of company chargeable gains under *TCGA 1992 ss 185–187*. It may be necessary for the company to secure payment of any outstanding tax under the provisions of *FA 1988 s 130* and if it fails to do so it may be liable to a penalty equal to the tax outstanding, *FA 1988 s 131*, and the Revenue may collect the tax from another member of the same group, or a controlling director of the company, under *FA 1988 s 132*.

## UK representatives of non-residents

**15.10** Subject to the terms of any double tax agreement, liability to tax on UK trading profits arises on non-residents irrespective of whether or not they are trading through a branch or agency, or permanent establishment in the UK. However, so far as collection of tax is concerned, the Revenue generally have to look to UK agents of non-residents. Under the old system the Revenue had wide powers to assess any person acting for a non-resident, the broad effect being to make any person who acted for a non-resident answerable for the latter's tax affairs. This could impose a heavy burden on persons who acted for non-residents in a restricted capacity, and the old provisions were only invoked in practice in limited areas.

**15.11** New rules were introduced by *FA 1995 ss 126* to *129* from 1 April 1996 to replace those contained in *TMA 1970 ss 78–85*. They apply only where the non-resident is carrying on a trade in the UK through a branch or agency. The objective is to make the UK branch or agent jointly responsible with the non-resident for all tax matters. The rationale for this approach is that such branch or management is part of the business of the non-resident, so it is reasonable to place full responsibility on that branch or management in relation to tax. This is in contrast to independent agents, who are not wholly responsible for the non-resident's affairs, and those who do not carry on the regular agency of the non-resident. Their position and that of brokers and investment managers, is dealt with in 15.25 et seq.

**15.12** From 1 April 1996, in the case of companies, a branch or agency through which a non-resident carries on any trade, profession or vocation (whether solely or in partnership) is designated as the non-resident's 'UK representative' for income tax, corporation tax and CGT purposes under *FA 1995 s 126(2)* in relation to the following:

(a)   the income from the trade, profession or vocation arising directly or indirectly from the branch or agency;

## 15.13 Other Overseas Aspects

(b) income from property or rights such as patents, copyrights, etc. which are used by or held by the branch or agency;

(c) capital gains on assets situated in the UK used for the purposes of a trade, profession or vocation or by the branch or agency within *TCGA 1992 s 10*;

(d) the chargeable profits of an overseas life insurance company, subject to tax under *TA 1988 19AC Sch 3*.

**15.13** For these purposes a branch or agency is defined by reference to *TMA 1970 s 118(1)* as 'any factorship, agency, receivership, branch or management.' [*FA 1995 s 126(8)*]. The UK representative is treated as a separate and distinct person from the non-resident, which allows notices to be served on it and tax collected from it. Moreover, it remains the representative for the income or capital gains which it has received even though it ceases to be the branch or agent. [*FA 1995 s 126(3)(4)*].

### Non-resident partners

**15.14** Where the non-resident company is carrying on the trade or profession through a branch or agency in the UK as a partner in a partnership, the trade or profession carried on through the branch or agency includes the deemed trade or profession arising from the non-resident's share in the partnership under *TA 1988 ss 111–114*. The partnership, as a deemed entity, is then the non-resident's UK representative. [*FA 1995 s 126(5)(6)*]. Where there is a UK resident partner, the partnership is treated as the branch or agent of each non-resident partner in respect of his share of partnership profit. [*FA 1995 s 126(7)*]. The effect is to make any partners present or resident in the UK jointly liable for tax on the non-resident's share of partnership profits, which overcomes the difficulty of collecting tax from a non-resident partner. It also has the effect of retaining the previous liability of partners for the tax liabilities of non-resident partners, even though the joint liability no longer applies under self-assessment for a UK resident partner in respect of the tax liabilities of his partners, in view of *TA 1988 s 111*. [See Chapter 12].

### Obligations imposed upon UK representatives

**15.15** All the general reporting obligations and charging provisions continued in the various Tax Acts apply equally to non-resident companies and their UK representatives. Such obligations may be discharged either by the non-resident or his UK representative, and any acts or omissions of the UK representative are treated as acts or omissions of the non-resident. [*FA 1995 23 Sch 1, 2*]. In order to make a non-resident's UK representative liable for the discharge of these obligations, where the liability depends on the service of a notice, or other documents, or the receipt of a request or a demand, it is necessary to serve these on the representative, or to supply him with a copy. [*FA 1995 23 Sch 3*]. This is the equivalent for self-assessment to the old rules under which the agent only became liable to tax where an assessment had been made on him.

**Independent agents**

**15.16** The obligations to supply information to the Revenue are limited in the case of an independent agent, being a person acting on the non-resident company's behalf in an independent capacity, i.e. where the relationship is at arm's length having regard to its legal, financial and commercial characteristics. [*FA 1995 23 Sch 7; FA 1995 s 127(18)*]. Such an independent agent has to discharge his obligations only so far as is practicable to do so by acting to the best of his knowledge and belief, after having taken all reasonable steps to obtain the necessary information. The agent would therefore be exonerated where, for example, the non-resident company withheld information. In such cases the non-resident company would be obliged to supply the relevant additional information. Moreover, a non-resident company is able to correct any error or mistake made by the independent agent which was not an act or omission of its own, one to which it consented, or one in which it connived.

**15.17** Information for the purposes of these provisions includes anything contained in a return, self-assessment, account, statement or report that is required by the Revenue. [*FA 1995 23 Sch 4(3)*]. An independent agent is entitled to be indemnified in respect of any tax obligation of the non-resident which he discharges, and to make an appropriate retention from any sums due to the non-resident, in a similar manner as a property agent under *FA 1995 s 40(1)*. [*FA 1995, 23 Sch 6*]. Moreover, an independent agent is not liable to any civil penalty or surcharge if the act or omission in question is not his, or one to which he did not give consent, or in which he did not connive, and in respect of which he is able to show that he cannot obtain indemnification. [*FA 1995 23 Sch 5*].

**Criminal offences**

**15.18** For the purposes of these provisions a person is not guilty of a criminal offence unless he committed the offence himself, or consented to, or connived in its commission. This will protect either the agent or the UK representative as appropriate, if criminal offences are committed by the other party.

## 15.19 Other Overseas Aspects

# Persons not treated as UK representatives – investment managers and brokers

**General**

**15.19** The extensive obligations imposed on a UK branch or agent in trading cases are based on the premise that the branch or agent is in effect an arm of his overseas principal, and therefore should be responsible for his tax affairs. Agents who do not carry on the regular agency of the non-resident, notably brokers and investment managers, fall into a separate category, and are hence faced with considerably reduced obligations subject to certain conditions being satisfied.

**15.20** In devising the self-assessment rules for agents of non-residents involved in financial trading transactions in the UK, a substantial degree of protection was accorded to agents in the investment management industry. This was in recognition of the importance to the UK economy of the London capital markets in particular and the wish to attract further investment management business to the UK. The expressed objective also was to ensure that non-residents engaged in such activities were not exposed to UK tax beyond the amount, if any, deducted at source on income from transactions carried out by investment mangers or brokers in the normal course of their business.

**15.21** The new provisions are in any event only relevant to those non-residents whose activities amount to trading in the UK. Thus UK-based agents generally do not need any protection where the transactions of the overseas resident give rise to capital gains, which are exempt from CGT in the hands of a company which is not resident in the UK. This covers, for example, non-resident investors in venture capital funds, where the Revenue generally accept that there is no trading. But it might well not extend to, say, hedge funds which are likely to be regarded by the Revenue as engaged in a trade.

**15.22** The general body of case law remains relevant in determining whether a person is an investor or a trader. In this regard the buying or selling of quoted shares and securities by a company which is not a share dealing company will generally be treated as an investment activity regardless of the timing and volume of the transactions, not least from the Revenue's point of view to avoid the generation of allowable trading losses; see for example, *Salt v Chamberlain (1979) 53 TC 143*. The position is likely to be otherwise in the case of commodities; see for example, *Wisdom v Chamberlain (1968) 45 TC 92*.

**15.23** There are certain general definitions which are applied for the purposes of the rules. First, a branch or agency is defined as 'any factorship, agency, receivership branch or management' [*TMA 1970 s 118(1)*]; and connected persons are defined by reference to *TA 1988 s 839*. [*FA 1995 s 127(17)*]. Secondly, an agent is deemed to carry out a transaction where he undertakes a transaction himself or gives instructions for it to be carried out by another person. Third, references to income arising from a business carried on through a branch or agency include income from property or rights used or held by the branch or agency. [*FA 1995 s 127(15)*]. The new provisions apply for income tax from 1996/97 for non-resident companies without a branch in the UK and for corporation tax for accounting periods beginning after 31 March 1996 [*FA 1995 s 127(19)*], where there is a branch in the UK.

**Persons not regular agents of non-residents**

**15.24** The previous exception to the normal agency rules for those persons who do not carry on the regular agency of the non-resident is continued under the new rules. This provides that where the trading income in question, or capital gains from the trading business, arise from transactions carried out through a person who does not carry on a regular agency for the non-resident, that person is not to be treated as his UK representative. [*FA 1995 s 127(1)(a)*]. The Revenue regard the words 'regular agency' as having the same meaning as habitual agent in the OECD Model Tax Convention.

**Brokers**

**15.25** A broker is not treated as the UK representative of a non-resident company in respect of income or capital gains from business transactions carried out through him, provided that:

(a) at the time of the transaction the broker was carrying on the business of a broker;

(b) the transaction was carried out on behalf of the non-resident company in the ordinary course of the broker's business;

(c) the remuneration received by the broker from the non-resident company was not less than the customary charge for that class of business; and

(d) the broker is not otherwise the non-resident company's UK representative. [*FA 1995 s 127(1)(b), (2)*].

**15.26** A broker who provides other services is deemed to carry on a separate business for these purposes. [*FA 1995 s 127(14)*]. The Revenue have confirmed that the term broker is to have the same meaning as in *TMA 1970 s 82(1)*. The wording in (a) and (b) above reproduces the *section 82* definition of 'sales or transactions carried out on behalf of a non-resident company through a broker in the ordinary course of his business as such'.

**15.27** It was established in *Wilcock v Pinto (1924) 9 TC 111* that the word 'broker' has a limited meaning, where Bankes LJ stated at pages 129 and 130:

## 15.28 Other Overseas Aspects

'As I understand that expression, it is used technically, and is used in reference to a class of persons who, by the custom of certain markets, are entitled and recognised as being entitled, to act for both purchaser and seller; and it is to that class of persons, as I understand it, that the expression "broker" is used, both in the cases in which reference has been made to that class of business, and in the statute.'

**Investment managers**

**15.28** Under the previous provisions, an investment manager who acted for overseas based financial traders enjoyed exemption from liability as an agent under *TMA 1970 s 78(2)* for services rendered in the normal course of trade as an investment manager and for full remuneration provided that certain conditions were complied with. These provisions have now been revised to exclude investment managers from the definition of UK representatives, and hence from liability as agents to account to the Revenue for tax on gains made by non-resident financial traders, in cases where the investment manager is independent of the non-resident or otherwise acts on customary commercial terms.

**15.29** Under the legislation contained in *FA 1995 s 127(1)(c), (3)* which came into effect from 6 April 1995, an investment manager is not treated as a non-resident company's UK representative in respect of income or capital gains from business transactions carried out through him, provided that:

(a) the investment manager is carrying on a business of providing investment management services;

(b) the investment transaction was carried out in the ordinary course of that business;

(c) the manager, when he acted on behalf of the non-resident in relation to the transaction, did so in an independent capacity;

(d) the remuneration received by the investment manager is not less than the customary charge for that class of business; and

(e) the investment manager is not otherwise the non-resident's UK representative. [*FA 1995 s 127(1)(c), (3)*].

**15.30** For the purposes of condition (b) an investment transaction is defined to include transactions in shares, stocks, futures contracts, options contracts, securities dealing in a foreign currency, or such other transactions as may be specified by regulations which may be made by the Treasury. An option for a futures contract includes one where the only obligation is to make payment of a sum of money in full settlement as opposed to an obligation to transfer assets. [*FA 1995 s 127(12)(13)*].

**15.31** For the purposes of condition (c) the relationship between the investment manager and the non-resident company must have the same legal, financial and commercial characteristics as one between independent businesses dealing at arm's length. [*FA 1995 s 127(18)*]. In the Revenue Press Release (17 February 1995) it was stated that where the (other) conditions in *section 127(3)* set out above, are satisfied, this 'independent relationship' will be satisfied if services for the non-resident company and persons connected with the non-resident company, are not a 'substantial part' of the investment management business.

**15.32** This condition is regarded as satisfied where no more than 70 per cent of the investment management business is with the non-resident and connected persons, either by reference to fees or some other measure where that would be more appropriate. An eighteen month grace period is allowed from the start of a new investment management business to permit this 'substantial part', i.e. 70 per cent, test to be satisfied. Moreover the condition will not be regarded as breached where the investment manager intended to satisfy it but did not do so for reasons beyond his control, having taken reasonable steps to fulfil the intention.

**15.33** If fee income exceeds 70 per cent, consideration will have to be given to whether the fee income is indeed a fair measure of the proportion of the business with the non-resident. Thus even if the 70 per cent level is exceeded the relationship might nevertheless be independent if, say, special deals have been reached on fees. Moreover, regardless of the normal 70 per cent rule, the relationship will still be considered to be independent where the investment management services are provided to a collective investment scheme which is quoted on a recognised stock exchange, or otherwise fully marketed (seemingly meaning offered to the public), such as units in a unit trust or widely held. It is regarded as widely held if either no majority interest in the fund is held by five or fewer persons and persons connected with them or no interest of more than 20 per cent is held by one person and persons connected with him.

**15.34** The Revenue Press Release further states that cases falling outside the above categories will have to be considered on their own facts to determine whether the independence requirement is satisfied and in this regard a parent's ownership of the share capital of the subsidiary will not in itself, mean that the subsidiary is not independent. It is to be hoped that even where the strict criteria are not satisfied there will be no charge to tax on the investment manager where the arrangements are commercial with no tax avoidance motive.

**Participating investment managers – the 20 per cent rule**

**15.35** Further conditions must be satisfied for those investment managers that take a share in any overseas fund. The Revenue concern here was that by establishing a fund in a tax haven and investing in that fund, the manager might otherwise be able to avoid or defer UK tax on his share of any profits generated. Yet at the same time it was considered that it would be commercially desirable to allow financial groups to place

## 15.36 Other Overseas Aspects

seed money into offshore funds they were promoting and to permit cross holdings without exposing the fund to UK tax, or to have an incentive arrangement through a 'carried interest' in the capital of a managed fund, for example, a performance fee structured as a special share in the fund. This has been accomplished by permitting investment up to a 20 per cent share in the fund without endangering the fund's tax status.

**15.36** In such cases further conditions, in addition to those outlined in 15.29 need to be satisfied. Throughout a qualifying period (essentially not more than five years), the investment manager (and any connected persons) must intend that his share of profits or gains of the non-resident company from transactions carried out through him should not exceed 20 per cent thereof. Professional fees paid to the investment manager, and connected persons, are to be netted off before the 20 per cent test is applied, provided they are allowable as deductions in arriving at taxable income. The requisite intention on the part of the investment manager must actually be fulfilled save to the extent that any failure is attributable to matters outside the control of the investment manager (and any connected persons) and does not result from a failure to take reasonable steps in mitigation. [*FA 1995 s 127(4)(5)*].

**15.37** Hence there is a certain amount of flexibility if markets move in an unexpected way and the 20 per cent limit is temporarily breached. Moreover, where the 20 per cent rule is not satisfied but the other investment manager conditions in 15.29 are complied with, only that part of the income belonging to the investment manager will be subject to a tax charge. [*FA 1995 s 127(8)*].

**15.38** For the purpose of determining what the profits and gains are in which the investment manager has a 20 per cent share, the profits or gains in question are those in which he has (or may acquire) a beneficial entitlement by virtue of an interest in reinvested securities, including rights to an immediate payment for a share in the profits and gains, and any other rights in relation to the non-resident which are attributable to those profits or gains. [*FA 1995 s 127(6)*]. An investment manager who provides other services is deemed to carry on a separate business for the purpose of those provisions. [*FA 1995 s 127(14)*].

### Collective investment schemes

**15.39** Where investment management services are provided to a collective investment scheme, as defined in the *Financial Services Act 1986*, which is financially transparent, the 20 per cent rule is applied by looking at the scheme as a whole, rather than by each participant separately. The rule is treated as satisfied by each participant in the scheme:

(a) where the scheme, if it were taxed as a separate entity, would not be regarded as carrying on a trade in the UK, regardless of the level of beneficial entitlement; and

(b) where the scheme, if it were taxed as a separate entity, would be regarded as carrying on a trade, provided that the 20 per cent rule is satisfied with regard to the beneficial entitlement of the investment manager (and connected persons) to the taxable income of the scheme. [*FA 1995 s 127(9)–(11)(17)*].

**15.40** The provision in (a), which excludes transparent schemes where the activities are investments rather than trading, is somewhat puzzling in that non-resident companies which invest, rather than carry on a trade, through a UK manager are generally not liable to tax in any event.

**Non-resident members of Lloyd's**

**15.41** Where the non-resident company is a member of Lloyd's, and the income arises from underwriting, the member's agent or the managing agent of the syndicate in question is excluded from being the non-resident company's UK representative. [*FA 1995 s 127(1)(d)*]. This matches changes made to the taxation of Lloyd's underwriters in *FA 1994 ss 219–230*, which repealed the provisions relating to deduction of tax at source by member's agents and managing agents. Lloyd's terms are defined by reference to *FA 1993 ss 171–174* and *FA 1994 ss 219–230, FA 1995 s 127(16)*.

**Certain overseas funds in existence at 29 November 1994**

**15.42** There may be some overseas funds which qualified for exemption under the rules in *TMA 1970 ss 78(2)–(5), 82(1)*, but would not do so under the new rules. The Revenue intend to introduce 'grand-fathering' arrangements in such cases. In the meantime Extra Statutory Concession B40 relating to UK investment managers acting for non-resident clients continued to apply up to 5 April 1996 and in certain cases will continue to apply up to 5 April 2005. [Revenue Press Release, 17 February 1995].

# Schedule D, Case VI

**15.43** Non-resident companies generally remain subject to tax in respect of income falling within Schedule D, Case VI but there are no specific provisions dealing with these sources of income.

# Income from land in the UK: Schedule A

**Background**

**15.44** Non-resident companies are subject to tax on income from property situated in the UK. In cases where the non-resident company has an agent in the UK, the agent under the old system could be charged

**15.45** *Other Overseas Aspects*

in the taxpayer's name. [*TMA 1970 Part VIII*]. He was obliged to notify chargeability and could be required to complete a tax return and pay the tax on behalf of the non-resident company. This was unsatisfactory in that the agent was often not sufficiently well aware of his principal's affairs to enable him to complete a full return. In other cases, where the rent was paid directly by the tenant, the tenant was obliged to deduct tax at basic rate from the rent, and account for it to the Revenue. This was also rather unsatisfactory, particularly where there was no liability.

**15.45** Under self-assessment, those non-resident landlords including companies who can demonstrate compliance with their responsibilities under self-assessment are permitted to receive rents without deduction at source. Otherwise tax at the basic rate will have to be deducted from net rental income, after certain permitted expenses, and paid to the Revenue.

**15.46** The new provisions were enacted by *FA 1995 s 40*, inserting a new *TMA 1970 s 42A*, setting out the statutory framework and enabling the Board to issue regulations for the implementation of the new system. The *Taxation of Income from Land (Non-residents) Regulations 1995 (SI 1995 No. 2902*) were duly issued in November 1995. The Revenue has since issued detailed guidance notes for letting agents and tenants to what is described as the 'non-resident landlord's scheme' ('NRLS'). Those involved in such schemes should refer to these guidance notes. What follows is a summary of their provisions. The new provisions are administered by FICO in Bootle. Another useful Revenue publication is booklet IR 150 which sets out the tax treatment of property income.

**Non-resident landlords**

**15.47** A company with its main office or other place of business outside the UK, and a company incorporated outside the UK, is within the provisions. A company treated as UK resident for tax purposes is not within the provisions. Neither is a non-resident company with a UK branch chargeable to corporation tax, even if the rental income has nothing to do with the branch.

**Knowledge of landlord's status by letting agents and tenants**

**15.48** Should letting agents and tenants have reason to believe that a landlord may be a non-resident company, for example where it has an overseas address, they should satisfy themselves as to the position, consulting FICO if in difficulty. Unless they are satisfied that the landlord is not a non-resident company they should deduct tax.

## Landlords' ability to apply for rent to be paid gross

*Application procedure*

**15.49** Non-resident company landlords may apply to FICO for rent to be paid without any deduction of tax at source. There are standard forms for companies (NRL 2). The application may be made at any time. It will be a requirement that:

(a) the company's tax affairs are up to date; or
(b) it has never had any UK tax obligations; or
(c) it does not expect to be liable to UK tax in the tax year in which the application is made.

**15.50** The company's registered office address should be provided. Where tax affairs have previously been dealt with via a letting agent or tenant, the latter's tax particulars should be given. These should assist in establishing that the non-resident company's tax affairs were up to date.

*Approval of application*

**15.51** In cases where the application form is complete and correct, and FICO are satisfied that the non-resident landlord will comply with its tax obligations, they will approve an application. FICO aim to deal with applications speedily. There will be an initial check, after which approval should normally be granted, followed by a later, detailed check. At that stage additional information may be required.

**15.52** Notice of approval to receive rental income without deduction of tax will be sent to the non-resident landlord, with a copy to the non-resident landlord's accountant or tax adviser where they hold written authority, showing a reference number. A separate notice will be sent to the letting agents or tenants named on the application form authorising them to pay rental income to the non-resident landlord without deducting tax, again with a reference number. Such notices of approval will specify the date from which rental income should be paid without deducting tax, normally the first day of the quarter in which the notice is issued.

*Refusal/withdrawal of approval*

**15.53** An application may be refused if FICO are not satisfied that the information provided in the application is correct; or they are not satisfied that the non-resident landlord will comply with its tax obligations. This will be by notice in writing. There is an initial right of appeal to FICO within 90 days of the date of the notice. There is then a further right of appeal to the General Commissioners or, if the landlord elects, the Special Commissioners.

## 15.54 Other Overseas Aspects

**15.54** An approval may be withdrawn if FICO cease to be satisfied that the information provided in the application is correct; or they are no longer satisfied that the non-resident landlord will comply with its tax obligations; or the non-resident landlord fails to supply information requested by FICO. A notice withdrawing approval will be issued by FICO stating the reason for the withdrawal and the date from which it is effective. The letting agent or tenant will also be notified of the date from which they should start deducting tax from rental income. The same appeals procedure applies as for refusals.

*Changes of letting agent or tenant*

**15.55** Where a non-resident landlord changes letting agents, or tenants where there is no letting agent, it is not permissible to transfer a notice held by the old letting agent or tenant to the new letting agent or tenant. The landlord should write to FICO with details of the new letting agent or tenant, who will then send a notice to them. New letting agents or tenants must deduct tax until they receive such a notice.

### Deduction at source

**15.56** In the absence of an authority to pay rent to an 'approved' non-resident landlord under the provisions outlined above, a letting agent or tenant must deduct basic rate tax from all property income, net of certain allowable expenses paid by the agent or tenant out of that income, and account quarterly for the tax to the Revenue. No deduction is required where the rental income does not exceed £5,200 per annum in aggregate.

### Letting agents

*Meaning of the term*

**15.57** A letting agent is a person whose usual place of abode is in the UK; who acts on behalf of a non-resident landlord in connection with the management or administration of his UK rental business; with power to receive income of that rental business, or control the direction of that income; and who is not an 'excluded person' as set out below. The category includes people acting in a professional capacity, such as estate agents, solicitors and accountants.

*Excluded persons*

**15.58** An excluded person is one whose activity on behalf of the non-resident landlord is confined to the provision of legal advice or legal services. [*Reg 4(1)* of the *1995 Regulations*; see 15.46]. The Revenue consider that solicitors who do no more than receive apportioned rental income in the course of a conveyance, or take legal proceedings for the recovery of arrears of rental income, are excluded persons. But solicitors who draw up a lease and collect the rent for the first period are not excluded persons. Whilst drawing up a lease would be the provision of a legal service, in collecting the rent the solicitor would be going beyond the provision of legal services and acting as a letting agent.

**15.59** Banks and building societies who only provide an account into which rental income is paid and from which withdrawals are made are likewise not treated as letting agents. The same applies to other persons who merely receive income. Those who find tenants for non-resident landlords and who receive fees for that service but do not handle or control any rental income, or handle or control income only for short periods (described as 'tenant finders'), are outside the scheme. [See 15.66].

### Chains of letting agents

**15.60** In cases where a non-resident landlord has more than one letting agent in the UK in respect of the same source of rental income, this is referred to as a chain of letting agents. In such cases, the last agent in the chain (being the agent who pays the income directly to the landlord) must generally operate the scheme. So if one letting agent collects rents and passes them on to a second letting agent, the second letting agent must operate the scheme. However, the last letting agent in the chain and any other letting agent can jointly elect to transfer the responsibility for operating the scheme from the last letting agent to the other letting agent making the election. [*Reg 4*]. Such an election should be made in writing to FICO with the following information: the name and address of the elected agent; the name and address of the other letting agent; the name and address of the non-resident landlord or landlords; and the date from which the election is to take effect (not earlier than the first date of the quarter in which the election is made). An election may be made in respect of only part of a landlord's rental business by identifying the property to which the election relates. Such an election may be revoked subsequently.

### Branches of letting agents

**15.61** Letting agents with several branches may apply to FICO to register each branch as a separate letting agent on form NRL 5, but only if the branches deal with an average of five or more non-resident landlords each. The term 'branches' means the units into which the letting agent divides his or her business and includes areas, regions and other administration centres. [*Reg 6(1)*]. On the form, letting agents must provide details of their name and head office address; their Tax Office and reference number; the name and address of each branch to be registered; the number of non-resident landlords dealt with by each

## 15.62 Other Overseas Aspects

branch; and a declaration that they do not act on behalf of any non-residents other than those whose business is managed by the branches listed on the form. [*Reg 6(2)*].

**15.62** When approval has been granted each branch will be able to operate the scheme separately from the first day of the quarter following the quarter in which the approval is given and for any subsequent quarter. [*Reg 6(3)*]. Letting agents may revoke approval for branches to operate the scheme separately by giving notice in writing to FICO, which will take effect from the first day of the quarter following the quarter in which the revocation is made. [*Reg 6(4)*]. FICO should be notified where a branch closes or ceases to act for non-resident landlords, and similarly, when a new branch opens or starts to act for non-resident landlords.

**15.63** An application may be refused by FICO where they have reason to believe that the average number of non-residents per branch is less than five; or the letting agent is likely to fail to comply with the obligations imposed on him by the rules of the scheme; or the declaration on form NRL 5 is incorrect. [*Reg 6(6)*]. A refusal will be given by notice in writing to the letting agent, specifying the reasons. The letting agent may appeal against the refusal to FICO within 30 days of the date of the notice. If the appeal cannot be settled by agreement it will be referred to the General Commissioners or, if the letting agent elects, the Special Commissioners. [*Reg 6(8)(9)*].

**15.64** There are similar provisions enabling FICO to withdraw approval, with a similar procedure to be followed regarding written notice and the right of approval.

### Notices from FICO to operate the scheme

**15.65** A notice may be issued by FICO to a letting agent requiring the letting agent to operate the scheme. The notice will usually specify the landlord(s) in respect of whom the letting agent must operate the scheme, and the commencement date. A letting agent who receives such a notice must operate the scheme until the notice is withdrawn or until he ceases to act for the non-resident landlord(s), if earlier.

### Tenant finders

**15.66** Some persons simply enter into arrangements with a non-resident landlord to find a tenant for the landlord's property. Having done so they may collect rent for a period, from which they recover the fee. The tenant subsequently pays rental income directly to the landlord. In such cases, the tenant finder does not have to operate the scheme in respect of the landlord, provided the period for which rent is collected is no more than three months, and the tax which would be payable would be no more than £100.

*Other Overseas Aspects* **15.71**

**15.67** In cases where tenant finders collect the initial rent but do not have to operate the scheme, the non-resident landlord will receive rental income gross for that period. Subsequently tenants paying the rent direct to the landlord may have to operate the scheme. The tenant finder should then notify the tenant of his obligations under the NRL scheme.

## Registration

**15.68** Letting agents who have to operate the scheme must register with FICO within 30 days of the date on which they are first required to operate the scheme, giving their name and address, their tax reference number and the name of their Tax Office. They will then be allocated a registration number, and the appropriate forms and information will be issued to them by FICO.

## Calculation of payment of tax by letting agents

*Obligations and tax calculation*

**15.69** Unless they have been informed in writing by FICO that the landlord is approved to receive the rental income with no tax deducted, letting agents must calculate the tax for each quarter and pay the tax due to the Inland Revenue within 30 days of the end of the quarter, being the last day of March, June, September and December. [*Reg 9*]. Letting agents must not accept merely a non-resident landlord's statement that rental income may be paid without deduction of tax.

**15.70** Tax should be calculated at the basic rate on rental income less expenses. Rental income actually received in the quarter is to be included, and also rental income which was income which the letting agent had the power to receive and was paid away in the quarter at his direction to another person without being received by him. Deductible expenses are those which the letting agent actually paid in the quarter and also those paid away in the quarter at his direction by another person.

*Excess expenses*

**15.71** Where the deductible expenses for any quarter exceed the rental income to be taken into account for the quarter, the excess is first to be carried back and deducted from rental income of the same landlord for previous quarters in the same year to 31 March, taking later quarters before earlier quarters. Any balance is to be carried forward and deducted from rental income of the same landlord for subsequent quarters, taking earlier quarters before later quarters. This carry forward is not restricted to quarters within the same year to 31 March. [*Reg 9(5)*]. It should be stressed that any excess expenses paid in respect of one

**15.72** *Other Overseas Aspects*

landlord cannot be deducted from the rental income of another landlord.

*Repayable amounts*

**15.72** Excess expenses carried back to an earlier quarter will reduce the letting agent's tax liability in respect of that earlier quarter, this reduction being called a 'repayable amount'. This is recoverable by a set off against the total tax due to the Inland Revenue in respect of the letting agent's other non-resident landlords for the same payment quarter as that in which the excess expenses arise. If the entirety cannot be recovered in this way, the letting agent may claim a repayment from the Revenue on the form NRLQ, which is to be completed for the quarter in which the excess expenses arise. [*Reg 9(6)*].

**15.73** Tax due must be paid each quarter to the Inland Revenue with return form NRLQ. Letting agents who are not required to pay tax for any quarter do not need to complete a form for the quarter, unless specifically required by FICO. The following details must be shown on the return form: the quarter to which the return form relates; the total amount of tax due in respect of all their non-resident landlords for that quarter; or where there is no tax due in the quarter but the letting agent is due a repayment, the amount of the repayment claimed. The declaration on the form stating that the particulars given are, to the best of the letting agent's knowledge, correct and complete must also be signed. [*Reg 10*].

**15.74** Letting agents acting for more than one non-resident company should calculate the tax due for each landlord separately, then add together the amounts due and subtract any repayable amount. Payment for the amount due with the completed return form should be sent to the Revenue Accounts Office at Cumbernauld. This must be sent in time to arrive no later than 30 days after the end of the quarter to which it relates. For example, form NRLQ for the quarter to 30 September 1999 must arrive at Accounts Office by 30 October 1999. Interest may be charged on late payment from the due date. [*Reg 10(6)*]. Where interest is so charged and that tax is subsequently repaid, the letting agent is not entitled to recover any of the interest. [*Reg 10(7)*].

*Assessments to recover tax*

**15.75** Under the NRL scheme tax is payable by letting agents without the need for the Inland Revenue to make tax assessments. But, where FICO has reason to believe that an amount should have been paid but was not, or a quarterly return is incorrect, they can make an assessment. In these circumstances FICO will ask the letting agent's own Tax Office to make the assessment. [*Reg 10(9)*]. The letting agent has the right of appeal, which should be made in writing, either to FICO or to the Tax

Office, within 30 days of the date of the assessment. If the appeal cannot be settled by agreement it will be heard by the General Commissioners, or if the letting agent elects, the Special Commissioners. Interest on assessed income may be charged from the date when the amount of tax became due until the date it is paid.

*Annual returns*

**15.76** An annual return must be made by all letting agents who have to operate the NRL scheme by 5 July each year in respect of the year to 31 March. The following details must be shown separately for each non-resident landlord:

(a) the landlord's name and address;

(b) the amount of rental income for the year to 31 March before the deduction of expenses;

(c) if the letting agent is not authorised to pay rental income to the landlord with no tax deducted, the deductible expenses for the year to 31 March, and the total of the tax shown as payable in the letting agent's quarterly returns for the year to 31 March; and

(d) if the letting agent is authorised to pay rental income to the landlord with no tax deducted, the landlord's approval reference number. [*Reg 11*].

**15.77** The letting agent must also sign a declaration that the return is, to the best of his knowledge, correct and complete. Returns submitted on magnetic media conforming to the Revenue's guidelines will be acceptable. Penalties are eligible for failure to make a return, or for making an incorrect return.

*Certificate to be provided by letting agents*

**15.78** Letting agents liable to pay tax in any year in respect of a non-resident landlord must provide the landlord with a certificate by 5 July following the end of the year to 31 March. The certificate must show the non-resident company's name and address; the letting agent's name and address; the year ended 31 March to which the certificate relates; and the letting agent's total liability to tax for the particular year in respect of the landlord. The certificate must also contain a declaration by the letting agent that the particulars contained in the certificate are, to the best of his knowledge, correct and complete. [*Reg 12*].

**15.79** Non-resident landlords should keep certificates. When they complete their UK Tax Return as non-resident companies they can set off the tax shown on the certificate against their overall UK tax liability, subject to the letting agent actually deducting the tax shown. Landlords may be asked to provide the certificate to their Tax Office as evidence in support of their self-assessment.

## 15.80 Other Overseas Aspects

**Tenants of non-resident landlords**

*Tenants who must operate the scheme*

**15.80** Tenants of a non-resident landlord generally have to operate the scheme where they pay rent direct to a non-resident landlord; or where they pay rent to a person outside the UK; or where they pay rent to a person who is not a letting agent; or where they receive a notice from the Inland Revenue. Rent paid into a non-resident landlord's UK bank or building society account is treated as paid direct to the non-resident landlord.

**15.81** FICO may issue a notice to a tenant requiring the tenant to operate the scheme. This will usually specify the landlord in respect of whom the scheme must be operated and the date of commencement. Tenants in receipt of such a notice must operate the scheme until the earlier of either FICO withdrawing the notice, or their ceasing to be a tenant of the non-resident landlord. [*Reg 3(1)*].

*Tenants who do not have to operate the scheme*

**15.82** Tenants do not have to operate the scheme if they pay rent to a letting agent in the UK. They also do not have to operate the scheme if they pay rent of £5,200 or less per year, unless they receive a notice from FICO requiring them to do so. Where a tenant occupies property for part of the year, the figure of £5,200 is proportionately reduced. For example, a tenant who occupies property for six months in the year ended 31 March 2000 is not required to operate the scheme if he is due to pay £2,600 or less. But if the amount is greater than this the scheme must be operated. The limit of £5,200 applies in respect of each landlord. So, where a tenant has several non-resident landlords, he is required to operate the scheme only in respect of those landlords to whom he is due to pay more than £5,200 a year.

*Notification*

**15.83** Tenants who have to operate the scheme should write to FICO providing their name and address, and the names and addresses of their non-resident landlords. FICO can then issue the appropriate forms and information in time for the tenant to complete returns and make payments of tax on time.

*Tenant's obligations regarding calculation and payment of tax*

**15.84** Tenants should calculate the tax each quarter, ending with the last day of March, June, September or December. They must pay the tax due to the Inland Revenue within 30 days of the end of the quarter. They are not required to calculate or pay tax on the rental income of a non-resident landlord if FICO have told them in writing that the landlord is approved to receive the rental income gross. A mere statement from the non-resident landlord that rental income may be paid without deduction of tax will not suffice.

**15.85** Tenants should calculate tax at the basic rate on rental income they pay to the landlord in the quarter, plus rental income they pay to third parties in the quarter which are not deductible expenses. [*Reg 8*]. A tenant who deducts insufficient tax will be able to recover tax from future rents. [*TMA 1970 s 42A (3)(b)*].

*Quarterly returns and payment*

**15.86** The tax due must be paid each quarter to the Inland Revenue Accounts Office, Cumbernauld with return form NRLQ. Quarterly returns are due for the periods ending 30 June, 30 September, 31 December and 31 March. Tenants who are not required to make a payment for any quarter do not need to complete a quarterly return form for the quarter, unless they are required to do so by a notice in writing from FICO. The return form must give details of the quarter to which the return form relates and the total amount of tax due on rental income. The declaration on the form must also be signed by the tenant stating that the particulars given therein are, to the best of his knowledge, correct and complete. [*Reg 10*].

**15.87** Tenants of more than one non-resident landlord should calculate the tax due for each landlord separately, adding together the amounts due and showing the total for the quarter on form NRLQ. The form and payment must be sent in time to arrive at the Accounts Office no later than 30 days after the end of the quarter to which it relates. For example, the quarterly return form NRLQ for the quarter to 30 September 2000 must arrive at the Accounts Office by 30 October 2000. Interest may be charged on late payment. [*Reg 10(6)*].

**15.88** Although it is the tenant's responsibility to pay the tax without a tax assessment by the Revenue, FICO have the same powers to make an assessment on tenants as they have on letting agents as described in 15.75 and in the same circumstances. The same appeals procedure and liability to interest on late payment applies.

*Annual returns*

**15.89** An annual return must be made by all tenants within the NRL scheme by 5 July each year in respect of the year to the previous 31 March. The following details must be shown separately for each non-resident landlord:

(a) the landlord's name and address;

## 15.90  Other Overseas Aspects

(b) the total amount of rental income paid to the landlord and rental income paid away to third parties in the year;

(c) if the tenant is not authorised to pay rental income to the landlord with no tax deducted, the deductible expenses for the year to 31 March; and the total of the tax shown as payable in the tenant's quarterly returns for the year to 31 March; and

(d) if the tenant is authorised to pay the landlord with no tax deducted, the landlord's approval reference number. [*Reg 11*].

**15.90**  The tenant must also complete the declaration that the return is, to the best of his knowledge, correct and complete. Where tenants have received notification from FICO that rental income may be paid to all their non-resident landlords with no tax deducted, they are not required to submit annual returns. Hence a person who is a tenant of only one non-resident landlord and who has the authority to pay rental income gross is not required to submit annual returns. A tenant of two non-resident landlords who has authority to pay rental income gross is not required to submit annual returns. But a tenant of two non-resident landlords who has authority to pay rental income to only one with no tax deducted must submit a return with details for both non-resident landlords. [*Reg 11(3)*]. Penalties may be charged for failure to make a return or for making an incorrect return.

*Certificate to be provided by tenants*

**15.91**  Tenants liable to pay tax in any year in respect of a non-resident landlord must provide each landlord with a certificate by 5 July following the end of the year to 31 March. The certificate must show the following information: the non-resident company's name and address; the year ended 31 March to which the certificate relates; and the tenant's total liability to tax for the year ended 31 March in respect of the landlord. The certificate must also contain a declaration by the tenant that the particulars contained in the certificate are, to the best of his knowledge, correct and complete. [*Reg 12*].

**15.92**  Non-resident landlords should keep certificates. When they complete their UK tax return they can set off the tax shown on the certificate against their overall UK tax liability subject to the tenant actually deducting the tax shown. Landlords may be asked to provide the certificate to their Tax Office as evidence in support of their self-assessment.

**Rental income**

*Tax deduction calculation*

**15.93**  Letting agents who have to operate the NRL scheme must calculate tax each quarter on the rental income received, less deductible expenses paid in the quarter. They should take into account all rental income they receive in the quarter, and rental income they do not receive in the quarter, but which is paid away to a third party (including the non-resident landlord) at the direction of the letting agent. Tenants must calculate tax each quarter on the rental income they have paid in the quarter. They should take into account all rental income they pay to the non-resident landlord in the quarter, and all rental income they pay to third parties in the quarter, unless the payments are deductible expenses.

**15.94** Letting agents and tenants should take into account all rental income received or paid in the quarter notwithstanding that it relates to rent due for an earlier, or later, period. They should not calculate tax for a quarter on rental income which fell due in the quarter but was not paid in the quarter.

*When rental income is received or paid*

**15.95** In the case of cheques for rent, letting agents are treated as receiving the income on the day it is banked or cleared. But if the cheque is subsequently dishonoured it may be disregarded in calculating the tax due. Tenants paying rental income by cheque are treated as making the payment on the day they give the cheque to the landlord and not on the day the cheque is cashed or cleared.

But if the cheque is subsequently dishonoured it may likewise be disregarded in calculating the tax due.

*Examples of rental income*

**15.96** Rental income includes a wide variety of receipts arising from land and property, as described in Chapter 7. In particular, rental income includes:
(a) income from furnished, unfurnished, commercial and domestic premises, and from any land;
(b) where property is let furnished, any separate sums from the tenant for the use of the furniture;
(c) rent charges, ground rents and feu duties;
(d) part of the premiums and other similar lump sums received on the grant of certain short leases;
(e) income arising from the grant of sporting rights, such as fishing and shooting permits;
(f) income arising from allowing waste to be buried or stored on land;
(g) income from letting others use land – for example, where a film crew pays to film inside a person's house or on their land;

### 15.97 Other Overseas Aspects

(h) grants received from local authorities or others contributing to expenditure, such as repairs to a let property;
(i) rental income received through enterprise investment schemes;
(j) income from caravans or houseboats where these are not moved around various locations;
(k) service charges received from tenants in respect of services ancillary to the occupation of property; and
(l) insurance recoveries under policies providing cover against non-payment of rent.

*Income which is not rental income*

**15.97** There are certain receipts which arise out of the use of the land which are not rental income, also as described in Chapter 7. These include:

(a) yearly interest;
(b) income from woodlands managed on a commercial basis; and
(c) income from the following types of concerns:

 (i) mines and quarries (including gravel pits, sandpits and brickfields);
 (ii) ironworks, gasworks, salt springs or works, alum mines or works and waterworks and streams of water;
 (iii) canals, inland navigations, docks, and drains or levels;
 (iv) rights of markets and fairs, tolls, bridges and ferries;
 (v) railways and other ways; and
 (vi) lettings of tied premises by traders.

**Deductible expenses**

*Test for deductibility*

**15.98** In determining tax due under the NRL scheme, letting agents and tenants should take into account expenses they pay in a quarter which they can reasonably be satisfied are allowable expenses in computing the profits of the landlord's rental business. [*Regs 8(2), 9(4)*]. It is to be noted that the payment of the expenses must be made by the letting agent or tenant himself, or at his direction. Any payments made directly by the landlord are not deductible in computing the tax due to the Revenue by the letting agent or tenant. Moreover, a deduction is not available for expenses accrued in a quarter but not paid.

**15.99** The test of reasonable satisfaction is considered by the Revenue to provide protection for letting agents and tenants in two ways:

(a) where they are uncertain whether an expense is an allowable expense they are justified under the rules in not deducting it when computing the tax due; and

(b) where they can reasonably be satisfied that an expense is an allowable expense they can deduct the expense without fear of being penalised if it is later found that the expense is not in fact allowable.

**15.100** Expenses are broadly allowable where they are incurred wholly and exclusively for the purposes of the rental business, and they are not of a capital nature. Expenditure on improvements and extensive alterations will be capital.

*Examples of deductible expenses*

**15.101** The Revenue have said that the following expenses will normally be deductible:

(a) accountancy expenses (incurred in preparing rental business accounts but not for preparing personal tax returns);
(b) advertising costs of attracting new tenants;
(c) cleaning;
(d) costs of rent collection;
(e) Council Tax while the property is vacant but available for letting;
(f) gardening;
(g) ground rent;
(h) insurance against loss of rents;
(i) insurance claim fees;
(j) insurance on buildings and contents;
(k) interest paid on loans to buy land or property (but see 15.104 below);
(l) legal and professional fees;
(m) letting agents' fees;
(n) maintenance charges made by freeholders, or superior leaseholders, of leasehold property;
(o) maintenance contracts (e.g. Gas Board servicing);
(p) provision of services (e.g. gas, electricity, hot water);
(q) rates;
(r) rental warranty and legal expenses insurance;
(s) repairs which are not significant improvements to the property, including:

**15.102** *Other Overseas Aspects*

    (i) damp and rot treatment;

    (ii) mending broken windows, doors, furniture, cookers, lifts, etc.;

    (iii) painting and decorating;

    (iv) replacing roof slates, flashing and gutters;

    (v) repainting; and

    (vi) stone cleaning;

(t) water rates.

**15.102** A letting agent's own fees are deductible notwithstanding that they are retained by the agent from rent received, rather than paid out by him.

*Interest paid on borrowings for the rental business*

**15.103** Interest paid directly by the landlord to a lender will not be taken into account in computing tax deductible by letting agents or tenants. This will therefore mean that a landlord company will only be able to obtain a deduction for such interest if it satisfies the procedure for payment of rent to be paid without deduction of tax or if it later files a tax return and self-assessment, in which case it may receive a repayment.

**15.104** When the letting agent or tenant pays loan interest on behalf of a non-resident landlord the interest should rank as a deductible expense.

**Record keeping and audit**

**15.105** Sufficient records are to be kept by letting agents and tenants to be able to satisfy the Revenue that their obligations under the NRL scheme have been complied with. [*Reg 15*]. They should keep the following records for each non-resident landlord separately: a record of rental income received by the letting agent or paid by the tenant; and copies of any correspondence with the landlord regarding his usual place of abode. Moreover, unless a letting agent is authorised to pay rental income with no tax deducted it should keep a record of expenses paid and invoices and receipts (or copies) to provide evidence of expenses paid.

**15.106** A detailed audit procedure is set out in the Revenue guidance notes, containing their proposed practice on the conduct of audits, including sample reviewing and extrapolation to quantify any tax underpaid. Interest and penalties are eligible for default.

*Other Overseas Aspects* **15.110**

**Practical implications of transfer pricing legislation**

**15.107** Transfer pricing issues are considered generally in Chapter 14. These can be relevant to non-resident landlord companies, particularly in respect of rents received from and interest paid to associates, or to a bank where a guarantee or similar has been given by an associate. In such cases the profits will have to be self-assessed in accordance with the arm's length principle. Some of the particular issues arising in respect of non-resident landlords have been considered in Tax Bulletin, Issue 46, April 2000 pp 740–742 (see Appendix 1).

# Investment income

**15.108** Under the old system non-resident companies could be assessed to basic rate tax on UK source investment income such as dividends and interest income. In practice the imposition of tax was largely restricted to tax deducted at source, with relief under ESC B13 (which exempted interest paid gross from assessment), ESC B40 (which exempted income under the investment manager and broker provisions from assessment) and double tax agreements (which limited taxing rights to nil, or a reduced rate of withholding tax).

**15.109** Under CTSA, statutory effect is given to the old de facto position by restricting the tax charge on non-resident companies to any tax which is deducted at source in the case of the following types of income, under *FA 1995 s 128(1)–(3)*, (described as 'excluded income'):

(a) income from government securities;

(b) deposit interest and other income taxable under Schedule D, Case III;

(c) dividends taxable under Schedule F;

(d) income from certificates of deposit with financial institutions and banks taxable under Schedule D, Case VI under *TA 1988 s 56*;

(e) social security benefits (notably retirement pensions and unemployment benefit) taxable under Schedule E under *TA 1988 s 150* or *s 617* and incapacity benefits taxable under *FA 1994 s 139*;

(f) income received through a broker or investment manager that meets the requisite conditions for exemption in *FA 1995 s 127* (such as commodity dealing or trading in derivatives) other than underwriting profits of a Lloyd's name [*FA 1995 s 129*]; and

(g) any other income that may be designated by the Treasury by statutory instrument.

**15.110** It follows that normally a non-resident company, the UK source income of which is wholly derived from investments, will have no need to self-assess except where a repayment is due. Excluded income taxed at

**15.111** *Other Overseas Aspects*

source includes income where tax is deducted or treated as deducted, paid or treated as paid, or in respect of which there is a tax credit and the amount of tax is the amount deducted, paid or credited as appropriate. [*FA 1995 s 128(4)*].

## Intellectual property

**15.111** The categories of excluded income outlined in 15.109 do not extend to intellectual property, for example royalties from a UK patent, trademark or copyright. Moreover, it is understood that it is not presently planned for there to be any Treasury designation to this effect under the provisions referred to in 15.109(g). Royalties from a UK patent are in any event subject to deduction of tax at source at the basic rate under *TA 1988 s 349(1)(b)*. Copyright royalties are similarly subject to deduction at source under *TA 1988 s 536*. There are similar provisions for public lending rights under *TA 1988 s 537*. There is, however, no withholding tax on royalties paid for the licensing of trademarks or know-how, although the sale of know-how is a trading receipt. However these rules are likely to change, following the publication of the Revenue Technical Note on 9 March 1999 entitled 'Reform of the Taxation of Intellectual Property'.

**15.112** In so far as royalties accrue to a corporate originator of the patent, trade marks or copyright, they are likely to be derived from a trade or profession carried on by it. The exploitation of the patents etc., might indicate that the trade or profession was being carried on partly in the UK, in which case it would be taxable. If the trading took place through a branch or agency, the UK representative would be jointly liable with the non-resident under *FA 1995 s 126* and *23 Sch*. If the trade or profession was carried out wholly abroad there would be no UK income tax liability.

**15.113** Where the royalties constituted investment income, say in the hands of the assignee of a trader, because the income would not be within the category of excluded income the royalties would be subject to basic rate tax in the hands of a non-resident company, unless they constituted pure income profit of the recipient taxable under Schedule D, Case III and subject to deduction of tax at source as an annual payment under *TA 1988 ss 348–350*.

## E-commerce

**15.114** E-commerce is the name normally given to business conducted through or with the assistance of the Internet. It can take a variety of forms, the most basic of which is nothing more than advertising for business through a web-site with any orders being dealt with by traditional means. It may, however, be sale of entirely digitised products which can be electronically transferred from the producer to the consumer. There are a number of intermediate operations where, for

*Other Overseas Aspects* **15.118**

example, an interactive web-site will offer a facility to search for the appropriate product and to enable the order to be placed electronically, and for payment to be made electronically through a credit card, as a result of which the product itself could be delivered physically through normal channels.

**15.115** The essence of the Internet is that it is world-wide and the customer can be almost anywhere. In business to business e-commerce a number of companies are not only selling but buying through the Internet, by inviting tenders for the supply of raw materials or services. It is the nature of e-commerce that the information on the Internet web-site can be posted from anywhere and likewise, orders processed from anywhere. This makes it difficult to fit e-commerce activities within the normal rules of a company where it has a permanent establishment making it liable to tax in a jurisdiction. It may be difficult to determine whether there is a taxable presence in a country, and whether withholding taxes should be applied to digitised products, on the grounds that it is a royalty, or only taxed if there is a permanent establishment, on the grounds that it is a supply of business services. There are also traditional transfer pricing problems of attribution of profit even where there is a physical supply of goods, because the actual physical activities requiring a permanent establishment may be little more than warehousing and distribution, with the marketing and processing of orders being done electronically.

**15.116** The position with regard to direct taxes such as VAT, sales taxes and customs duties is also difficult, although where physical goods are concerned these may be collected at the point of importation.

**15.117** The trouble with global business, such as may be carried out through the Internet, is that there is no global system of taxation. The ability to trade through the Internet is regarded as a threat to the tax base in a number of high tax jurisdictions, which has resulted in a number of international studies led independently, and not always consistently by the OECD, the European Union and the G8 countries. In this connection the Commission of the European Communities published on 7 June 2000 Proposals for a Regulation of the European Parliament and of the Council, amending *Regulation EEC No. 218/92* on administrative co-operating in the field of indirect taxation (VAT) and a Proposal for a Council Directive, amending *Directive 77/388/EEC* as regards the value added tax arrangements applicable to certain services supplied by electronic means.

**15.118** Little effective action has been taken, although countries such as Bermuda with its Electronic Transactions Act introduced in 1999, have taken steps which go some way to regulating the trade. Many other jurisdictions are contemplating further regulation but little has yet been enacted in tax terms, and the US has recently extended its moratorium on new taxes for e-commerce business until 2006.

## 15.119 Other Overseas Aspects

**15.119** In interpreting permanent establishment it is obviously necessary to consider whether this is restricted to the physical world, or whether a web-site on a server could be regarded as a permanent establishment. So far as the UK is concerned, in the Inland Revenue Press Release of 11 April 2000, Appendix 6, it has been confirmed that the UK Revenue take the view that a web-site of itself is not a permanent establishment and that a server is insufficient to constitute a permanent establishment of a business that is merely conducting its own e-commerce through a web-site on the server. This is so, regardless of whether the server is owned, rented or otherwise at the disposal of the business.

**15.120** Other tests of residence, such as central management and control, are also made more difficult with the use of electronic communication. It is difficult to say where a decision is taken where a number of directors in different jurisdictions hold a directors' meeting through video-conferencing links. It seems likely that in the direct tax field in the short term, Revenue authorities world-wide will move towards controlled foreign company type legislation if they do not already have it in place to pick up a tax charge on profits arising through group vehicles overseas. It also seems likely that the countries that already have such legislation will be looking to reinforce its efficacy to take account of potential avoidance through areas such as trading trusts and cellular companies, although the extent to which this is going to be successful is likely to be very mixed given the vast differences in the sophistication of the tax legislation in different jurisdictions, the substantial differences in tax rates, encouraging tax arbitrage, and substantial differences in the practical application and enforcement of those rules that do exist.

**15.121** Governments, at the time of writing, have a love-hate relationship with e-commerce because, on the one hand they need to protect the tax base in order to provide the services expected by their inhabitants, and on the other they wish to encourage employment and prosperity which a global marketplace can provide, and to ensure that they obtain at least their fair proportion, and if possible more than their fair proportion, of the world-wide electronic business. At the present time, therefore, e-commerce is being squeezed to fit within the existing rules of residence by reference to incorporation and central management and control and trading with a country rather than carrying on trade in that country with or without a permanent establishment. Similarly, the rules relating to controlled foreign companies (Chapter 13) and transfer pricing (Chapter 14) have to be applied to e-commerce under the existing rules. The fact that e-commerce transactions do not fall easily within existing definitions offers opportunities for effective tax planning.

## Double taxation relief

### Unilateral relief

**15.122** Credit for corporation tax may be claimed for foreign taxes suffered as unilateral relief under *TA 1988 s 790(1)* and *(2)*. Unilateral relief is given as if there were a double taxation treaty in force, computed by reference to the foreign tax rules, subject to an overriding restriction of the UK corporation tax due on that income. [*TA 1988 s 790(3)* and *(4)*, *Yates v GCA International Ltd [1991] STC 157*, *George Wimpey International v Rolfe [1989] STC 609*, SP7/91]. The credit for foreign tax against UK corporation tax is, except for the Channel Islands and the Isle of Man, limited to the income arising in the foreign territory, so that indirect foreign tax, for example on foreign branch profits of the overseas company would not be relieved. [*TA 1988 s 790(5)(a)*]. Where there is a treaty in force, relief has to be claimed under the treaty so far as possible, which may mean reclaiming tax from the overseas Revenue authority, rather than as a credit against the UK tax liability. [*TA 1988 s 790(5)(b)*].

**15.123** Unilateral relief is available for foreign withholding taxes on dividends under *TA 1988 s 790(5)(c)(i)*. It also applies to dividends paid to UK insurance companies trading overseas [*TA 1988 s 790(5)(c)(iii)* and *s 802*], or dividends paid to a UK company which either directly or indirectly controls, or is a subsidiary of a company which directly or indirectly controls, not less than 10 per cent of the voting power in the company paying the dividend, or would have, had it not been reduced through force majeure. [*TA 1988 s 790(5)(c)(ii)*, *(6–10)*]. A subsidiary for this purpose means not less than 50 per cent of the voting power is held by the parent company. [*TA 1988 s 792(2)*].

**15.124** Although *TA 1988 s 790(4)* restricts the credit available to the foreign tax on the income arising or chargeable gain accruing in the foreign territory, it is extended by Extra Statutory Concession B8 to include royalties and know-how payments subject to overseas withholding taxes, even though technically the source of income may be in the UK. A distribution from a German silent partnership is not a dividend for which relief is available under these provisions. [*Memec plc v IRC [1998] STC 754*]. Unilateral relief for chargeable gains is given by *TCGA 1992 s 277*.

### Treaty relief

**15.125** Double taxation agreements may be entered into with other countries under the provisions of *TA 1988 s 788*. As an international agreement, a double tax treaty overrules any of the provisions of the Taxes Acts. [*Ostime v Australian Mutual Providence Society (1959) 38 TC 492*, *Padmore v IRC [1989] STC 493*]. Relief is normally given on

**15.126** *Other Overseas Aspects*

income and gains where overseas taxes are similar in nature to income or corporation tax. Deemed income is not relievable under a double taxation treaty so that relief is not available for deemed corporation tax under the controlled foreign company provisions of *TA 1988 s 747(4)(a)*. [*Bricom Holdings Ltd v IRC [1997] STC 1179*].

**15.126** The provisions of the double taxation treaty may exempt income or gains of a treaty partner from UK taxation in whole or in part, or may provide a reduced level of taxation, or provide a mechanism for attributing income or gains to the UK branches of non-residents.

**15.127** The UK has a large number of double taxation agreements which differ materially in detail, although most modern agreements tend to follow the OECD Model Tax Convention. A number of treaties of limited application do not apply, for example, to dividends, interest and royalties, or to capital gains, whereas others are limited to shipping and air transport profits. Many treaties provide a tie-breaker clause under which a company resident in both states under local laws would be deemed to be resident only in the country where the place of effective management is carried on. [*FA 1988 s 66* and *FA 1994 s 249*].

**15.128** Some treaties contain anti-avoidance provisions limiting the benefit of the relief to companies beneficially owned by residents of the other jurisdiction while others are subject to a protocol denying relief for tax favoured entities in the other jurisdiction. A taxpayer who is entitled to relief under a double taxation agreement must claim relief from the foreign tax or a credit in respect of the foreign tax paid under the treaty, and not as unilateral relief under *TA 1988 s 790*. This applies to claims made on or after 21 March 2000. Further restrictions apply to treaties entered into on or after this date. [*TA 1988 s 793A;* Inland Revenue Press Release, 3 March 2000]. Credit for foreign tax will be given for foreign tax paid after all reasonable steps have been taken to reduce to a minimum the foreign tax liability, by claiming any treaty entitlement or reliefs or allowances available under the domestic law of the foreign country. These provisions apply to claims made on or after 21 March 2000. [*TA 1988 s 795A*].

**15.129** Where an agreement confers on non-residents the right to a tax credit, the credit is calculated in accordance with *FA 1989 s 115*, which overruled *Union Texas Petroleum Corpn v Critchley [1990] STC 305* with retrospective effect. [*Getty Oil Co v Steele [1990] STC 434*]. The UK tax deductible under the UK/US double taxation treaty is based on the aggregate of the dividend and the gross tax credit payable, so that from 5 April 1999, a dividend of £90 which gives rise to an ACT payment of £10 produces a tax credit payment of 1/2 of this, which amounts to £5, less 5 per cent of £95, £4.75, leaving a net credit of £0.25 on the dividend. Not surprisingly the US Government has given notice to cancel the existing agreement and a new double tax treaty between the UK and the US is under negotiation. The changes to the imputation system arising from the abolition of ACT and withdrawal, in most circumstances, of payable tax credits, means that the entitlement to any material credit, other than for the underlying tax, is denied under most double tax treaties.

**15.130** Where a non-resident is given a right to a tax credit, that includes any repayment supplement. [*R v IRC, ex p Commerzbank AG [1993] STC 605*].

**15.131** Where an overseas country grants pioneer relief, to encourage developing industries through tax exemption for a period, the benefit of this relief would be lost to a UK resident company liable to corporation tax on its profits, or dividends from an overseas branch or subsidiary, where foreign tax had been spared under such provisions. Therefore double taxation treaties with such countries typically provide that the tax forgone under the pioneer provisions is nonetheless deemed to have been paid for the purpose of giving credit under the treaty to UK residents. [*TA 1988 s 788(5)*]. From 20 March 2000 this relief is restricted to first tier subsidiaries or second or greater tier subsidiaries in the same jurisdiction. [*FA 2000 30 Sch 1–3*]. Excess credit may be recovered by means of an assessment under Schedule D, Case VI. [*TA 1988 s 788(7)*].

**15.132** The Inland Revenue publish a list of taxes they consider to be admissible under double taxation treaties or for unilateral relief, IR146. Powers are given to the Revenue to make regulations by Statutory Instrument to ensure the double taxation relief, and these include *SI 1970 No. 488* and *SI 1973 No. 317*.

**15.133** Double taxation agreements include foreign tax, UK tax and underlying tax. Double taxation relief is normally given by way of a credit for the tax suffered abroad against the UK corporation tax charge on those profits.

**15.134** Only a UK resident used to be able to claim relief for foreign tax credits against UK taxes, although this was extended to the UK branch of a foreign bank in appropriate circumstances, under *TA 1988 s 794*. The provisions of foreign tax credits for banks and insurance companies is a specialised area outside the scope of this book. [See for example, *TA 1988 ss 797A, 798, 798A, 798B, 802, 803, 804A to F* and *19AC Sch*]. However, the unilateral relief provisions in *TA 1988 s 790* are modified by *FA 2000 30 Sch 4* to allow a non-resident with a branch or agency in the UK to claim unilateral relief for foreign tax where a foreign dividend forms part of the UK branch profits. Relief extends to underlying tax and effectively treats the UK branch of a non-resident as a UK company. These changes apply in relation to accounting periods ending on or after 21 March 2000.

**15.135** *TA 1988 s 797* limits the credit for double taxation relief available against corporation tax on any income or chargeable gains to the UK

**15.136** *Other Overseas Aspects*

corporation tax on that income or gain. [*Yates v GCA International Ltd [1991] STC 157*].

**15.136** In the case of tax payable on chargeable gains SP6/88 confirms that there is no requirement that the respective tax liabilities should arise at the same time, or be charged on the same person. If therefore, there is, for example, an intra-group disposal within *TCGA 1992 s 171* which is subject to foreign tax on the chargeable gain arising, there would be no immediate UK corporation tax liability against which to set the foreign tax paid because of roll-over. When, however, the transferee disposes of the asset outside the group, the overseas tax previously paid would be credited against the corporation tax on the chargeable gain.

**15.137** A company may allocate charges on income, management expenses and non-trading deficits on loan relationships in the most beneficial manner to maximise the double tax relief available. [*TA 1988 s 797(3)*]. The amount of charges etc. which may be set against profits from a particular source can reduce those profits to zero, but cannot create a loss. [*Commercial Union Assurance Co plc v Shaw [1998] STC 386*].

**15.138** *TA 1988 s 797(4)* allowed foreign tax credits to be set against the mainstream liability before deducting ACT. As foreign tax credits could not be carried back or forwards or surrendered, this provision helped to minimise the loss of foreign tax credits, but often at the expense of creating irrecoverable ACT surpluses.

## Offshore pooling

**15.139** Because the UK restricts the foreign tax credit to the UK tax on that income, it was common practice to set up a foreign holding company to hold investments in overseas subsidiaries so that the tax paid out from the subsidiaries to the foreign holding company might be aggregated and apportioned to the dividend paid to the UK parent. Such foreign holding companies have typically been set up in the Netherlands, and are therefore known as 'Dutch Mixers'. The Revenue seemed to regard this as acceptable tax planning and not a structure interposed for purely tax planning purposes, capable of being disregarded on the basis of *WT Ramsay Ltd v IRC [1981] STC 174*. However, *TA 1988 s 801* is amended by *FA 2000 30 Sch 11* to remove the benefit of using mixer companies. The relief for underlying tax in respect of dividends out of profits of sub-subsidiaries, paid to the United Kingdom is, in each case, limited to a credit at the standard rate of corporation tax. The maximum credit for underlying tax is the net dividend grossed up at the standard rate of corporation tax. The restriction applies to claims made on or after 31 March 2001 in respect of dividends paid on or after that date. [Inland Revenue Press Release, 3 May 2000]. These restrictions do not normally apply to dividends within the same jurisdiction. There are, however, provisions introduced to allow a limited form of onshore pooling where this involves genuine business activities (see below). [Inland Revenue

*Other Overseas Aspects* **15.142**

Press Release, 16 June 2000]. Mixing CFC dividends to meet an acceptable distribution policy is prohibited. [*TA 1988 s 801C*]. Non-CFC dividends with underlying tax above the 30 per cent corporation tax cap may be credited against UK tax payable on uncapped non-CFC dividends under the onshore pooling provisions.

**15.140** In the case of non-trading loan relationships, for the purpose of computing double taxation relief, *TA 1988 s 797A* provides that corporation tax is based on the company's gross non-trading relationship credits without deducting non-trading loan debits, which may then be deducted in the manner most beneficial to the company, in order to maximise the double taxation relief available. Unused non-trading deficits brought forward are allocated against non-trading profits.

**Underlying tax**

**15.141** Relief for underlying tax on the profits out of which dividends are paid is given by *TA 1988 s 799*. The underlying tax attributable to a dividend is the tax payable on the relevant profits represented by the dividend [*TA 1988 s 799(1)*] subject to an overriding limit of the standard rate of corporation tax on the grossed up equivalent of the dividend. [*FA 2000 30 Sch 8*]. Where the foreign country has an imputation tax system the dividend tax credit is ignored in order to avoid the underlying tax being credited twice. [*TA 1988 s 799(2)*]. The relevant profits which relate to the dividend are those of any specified period covered by the dividend or any specified profits out of which the dividend is paid, otherwise it is the profits of the last period of account made up to the date before the dividend becomes payable. [*TA 1988 s 799(3) and (4)*]. The Courts considered the allocation of the overseas tax to the profits computed for accounting purposes in *Bowater Paper Corpn Ltd v Murgatroyd (1969) 46 TC 37*, and the CCAB published clarification on 19 October 1979 of the calculation of underlying relief. *TA 1988 s 799* is amended to clarify the meaning of relevant profits out of which a dividend is paid to a UK company. The profits are those available for distribution, as shown by the commercial accounts of the overseas company, without any adjustment for reserves, bad debts and contingencies, other than those which are obligatory under the appropriate foreign law. This applies to claims for relief for underlying tax in respect of dividends paid to a UK company on or after 21 March 2000. [*FA 2000 30 Sch 9*]. Where a group of overseas companies is taxed as a single entity, for example under the Dutch fiscal entity provisions, the underlying tax is calculated as if the overseas group were a single company. These provisions apply in respect of credit relief claims for dividends paid to a UK company on or after 21 March 2000. [*TA 1988 s 803A*].

**15.142** Where a double taxation treaty restricted relief for underlying tax on dividends to certain classes of shares, *TA 1988 s 800* gave credit for underlying tax where the shareholding was not less than 10 per cent in the voting power of the foreign company paying the dividend, in the same

**15.143** *Other Overseas Aspects*

way as unilateral relief was granted by *TA 1988 s 790(6)*, but this is now repealed as obsolete, from 1 April 2000, by *FA 2000 30 Sch 9*. Where a UK company receives a dividend from an overseas company and that dividend is paid out of profits which include dividends from related companies in other countries, the underlying tax of the entire chain is available for relief, provided that each company in the chain controls directly or indirectly, or is a subsidiary of a company which controls directly or indirectly, the company paying the dividend in each case. [*TA 1988 s 801*]. There is, however, an anti-avoidance provision in *TA 1988 s 801A* which denies a double taxation credit for underlying tax in respect of a dividend if there is a scheme or arrangement, the purpose, or one of the purposes, of which, is to have an amount of underlying tax taken into account where the non-resident company is not under the control of the UK company before the scheme or arrangement was entered into. [Tax Bulletin, Issue 29, June 1997, p 441]. Profits of one foreign company may have become profits of another foreign company other than by way of dividend, for example on a merger or where payment is made through a fiscally transparent entity such as a US limited liability company. In such cases underlying tax credit relief will be allowed in respect of dividends paid by the transferee of the foreign profits to the UK resident company on or after 21 March 2000, subject to the same limitation that would apply as if the profits had actually been transferred by way of dividend. [*TA 1988 s 801B*].

**15.143** In certain cases it actually pays not to claim a foreign tax credit, and *TA 1988 s 805* allows this. In such cases the foreign tax may be treated as a trading expense, under *TA 1988 s 811* or *TCGA 1992 s 278*. [*Harrods (Buenos Aires) Ltd v Taylor-Gooby (1964) 41 TC 450, IRC v Dowdall O'Mahoney & Co Ltd (1952) 33 TC 259*]. Where foreign tax is treated as an expense because no credit is allowable and there is a subsequent adjustment to the foreign tax payable, the UK tax charge may be revised within six years from the date of the foreign tax adjustment, and written notice that a deduction has become excessive has to be given to the Revenue. This applies to foreign tax adjustments made on or after 21 March 2000. [*FA 2000 30 Sch 20*].

**15.144** The time limit for double taxation relief claims is six years from the end of the accounting period, under *TA 1988 s 806(1)(b)*, but this period can be extended where the tax is subsequently adjusted either in the UK or overseas. [*TA 1988 s 806(2)*]. *TA 1988 s 806* is amended in respect of claims made on or after 21 March 2000, to enable claims for foreign tax to be made within one year of the actual date of payment of the tax, if this is later than the normal six year time limit. [*FA 2000 30 Sch 21, TA 1988 s 806G*]. This will help to alleviate timing mismatches where, for example, the foreign tax is paid on a payment basis but the UK income is taxed on an accruals basis. If excessive relief has been claimed as a result of the adjustment to the overseas taxation, the company must notify the Revenue or face a penalty. [*TA 1988 s 807(3) to (6)*].

**15.145** Eligible unrelieved foreign tax paid in excess of the credit that is allowable, up to a maximum of 45 per cent on the grossed up dividend, may be carried forward without limit, or backwards for three years, and set against UK tax chargeable on income from the same source provided that a claim is made within six years of the accounting period in which the excess arises. Where the mixer cap under *FA 2000 39 Sch 8* applies, the eligible unrelieved foreign tax is the difference between the credit allowed and the foreign tax suffered on the ultimate dividend to the holding company as if it had been grossed up at the foreign tax rate, subject to a maximum of 45 per cent. This does not apply to lower level dividends, however. Under these carrying backwards and forwards provisions the excess foreign tax is treated as if it were paid in the previous or following accounting period. These provisions apply both to overseas branch or agency profits taxable under Schedule D, Case I or VI and qualifying dividends chargeable under Schedule D, Case V. The sources are the particular branch, agency or shareholding in respect of which the excess credit arises. The new rules apply in respect of accounting periods ending on or after 1 April 2000 or dividends arising on or after 31 March 2001, including those received by a UK branch of a foreign company. [*TA 1988 s 806K*]. However, the carry back provisions cannot be applied to accounting periods ending on or before 31 March 2000 or dividends arising on or before 31 March 2001. [*TA 1988 s 806A and B*; Inland Revenue Press Release, 16 June 2000]. There are provisions to deal with cases where two or more dividends from the same qualifying source are received in an accounting period. Where a particular qualifying source ceases, the amount of any unrelieved foreign tax credit in respect of it that remains unrelieved is reduced to nil, even if another similar source in the same country is subsequently acquired. Formal claims specifying the allocation of the unrelieved foreign tax must be made within six years of the end of the accounting period in which the excess credit arises. [*TA 1988 s 806G*]. In respect of accounting periods ending on or after 21 March 2000, the carry forward/carry back rules, so far as they relate to dividends, include unrelieved foreign tax arising on the profits of the UK branch. [*TA 1988 s 806L*]. Where a branch or agency is closed and another branch or agency is opened they are treated as different businesses and credit cannot be carried between the old and new businesses. A number of overseas branches or agencies may be aggregated for tax credit relief purposes. Relief must be claimed within six years of the end of the relevant accounting period or one year after the end of the period in which the foreign tax is paid. [*TA 1988 s 806M*].

## Onshore pooling

**15.146** A qualifying foreign dividend is one other than from a CFC pursuing an acceptable distribution policy, or in respect of which an eligible unrelieved foreign tax credit arises under *TA 1988 s 806B*. A related qualifying dividend is one paid to a UK resident company by a related company (see *TA 1988 s 806J*). Tax credit relief is available for

**15.147** *Other Overseas Aspects*

the aggregate foreign underlying tax applicable to the aggregate related qualifying foreign dividends, and the aggregate foreign non-underlying (withholding) tax applicable to the aggregate unrelated qualifying foreign dividends, as if each group were a single dividend, so giving effect to a form of onshore pooling. [*TA 1988 s 806C*]. Eligible underlying tax can be treated as underlying tax in respect of the aggregate related dividend in the same or next accounting period or carried back in respect of the related dividend of previous accounting periods, and eligible withholding tax can be treated as withholding tax in respect of the aggregate unrelated dividend of the same accounting period, or carried forwards, or backwards. [*TA 1988 s 806D*]. Carry-back of relievable tax is restricted to accounting periods beginning no more than three years before the accounting period in which the relievable credit arises. Relief is given against later accounting periods first, but after relief for each current accounting period has been given. [*TA 1988 s 806E*]. Credit is given for underlying tax before withholding tax for any dividend, and before credit is given for tax treated as underlying tax or withholding tax. [*TA 1988 s 806F*]. Regulations may be made to enable one company in a group to surrender any part of its relievable tax in an accounting period to another group company. [*TA 1988 s 806H*].

**15.147** *TA 1988 s 807A* allows double taxation relief on non-trading interest in certain limited circumstances. Thin capitalisation provisions are given effect to by *TA 1988 s 808A*, where, under the treaty, excessive interest will not qualify for relief as an expense if it is only incurred because of a special relationship between the payer and recipient. [ICAEW guidance note, 19 March 1993 (Tax 5/93)]. These provisions are in addition to any thin capitalisation attack under the transfer pricing provisions. [See Chapter 14]. Similar restrictions apply to royalties under *TA 1988 s 808B*. It is made clear that in addition to considering the rate or amount of royalties and the terms which would have been agreed, it is also necessary to consider whether any royalties would have been paid in the absence of the special relationship, and where there has been a series of transactions transferring the entire intangible property rights giving rise to the royalties, whether those transactions could have taken place in the absence of the special relationship. These provisions apply in respect of royalties payable on or after 28 July 2000, except where the special relationship provision in the royalty article in the appropriate treaty expressly limits the factors to be taken into account in determining whether tax credit relief is to be restricted or denied.

**15.148** Foreign tax credits are sometimes lost because of a mismatch in the calculation of the taxable profits in the foreign country and the UK. To the extent that these arise from capital allowances, *TA 1988 s 810* allowed the UK company to postpone capital allowances in order to avoid loss of double taxation credits. In view of the carry forward and carry backward provisions in *TA 1988 s 806A–806M*, the provisions are repealed from 1 April 2000, as they are no longer required. [*FA 2000 30 Sch 26*].

## Record Keeping  16.13

**16.13** Most limited companies are governed by *Companies Act 1985 ss 221* and *222* and the Revenue has confirmed that a company complying with its Companies Act requirements as to record keeping will satisfy the requirements to keep records for tax purposes. The Companies Act provisions are:

### Duty to keep accounting records

*Section 221*

(1) Every company shall keep accounting records which are sufficient to show and explain the company's transactions and are such as to:
   (a) disclose with reasonable accuracy, at any time, the financial position of the company at that time; and
   (b) enable the directors to ensure that any balance sheet and profit and loss account prepared under this Part complies with the requirements of this Act.

(2) The accounting records shall in particular contain:
   (a) entries from day to day of all sums of money received and expended by the company, and the matters in respect of which the receipt and expenditure takes place; and
   (b) a record of the assets and liabilities of the company.

(3) If the company's business involves dealing in goods, the accounting records shall contain:
   (a) statements of stock held by the company at the end of each financial year of the company;
   (b) all statements of stocktakings from which any such statement of stock as is mentioned in paragraph (a) has been or is to be prepared; and
   (c) except in the case of goods sold by way of ordinary retail trade, statements of all goods sold and purchased, showing the goods and the buyers and sellers in sufficient detail to enable all these to be identified.

(4) A parent company which has a subsidiary undertaking in relation to which the above requirements do not apply shall take reasonable steps to secure that the undertaking keeps such accounting records as to enable the directors of the parent company to ensure that any balance sheet and profit and loss account prepared under this Part complies with the requirements of this Act.

(5) If a company fails to comply with any provision of this section, every officer of the company who is in default is guilty of an offence unless he shows that he acted honestly and that in the circumstances

## 16.13  Record Keeping

in which the company's business was carried on the default was excusable.

(6) A person guilty of an offence under this section is liable to imprisonment or a fine, or both.

**Where and for how long records are to be kept**

*Section 222*

(1) A company's accounting records shall be kept at its registered office or such other place as the directors think fit, and shall at all times be open to inspection by the company's officers.

(2) If accounting records are kept at a place outside Great Britain, accounts and returns with respect to the business dealt with in the accounting records so kept shall be sent to, and kept at, a place in Great Britain, and shall at all times be open to such inspection.

(3) The accounts and returns to be sent to Great Britain shall be such as to:

    (a) disclose with reasonable accuracy the financial position of the business in question at intervals of not more than six months; and

    (b) enable the directors to ensure that the company's balance sheet and profit and loss account comply with the requirements of this Act.

(4) If a company fails to comply with any provision of subsections (1) to (3), every officer of the company who is in default is guilty of an offence, and liable to imprisonment or a fine or both, unless he shows that he acted honestly and that in the circumstances in which the company's business was carried on the default was excusable.

(5) Accounting records which a company is required by *section 221* to keep shall be preserved by it:

    (a) in the case of a private company, for three years from the date on which they are made; and

    (b) in the case of a public company, for six years from the date on which they are made.

This is subject to any provision contained in rules made under *section 411* of the *Insolvency Act 1986* (company insolvency rules).

(6) An officer of a company is guilty of an offence, and liable to imprisonment or a fine or both, if he fails to take all reasonable steps for securing compliance by the company with subsection (5) or intentionally causes any default by the company under that subsection.

## Transfer pricing records

**16.14** In the case of pricing of goods and services between UK companies and connected parties overseas, the transfer pricing information required to support arm's length prices may exceed the strict Companies Act requirement. [Tax Bulletin, Issue 37, October 1998, pp 579–582, see Appendix 1].

**16.15** The Revenue expect taxpayers to prepare and return for transfer pricing purposes such documentation as is reasonable given the complexity or otherwise of the transactions and which identify the relationship bringing the case within transfer pricing considerations, the nature and terms of the relevant transactions, the method or methods by which the prices used were arrived at, including any study of comparables or functional analysis. [See Chapter 14]. It is also necessary to show how the chosen method has resulted in an arm's length price or what adjustment has been included and the full terms of the commercial arrangement between arm's length and connected parties.

## Period for retention of records

**16.16** In the case of a company all records have to be preserved until the sixth anniversary of the end of the accounting period in question. [*FA 1998 18 Sch 21(2)*]. Where enquiries are being made into the company's return the records must be kept until the enquires are completed. Moreover, if the time limit for enquiries expires after the sixth anniversary, the records have to be kept until the expiry of the time limit. Furthermore, where the company is required to submit a return after the time limits have expired, perhaps as a result of Revenue enquiries, any records that it has retained must be preserved until any Revenue enquiries have been completed, or until the time limit for making such enquiries has expired. [*FA 1998 18 Sch 21(3) to (5)*].

**16.17** The period for which minor records such as till rolls and petty cash vouchers need to be kept is unclear, and it is probable that in the event of dispute the Court would come down on the side of a common sense interpretation of whether the records retained are sufficient to enable the company to meet its obligations to make a complete and correct return. This will depend on the circumstances and therefore a prescriptive list of what is, and is not required is neither practicable nor desirable. Where, however, a document is required to be preserved it can be done so on computer using an optical imaging system which is capable of reproducing a complete and accurate record of the information in the original document, for example, through optical scanning.

**16.18** Penalties for record-keeping failures are limited to £3,000 in respect of all record-keeping offences in respect of a particular accounting period, which is the same as for personal self-assessment. The Revenue have confirmed that penalties will only be charged in serious

**16.19** *Record Keeping*

cases, such as where there is a history of record-keeping failures or where records have been deliberately destroyed to obstruct a Revenue enquiry.

**16.19** Pay As You Earn records need to be preserved for three years after the end of the tax year to which they relate under *para 55(12)* of the *Income Tax (Employments) Regulations 1993 (SI 1993 No. 744)*.

**16.20** In relation to records relating to claims, the information has to be kept until the latest of the day on which any Revenue enquiries into the claim, or any amendment of it, are completed, and the day on which the Revenue no longer have power to make such enquiries. Revenue enquiries are completed when so confirmed by the Revenue by notice under *TMA 1970 1A Sch 7(4)*.

Chapter 17

# Finality and Certainty, Powers of Enquiry and Discovery

## Finality and certainty

**17.1** The achievement of finality and certainty for any period is a necessary ingredient in the corporate tax system. Given full disclosure, once a company's liability for a particular year or period has been ascertained, it should not be possible for the issue to be reopened and reviewed at a later date. For many years this was accomplished by the inefficient system of estimated assessments, appeals, correspondence and, if the liability could not be agreed, a right of appeal to the Commissioners. A measure of simplification came with Pay and File, but this did not conclude the process as the assessing responsibility remained with the Revenue. Moreover, the Revenue considered that the absence of automatic comprehensive rights of access to company records fettered their ability to ensure the correct tax liability had been assessed, often causing unnecessary delays and limiting their powers of enquiry. In particular, in accordance with the 1977 agreement with the Consultative Committee of Accountancy bodies, the Revenue had to state their grounds for dissatisfaction with a return at the commencement of any investigation.

**17.2** The structure which has been devised to replace the old system and give the Revenue the broader powers they considered necessary may be summarised as follows. The responsibility is placed on companies themselves for determining their tax liability and making the tax assessment. At the same time the Revenue are given carte blanche to open a formal enquiry into a company's return within a year of the filing date. They then have extensive powers of investigation and access to the company's records to check the validity of the return. However, if an enquiry is not opened within the one year period the company's liability becomes final and conclusive, subject only to the ability of the Revenue to reopen the matter in cases of fraud or neglect, or where they 'discover' an error or mistake.

**17.3** *Finality and Certainty, Powers of Enquiry and Discovery*

## Revenue enquiry/audit

### Revenue powers of enquiry: introduction and time limits for notice of enquiry

**17.3** The enquiry provisions apply to companies for accounting periods ending on or after 1 July 1999 and are contained in *FA 1998 18 Sch 24–35*. The period within which an enquiry can be commenced is twelve months from the filing date if the return was delivered on time. Otherwise it is 31 January, 30 April, 31 July or 31 October next following the anniversary of the actual date the return was delivered (or the date an amendment to the return was made in the case of an enquiry into an amendment to a return). [*FA 1998 18 Sch 24*]. In the case of a return made for the 'wrong' accounting period, the time limit for commencing an enquiry is based on what the deadline would have been if the chosen period had been correct. A return is for the wrong period if (a) the selected period is not actually an accounting period, or (b) the return has been submitted on the basis of no accounting period but there is in fact one. [*FA 1998 18 Sch 26*]. There is no formal time limit for completing an enquiry, this being dependent on the nature and complexity of each case. However, if the company believes that the enquiry is overly protracted, it can apply to the Commissioners for the enquiry to be terminated. [See 17.41].

**17.4** In the context of self-assessment for individuals, where the filing deadline is 31 January from the end of the year of assessment, the Revenue had considered that the 12 month period for giving notice of their intention to raise an enquiry expired on 30 January and that they were simply required to place the notice in the post by then. Their view on posting was successfully challenged by taxpayers in the Special Commissioner's cases *Wing Hung Lai v Bale [1999] STC (SCD) 238* and *Holly v Inspector of Taxes [2000] STC (SCD) 50*. The Revenue now accept that for returns filed on time by individuals, an enquiry is only valid if the notice was actually delivered to the taxpayer no later than 30 January. See Tax Bulletin Special Edition, April 2000 (Appendix 1) for details of Revenue practice in relation to individuals. Similar issues will apply in relation to the time limit for serving enquiry notices on companies.

**17.5** The enquiry may extend to anything contained in the return, or which should have been contained in it. No reason has to be or will be given for opening the enquiry, although the Revenue may identify particular areas on which the enquiry will focus. Specifically included are claims or elections included in the return and any amount that affects the tax payable by the company for another accounting period, or which affects the tax liability of another company for any accounting period. However, where an amendment to a return is made after the time the Revenue may enquire into a return, the enquiry must be limited to matters relating to, or affected by, the amendment. [*FA 1998 18 Sch 25*].

# Finality and Certainty, Powers of Enquiry and Discovery  17.9

**17.6** In the initial processing period the Revenue will only check a return for obvious errors. Any consequent corrections will not be regarded as pursuant to an enquiry. During the remainder of the year from the filing date, the Revenue will not give a company any assurance or clearance that it will not be subject to an enquiry, as they consider this would be unfair on other companies who could not be given such an assurance. The nature of any particular enquiry will depend upon the particular case, and could range from a straightforward computational question to a full, in-depth, investigation, although the Revenue expect that the number of full enquiries will be small. Random selection will play a part, but the majority of enquiry cases will be selected by reference to information in the return or in the Revenue's possession.

**17.7** Recent governments have emphasised their belief that there has been an unjustifiable loss of tax in the corporate sector, notably by the larger multi-nationals. This was reflected in the Conservative Government 1997 'Spend to Save' initiative. The new enquiry regime forms part of the Revenue's armoury in this drive against tax avoidance. But as well as targeting public companies and multi-nationals, greater challenges in the future may be expected to the larger owner-managed business.

## Outline of enquiry procedure

**17.8** The Revenue are required to give formal written notice of their intention of enquiring into a return within the time limits set out in 17.3. Having done so the enquiry will be conducted in accordance with the framework described in 17.9. During the course of the enquiry the Revenue may amend the company's self-assessment if they think there is likely to be a loss of tax to the Crown, known as a jeopardy amendment. If the company thinks that the enquiries are becoming overly protracted it may apply to the Commissioners for a direction to bring the enquiry to an end. The normal procedure, however, is that once the Revenue enquiries are completed the Inspector will inform the company and agent of his conclusions. If the Inspector considers there has been an underpayment, he will seek to negotiate a contract settlement. The enquiry must be formally completed by the issue of a closure notice, following which the company has thirty days to amend its self-assessment to reflect the Revenue's conclusions. If the company fails to do so the Revenue may make the appropriate amendment. The company then has a right of appeal to the Commissioners.

**17.9** The time taken to carry out a Revenue enquiry will depend upon the circumstances of each case, in particular whether there is to be a full investigation or an aspect enquiry as set out below. Moreover, a 'fast tracking' procedure may be adopted in appropriate cases. The framework, which will be common to all enquiries, will be as follows:

(a) full review of the return, compliance history and any other information held;

**17.10** *Finality and Certainty, Powers of Enquiry and Discovery*

(b) identify the information necessary to check the return;
(c) issue opening letter incorporating notice of enquiry;
(d) obtain the information;
(e) examine the information;
(f) draw conclusions, identify what further information is required;
(g) issue closure notice or settle by contract.

**17.10** The Revenue are not required to give any reasons for the opening of enquiries, and are adamant that they will not do so. In a small number of cases, the enquiries will be randomly generated by the Revenue computer. The enquiry procedure will follow the same lines in such cases, albeit tailored to the size and complexity of the affairs of the company selected.

### Code of Practice

**17.11** The Revenue have drawn up a code of practice (COP 14) for enquiries into company tax returns. [See Appendix 7]. This emphasises the Revenue's commitment to ensuring that companies pay the right amount of tax, no more no less. COP 14 sets out the procedure for starting an enquiry, the right to professional representation, the provision of information and the conduct of any meetings. It also deals with the payment of tax during the course of enquiry to reduce interest charges if an error is found and the Revenue's power to make a jeopardy amendment to the company's self-assessment, as well as the procedure to agree revised tax figures and, in the absence of agreement, the appeals system.

**17.12** Reference is made to an exposure to interest and penalties for default, and the possible requirement of a certificate of full disclosure at the end of enquiries. There is a warning of the serious view taken against falsehood, i.e. the dangers of a prosecution for a certificate of disclosure that turns out to have been knowingly incorrect. The code contains Revenue undertakings to be courteous, fair and professional and to deal with the issues arising on a timely basis. The Revenue also undertake to keep the company fully informed and to protect confidentiality, as well as to be mindful of the cost implications. There is also a complaints procedure.

### Aspect enquiries

**17.13** A significant change is to what are known as 'aspect enquiries', where the Revenue are not commencing a full investigation but where there are areas where they require further information, or disagree with the tax treatment put forward by the company. Previously these would have been dealt with informally by a letter to the agent or by a telephone

## Finality and Certainty, Powers of Enquiry and Discovery  17.17

call but casual enquiries of this nature are impossible under self-assessment. The concern about such enquiries is that once the Inspector has gone to the trouble of opening a formal enquiry, instead of merely asking the one question as he would have done previously, he must consider carefully all possible questions that he could ask, because once having commenced his enquiry on any particular aspect, and brought that enquiry to conclusion, he cannot reopen the case should another matter occur to him, unless he can invoke the discovery procedure under *TMA 1970 s 29*.

**17.14**  The Revenue seem to believe that there is no reason why the introduction of the new self-assessment procedures should require Inspectors to ask any more questions in an aspect enquiry than they would have done as a result of a review under the old system. It should be observed that if an aspect enquiry has been initiated and concluded, another officer cannot then commence a full enquiry for the same year of assessment unless a discovery is made.

### District enquiries

**17.15**  In the case of a normal district enquiry (which is not a mere aspect enquiry) the Revenue can be expected to make a full review of the return, the company's compliance history and any third party information. They will identify the information needed to check the correctness and completeness of the return. In business enquiries of any substance the Revenue may suggest examining the records and having a meeting with the company's representatives at the business premises, provided that the company so agrees. In some cases it may be preferable for the business records to be examined at the agent's premises, particularly where it is not practical to send the papers direct to the Revenue.

**17.16**  The Revenue have no power to demand a site visit, other than with an appropriate judicial authority on a sworn statement by an Officer of the Board who is granted a search warrant, enabling the Revenue to enter premises and seize and remove evidence of a serious tax fraud. It is not necessary for such a warrant to specify the document to be seized [*IRC v Rossminster Ltd [1980] STC 42*], nor need they name the Board Officers concerned. [*R v Hunt [1994] STC 819*]. The appropriate judicial authority in England is a circuit judge. Where documents are removed under such a warrant the Revenue must, if required, provide a record of them and must not retain them longer than is necessary to copy them, unless the originals are needed as evidence for a trial or for examination. These proceedings under *TMA 1970 ss 20C, 20CC, 20B* are only used very rarely in cases of suspected serious fraud (IH 5101).

**17.17**  If the Revenue, as a result of the information they receive, decide that they require further information, they will make the appropriate request for it. They will then draw their conclusions as to the amount of tax under-declared, if any, and present these to the company.

## 17.18  Finality and Certainty, Powers of Enquiry and Discovery

These proceedings may be subject to negotiation to arrive at an agreed settlement and the Revenue may suggest that this may best be done at a meeting with a representative from the company and its agent. Many agents will prefer to attend the meeting without a representative from the client company present, and accede to a final interview only when all matters in dispute have been satisfactorily resolved. Where tax has been underpaid, it may be settled by a contract settlement, under which the company agrees to pay a certain amount by way of tax, interest and penalties in consideration for the Revenue taking no further action as a result of the incomplete return. In less serious cases the Revenue may merely request the company to amend its self-assessment under *FA 1998 18 Sch 31*.

**17.18**   Obviously at any stage in an enquiry, if the company has understated its tax, its co-operation in admitting this fact will be reflected in a reduced penalty at the end of the day. Once the Revenue have started a general enquiry the company has little option but to provide the Revenue with the information requested, attend meetings via its officers or appointed agents and try and resolve the problems as cheaply as possible. Generally it will be well advised to engage a professional, well versed in investigation procedures, to handle the case, with a view to convincing the Revenue that the accounts are correct, or in cases of default, agreeing a negotiated settlement as expeditiously and fairly as possible.

**Preventing an enquiry starting**

**17.19**   If there is any aspect of the return that causes the Inspector to have a concern, he may commence a general enquiry or look very closely to see whether other aspects of the return need investigation. It is clearly in the company's interest to try and anticipate areas where the Revenue are left with no real option but to commence enquiry procedures in order to obtain explanations for unusual items, which are not adequately explained in the return or accompanying notes.

**17.20**   The Revenue do not require companies to complete what is generally known as the 'standard accounts information' relevant for individuals. But accounts and computations will still be required. The Revenue will be able to compare the company's figures and ratios with other similar businesses, as well as comparing the results with previous years. Abnormalities may well be identified by computer to assist the Inspector in determining which returns to open up for enquiry. It is obviously in the company's interest to ensure that anomalies are avoided where possible, or explanations are provided for the causes of variations that are otherwise not readily apparent.

**17.21**   In order to reduce the likelihood of an enquiry, it may be appropriate to err on the side of over-disclosure rather than force the Revenue into having to make an aspect enquiry. In particular it may be

## Finality and Certainty, Powers of Enquiry and Discovery  17.26

sensible to enclose supplemental schedules and computations giving more detailed information about possibly questionable items.

**17.22** A company which has a history of non-compliance, either in its own affairs, in the PAYE or in its VAT returns, is more likely to be identified for enquiry, as is a company using what the Revenue regard as an unreliable agent. Unfortunately the company may be unaware of the reputation of his agent in the local district, and this may present the company with unforeseen difficulties.

### Special Compliance Office Enquiries

**17.23** The old Inland Revenue Special Offices and Enquiry Branch have been merged into the Special Compliance Unit. Complex enquiry cases, where serious fraud is not suspected, are dealt with as Special Compliance Unit Investigations under COP 8, and cases involving suspected serious fraud are dealt with as Special Compliance Unit Investigations under COP 9.

**17.24** COP 9, dealing with suspected fraud cases, sets out the *Hansard* policy with the warning that deliberate failure to admit any irregularities or to make a disclosure of them or the submission of a false certificate or statement might lead to prosecution. [Revenue Press Release, 18 October 1990]. The standard questions under the *Hansard* procedures are:

1. Have any transactions been omitted from or incorrectly recorded in the books of the company?
2. Are the accounts of the company as supplied to the Revenue correct and complete to the best of your knowledge and belief?
3. Are all the taxation returns of the company correct and complete to the best of your knowledge and belief?
4. Are your own personal tax returns correct and complete to the best of your knowledge and belief?

**17.25** Normally, a company (and its directors) which is being justifiably investigated, will be advised to answer, yes, no, no and no to the questions and to commission a report from a firm experienced in dealing with Special Compliance Unit fraud enquiries of this nature. The timetable for the disclosure report so commissioned will be agreed with the Revenue, and it is obviously prepared at the taxpayer's cost. It is clearly in the company's interest to show full co-operation as not only will this mitigate penalties but it should, in practice, avoid prosecution for the directors. *Hansard* procedures are not used at district level, EH 305.

**17.26** The theory is that once the taxpayer company has been caught it will divulge everything to its adviser, who will complete the disclosure report and negotiate the minimum penalties, in addition to the tax and interest, with the Revenue. In practice it is rather more difficult as the

**17.27** *Finality and Certainty, Powers of Enquiry and Discovery*

truth usually has to be extracted from the taxpayer company, painstakingly, over a protracted period. But it is important for the company's own protection that the report is correct and complete, so far as it possibly can be given the period of time it covers and the records available.

**17.27** COP 9 then refers to keeping the taxpayer informed, providing information, records, payments on account, appeals, interest, surcharges and penalties and the conclusion of the investigation. Reference is made to a certificate of full disclosure which the Revenue will require if there have been errors or omissions in the accounts or returns. The Revenue will usually prosecute a taxpayer who has signed a certificate of full disclosure which subsequently proves to be false.

**Production of documents**

**17.28** The investigating officer may require the company (on no less than 30 days written notice) to produce such documents as are in the company's possession or power, and to provide such information, as the officer may reasonably require for the purpose of the enquiry. In cases of genuine difficulty in obtaining the documents the Revenue will agree an extension to the 30 days. Such a notice may be issued at the same time as the notice of enquiry or later. The period of 30 days starts from the receipt of the notice by the company, rather than 30 days from the date stated in the notice: *Self-assessed v Inspector of Taxes [1999] STC (SCD) 253*. The Revenue's practice in relation to the delivery of such a notice is set out in Tax Bulletin Special Edition, April 2000 (see Appendix 1).

**17.29** The Revenue have indicated that the nature and quantity of documents requested will depend on the nature of the enquiry. Thus a simple technical enquiry into expenditure qualifying for capital allowances may be limited to the documents detailing that expenditure. But for a full in-depth review the request might cover all the business records. It is in order for the company to supply photographic or other facsimile copes of documents, but the Revenue can require (on not less than 30 days notice) to see the originals and take copies or make extracts. [*FA 1998 18 Sch 27(1)(2)(3)*]. There are penalties for failure to comply, considered in Chapter 18. A document includes anything in which information of any description is recorded. [*FA 1998 s 122*]. In the Revenue's view their right to obtain 'information' enables them to require a company to provide information beyond that contained in existing documents. For example it could include analyses of accounting entries, computations, explanations or translations of foreign documents.

**17.30** The Revenue already have powers of investigation under *TMA 1970 s 20*, but these are subject to particular safeguards. They evidently considered that they required an almost unfettered right to examine prime records, and that the existing *s 20* powers were too cumbersome for general use in policing self-assessment. The Revenue's powers stop short

## Finality and Certainty, Powers of Enquiry and Discovery   17.34

of a right of entry into the company's premises, although it may be appropriate to suggest that the Revenue inspect records at the company's premises. The Revenue may even suggest this. The Revenue's powers under *s 20(3)* may still be invoked to obtain documents from third parties (e.g. a director of the company or another company which has been party to a transaction with the company being investigated).

**17.31** A company is not obliged to produce documents, or provide information, relating to the conduct of any pending appeal. *[FA 1998 18 Sch 27(5)]*. The value or the relevance of this is debatable since under self-assessment it is unlikely that an appeal will be pending.

### Right of appeal against notice to produce documents

**17.32** The company has the right of appeal to the Commissioners against a notice to produce documents, or provide information. The appeal has to be made in writing within 30 days after the notice was given. The same appeals procedure then applies as if it were an appeal against an assessment to tax. *[FA 1998 18 Sch 28(1)(2)(3)]*. The Commissioners are empowered to confirm the notice if it appears to them that the production of the documents etc., was reasonably required. Otherwise they are to set it aside. *[FA 1998 18 Sch 28(4)]*. How this ties in with the limitation on the obligation to produce documents when an appeal is pending or documents contain legal advice is not clear.

**17.33** There is no further right of appeal by way of case stated. *[FA 1998 18 Sch 28(6)]*. It would seem that the aggrieved company's only remedy would then be by way of judicial review. The Revenue accept that there is no limitation on the terms of an appeal to the Commissioners against a notice to produce documents. However, they consider that the potential grounds for appeal are limited since the points which are to be considered by the Commissioners are only whether the production of the documents etc. requested was reasonably required for the purposes of the enquiry, and whether the company had sufficient time to comply with the notice.

### Jeopardy amendment of assessment by Revenue after opening of enquiry

**17.34** Where an enquiry into a company's return has been opened, if it appears to the Revenue Officer that the amount of tax stated in the self-assessment was insufficient, and that unless there was an immediate amendment there was likely to be a a loss of tax to the Crown (e.g. a possibility of the company disposing of its assets and going into liquidation), he is entitled to amend the assessment by notice served on the company. *[FA 1998 18 Sch 30(1)]*. In the case of an enquiry limited to matters relating to amendment of a return (see 17.5), this ability is limited

**17.35** *Finality and Certainty, Powers of Enquiry and Discovery*

to apparent deficiencies attributable to the amendments. [*FA 1998 18 Sch 30 (2)*].

**17.35** The purpose of this power is to enable the Revenue to move quickly, well before the enquiries are completed, to try and forestall any possible loss of tax. In normal enquiry cases, where the Revenue consider there is an underpayment of tax they would generally seek to recover this by requesting a further payment on account. It will only be in cases of perceived risk that a jeopardy amendment of assessment will be required. The company has the right of appeal against such an amended assessment but the appeal is not to be heard until the enquiries are completed. However, the tax payable under the amendment can be the subject of a postponement appeal. Otherwise the company's only interim remedy to expedite the matter is to apply to the Commissioners to direct the Officer to bring the enquiries to an end (see 17.41).

### Amendment of return by company during enquiry

**17.36** A company is permitted to amend its return when an enquiry is in process. Such an amendment is not to take effect until after the enquiry is completed, in so far as it affects (a) the tax shown as payable in the company's self-assessment for that accounting period, (b) the company's tax liability for another accounting period, or (c) the tax liability of another company for any accounting period. [*FA 1998 18 Sch 31(1)(2)(3)*]. But it is a factor which the Revenue may take into account in the enquiry, for example it might go to reduce penalties. Moreover, a claim for repayment of corporation tax made under *TMA 1970 s 59DA* will not be affected where the amount already paid exceeds the possible liability.

**17.37** Where an amendment has been deferred in this way, it takes effect on completion of the enquiry, provided that it was not taken into account during the enquiry or no amendment of the return arose out of the enquiry. Otherwise, it is to be taken into account as part of any amendments arising from the enquiry itself in accordance with the conclusions in the closure notice; see below. [*FA 1998 18 Sch 31*].

### Conclusion of enquiry and amendment of return

**17.38** An enquiry is completed when the Revenue issues a closure notice informing the company that the enquiry is completed and stating their conclusions. If the Revenue conclude that the return was for the wrong period, the closure notice is to designate the correct period, specifying the date upon which the period begins and ends. If there is more than one accounting period ending in the period specified in the return, the closure notice only has to designate the first of those accounting periods for which no return was delivered. [*FA 1998 18 Sch 32*].

## Finality and Certainty, Powers of Enquiry and Discovery  17.42

**17.39** Upon issue of the closure notice the company has 30 days to amend the particular return and any other returns which may have been affected, to accord with the conclusions in the closure notice. For example, a return for a subsequent period can be varied to reflect a change in the amount of losses carried forward as a result of the enquiry even though the normal time limit for amending the later return has expired. Also where the return was for the wrong period, it has to be amended within 30 days so that it is appropriate to the correct period. If this is not done to the Revenue's satisfaction, they may within the following 30 days, make the amendments they consider necessary. The company then has the right of appeal. [*FA 1998 18 Sch 34*]. It is, however, expected that in the vast majority of cases settlement will be by agreement and the company will amend its self-assessment to accord with the settlement figure. The facility to agree a contract settlement for all outstanding liabilities in appropriate cases will remain broadly as under the old system, including penalties.

**17.40** Where a return has been made for the wrong period, and the enquiry has determined the correct period, this is likely to result in a return being due for a further period. If there is no return for that period which could be amended, a return must be filed by the later of the original filing date and 30 days after the matters in the closure notice have been finally determined. [*FA 1998 18 Sch 35*].

**Direction to complete enquiry**

**17.41** At any time during the enquiry period the company is entitled to apply to the Commissioners to direct the Officer to give a closure notice, bringing the enquiry to an end. The issue is then heard and determined in the same way as an appeal, and the Commissioners are to give such a direction unless they are satisfied that the Officer has reasonable grounds for continuing his enquiries. [*FA 1998 18 Sch 33*]. There is thus some protection against the Revenue prolonging their enquiries beyond a reasonable period.

**17.42** It has been suggested that a taxpayer might upon the opening of an enquiry make an application to the Commissioners for such a direction as an indirect means of eliciting information from the Revenue about the reasons for their enquiry. In this regard, it is to be noted that the onus of persuading the Commissioners to allow the enquiry to continue effectively falls upon the Revenue, and the information they adduce is likely to be very helpful to the taxpayer company. However, the Revenue can be expected to try and resist any attempts by taxpayers to circumvent their right of enquiry by applying prematurely for a closure notice, albeit that the decision in any case rests with the Commissioners. Moreover, where the Commissioners have made such a direction, the closure notice subsequently issued will be based on the information then available to the Revenue and will represent what the Revenue consider to be the correct amounts to be included in the return on the basis of that information.

**17.43** *Finality and Certainty, Powers of Enquiry and Discovery*

## Revenue enquiry into claims

### General position

**17.43** The Revenue's general powers to enquire into a return and self-assessment as described above extend to any claim which forms part of that return or an amendment to it. There are similar powers to enquire into other claims made by a company, being those not within *FA 1998 18 Sch 57* and *58*; see 4.9 and 4.10. [*FA 1998 18 Sch 59*]. A formal notice in writing must be served on the company within the specified time limit, being the period ending with the quarter day following the first anniversary of the day on which the claim or amendment was made. Once such an enquiry has been made into a claim there cannot be a further enquiry. [*TMA 1970 1A Sch 5(1)(2)(3)*].

**17.44** Where such an enquiry has been opened, the Revenue may require the company (on not less than 30 days' notice) to produce such documents as are in its possession or power and are reasonably required for the purpose of determining whether the claim or amendment is incorrect. There are similar powers to request accounts or particulars. All the provisions which apply in a case of a Revenue enquiry into a company's return, as outlined in 17.28 et seq. above, are then to apply. [*TMA 1970, 1A Sch 6, 6A*].

**17.45** The Revenue have intimated that such enquiry will require the same sort of dialogue between the Inspector and the company as is applicable to enquiries in general. In the progression towards agreement, it is anticipated that points would be agreed along the way and that the Inspector's conclusions at the end of the enquiry would summarise the agreed positions and the Inspector's position in respect of any items in dispute. As set out below there would then be 30 days for the company to deal with the mechanics of any amendments, such as additional or amended claims, in line with the procedures relating to enquiries into tax returns.

### Conclusion of enquiry and amendment of claim

**17.46** As with Revenue enquiries into a company's return, once the enquiries have been completed, the Revenue officer must inform the company and state his conclusions as to the amount which should have been in the claim. The company is then allowed 30 days, to amend its claim to eliminate or make good any excess or deficiency, or to give effect to any amendments to the claim which it has notified to the officer. [*TMA 1970 1A Sch 7(2)(4)*].

**17.47** The company thus has the opportunity to amend its claim, so as to reflect the conclusions of the Revenue officer. Should it not do so, the officer is permitted, within the next 30 days, to amend the claim as appropriate. [*TMA 1970 1A Sch 7(3)*]. The company has the right of

## Finality and Certainty, Powers of Enquiry and Discovery   17.51

appeal against such amendment by the Revenue officer. [*TMA 1970 1A Sch 9*]. After a claim has been so amended, effect is to be given to the amendment within 30 days either by way of an assessment on the company, or by a discharge of tax, or a repayment of tax as the case may be. [*TMA 1970 1A Sch 8(1)*].

**17.48**   As with the provisions relating to enquiries into a company's return, at any time during the enquiry period, the taxpayer may apply to the Commissioners to direct the Officer to bring the enquiries to an end. The provisions set out in 17.41 are to apply as regards the handling of the matter thereafter. [*TMA 1970 1A Sch 7(5)*].

# Discovery

### Previous position and background

**17.49**   The previous rules relating to discovery (contained in a combination of statute and case law, Revenue practice and concession) developed from two apparently contradictory provisions in *TMA 1970*, and were a continuing source of controversy. Outside the fields of fraud and neglect, *TMA 1970 s 29(3)* gave the Inspector an ostensibly untrammelled right to raise a further assessment, within six years of the end of the year of assessment in question, if he 'discovered' that the original assessment was incorrect. But where an assessment had been determined by agreement under *TMA 1970 s 54*, following an appeal by the taxpayer, the determination was treated as final and conclusive under *TMA 1970 s 46(2)*. Where there was new evidence, the matter could be reopened. But where there was merely a change of mind by the Inspector (or his successor) there was a limitation on the right to make further assessments.

**17.50**   The issues were considered in two leading cases. It was held in *Cenlon Finance Co Ltd v Ellwood (1962) 40 TC 176* that where the Inspector had explicitly agreed the point in issue, a further assessment was not possible. *Scorer v Olin Energy Systems Ltd [1985] STC 218* concerned a company's computation in which the point at issue was identified, but was not explicitly addressed by the Inspector, and which was technically incorrect. Losses which had arisen from one trade were carried forward and set against the profits of another trade in the following year. This was not in fact permissible under the relevant corporation tax provisions. It was held that the matter could not be reopened since it was reasonable to assume that the Inspector had *implicitly* considered and accepted the position put forward by the company in the computation.

**17.51**   In the light of these cases and after considerable debate the Revenue issued Statement of Practice, SP 8/91, which set out their interpretation of the position where there had been an appeal by the taxpayer against an assessment which was determined by a *TMA 1970 s 54*

**17.52**   *Finality and Certainty, Powers of Enquiry and Discovery*

agreement. The stance taken by the Revenue, in cases where there had been no *explicit* agreement, was to accept that discovery could not be made if:

(a) the point was fundamental to the basis of computation of the taxpayer's liability; and

(b) it was so clearly and fully described in the accounts or computations that its significance was clearly apparent and the Inspector was put on notice of the point. Moreover, the Inspector must not have been given misleading information.

**17.52**   By concession the Revenue took the same line in cases where there had been no formal appeal and determination. Furthermore where the point was not fundamental, they did not seek to raise a further assessment if the position taken by the original Inspector was a tenable one.

**Discovery under self-assessment**

*Disclosure by taxpayer*

**17.53**   Under self-assessment the agreement of the Revenue to a particular point in issue, whether explicitly or implicitly, is not in point. The Inspector is no longer required to be satisfied as to the information in the tax return and to raise the requisite assessment. The responsibility is left entirely to the company. So the only area which can be relevant to the question of discovery is that of full disclosure, namely whether the return submitted, including any documents, provides a complete picture of all the matters relevant to the company's liability.

*Codification in new statutory provisions*

**17.54**   Given this narrowing down and simplification of the position, the Revenue have sought to codify in statutory form the essence of the old law and practice. Their expressed intention was to follow the tests which they considered emerged from the judgments in the *Olin* case, namely that for a taxpayer to avoid any possibility of a discovery assessment raised at a later date, the disclosure of a particular point had to be sufficiently full and clear to put an ordinarily competent Inspector on notice of precisely what issues needed to be considered and the stance to be taken on them.

**17.55**   The new provisions apply for accounting periods ending on or after 1 July 1999. If the Revenue discover as regards an accounting period that any amount which should have been assessed to tax has not been assessed, or that an assessment has been insufficient, or excess relief has been given, they may make the appropriate assessment to make good the loss of tax. Moreover, where the Revenue discover an error which affects

## Finality and Certainty, Powers of Enquiry and Discovery 17.57

the tax payable by the company for another accounting period, or the tax liability of another company for any period (e.g. a change in an amount of group relief), they may make a discovery determination. Such a discovery assessment or determination can only be made if one of the alternative conditions considered below is satisfied (except where the assessment or discovery gives effect to a discovery made in another company's return). [*FA 1998 18 Sch 41, 42*].

*First alternative condition for discovery: fraud or neglect*

**17.56** The first alternative condition is that the loss of tax is the result of fraudulent or negligent conduct by the company, or any person acting on its behalf, or a person who was a partner of the company at the relevant time. [*FA 1998 18 Sch 43*]. 'Fraudulent or negligent' conduct would extend to a failure to observe the standards to be expected of a reasonable person in the circumstances. An arithmetical error, a double deduction, or such other obvious error would possibly amount to negligence, and certainly in the Revenue's view would be sufficient to enable them to raise a discovery assessment. The Revenue do, however, accept, in the context of lost records, that a genuine mistake, made in good faith, must be regarded as an innocent error (IH 5066).

*Second alternative condition for discovery: inadequate information*

**17.57** The second alternative condition is that when the Revenue ceased to be entitled to enquire into a return or, in the event of any enquiry, completed their enquiries, they could not reasonably have been expected to be aware of the tax deficiency on the basis of the information made available to them. [*FA 1998 18 Sch 44(1)*]. For this purpose information is treated as made available to the Revenue if:

(a) It is contained in the company's tax return for the period in question or either of the two immediately preceding accounting periods, or in documents accompanying such return. [*FA 1998 18 Sch 44(2)(a), (3)*].

(b) It is contained in any claim made by the company, or in any accounts, statements or documents accompanying the claim. [*FA 1998 18 Sch 44(2)(b)*].

(c) It is contained in any documents, accounts or information which are produced or provided by the company during the course of any Revenue enquiry. [*FA 1998 18 Sch 44(2)(c)*].

(d) It is information, the existence and relevance of which could reasonably be expected to be inferred by the Revenue from the information in (a)–(c), or which is notified in writing by the company to the Revenue. [*FA 1998 18 Sch 44(2)(d)*].

## 17.58 Finality and Certainty, Powers of Enquiry and Discovery

**17.58** Provided that the information submitted to the Revenue is sufficiently comprehensive, and either any controversial point is specifically raised, or its relevance can clearly be inferred, discovery will not be possible under these new rules. The 'reasonably' test in the opening words of the condition indicates that an objective standard is appropriate. Thus a change of opinion on information previously made available in a relevant return, and whose relevance was clear, will not be grounds for a discovery.

*Accompanying documents*

**17.59** Although strictly any documentation is to accompany the return, the Revenue accept that any documents submitted within one month of the return 'accompany' it, provided that the return indicates that the documents have been or are to be submitted. Where they have been sent outside that time limit, the Revenue will consider sympathetically a request for them to be treated as supporting the return.

*Information submitted on past returns*

**17.60** There is a limited extent to which information given to the Revenue in past periods is to be assumed to be known to them in the current period, only the two prior returns being taken into account. In this regard, even a permanent note on the company's file would not suffice. The Revenue have observed in the context of individuals that it cannot be assumed that a Revenue Officer will always make systematic permanent notes regarding a particular taxpayer. It would seem that some form of cross-referencing to past periods might be in order, but to be sure, any potentially controversial areas would have to be dealt with explicitly, at least once every three years.

**Practical aspects**

**17.61** The question then arises as to precisely what a company should do to protect itself from the risk of a discovery assessment, both as regards the actual documentation which should be submitted with the return and also the extent to which any possible grey areas should be specifically highlighted. In the context of self-assessment for individuals this was the subject of considerable debate between the Revenue and the Consultative Committee. The issue arose acutely in the context of the preparation and submission of business accounts and computations. The Revenue's initial stance was that other than in the cases of the larger business, where full accounts might be submitted, the usual approach would be for the taxpayer merely to complete the standard accounts information part of the return and then separately highlight on the return in the space provided, or in a separate letter, any potentially controversial areas.

## Finality and Certainty, Powers of Enquiry and Discovery  **17.66**

**17.62** A related issue was the extent to which filing full accounts alone would protect the taxpayer, if the tax treatment adopted in any potentially questionable areas was clear from an examination of the accounts, say by a specific note included therein. Seemingly this would suffice in view of the express provisions of *TMA 1970 s 29* [the corresponding provisions for companies being in *FA 1998 18 Sch 44(2)* set out in 17.57] that information is treated as made available to the Revenue if it is contained inter alia in any accounts accompanying the return. Here the Revenue's initial view was that this alone might not be enough, and that particularly in cases where the accounts were lengthy, any questionable issue should be separately highlighted in the return.

**17.63** The culmination of the Consultative Committee debates on the subject was the issue by the Revenue of a press release on 31 May 1996 setting out their views, reported in Tax Bulletin, Issue 23, June 1996, pp 313–315. The Revenue again stated that the majority of income tax cases involved reasonably straightforward accounts, and that in such cases the fully completed return and standard accounts information should enable a full and fair picture of the taxpayer's affairs to be presented. In so far as there was the odd point of difficulty needing further explanation, this could be dealt with by setting out further information within the areas provided on the return.

**17.64** The Revenue did, however, acknowledge that in larger or more complex cases, this might not provide adequate disclosure, and the submission of further information including perhaps the submission of accounts might be considered appropriate. The Revenue also accepted that taxpayers and practitioners were entitled to send in additional material if they considered it added relevant information. Applying this general approach to companies (where there is no standard accounts information requirement, but where formal accounts in any event need to accompany the return), there should be adequate disclosure with regard to the figures in the accounts, provided that it is evident from an examination of the accounts that any questionable points had been dealt with therein, by a note if appropriate.

**17.65** As regards other information, the Revenue have made the point that merely including with the return, a mass of additional material of a voluminous nature and whose relevance is not immediately apparent, might not alone suffice. In particular, there might be so much material that the Revenue 'could not have been reasonably expected, on the basis on the information made available to them, to be aware' [*FA 1998 18 Sch 44(1)*] of the particular point of liability, unless the company or its agent had explained its relevance.

**17.66** In the Revenue's view, the company has the onus to draw the Revenue's attention to any important information that is relevant to a tax liability, particularly if there is some doubt as to the interpretation which could be placed on that information. Merely providing the information somewhere in the return or the accounts or other documents is insuffi-

**17.67** *Finality and Certainty, Powers of Enquiry and Discovery*

cient if it is hidden away, is obscure or its relevance is unclear. Both the existence and the relevance of the information have to be notified by the company, or must reasonably be expected to be inferred.

**17.67** In the light of the above, the following may be regarded as the prudent approach to adopt in relation to the provision of information to the Revenue as part of the return:

(a) The accounts submitted with the return should explicitly deal with any potentially controversial areas in the figures by a suitably unambiguous note.

(b) In other areas further documentation should be filed where it may be relevant to a determination of the proper tax treatment, e.g. a sales contract, but its relevance should be explained and the particular parts of the document which have a bearing on the issues should be highlighted.

**17.68** It should also be noted that information is 'made available' to the Revenue as referred to in 17.57 if it is provided by the company. The Revenue therefore consider that they will not be prevented from making a discovery assessment if the information has been provided by another person, e.g. another company in the same group or a return of one of the directors. Finally, if there is still any real doubt about whether the approach adopted by the company is correct, it would be advisable for the company or its agent to use the post transactions ruling system described in Chapter 2.

**Discretionary and judgmental issues**

**17.69** As described in 4.33 et seq. the move to self-assessment has radically changed the procedure in areas where a company's tax position previously depended on the Revenue formally accepting a state of affairs or exercising their discretion in favour of the company in a particular way. This particularly applied to special reliefs, where generally specific claims had to be made. *FA 1996 s 134* and *Sch 20* have amended a large number of different provisions in the Taxes Acts to transfer complete onus in deciding the issue on to the taxpayer. To avoid the risk of discovery assessments being made at a later date, where advantage has been taken of reliefs in such circumstances where entitlement may be open to question, the issue should be highlighted in the return.

**Valuations**

**17.70** In cases where liability is determined by reference to valuations, for example, a CGT computation where a 31 March 1982 value was relevant, it seems that if a professional valuation has been included in the return, which is within a reasonable range, the matter cannot be reopened under a discovery assessment after the twelve month period has

## Finality and Certainty, Powers of Enquiry and Discovery  17.73

elapsed. This assumes that the information given to the valuer is sufficiently comprehensive.

**17.71**  In straightforward cases it may be possible to submit details of disposals requiring valuations to the Revenue prior to filing and ideally to agree the figures to be submitted before the final filing date for the return under the procedure outlined in 8.21 et seq. Even where it is not possible to agree figures by this time, the dialogue with the Revenue valuation department will have commenced leading to a speedier resolution of an acceptable valuation with the subsequent reduction in any interest adjustment (see Revenue Press Release 4 February 1997). Where, as would normally be the case in the material valuation, the Revenue have opened an enquiry and referred the case to the Share Valuation Division or the Valuation Office, and as a result the enquiry remains open at the end of the normal enquiry period, the Revenue will not, as a matter of practice, raise further enquiries unrelated to the valuation and associated capital gains tax computation, unless they could have made a discovery had the enquiry been formally closed.

### Error and prevailing practice

**17.72**  Where a return has been filed and the tax shortfall results from an error or mistake as to the basis on which the liability should have been computed, the shortfall is not recoverable if the return was made on the basis of, or in accordance with, the practice generally prevailing at the time when it was made. [*FA 1998 18 Sch 45*].

### Time limit for discovery assessment

**17.73**  There is a general time limit of six years from the end of the accounting period to which the assessment relates. However, in the case of fraud or negligence (whether by the company, a person acting on its behalf, or a partner of the company) the time limit is 21 years from the end of the accounting period. [*FA 1998 18 Sch 46*].

Chapter 18

# Interest and Penalties

## Interest

### Summary of basic provisions

**18.1** Any corporation tax which is unpaid on the due date (generally nine months and one day after the end of the accounting period) automatically carries interest. The rate is 2.5 per cent above a 'reference' rate linked to the base rates of the principal clearing banks. In the case of larger companies where corporation tax is payable by instalments, interest is charged at a lower rate on unpaid or inadequate instalments, being 2 per cent above the reference rate, until the normal due date for payment of corporation tax has passed. In both cases the interest is deductible in computing profits chargeable to corporation tax.

**18.2** Where there has been an overpayment of tax resulting in a repayment, the company is entitled to receive 'repayment' interest on the overpayment. For corporation tax, this runs from the later of the date the tax was paid and the normal due date. For repayment of income tax or payment of a tax credit, interest runs from the end of the accounting period. Such interest is generally payable at the reference rate less 1 per cent and is chargeable to corporation tax. Furthermore, a company is entitled to received 'credit' interest in certain cases if tax is paid early or an instalment payment turns out to have been excessive, such interest being payable at the reference rate less 0.25 per cent. The detailed rules are now considered.

### Interest chargeable on tax paid late ('late payment interest')

**18.3** The general provisions for charging interest on tax paid late, described by the Revenue as 'late payment interest', are contained in *TMA 1970 s 87A*. Any unpaid corporation tax carries interest from the date the tax becomes due and payable (for which see Chapter 5 but generally nine months and one day after the end of the accounting period), even if the date is a non-business day. The rate of interest is 2.5 per cent above the reference rate (see 18.19). Late payment interest automatically arises on tax in arrears, irrespective of the cause and when the tax liability is determined. It is regarded simply as 'commercial restitution' for the payment being late.

**18.4** Late payment interest is to be paid without deduction of tax. Where it is payable by a company within the charge to corporation tax, and it relates to a CTSA period (i.e. an accounting period ending on or after 1 July 1999) the interest is deductible in computing profits. [*TMA 1970 s 90*]. The Revenue have stated that in most cases payment applications will show the amount of any interest that has accrued. But where exceptionally the computer cannot calculate interest correctly the Revenue will try to ensure that the application shows the accrued interest as nil rather than as a positive but incorrect amount. A proper interest calculation will be carried out once the tax has been paid in full.

**18.5** Where the corporation tax charge is reduced and tax is repaid, there is an appropriate adjustment to the interest charge. The actual interest charge is based on the adjusted corporation tax figure. [*TMA 1970 s 91(1A)(1B)*]. Although the legislation places the onus on the company then to 'require' the repayment of overpaid interest, the Revenue have stated that their aim will be to repay any overpaid interest automatically, along with the tax and any repayment interest that may be due.

**18.6** There is a limitation on the right to be refunded overpaid interest as mentioned in the previous paragraph where the right to the corporation tax repayment results from the carry back of trading losses under *TA 1988 s 393A(1)*. Unless the loss is carried back more than twelve months, the relief is not normally effective for interest purposes until the due date for the accounting period in which the loss was incurred, i.e. nine months after the end of the period. [*TMA 1970 s 87A(6)(7)*]. There is a similar restriction where a non-trading deficit on a company's loan relationship is carried back on a claim under *FA 1996 s 83(2)*.

---

*Example 1*

---

For the year to 31 December 2001, Oak Ltd has a corporation tax liability of £60,000 on profits of £300,000, including non-trading loan relationship profits of £100,000. Oak Ltd pays £30,000 by the due date of 1 October 2002. In its next year to 31 December 2002 Oak Ltd has a non-trading loan relationship deficit of £200,000 and claims relief on £100,000 by carry back against the non-trading loan relationship profits of the previous year.

Whilst the tax relief is £20,000 (£100,000 × 20%) this is only effective for interest purposes from 1 October 2003. Consequently Oak Ltd is liable to late payment interest on £20,000 from 1 October 2002 to 1 October 2003 and on £10,000 from 1 October 2002 to the date of payment.

---

**18.7** Where a tax charge has arisen under *TA 1988 s 419* (loans to participators) and relief is given under *s 419(4)* following the repayment,

## 18.8 Interest and Penalties

release or write off of the loan, interest on any outstanding tax is not chargeable beyond the date of such repayment, release or write off. The Revenue have stated that for the purpose of applying this rule, any tax unpaid on the date of repayment etc. is assumed to be *s 419* tax rather than corporation tax so far as possible.

**18.8** Under Pay and File, interest may be charged in advance of the receipt of a return if a late payment of tax has been made. The Revenue have stated that this will cease when their new computer system starts. Thereafter interest will not be calculated until a return is made or some other charge to tax arises.

**Interest payable on tax repaid ('repayment interest')**

**18.9** Tax which is repaid to a company, whether corporation tax, income tax or tax credit comprised in any franked investment income, carries repayment interest from the 'material date' until the payment order is issued. [*TA 1988 s 825*]. The rate of interest is the reference rate less 1 per cent (see 18.20). The interest is payable without deduction of tax and is chargeable to corporation tax.

**18.10** For corporation tax, the material date is the later of the date the corporation tax was paid and the date on which it became due and payable. For income tax repayments and payments of tax credits, the material date is the day after the end of the accounting period in which the payment was received by the company. Where tax has been paid on more than one date, any repayment is treated as a repayment of tax paid on a later rather than an earlier date, for the purposes of calculating repayment interest.

**18.11** There are parallel provisions to those described in 18.6 where a tax repayment is generated by a claim to carry back a trading loss or a non-trading deficit on loan relationships to an earlier accounting period. Unless a trading loss is carried back more than twelve months, repayment interest only runs from the normal due date for the accounting period in which the loss or deficit is incurred.

---

*Example 2*

---

For the year to 31 December 2001, Elm Ltd has a corporation tax liability of £60,000 on profits of £300,000, including non-trading loan relationship profits of £100,000. Oak Ltd duly pays the £60,000 tax on 1 October 2002. In its next year to 31 December 2002, Elm Ltd has a non-trading deficit on loan relationships of £200,000 and claims relief on £100,000 by carry back against the profits of the previous year.

Tax of £20,000 is repaid by the Revenue in (say) July 2003. Interest on the repaid tax runs from 1 October 2002, being the normal due date for the accounting period in which the deficit arose.

**18.12** As referred to in 18.7, relief is given under *TA 1988 s 419(4)* following the repayment, release or write off of a loan to a participator. Where the repayment etc. takes place more than nine months after the end of the accounting period in which the loan was made, repayment interest does not arise until the normal due date for the accounting period in which the repayment etc. occurs. [*TA 1988 s 826(4)*].

**Revenue practice regarding computer treatment of losses and deficits carried back (and of relief to which *s 419(4A)* applies)**

**18.13** In order to handle the interest consequences mentioned at 18.6 and 18.12, the Revenue's computer system calculates the tax effect of the carry back of a loss or deficit, then adds the result of that calculation to the tax liability shown in the assessment or other calculation of liability, and treats the tax effect of the loss as a payment made on the date on which the relief is effective for interest purposes. This approach will be reflected in payment applications.

**18.14** Thus in *Examples 1* and *2* above, any payment applications issued would show the tax charge as £60,000 both before and after relief has been given for the non-trade deficit. Once the relief has been given, the tax effect of the relief, £20,000, would be shown as tax paid. The computer handles relief for trading losses carried back for twelve months or less in the same way. The computer will treat relief to which *s 419(4A)* applies in the same way.

**Interest on late and inadequate instalment payments ('debit interest')**

**18.15** Late and inadequate instalment payments attract interest, described by the Revenue as 'debit interest'. This carries a lower rate than that generally applicable under *TMA 1970 s 87A*, being the reference rate plus 2 per cent (see 18.20). The lower rate applies to interest that accrues at any time from an instalment due date until the normal due date for the payment of corporation tax (i.e. nine months and one day after the end of the accounting period). As with other interest chargeable under *TMA 1970 s 87A*, debit interest is deductible in computing profits for corporation tax purposes.

**Interest on early paid tax and overpaid instalments ('credit interest')**

**18.16** Under the instalment payments regulations (*SI 1998 No. 3175*) all companies (whether large or small) are entitled to be paid credit interest on tax paid earlier than the normal due date, whether tax is payable in one amount or in quarterly instalments.

## 18.17 Interest and Penalties

**18.17** For corporation tax payable in one amount, credit interest runs from the date on which tax is paid (provided this is not earlier than the date on which a first instalment payment would have been due for the accounting period if the company were due to make quarterly instalment payments) to the normal due date, or the date on which the tax is repaid if earlier. For instalments, credit interest runs from the date on which the amount is paid (or from the due date for the first instalment payment, if later) to the normal due date for corporation tax. Credit interest is payable at reference rate less 0.25 per cent. [See 18.20].

### Handling debit and credit interest: Revenue practice

**18.18** The Revenue have stated that they will not calculate debit or credit interest, or post the amounts to company accounts until the company's self-assessment is recorded (or exceptionally a determination of the tax payable is made in the absence of a return) and the normal due date for the payment of corporation tax has been recorded. The Revenue will then calculate debit and credit interest on a daily basis by reference to the extent to which the cumulative amount of the tax paid (after taking into account any repayments) exceeds or falls short of the cumulative amount the company had become liable to pay, and will post separate totals of debit and credit interest to the company's account. The Revenue calculate debit interest on the basis that there are 366 days in a year and credit interest on the basis of 365 days in a year whether or not the year is a leap year.

---

*Example 3*

---

Having been required to make quarterly instalment payments for the three years to 31 December 2002, Ash Ltd anticipates that there will be the same requirement for 2003. It duly makes estimated instalment payments in July and October 2003. In January 1994 Ash Ltd concludes that it is not liable for instalment payments for 2003.

Ash Ltd makes a repayment claim, and the tax is repaid by the Revenue on 20 January 2004, but no credit interest is then added. When the 2003 accounts are finalised they confirm that there was no liability to make quarterly instalments and this is reflected in the return filed in August 2004. Credit interest will accordingly be due on the full amount of the two instalment payments from the date they were repaid until the date of repayment, 20 January 2004.

---

*Example 4*

---

Hazel Ltd calculates that its corporation tax liability for the year to 31 December 2000 will be £150,000, and it pays this on 20 September 2001, i.e. eleven days before the due date. Hazel Ltd completes its tax return in November 2001 which shows a tax liability of £160,000, and it pays the balance of £10,000 on 25 November 2001.

Hazel Ltd is entitled to credit interest on £150,000 for the eleven days from 20 September to 1 October 2001, and is liable to late payment interest on £10,000 from 1 October to 25 November 2001.

*Example 5*

Spruce Ltd's corporation tax liability for the year ended 31 December 2005 is in fact £144 m. Accordingly this should have been paid by equal quarterly instalment payments of £36 m on 14 July 2005, 14 October 2005, 14 January 2006 and 14 April 2006. In fact Spruce Ltd's initial estimate of the liability, made in July 2005, was £72 m and it duly paid its first instalment of £18 m on 10 July, 4 days before the due date. In October 2005, Spruce Ltd's revised estimate of its liabilities was £120 m and it paid a second instalment of £42 m on 14 October, bringing the total tax paid to £60 m. The recalculation for the third instalment due in January 2006 showed tax of £136 m, so £42,000 was paid on 14 January. The fourth instalment due in April 2006 showed tax of £140 m, so a further amount of £38 m was paid on 14 April. The balance of £4 m was paid on 20 September 2006. Assume that the reference rate is 5 per cent, so credit interest is 4.75 per cent and debit interest is 7 per cent.

|   |   | **Credit** | **Debit** |
|---|---|---|---|
| 1. | The first instalment paid on 10 July is early, and it results in an underpayment of £18 m (£36 m − £18 m). The consequences are that: | | |
| | (a) there is no credit interest, since this only starts to run on the due date for the first instalment, i.e. 14 July; | Nil | |
| | (b) the underpayment of £18 m carries debit interest from 14 July to 14 October (92 days). | | £316,721 |
| 2. | The second instalment is paid on time but results in an underpayment of £12 m (£72 m − £60 m) which carries debit interest until 14 January (92 days). | | £211,147 |
| 3. | The third instalment is also paid on time but this results in an underpayment of £6 m (£108 m − £102 m) until 14 April (90 days). | | £103,278 |

**18.18** *Interest and Penalties*

| | | |
|---|---|---|
| 4. | The final instalment paid on 14 April was on time but also results in an underpayment of £4 m (£144 m − £140 m) until 20 September (159 days). | £121,639 |
| | Total | £752,785 |

The interest is posted to Spruce Ltd's account and payment applied for.

---

*Example 6*

---

Alder Ltd's corporation tax liability for the year ended 31 December 2005 is in fact £32 m. Accordingly, Alder Ltd should have paid equal quarterly instalments of £8 m on 14 July 2005, 14 October 2005, 14 January 2006 and 14 April 2006. Alder Ltd's initial estimate of the liability, made in July 2005 was £80 m and it duly paid £20 m on 14 July 2005. By the time of the second instalment, the estimated liability had been revised to £72 m, and Alder Ltd paid a second instalment of £16 m on 14 October. There was a further revision of the estimated liability to £28 m when the third instalment was due on 14 January, and Alder Ltd made a repayment claim of £11 m (although it could have claimed £15 m) which was paid on 23 January. When the fourth instalment was due in April 2006, Alder Ltd still considered that the tax would be £28 m and it made a payment of £3 m on 14 April. Alder Ltd files its return and self-assessment in November 2006 (indicating a total tax liability of £32 m). Assume that the reference rate is 5 per cent, so credit interest is 4.75 per cent and debit interest is 7 per cent.

| | | Credit | Debit |
|---|---|---|---|
| 1. | The first instalment of £20 m on 14 July results in an overpayment of £12 m (£20 m − £8 m) on which credit interest is due to 14 October (92 days). | £143,671 | |
| 2. | The second instalment of £16 m paid on 14 October results in an overpayment of £20 m (£36 m − £16 m) on which credit interest is due to 14 January (92 days). | £239,452 | |
| 3. | No third instalment was paid, but a repayment claim was made for £11 m which was paid on 23 January. Total tax paid was therefore £25 m. The consequences are: | | |

294

|   |   |   |   |
|---|---|---|---|
| (a) | credit interest on an overpayment of £12 m (£36 m − £24 m) until 23 January (9 days). | £14,054 | |
| (b) | credit interest on a net overpayment of £1 m (£25 m − £24 m) from 23 January till 14 April (81 days). | £10,541 | |
| 4. | The payment of the fourth instalment of £3 m on 14 April (which brought the total payments up to £28 m) resulted in an underpayment of £4 m, on which debit interest is payable until 1 October, the normal due date (170 days). | | £130,054 |
| | Total | £407,718 | £130,054 |

The amounts of credit and debit interest are posted to Alder Ltd's account. The net credit of £277,664 is set against the outstanding tax of £4 m, leaving a net liability of £3,722,336. Late payment interest accrues on this until it is paid.

**Interest rate-setting arrangements and formulae**

**18.19** The procedure and formulae for calculating the rates of interest on the four kinds of interest (late payment interest, repayment interest, debit and credit interest) are set out in *FA 1989 s 178* and various regulations (*SI 1989 No. 1297, SI 1993 No. 2212* and *SI 1998 No. 3176* (see Appendix 3)). There is a reference rate, being the average base lending rate of six clearing banks specified in *SI 1989 No. 1297* which is rounded to the nearest whole number, with 0.5 rounded down, for ordinary late payment interest and repayment interest (but not for debit or credit interest). When the rate for credit interest produced by the formula is not a multiple of a quarter, it is rounded down to the nearest quarter. When the rate for debit interest produced by the formula is not a multiple of one quarter, it is rounded up to the nearest quarter.

**18.20** Rates of late payment and repayment interest are reviewed monthly, with changes taking effect on the sixth day of the calendar month. Rates of debit and credit interest are reviewed twice monthly. The rate for late payment interest is the reference rate plus 2.5 per cent, and for debit interest, the reference rate plus 2 per cent. For repayment interest the rate is the reference rate minus 1 per cent, and for credit interest, the reference rate minus 0.25 per cent.

## 18.21 Interest and Penalties

**ACT and income tax deducted from payments by a company**

**18.21** A company suffers an interest charge if it is late paying ACT (for accounting periods beginning before 6 April 1999) and income tax deducted from yearly interest and other payments. The due date for payment of interest in such cases is 14 days after the expiry of the return period in which the dividends or other payments were made. [*TMA 1970 s 87*].

# Penalties

**Introduction**

**18.22** The penalties regime of *TMA 1970 Part X* applied to companies as well as to individuals and trustees. With the introduction of CTSA, the applicable provisions relating to companies are contained in *FA 1998 18 Sch*, which are now considered. Such penalties are charged by determination under *TMA 1970 s 100* and the general right of appeal to the Commissioners under *TMA 1970 s 100B* remains under CTSA.

**Failure to notify Revenue of chargeability**

**18.23** Where a company which is chargeable to tax for an accounting period, but which is not on the records of the Revenue and hence has not received a tax return, fails to notify the Revenue as to its chargeability within twelve months of the end of the accounting period, it is liable to a tax-related penalty. [*FA 1998 18 Sch 2(2)(3)*]. For this purpose 'tax' means corporation tax, including any amount assessable or chargeable as if it was corporation tax, notably tax due under *TA 1988 s 419(1)* (loans to participators) and *TA 1988 s 747(4)(a)* (controlled foreign companies). For a 'reasonable excuse' defence see 18.39.

**18.24** The penalty is not to exceed the amount of tax payable for the accounting period in question that remains unpaid twelve months after the end of the period. In computing the tax unpaid, no account is to be taken of any relief under *TA 1988 s 419(4)* (relief in respect of repayment etc. of loan to participator) which is deferred under *s 419 (4A)*. [*FA 1998, 18 Sch 2(3)(4)*].

---

*Example 7*

---

Cobb Ltd failed to give notice of its chargeability to tax for its accounting period ending 31 December 2000. It is liable to tax of £3,000, but had only paid £2,300 by 31 December 2001. The maximum penalty is therefore £700. The liability includes a *s 419* charge of £400 on a loan made in the period to 31 December 2000 and repaid in full in November 2001. Relief

*Interest and Penalties* **18.26**

is due under *s 419(4A)* but this is deferred until 1 October 2002, being the due date for the accounting period in which the loan was repaid. This £400 is not deductible in calculating the unpaid tax for the purposes of the penalty.

**Late filing of or failure to make return**

**18.25** There is a £100 flat rate penalty for failure to file the corporation tax return on time, increased to £200 after three months. Unlike income tax self-assessment there is no provision for reducing this if the tax is less than the penalty. Where the company is persistently late in filing (i.e. where this is the third occasion of default), the penalties are increased to £500 and £1,000 respectively. [*FA 1998 18 Sch 17*]. For a 'reasonable excuse' defence see 18.39.

*Example 8*

Walnut Ltd draws up accounts to 30 September, and its return for the accounting period to 30 September 2001 is only filed on 10 November 2002 (the deadline being 30 September 2002). It incurs a flat rate penalty of £100.

*Example 9*

The facts are as in *Example 8*, save that the return is filed on 5 January 2003. There is a flat rate penalty of £200.

*Example 10*

The facts are as in *Example 8*, save that Walnut Ltd files its next two returns (for the years to 30 September 2002 and 30 September 2003) on 3 February 2004 and 28 December 2004 respectively. The flat rate penalty for the year to 30 September 2002 is £200 and for the year to 30 September 2003 is £500.

**18.26** In addition, there is a further penalty of 10 per cent of the tax if the return is not filed within 18 months after the end of the accounting period (or the due date for filing if this is later). This is increased to 20 per cent if the delay in filing is more than two years after the end of the accounting period. In calculating the unpaid tax no account is taken of any deferred relief under *TA 1988 s 419A* where a loan to a participator

## 18.27 Interest and Penalties

has been repaid in the period. [*FA 1998 18 Sch 18*]. In the event that extensions to the Companies Acts filing dates are allowed by the Registrar (e.g. companies carrying on business outside the UK) the filing date for the tax return is also extended. [*FA 1998 18 Sch 19*].

*Example 11*

Pine Ltd's return for the year ended 30 September 2001 is due for filing by 30 September 2002. It is in fact not filed until 1 June 2003. Unpaid tax is £35,000 so the tax related penalty (10 per cent) is £3,500.

*Example 12*

The facts are as in *Example 11*, save that Pine Ltd did not file the return until 30 November 2003. The tax related penalty (20 per cent) is £7,000.

**Late filing penalties: practical issues**

**18.27** The Revenue have stated that although they may require a return for a period during which a company is outside the charge to corporation tax, they will not knowingly issue a Notice to file that specifies such a period. Once the Inspector is satisfied that a period for which a return has been made is such a period he will not impose a penalty for delay in making such a return. If a penalty has already been charged, it will be discharged on appeal.

**18.28** Under Extra Statutory Concession B46, the Revenue do not charge a penalty in respect of a return received on or before the last business day within seven days following the statutory filing date. A business day, for this purpose, is any day other than a Saturday, a Sunday, Christmas Eve, Good Friday or any Bank or Public Holiday. The Revenue have stated that whilst this concession, which is couched in terms of the Pay and File provisions, is kept under review, they have no plans to disapply it to returns for CTSA periods. This does not apply to any other statutory date which may trigger higher or additional penalties under *18 Sch 17* or *18*, and should not be regarded as an extension to the statutory time limit. But see also 18.39 in relation to exoneration from penalty for late filing where the company has a reasonable excuse.

*Example 13*

Teak Ltd receives a Notice to file a return for its accounting period ending 31 December 2000, the filing date being 31 December 2001. Teak Ltd's return is received by the Revenue on 4 January 2002.

No penalty is charged on Teak Ltd by reason of the concession.

*Example 14*

Iroko Ltd also receives a Notice to file a return for its accounting period ending 31 December 2000. It posts its return by first class post on Thursday 4 January 2002 but the return is not received by the Inspector until Monday 8 January 2002.

Iroko Ltd does not benefit from the concession because its return is not received by Friday 5 January, the last business day within the seven days following the filing date.

**Incorrect or uncorrected return etc.**

**18.29** A tax related penalty is imposed on companies for (a) fraudulently or negligently delivering an incorrect corporation tax return or (b) within a reasonable time of discovering the error, failing to rectify a return that the company mistakenly (but not fraudulently or negligently) filed. The penalty is an amount up to the additional tax due, and no account is to be taken of any deferred relief under *TA 1988 s 419(4A)*.

**18.30** There is a similar penalty for fraudulently or negligently (a) making any incorrect return, statement or declaration in connection with a claim for any allowance, deduction or relief in respect of tax or (b) submitting to the Revenue, or to the Special or General Commissioners, any incorrect accounts in connection with ascertainment of the company's tax liability. [*FA 1998 18 Sch 89*].

*Example 15*

Birch Ltd files its return for the year ended 30 September 2000 on 1 August 2000 which shows tax payable of £10,000. Enquiries into the return establish incorrect accounts delivered negligently, with revised tax payable for the period of £18,000. The maximum penalty is the understated tax of £8,000.

**18.31** In a case where a company incurs more than one tax related penalty for the same accounting period which is determined by reference to the same part of the tax liability, the total penalty on that part of the tax is not to exceed the largest penalty on that part. Hence in such cases only one penalty will be charged.

**18.32** *Interest and Penalties*

*Example 16*

Burr Ltd files its return for the year ended 30 September 2000 on 1 May 2002. This showed tax payable of £25,000, but only £5,000 had been paid by 31 March 2002. The tax related penalty under Paragraph 18, based on the unpaid tax at 31 March, is £20,000 × 10% = £2,000.

Enquiries made by the Revenue reveal a negligent submission of incorrect amounts. The actual amount of tax due is £30,000, so £5,000 tax has been understated. The maximum Paragraph 20 penalty is £5,000. Applying an agreed abatement for the Paragraph 20 penalty, the calculation would be:

| | | |
|---|---|---|
| Paragraph 18 penalty: £20,000 × 10% | = | £2,000 |
| Paragraph 20 penalty: £5,000 × say, 30% | = | £1,500 |
| Total | | £3,500 |

If there had been no Paragraph 20 culpability with regard to the additional £5,000, the total Paragraph 18 penalty would have been £25,000 × 10% = £2,500.

**Failure to produce documents during enquiry**

**18.32** Penalty provisions are contained in *FA 1998 18 Sch 29* for failure to provide documents requested during a Revenue enquiry in accordance with the procedure set out in 17.28. The company has 30 days to comply, this period starting from the receipt of the notice by the company, rather than 30 days from the date stated in the notice. [*Self-assessed v Inspector of Taxes [1999] STC (SCD) 253*]. The Revenue's practice in relation to the delivery of such a notice is set out in Tax Bulletin Special Edition, April 2000 (see Appendix 1). Where a company fails to comply with a notice to provide the documents or other information it is liable to an initial penalty of £50. If the failure continues, a Revenue Officer may directly impose a further penalty of up to £30 per day for each day on which the failure continues under the determination provisions of *TMA 1970 s 100*. [*FA 1998 18 Sch 29(2)(a)*]. Alternatively, the officer may commence penalty proceedings before the General or Special Commissioners, in which case the Commissioners may, if satisfied, impose a penalty of up to £150 per day. [*FA 1998 18 Sch 29(2)(b)*]. In either event no penalty is to be imposed after the failure has been remedied.

**18.33** The Revenue accept that there can be no question of a penalty in any case in which it is genuinely impossible, for whatever reason, to comply with the notice. Moreover, a company cannot be penalised for failing to produce documents that do not exist. So if the company has failed to keep the records required by Paragraph 21 a penalty may arise

*Interest and Penalties* **18.37**

for that failure as described below, but not for any consequential failure to produce those records in response to a notice issued under Paragraph 27. However, where the company has kept some but not all required records and fails to comply with a request to produce them, penalties could be sought for the failure to comply with a Paragraph 27 notice.

**18.34** The Revenue consider that requesting information, as opposed to documents, may require the company to provide information beyond that contained in documents which already exist. For example, information could include an analysis showing how a particular entry in the company's accounts or return is made up, computations or calculations, an explanation of how certain items have been categorised in the company's return, or a translation of documents written in a foreign language. A penalty can be sought for a failure to provide such information in response to a notice.

### Failure to retain and preserve records

**18.35** The new record keeping provisions of *FA 1998 18 Sch 21* impose an obligation on a company to retain and preserve its records. Generally these have to be kept for six years after the end of the accounting period. A penalty of up to £3,000 is exigible for any company which fails so to do. The penalty provisions relate to an accounting period, so there is a maximum penalty of £3,000 for one accounting period. [*FA 1998 18 Sch 23(1)*]. There is no penalty for failure to preserve records needed only for the purposes of claims and elections not included in the corporation tax return. There is likewise no penalty if the records relate to *TA 1988 s 234(1)* (dividend vouchers) or *352(1)* (certificates of income tax deducted) so long as the Revenue are satisfied that reasonable alternative documentary evidence is available. [*FA 1998 18 Sch 23(2)(3)*].

**18.36** The Revenue have stated that penalties under this head will not be sought routinely. They will only be sought in the more serious cases where, for example, records have been destroyed deliberately to obstruct an enquiry or there has been a history of serious record keeping failures.

### Penalty for unpaid tax instalments by larger companies

**18.37** Where a company is liable to debit interest on late instalments of corporation tax (see Chapter 5) there is authority under *TA 1998 s 30(4)* for prescribing circumstances in which the company may be liable to a penalty not exceeding twice the amount of that interest. The prescribed circumstances are set out in Regulation 13 of *SI 1998 No. 3175*, which are that the company or a person acting on its behalf deliberately or recklessly fails to make the required instalment payments, or the company or a person acting on its behalf makes a fraudulent or negligent repayment

## 18.38 Interest and Penalties

claim. The Revenue have issued guidance on their practice in relation to this penalty in Tax Bulletin, August 1999, p 683 (see Appendix 1).

### Failure to provide information regarding instalment payments

**18.38** Under the regulations regarding instalment payments for large companies the Revenue may require the company to provide documentary or other information. If the company fails to do so there is an initial penalty of up to £300, with daily penalties thereafter; and up to £3,000 for fraudulently or negligently providing incorrect particulars [*TMA 1970 s 98* as amended by *FA 1999 s 80*]. The Revenue have stated that they will only seek to use their information powers where a company has deliberately or recklessly failed to comply with its payment obligations, or fraudulently or negligently made a repayment claim.

### Reasonable excuse for failure

**18.39** A person who has a reasonable excuse for not doing something he was required to do is deemed not to have failed to do it, provided the failure is remedied without unreasonable delay after the excuse has ceased. [*TMA 1970 s 118(2)*]. The Revenue's approach to 'reasonable excuse' cases is set out in Company Taxation Manual CT 10412. The question of reasonable excuse within context of late filing of an individual's self-assessment return was considered by the Special Commissioners in *Steeden v Carver [1999] STC (SCD) 283*. The issues are discussed in Tax Bulletin Special Edition, April 2000 (see Appendix 1).

### Time limit for tax related penalties

**18.40** As under the previous rules, a penalty determination must generally be made or proceedings commenced within six years of the date on which the penalty was incurred, or at any later time within three years of the final determination of the tax liability. [*TMA 1970 s 103(1)*].

### Interest on penalties

**18.41** Penalties carry interest from the date on which they become due and payable. [*TMA 1970 s 103A*]. Full effect is given to this charge by new regulations [*SI 1998 No. 310*] inserting the penalty interest provisions into the existing regulations relating to the charging of interest (Revenue Press Release, 16 February 1998).

Chapter 19

# Appeals: Collection and Recovery

## Appeals under self-assessment

### General position

**19.1** The old system, based on the Revenue raising a tax assessment and the matter being resolved either by agreement or by an appeal to the General or Special Commissioners, largely disappears. Under CTSA a company self-assesses its own tax liability and in the majority of cases that is likely to be the end of the matter. The Revenue's role shifts to one of investigation and policing. The company's rights are then safeguarded by entrusting supervisory powers to the Commissioners, notably their ability to review the imposition of penalties and to monitor Revenue investigations, whilst also giving a right of appeal in respect of discovery assessments by the Revenue.

### Appeals on substantive grounds in relation to Revenue enquiries

**19.2** As explained in Chapter 17, during an enquiry the Revenue are empowered to amend a company's self-assessment to make good a perceived deficiency if they consider that without an immediate amendment tax is likely to be lost. In such a case the company may appeal to the Commissioners although the appeal is not to be heard until the enquiry is completed. [FA 1998 18 Sch 30]. Once the enquiry has been completed the Revenue may also amend a company's tax return if the company refuses to do so of its own volition in order to accord with the Revenue's conclusions. This is tantamount to a Revenue assessment. Again the company has the right of appeal to the Commissioners. [FA 1998 18 Sch 34]. In both cases the notice of appeal has to be given in writing to the officer by whom the notice of amendment was given, within 30 days of the issue of that notice.

**19.3** As claims will generally be included in returns, any proposed amendments to such claims during an enquiry will likewise be reflected in an amendment to the company's self-assessment and return, and hence open to a company's appeal under this procedure. However, the Revenue have separate enquiry powers into other kinds of claim as described in 17.43, and also powers to amend such claims. There is again a right of

**19.4** *Appeals: Collection and Recovery*

appeal to the Commissioners against such amendments. [*TMA 1970 1A Sch 9*].

**Appeals in relation to group relief and capital allowances**

**19.4** The Revenue are given certain powers in relation to group relief claims, notably to give directions in cases where the amount available for surrender is reduced and also to make an assessment should they discover that group relief which has been given is excessive. [See 4.28 and 4.29]. In such cases the company has a right of appeal. [*FA 1998 18 Sch 75(8)* and *48*].

**19.5** With regard to capital allowances, a claim may reduce the amount available for allowances for another period for which a return has already been filed. In such a case the Revenue may amend the return for that other period. [See 4.33]. The company has the right of appeal against such an amendment. [*FA 1998 18 Sch 83*].

**Appeals in relation to discovery assessments and determinations**

**19.6** The Revenue's rights to make discovery assessments or determinations are considered in Chapter 17. The Revenue are empowered to make a discovery assessment in certain cases where they consider that there has been an under-assessment or excessive relief has been given. They may make a discovery determination where they discover that a company's tax return incorrectly states an amount affecting the tax for another period of the same company, or which affects the tax liability of another company. There is a right of appeal to the Commissioners in both such cases. Again, the appeal has to be given in writing within 30 days to the officer who made the assessment or determination. [*FA 1998 18 Sch 48, 49*].

**Appeals against penalties**

**19.7** There are specific rights of appeal against a penalty imposed for failure to keep proper records. [*FA 1998 18 Sch 23*]. The various CTSA penalties set out in *FA 1998 Sch 18* and covered in Chapter 18 relating to failure offences and for the delivery of an incorrect return, claim or accounts, are charged by determination under *TMA 1970 s 100*. Hence, they are penalties determined by an officer of the Board. The general right of appeal to the Commissioners against such penalty determinations under *TMA 1970 s 100B* remains under CTSA, with the normal *TMA 1970* rules relating to appeals applying except for *s 50(6)–(8)* (Commissioners' powers to reduce, confirm or increase an assessment). Instead, in the case of a penalty the amount of which is fixed by the relevant statutory provision (e.g. flat rate penalty for late filing), the Commissioners may confirm the penalty, set it aside, or increase or reduce it to the correct amount. Where the penalty is not to exceed a statutory maximum (e.g. the £3000 which may be imposed for record keeping deficiencies) the Commissioners may likewise confirm or set the penalty aside. They can also increase or reduce it to what they consider is an appropriate amount.

**Supervisory powers over Revenue investigations**

**19.8** The new system for Revenue enquiries is described in Chapter 17. As set out in 19.2, a company has a substantive right of appeal against any assessments made to its self-assessment by the Revenue as a result of an enquiry. As an entirely separate matter, the company effectively has some recourse to the Commissioners against the conduct of an enquiry. This is accomplished by giving the company the right to apply to the Commissioners' for a direction that the Revenue give a closure notice within a specified period. The direction must be granted unless the Revenue can show reasonable grounds for not giving a closure notice. [*FA 1998 18 Sch 33*].

**19.9** There is no time limit for the making of such an application nor any limit on the number of times a company can apply. Moreover, an application can be made immediately after the company has received notice that an enquiry is about to be commenced. In appropriate cases this may be an indirect means of trying to establish whether the Revenue has real grounds for making an enquiry or whether the company has been selected for enquiry at random.

**19.10** Once the Revenue have notified a company as to the commencement of an enquiry, they have wide powers to require documents and information. A company may appeal to the Commissioners against such a requirement, which is to be set aside to the extent that the Commissioners conclude that the documents or information are not reasonably required for the purposes of the enquiry. [*FA 1998 18 Sch 28*].

**Whether appeal heard by General or Special Commissioners**

**19.11** Under the previous system, there was generally a choice as to whether appeals against assessments were heard by the General or Special Commissioners, although certain appeals had to go to the Special Commissioners. Moreover, appeals against assessments in respect of chargeable gains involving a question of the value of land had to be referred to the Lands Tribunal. Under CTSA the principle of the company's choice between the General or Special Commissioners is maintained, but with the requirement that certain important or difficult matters are only heard by the Special Commissioners or the Lands Tribunal.

**19.12** Appeals against (a) an amendment by the Revenue to a self-assessment during the course of an enquiry, (b) an amendment by the

**19.13** *Appeals: Collection and Recovery*

Revenue to a company return at the conclusion of an enquiry, (c) an assessment to tax other than a self-assessment, or (d) a discovery determination, are generally to be heard by the General Commissioners. However they are to be heard by the Special Commissioners if the appeal is against a decision of the Board of Inland Revenue, or it is expressly within the jurisdiction of the Special Commissioners or the Lands Tribunal under the provisions set out in 19.14 to 19.17, or the company so elects.

**19.13** Such an election may, however, be disregarded if the taxpayer and the Revenue agree in writing before the determination of the appeal, or alternatively if the General Commissioners so direct. A direction from the General Commissioners may be made if following an application by the Revenue, the General Commissioners decide that they are not satisfied that the company has arguments to present or evidence to adduce on the merits of the appeal. [*FA 1998 18 Sch 93, 94*].

**Questions to be determined by Special Commissioners**

**19.14** Under a new *TMA 1970 s 46B*, certain questions on the matters set out in 19.15 arising in respect of any of the following appeals must be determined by the Special Commissioners:

(a) an appeal against a Revenue amendment to a self-assessment under *FA 1998 18 Sch 30 or 34(2)*;

(b) an assessment which is not a self-assessment;

(c) an amendment to a claim or election not in a return under *TMA 1970 Sch 1A Sch 9(3)*; and

(d) an appeal against the disallowance of a claim or election under *TMA 1970 1A Sch 7(3A)*.

**19.15** The questions relevant to companies which are only to be determined by the Special Commissioners are those relating to:

(a) the valuation of shares or securities in an unquoted company;

(b) the taxation of chargeable gains or in relation to a claim under *TCGA 1992*;

(c) a controlled foreign company, under *TA 1988 s 747(4)(a)*; and

(d) the territorial sea and designated areas, under *TA 1988 s 830* or *TCGA 1992 s 276*.

**Jurisdiction of Special Commissioners over certain claims included in returns**

**19.16** Under a new *TMA 1970 s 46C*, in the case of an appeal against an amendment to a self-assessment under *FA 1998 18 Sch 30 or 34(2)*, questions relating to the following must be determined by the Special Commissioners:

(a)  a claim made to the Board;

(b)  a claim for management expenses for owners of mineral rights under *TA 1988 s 121*;

(c)  a claim for exemption for certain friendly societies under *TA 1988 ss 459* and *460*;

(d)  a claim for exemption for certain trade unions and employers' associations under *TA 1988 s 467*;

(e)  a claim for double taxation relief under *TA 1988 Pt XVIII Chapter I*.

**Questions to be determined by the Lands Tribunal**

**19.17**  Under a new *TMA 1970 s 46D* in respect of all appeals set out in 19.14, disputes in connection with the value of any land or lease of land for chargeable gains purposes must be determined by the relevant Lands Tribunal, but only in so far as it relates to that value.

**Rules for assigning proceedings to General Commissioners**

**19.18**  A substituted *TMA 1970 Sch 3* contains the rules for determining which body of General Commissioners hears a taxpayer's appeal. These rules come into effect for proceedings relating to companies for accounting periods ending on or after 1 July 1999. Appeals in connection with corporation tax, company income tax or tax liabilities in respect of loans to participators under *TA 1988 ss 419* and *420* may, at the company's election, be heard by the division of General Commissioners for the place where the company's business is carried on, or where its head office is situated, or where it resides, being its place of effective management. However, if the Board institute the appeal, or the company fails to elect, the Board chooses the appropriate divisions for one of these places. [*TMA 1970 3 Sch 4*].

**19.19**  The company should make the election to determine the appropriate division of General Commissioners by a notice in writing served on the Revenue. The time limit is when the company gives notice of appeal, or if the proceedings are not an appeal, when the company otherwise commences the proceedings, or later if the Revenue allow it. The election is irrevocable and cannot be withdrawn. However, it can be overridden by an agreement reached under *TMA 1970 s 44(2)*. [See Tax Bulletin, Issue 27, February 1997, p 387]. An election by the Revenue has to be notified in writing to the company. [*TMA 1970 3 Sch 5, 6*].

## 19.20 Appeals: Collection and Recovery

### Procedure on appeal

**19.20** The procedure for appeals to the Commissioners is contained in *TMA 1970 s 50*, the *Special Commissioners (Jurisdiction and Procedure) Regulations 1994 (SI 1994 No. 1811)* and the *General Commissioners (Jurisdiction and Procedure) Regulations 1994 (SI 1994 No. 1812)*. The basic provisions have not been changed. The appellant is to be given notice of the day for hearing the appeal. A Revenue Officer may attend every appeal, and is entitled to be present during the entire hearing and to give reasons in support of the assessment. The Commissioners are empowered to postpone the appeal for absence, sickness or other reasonable cause. The company may be represented by a barrister, solicitor or accountant, or by any other person unless the Tribunal is satisfied that there are good and sufficient reasons not to permit a particular person in the circumstances of the case. The Commissioners are directed to make the appropriate adjustments to any assessments, or any amendment to a self-assessment, whether upwards or downwards as the case may be, or to hold that the assessment etc. should stand good.

### Postponement of tax pending appeal

**19.21** Provisions are contained in *TMA 1970 s 55* dealing with the postponement of tax pending an appeal by the company to the Commissioners. For a summary of these provisions and the procedure, see Tolley's *Taxes Management Provisions* (6.37–6.43). *TMA 1970 s 55(1)* is amended by *FA 1994 19 Sch 18* to ensure that these rules for postponement of tax and the collection of tax which has not been postponed, apply to appeals to the Commissioners under CTSA.

### Collection and recovery

**19.22** The proceedings relating to the collection and recovery of tax are presently contained in *TMA 1970 ss 60–70*. The first of these deals with the Collector's powers to distrain upon the goods and chattels of a taxpayer in default, and the Revenue's prior claims over other creditors, and the separate recovery and priority procedures in Scotland. These provisions are unchanged under CTSA. Under *TMA 1970 s 65* small amounts of tax (corporation tax not exceeding £2,000) can be recovered summarily in the Magistrates Court. Proceedings are to be brought within twelve months from the time of default. [*TMA 1970 s 65(3)*]. The provisions in *TMA 1970 s 66*, regarding recovery in the county courts, remain unchanged.

**19.23** Interest which is due on unpaid tax is treated as tax for recovery purposes under *TMA 1970 s 69*. Under amended *TMA 1970 s 69*, penalties are also regarded as tax. A certificate from a Collector that such interest and penalties are payable is sufficient evidence of that fact for recovery purposes. [*TMA 1970 s 70(2)*].

# Appendix 1

# Inland Revenue Tax Bulletins

Issue 12, pages 137–138 (August 1994)

**MATRIX SECURITIES: GUIDANCE TO TAXPAYERS**

**Some readers will have seen the consultative document 'Post Transaction Rulings' published on 12 May. Although the document is mainly about post-transactions/pre-return rulings, it did trail the prospect of a subsequent consultative document about pre-transaction rulings – and it promised a Code of Practice, later this year, about the Department's current approach to the provision of advice to taxpayers.**

In the meantime, readers may be interested to see the following letter sent by the Deputy Chairman to the main representative bodies with whom we have regular exchanges. It picks up the same theme, commenting on the case of Matrix Securities Ltd and responding to enquiries put to us about the implications of that case for taxpayers seeking to rely on Inland Revenue guidance.

'From correspondence, discussion and press comment it is clear that there is some uncertainty following the speeches in the House of Lords in the Matrix Securities case, particularly concerning the extent to which taxpayers can rely on guidance provided by the Revenue. It may be helpful if I comment briefly on the position, as we see it, in relation to the provision, by the Revenue, of non-statutory guidance.

There are two things to say about the Matrix Securities case. First, it seems to us that, in the end, the Matrix case broke little new legal ground; for all their Lordships, whatever the individual differences in their reasoning, the case involved the application of established law (or legal principle) to the particular facts.

Second, however the case does provide further endorsement at the highest level of MFK and the guidelines set out in that case. In particular, the case underlines the need for complete frankness in circumstances where taxpayers expect to rely on guidance given by the Revenue; disclosure must be full, accurate and fair as to the facts and the complete context in which the ruling is sought.

My letter of 18 October 1990 therefore holds good; we would not wish to withdraw the help we have undertaken, in certain circumstances, to give. Indeed, as you will have seen from the recent Press Release on Rulings, we plan to build on the proposals for a post-transactions rulings system and in due course issue a consultative document exploring the options for an advance rulings system. In

## Inland Revenue Tax Bulletins

the meantime, we are working on a Code setting out our present practice on the provision of advice to taxpayers. We shall wish to seek your views on a draft of that code in a few months time.

I have been asked whether, following Matrix, taxpayers and their advisers are expected to judge for themselves the appropriate level of Revenue officials to whom they should address requests for guidance. It seems to me, on the basis of the case, that the question crucially arises where those seeking Revenue guidance are already aware of views held within the Department contrary to the confirmations being sought. That fact cannot be ignored if people are intending to rely on the advice they get; apart from that there is little to add to what I said in my letter of 18 October 1990.

In the ordinary way, it may be appropriate to write to the Inspector of Taxes who handles the affairs of the taxpayer concerned; but if it is known, for example, that Head Office have recently been considering the issue the appropriate course would be either to write to the relevant Inspector, pointing out the Head Office interest and the need for its clearance or, alternatively, to Head Office direct. In either event an answer should not be sought in an unreasonable time, bearing in mind the complexity of the issues involved and the volume of material to be examined.

Similarly, I have been asked how far taxpayers and their advisers are expected to go in disclosing not only the facts but also the main legal issues arising in particular circumstances. In answering that point I would refer back to my letter of 18 October 1990 when I said that we will provide guidance in certain circumstances and in particular where the operation of the law is uncertain. We are not setting out to give our comprehensive blessing to transactions and schemes put to us but rather responding to the uncertainties in the minds of taxpayers and their advisers on the specific points on which guidance is sought. By definition, therefore, it will invariably be appropriate to spell out those uncertainties and the legal issues on which comfort is being sought as well as it being made clear for what purpose the ruling is required.'

In case readers have not seen it (although it was published by most if not all of the bodies to whom it was sent) we also reproduce below an extract from the Deputy Chairman's earlier letter of 18 October 1990 to which reference was made in his recent letter.

'We have told our Head Office staff that they should be prepared when they can to answer requests for guidance on the Revenue's interpretation of tax law, not only where they involve the interpretation of recent legislation, Statements of Practice and other published information, but also in cases where there is a major public interest in developments in an industry or in the financial sector but where the operation of the law is uncertain. In addition, local Inspectors of Taxes will of course continue where practicable to inform practitioners about the Revenue's interpretation of tax law as it applies to any case which falls within the responsibility of that office.

In no case, however, whether at Head Office or local office, would a member of the Department seek to advise a taxpayer or a practitioner on the arrangement of a person's own affairs: that must remain the responsibility of his professional advisers. Still less of course could we advise in the area of tax planning.

Where guidance is sought, the enquirer will doubtless bear in mind the principles set out by Bingham LJ in the MFK case. In addition to providing details such as the tax district and the reference, the enquirer should bear in mind that if he wishes to rely on Revenue guidance he must:

- a.  put all his cards face upwards on the table;
- b.  indicate the guidance sought;
- c.  make it plain that it is fully considered guidance that is being sought; and
- d.  indicate the use which it is intended to make of the guidance, and in particular whether he proposes to tell others of it.

Where guidance is given it should not be relied on to the extent of any qualification it contains. Moreover the actual application of the law will depend on the precise way in which the transaction is carried out and of course on the precise terms of the law at the time.

There may occasionally be cases, in particular where a representative body would find it helpful to be given an informal view of the interpretation of new legislation, where it would be appropriate for a reply to be given on an explicitly non-binding basis. Such cases will of course be quite different from Statements of Practice on the one hand or the more formal guidance with which this letter is otherwise concerned.'

**Issue 17, pages 218–220 (June 1995)**

## INTRA-GROUP INTEREST AND SIMILAR SUMS TREATED AS DISTRIBUTIONS

The parts of Section 209 Income and Corporation Taxes Act (ICTA) 1988 repealed by Section 87 of this year's Finance Act had a different impact on the tax treatment of cross-border intra-group interest payments according to whether, and how, the terms of double taxation treaties interacted with the statute. The law itself characterised all interest paid to certain non-resident group members as a distribution. Where no treaty applied or where a treaty did not restrict the operation of the law, this remained the result. In other cases, treaty wording prevented the law applying and intra-group interest could only be characterised as a distribution to the extent that it was excessive as a result of the interest rate being too high. In the most frequently occurring case, however, only the amount of an interest payment which exceeded, for whatever reason, what would have been paid between companies acting at arm's length was characterised as a distribution.

Section 87 puts this arm's length approach into United Kingdom domestic law. Consequently, it leaves the tax treatment of most existing intra-group financial arrangements unchanged. It provides for less harsh treatment in cases where no treaty applies or where a treaty imposed no restriction on the operation of the old domestic law. It may also have an impact on some cases where a treaty prevented the old law applying. This will only be the case if, and to the extent that, the interest payment exceeds what would have been paid in the absence of the group relationship.

The new provisions, like their predecessors, are concerned with payments of

## Inland Revenue Tax Bulletins

interest and similar sums in respect of securities. For this purpose 'security' has the extended meaning set out at Section 254(1) ICTA 1988 and therefore covers most forms of indebtedness. The focus on the existence of certain 75% shareholding relationships also remains. Unlike the old domestic law, however, only that part of the interest or similar payment which exceeds what would have been paid in the absence of the group relationship is characterised as a distribution. (This could, of course, be the whole amount.) The previous restriction to non-resident companies has also been removed. Instead, all intra-group payments where the shareholding condition is satisfied are within the scope of the legislation, unless the recipient is within the charge to corporation tax in respect of the sum or is a charity.

Concerns have been expressed about the complexity of the new provisions and also the lack of certainty for taxpayers and potential investors to which some have felt they give rise. This article outlines the Revenue's approach to the new law and indicates how guidance on our likely reaction in specific cases may be obtained. A subsequent Tax Bulletin will deal with some of the more detailed points which have been raised about the new Section.

### THE ARM'S LENGTH APPROACH

The legislation requires taxpayers and Inspectors to consider what would have happened in the absence of the intra-group relationship between the issuer and holder of the securities in question. As a result, the focus is on the facts and circumstances at the time the actual security was put in place or assigned.

It is worth stressing that the legislation is extremely broad in its scope. It is capable of applying where, even though a loan could have been obtained from a third party on identical terms, the transaction would not have taken place but for the group relationship. Such a case might arise where, for example, a company has a fixed-term third-party loan bearing interest at LIBOR + 1.00 % which still has three years to run at the relevant time. This loan is repaid and replaced by a three-year intra-group loan carrying interest at LIBOR + 1.50 %, but which otherwise has terms and conditions identical to the third-party loan it replaces. It is accepted that, arm's length interest rates having increased since the original loan was obtained, LIBOR + 1.50 % is an arm's length rate for a three year loan at the time the new loan is made. Nonetheless, given the lack of commercial logic in this change, we would contend that the arrangement would not have been entered into but for the group relationship and that the legislation applies with the result that all of the interest will be a distribution.

This is one reason why there can be no blanket 'let-out' for intra-group loans satisfying some crude formulaic test. Although we are aware of the importance to arm's length lenders of ratios of debt to equity or pre-tax and pre-interest profit to total interest payable ('income cover') they are insufficient, in themselves, to determine what would have happened at arm's length. Moreover, ratios such as these are far from being the only factors which potential lenders take into account. Among the others probably the most important are:

- the business sector concerned;
- the nature of, and title to, any assets which might provide security;
- cash flow; and
- the general state of the economy.

# Inland Revenue Tax Bulletins

Nonetheless, the legislation will most often be relevant in cases of thin capitalisation (a high ratio of debt to equity) or insufficient income cover. Consequently it may be helpful to explain our approach to these two aspects of the arm's length test.

Commentators have suggested that the Revenue has been content to accept a 1:1 ratio of debt to equity and a 3:1 income cover ratio. Often the possibility of satisfying us that, in the circumstances of a specific case, arm's length ratios would have differed from these is also mentioned. While we understand why our approach has been construed in this way, it is to some extent misleading and certainly needs to be considered in context.

As with our approach to the legislation as a whole, when we consider such ratios, we focus on what would have been expected to happen at arm's length.

In our experience, third party lenders in the United Kingdom market almost always look at the consolidated debt to equity ratio of the group of companies to which the borrower belongs and the resources on which it could draw within that group to fund interest charges and capital repayments. Consequently, in the overwhelming majority of cases, we too look beyond the company issuing the security to the wider company grouping to which it belongs. Of course, the legislation is designed to protect the United Kingdom tax base. Accordingly, it limits the extent to which the wider group is taken into account by specifying that, for certain purposes, relationships with connected companies which are not part of the (defined) UK grouping as well as with the holder of the securities (except in respect of the securities in question) are to be disregarded.

It is also our experience that arm's length lenders in the United Kingdom revise their view of an acceptable level of gearing or income cover for particular groups at different times – although the variation has not been large in recent years. As a result, we may be able to say that a particular debt to equity ratio meets the arm's length standard today. We could not say that the same ratio would meet that standard even a year from now.

We are also aware that the relative importance of debt to equity ratios and other factors such as income cover or cash flow varies over time and between industries. In recent years, we have detected a trend away from simple debt to equity ratio criteria, perhaps reflecting the realisation that balance sheets can show flattering snapshots which are not representative of the position as a whole. This has been coupled with increased evidence of the continuing availability of loans being made subject to satisfying certain covenants – including meeting gearing and income cover targets at specified intervals. Our approach endeavours to reflect such trends.

As for the precise ratios themselves, arm's length lenders have always applied different standards when lending to different industries at any one time. So, for example, financial concerns and property holding groups have always been able to gear up to a greater extent than most other borrowers. Here too we follow the market pattern.

Despite the industry spread of acceptable ratios and the variation over time, we understand that the average debt to equity ratio of United Kingdom quoted companies has historically ranged around 0.6:1. It remains in that region at present. Similarly, we are aware of comment that lenders are currently concerned

## Inland Revenue Tax Bulletins

when the level of operating profit is less than four times the interest payable. Partly because an average is a point between the high and low positions and partly as a result of a desire to use our resources most effectively, we have in recent years tended to accept that, where a loan otherwise meets the arm's length test, if the United Kingdom grouping remains geared at something less than 1:1 and its income cover is at least 3:1, its financing should be regarded as satisfying the test as a whole. If not, further consideration would be appropriate. It must be stressed, however, that there are no hard and fast rules in this area and each case has to be considered on its own facts.

### THE NEGOTIATION PROCESS

Where detailed consideration of the position is necessary, we generally endeavour to advance matters by way of discussion with the group and its advisers, with a minimum of correspondence. This speeds the resolution of our enquiries and enables groups to understand the tax position at an early stage. We recognise that applying the arm's length test can never be a precise science. We are, therefore, able to show some flexibility in the course of the discussions, provided we are satisfied that the result is about right at the end of the day.

As a consequence of these discussions, groups sometimes restructure their investment entirely by putting in additional equity finance as well as the debt or by replacing part of the debt with an equity injection. In some cases, however, we are content if they simply make part of the loans interest-free: provided interest-bearing debt is repaid in preference to interest-free debt.

### PROCEDURAL MATTERS

In the past, enquiries have often been triggered either by an Inspector's examination of accounts showing the intra-group funding or by receipt of a tax treaty claim for exemption from, or reduction in, withholding tax on the payment to the non-resident group member. No doubt this will continue.

In future, when consideration of the legislation is triggered in one of these ways, the Inland Revenue will normally issue a letter commenting on the relevance of Section 209(2)(da) ICTA 1988 to the specific intra-group arrangement. If companies are concerned about the position and do not receive such a written notice they should contact us at the address given below.

Although the new legislation makes no difference to most existing intra-group funding arrangements, there could be some change where the funds have come from one of a dozen countries. These are:

Austria;
Barbados;
The Faroe Islands;
Fiji;
Germany;
Israel;
Japan;
Kenya;
Luxembourg;

South Africa;
The Sudan; and
Zambia.

We have attempted to identify such arrangements and have written to the groups concerned commenting on the legislation's impact in each case. Companies who have not received any communication from us about existing advances from group members in one of the above countries and who are concerned about the possible impact of the new legislation, should also contact us at the address below.

More generally, in recent years groups and their advisers have increasingly taken the initiative by approaching International Division at the time when finance is being put in place to obtain guidance on their plans. Where sufficient information to reach a view has been available, we have normally been able to give groups some certainty as to the tax treatment likely to apply to what they propose. (The Financial Secretary to the Treasury drew attention to this during the Committee Stage debate on this provision of the Finance Bill.) It is our intention to continue to offer this service to groups considering investment or reinvestment in the United Kingdom.

Guidance on this and other aspects of the new legislation may be obtained by writing to:

Inland Revenue
International Division 5/2
Melbourne House
Aldwych
LONDON WC2B 4LL

Correspondents should identify the parties to the transaction and supply as much information as possible about the group's existing financial structure and/or its proposals.

**Issue 18, pages 237–241 (August 1995)**

## NON-RESIDENTS TRADING IN THE UK: THE ARM'S LENGTH PRINCIPLE

The rules for taxing non-residents were revised in Sections 40, 124 to 129 and Schedule 23 of Finance Act (FA) 1995. The new rules simplify the procedures for taxing non-residents and align them with Self Assessment. The main effect is to codify the present practices by replacing the present patchwork of statutory rules, administrative procedures and extra statutory concessions with clear simple rules. The amount of tax charged is left broadly unchanged.

The new rules clarify the way in which non-residents will be taxed under Self Assessment and the extent of the tax charge. Non-residents are taxed in the UK on the shoreline principle, that is on income arising in or connected with the UK. The new rules divide this into three broad categories which can loosely be described as:

- income from property in the UK,

## Inland Revenue Tax Bulletins

- investment income (most types of income from investments in the UK other than land) and,

- earned income (income from an employment, trade, profession or vocation in the UK and any income not included in the previous categories).

Income from property will continue to be taxed in full either through deduction at source, with a final settling up with the non-resident through Self Assessment where necessary, or, where the non-resident chooses by agreement with the Inland Revenue, wholly through Self Assessment.

Earned income will also continue to be taxed in full. Income from employment will normally be taxed through PAYE, with a final settling up with the non-resident through Self Assessment where necessary. Income from a trade, profession or vocation will normally be taxed through Self Assessment by the non-resident or, where the trade is carried on through a branch or agency, by the branch or agent.

Investment income will continue to be taxed principally through deduction at source. The new rules limit the tax chargeable on investment income to the tax, if any, deducted at source. There will therefore normally be no need for non-residents whose UK income is wholly investment income to self assess, except where a repayment is due.

In the case of a non-resident trust where all the existing and potential beneficiaries are not ordinarily resident (or not resident in the case of corporate beneficiaries), there will be no charge at the rate applicable to trusts under Section 686 Income and Corporation Taxes Act (ICTA) 1988 in respect of income falling within Section 128(2) and (3) FA 1995.

These rules are in line with the agreed principles of international taxation as set out in the OECD model tax convention (MTC), which are also followed in double taxation agreements (DTAs) between the UK and other countries. The main difference is that there is no requirement, except where a DTA applies, for the non-resident to have a fixed presence in the UK before earned income may be taxed.

The new rules leave the provisions for charging tax on the income of non-residents from carrying on a trade, profession or vocation unchanged. The main rule is in paragraph (a)(iii) of Schedule D in Section 18(1) ICTA 1988 which limits the charge to trades, professions and vocations exercised within the UK.

Two main principles were established in early tax cases. First, trades carried on wholly or partly in the UK, including trades carried on by non-residents, are chargeable under Case 1 of Schedule D. Trades carried on wholly outside the UK are chargeable under Case V of Schedule D, which is limited by paragraph (a) to UK residents (*Colquhoun v Brooks* 2 TC 490, *San Paulo (Brazilian) Rly Co v Carter* 3 TC 407). Second, trades carried on by non-residents are chargeable only where the non-resident trades in the UK, which means broadly that economic activities are carried on in the UK that give rise to trading profits (eg sales or manufacture). Trading by non-residents with the UK, as opposed to in the UK, (eg purchases or delivery) is not chargeable (*Erichsen v Last 1* TC 351 and 4 TC 422, *Pommery and Greno v Apthorpe* 2 TC 182, *Werle v Colquhoun* 2 TC 402, *Grainger & Son v Gough* 3 TC 311 and 462, *Smidth & Co v Greenwood* 8 TC 193, *Firestone Tyre & Rubber Ltd v Lewellin* 37 TC 111).

# Inland Revenue Tax Bulletins

These principles are well understood. They are also in line with principles in the MTC which exempt trading functions of a resident of the other state from charge if they are solely of a preparatory or auxiliary nature.

It is also well understood that, where a non-resident carries on a trade partly in the UK and partly outside the UK, the charge is limited to the profits from the part of the trade carried on in the UK.

It is perhaps less obvious how the profits from the part of the trade carried on in the UK should be measured. They are required to be measured on the arm's length principle set out in the MTC where a DTA applies which includes the relevant provisions. It is considered that it also follows from the main rule in Schedule D that the same principle applies even if there is no treaty.

There is support for this principle in the early tax cases on non-residents trading in the UK. For example, in *Pommery and Greno v Apthorpe* at 2 TC 189, Denman J said, with regard to the profits chargeable in the UK from merchanting champagne produced in France, that:

'It may be that there may be some difficulty in some respects as to the manner of calculating the amount of expenditure to be put against the profits, whether it would be a proper course to look at the goods sent over to England and then to consider what profit they make, putting a fair valuation on them as they arrive, and as the money is transmitted, or whether it would be necessary in such a case to look more minutely into the profits and losses upon the whole trade carried on partly in France and partly in England. I do not think it is necessary at all at this stage of the case to decide that. That is a matter of quantum, a matter for the consideration of persons skilled in dealing with such matters as assessing profits of trade.'

This can be seen as an early description of the arm's length principle and as a recognition of the need to develop methods to apply that principle in practice. Such methods were developed in the OECD 1979 Report on 'Transfer Pricing and Multinational Enterprises' and have been reaffirmed and clarified in the recently published 1995 revision of that report by OECD 'Transfer Pricing Guidelines for Multinational Enterprises and Tax Administrations'.

The new rules in FA 1995 were developed in consultation with the Self Assessment Consultative Committee (SACC)*. We asked the Committee whether the application of the arm's length principle to the measure of trading profits should be made explicit in the statute. The Committee decided this was neither necessary nor desirable. They considered that it is well established that the arm's length principle applies as a matter of law and that this is accepted by taxpayers, tax advisers and the Inland Revenue as the correct basis for taxing non-residents in the UK.

The Committee also pointed to the lack of recent cases on the taxation of non-residents trading in the UK as confirmation of the principle. They were concerned that a new provision to put that beyond doubt could create uncertainty or have unforeseen consequences through the inevitable differences between the wording which would be used in the statute and that used in the MTC. They suggested that it would be better to confirm that the arm's length principle applies automatically through an article in Tax Bulletin.

The new rules in FA 1995 replace the whole of the existing rules in Part VIII

## *Inland Revenue Tax Bulletins*

Taxes Management Act (TMA) 1970. The rules which are still relevant, that is those in Sections 78, 82(1) and 83-85 TMA 1970, reappear in the new rules with any necessary modifications. The rules which are no longer relevant, that is those in Sections 79, 80, 81 and 82(2) TMA 1970, do not reappear. Nothing of significance is lost as a result. The rules which have disappeared did not affect the measure of charge on the non-resident. But they were also otiose as they were no more than a reflection of the arm's length principle. In particular, the double foreigner provision in Section 82(2) TMA 1970 was of no effect. In the cases which would have fallen within the subsection, the arm's length principle would have left no profits to tax in the UK once the arm's length fee payable to the agent had been deducted, leaving nothing for the subsection to bite on.

Sir George Young Bt MP, the former Financial Secretary to the Treasury, also reaffirmed that 'the arm's length principle applies generally to the measure of profits brought into charge on a non-resident' when these sections were debated in the Standing Committee on the Finance Bill.

To summarise, it is generally agreed by taxpayers, tax advisers and the Inland Revenue that the arm's length principle, as set out in the MTC and explained in OECD publications, applies to the measure of profits chargeable on a non-resident in respect of trading in the UK as a matter of law, irrespective of whether a DTA applies.

> \* The following bodies are represented on SACC – Chartered Association of Certified Accountants, Chartered Institute of Taxation, Confederation of British Industry, Federation of Small Businesses, Institute of Chartered Accountants of England and Wales, Institute of Chartered Accountants of Scotland, Institute of Directors, Law Society, Law Society of Scotland. This article was agreed with the members of the Committee.

### Issue 20, page 271 (December 1995)

### SELF ASSESSMENT: ASSESSMENT OF SCHEDULE A INCOME ARISING TO A PARTNERSHIP

We have been asked to clarify the circumstances in which the income from jointly owned property constitutes partnership income within the terms of Section 111 Income and Corporation Taxes Act (ICTA) 1988 (as substituted by Section 117(2) Finance Act (FA) 1995).

There are a number of possibilities. For example, consider Mr and Mrs Jackson who let a jointly owned property.

Where Mr and Mrs Jackson carry on a business in partnership, and that business comprises both a Case I Schedule D source and a Schedule A source, then Section 111(7) & (8) ICTA 1988 would apply. The income from the Schedule A source will be assessable using the basis periods that apply for the Case I Schedule D source.

But it may be that these two activities have been arranged in such a way that there are two separate businesses and two separate partnerships, albeit partnerships between the same two individuals. In such circumstances Section 111(10) ICTA 1988 would apply to the partnership with the Schedule A source. The income

# Inland Revenue Tax Bulletins

from the Schedule A source will be assessable on a tax year (6 April to 5 April) basis.

There is a further possibility. Joint ownership of property does not, of itself, create a partnership. There will only be a partnership if, exceptionally, the exploitation of the property constitutes the carrying on of a business jointly with a view to profit. Where the letting income is not ancillary to a Case I/II partnership source, and the letting activity cannot be described as the carrying on of a business, the income arising is not assessable as partnership income. Instead, each share will be assessable as the personal income of Mr and Mrs Jackson. In this context there is a distinction between the term 'business' as used in the Partnership Act 1890, and the new concept of a 'Schedule A business' introduced by FA 1995.

[Section 111 ICTA 1988]

**Issue 32, page 485 (December 1997)**

## RELATIONSHIP BETWEEN ACCOUNTANCY AND TAXABLE PROFITS

The relationship between accountancy and taxable profits is never a static one and of late it has attracted considerable interest. For example, the Tax Faculty of the Institute of Chartered Accountants in England and Wales recently made available to its members a note summarising a wide-ranging discussion on the subject with Revenue specialists.

The extent to which the business tax system uses accounting concepts of profit in the computation of what is to be taxed has always varied across the code. At one extreme, the computational rules for calculating chargeable gains are set out in the statute and no reliance is placed on accountancy concepts at all. On the other hand, the courts have long held that the starting point in calculating the profit taxable under Case I or II of Schedule D (trades, profession and vocations) is the profit shown in the accounts.

There is no direct reference to the use of the accounting profit in this way in current law but in the first Exposure Draft, issued as part of the Tax Law Rewrite project in July, we have suggested a clause for inclusion in the rewritten legislation which would make the use of the accounting profit as the starting point for the Schedule D tax computation explicit. (Clause 3.2.2)

A number of specific statutory provisions have long required adjustments to be made in moving from the accounting profit to the profit taxable under Schedule D. For example, commercial depreciation is disallowed (as a capital matter) and the statutory code for capital allowances applied instead. But the courts have also been prepared to over-ride for tax the commercially acceptable accounting treatment of an item, not by reference to a specific provision, but because the treatment violates some principle developed by the courts as part of the process of calculating 'the full amount of the profits', as required by the Taxes Act.

Two important cases decided in 1993 and 1994, *Threlfall v Jones* and *Johnston v Britannia Airways*, (66 TC 67 and 67 TC 99) were concerned, not with whether an item of income or expenditure is – ever – taxable or deductible, but when. In both, the courts were unwilling to identify and apply any such principle to over-ride generally accepted accounting treatment concerned with the timing of an item of income or expenditure. These cases illustrate the courts' reluctance nowadays to hold that general accepted accounting treatment should be over-ridden for tax in this way.

One factor at work here is the, relatively recent, codification and continuing refinement of accounting practice by means of accounting standards. As a result the expert evidence given before the Commissioners on the correct accounting treatment of an item can nowadays be seen not just as the expression of a single practitioner's opinion but, in effect, as the collective view of the profession. Accountancy evidence therefore carries greater weight than it once did.

It is worth noting that the development of the law in this field does not depend on the courts ignoring their own precedents where they deem them to be inconvenient. What is, or is not, commercially acceptable accounting treatment is a question of fact not law. Furthermore, the courts have recognised that accounting practice evolves over time. In principle, therefore, it is possible for a modern court to come to a different decision from one taken in the past on the sole grounds that the accounting treatment has changed. That is the case because the cases are distinguishable on their accountancy facts, even though the other facts in the two cases may be identical. The courts therefore have a mechanism to ensure that the law does not become yoked to superseded accountancy practice and to decisions, often taken a long time ago, where judges themselves were forced to take a view of commercial practice in the absence of any accountancy evidence at all.

A current practical illustration of how this approach may work is this. Last month the Accounting Standards Board published in final form its Financial Reporting Standard for Smaller Entities (FRSSE). For smaller companies this simplifies some of the accounting rules for the measurement of profit currently in force. On the assumption that the rules in the FRSSE become generally accepted practice for these concerns, we doubt whether the courts would ever accept the argument that the correct application of the FRSSE in the accounts of a small company should for tax give way to the measurement rules for larger entities on the grounds that the latter is more precise.

It has been suggested that the judgments mentioned above mean that commercially acceptable accounting practice can no longer ever be over-ridden by a judge-made tax principle. But some recent decisions of the Special Commissioners support our view that the law has not moved that far. (For example *Meat Traders Ltd v Cushing* [1997] STC (SCD) 245; *Herbert Smith (a firm) v Honour* [1999] STC 173.) But future litigation will doubtless throw further light on these issues.

Another relatively recent feature in the development of business tax law has been the willingness of Parliament to legislate to ensure that the accountancy treatment of certain types of transactions is closely followed for tax. Examples are the 1993 legislation on foreign exchange gains and losses, that in 1994 on financial instruments and last year's rule on companies' loan relationships (Section 125 onwards FA 1993; Section 147 onwards FA 1994; Section 80 onwards FA 1996). All these provisions are based on accounting principles but cannot always follow them precisely. So some departures from accounting practice will still occur.

# Inland Revenue Tax Bulletins

Examples include legislating specifically for bad debt provisions rather than following the accountancy concept of prudence and requiring either accruals or marking to market when accounting practice allows the lower of cost or market value.

The general alignment of tax with accounting discussed in the previous paragraph has not only been a matter of recognising items for tax at the same time as they are recognised in a company's accounts. It has also involved treating all the relevant credits and debits in the accounts, including those which would be capital on first principles, as items of an income nature. Furthermore, the new rules have applied as much to investment companies as trading companies.

Alignment of tax with the accounting treatment in the field of loan relationships has made it possible to repeal a considerable body of statutory provisions which set out free-standing tax rules for particular types of transactions. This has led some commentators to ask whether a more thoroughgoing alignment of tax with accounting might be desirable. This of course is ultimately a matter for Parliament but the drawbacks, as well as the advantages, would have to be carefully considered.

For example, for tax purposes it is the profit shown in a set of business accounts which is the predominant issue. But those accounts are as much concerned with a fair presentation of balance sheet assets and liabilities as of the profit. And in preparing any set of commercial accounts difficult judgements are required, for example over the likely useful life of assets. If these judgements were all simply followed for tax there would be significantly greater inconsistency in tax treatment between one business and the next than there is at present.

In the most recent Finance Acts there has been recourse on occasion not only to companies' own accounts but also to the figures in consolidated group accounts for specific, limited purposes. For example, the question whether a lease is a 'finance lease' has to be answered in applying particular provisions not only by the accounting treatment at individual company level but also by reference to that in consolidated accounts (see Schedule 12 FA 1997 and Section 47 F(No2)A 1997). It is clear that using consolidated accounts more generally for tax would raise some very difficult and complex issues. But, as a solution to particular problems, typically in the anti-avoidance field, this example illustrates how it may occasionally be expedient for tax law to make use of some of the figures reflected in the consolidated accounts.

## Issue 37, pages 579–582 (October 1998)

### THE NEW TRANSFER PRICING LEGISLATION

**The 1998 Finance Act (FA 98) introduced a comprehensive modernisation of the UK's transfer pricing legislation. The changes are part of a wider reform of the Corporation Tax regime which includes the introduction of self assessment for companies (CTSA). For accounting periods ending on or after 1 July 1999 and years of assessment 1999/2000 et seq., Sections 770 to 773 of the Income and Corporation Taxes Act (ICTA) 1988 will be replaced by Sections 108–111 and Schedule 16 FA 98, with the full text of the basic rule appearing at Schedule 28AA ICTA 1988. Two notable changes are that there will be no requirement for**

the Board of Inland Revenue to give a direction before the legislation applies – companies will be expected to self assess in accordance with the arm's length principle; and the new wording is more closely aligned than was the old with Article 9 (the 'Associated Enterprises Article') of the Organisation for Economic Co-operation and Development (OECD) Model Tax Convention on Income and on Capital.

The new legislation was the subject of extensive consultation with taxpayers, tax advisers, and representative bodies. During the consultations, requests were made for guidance on certain issues following the integration of transfer pricing into the CTSA system. Foremost among these issues were record keeping, financial transactions and arrangements ('funding'), and penalties.

Reproduced below is the text of guidance notes on record keeping and funding. The guidance on penalties will be published shortly. These notes will be incorporated into Departmental guidance manuals in due course.

The notes refer to 'the OECD Guidelines'. These are the 1995 Transfer Pricing Guidelines for Multinational Enterprises and Tax Administrations, available from HMSO in the UK or the OECD at 2 rue André-Pascal, 75775 Paris Cedex, France.

**RECORD KEEPING**

Under the new transfer pricing legislation, taxpayers are required to recognise the arm's length principle in reporting income, profits or losses for tax purposes. Where transactions within the scope of the new rules have taken place on other than arm's length terms to the disadvantage of the UK Exchequer, appropriate computational adjustments must be made in the Tax Return.

Section 12B Taxes Management Act 1970 and paragraph 21, Schedule 18 FA 1998 require taxpayers to keep and preserve the records needed to make and deliver a correct and complete Return for any chargeable period.

In interpreting those rules for transfer pricing purposes, the Inland Revenue will be guided by Chapter V of the OECD Guidelines. This is designed to assist tax administrations in developing their approaches to documentation rules, and taxpayers in identifying the records that would be helpful in demonstrating how their methodologies satisfy the arm's length principle.

The Inland Revenue does not want taxpayers to suffer disproportionate compliance costs, nor to be required to prepare and retain documentation which is out of keeping with the nature, size, and complexity of their business, or with the transaction (or series of transactions) in question.

At the same time, taxpayers will be required to self assess accurately, and may be called on by the Inland Revenue to justify their transfer prices and the quantum of income, profits or losses returned for tax purposes.

Taxpayers should therefore prepare and retain such documentation as is reasonable given the complexity or otherwise of the relevant transaction (or series of transactions), and which identifies:

- relevant commercial or financial relations falling within the scope of the new legislation;

## Inland Revenue Tax Bulletins

- the nature and terms (including prices) of relevant transactions (including transactions which form a series, and any relevant off-setting transactions). Transactions which are clearly in one family (e.g. regular purchases made by a distributor throughout a return period of the same or similar products for resale) may be aggregated, provided any significant changes during the period in the nature or terms of the transactions are recorded;

- the method or methods by which the nature and terms of relevant transactions were arrived at, including any study of comparables and any functional analysis undertaken;

- how that method has resulted in arm's length terms etc. or, where it has not, what computational adjustment is required and how it has been calculated. This will usually include an analysis of market data or other information on third party comparables;

- the terms of relevant commercial arrangements with both third party and affiliated customers. These will include commercial agreements (e.g. service or distribution contracts, loan agreements), and any budgets, forecasts or other papers containing information relied on in arriving at arm's length terms etc. or in calculating any adjustment made in order to satisfy the requirements of the new transfer pricing legislation.

Current arrangements need not be freshly documented for the first CTSA return period, provided the existing documentation is sufficient to enable the taxpayer to make a complete and correct Return for that period.

Where arrangements continue in force for more than one return period (e.g. a distribution agreement lasting several years), there is no need to prepare fresh documentation for each return period, provided the original documentation is sufficient to demonstrate that the taxpayer has made a complete and correct return for that later period. Any significant changes in the nature or terms of the transaction or transactions in question should be recorded.

The documentation should exist at the latest by the time the Return is made.

The rules governing the period for which records generally must be preserved are described on page 587 of this issue and apply as much to transfer pricing documents as to other records. In summary, this means that transfer pricing documents should be preserved until the later of:

- six years from the end of the chargeable period to which they refer or for which there could be a related tax effect; or

- the date on which enquiries to which the documents are relevant are complete.

## FINANCIAL TRANSACTIONS AND ARRANGEMENTS ('FUNDING')

Paragraph 1 of the new transfer pricing legislation is framed in terms of provision being made or imposed between two persons by means of a transaction or series of transactions. Paragraph 3 defines 'transaction' and 'series of transactions' in wide-ranging terms. The basic pricing rule works by substituting the provision which would have been made between independent enterprises ('the arm's length provision') for the actual provision in defined circumstances. This is a more broadly based formulation than the narrow transactional approach of Section 770 ICTA 1988, but the rule of construction in paragraph 2 of Schedule 28AA ensures that the legislation will not go further than the formulation of the arm's length principle contained in Article 9 of the OECD Model.

*Inward investment: interest reclassified as a distribution*

The new legislation applies to non-arm's length interest, discounts and other payments for the use of money which create a UK tax advantage, although for inward investment where the borrower is a company, an interest *rate* which exceeds a reasonable commercial return will continue to be reclassified as a distribution under Section 209(2)(d) ICTA 1988. Where the borrower is a partnership however an excessive rate of interest may be considered under Schedule 28AA where the requisite control relationship exists.

Interest or discounts payable on funds obtained from connected persons may be excessive for reasons other than the existence of an excessive rate. The amount of the loan or terms other than the rate may not reflect what would have been agreed if the parties had been unconnected and acting entirely at arm's length, or the transaction might not have taken place at all.

In this context the guidance on when transactions should be disregarded at 1.37 of the OECD Guidelines is particularly relevant. One example quoted is that of an investment in an associated enterprise in the form of interest-bearing debt when, at arm's length, and having regard to the economic circumstances of the borrowing company, the investment would not have been expected to be structured in that way. In such circumstances it is recognised that it might be appropriate to treat the loan as a subscription of capital.

Interest, discounts, etc. which are excessive for reasons other than the rate being excessive will continue to be reclassified as distributions under Section 209(2)(da) ICTA 1988 where the borrower is a 75% subsidiary of the lender or both are 75% subsidiaries of another company. Such excessive interest is not allowed as a deduction in the corporation tax liability of the paying company and, until its abolition, ACT will be payable at the time the payment is made.

The factors which we take into account to determine whether interest is excessive for any reason for the purposes of Section 209(2)(da) ICTA 1988 are discussed in Tax Bulletin Issues 17 and 35 (June 95 and June 98). The approach outlined in these articles will also apply for the purposes of Schedule 28AA – see below – including the normal focus on the UK grouping in determining borrowing capacity.

*Inward investment: where excessive interest is not reclassified*

Where subsections (d) and (da) of Section 209 ICTA 1988 are not in point, but loan funding has been provided between two parties which are connected within the terms of the new legislation, excessive interest is payable for whatever reason and this has conferred a tax advantage on one or both parties, the tax computation will require adjustment to eliminate the effect of the excessive interest or discount. However there are no ACT consequences as the excessive interest is not reclassified as a distribution.

As provision may be made by means of a series of transactions, the situation where a related party provides a guarantee to a bank which then, on the strength of this, makes a loan, or an additional part of a loan, available to a UK borrower will be within the scope of the legislation. If, however, the effect of the guarantee is solely to reduce the rate of interest being charged and the UK borrower is not thinly capitalised the legislation will not apply, since no tax advantage is being conferred.

Where there is a special relationship between the borrower and lender or between them and another person, in addition to the tax treatment of the interest expense incurred by the borrower, it is necessary to consider the liability of the non-resident lender in respect of UK source interest income. In these circumstances the terms of a particular double taxation treaty may not allow excessive interest to be paid without deduction of income tax at the UK domestic rate. Consequently, in such situations interest will both be disallowable in the borrower's tax computation and also suffer deduction of income tax at source without the benefit of any reduced rate which might otherwise have been available under the treaty. In the absence of a special relationship between the borrower and lender, interest paid to an unconnected bank would not fall foul of such a treaty provision even if the loan is backed by a parental guarantee.

*Off-setting transactions*

Some separately contracted transactions between associated enterprises may be evaluated together in order to determine whether a tax advantage arises. However this must involve the same associates and the separately evaluated transactions must form part of the same overall provision. So, for example, it may be argued that the 'margin' earned on loans routed through the UK is consistent with the arm's length standard despite both the inward price from one associate and the outward price to a different associate being non-arm's length. Nevertheless, because the same associate is not involved in both transactions, the two elements cannot be 'off-set'. To provide for off-setting in such circumstances would expose the UK exchequer in the event of Competent Authority intervention in relation to one of the transactions.

*Outward Investment: interest-free loans*

Loans provided to an overseas associate at a nil or low rate of interest have always been within the scope of Section 770 et seq., ICTA 1988, and will continue to be within the scope of the new legislation, so that the market rate of interest should be charged. However, until now, where it has been accepted that the Competent Authority process would result in agreement that the recipient would have been unable to obtain an interest-bearing loan at arm's length then the discretion which comes with the directional nature of the legislation has been exercised so as not to impute interest. This is often referred to as acceptance that the loan performs an 'equity function'. Importantly this treatment has depended on the existence of a double taxation treaty with the country concerned providing for a Mutual Agreement procedure and has involved consideration of the contention by the UK Revenue in every case. In future, the UK lender will have to consider only whether an outward interest-free loan is in practice standing in the place of equity when deciding whether a transfer-pricing adjustment should be made in its self-assessment. The existence of a double taxation treaty with the recipient's country will not be relevant and the Revenue will only become involved where we think the lender's conclusion may be incorrect.

*Foreign Exchange movements*

If an inward or outward loan is made in a currency other than sterling, there are likely to be foreign exchange movements which will normally result in debits or credits to the profit and loss account. Because these may distort the effects of an incorrect transfer-price they are not taken into account in calculating whether there is a UK tax advantage arising from the transaction. They will continue to be dealt with as a separate matter under existing Foreign Exchange and Financial Instruments legislation.

*Charities*

In principle the funding by UK charities of their UK trading affiliates falls to be considered under Schedule 28AA since it does not fall within the scope of the paragraph 5 exemption for UK-UK transactions. However charities are expected to follow the general advice and guidelines of the Charity Commission in considering the nature of their investments in trading affiliates. When reviewing the funding of charities and their associates, we will respect the fact that they are following these. This is consistent with paragraph 1.55 of the OECD Guidelines. Where, exceptionally, charities enter into financial arrangements which are other than in accordance with the Commission's advice or guidelines, or where avoidance is present, the provisions of Schedule 28AA could be in point. This is an area in which International Division will be willing to offer up-front advice.

*Interaction with other provisions*

There are various parts of both domestic legislation and treaties which are concerned with thin capitalisation and other ways in which interest paid or accrued may be excessive. This to some extent reflects the wide variety of ways in which loan finance can be provided to a company, but the Government recognises that the result is unattractive and may give scope for some uncertainty. Consequently a review will be undertaken of the full range of currently applicable legislation with a view to establishing whether there is scope for rationalising the law in ways that do not put the UK exchequer at risk.

*Help and advice*

International Division already operates a system offering pre-transaction assistance as publicised in the Tax Bulletin Issue 17 (June 1995). This enables groups and their advisers to approach International Division at the time when finance is in the process of being put in place to obtain guidance on their plans. Where sufficient information to reach a view has been available, we have normally been able to give groups some certainty as to the tax treatment likely to apply to what they propose. We are happy to confirm that this service will continue to apply to the new legislation in relation to proposed funding structures. While we are sensitive to the commercial deadlines to which groups are subject, we cannot guarantee delivery against unreasonably tight timetables and request early notification of proposed arrangements to enhance the quality of the service we are able to provide. The contact address for advice on particular cases is:

International Division, Room 311, Melbourne House, Aldwych, LONDON WC2B 4LL

Questions on the record keeping content of this note should be directed to:

Richard Coombes, International Division, Room 409, Melbourne House, Aldwych, LONDON WC2B 4LL, Tel: 0171-438 6842, Fax: 0171-438 7518

and on the funding guidance to:

Susan New, International Division, Room 307, Melbourne House, Aldwych, LONDON WC2B 4LL, Tel: 0171-438 7596, Fax: 0171-438 7511

The Revenue recognises that these are sensitive issues. It will monitor closely the use and usefulness of this guidance, and update or amend it as the need arises.

**Issue 37, pages 587–589 (October 1998)**

## RECORDS TO BE KEPT UNDER SELF ASSESSMENT

### INTRODUCTION

This article is mainly about the record keeping requirements for corporation tax purposes under self assessment. It is intended that the key points will in due course become the subject of a formal Statement of Practice. But the section on the preservation of records in an alternative form is also relevant to unincorporated businesses. We will revise the next edition of our booklet on record keeping for the self employed (SA/BK3) to record it.

Paragraphs 21 to 23 of Schedule 18 to Finance Act 1998 require companies and other concerns within the charge to corporation tax to keep and preserve records. The provisions mirror those in Section 12B Taxes Management Act (TMA) 1970, which brought in, for 1996-97 and subsequent years of assessment, a record keeping requirement for individuals and partnerships. Paragraphs 21 to 23 have effect for accounting periods ending on or after 1 July 1999.

As noted above, these rules apply not only to ordinary limited companies but to all concerns within the charge to corporation tax including for example industrial and provident societies, authorised unit trusts, clubs and societies as well as ordinary limited companies. Except in the paragraph referring to the Companies Act record keeping requirements we use 'companies' as convenient shorthand for all concerns within the charge to corporation tax.

### SUMMARY

The legislation requires companies to keep and preserve sufficient records to enable them to make a correct and complete company tax return. Should the

Revenue decide to make enquiries into a return, the company will need to be able to explain and substantiate the information it contains. Companies with systems in place to enable them to do that should be affected by the new legislation only to the extent that they may have to retain records for longer than they do at present.

## OUR APPROACH IN PRACTICE

Concern has been expressed that, on a strict interpretation, the legislation would impose an additional and unwarranted burden on companies by extending the requirement to preserve greater quantities of prime records than is currently the case. That is not the purpose of the legislation.

We issued guidance on how Section 12B TMA affects self employed taxpayers in leaflet SA/BK3, 'Self Assessment: a guide to keeping records for the self-employed', published in June 1995.

The leaflet gives guidance on the practical effect of the legislative requirement. In particular, it makes clear that:

- the taxpayer is required to keep sufficient records to make a correct and complete return;
- the taxpayer will also need to be able to demonstrate in response to Revenue enquiries that that is the case;
- the precise nature and extent of the records needed to discharge that obligation to be kept will be dependent on the type and size of business.

This statement is equally applicable to companies and other concerns within the charge to corporation tax.

## INTERACTION WITH THE RECORD KEEPING REQUIREMENTS OF THE COMPANIES ACT

Companies to which the Companies Act applies are already required by Section 221 Companies Act 1985 to keep and preserve specific accounting records in terms which are close to the tax requirements. We can confirm that any company satisfying the requirements of the Companies Act will have satisfied the requirement to keep and preserve records for tax purposes. This is subject to keeping adequate records for arm's length pricing purposes and to the rules on the period for which records must be preserved. These provisos are discussed further below.

## RECORDS FOR ARM'S LENGTH PRICING PURPOSES

A particular issue here concerns the 'transfer pricing' legislation. These provisions require taxpayers to apply the arm's length standard to certain arrangements and transactions for the purpose of making their tax returns and self assessments.

The legislation applies primarily to dealings between a UK taxpayer and an associate operating outside the UK. It will generally not be relevant where the parties are unconnected, unless the dealings in question constitute individual transactions within a 'series of transactions' to which the legislation applies. And – with very limited exceptions – the legislation is of no relevance where the parties to a transaction are both subject to UK tax in respect of it.

Where the transfer pricing legislation may be in point, the records required by Paragraph 21 of Schedule 18 to the Finance Act 1998 to enable a company to deliver a correct and complete return, and to substantiate the figures in the return on enquiry, may well go beyond those required for the purposes of Section 221 Companies Act.

Following extensive consultations, we are also issuing guidance in this issue of Tax Bulletin on how we will interpret and apply the SA documentation requirements for transfer pricing purposes.

## PERIOD FOR WHICH RECORDS MUST BE RETAINED

The Companies Act requires private companies to retain their accounting records for a period of only three years. For tax purposes, once Corporation Tax Self Assessment is introduced, such companies will need to preserve their records for the longer period prescribed in Paragraph 21 of Schedule 18.

Normally, records for an accounting period will have to be preserved for six years from the end of that period. But in three cases they have to be kept for longer. The second and third cases in particular will be very rare in practice.

First, if an enquiry into the return for an accounting period remains open at the six year point the records for that period must be retained until that enquiry is completed.

Secondly, where no such enquiry has been started but the statutory period for doing so has not expired at the six year point (because the return is late) the records for that accounting period must be retained until the latest date for starting an enquiry has passed or, if later, the date such an enquiry is completed.

The third case is where, contrary to the first two situations, the date on which a company is requested to complete a tax return for an accounting period is itself more than six years after the end of that period. In that case the records in existence at that date must be retained as in the second situation, that is until the latest date for starting an enquiry has passed or, if later still, the date such an enquiry is completed.

Preservation of records in an alternative form (see below) should make it easier for some companies to retain their records for this longer period.

## RECORDS PRESERVED IN AN ALTERNATIVE FORM

For unincorporated business we have already indicated in Tax Bulletin Issue 21 (February 1996) that records may be preserved on optical imaging systems, and the originals discarded, provided that what is retained in digital form represents

## Inland Revenue Tax Bulletins

a complete and unaltered image of the underlying paper document. We are now able to go further. Both in the case of companies and unincorporated businesses we can accept other methods which preserve the information in the records in a different form. This is so long as those methods capture all the information needed to demonstrate that a complete and correct tax return has been made and are capable of yielding up that information in legible form. Businesses need to bear in mind this second condition when they change or up-date computerised accounting packages and ensure they have the software to access the old data.

Precisely what information needs to be preserved in this way will vary from business to business. But standard information, such as contractual terms and conditions printed on all invoices, need not be reproduced as part of the record of each transaction.

We accept of course that companies which store information in accordance with the Code of Practice on the Legal Admissibility of Information stored in Electronic Document Management Systems (BSI 1996 DISC PD 0008) will thereby automatically satisfy the tax requirements.

The exceptions, where the original record must be retained, are set out in Paragraph 22 of Sch 18 to Finance Act 1998. In essence they consist of vouchers for tax suffered or for tax credits in respect of incomings. But photocopies of foreign tax assessments, rather than the assessments themselves, will remain acceptable for the purposes of claims to double taxation relief in respect of foreign tax underlying dividend income from abroad.

### PENALTIES FOR RECORD KEEPING FAILURES

We have been asked to clarify what constitutes a failure for the purpose of the penalty provisions in the record keeping rules (Paragraph 23 of Sch 18 to Finance Act 1998 and Section 12B(5) TMA 1970). These penalty provisions relate the penalty to a year of assessment (for income tax) or to an accounting period (corporation tax). The effect is that there can only be one penalty of a maximum £3,000 in relation to all the offences relating to that year of assessment or accounting period.

We have given assurances in connection with self assessment for individuals and partnerships that penalties under S12B(5) will only be sought in the more serious cases – where, for example, records have been destroyed deliberately to obstruct an enquiry, or where there has been a history of serious record keeping failures. We are now able to offer equivalent assurances to companies. We can also confirm that a penalty would only be sought from companies, as in the case of individuals and partnerships, following approval by Compliance Division.

### PAY AS YOU EARN (PAYE) RECORDS

The requirement to create and preserve records to enable a correct and complete tax return to be filed applies to records relating to employee costs in the same way as other business costs. Some employee records will almost automatically be required for Company Tax Return purposes. Where records of employee costs are used for this purpose they must be preserved for the longer period specified in Paragraph 21 of Sch 18 to the Finance Act 1998, described above.

*Inland Revenue Tax Bulletins*

But companies which are employers must also preserve PAYE records, that is those additional records created to show that the PAYE system has been operated in a satisfactory manner. Regulation 55(12) of the Income Tax (Employments) Regulations 1993, SI 1993 No. 744, requires these additional PAYE records to be preserved for three years after the end of the tax year to which they relate.

Unlike Paragraph 22 of Sch 18 to the Finance Act 1998, the PAYE regulations do not provide for preservation of information in the records in another form. To help employers we have recently changed our view on the use of optical imaging to preserve such records which were originally created in paper form. Any paper records may now be preserved by the use of optical imaging systems, provided that what is retained is a complete and unaltered image of the underlying paper document.

**Issue 37, pages 593–596 (October 1998)**

## SELF ASSESSMENT: (1) INCOMPLETE RETURNS (2) THE USE OF PROVISIONAL FIGURES IN RETURNS

We have been asked to clarify our position regarding 'incomplete returns' and the use of provisional figures in self assessment (SA) tax returns.

### STATUTORY BACKGROUND

Section 8(1) TMA 1970 allows the Revenue to issue a notice requiring the taxpayer to deliver a return of *'such information as may reasonably be required'* to establish the tax due for any year of assessment. Section 113(1) TMA 1970 provides that any such return shall be *'in such form'* as the Board prescribe. And Section 8(2) TMA 1970 requires that the taxpayer make a declaration to the effect that *'the return is to the best of his knowledge correct and complete'*.

This means that whenever a tax return form is issued the statutory notice incorporated in that form places a obligation on the recipient to make a return of the information required, in the manner specified. If the completed tax return form delivered to the Revenue is not *'correct and complete'* the statutory notice has not been complied with and the relevant sanctions may apply. The relevant sanctions are penalties under either Section 93 TMA 1970 or Section 95 TMA 1970, depending on the nature of the failure and the circumstances in which the failure is identified.

### (1) INCOMPLETE RETURNS

In many cases it will be obvious that a tax return form is incomplete **when it is received**. For example, the signature required to satisfy the mandatory declaration may be missing. Or it may be that there is a tick, or note, to the effect that a particular set of pages have been attached to the form, but in fact they are missing. In such cases the return submitted by the taxpayer is clearly deficient in form and the taxpayer has clearly failed ' ... *to comply with the notice* ... ' (Section 93(1)(b) TMA 1970). A failure of this sort should be identified during the initial screening of the return and in such cases we will send back the

## Inland Revenue Tax Bulletins

incomplete return almost immediately, to give the taxpayer the opportunity to rectify the omission.

In other cases the fact that the tax return form is incomplete may not come to light until the information in the return is being systematically transferred to our computer database. If so we may try to obtain the missing information from the taxpayer without sending back the return. This would be appropriate where, say, it is clear that there should be an entry in a particular box. But where there is a major omission we send the return back. This might be the case where, for example, we believe the necessary accounts information is incomplete. Whether we send the return back or not, the action we take has but a single purpose – to give the taxpayer the opportunity to rectify the omission.

Giving the taxpayer an opportunity to rectify an omission in such cases is a means of enhancing voluntary compliance. This is because by sending the incomplete tax return form back we are, in effect, opting to help taxpayers meet their obligations rather than penalising them for not doing so.

**Incomplete returns delivered to the Inland Revenue on or before 31 January but sent back close to, or after, the 31st January filing deadline**

One of the issues that arose during the first year of self assessment was the treatment of returns delivered to the Inland Revenue on or before 31 January but sent back to taxpayers or their agents, as incomplete close to, or after, the 31 January deadline. If an incomplete return is sent back in these circumstances it may be too late for the omission to be rectified before the filing deadline. If so the taxpayer will face an automatic late filing penalty under Section 93(2) TMA 1970.

In the Inland Revenue Press Release of 3 February 1998, Dawn Primarolo, the Financial Secretary to the Treasury announced a concession addressing this issue. The concession provided that taxpayers whose returns were sent back to them (or their agents) in the circumstances described above would still be treated as having met the filing deadline **provided they sent back a corrected return within a specified period.**

A similar concession will apply for 1997–98 returns. **The concession will apply where**:

- **a return is delivered to the Inland Revenue on or before 31 January 1999, and**
- **the return is subsequently found to be incomplete, and**
- **it is sent back to the taxpayer (or agent) for completion on or after 18 January 1999.**

**In such circumstances the taxpayer will be given 14 days in which to complete the return and deliver it back to the Inland Revenue. If a completed return is delivered to us before the end of this 14 day period the taxpayer will be treated as having met the filing deadline.**

The concession will also apply to those who file by electronic lodgement. Any rejection is carried out automatically. Accordingly, if a return is rejected shortly

# Inland Revenue Tax Bulletins

before the filing deadline and resubmitted successfully within the 14 day period, the agent will need to take a print-out of the rejection and send it to the office dealing with the return together with an explanation.

We will be monitoring the operation of the concession this year and, depending on the outcome, may recommend that it is established as a formal Extra Statutory Concession. For the avoidance of doubt it ought to be mentioned that the concession will only apply where the return is incomplete as a result of a genuine oversight. It will **not** apply where the return is deliberately incomplete, in an attempt to take advantage of the concession. For example, the concession will not apply if a return is deliberately sent in without a relevant set of pages, to buy a little more time to complete those pages. Nor will it apply if a return is deliberately sent in without a signature, to buy a little more time to obtain the signature.

**Examples:**

Return submitted on 20 October 1998 and sent back to taxpayer as incomplete on 10 November 1998. **Concession not relevant** because taxpayer still has until 31 January 1999 to meet filing deadline.

Return submitted on 20 January 1999 and sent back to taxpayer as incomplete on 21 January 1999. Concession means that providing the completed return is sent back to the Revenue by **4 February 1999** the taxpayer will be treated as having met the filing deadline.

Return submitted on 20 January 1999 and sent back to taxpayer as incomplete on 10 February 1999. Concession means that providing the completed return is sent back to the Revenue by **24 February 1999** the taxpayer will be treated as having met the filing deadline.

Return submitted on 20 February 1999 and sent back to taxpayer as incomplete on 21 February 1999. **Concession not relevant** because return was not sent in on or before the 31 January 1999 filing deadline.

## (2) USE OF PROVISIONAL FIGURES IN RETURNS

Given that the purpose of the SA tax return is to establish the tax chargeable for a particular year of assessment it is neither surprising, nor unreasonable, that taxpayers are asked to include correct and final figures of income and gains in their returns.

But it has long been realised that there is an unacceptable tension between an *absolute* requirement to provide correct and final figures and a requirement to provide such information *by a certain date*. Prior to self assessment the Courts supported the view that the paramount requirement was to comply with the statutory filing obligation and that this may require the taxpayer to use provisional figures in the return (*Dunk v Havant General Comrs*, 51 TC 519; *Alexander v Wallington General Comrs* 65 TC 777). For example:

> 'If a taxpayer finds particular circumstances that make the best of his knowledge more than usually unreliable, it is open to him to put against his figure for a particular item of income such words as "estimated – see accompanying memorandum", or something of that kind, and explain the circumstances. If he has done his best, and, of course, he is under a duty to use all proper sources of knowledge – he will not, in my view, be guilty of making a false statement,

*providing, as I say, he puts in a genuine estimate and, if necessary, explains that it is not very reliable.'* [Goulding, J, in *Dunk v General Commissioners for Havant*, 51 TC at p 521].

## APPLICATION OF DUNK PRINCIPLES TO SA RETURNS

We would argue that the time limits for filing an SA tax return are such that it is reasonable to expect the vast majority of taxpayers to be able to provide correct and final figures by the statutory filing date. Nonetheless, we recognise that there will still be some circumstances in which it is impossible for the taxpayer to provide final figures, despite their best efforts to do so. So it is the Inland Revenue's view that the 'Dunk principles' apply equally well to SA returns. Indeed, these principles are clearly identifiable in the guidance published in 1994, at paragraph 2.53 of SAT 2:

*'There will be occasions on which some information cannot be finalised within the formal self assessment time limits despite the taxpayers best efforts to do so. In such cases the taxpayer should include a "best estimate" of the information in the return and, if appropriate, a corresponding estimate of the tax due . . . . . . A return containing any such provisional figure will not be regarded as incomplete.'*

Our views on the use of the continuing application of the Dunk principles are also reflected in the guidance material provided with the SA tax return. For example, there is general advice on the use of provisional figures at page 27 of the main Tax Return Guide:

*'Do not delay sending your Tax Return just because you do not have all the information you need. You must do your best to obtain the information, but if you cannot provide final figures by the time you need to send your Tax Return, then estimate the amount.'*

## CIRCUMSTANCES IN WHICH THE INLAND REVENUE COULD REGARD A RETURN CONTAINING PROVISIONAL FIGURES AS 'INCOMPLETE'

Despite the general guidance provided in the 1996-97 tax return there appears to have been some confusion as to the circumstances in which the Inland Revenue could regard a tax return as incomplete simply because it contains provisional figures.

The general guidance in the Tax Return guidance tells the taxpayer that *'You must do your best to obtain the information'* and goes on to say that we *'. . . will not normally regard a Tax Return as incomplete simply because it contains provisional figures, provided you have taken all reasonable steps to get the final figures, and you ensure that they are sent as soon as they are available'*.

It should be clear from this that we expect the taxpayer to have done all they reasonably can to obtain the final figures, or, in the words of Goulding, J., the taxpayer must have ' *. . . .done his best . . .* '. If a taxpayer **has made little or no effort** to obtain the final figures before the filing deadline we would argue that a key element of the 'Dunk' principles is absent and the taxpayer has failed to comply with the notice to make a return. Similarly, we would not accept that **general pressure of work or the complexity of a taxpayer's affairs** justify the use

## Inland Revenue Tax Bulletins

of provisional figures. The onus is on the taxpayer (and his agent) to take such factors into account, for example, when considering how long it will take to complete the return.

There is further guidance on the use of provisional figures in the Self-employment pages. This guidance (on page SEN3) allows for the return of a single figure of estimated profit, rather than standard accounts information:

> 'If you cannot complete the income and expenses section of your Self-employment pages because it is impossible to prepare the figures from which your taxable profit is to be calculated before the latest date for sending your Tax Return, you should provide an estimate of your taxable profit in box 3.88 .........'.

As is made clear this guidance is to be read in conjunction with the general advice on the use of provisional figures in the main Tax Return Guide. It follows that we expect taxpayers to have done all they reasonably can to obtain the final figures. It was certainly not our intention to accept a single figure of profit when, for example, it was only 'impossible' to prepare final figures because the taxpayer had made little or no effort to have the final figures prepared in time to meet the filing deadline. In such circumstances we would argue that a key element of the 'Dunk' principles is absent and the taxpayer has failed to comply with the notice to make a return. In fact we would expect there to be very few circumstances in which, despite the taxpayer's best efforts, it is genuinely *'impossible'* for the taxpayer to provide us with accounts information. The only common circumstance would be where, in the case of a newly commenced business, the first accounting period does not end until close to, or after, the statutory filing date. (By 'close to' we mean within 3 months of the filing date, so for the normal 31 January deadline, that means accounting periods ending on or after 1 November.)

Even though there are relatively few circumstances in which it would be acceptable for a single provisional figure of profit to be returned there may be circumstances in which it is acceptable for some, or all, of the standard accounts information to be completed on a provisional basis. For example, there may have been a change of accounting date requiring two sets of accounts to be prepared. If only the earlier set of accounts were final then provisional standard accounts information would be required, pending completion of the second set of accounts. In these and similar circumstances (that is where a provisional figure of profit is estimated by reference to an earlier period of account) we would expect provisional figures **for each of the anticipated entries in the standard accounts information**.

In practice it is unlikely that we will send back a 1997–98 tax return as incomplete simply because it contains provisional figures. We would prefer to process the return as received and then hold the taxpayer to the obligation to provide final figures as soon as they are available. We will do this by identifying all those returns which contain provisional figures. If the final figures are not provided by the expected date we will take appropriate action to obtain them and in some cases this will mean opening an enquiry. (The guidance in the 1998–99 returns has been clarified along the lines described above.)

*Inland Revenue Tax Bulletins*

**Issue 38, pages 603–605 (December 1998)**

## PENALTIES AND THE NEW TRANSFER PRICING LEGISLATION

The 1998 Finance Act ('FA 98') introduced new transfer pricing legislation, affecting all accounting periods ending on or after 1 July 1999 and years of assessment 1999/2000 et seq. At the time of the Budget the Revenue undertook to provide guidance on a number of issues raised by these changes. Notes on record keeping and funding were published in October's *Tax Bulletin*; this third guidance note concerns penalties.

Among the changes made by FA 98 is the abolition of the direction requirement at Section 770 (2)(d) Income and Corporation Taxes Act 1988 ('ICTA 1988'). The removal of this requirement means that, for the first time, taxpayers entering into transactions and arrangements covered by the new legislation will be obliged to make tax returns in accordance with the arm's length principle. This in turn raises the possibility, again for the first time, of penalties under Section 95 or 95A Taxes Management Act 1970 ('TMA 1970') or Paragraph 20, Schedule 18 FA 98 where:

- a return is made which is not in accordance with the arm's length principle;
- it can be shown that the return was submitted fraudulently or negligently by the taxpayer; and
- UK tax is lost as a result.

This is consistent with the Government's desire to create a fairer transfer pricing regime, one which encourages voluntary compliance and deters, and if appropriate penalises, non-compliance.

It is worth saying first of all that although penalties arising from fraudulent or negligent conduct have not previously been imposed in a transfer pricing context, they are not in themselves new. The Revenue has already published guidance on them in the Investigation Handbook at paragraphs 4720 ff. That general guidance holds good for transfer pricing purposes; there are, however, one or two extra points to be made which are specific to transfer pricing. This note deals first with the main general issues, then turns to those particular to transfer pricing.

### GENERAL

A penalty can only be charged under Section 95 or 95A TMA 1970 or Paragraph 20, Schedule 18 FA 98 where UK tax has been lost through fraudulent or negligent conduct by the taxpayer.

The maximum penalty which may be charged is an amount equal to the tax lost by reason of the offence. However, an officer authorised by the Board can, under Section 100(1) TMA 1970, determine the penalty at such amount as is, in his opinion, appropriate. The Board's policy in negotiated settlements is to abate any penalty to an appropriate percentage of the culpable tax recoverable by assessment for all years which are not time-barred for penalty action. A penalty

# Inland Revenue Tax Bulletins

measured by reference to tax lost is called a 'tax-geared' or 'tax-related' penalty. This guidance deals with tax-geared penalties only (as opposed to flat rate penalties, such as those chargeable under Paragraph 23, Schedule 18 FA 98 for a failure to keep proper records).

The factors which the Board takes into account when considering abatement are described in leaflet IR 160 and at Investigation Handbook paragraphs 5525 ff. These will apply to penalties arising from transfer pricing adjustments. See also the further comments under 'Size and gravity' below.

**TRANSFER PRICING**

*Importance of OECD Guidelines*

The Revenue's approach to the matter of penalties will be consistent with that set out in Chapter IV of the 1995 *Transfer Pricing Guidelines for Multinational Enterprises and Tax Administrations*, published by the Organisation for Economic Co-operation and Development ('OECD') and available from HMSO in the UK or the OECD at 2 rue André-Pascal, 75775 Cedex, France.

*Negligence*

One of the main concerns of business in relation to transfer pricing and penalties is what is meant by 'negligence', given that to some extent what is an arm's length price is a matter of judgement and there is not always one 'right' answer. Where taxpayers can show that they have made an honest and reasonable attempt to comply with the legislation, there will be no penalty even if there is an adjustment. Indeed, the onus will be on the Revenue in this area, as it is more generally, to show that there has been fraudulent or negligent conduct by the taxpayer before any penalty can be charged. Examples 3 and 4 below illustrate adjustments which will not give rise to a penalty.

Neither the Courts nor the Revenue have ever attempted a detailed definition of 'negligence'. Each case is to be judged on its own facts and merits, with the guiding principle being that a person is not negligent if he or she has done what 'a reasonable person would do'. There is therefore an obligation on taxpayers to do what a reasonable person would to ensure that their returns are made in accordance with the arm's length principle. This would involve, but not be limited to:

- using their commercial knowledge and judgement to make arrangements and set prices which conform to the arm's length standard (or to make computational adjustments in their returns where they do not);
- being able to show (for example, by means of good quality documentation) that they made an honest and reasonable attempt to comply with the arm's length standard and with the legislation;
- seeking professional help where they know they need it.

Taxpayers will want to document what they do to the extent necessary to enable them to sustain the arm's length nature of their arrangements and prices in any discussions with the Revenue. Guidelines on what records should be kept were published in October's *Tax Bulletin*; taxpayers who act in accordance with that

# Inland Revenue Tax Bulletins

guidance should not find themselves facing penalties on account of fraudulent or negligent conduct. Taxpayers should bear in mind, though, that detailed documentation will not *in itself* free them from the possibility of a penalty, if that documentation does not show that they had good grounds for believing their arrangements and prices to be in accordance with the arm's length principle.

*Negligence: examples*

The following examples are designed to give a broad understanding of how the Revenue will interpret 'negligence' in transfer pricing cases. They are not exhaustive, and it cannot be stressed too strongly that each case can only be properly judged on its own facts and merits. The examples address only the issue of what constitutes negligence in transfer pricing cases, and do not duplicate or replace the general guidance on penalties found in the Investigation Handbook and IR 160.

It should also be made clear that the percentage mark-ups mentioned in the examples are not to be taken as indicative of the Revenue's view of the 'right' or 'wrong' mark-up in particular real life cases. All figures used are illustrative only.

**Example 1**

A company whose business is to provide services to other group members charges out its services at cost plus 5%. 5% accords with a policy in place throughout the group, and is documented in correspondence involving members of the main Board, the Finance Directorate, and the Tax Department; and in a group agreement. It is established in discussion with the Revenue that the arm's length range for the services in question is 10%–15%. The company cannot show from its records that it even considered whether its own 5% rate complied with the arm's length principle. The Revenue would view any tax lost as a result of the undercharge as having been lost through negligence, and would wish to consider a penalty.

**Example 2**

As example 1, except that in the correspondence it is asserted several times that the group's policy is to comply with the arm's length standard, and that 5% is an arm's length price. However, the company is unable to bring forward any convincing evidence in support of its assertions, while the Revenue is able to show that an arm's length price would be in the 10%–15% range. The Revenue would wish to consider a penalty.

**Example 3**

As example 1, except that the company charges out at cost plus 8%, and can show that at the time the rate was set it had run a check of available industry data, and had found what it considered to be a comparable uncontrolled price supporting the 8% rate. In discussion with the Revenue, the company agrees that the comparable it used was flawed, and that the weight of evidence points towards a price in the 10%–15% range. The Revenue accepts that the company had made an honest and reasonable attempt to comply with the arm's length principle. There is an adjustment but no penalty.

**Example 4**

A company whose business is to provide services to other group members charges at cost plus 5%. As in example 1, 5% accords with a policy in place throughout the group, and is documented in correspondence and a group agreement. The company includes an adjustment in its computation, bringing the effective rate of charge-out up to 8%. It did so after searching available industry data for possible comparable uncontrolled prices, this search being made at the time the tax computation was being prepared. As with example 3, the company sees this information as supporting its opinion that 8% accorded with the arm's length principle, but it later agrees that the price should have fallen in the 10%–15% range. Once again, the Revenue accepts that the company had made an honest and reasonable attempt to comply with the arm's length principle, and there is an adjustment but no penalty.

*'Size and gravity'*

In considering what abatement should be available in respect of 'size and gravity', the Revenue will take into account all of the following:

- the absolute size of the adjustment;
- the size of the adjustment relative to the turnover and profitability of the business against which the adjustment is being made; and,
- where this is possible, the size of the adjustment in relation to the volume and value of the related party transactions giving rise to the adjustment.

*Head Office monitoring*

The Revenue recognises that the issue of penalties on transfer pricing adjustments will be a sensitive one, especially in the early years of the new regime. As a result, and to ensure that a consistent approach is taken across the department, all potential penalty cases will be monitored by International Division, working in conjunction with Compliance Division.

Any questions on this guidance should be directed to:

Richard Coombes, International Division, Room 409, Melbourne House, Aldwych, London WC2B 4LL Tel: 0171-438 6842 Fax: 0171-438 7518

**Issue 39, pages 623–625 (February 1999)**

## RELATIONSHIP BETWEEN ACCOUNTANCY AND TAXABLE PROFITS: CURRENT POINTS OF INTEREST

An article on this subject appeared in the December 1997 Tax Bulletin (page 485). We have been asked to clarify a few points. This article applies to both unincorporated businesses (individuals and partnerships) and companies.

### 'DEFERRED' REVENUE EXPENDITURE

In a number of circumstances UK generally accepted accounting practice ('GAAP') either permits or requires expenditure to be 'spread' or 'deferred' in accounts; in other words, the expenditure is charged to the profit and loss account of more than one year. For example Statement of Standard Accounting Practice 13 'Research and development' permits development expenditure, under certain conditions, to be deferred to future periods. Similarly Financial Reporting Standard ('FRS') 10 'Goodwill and intangible assets' requires expenditure on the purchase of intangible assets to be spread over the expected useful economic life of the asset. Finally, recent and forthcoming changes in GAAP may make it more common for expenditure on major overhauls of plant and machinery to be spread over a number of years after the overhaul has been carried out. (The changes in GAAP are FRS 12 'Provisions, contingent liabilities and contingent assets', issued in September last year, and a forthcoming Accounting Standard based on Financial Reporting Exposure Draft 17 'Measurement of tangible fixed assets'.)

The accountancy treatment is not relevant for expenditure which is 'capital' in tax terms. But we have been asked whether revenue expenditure which is 'capitalised' by accountants is also disallowable for tax. Generally, the answer is 'no'.

Accountants often refer to 'capitalising' expenditure without implying anything about its treatment as revenue or capital expenditure for tax. They simply mean that expenditure is taken to the balance sheet because it relates to a later year. An alternative description for capitalised revenue expenditure is 'deferred revenue expenditure'.

The question of whether expenditure is capital or revenue **for tax purposes** is one of tax law. It follows that expenditure which is revenue for tax purposes does not, and cannot, lose that character whether or not it is charged wholly in one year's accounts, or spread over the accounts of more than one year. In other words expenditure does not become **capital** expenditure by being 'capitalised'; 'capitalised' revenue expenditure is still revenue. Equally, capital expenditure does not become revenue expenditure when, say, depreciation is charged to the profit and loss account.

Taking FRS 10 and intangible assets as an example, the cost of purchasing some intangibles such as patents will often be capital expenditure for tax purposes (and for which tax relief depends on whether capital allowances are available). On the other hand, the cost of other intangibles such as the 'locked-in' services of an employee are likely to be revenue. In neither case is the accounts treatment prescribed by FRS 10 of relevance to the nature of the expenditure as *capital or revenue*.

Accounting standards will be relevant for tax when it comes to deciding in which periods revenue receipts and expenses fall, unless there is a specific tax rule which provides to the contrary. Examples of specific rules are the Section 592(4) Income and Corporation Taxes Act (ICTA) 1988 rule on contributions to exempt approved pension schemes and the Section 43 FA 1989 rules about late paid emoluments.

Leaving aside these specific tax provisions, there is no rule of tax law that the 'right' time to deduct revenue expenditure for tax purposes is the year in which it is incurred, or the year in which there is a legal liability to pay it. (*Threlfall v Jones*, 66 TC 77.) It follows that where revenue expenditure is spread over the accounts of more than one year, and this treatment accords with GAAP, there is

# Inland Revenue Tax Bulletins

no rule of tax law which entitles a taxpayer to deduct it all 'up-front'. Equally, the fact that the accounts describe some deferred revenue expenditure as having been 'capitalised' does not mean that it cannot be allowed for tax as a business expense.

Generally speaking there will be no reason for the tax treatment to differ from the accounts treatment, so no computational adjustments will be justified.

## CHANGES OF ACCOUNTING POLICY

A business may change its accounting policy either voluntarily, because it considers a new policy will give a fairer presentation of its results and financial position, or as a result of a change in GAAP. For example FRS 10 (above) requires the cost of purchasing intangible assets to be spread; for many businesses this will mean a change from their former accounting policy of writing off such costs as incurred. (FRS 10 is mandatory for accounting periods ending on or after 23 December 1998, except that for businesses which are entitled to, and do, adopt the Financial Reporting Standard for Small Entities ('FRSSE') essentially similar provisions are mandatory for accounting periods ending on or after 23 March 1999.) Similarly FRS 12 'Provisions, contingent liabilities and contingent assets' may require businesses to make substantial changes to their accounting policies on the circumstances in which provisions may be made. (FRS 12 is mandatory for accounting periods ending on or after 23 March 1999, except that for businesses which are entitled to, and do, adopt the FRSSE no date has yet been fixed for similar provisions to become mandatory.) For example, FRS 12 prohibits provisions for **future** overhauls and plant and machinery. Such provisions formerly accorded with GAAP and *Johnston v Britannia Airways Ltd*, 67 TC 99, established that there was no rule of tax law which overrode the accountancy treatment. Now they will no longer accord with GAAP and it follows that they will no longer be acceptable for tax purposes.

Where there is a change of accounting policy FRS 3 requires not only entries in the profit and loss account to be made in accordance with the new policy, but also balance sheet figures to be adjusted so that the closing figures fully reflect the effect of the new policy. For example, sometimes a provision has been made in an earlier year which would not be permitted under FRS 12 and so that provision must be removed from the closing balance sheet. The adjustment is reported as a 'prior year adjustment' and is added to, or deducted from, the owners' interest in the business (shareholders' funds or proprietors' capital accounts).

In our view case law (*Pearce v Woodall-Duckham Ltd*, 51 TC 271) establishes that a 'prior year adjustment', so far as it relates to transactions previously brought into account for Case I or II purposes, is treated as a taxable receipt (if positive) or a deductible expense (if negative) in the year the accounting policy is changed. It is immaterial whether the change of accounting policy is voluntary or as a result of a change in GAAP. It is also immaterial that 'prior year adjustments' do not appear in the profit and loss account. This rule does not, however, apply if the former accounting policy did not comply with GAAP or conflicted with the requirements of tax law in some other way.

Suppose, for example, a business was intending to reorganise its operations and made a reorganisation provision of £500,000 for the year ended 31 March 1998 on a basis which accorded with GAAP. Suppose, further, that on the same basis it

## *Inland Revenue Tax Bulletins*

would have been entitled to make a further £200,000 provision for the year ended 31 March 1999. And finally, suppose that neither provision would have been permitted under FRS 12 (FRS 12 contains stringent requirements for reorganisation provisions).

For the year ended 31 March 1999 the business must change its accounting policies to accord with FRS 12 (assuming it is not entitled to the benefit of the FRSSE). It is not therefore entitled to make the £200,000 provision. But it must also make a 'prior year adjustment' of £500,000 to remove the earlier provision from its balance sheet. That £500,000 is treated as a taxable Case I or II receipt. *Woodall-Duckham* applies for accounting periods ending up to and including 5 April 1999.

For changes of accounting basis taking effect on or after 6 April 1999 the case-law rule is made statutory (for companies as well as for income tax payers) by Section 44 and Schedule 6 FA 1998. The only difference of substance is that positive prior year adjustments are charged as Case VI income rather than as Case I or II receipts; this means that for individuals they do not count for Class 4 NIC purposes. They continue, however, to be 'earned income' and relevant earnings for pension purposes, and loss relief brought forward can be set against them as if they were trading income. Negative adjustments continue to be treated as deductible Case I or II expenditure.

We hope to publish further guidance on this area, in particular on the implications of FRS 12, in the coming months.

### Issue 40, pages 636–641 (April 1999)

### INTERACTION OF TAX LAW AND ACCOUNTANCY PRACTICE: RECENT DEVELOPMENTS

This note covers:

- the new Accounting Standard on provisions, Financial Reporting Standard ('FRS') 12;
- the new Accounting Standard on goodwill and intangible assets, FRS 10;
- developments on the Financial Reporting Standard for Small Entities ('FRSSE');
- the recent tax case, *Herbert Smith v Honour*.

All of these have implications for Schedule D Case I and II profits; FRS 12 in particular is of major importance.

This note was originally drafted mainly for the guidance of Inspectors but we are happy to publish it to a wider audience.

**This note is written on the basis of the Revenue's understanding of current accounting practice at the time of writing. Except in the discussion of the Herbert Smith case, and elsewhere where tax treatment is specifically mentioned, it is not intended to indicate the Revenue's views of tax law, nor to set out Revenue**

practice. Nor is it intended as an authoritative guide to accountancy practice; if correct accountancy practice is an issue in a tax appeal it will normally have to be determined by expert evidence.

This note applies to unincorporated businesses as well as to companies. In particular a business, which if it were a company would satisfy the conditions in UK company law for being a 'small' company, is entitled in computing its profits for tax purposes to apply the FRSSE as if it were a company.

## FRS 12 'PROVISIONS, CONTINGENT LIABILITIES AND CONTINGENT ASSETS'

FRS 12 was issued by the Accounting Standards Board ('ASB') in September 1998 and is mandatory for accounting periods ending on or after 23 March 1999. No date has yet been announced at which its provisions will become mandatory for businesses which are entitled to, and do, adopt the FRSSE (see 'Updating the FRSSE', below); this is likely to be only a matter of time.

FRS 12 had its origin in the ASB's concern that businesses were making large provisions for future restructuring/reorganisation (called 'big bath' provisions since everything was thrown into them) where in many cases the only event that had occurred at the balance sheet date was an unpublished decision of the directors. However, FRS 12 goes much wider than restructuring provisions; its basis is that provisions must satisfy the definition of liabilities: 'obligations of an entity to transfer economic benefits as a result of past transactions or events'. Mere anticipation of future expenditure, however probable and no matter how detailed the estimates, is not enough, in the absence of an obligation at the balance sheet date.

FRS 12 lays down a complete code prescribing when provisions must be made, and when they must not, and also lays down rules for the quantification of provisions. Where businesses have made, or not made, provisions in the past on a basis which does not accord with FRS 12 they will need to change their accounting policies. This is likely to affect a substantial number of businesses. The tax consequences of changes of accounting policies are dealt with in an article in the February 1999 Tax Bulletin.

This note can only be a brief summary of FRS 12. Although it will be included in the annual collected volume of Accounting Standards this will not be until this summer. Until then you can buy a copy for £8 (post free) from:

ASB Publications PO Box 939 Central Milton Keynes Milton Keynes MK9 2HT Tel: 01908 230344

'Provisions' are defined by FRS 12 as 'liabilities of uncertain timing or amount'. FRS 12 does **not** apply to:

- 'trade creditors', which are defined as 'liabilities to pay for goods or services that have been received or supplied and have been invoiced or formally agreed with the supplier';
- 'accruals', which are defined as 'liabilities to pay for goods or services that have been received or supplied but have not been paid, invoiced or formally agreed with the supplier, including amounts due to employees (for example, amounts related to accrued holiday pay)';

- adjustments to the carrying value of assets such as stock 'provisions', bad debt 'provisions' and 'provisions' for depreciation;
- insurance company provisions arising from contracts with policyholders;
- provisions which are specifically addressed by other Accounting Standards, such as:
  - losses on long-term contracts (Statement of Standard Accounting Practice ('SSAP') 9);
  - provisions relating to leases (SSAP 21) other than operating leases that have become 'onerous' (see below);
  - pension costs (SSAP 24).

There are other exceptions which are not relevant for tax purposes.

A provision must be made when, and only when, at the balance sheet date:
- a business has a **present** obligation (legal or constructive) as a result of a **past** event,
- it is **probable** that a 'transfer of economic benefits' (i.e. expenditure) will be required to settle the obligation, and
- a **reliable estimate** can be made of the amount of the obligation.

In practice it is the first two conditions that are of most importance, since the ASB considers that it will be 'extremely rare' for it to be impossible to make a reliable estimate if the first two conditions are satisfied.

The key to FRS 12, and what distinguishes it from earlier Accounting Standards, is the concept of 'present obligation as a result of a past event' (referred to in FRS 12 as an 'obligating event'). An obligating event has occurred only if the business has 'no realistic alternative' to settling the obligation created by the event. An obligation always involves another party to whom the obligation is owed. FRS 12 contains a number of examples designed to show when an obligating event has occurred and when it has not.

For tax purposes the most important consequences of FRS 12 are:
- provisions for future repairs and overhauls of plant and machinery (i.e. provisions of the sort that were in issue in *Johnston v Britannia Airways Ltd*, 67 TC 99) are not permitted (except where an asset is held under an operating lease which contains a repairing obligation);
- provisions for future restructuring or reorganisation are permitted only where at the balance sheet date the business has a 'detailed formal plan' for the restructuring **and** has raised a 'valid expectation' among those affected (e.g. employees and/or customers) that it will carry out the restructuring, either by starting to implement the plan or by announcing its main features to those affected by it;
- provisions cannot be made for future expenditure required by legislation where the business could avoid the obligation by changing its method of operation (for example, by stopping doing whatever is affected by the legislation);

- provisions cannot be made for 'future operating losses': for an example of a 'future operating loss' see *Meat Traders Ltd v Cushing* [1997] STC (SCD) 245; at the time the provision was made in that case it was acceptable accounting, but where FRS 12 applies it would no longer be acceptable;
- a provision must be made where an existing contract becomes 'onerous', for example, where a business vacates property held under a lease, but the obligation to pay rent continues and the lease cannot be surrendered or assigned (this is a change from previous practice where as a general rule 'rent provisions', although often best practice, were not mandatory). Whether such a provision is permitted by tax law depends on the final outcome of *Herbert Smith v Honour* (see below).

FRS 15 'Tangible fixed assets' was issued in February 1999 and is mandatory (except for businesses which are entitled to, and do, adopt the FRSSE) for accounting periods ending on or after 23 March 2000. As a result there are likely to be further changes to the way in which expenditure on tangible fixed assets, such as overhauls of plant and machinery, is dealt with in accounts. This will probably result in expenditure on overhauls being spread over a number of years more often than it is now. However, because FRS 12 prohibits provisions for **future** overhauls this spreading will have to be achieved by:

- initial depreciation of the part of the asset that needs regular overhaul to reflect that need, followed by;
- debiting the overhaul expenditure in the balance sheet, followed by;
- amortising that expenditure over a number of years **after** the overhaul has been carried out.

We will give more guidance on this in due course.

FRS 12 also has important consequences for revenue 'decommissioning provisions' made (for example) by companies in the nuclear, oil and mining sectors.

Where it is not **probable** that there will be a 'transfer of economic benefits' then a provision must not be made, although it may be that a 'contingent liability' should be disclosed in a note to the accounts. As usual SSAP 17 'Post balance sheet events' applies, so in deciding what is 'probable' in relation to assets and liabilities in existence at the year end the directors or business proprietors should have regard to the information available to them at the time they prepare the accounts. In appropriate cases (for example, in considering whether it is probable that a court case will give rise to liability) they should take professional advice.

On quantification FRS 12 requires provisions to be a 'best estimate', again having regard to the information on assets and liabilities in existence at the year end available to the directors or business proprietors at the time they prepare the accounts. More importantly FRS 12 requires provisions to be **discounted** 'where the effect of the time value of money is material'. This will clearly be so for many long-term liabilities such as the cost of decommissioning nuclear power stations, but the effect of the time value of money may be material for provisions for shorter terms, in which case they too should be discounted. We do not consider there is any rule of tax law which would permit a provision to be brought to account for tax purposes without a discount where the figure in the accounts has been, or ought to be, discounted in accordance with FRS 12.

However as 'materiality' is an accountancy concept, and one on which different accountants might take different views, whether a provision should be discounted will normally depend on the opinion of accountants. FRS 12 gives guidance on the rate of discount and on the way in which the 'unwinding' of the discount (that is, the way in which the provision builds up from its discounted value to the eventual cash liability) should be recognised in accounts. For tax purposes the 'unwinding' of the discount should be treated as a further provision; in particular it is not a financial item within the scope of the 'loan relationship' legislation in FA 1996.

FRS 12 supersedes SSAP 18 'Contingencies'. FRS 12 distinguishes between 'provisions' which are liabilities that must be recognised and 'contingent liabilities' which must not be recognised but may be disclosed in a note to the accounts. Broadly speaking 'contingent liabilities' arise from events where it is **possible** but not probable that there will be a 'transfer of economic benefits' and from the 'extremely rare' case where a reliable estimate of the liability is not possible. 'Contingent assets' must not be recognised; this is similar to the rule in SSAP 18 which prohibited recognition of 'contingent gains'.

What consequences does all this have for tax purposes? Our view continues to be that a provision will be allowable for tax purposes if, and only if all the following conditions are met:

- the expenditure for which it provides is admissible for tax purposes (e.g. revenue and not capital);
- the making of the provision accords with UK generally accepted accounting practice ('GAAP');
- the provision is a sufficiently accurate estimate of the liability;
- the making of the provision does not cause a loss to be anticipated or violate any other rule of tax law (the scope of the non-anticipation principle depends on the final outcome of *Herbert Smith v Honour*, discussed below);
- the timing of the expenditure is not prescribed by statute (e.g. contributions to exempt approved pension schemes).

FRS 12 does not change our view of tax law, but it clearly changes UK GAAP. In particular many provisions which formerly accorded with UK GAAP will no longer do so. It follows that those provisions, even if they were formerly allowable for tax purposes, will no longer be so. **In our view there is no rule of tax law which permits provisions made on a now superseded basis to be 'run off' on that basis for tax purposes when the accounts now adopt a new basis.** This is discussed further in the February 1999 Tax Bulletin article referred to above.

FRS 12 has novel features for accountants as much as for tax practitioners. Because of this it is likely that in the first few years of its existence there will be real doubts over its effect.

On quantification the 'best estimate' test of FRS 12 could well be the same as the 'sufficiently accurate estimate' test of tax law. However it remains to be seen whether the adoption of FRS 12 causes a general tightening-up of the level of accuracy of provisions in accounts; it is arguable that 'best estimate' is already implicit in UK GAAP. In our view the Courts are still perfectly entitled to consider the factual accuracy of provisions, by reference to both the FRS 12 test and the tax law test.

## FRS 10 'GOODWILL AND INTANGIBLE ASSETS'

FRS 10, issued in December 1997, is mandatory for accounting periods ending on or after 23 December 1998. For businesses which are entitled to, and do, adopt the FRSSE broadly similar provisions (with some simplification) are mandatory for accounting periods ending on or after 23 March 1999.

FRS 10, prescribes a new code for the treatment of **purchased** goodwill and intangible assets, which by and large ensures that they appear in the balance sheet rather than being written off directly to reserves. The treatment of **internally created** goodwill and intangibles is generally unaffected; FRS 10 continues to prohibit the recognition of these in the balance sheet (there is an exception for a very limited class of internally created intangibles; this is likely to be rare in practice).

The significance of this for tax purposes is limited. Some expenditure affected by FRS 10 is **capital** expenditure for tax purposes, so that the accounting treatment does not affect the tax treatment. For example, when a business is acquired a payment for the goodwill of the business is capital expenditure, and no income tax relief is available. Similarly payments to purchase trademarks or patents are often capital expenditure (and capital allowances may be available for payments to purchase patents). (A Revenue technical note published on 10 March 1999 considered whether a reform of intellectual property in 2000 might affect the capital-revenue distinction.)

On the other hand some payments for intangible assets may be revenue expenditure. A common example is transfer fees for football players, which are payments for the intangible asset of the rights to the service of an employee. It would be hard to argue that rights to the service of an employee are on capital account. Another example is payments to purchase copyright which, because of the wasting nature of copyright, are often revenue expenditure.

FRS 10 requires expenditure on purchased goodwill and intangible assets to be written off over the expected useful economic life of the asset. For many businesses this will require a change of accounting policy. The expected useful economic life of the asset will normally not exceed 20 years, but there are special provisions which permit a business to write off an asset over more than 20 years, or to keep it in its balance sheet without writing it off at all, subject to certain strict tests.

For example, most football clubs used to write off transfer fees as incurred; they will now be required to write them off (generally) over the term of the player's contract. The 'unexpired' part of previous transfer fees will have to be brought back onto the balance sheet, with an appropriate prior year adjustment. This adjustment is taxable under current law for the reasons set out in the February 1999 Tax Bulletin article but the Budget contains proposals which 'grandfather' the past treatment of expenditure on players held before Budget day.

We do not consider that there is anything in FRS 10 which offends against a rule of tax law. Accordingly, where **revenue** expenditure is written off over several

## Inland Revenue Tax Bulletins

years in accordance with FRS 10 there is no rule of tax law which entitles the business to deduct the whole amount up front for tax purposes. The tax treatment should follow the accounts treatment.

**THE FRSSE**

There are two issues arising from the FRSSE which have consequences for tax purposes.

Updating the FRSSE

Because the FRSSE is self-contained it is not automatically updated when new Accounting Standards are issued. Instead the FRSSE is reviewed from time to time and revised to incorporate those parts of new Accounting Standards that are thought appropriate to small businesses. There may therefore be a time-lag before new Accounting Standards apply to businesses that are entitled to, and do, adopt the FRSSE.

This happened most recently in December 1998; the revision is mandatory for accounting periods ending on or after 23 March 1999. The important revision for tax purposes is that FRS 10, with some simplification, was incorporated in the FRSSE. However FRS 12 was not incorporated in the FRSSE because it had not been issued when the draft revision was issued for consultation. It is likely that elements of FRS 12 will be incorporated in the next revision, which will be issued towards the end of 1999 or shortly thereafter.

Issues not addressed by the FRSSE

An area of more long-term concern is issues that are not addressed by the FRSSE. This is not an easy area to deal with, and the opinion of accountants will normally be relevant.

Smaller entities applying the FRSSE are exempt from all other Accounting Standards and UITF Abstracts and therefore there is no explicit requirement to apply them. However, paragraph 2.1 of the FRSSE says that financial statements to which the FRSSE applies are required to show a true and fair view, and to achieve such a view regard should be had to the substance of any arrangement or transaction into which the business has entered. In addition, the introductory 'Status of the FRSSE' section of the FRSSE says that financial statements will generally be prepared using accepted practice and accordingly, for transactions and events not dealt with in the FRSSE, businesses should have regard to other Accounting Standards and UITF Abstracts, 'not as mandatory documents, but as a means of establishing current practice'.

It would therefore be wrong to say that other Accounting Standards and/or UITF Abstracts **must** apply if there is no guidance in the FRSSE. However, it would be equally wrong to disregard that evidence when considering the substance of the transaction or event in order to determine the appropriate treatment for a true and fair view. Generally, the principles in the exempt standards and extracts are the same as those in the FRSSE. However, the exemption from the specific Standard and/or Abstract gives entities the latitude to apply a simpler approach, presentation and/or disclosures, where appropriate.

A specific example is the treatment of employee share ownership trusts (ESOTs).

## Inland Revenue Tax Bulletins

This is dealt with in UITF Abstract 13, from which companies applying the FRSSE are exempt, and is not covered by the FRSSE. The question then is whether a company which is entitled to, and does, adopt the FRSSE should treat the assets and liabilities of its ESOT as its own. Where the company has control of the shares held by its ESOT and bears their benefits or risks, the substance of the transaction is that the assets and liabilities of the ESOT would be treated as the entity's own. This would lead to a treatment that was consistent with UITF Abstract 13. These issues are relevant in deciding when the entity can have a tax deduction for contributions to the trust: this was discussed in the Tax Bulletin Issue 27 (page 399, February 1997).

### HERBERT SMITH v HONOUR

This case, decided in the High Court on 12 February and reported at [1999] STC 173, is likely to be a leading case on the interaction between tax law and accountancy practice. The facts were that the taxpayers, a large firm of solicitors, decided in Autumn 1989 to rationalise their four London offices into a single one. Accordingly in January 1990 they took a lease of new premises and, during 1990, vacated their four existing offices. Two of those offices were held under leases which were not capable of being terminated.

The firm's accounts for the year ended 30 April 1990 were drawn up to give a true and fair view of the state of affairs of the firm at 30 April 1990, and of its profit and source and application of funds for the year then ended, and were audited. In those accounts the firm made a provision of some £5.5 million for the expected loss on the two leases (in the case of one of them, the expected loss only up to the period of the next rent review). Although this was disputed the judge held that on the evidence the only conclusion open to the Commissioners was that the making of the provision was the **only** accounting treatment which would have given a true and fair view.

The Revenue argued that there was a rule of tax law that neither a profit nor a loss could be anticipated, and that this overrode UK GAAP if the application of GAAP resulted in a profit or a loss being anticipated. The judge held that:

- in this case it was not open to the Revenue to replace a treatment which accorded with GAAP, and indeed was the **only** treatment which so accorded, by one that did not;

- there was no general rule of tax law which prohibited provisions made on the grounds of prudence where the making of the provision was **required** by GAAP.

The judge accepted, as had the taxpayers, that provisions were vulnerable to challenge under tax law if the making of the provision was inconsistent with the true facts, or if the provision was not estimated with sufficient accuracy. By the time the case reached the High Court it was common ground that neither of these prohibitions applied.

The Revenue have appealed against the decision; the hearing before the Court of Appeal will be some time in 2000. We will comment on the implications of the case once the appeal has been finally determined.

*Inland Revenue Tax Bulletins*

**Issue 40, page 645 (April 1999)**

## A MODERN SYSTEM FOR CORPORATION TAX PAYMENTS: QUARTERLY INSTALMENT PAYMENTS AND GROUP PAYMENT ARRANGEMENTS

The 1998 Finance Act ('FA 98') introduced a new way for large companies to pay Corporation Tax – in quarterly instalments. FA 98 also allows the Inland Revenue to enter into arrangements with groups of companies so one company in the group can pay the Corporation Tax liabilities of the others. The changes are part of a wider reform of the Corporation Tax regime, which includes the introduction of Corporation Tax Self Assessment for accounting periods ending on or after 1 July 1999, and the abolition of Advance Corporation Tax on 5 April 1999.

**QUARTERLY INSTALMENT PAYMENTS**

Around 20,000 large companies will have to start paying their Corporation Tax in four quarterly instalments. The Quarterly Instalment Payment regime will be phased in over four years, starting with accounting periods ending on or after 1 July 1999.

A company is 'large' if, broadly, its profits in an accounting period are more than the Upper Relevant Maximum Amount (URMA) in force at the end of the accounting period so that it pays Corporation Tax at the main rate. At the moment, URMA is set at £1.5 million and the main rate of Corporation Tax – from 1 April 1999 – is 30%. (URMA is reduced where a company has associates, or where there are short accounting periods.)

Companies that are not large do not have to pay in instalments, so the overwhelming majority of companies will carry on paying their Corporation Tax nine months and one day after the end of their accounting period, as they do now. And companies with a net tax liability below £5,000 (reduced proportionately for an accounting period of less than 12 months) will not be affected. So companies with small liabilities in large groups will not have to make Quarterly Instalment Payments.

To ensure that growing companies do not unexpectedly find that they have to pay by instalments, and to give them time to prepare for paying, Quarterly Instalment Payments will not have to be paid for an accounting period if the company's taxable profits for that period are less than £10 million (reduced proportionately for an accounting period of less than 12 months) and it was not large in the previous year. Where there are associated companies, that £10 million threshold will be divided by one plus the number of associates at the end of the previous accounting period.

*The transition to quarterly instalments*

To help companies adapt to the new system, Quarterly Instalment Payments will be phased in over the next four years. So large companies will pay:

- 60% of their Corporation Tax in instalments for accounting periods

# Inland Revenue Tax Bulletins

ending between 1 July 1999–30 June 2000, and the other 40% nine months and one day after the end of the accounting period;

- 72% of their tax in instalments for accounting periods ending between 1 July 2000–30 June 2001, and the remaining 28% nine months and one day after the end of the accounting period;
- 88% of their tax in instalments for accounting periods ending between 1 July 2001–30 June 2002, with the rest nine months and one day after the end of the accounting period, and
- 100% of their tax in Quarterly Instalment Payments for accounting periods ending on or after 1 July 2002.

*When Quarterly Instalment Payments will be due*

After the phasing-in period, a large company with a 12 month accounting period will be due to pay its Corporation Tax in four equal instalments. The due dates of payment will be:

- six months and 13 days after the start of the accounting period;
- then nine months and 13 days;
- then twelve months and 13 days, and
- finally fifteen months and 13 days after the start of the accounting period.

So, for a company with a 12 month accounting period starting on 1 January, Quarterly Instalment Payments will be due on 14 July, 14 October, 14 January and 14 April.

Where an accounting period lasts less than 12 months, the last instalment will be three months and 14 days from the end of the accounting period and there may be more instalments (up to a maximum of four in all) every three months, starting six months and 13 days from the start of the accounting period. So, for a company with an eight month accounting period starting on 1 January, Quarterly Instalment Payments will be due on 14 July and 14 October, with a final instalment on 14 December.

*Deciding whether Quarterly Instalment Payments are due*

The onus is on companies to determine whether or not they have to make Quarterly Instalment Payments. As a customer service, we will send a reminder and a payslip to every company whose last return showed profits of more than £1.25 million (reduced proportionately for any associated companies, or if the accounting period was shorter than 12 months) and whose tax liability was over £5,000. We will do this between one or two months before each instalment is due. But because the regime only applies to some 5% of companies in any one year, and the profits of companies are neither fixed nor certain in advance, it may be that a company will not get a reminder or payslip even though it has to pay by instalments.

Remember, it is still the company's responsibility to make Quarterly Instalment Payments if they are due.

## Inland Revenue Tax Bulletins

The Accounts Offices at Cumbernauld and Shipley will provide payslips if companies ask them to. But they cannot help with general questions about Quarterly Instalment Payments. If a company needs help and advice, it should telephone its own tax office.

### Working out Quarterly Instalment Payments

Instalment payments are based on estimates of a company's tax liability for each accounting period (net of reliefs and set offs).

The amount of each instalment is worked out by:

- forecasting the tax payable by instalments for the accounting period (CTI);
- working out $3 \times CTI/n$, where n is the number of months in the accounting period;
- paying the smaller of that amount and CTI at the first quarterly instalment due date; and
- paying the smaller of that amount and the unpaid balance of CTI at each later instalment due date (remembering to revise the forecast and adjust payments accordingly as appropriate).

There are examples of how to calculate Quarterly Instalment Payments in our leaflet, *A Modern System for Corporation Tax Payments – A Guide to Quarterly Instalment Payments* (inst1) available free from any tax office or Tax Enquiry Centre.

A company's forecast of its tax liability may go up and down during the Quarterly Instalment Payment period. But the new regime is flexible and companies should make top-up payments if they believe at any stage that not enough tax has been paid in previous instalments. On the other hand, if companies find that they have paid too much, they will normally be able to claim a repayment.

### Interest and Penalties

Interest on late paid tax will be calculated only after a company has filed its Company Tax Return (or we have made a determination of its Corporation Tax liability in the absence of a return) **and** the normal due date (nine months and one day after the end of the accounting period) has passed. The rates which apply during the period up to the normal due date are more favourable to the company than the rates which apply after the normal due date.

Interest receivable by companies will be chargeable to tax; interest paid will be deductible for tax purposes. 'Debit interest' will be charged on underpaid tax, and 'credit interest' will be paid on tax overpaid (or paid early) after the first instalment date has passed and up to the normal due date.

Although companies will be making Quarterly Instalment Payments based on forecasts of liability, by the time of the normal due date they should have a good idea of what their liability will be. (In the case of a 12 month accounting period the third and fourth instalments will be paid after the end of the accounting

# Inland Revenue Tax Bulletins

period.) The normal late payment and repayment interest rates will apply to companies within the Quarterly Instalment Payment regime, as to other companies, from the normal due date.

Under CT Pay and File, groups of companies could surrender overpayments between group members to minimise liability to interest on tax paid late. This will not change. Groups who make Quarterly Instalment Payments will also be able to benefit from Group Payment Arrangements (see below).

As well as interest, a penalty may be charged if a company deliberately or recklessly fails to make adequate instalment payments and where a company fraudulently or negligently makes a claim for repayment. Like interest, a penalty will be charged only after a company has filed its Company Tax Return, or the Inland Revenue have made a determination of its Corporation Tax liability and the normal due date has passed. Guidance on use of the penalty will be published early in the summer.

*More information*

Apart from the leaflet already mentioned, there is more information about Quarterly Instalment Payments in *A Guide to Corporation Tax Self Assessment for Tax Practitioners and Inland Revenue Staff*, to be published later this month.

## GROUP PAYMENT ARRANGEMENTS

Section 36 FA 1998 gives the Board of Inland Revenue the power to enter into an arrangement with groups of companies under which one company in the group (the 'nominated company') undertakes to pay the Corporation Tax liabilities of all companies in the group which are part of the arrangement (the 'participating companies').

The new facility – which is voluntary – responds to representations made on the Consultative Document, A Modern System for Corporation Tax Payments (issued in November 1997).

Respondents felt that such a facility would help groups with the switch to Quarterly Instalment Payments by helping groups containing large companies manage any uncertainty over Corporation Tax liabilities in the period between their falling due and the filing by individual companies of their Company Tax Returns.

Group Payment Arrangements apply to accounting periods ending on or after 31 December 1999. So most grouped companies within the Quarterly Instalment Payment regime will be covered by Group Payment Arrangements for their first accounting period under Group Payment Arrangements. The first payment within the arrangements will fall due on 14 July 1999. A minority of groups that have an earlier year-end will not be able to take advantage of Group Payment Arrangements until their second accounting period under Quarterly Instalment Payments.

Groups will still have to pay the right amount of tax at the right time. But the new

## Inland Revenue Tax Bulletins

arrangements mean that, in estimating what is due to be paid, they will be able to forecast at the group rather than the individual company level, and pay on that basis. This means they do not have to worry about dividing up payments between the companies in the group until the closing date (defined below). These arrangements will also mitigate the effect on a group of the differential between interest rates on overpaid and underpaid tax.

*Eligible companies*

Parent companies, their 51% subsidiaries, and the 51% subsidiaries of those subsidiaries, and so on, are eligible to enter into the Group Payment Arrangements. The group must be reasonably sure, at the time the arrangement is entered into, that at least one of the companies covered by it will be liable to pay Quarterly Instalment Payments. The nominated company must be UK resident, but the other participating companies do not need to be. And UK branches of non-resident companies can also be covered by the arrangement. Not all members of the group need be covered by the Group Payment Arrangement, and a group may apply to set up more than one arrangement for different sub-sets of companies in the group.

We will only be prepared to enter into the arrangement with companies which have filed returns and paid tax due in respect of their last but one accounting period.

*Periods covered by arrangements*

The arrangement will relate to one or more periods of account of the nominated company, which must last for no more than 12 months. Generally, this period of account will also be the accounting period of all the participating companies. But a company which joins a group will be able to take part in the group's Group Payment Arrangement provided that it aligns its period of account with that of the group. It will not, though, be able to join an existing arrangement after the first tax payable under the arrangement for the period is due. And it cannot be covered by the arrangement in respect of an accounting period which started before the period of account covered by the arrangement.

If a participating company proves to have an accounting period which ends during the period of account covered by the arrangement, it can remain part of the arrangement as long as its accounts are drawn up for the same period as the rest of the group. For example, if a participating company in a group with a 31 December 1999 accounting date stops trading on 31 August (triggering the end of an accounting period) it can remain part of the Group Payment Arrangement as long as its accounts cover the period to 31 December 1999. It will then have two accounting periods within the arrangement, one from 1 January 1999 to 31 August 1999, the second from 1 September 1999 to 31 December 1999.

The arrangement will generally roll forward automatically to subsequent periods of account. The nominated company will have to tell us if there are any changes to the set of participating companies, and if it plans to change its accounting date.

# Inland Revenue Tax Bulletins

*Taking companies out of the arrangements*

The nominated company must remove from the Group Payment Arrangement a participating company which ceases to be a member of the group, or which turns out not to have an accounting period aligned with the rest of the group. In cases like this, the nominated company may apportion payments – or parts of payments – to the departing company. The nominated company will not retain any liability in respect of the departing company after it has left the arrangement (including in respect of its liability for the accounting period for part of which it was a member of the group).

We will have the right to remove from a Group Payment Arrangement any company which ceases to be a member of the group, or turns out not to have an accounting period aligned with the rest of the group, or turns out never to have been a member of the group. We will also have the right to terminate the arrangement if the nominated company breaches the terms of the agreement, or if any of the companies covered by the arrangement is likely to become liable to tax under the provisions of Section 767A or Section 767AA Income and Corporation Taxes Act (ICTA) 1988 (anti-avoidance legislation concerned with changes in ownership of a company).

*Deadline for signing-up*

Groups who wish to enter into a Group Payment Arrangement for accounting periods ending on 31 December 1999 should contact us by telephone or fax straight away and we will send full documentation for the group to consider before taking a final decision. We will be entering into arrangements with groups from April 1999. Groups with 31 December 1999 accounting periods will need to deal quickly with the arrangement documentation so that they can get the signed agreement back to us before 15 May 1999.

The arrangement document has been drawn-up with input from the Self Assessment Consultative Committee. Its terms are non-negotiable and will be identical for all Group Payment Arrangements.

A group may register its interest, and get the answers to any questions about Group Payment Arrangements, by contacting the Group Payment Team at the Inland Revenue Accounts Office to which it normally makes its payments. **Groups should not contact their local tax offices**. The Group Payment Team contact details are as below:

Group Payment Team, Accounts Office Cumbernauld, St Mungo's Road, Cumbernauld, Glasgow G70 5TR, Telephone: 01236 783488, Fax: 01236 783387

Group Payment Team, Accounts Office Shipley, Victoria Street, Shipley, West Yorkshire BD98 8AA, Telephone: 01274 539561, Fax: 01274 539669.

The Group Payment Team will need to know:
- the name of the group;
- a contact point for the group;
- the number of Group Payment Arrangements the group is thinking of applying to set up, and

## Inland Revenue Tax Bulletins

- the dates of the first period of account to be covered by the arrangement.

We will normally only agree to enter into a Group Payment Arrangement for an accounting period if the group delivers its signed arrangement document to one of our Group Payment Teams at least two months before the first Quarterly Instalment Payment is due. This is to allow time for the necessary administrative processes.

The Group Payment Teams will send every group expressing an interest a pack containing:

- an Arrangement Document and schedule, and
- information and guidance notes.

If we agree to enter into an arrangement, the Group Payment Team will sign the Arrangement Document on behalf of the Revenue and return it to the nominated company contact point with:

- a standard covering letter, and
- any further information the group may need.

The Group Payment Teams are also happy to handle any enquiries about the new arrangements.

*The undertaking*

Under Group Payment Arrangements, the nominated company must undertake to pay the Corporation Tax liability of all the companies covered by the arrangement. And we will not look to each of the companies individually to pay its own Corporation Tax during the period up to the date when all the companies covered by the arrangement have either filed their returns or had their Corporation Tax determined by us. (This is known as the closing date which cannot be earlier than the filing date.)

Payment of Corporation Tax under the Group Payment Arrangements must be made by electronic funds transfer. This means BACS, CHAPS or Bank Giro Credit.

The nominated company must undertake to make payments of tax on the quarterly instalment due dates on the basis of the most recent forecast of the level of group profits. That will mean adjusting its payments throughout the Quarterly Instalment Payments period if that forecast changes, increasing or reducing payments as needed. If a revised forecast shows that the nominated company has paid too little tax in respect of one or more earlier instalments, it should make a top-up payment to meet the shortfall, as well as increasing the payment for later instalments. If the nominated company believes it has overpaid on previous instalments because the group's forecast profits are down, it can claim a repayment.

A company can amend its return, and have the amendment taken into account for the purposes of working out what is due from the nominated company under the arrangement, up until the closing date. Any adjustments made to the liabilities of participating companies after that point will be dealt with on an individual company basis.

The Group Payment Arrangement does not affect the actual liability of any company. Entering into the arrangement will not absolve any company of its liability to Corporation Tax, nor mean that it cannot be pursued for payment of Corporation Tax should legal proceedings to enforce payment be required after the closing date. Corporation tax for these purposes includes tax under Sections 419 and 747 ICTA 1988 (tax due on loans by close companies to participators, and the rules covering Controlled Foreign Companies respectively).

*Apportionment of payments*

After the Group Payment Arrangement closing date, we will send a notice to the nominated company showing what it has paid on behalf of the participating companies and the liability at the closing date. We will ask the nominated company to make good any shortfall of Corporation Tax, and to apportion payments made to the companies covered by the arrangement. A shortfall may be allocated by the nominated company if it has reason to believe that the liability of the company to which it allocates the shortfall is likely to decrease after the closing date. The nominated company may also allocate any surplus to one or more participating company, or request its repayment. Interest will be the liability of the individual participating company. So will any late-filing penalty which may be incurred.

The Board of Inland Revenue will have the right to override the nominated company's apportionment of the payments if payment could not be secured from the company to which any shortfall was ultimately allocated.

The text of the arrangement document and the guidance notes has been posted on the Internet on our Corporation Tax Self Assessment website at www.inlandrevenue.gov.uk.

And some information on Group Payment Arrangements will be published in A Guide to Corporation Tax Self Assessment for Tax Practitioners and Inland Revenue Officers, available later this month. (The text of the Guide will also be reproduced on the website.)

If you need more information about Quarterly Instalment Payments, please contact your own tax office. If you need to know more about Group Payment Arrangements, please get in touch with the Group Payment Team at the Accounts Office dealing with the nominated company.

**Issue 14, page 667 (June 1999)**

# CONSTRUCTION INDUSTRY SCHEME

This second article of two is intended to try and cover some more of the questions that have been raised about the introduction of the new Construction Industry Scheme (CIS) on 1 August 1999.

## Inland Revenue Tax Bulletins

**CURRENT CERTIFICATES THAT EXPIRE AFTER 1 AUGUST 1999**

There is no transitional period for the introduction of the new Scheme. All existing documentation becomes obsolete when CIS starts on 1 August 1999. Current certificate holders are not automatically entitled to a Subcontractors Tax Certificate under the new Scheme but will need to pass the business, compliance and turnover tests in order to qualify. Further information can be found in the leaflet IR40(CIS).

**TURNOVER TEST AND CHANGE IN TYPE OF CONCERN**

*General*

By 'concern' we mean whether a business is a sole trader, a partnership or company.

**How is the turnover test applied where the applicant's business changes?**

*No change*

Where the number of partners within an existing partnership, or directors/shareholders in an existing company, changes, there is no change in the type of concern. New partners/directors should apply for additional certificates, but there is no need for the partnership or company to go through the turnover test again. When the certificate needs to be renewed, the change in the number of persons will need to be taken into account in determining the turnover threshold.

*Changes*

However, where for example:

- a partnership becomes a sole trader;
- a sole trader or partnership becomes a company;
- a sole trader becomes a partnership;
- two or more sole traders or partnerships merge to form a new partnership;

there is a change in the type of concern. If the subcontractor already holds a certificate under the new Scheme, the new concern will need a new certificate. The applicant should inform the Revenue of the details of the change and make an application on the appropriate form:

– CIS2 for new sole trader concerns and partnerships

– CIS3 for new companies

The applicant might not be able to use the turnover test grids on the CIS2 or CIS3 in every case. For example, two sole traders forming a new partnership might have had different accounting periods over the 3 test years. In such cases, the applicant should set out their figures on a separate sheet of paper.

# Inland Revenue Tax Bulletins

In the first applications for certificates under the new Scheme, if there has been a change during the 3-4 years up to the date of application, the applicant should use the form appropriate to the current type of concern, and give details of the change separately.

Which test the new concern uses depends on whether it needs to be treated as a new concern (and use the six month test) or can be treated as an established concern (and hence use a three year test).

The questions we ask will be:

- is the business itself unchanged apart from the type of concern?
- does it have the same assets, goodwill, and largely the same personnel?
- is it carrying out the same sort of work?

If the business itself is essentially unchanged from before the change in type of concern, we will treat it as an established business, and so the new concern may apply on the basis of a three year test, as long as each old concern involved has a 3-4 year history.

If the business itself has changed, we will treat it as a new business, and the new business will have to use the six month test as soon as it can.

*Partnership becoming sole trader*

If the new concern is essentially the same business as the old one, i.e. it has the same assets and goodwill and does the same type of work, then an application can be made using the three year test. The multiplier rule would not apply, as the business is a sole trader at the date of application, and the business's turnover would be measured against the individual threshold throughout. For example, a husband and wife partnership ceases when the wife leaves the partnership, but the business remains unchanged.

If the new concern is not carrying on the same business as the old one, we will treat it as a new business. For example, a partnership of 3 builders becomes a sole trader concern, and the nature of the business and its ownership is dramatically changed. The new business can use the six month test as soon as it has built up an appropriate level of turnover over a period of up to six consecutive months from its inception.

*Sole trader becomes partnership*

This is where a sole trader takes on a new person as a partner, without also taking on other business activities belonging to the new partner.

If the nature of the business and its assets are largely unchanged, the new partnership can use the standard or alternative three year test. For the standard partnership test, the multiplier rule would be applied to each test year. For example, if the change occurred half way through the three year test period when the sole trader became a partnership of 2, the multiplier for the threshold would be as follows:

## Inland Revenue Tax Bulletins

year 1:1
year 2:2  (maximum number of partners at any time during the test year)
year 3:2

If the new concern is not carrying on the same business as the old one, the applicant can use the six month test as soon as it has built up an appropriate level of turnover over a period of up to six consecutive months from the start of the new business. The applicant is a partnership at the date of application, and the multiplier for the six month test is the maximum number of partners at any point during the period chosen.

*Sole traders or partnerships merging to form new partnerships*

Where two or more existing businesses merge, the new partnership created would normally be treated as a new business. The six month turnover test can be used with figures from the new partnership's turnover. The number of partners will be the maximum number of partners at any point during that six month period.

Where the partnership claims to use a three year test because using the six month test would be a severe disadvantage, it should set out its proposed turnover test figures with an explanation.

We may consider such claims on the following basis:

- the new business is essentially the sum of the operations of the original business;
- the multiplier is the maximum number of 'partners' in each test year;
- for 'partners' we will count all sole traders and all partners involved in all the concerns in each year.

For example, 2 sole traders plus a partnership of 2 individuals form a new partnership of 4. The multiplier for each year is as follows:

year 1:4
year 2:4
year 3:4

*Sole trader or partnership becomes a company*

Where a sole trader or partnership incorporates, it is likely that the new concern will be essentially the same business as the old one, despite the change in type, and the new company may use a three year test, as long as the old concern was running for 3–4 years.

If the nature of the business and its assets are largely unchanged, the new company can use the standard or alternative three year company test. For the standard company test, the multiplier rule would be applied to each test year. For example, if the change occurred half way through the three year test period when a sole trader became a company of 3 relevant persons, the multiplier for the threshold would be as follows:

year 1:1

year 2:3 (maximum number of relevant persons* at any time during the test year)
year 3:3

* 'Relevant persons' in this context means any director (and beneficial shareholder in the case of close companies) or partner who was carrying on the business at the relevant time.

However, for applications made before 1 August 2001, the multiplier for all three years can be based on the maximum number of relevant persons at any point in the final six months of the three year period if that is beneficial under the extra-statutory concession B52.

If the business has essentially changed, the applicant can use the six month test as soon as it has built up an appropriate level of turnover over a period of up to six consecutive months from the start of the new business. The applicant is a company at the date of the application and the multiplier for the six month test is the number of relevant persons during the period chosen. (See Chapter 5.)

**Issue 41, page 669 (June 1999)**

## DOUBLE TAXATION RELIEF ON UK COMPANY INTEREST PAYMENTS: PROVISIONAL TREATY RELIEF (PTR) SCHEME

### BACKGROUND

Any person who receives interest arising in the UK is liable to tax on that income. Generally if the recipient is resident abroad this UK tax liability is collected via the payer. Under Section 349(2)(c) of the Income and Corporation Taxes Act (ICTA) 1988, the payer must deduct the relevant amount from each payment of interest made and pay this over to the appropriate Accounts Office.

Most double taxation agreements contain provisions that can relieve all or some of this tax. These are invoked by the overseas owner of the interest making a claim for repayment of the tax so deducted from the Financial Intermediaries and Claims Office (FICO) at Nottingham. Alternatively, the overseas resident can ask FICO to authorise the UK payer of the interest to give the treaty relief itself when making payments, under SI 1970/488. If the application is successful the payer will receive a notice from FICO authorising it to make future payments on this basis. The overseas resident needs to send the application via its own tax authorities for certification.

However relief may not always be due, and until such time as the payer receives notification from FICO that interest may be paid gross or with a reduced rate of tax deducted, it should deduct the full rate of tax from payments. The eventual notice authorising treaty relief will normally be retrospective to the date that FICO received the application to pay gross from the relevant overseas tax authority – as explained in Tax Bulletin Issue 12, published in August 1994.

It can take some time for the certified application to reach FICO in the first place. Only then will the Inland Revenue normally be in a position to start processing it (this will typically involve liaising with the tax office for the payer of the interest). The cumulative time-lag involved can create difficulties if the first payment date

## Inland Revenue Tax Bulletins

is soon after the loan in question starts, as the payer may be unaware of the progress of an application, or even if one has been made at all. These problems can be worsened where there is more than one beneficial owner of interest paid under a loan. For example, where there is a syndicated loan involving a number of lenders, which may include a mix of UK and overseas lenders. Each overseas lender seeking treaty relief is required separately to claim it in their own right. It is common for individual lenders to sell their debt-rights on the 'secondary loan market', which can mean the automatic cancellation of an existing authority, pending reissue once the new owner has itself successfully applied for relief.

FICO has received a number of representations asking for the whole relief process to be speeded up as an aid to British business and giving quicker effect to the UK's treaty obligations. It has accepted that a good case has been made for streamlining procedures in low-risk cases, and over the course of the past year has discussed this with a number of interested parties. With due regard to the interests of the UK Exchequer and taxpayers, FICO can now offer the following Provisional Treaty Relief (PTR) scheme. They aim to make this available from 1 September 1999.

### OUTLINE OF THE PTR SCHEME

The scheme is entirely voluntary, and complements rather than replaces existing arrangements. It is limited to two types of loan where there is only a negligible risk that an application for relief would fail:

- **'one to one' company loans** where there is no shareholding relationship or common ownership between the parties involved, for example where the lender is an overseas lending institution;
- **syndicated loans**, where there is a Syndicate Manager.

But the acceptance of a loan in the PTR scheme does not necessarily imply that treaty relief will automatically be due, and will have no bearing on the allowability of the interest paid for the purposes of the *borrower's* corporation tax liability.

### ONE TO ONE COMPANY LOANS

For a loan to qualify, it is important to note that there must be no common shareholding or ownership between the parties to it. If there is no link of this sort, then as soon as a loan commences, or the lender changes, the borrower can, if they wish, approach FICO to ask for its provisional authority to incorporate treaty relief in its payments.

FICO keeps a database of overseas concerns which it has had recent dealings with. Where such dealings have involved a formal consideration of the overseas lender within the preceding three years, then a loan made by that company to a UK company will be eligible for consideration under the new scheme. The most typical cases will be where there has been a successful application for relief at source, or a paid repayment claim. UK companies wanting to know whether an overseas lender is included on that database can seek confirmation from FICO (if necessary, by telephoning 0115 974 1904). If it is, then the borrower can then seek FICO's provisional authority to give relief right away, applying to do so on a form PTRPAY1.

This provisional authority is strictly conditional on FICO getting a normal double taxation treaty application from the recipient within three months of this provisional authority. If such a certified application is not received within three months, or relief is found not to be due, or due in some restricted manner only, then the provisional authority will be withdrawn. FICO would then look to the UK company for the tax that should have been deducted from any payments made and, if applicable, interest arising thereon.

FICO will process the formal treaty relief application as usual, although the information received at the initial provisional relief stage will help to shorten the time needed for this. Ultimately, FICO will send a formal SI 1970/488 authority to the UK payer, assuming relief is appropriate.

**SYNDICATED LOANS**

These will have more than one lender participating in the loan, and are administered by Syndicate Managers. In recognition of these factors FICO will in future concentrate on the loan itself rather than the separate participators within it, treating the Syndicate Manager as representing to a far greater degree the members of the syndicate. In return the Syndicate Manager will be expected to assume a greater role in providing information about – and assurances concerning – the syndicate's members and the loan.

- The Syndicate Manager will first apply to FICO for provisional relief, summarising the main details about the loan on a form PTRSM1. An undertaking must be given that a composite treaty application in the syndicate's name, and on behalf of all its qualifying overseas members, will be delivered to FICO by the *Syndicate Manager* within three months of any provisional authority.

- If all is in order, FICO will issue the Manager with a provisional authority allowing the incorporation of treaty relief into interest payments. The Syndicate Manager will in turn pass on a copy of this provisional authority to the UK borrower which can, if it chooses, act on it when making payments.

- A formal application for relief, in normal form, must then be received within the three months. This will be sent direct to FICO by the Syndicate Manager, without the need for foreign revenue certification.

- The Revenue will liaise with the overseas tax authorities for exchange of information purposes, and FICO will ultimately issue the UK borrower with the formal authority under SI 1970/488, assuming relief is appropriate.

- Thereafter, arrangements will be made between FICO and the Syndicate Manager to keep that authority under review from time to time. Any changes in the composition of the syndicate – for example, as a result of the trading-on of debt-rights – can then be dealt with speedily and easily between FICO and the Syndicate Manager, adjusting the scope of the SI authority as required.

**FURTHER INFORMATION**

A copy of the PTR scheme's explanatory 'Guidelines' can be obtained from: Complex Claims Group (Provisional Treaty Relief Scheme), FICO, Fitz Roy

## Inland Revenue Tax Bulletins

House, PO Box 46, Nottingham NG2 1BD; Helpline 0115 974 1904; Fax 0115 974 1918, to whom any requests should be made for copies of the PTR application forms PTRPAY1 (for one-to-one loans) and PTRSM1 (syndicated loans).

The operation of the scheme will be monitored, and FICO welcomes any comments on it. Please address these to Brian Place of FICO's Technical Advice Group, at the above address, or by fax on 0115 974 2063. Brian's telephone number is 0115 974 2025. (See Chapter 10.28.)

## DOUBLE TAXATION RELIEF: ADJUSTMENTS TO FOREIGN TAX PAID

Section 107 FA 1998 introduced amendments to Section 806 Income and Corporation Taxes Act 1988. The new provisions require taxpayers (both individuals and companies) to notify the Inland Revenue within one year of any adjustment to the amount of foreign tax in respect of which they have claimed credit relief against United Kingdom tax. This article seeks to clarify what is meant by an adjustment and when it should be considered to have been made for the purposes of Section 107.

The requirement only applies however in circumstances where the adjustment is such that it results in a claim to relief becoming excessive.

The notice must be given in writing within one year from when the adjustment was made. A person who fails to give the required notice within the time limit is liable to a penalty of an amount not exceeding the amount by which the credit allowed has been rendered excessive by reason of the adjustment. Any penalty chargeable is subject to the provisions of Section 100, Taxes Management Act 1970 and to the normal abatement procedure.

### WHAT IS AN ADJUSTMENT?

This new provision relates to foreign tax paid under a wide variety of systems and methods of collection. It is not possible therefore to define precisely what constitutes an adjustment of the tax paid. However, in most cases this will involve the foreign tax authority formally accepting that the amount of tax paid is excessive and agreeing to repay the excessive tax, either directly, or indirectly by setting it off against other liabilities that the taxpayer may have.

### WHEN IS AN ADJUSTMENT MADE?

An adjustment should be considered to have been made when the foreign tax authority issues a notification, in writing to the person (or their advisers) who has paid the tax in respect of which the claim to relief has been made, that it accepts that the amount of tax paid is excessive. Where the foreign tax authority does not issue such a notification but simply repays or sets off the excessive tax, the date when the repayment was issued or the set off carried out should be taken as the date when the adjustment was made.

In some circumstances, for example where underlying tax is involved, claims may be made in respect of foreign tax paid by a person other than the person claiming relief in the United Kingdom. Notification of any adjustment to the amount of tax paid will normally be sent only to the person who has paid that tax. Persons who have claimed relief in the United Kingdom in respect of foreign tax paid by another person should therefore ensure that they will be made aware of any subsequent adjustment to the amount of foreign tax on which their claim is based. (See Chapter 5.)

**Issue 42, page 682 (August 1999)**

**CORPORATION TAX: NEW RETURN FORMS**

Corporation Tax Self Assessment (CTSA) applies to all company accounting periods ending on or after 1 July 1999. Most of the legislation for CTSA is in Finance Act 1998 and supporting Regulations. Among the changes are the inclusion of tax under Sections 419 and 747 Income and Corporation Taxes Act (ICTA) 1988 in the calculation of tax payable.

We have introduced new return forms, which must be used for accounting periods ending on or after 1 July 1999, to take account of these provisions.

A Press Release, announcing the new forms, was issued on 30 June 1999.

The new forms are:

Company Tax Return Form – CT600 (1999)

Company Tax Return Guide – CT600 Guide

Supplementary Pages:

Loans to participators by close companies – CT600A

Controlled foreign companies – CT600B

Group and consortium relief (claims and surrenders) – CT600C

Insurance (overseas life assurance business, and claims under Schedule 19AB ICTA 1988) – CT600D

Charity (where exemption on any part of income or gains is claimed) – CT600E.

The new CT600 and CT600 Guide will be issued automatically, for accounting periods that end on or after 1 July 1999, from November 1999, but only to companies that do not have agents and do not use Revenue-approved substitute forms. Supplementary Pages will not be sent automatically to any company.

If any agent or company needs the new forms to complete, and does not use approved substitutes, they can get them by making a note of the form number(s) shown above and contacting: CTSA Orderline, telephone 0845 300 6555, or fax 0845 300 6777.

The CTSA Orderline is open seven days a week between 8.00 am and 10.00 pm. All calls are charged at local rates.

The forms can also be downloaded from the Internet at: www.inlandrevenue.gov.uk (see Chapter 2).

*Inland Revenue Tax Bulletins*

## CORPORATION TAX SELF ASSESSMENT (CTSA): NEW CODE OF PRACTICE FOR ENQUIRIES INTO COMPANY TAX RETURNS

Last month we published our new Code of Practice for enquiries into company tax returns (COP14) under Corporation Tax Self Assessment (CTSA). A copy of COP14 is bound in the middle of this edition of Tax Bulletin.

The Code was produced after consultation with representatives of companies and their professional advisors and with Inland Revenue staff. It applies to enquiries which the Inland Revenue make into CTSA company tax returns, that is for accounting periods ending on or after 1 July 1999. It replaces the existing Code of Practice 2 (COP2), which will still be used for investigations into company tax returns for accounting periods ending before 1 July 1999.

The Code sets out companies' rights and how our staff will conduct enquiries. There are separate Codes of Practice for cases dealt with by our specialist offices (COP8 and COP9).

As well as the full Code, we have produced a single page shortened version. We will use this for the simplest enquiries which we consider we will be able to settle by a brief exchange of correspondence. The full text of the shortened version is reproduced at the end of this article. Even when we issue the shortened version our staff will act in accordance with the procedures set out in the full Code.

We will always send out the appropriate version of the Code with our enquiry notice.

You can get further copies of the Code of Practice:

- by calling our Orderline on 0845 900 0404 (between 8.00 am and 10.00 pm)
- by fax on 0845 900 0604
- by e-mail on saorderline.ir@gtnet.gov.uk
- by writing to PO Box 37, St Austell, Cornwall, PL25 5YN
- from the Internet at www.inlandrevenue.gov.uk
- from any Inland Revenue Enquiry Centre or Tax Office.

The following text reproduces the short Code of Practice that we will issue in the very simplest enquiries.

### SHORT CODE OF PRACTICE FOR USE IN COMPANY ENQUIRIES

#### Enquiries into company tax returns

When we receive tax returns we use the figures provided to establish the tax due or payable. If we find any obvious mistakes we may correct them without making an enquiry.

We enquire into a selection of returns to make sure they are correct, or if we need further information to understand the figures.

*Inland Revenue Tax Bulletins*

We tell the company in writing if we intend to start enquiries. Where professional advisers are acting we also notify them.

We end our enquiries once we have determined that the return is correct or that all errors have been corrected. When our enquiries are completed we say so in writing and set out any adjustments that we think are necessary.

For further information about enquiries into tax returns, ask your tax office for our Code of Practice 14 – 'Enquiries into company tax returns'.

You can ask us at any stage why we are continuing our enquiries if you believe we have all the information and explanations necessary to check your return. If you think that our enquiries are not relevant or reasonable or are being prolonged unnecessarily you may ask independent Appeal Commissioners to consider whether they should be brought to an end.

In all our dealings with you we will adhere to 'Our Service Commitment to You'. This and other information on customer service is available at Inland Revenue offices, set out in our Charters, complaint leaflet (IR120) and full Codes of Practice. (See Chapter 17).

## Issue 42, pages 683–684 (August 1999)

## GUIDANCE ON USE OF INFORMATION AND PENALTY POWERS IN QUARTERLY INSTALMENT PAYMENTS CASES

In a Press Release on 8 June, the Inland Revenue published guidance explaining how the information and penalty powers in the Corporation Tax (Instalment Payments) Regulations 1998 (SI 1998 No 3175) will be used.

There have been suggestions in newspaper reports that the guidance applies to Inland Revenue practice in respect of a much wider range of information and penalty powers. This is not the case. It applies only to the information and penalty powers contained in the instalment payments regulations. Other information and penalty powers are not affected by the guidance.

We reproduce that guidance here.

### USE OF INFORMATION POWERS

The information powers are in regulations 10, 11 and 12 of the instalment payments regulations. They require a company to provide the Inland Revenue with information to support the payments made on the instalment due dates, or the lack of such payments, or to support a claim for repayment. They are described in more detail below.

Where companies file their returns by the statutory filing date, a review of the quarterly instalment payment (QIP) position will be undertaken at the same time as the review of the return. Information about the basis upon which QIPs have been estimated will not be sought as a matter of routine. Where the amounts paid on the instalment dates do not correspond to the amounts required under the regulations interest will be charged or paid accordingly. In cases where the Inland

## Inland Revenue Tax Bulletins

Revenue make a determination of the tax payable because a company has failed to file its return on time, the Inland Revenue also have the power to make a determination of the dates on which amounts should have been paid under the regulations.

The Inland Revenue will seek to make use of the information powers in regulations 10, 11 and 12 only where there are indications that a company may have deliberately or recklessly failed to comply with its payment obligations under the regulations, or fraudulently or negligently made a claim for repayment. In such a case, all the necessary evidence will be requested from the company in respect of its instalment payments (or absence of them) or claim. This will enable the Inland Revenue to establish the extent to which the company failed to pay in accordance with its most recent estimate of its total liability, and to form a judgement as to whether the company, or persons acting on its behalf, acted deliberately or recklessly in failing to make its payments as they fell due, or in later failing to correct the position as newer and more accurate information became available.

### APPLICATION OF PENALTY REGULATION

The penalty power is in regulation 13 of the instalment payments regulations. It provides for a penalty (under Section 59E(4) Taxes Management Act 1970 (TMA)) of not more than twice the amount of interest charged in respect of the total liability of the company for that accounting period. Total liability includes liability to corporation tax, and tax under Sections 419 and 747 ICTA 1988 (provisions dealing with loans by a close company to its participators, and controlled foreign companies, respectively).

The majority of cases of inadequate or late payments, or the miscalculation of a repayment, will involve only an interest charge:

- inadequate payments: a penalty position will apply where there is evidence that the company failed to pay in accordance with its most recent estimate of its total liability (including failing to make a top-up payment) or failed to pay the right amount at the right time. Such a failure by a company or by a person acting on its behalf must be more than negligent – it must be deliberate or reckless;

- claims to repayment: a penalty will apply in respect of a claim to repayment under regulation 6 if the company or a person acting on its behalf has acted fraudulently or negligently.

A penalty under Section 59E(4) TMA will be sought in only the most serious cases involving flagrant abuse of the regulations. Before seeking a penalty the case must be submitted to Head Office for approval. The normal appeal rights of Section 100B(1) TMA will apply to any such penalty.

### INTEREST

New interest rates have been introduced for tax over- and underpaid during the instalment payments period. This is provided for in the Taxes (Interest Rate) (Amendment No 2) Regulations 1998 (SI 1998 No 3176). The new rules are more generous to companies than those that apply outside that period. The rates also

*Inland Revenue Tax Bulletins*

have a smaller spread and are more sensitive to base rate movements than the ordinary rates. Interest on underpaid corporation tax is also deductible in arriving at a company's chargeable profits. The interest represents no more than compensation for the Exchequer's (or the company's) loss of use of the money.

## INFORMATION POWERS

Regulation 10 of the Corporation Tax (Instalment Payments) Regulations (SI 3175/1998) requires a company to furnish information to the Board of Inland Revenue, and regulation 11 requires a company to produce books, documents and other records in its possession or power, relating to:

- the estimation of amounts paid in respect of the company's total liability for an accounting period in accordance with regulation 5 of SI 3175/1998;
- the non-payment of any amount in respect of the company's total liability for an accounting period in accordance with regulation 5 of SI 3175/1998; and
- a claim for repayment under regulation 6(2) SI 3175/1998.

Such details can be required within a period of not less than 30 days, by notice, at any time following the fixed filing date for the company.

In addition, regulation 12 requires a company to make available for inspection all such books, documents and other records in its possession or power as could be required to be produced under regulation 11. Where such records are maintained by computer, the company must provide the officer making the inspection with all the facilities necessary for obtaining information from them.

### PENALTY

Regulation 13 provides for a penalty under Section 59(E)(4) Taxes Management Act 1970 (TMA) where:

- a company, or a person acting on its behalf, deliberately or recklessly fails to pay the right amount on a particular instalment date in accordance with the regulations; or
- a company, or a person acting on its behalf, fraudulently or negligently makes a claim for repayment under the regulations

the amount of the penalty is a sum not exceeding twice the amount of interest charged in respect of the total liability of the company for that accounting period. (See Chapter 18.)

**Issue 42, pages 684–685 (August 1999)**

## GROUP PAYMENT ARRANGEMENTS: A REMINDER FOR COMPANIES WITH 31 MARCH ACCOUNTING PERIOD END-DATES

Time is nearly up for some groups of companies if they wish to enter into a Group Payment Arrangement with the Inland Revenue for their first CTSA year. Groups who need to act now are those which:

## Inland Revenue Tax Bulletins

- have an accounting period ending on 31 March 2000;
- contain large companies required to pay their corporation tax in quarterly instalments.

Group Payment Arrangements are voluntary. Groups with accounting periods ending on 31 March who would like to take part must get their signed Arrangement document to the Inland Revenue Accounts Office no later than 14 August. This is to allow time for the Arrangement to be set up before their first Quarterly Instalment Payment becomes due on 14 October 1999.

To register interest, and to get hold of an information pack which includes the Arrangement document, the groups must contact the Group Payment Team at the Accounts Office to which their Corporation Tax payments are normally made: Group Payment Team, Accounts Office Cumbernauld, St Mungo's Road, Cumbernauld, Glasgow G70 5TR; telephone: 01236 783488; fax: 01236 783387; Group Payment Team, Accounts Office Shipley, Victoria Street, Shipley, West Yorkshire BD98 8AA; telephone: 01274 539561; fax: 01274 539669.

Details of Group Payment Arrangements are in Tax Bulletin, Issue 40 (April 1999, pages 645 – 650), an Inland Revenue Press Release ('A Modern System for Corporation Tax Payments: Group Payment Arrangements') issued on 26 February 1999, and A Guide to Corporation Tax Self Assessment for Tax Practitioners and Inland Revenue Staff, issued to all agents in April.

The Group Payment Arrangement document and guidance notes may be downloaded from the Internet at www.inlandrevenue.gov.uk.

The Group Payment Arrangement document must be signed by a director of the company that is nominated to meet the Corporation Tax liabilities on behalf of the others in the group.

And groups need to make sure that companies within the group which are not eligible to take part in the Arrangement are not included in the list of those taking part. For example, companies which are dormant at the time the Arrangement is made, and are likely to remain dormant, will not have a 'relevant accounting period' which is a condition for inclusion in the Arrangement.

The Accounts Office Group Payment Teams will be happy to help with any questions about Group Payment Arrangements. (See Chapter 5.)

**Issue 42, pages 685–686 (August 1999)**

### DEDUCTION OF TAX AT SOURCE: LOAN RELATIONSHIPS FOR TRADING PURPOSES

We have been asked to clarify whether, or how, the obligation to deduct income tax from payments of yearly interest has been affected by the enactment of the loan relationships legislation at Part IV, Chapter II, Finance Act 1996. In particular we have been asked to comment on the suggestion that, where interest received is being taxed as part of the Case I profit of a company, this removes the obligation to deduct tax imposed by Section 349(2) Income and Corporation Taxes Act (ICTA) 1988 on the payer.

Subsection (2) of Section 349 provides that where annual interest chargeable to tax under Case III of Schedule D is paid by a company, a partnership of which a company is a member, or any person to another person whose usual place of abode is outside the United Kingdom, the payer is obliged to deduct income tax. This obligation is subject to subsection (3) of the Section which provides that, in the case of certain specified payments (including payments to a person within the charge to corporation tax in respect of interest on an advance from a bank), there is no obligation to deduct tax on making the payment. Such exceptions to the rule in subsection (2) of Section 349 are not addressed further in this note.

Where interest is paid to a company within the charge to corporation tax the receipt will be taxed under the provisions of the loan relationships legislation. If the loan relationship is for trade purposes, yearly interest received will be a credit which falls to be taxed as part of the Case I profit of the company. It would not be taxed under Case III. It has been suggested that in such circumstances, where no Case III charge arises, there can be no obligation to deduct income tax in accordance with Section 349. This is not the case.

The test in Section 349(2) to establish whether there is an obligation to deduct tax is based on whether the yearly interest is:

> '*chargeable to tax under Case III of Schedule D (as that Schedule has effect apart from the modification made for the purposes of corporation tax by Section 18(3A))*'.

The payer of the interest therefore has to decide whether the interest falls into the categories of income referred to in Section 18(3) ICTA 1988 under the heading 'Case III'. The test is carried out with no reference to the actual treatment of the interest in the hands of the recipient. Clearly it is possible for interest to be within the categories of income referred to in Section 18(3) but actually to be taxed as part of the Case I profit of a corporate creditor. In such circumstances the obligation to deduct income tax remains. (See Chapter 10.26.)

### Issue 42, pages 686–687 (August 1999)

## LATE PAYMENT OF COMMERCIAL DEBTS (INTEREST) ACT 1998: WHETHER INTEREST PAYABLE UNDER THE ACT IS 'YEARLY INTEREST'

The purpose of this article is to provide guidance on whether interest under the above Act is 'yearly' interest within the meaning of Section 349(2) Income and Corporation Taxes Act (ICTA) 1988.

The Late Payment of Commercial Debts (Interest) Act 1998 came into force on 1 November 1998. It provides for statutory interest to run where payment is delayed on certain contracts for goods or services. It does not apply where there is a prior right to interest under the terms of the contract itself, or under statute.

The question arises as to whether interest under the Act is 'yearly' interest and so subject to deduction of income tax by the payer in accordance with Section 349(2). The leading case law authorities in this area explain that, in deciding whether interest is 'yearly', it is of primary importance to establish whether the parties intend or contemplate that the debt will, or may, remain outstanding for a year or more. It is our understanding that the Late Payment Act was introduced primarily to encourage prompt payment, and that it is not its intention, nor will it normally be its effect, to provide interest of money over a long period. Accordingly we consider that interest payable under the Act will not constitute 'yearly' interest, and that no obligation therefore arises to the payer to deduct tax from the payment under Section 349(2). This same view extends to interest expressly provided for under the terms of a contract for goods or services, where that contract is one to which the Act would have applied but for the prior contractual right to interest.

More generally, all relevant provisions of the Taxes Acts will apply to interest payable under the Late Payment Act as they apply to any other interest chargeable under Case III of Schedule D. This means for instance that, in the case of a company chargeable to corporation tax, the relevant interest will rank as interest on a 'money debt' which by virtue of Section 100(2) Finance Act 1996 should be brought into account on an accruals basis in accordance with the loan relationships regime. Section 100(4) will apply to determine whether the corresponding debits or credits fall to be brought into account as trading or non-trading items. In the case of a business outside the scope of the corporation tax rules we will normally expect to follow the timing of recognition of receipts and payments given by correct accounting treatment. In such a case interest payable will normally qualify as a business expense on ordinary principles; interest receivable will be a component of the Case I profit where it is received in the course of an activity forming an integral part of a trade, otherwise it will be charged under Case III as it arises. (See Chapter 10.27.)

**Issue 43, pages 697–698 (October 1999)**

## ADVANCE PRICING AGREEMENTS: THE INLAND REVENUE'S EXPERIENCE AND EXPECTATION OF THE BILATERAL PROCESS FOR GUIDANCE TO ITS TAXPAYERS

### GENERAL

This guidance about the procedures relating to bilateral Advance Pricing Agreements ('APAs') draws on the experiences and observations of the Inland Revenue in concluding APAs with its treaty partners under the authority of the Mutual Agreement Procedure of Double Tax Treaties. The introduction of a statutory basis for APAs in the UK (see Sections 85–87 Finance Act 1999 and the Statement of Practice issued 31 August 1999) will not in itself affect these procedures for reaching bilateral agreement, and the purpose of this guidance is to provide an outline of what might be expected to happen in the generality of bilateral APA applications in order to assist UK taxpayers in considering whether to make such an application. While this document expresses the views of the Inland Revenue, the contents have been discussed with the US Internal Revenue Service, which concurs that these guidelines broadly reflect our mutual experience.

The guidelines that follow are structured around the main stages of a typical APA. However, five major principles are fundamental:

1. Simultaneous procedures: applications should be submitted to affected tax administrations at approximately the same time. It is the applicant's responsibility to ensure that all information is provided promptly to affected tax administrations and, where meetings are held with one tax administration, to make notes which can be forwarded to the other tax

# Inland Revenue Tax Bulletins

administration as soon as practicable and ideally within 4 weeks of the meeting.

2. Co-ordinated approaches: the affected tax administrations should seek to co-ordinate their respective approaches as much as practicable to improve efficiency.

3. Timetable: the affected tax administrations should agree to a joint target timetable for dealing with the various stages of the application, and will, depending on the applicant's ability to provide information timeously, aim to complete the APA within 18 months of formal application.

4. Continuous contact: the affected tax administrations should keep each other informed of progress through regular exchanges in correspondence, by telephone and video case conferences, and in face-to-face meetings.

5. Competent Authority role: negotiations to conclude the APA are conducted by the Competent Authorities of the affected tax administrations. The exchanging of information between the tax administrations is also conducted under the authority of the Competent Authority. APA information is confidential and subject to the safeguards against disclosure provided by the terms of the Exchange of Information Article of the Double Tax Treaty. The affected tax administrations should begin Competent Authority negotiations as soon as practicable, and develop provisional agreements which can be adapted as additional facts are obtained.

**PRE-FILING MEETINGS**

The Inland Revenue and other tax administrations have procedures for pre-filing meetings at which the potential for an APA can be discussed with the taxpayer. In the case of a potential bilateral APA the IR would expect that:

1. The same information is provided to each tax administration in advance of and in the course of such a meeting.

2. The meetings take place within a short time of each other.

3. The taxpayer makes notes of each meeting which can be forwarded to affected tax administrations as soon as practicable and ideally within 4 weeks of the meeting.

There is no objection in principle to the holding of joint pre-filing meetings, although practical difficulties may prevent such arrangements being made. The tax administrations may be prepared to participate in a joint pre-filing meeting by video conferencing arranged by the applicant.

The IR recognises that the taxpayer may decide to make an application for a bilateral APA after a pre-filing meeting with only one of the affected tax administrations. In such circumstances any pre-filing meeting with the other tax administration should be held as soon as possible after the first meeting with the same information being provided.

**FORMAL APPLICATION**

The simultaneous submission of an application, as required by the respective governments, is preferred. The date of the formal application is the starting point

## Inland Revenue Tax Bulletins

for the target timetable. The timetable outlined below is illustrative and may need to be modified to meet the demands of particular cases.

### MONTHS 1–3

The IR and affected tax administrations aim to complete an initial review of the submission within 3 months, and to hold a discussion (possibly using conference link) to share preliminary conclusions and concerns.

### MONTHS 4–9

The IR and affected tax administrations will then pursue enquiries independently, but will liaise with each other in order to co-ordinate enquiries as much as possible. Information received by one tax administration in response to enquiries will be made available by the applicant to the other tax administration. It may be possible to hold joint meetings, although practical difficulties may prevent such arrangements. Some tax administrations may be prepared to participate in joint meetings by video conferencing arranged by the applicant if appropriate. During this period, informal discussions between the tax administrations will take place to provide updates on progress. By the end of Month 9 the two tax administrations should be in a position to exchange formal position papers.

### MONTHS 10–12

The IR and affected tax administrations will evaluate each other's positions, obtain further information as appropriate, and aim to complete their respective analyses by the end of Month 12.

### MONTHS 12–18

Negotiations to conclude the terms of the bilateral APA by the Competent Authority staff should aim to be concluded by the end of Month 15, with formal agreement completed by the end of Month 18. The Competent Authorities will keep each other informed of the progress of APAs, and will participate in audio and video case conferences as well as face-to-face meetings in order to resolve negotiations effectively.

## ADVANCE PRICING AGREEMENTS: A NOTE ABOUT THE SCOPE OF AGREEMENTS

During the consultation process about the introduction of a statutory basis for APAs some concerns were raised that an APA which determines how the arm's length provision of Schedule 28AA ICTA 1988 is to be applied might not protect a business against a challenge from the Revenue which seeks to apply the same arm's length standard but under another legal heading. During the term of an APA which agrees how matters within Schedule 28AA ICTA 1988 are to be determined in relation to specified arrangements, the Revenue would not invoke other rules bearing on arm's length pricing in relation to those arrangements in order to argue for a different interpretation of the arm's length principle. Those other rules include the application of Section 788(3)(c)(ii) ICTA 1988 and case law principles deriving from *Sharkey v Wernher* 36 TC 275 and *Petrotim Securities v Ayres* 41 TC 389.

For further information about APAs contact: Andrew Hickman, International Division, Inland Revenue, Victory House, 30–34 Kingsway, London WC2B 6ES; Telephone 0207 438 6916. (See Chapter 14.)

**Issue 44, page 707 (December 1999)**

## INTERACTION OF TAX LAW AND ACCOUNTANCY PRACTICE

The last article on this subject appeared in Tax Bulletin 40 (April 1999, page 636). We have been asked to clarify some points arising from that article, and also from our Press Release of 20 July 1999 concerning the decisions in *Herbert Smith v Honour* (Tax Leaflet 3576) and *Jenners Princes Street Edinburgh Ltd v CIR [1998] STC (SCD) 196*.

### Allowability of provisions for tax purposes

Our view can be summarised as follows. A provision made in accounts will be allowable for tax purposes if (and only if):

- it is in respect of allowable revenue expenditure (and not, for example, in respect of capital expenditure);
- it is required by UK generally accepted accounting practice ('GAAP');
- it does not conflict with any specific tax rule governing the time at which expenditure is allowed;
- it is estimated with sufficient accuracy.

Where the first three bullets are satisfied but the fourth is not then only a sufficiently accurate estimate is allowable for tax purposes.

### Accuracy of provisions and other estimates

Whether provisions and other estimates included in accounts are sufficiently accurate is ultimately a question of fact for the Commissioners, to be determined by them after considering all relevant evidence. This means that it is in the first instance a matter for Inspectors, in the course of any enquiry they make into a return, to consider the accuracy of provisions and other estimates. Inspectors may wish to ask what factors the directors or business proprietors took into account in arriving at the figure, and what information was available to them.

Some practitioners have suggested that one effect of the *Herbert Smith* decision is that the Inland Revenue has no right to enquire into the factual accuracy of entries in company accounts which have been signed off by directors and auditors. We do not accept this.

For self-assessment tax years or accounting periods we have an explicit right to enquire into any return to check that it is correct and complete. For pre-SA periods the Inspector had to be satisfied that a return was correct and complete before making an assessment. Usually the only way we can check if a return is correct and complete is by looking at the underlying evidence.

Paragraph 25 of Schedule 18 FA 1998 governs the scope of an enquiry into a company return for CTSA accounting periods. It extends to anything contained in the return or required to be contained in the return. Accounts form part of the return and entries in the accounts can be included in the scope of an enquiry.

We can therefore check for the factual accuracy of any entry in the return, but ultimately, matters of fact are for the Commissioners to determine, whatever certificates or reports appear on accounts.

We accept that sometimes absolute accuracy is impossible, so that there is no single 'right' figure. Directors and business proprietors have a responsibility when preparing accounts to make judgements, and there will often be a range of possible answers within which their own business expertise will be the main factor affecting the final answer. What we expect them to do in arriving at an estimate is to exercise their judgement in a reasonable manner, taking into account the information reasonably available to them and other relevant factors including their own business expertise. If they have done this, and arrived at a result that accords with the requirements of UK GAAP, then Inspectors cannot substitute a different figure just because they might have exercised their own judgement differently.

### UK GAAP AND ENTRIES IN ACCOUNTS

Whether entries in accounts accord with UK GAAP is also, so far as relevant to the computation of taxable profits, a question of fact for determination by Commissioners. If there is a dispute on this issue the Commissioners would expect to hear expert accountancy evidence, as they did in cases such as *Johnston v Britannia Airways Ltd* (67 TC 99). Thus the same considerations apply to this issue as regards enquiries by Inspectors as to the issue of accuracy (see above). Whatever certificates or reports appear on accounts are not conclusive as far as the computation of taxable profits is concerned.

### PROVISIONS AND SPECIFIC TAX RULES

Taxpayers may need to consider whether a provision includes elements that are affected by specific tax rules. For example, Section 43 FA 1989 provides that in computing taxable profits no deduction may be made for the remuneration of directors or employees unless that remuneration is 'paid' (as defined for Schedule E/ PAYE purposes) during the accounting period or within 9 months of the end of the accounting period. This means that if a provision, such as a provision for foreseen losses on a long-term contract, includes an element in respect of employees' remuneration, that element must be disallowed to the extent that the remuneration is not 'paid' within 9 months of the end of the accounting period.

### PROVISIONS DISALLOWED IN SETTLED YEARS

There may be cases where provisions have been disallowed in computing profits for years which are now settled, but where on our view of the law following *Herbert Smith* and *Jenners* an accurately computed provision ought to have been

# Inland Revenue Tax Bulletins

allowed. Where this has been done we accept that an adjustment can be made to the earliest open year so that at the end of that year the cumulative position reflects our current view.

> **Example**
>
> (This example assumes that all provisions have been estimated with sufficient accuracy.)
>
> A construction company enters into a long-term contract in 1995. By the time the directors come to prepare the 1996 accounts it is clear that the contract will make a loss. In those accounts they make a provision of £100,000 which on our current view of the law ought to have been allowed. However, after negotiations only £15,000 was allowed for tax, on the grounds that the remaining £85,000 was an 'anticipation of loss'. The tax position for 1996 was finally settled in 1998.
>
> In the 1997 accounts the directors make a further provision of £50,000, and in the 1998 accounts a further provision of £20,000, both of which ought to be allowed on our current view of the law. The tax position for both years is still open.
>
> For 1997 the company can claim not only the provision of £50,000, but also (by way of a computational adjustment) the £85,000 disallowed for 1996. For 1998 the company can claim the provision of £20,000.

## ERROR OR MISTAKE RELIEF CLAIMS FOR SETTLED YEARS

Where there has been an error or mistake in a claim a supplementary claim may be made under Section 42 TMA 1970 within the time limit for making the original claim. For example where a claim has been made to carry forward a trading loss it may be possible to make a supplemental claim to increase the amount of loss carried forward. The normal rules apply to any such claim.

Where tax has been overpaid as a result of an 'error or mistake' in a return, a claim for relief may be made under Section 33 TMA 1970. The normal conditions will apply to any such claim. One of these conditions is that no relief shall be given where a return was made in accordance with the 'practice generally prevailing' at the time the return was made. We have been asked how this applies to returns made before the *Herbert Smith* and *Jenners* decisions.

*Herbert Smith* concerned the supposed rule that neither a profit nor a loss could be anticipated. We accept that owing to the uncertainty as to the scope of this rule there was no 'practice generally prevailing' on this issue. Thus where a provision was disallowed in the past on the grounds that it caused a loss to be anticipated we will not refuse a claim under Section 33 on the grounds of 'practice generally prevailing'. The remaining conditions of Section 33 will have to be satisfied before any relief is given.

*Jenners* concerned the interpretation of Section 74(1)(d) ICTA 1988: the Revenue argued that this subsection prohibited provisions for repairs to premises. This view was shared by most leading textbooks and commentators. In our view, therefore, there was a 'practice generally prevailing' to this effect up to the time the *Jenners* decision was given on 29 June 1998. This means that in our view the *Jenners* decision cannot be used to support a claim under Section 33 where the relevant return was submitted before 29 June 1998. (See Chapter 7.)

**Issue 44, page 709 (December 1999)**

## E-COMMERCE – TAX IN THE ELECTRONIC AGE

E-commerce is revolutionising the way in which business and Government is conducted, a revolution that is happening at an unprecedented pace. The Government is committed to ensuring that business in the UK is able to benefit from the changes taking place and to achieving the Government's goal of 'creating in the UK the best environment in the world in which to trade electronically by 2002'.

The Government has set out clear aims for e-commerce and for e-government in the UK. And it has drawn up strategies to achieve them. Its broad policies on the taxation of e-commerce and the principles which should be applied to it have been supported by business.

On 26 November the Government published a paper, 'Electronic Commerce: The UK's Taxation Agenda', detailing the work the Inland Revenue and HM Customs and Excise are doing to meet these objectives. A copy of the paper is enclosed in CD ROM format for subscribers of Tax Bulletin. The paper can also be accessed on both the Revenue's and Customs' web sites at: Inland Revenue: www.inlandrevenue.gov.uk/ebu/ecom.htm; Customs and Excise: www.hmce.gov.uk/bus/info/e-comm.htm.

### CREATING THE CLIMATE FOR GROWTH

The Government is committed to making sure that taxation is not a barrier to the growth of e-commerce, but rather fosters a climate in which e-commerce can grow. A package of measures has been introduced, and more are proposed, which demonstrates the strength of this commitment and ensures that enterprise, growth and investment are encouraged in the UK. These play a vital part in working towards the Government's goal.

### INTERNATIONAL CO-OPERATION

But e-commerce is a truly global phenomenon, and international debate and co-operation have been crucial to the progress which has been made on finding global solutions to the taxation issues thrown up by e-commerce. The Government recognises that international consensus is needed to give business certainty and avoid double and unintentional non-taxation and has been playing a leading role in work in international fora.

### MODERNISING TAX ADMINISTRATION

The Inland Revenue and Customs are in the forefront of the move to Information Age Government outlined in the *Modernising Government* White Paper. Along with making greater use of technology to help deliver the Government's vision of services available 24 hours a day seven days a week where there is demand, they are acutely conscious of the need to improve the content of the information and services they deliver, as well as the channels through which it is delivered. And the plans for the introduction of contact centres providing customers with interactive, multi-media access to Government are a clear illustration of this drive.

Both the Inland Revenue and Customs are introducing Internet filing of customers' returns, and the first electronic submissions will be possible during 2000–2001. And the Government intends to offer a discount on tax returns filed over the Internet as announced in Budget 1999. Further details will be announced in Budget 2000.

The pilot partnership represented by Business in Government aims to provide a 'one-stop-shop' for people setting up in business. This interactive, web-based service provides step by step guidance through customers' obligations and entitlements, making government more user friendly. It is only one example of the close co-operation between the Inland Revenue and Customs in the development of electronic services and demonstrates joined-up government in action; a way of making it easier for their customers to do business with them – saving everyone time and money.

## CHALLENGES TO TAX COMPLIANCE

The development of e-commerce does not just present opportunities for governments and business — there are also challenges. And the Government recognises that e-commerce poses risks to tax administration and compliance.

The Government will continue to work on these issues to ensure that a robust compliance regime can be applied to the e-commerce environment. And more positively, the use of developing technology will make it easier for taxpayers to comply with their tax obligations, complementing the Government's view that encouraging and assisting taxpayers is the most effective way of maximising voluntary compliance.

The risks to compliance are not solely a concern of the Government. Business too has an interest in ensuring a level playing field where all are aware of their rights, but at the same time comply with their obligations. The role of business in consultation with the Government has been important in tackling the issues raised by e-commerce.

## THE TAX RULES

A consistent message from business has been that clarity of the tax rules for e-commerce is a top priority, and businesses that trade internationally need to be certain what rules will apply and how they will be applied. At the same time Government needs to ensure the rules work in a way that protects tax revenues. But the globalisation of trade brought about by e-commerce, and the question of achieving effective application of the tax rules to international e-commerce mean

## Inland Revenue Tax Bulletins

that it is not possible for any country to act unilaterally to provide this certainty.

The Government is working with its international partners to provide clarification in a number of areas by the end of 2000. It is, for example, playing a leading role in work with them to agree a clear definition for place of consumption — a key concept in the operation of VAT, to ensure consistency in treatment of electronic and conventionally delivered services; and to clarify the interpretation of the 'permanent establishment' concept in an electronic environment and how certain income should be classified for direct tax purposes.

The business community has indicated that some of these issues need speedy clarification but in other areas the Government should not act too hastily to change long standing and widely accepted concepts, since changes brought in too rapidly might work inappropriately as technology develops. The Government agrees with this analysis and is continuing to work to resolve immediate issues while monitoring closely how developments in technology will affect the international tax rules and UK tax revenues, so as to be ready to adapt any of the rules in the future should this become necessary.

**SUMMARY**

The Government recognises that e-commerce presents both challenges and huge opportunities for taxation and tax administration. It is actively exploring and introducing ways in which the tools and techniques of e-commerce can assist taxpayers in their dealings with government, while also contributing fully to the targets for digital government. At the same time the Government has developed its policy for the taxation of e-commerce and is working, with business and its international partners, to resolve and clarify particular issues and establish consensus on those of international significance. This work is playing an important part in achieving the Government's strategy for the success of e-commerce in the UK. (See Chapter 15.)

**Issue 45, pages 723–726 (February 2000)**

### CORPORATION TAX: QUARTERLY INSTALMENT PAYMENTS

Some 20,000 of the largest companies now have to pay their corporation tax by instalments, starting in-year. The rules are in Statutory Instrument 1998 No. 3175 – the Corporation Tax (Instalment Payments) Regulations 1998. They are outlined in Revenue leaflet 'inst. 1 – A Modern System for Corporation Tax Payments'.

The Revenue is monitoring the transition to this 'Quarterly Instalment Payment' ('QIP') system. Early indications are that companies are coping with the change,

## Inland Revenue Tax Bulletins

but we are continuing to consult companies' and tax advisers' representative bodies. It will be some time before we can draw firm conclusions.

There is detailed guidance on the operation of QIPs, and the special group payment arrangements, in Chapters 12 and 13 of 'A Guide to Corporation Tax Self Assessment'. (The text of this guide is available on the Internet at www.inlandrevenue.gov.uk). But our consultations have identified some areas where it may be helpful to further clarify the rules now to help companies adapt to the new system. This article deals with those areas.

**Over- and under-payments of early QIPs**

Some people have taken a very cautious view of the interaction between Regulation 5 (the principal instalment payment rule) and Regulation 6 (the repayment rule) particularly where the best view of the ultimate liability changes. They have:

- viewed each instalment as a separate liability, to be paid at its due date regardless of any balance over- or under-paid at previous instalment dates;

- assumed that they had to claim repayment under Regulation 6 to recover (by repayment or set-off) any over-payment at an individual instalment due date.

The system is intended to operate more flexibly than that.

The QIP system is best thought of as creating a running balance of payments and liabilities, not a series of free-standing liabilities. The effect of Regulation 5 is to require the company to:

- make its best estimate of its total liability for the accounting period about six months after its start, and pay a specific proportion of that amount at the first instalment date

- keep that estimate under review and

    – make a top-up payment if the estimate increases

    – base subsequent instalment payments upon the latest estimate, taking account of the current balance of payments already made against the percentage of the estimated liability which is due by that instalment date.

Where the estimated liability for the accounting period goes down, and the cumulative amount paid to date exceeds the proportion of the latest estimated liability which should have been paid to date, the company has a choice: it can either leave the balance with the Revenue and reduce the next instalment payment accordingly, or it can claim a repayment under Regulation 6.

## Inland Revenue Tax Bulletins

> **Example** (set after full transition to QIPs, for clarity)
>
> Quartermaster Ltd has an accounting period 1.1.2004–31.12.2004. In early July 2004, it estimates its total liability for the accounting period to be £10 Million.
>
> The company pays £2.5M on 14 July 2004.
>
> It pays a further £2.5M on 14 October, as its estimate has not changed.
>
> By the year end, the company realises that its results have not fulfilled its expectations. Its provisional results show a total liability of just £8M. Quartermaster Ltd has paid £5M to date, but it only needs to have paid £4M until the third instalment falls due. As the third instalment due date is close, it decides not to seek a repayment under Regulation 6.
>
> On 14 January, the company pays just £1M. That is correct, as:
>
> - 75% of the total liability should be paid by the third instalment due date
> - the current estimate of the total liability is £8M
> - so 75% × £8M = £6M is due, and £5M has been paid already.

**TOP-UP PAYMENTS**

Where the estimated liability increases, the company can minimise its exposure to interest by making a top-up payment at any time. It does not have to wait for the next instalment due date to do this.

> **Example**
>
> Goodhead Ltd also has an accounting period 1.1.2004 – 31.12.2004. In July and October 2004, it estimates its total liability for the accounting period to be £20M and so the company pays £5M on 14 July and another £5M on 14 October.
>
> In November, the company has an unexpected opportunity to sell a major capital asset, and realises a considerable capital gain. As a result, its estimate of total corporation tax liability increases to £30M. On this latest view, it has underpaid by £5M (£2.5M at each of the first two instalment dates). To minimise the eventual interest charge, the company makes a top-up payment of £5M at the end of November, bringing its total payments to date up to £15M. It then increases its instalment payments, paying £7.5M in January and a further £7.5M in April.

This is perfectly acceptable. However, it is important to quote the correct collection reference number when making the payment (whether electronically via BACS, CHAPS or Bank Giro, or by cheque). This helps us to allocate the payment to the correct period. See 'Making QIP Payments' below.

## REVENUE COMPLIANCE ACTION

The QIP system leaves it entirely to the company to estimate its liability and calculate what payments to make. We will try to identify companies likely to have to pay QIPs and issue payslips at appropriate times to facilitate payment, but we will not issue demands or take any form of collection action until a tax charge is established for the accounting period — usually when the company return reaches us and we record the self-assessment.

So, if a company finds at the final instalment due date that its earlier estimates have been excessive and it has already paid enough to cover its total liability, it should not pay any more. We do NOT expect it to pay the amount that falls due at the fourth instalment and also seek repayment of earlier over-payments.

## MAKING QIP PAYMENTS

Where possible, we recommend that companies pay using the electronic BACS or CHAPS systems. Payments made under a group payment arrangement MUST be made electronically. Companies which are not within a group payment arrangement can choose to pay by cheque if they prefer, though we recommend the more secure and modern payment methods, rather than cheques, which are susceptible to theft when in the post.

Whatever method of payment is chosen, it is important to use the correct collection reference number. This reference appears near the centre of the payslip. It is specific to the accounting period, so it is important to use the reference from the correct payslip, or there is a risk that the payment will not be allocated to the intended accounting period.

Although we do our best to send QIP payslips to companies which need them, there are some cases — particularly new cases — where our computer may not be able to identify the need to do so.

That does not affect the obligation to pay QIPs. Companies should tell their Inspector if they do not receive payslips. The Inspector can set an indicator on our computer system so that it will start to issue payslips at the appropriate times.

If you do not have the appropriate payslip when you need to make a payment, please telephone the Revenue Accounts Office to which you make your payments and ask them to tell you what reference to use. The telephone numbers are:
  Accounts Office Cumbernauld: 01236 783077
  Accounts Office Shipley: 01274 539536

## CREDIT AND DEBIT INTEREST

Regulations 7 and 8 provide for interest on over- and under-paid balances during the period from the first QIP due date (6 months and 13 days after the accounting period begins) to the normal tax due date (9 months and a day after it ends). We only calculate and pay – or charge this interest once the tax charge is established and the normal due date is passed.

*Inland Revenue Tax Bulletins*

Again, it is best to think of the running balance of payments and liabilities.

We pay interest (credit interest) for each day on which the total amount paid to date exceeded the amount which should have been paid by that date.

We charge interest (debit interest) for each day on which the total amount paid to date was less than the amount which should have been paid by that date.

---

**Example**

Stores Ltd is within the QIP rules for its accounting period 1.1.2005 – 31.12.2005. The company had initially estimated its total liability as £4M. An upturn in business later in the year led it to revise the estimate to £6M at the end of the accounting period. Due to unforeseen group relief, its final self assessed liability was £5M. So the company's liability was in fact £1.25M at each instalment date (14 July and 14 October 2005, and 14 January and 14 April 2006).

Stores Ltd actually made the following payments:

| Date of payment | Amount paid | Total Paid |
| --- | --- | --- |
| 10 July 2005 | £1M | £1M |
| 14 October 2005 | £1M | £2M |
| 5 January 2006 | £2.5M | £4.5M |
| 14 April 2006 | £1.5M | £6M |

The resulting interest position can be expressed as follows:

| Period | Total due | Total paid | Balance over/(under) paid | Interest accruing |
| --- | --- | --- | --- | --- |
| 10–13 July | Nil | 1M | 1M | None |
| 14 July – 13 October | 1.25M | 1M | (0.25M) | debit on 0.25M |
| 14 October – 4 January | 2.5M | 2M | (0.5M) | debit on 0.5M |
| 5 January – 13 January | 2.5M | 4.5M | 2M | credit on 2M |
| 14 January – 13 April | 3.75M | 4.5M | 0.75M | credit on 0.75M |
| 14 April – 30 September | 5M | 6M | 1M | credit on 1M |

Stores Ltd files its return in November 2006. The relevant amounts of credit and debit interest will be posted to its account on our computer system when the self assessment is recorded from the return. We will then repay the overpaid balance (£ 1M tax, plus credit interest, less debit interest). We will add repayment interest to this repayment, calculated from the normal due date (1 October 2006) to the date of repayment.

## GROUP PAYMENT ARRANGEMENTS

A large number of grouped companies affected by QIPs have already taken advantage of the arrangements for payment of tax on a group-wide basis. The arrangements are explained in detail in Chapter 13 of 'A Guide to Corporation Tax Self Assessment'. The text of the arrangement contract and the accompanying notes, as well as the guide itself, are available on the Internet at: www.inlandrevenue.gov.uk.

Only groups of companies whose first CTSA accounting period ends on or after 31 December 1999 have so far been able to take advantage of group payment arrangements. Other groups of companies are invited to enter into an arrangement for their first accounting period ending after 31 December 1999. This is entirely voluntary, but the arrangements make the administration of QIPs easier for all concerned. They can also save companies interest. If you would like more information, please contact the special group payment team at the Revenue Accounts Office to which your company makes its payments: Group Payment Team, Accounts Office Cumbernauld, St Mungo's Road, Cumbernauld, Glasgow, G70 5TR; Tel: 01236 785228; Fax: 01236 785341; Group Payment Team, Accounts Office Shipley, Victoria Street, Shipley, West Yorkshire BD98 8AA; Tel: 01274 539561; Fax: 01274 539669.

Groups should make contact as early as possible. We will only normally agree to enter into a group payment arrangement for an accounting period if we receive the completed arrangement document at least two months before the first quarterly instalment payment is due.

Groups which have already entered into an arrangement do not need to reapply. Once made, the contract automatically applies to subsequent accounting periods unless it is expressly terminated by either side. However, you should provide the group payment team with an amended schedule of participating companies if you wish to remove a company from, or add a company to, the arrangement. (See Chapter 5.)

**Issue 45, page 728 (February 2000)**

## CORPORATION TAX ON CHARGEABLE GAINS–POST TRANSACTION VALUATION CHECKS

On 1 April 1997 we introduced a new service that provides individuals or trustees with the opportunity to submit capital gains tax valuations to their tax office for agreement before the filing date for making their return. We are now able to offer the service to companies as well as individuals and trustees.

The aim of the service is to help with the preparation of the Self Assessment return. As before we will consider valuations only after the relevant transaction has taken place.

The details of the service for companies are essentially the same as for individuals and trustees. No charge will be made for the service. Applications to use the service must be made on form CG34.

If we cannot agree the proposed valuations we will put forward an alternative figure that we would accept. If this is not agreed we will be happy to try to negotiate an acceptable valuation. We will try to put forward an alternative and, if time allows, enter into negotiations before the deadline for filing returns. In some cases this may not be possible, either because of the complexity of the valuation or if the application to use the service is made late. The return must still be filed within the time allowed.

The press release dated 10 January 2000 gives more details. New guidance notes relating to the service have been prepared and these will form an attachment to a revised form CG34. Forms CG34 and the notes will be available from the company's Inland Revenue office or any Inland Revenue Enquiry Centre. (See Chapter 8.)

**Issue 46, pages 740–742 (April 2000)**

## NON-RESIDENT LANDLORDS: PRACTICAL IMPLICATIONS OF NEW TRANSFER PRICING LEGISLATION AT SCHEDULE 28AA OF ICTA 1988

The 1998 Finance Act introduced a comprehensive modernisation of the UK's transfer pricing legislation. This has been incorporated into the Taxes Acts at Schedule 28AA of the Income and Corporation Taxes Act (ICTA) 1988 (Sch 28 AA). For non-resident landlord companies and partnerships liable to income tax the first year of assessment affected is 1999–2000.

Non-resident landlords will be required to self assess their profits in accordance with the arm's length principle. This means that if provision has been made:

- between any two persons which are in the required control relationship;
- by means of a transaction or a series of transactions;
- which differs from that which would have been found between independent enterprises;
- which confers a potential UK tax advantage on one or both of those persons;

then the profits/losses of the potentially advantaged person(s) must be recomputed as if the arm's length provision had been made. The arm's length provision is that which would have been found between independent enterprises acting entirely at arm's length.

Although the legislation covers all provisions, the most common ones likely to be affected for landlords are rents received from and interest paid directly to associates, or to a bank where a guarantee or similar has been given by an associate. It looks at every aspect of the provision, not just its price.

The October and December 1998 Tax Bulletins, Issues 37 and 38, contained articles covering record-keeping, financial transactions and penalties under the new legislation. However, we continue to receive a considerable number of queries specifically in connection with interest paid and rents received by non-residents letting property in the UK. This article deals with the most common questions we have received from such landlords, although many of the answers will be relevant to any company taking out a loan to purchase property.

# Inland Revenue Tax Bulletins

**Who does the legislation apply to?**

Sch 28AA applies where one of the affected persons directly or indirectly controls the other or the same person controls both. The person who is controlled must be a body corporate or a partnership, but the person controlling may be any person. A joint venture company or partnership that has at least two 40% participants is within the legislation in respect of provisions between it and each of these.

Provisions are exempt where they are made between persons who are each, either liable to corporation tax (whether resident or not) on the relevant activities or, resident **and** liable to income tax on them.

In the following questions 'an associate' refers to another person which has the required control relationship with the non-resident landlord company or partnership.

**How does Schedule 28AA differ from previous transfer-pricing legislation?**

There are several differences but the most crucial for non-resident landlords is that all aspects of a provision made between associates must be as would be found between independent enterprises acting entirely at arm's length, not just the price. This is particularly relevant to loan interest claimed against rents as this is determined by the amount lent as well as the interest rate.

**Interest arising on a bank loan obtained by means of a guarantee from an associate is within the legislation. Why — isn't the loan between third parties?**

The loan granted by the bank is one transaction but there is also another transaction involved, i.e. the associate giving a guarantee to the bank. So there is a provision (of funding) which has been made between associates by means of a series of transactions and this is therefore within the scope of Sch 28AA. If the interest arising is more than would have been obtained without the guarantee, e.g. because the principal loaned is more, then the amount claimed should be recalculated as if no guarantee had been given.

The same applies if the loan has been advanced because of a backing deposit, etc from an associate (a 'back-to-back' loan), a letter of comfort or similar.

**How do I know what amount would have been lent at arm's length?**

This will vary with the facts and circumstances of each case. If no other persons are involved, a third party lender will determine the amount it would lend by looking at the assets and income of the prospective borrower. In our experience third party lenders are primarily concerned with the value of the property they are being asked to lend against and currently offers of advances appear typically to be in the range of 65–80% if there is a satisfactory projected income stream. In reviewing projected rental streams a third party lender would have regard to both the quality of the tenant and the duration of the leases, and as always lending decisions are the result of the evaluation of a number of general economic and specific commercial factors.

## Inland Revenue Tax Bulletins

Companies paying corporation tax have had to consider broadly parallel legislation at S 209(2)(da), ICTA 1988 for some time. Non-resident landlords may find it useful to consult the articles on 'Intra-group payments: deemed distributions: interest and similar sums' in Tax Bulletins Issues 17 and 35 as the practical considerations are largely the same.

**Surely if a bank *had* lent 100%, this would be at a greater interest rate to reflect this increased risk?**

It is true that a higher risk may well justify a higher interest rate. However the arms' length price is a bargain, arrived at between two parties acting independently. Even if a 100% loan were on offer from a bank, which in our experience is not nowadays normally the case, a prospective borrower would not necessarily take this up if they considered the price would not give an adequate return.

**Suppose the loan provided by an associate was 100% of the original purchase price, but the value of the property has risen since so that the loan now represents only, say 65% for 1999–2000?**

The provision giving rise to the interest, i.e. the loan, was made when the property was purchased, and this is the date that must be considered when considering whether the interest payable would have arisen at arm's length in any particular year.

In the same way, if the value of a let property has decreased in the interim but the original loan would have been obtained at arm's length and would still be in place interest arising will not be challenged under Sch 28AA.

**What if the original loan is refinanced by a provision made between associates?**

If such refinancing reflects what would have happened between parties at arm's length, for example because a better deal is available on interest rates, and the replacement financing is on terms that would have been agreed by such parties, no limitation under Sch 28AA will be necessary. If the refinancing is also an occasion on which there is an increase in the amount borrowed — perhaps because the value of the property has increased the borrowing capacity of the company — then the purpose of the additional borrowing will need to be examined on its own merits under the normal rules of Schedule A and Sch 28AA.

If such refinancing is on terms worse than the original loan, for example because it is based on interest rates which have risen since the original loan was made, the company or partnership will need to establish to the Revenue's satisfaction that the refinancing would nevertheless have taken place at arm's length. Where this is not so, or not fully so, the arm's length provision must be substituted. Normally, in the absence of other considerations, the arm's length provision would be based on a refinancing at the previous interest rate or on a discount by the lender of the principal lent to reflect the new, higher interest rate. In both cases the net interest payable would remain the same.

It should be noted that this description of the Revenue's approach to such refinancing applies generally and are reflected in Tax Bulletin Issue 17 of June 1995.

**If a mortgage loan were taken from a bank, they would take a charge over the property. Does this mean a loan directly or indirectly provided by an associate is also deemed to involve a charge over the property?**

When considering the amount which would have been advanced and the rate of interest which would have been charged, yes, as this is what would have happened at arm's length. However this does not mean a charge over the property is deemed for any other reason, such as considering whether the interest has a UK source.

**Who has responsibility for determining the arm's length amount of rents and interest paid when a managing agent prepares the return?**

Returns should only be signed by a proper officer of the company or any other person authorised by the company. It is therefore the company's responsibility to determine this information.

**Will a charge be imputed on a non-resident landlord providing rent-free residential accommodation within the UK to a UK individual who is a participant?**

It will not be Inland Revenue practice to impute a charge under Sch 28AA in these circumstances.

**Where can I get further help or advice?**

Any general enquires relating to the tax affairs of non-resident company landlords may be sent to: FICO Audit and Compliance, Fitz Roy House, P O Box 46, Nottingham NG2 1BD; Tel: 0115 974 2041/2049.

Specific technical enquiries on Sch 28AA should be addressed to: Susan New or Colin Clavey, International Division (BTG), Victory House, 30–34 Kingsway, London WC2B 6ES; Tel: 0207 438 7596 (Susan New) and 0207 438 6911 (Colin Clavey). (See Chapter 15.)

## Issue 46, page 742 (April 2000)

## S703 ICTA 1988 AND SELF ASSESSMENT

We have received a number of enquiries from taxpayers and their advisers about how to return the proceeds of transactions in securities which have taken place either without any application being made for advance clearance under s 707 ICTA 1988 or where such an application was refused by the Board of Inland Revenue.

The anti-avoidance legislation at Sections 703–9 ICTA 1988, which is operated by the s 703 Compliance Unit (s 703CU) under powers devolved by the Board of Inland Revenue, is outside the self assessment regime and operates independently of the self-assessment provisions at TMA 1970. No liability under s 703 therefore arises unless and until the Board serves a notice under s 703(3) specifying the appropriate adjustment.

Taxpayers should therefore complete their returns on the basis which they consider to be correct without having regard to s 703–9. They may, however, wish to draw the attention of the district to whom the return is sent to any correspondence with s 703CU in connection with the transactions in question.

As s 703 is outside SA, any enquiries by s 703CU into the possible application of s 703 to the transactions in question will be carried out independently of any enquiry into the self assessment tax return for the period in which the transactions took place.

S 703CU may therefore begin enquiries into the possible counteraction under s 703 of a tax advantage obtained in one of the prescribed circumstances at s 704A-E outside the time limits for making an enquiry under Section 9A TMA 1970 and may instigate or continue such enquiries after the issue of a closure notice under Section 28(5) TMA 1970 in respect of the tax return for the year in which the tax advantage arose.

In accordance with s 703(12), Section 29(2) and (3) TMA 1970 do not restrict the Revenue's ability to make any assessment under s 703(3) necessary to counteract the tax advantage provided that the assessment in question is made within six years of the chargeable period to which the tax advantage relates.

Anyone wishing to ascertain whether a transaction for which no advance clearance was obtained under s 707 is considered by the Board of Inland Revenue to fall within s 703–9 ICTA 1988 before completing a 1999–2000 SA return may apply for s 707 clearance in the usual way by writing direct to s 703CU at the following address giving full details of the transaction(s) in question: S 703 Compliance Unit, Room 522, 22 Kingsway, London WC2B 6NR. (See Chapter 2.)

**Issue 46, page 743 (April 2000)**

## INFORMATION POWERS AND LEGAL ADVICE

This is the article on Information Powers and Legal Advice foreshadowed in Tax Bulletin Issue 41 (June 1999, page 676). Its purpose is to explain our view on the question of claims to professional or legal privilege which are sometimes made in response to requests for information. This subject has attracted significant interest following the recent Special Commissioner's decision in *An Applicant and An Inspector of Taxes [1999] STC (SCD) 128* and was debated by the Finance Bill Standing Committee in the House of Commons on 28 June 1999.

Situations where deliberate tax evasion is suspected are outside the scope of this article. As usual, tax evasion or tax fraud, both of which are illegal, destroy legal privilege.

The main information powers available under the Taxes Acts (other than those concerned with self assessment) are in Section 20, Taxes Management Act 1970 and its related sections. These provisions provide for four specific circumstances in which production of documentation cannot be compelled by an inspector. The first relates to notices addressed to a particular taxpayer (under Section 20(1)) as well as notices addressed to a 'third party' (under subsections (3) or (8A) and Section 20A:

- **Section 20B(2)** — a person is not bound to deliver documents or furnish particulars which relate to the conduct of a pending appeal by him, nor is a person bound to deliver or make available documents relating to the conduct of a pending appeal by the taxpayer.

The others relate only to third party notices:

- **Section 20B(8)** — a barrister, advocate or solicitor is not bound to deliver or make available documents for which professional privilege could be claimed, that is, broadly speaking, documents containing communications between lawyer and client for the purpose of obtaining or giving legal advice or other legal services.

- **Section 20B(9)** — a person appointed as auditor is not bound to deliver or make available documents which are his property and which were created for his duties as auditor; and

- also **Section 20B(9)** — a tax adviser is not bound to deliver or make available documents which are his property and which consist of communications for the purpose of giving or obtaining tax advice.

The same principles apply equally to advice provided by lawyers and that from tax advisers. References to 'legal advice' in this article should therefore be read as covering all tax advice whether or not it is given by lawyers.

It has sometimes been suggested that there is a principle of privilege in general law which overrides or operates in addition to the specific exceptions in Section 20 mentioned above. We have always taken the view that Section 20 is a complete, self contained information power, and that the only exemptions from it are those specifically provided. (See paragraph 8117 of the Investigation Handbook.) In *An Applicant and An Inspector of Taxes* the Special Commissioner confirmed our view though his decision is now the subject of a judicial review.

It does not follow from this view of the law that all the professional advice which is specifically exempted from disclosure in the hands of the adviser, whether under Section 20B(8) or (9), is subject to disclosure if it is held by the taxpayer. That is because, in addition to those specific exemptions for legal advice and documents relating to a pending appeal, Section 20 provides further safeguards.

In particular, the inspector seeking consent to issue a notice under Section 20 must satisfy a Commissioner that, in the inspector's reasonable opinion, the documents 'contain or may contain information relevant to any tax liability to which the person is or may be subject'.

We recognise that this test of relevance will not often be satisfied where legal advice is concerned. 'Pure' legal advice, that is advice concerned with whether specific pieces of legislation apply to a given transaction, is simply opinion on the law and will be exempt from disclosure save in wholly exceptional circumstances.

*Inland Revenue Tax Bulletins*

Advice given after a transaction has taken place will almost invariably fall into this category. In particular, once a point has been raised by us about a completed transaction, subsequent legal advice on that point will never be sought by means of a Section 20 notice.

Sometimes, however, legal advice (and the papers prepared to obtain that advice) may not be concerned solely with legal arguments and may include factual information. In these circumstances the advice is likely to contain material which satisfies the 'relevant information' test described above. In particular, the factual information may set out the purpose in entering into the transaction where statutory provisions containing a specific reference to purpose or importing a motive test need to be considered. For example, paragraph 13, Schedule 9, FA 96 (a loan relationship anti-avoidance rule) depends on the taxpayer's purpose in entering into a transaction.

Likewise, the legal advice may contain information about purposes relevant to the 'Ramsay' principle. Ramsay may be in point, if on enquiry there appears to be no convincing commercial purpose for a transaction which is one step in a composite whole.

**Practical issues**

We recognise that there can be practical difficulties in this area but we would hope that the following practices and procedures should resolve most of them.

- Information notices designed to obtain details of legal advice will specifically mention that intention (and we will have explained prior to the formal notice or in the summary of reasons required under S 20(8E) why the advice is considered relevant to the point at issue).

- Approval must always be obtained from Compliance Division before an Inspector can proceed.

- Applications for consent for any such notice will be made to a Special Commissioner, save in wholly exceptional circumstances.

- Copies of documents containing both disclosable material and 'pure' legal advice may blank out the latter (as the Economic Secretary to the Treasury indicated in the debate mentioned above) and any dispute may be referred to the Special Commissioner who gave consent to the issue of the notice.

Similar issues can arise in connection with the information powers relating to certain special areas of tax law and in particular in connection with the information powers for self assessment (in Section 19A Taxes Management Act and, for companies, in Paragraph 27, Schedule 18 Finance Act 1998).

Generally in these other contexts our approach will be as described in this article.

## Inland Revenue Tax Bulletins

And specifically as regards the self assessment information powers two comments may be helpful.

First, the test governing the use of those powers is whether the information sought is reasonably required for the purposes of our enquiry into a SA return. We accept here that information which is not relevant to a tax liability (the test in Section 20) will also necessarily fail the self assessment test.

Secondly, no prior consent to the issue of an SA information notice is needed from a Commissioner. There is instead a right of appeal (to the General or Special Commissioners as the appellant wishes) against its requirements. In addition, the practices described in the first, second and fourth bullets above will be followed.

The following examples are intended to assist practitioners in understanding our approach. They should be read in that spirit. They are not definitive and changes to the facts that at first sight seem quite minor could occasionally lead us to take a different view.

---

**Example 1**

We inform the UK parent of a multinational group that we wish to review its transfer pricing policies in detail. The company's board responds by commissioning a report from a specialist legal firm to assess its transfer pricing methodologies and any possible weaknesses. We accept that the report is not likely to be relevant for the purposes of Section 20(1) TMA 1970. On the other hand, Section 20(1) could be used to require production of the raw data and background documentation from which the report was prepared as well as requiring a person to furnish the Inspector with such particulars as may meet the requirements of Section 20(1)(b).

---

**Example 2**

An entrepreneur wishes to sell a business that he has carried on through an owner-managed company. He seeks legal advice as to whether it would be advantageous to sell the shares in the company or the business assets themselves and, subsequently, follows that advice. Although the advice may be tax driven there is no reason for us to suspect a preordained composite transaction with steps inserted for tax avoidance purposes which might bring the **Ramsay** principle into play and no purposive test requiring us to look into the mind of the person taking the decision appears relevant. We therefore accept that the advice is not relevant to the person's tax affairs and that Section 20(1) TMA 1970 could not be used.

## Inland Revenue Tax Bulletins

**Example 3**

A UK group wishes to expand its operations by purchasing the business of an overseas company in a joint venture with another non resident group. Legal advice is taken and a number of possible structures are considered involving the creation of structures which are fiscally transparent in one country and opaque in another and alternative methods of funding. Eventually, one such structure is picked and the transaction goes ahead. We however suspect that the UK group is seeking a double deduction for finance costs, in the UK as well as a further deduction overseas. Here, several steps are inserted before the purchase of the business and the Ramsay principle may apply if the steps have no commercial purpose other than the avoidance of tax. In addition, paragraph 13 Schedule 9 FA 1996 may apply to the loan relationships if there are unallowable purposes. The legal advice relating to the transaction which was given to the UK group may provide evidence of purpose and may therefore be relevant. We would be prepared to use Section 20(1) TMA 1970 in these circumstances.

**Example 4**

A company wishes to pay its directors substantial bonuses but does not wish to account for tax under PAYE or pay employer's NIC. It seeks legal advice and is recommended a scheme involving a number of offshore trusts. The scheme is implemented and the directors receive their bonuses without deduction, although they offer to pay the tax under Schedule E. Again, several steps have apparently been inserted into a composite transaction in the means whereby the bonuses leave the company and reach the directors so the **Ramsay** principle may apply. The legal advice may provide evidence of the purpose of these inserted steps and we would be prepared to use Section 20(1) TMA 1970 to require its production.

**Example 5**

A UK group decides to restructure itself after making heavy losses and instructs tax advisers to ensure that the restructuring is tax efficient. They suggest a series of transactions which achieve the necessary restructuring and also enables ACT to be paid on an intra-group dividend in a way which gives rise to both a repayment of mainstream CT and a dividend against which losses can be set to give rise to a claim to payment of a tax credit. The Group claims that the transaction was a commercial restructuring carried out in a tax efficient manner. We need to consider whether there is a preordained composite transaction and, if so, whether there are any steps inserted solely for tax purposes. In these circumstances it is necessary to look at the transactions as a whole and the intentions of the directors as evidenced in the advice from their advisers. We would therefore be prepared to use Section 20(1) TMA 1970 to require production of the tax advice to the extent it was evidence of those intentions as well as other contemporary documentation.

> **Example 6**
>
> A company occupies a building that is badly damaged in a storm. Architects are instructed and produce three alternative proposals, all of which involve extensive alterations. The directors are concerned that expenditure on one or more of the proposals might be considered to be capital expenditure and not allowable as a deduction in computing profits for tax purposes. The directors seek advice from a specialist tax adviser. This advice would not be relevant to the company's tax affairs because it would be no more than an opinion. We accept that Section 20(1) TMA 1970 would not be used in these circumstances.

> **Example 7**
>
> A person buys a plot of land and sells it three months later at a large profit. He claims that the land was bought as a medium term investment and there was no particular intention to sell it quickly at the time of purchase. Immediately prior to the purchase legal advice was taken about the tax implications of the transaction. The request for legal advice and the advice itself may contain information about the intention of the person at the time the land was purchased. As such it may be relevant in deciding whether the transaction is to be taxed as a capital gain or as an adventure in the nature of trade. We would be prepared to use Section 20(1) TMA 1970 in these circumstances. (See Chapter 17.)

## Issue 46, page 746 (April 2000)

## INTERPRETATIONS

### SECTIONS 765 AND 765A ICTA 1988

Section 765 requires UK companies with overseas subsidiaries to obtain the consent of the Treasury before certain transactions involving those subsidiaries are carried out. In line with European Union law, Section 765A disapplies Section 765 where the transactions are capital movements within the European Economic Area, substituting a reporting requirement instead. This article clarifies the position concerning three issues on which we have received questions from taxpayers and practitioners.

The first issue concerns a proviso that used to mean that the disapplication of Section 765 by Section 765A was relevant only where the transaction was carried out 'with a view to establishing or maintaining lasting economic links'. Its effect was that, if no such links existed, Section 765 applied in the normal way. This was explained in paragraphs 8 and 9 of Inland Revenue Statement of Practice 2/92.

Changes made by the Maastricht Treaty removed the requirement for such links to exist. Paragraphs 8 and 9 of SP2/92 do not apply therefore to transactions carried out on or after 1 January 1994.

# Inland Revenue Tax Bulletins

The second issue concerns the Treasury General Consents. To ease the administration of Section 765, the Treasury is empowered to give a general consent to transactions that might otherwise need its special consent. Known as the Treasury General Consents, these were last issued in 1988. One of them (at paragraph 3(c)(ii)) is subject to conditions at paragraph 7. One of the conditions (at sub-paragraph (2)(c)), states that there should not be a loan associated with the transaction that has been made to a UK company by a non-UK company.

As a matter of practice, the loan condition is now regarded as being satisfied where a non-UK lender makes a loan from its UK branch, or where it is resident in a country within the European Economic Area.

The third issue also concerns the Treasury General Consents. Two of them (paragraph 3(b)(i) and paragraph 8(c)) apply to transactions between members of groups of companies wholly within another country. Definitions of these two types of group — an 'overseas group' and 'territorial group' respectively — are given at paragraph 2. Very broadly, they rely on the definition of a UK group for group relief purposes at Section 413 ICTA 1988.

South African groups did not previously satisfy either definition, because of the way they were taxed in South Africa. It has been put to us that changes to South African law in 1997 mean that such groups can now form an 'overseas group' or a 'territorial group' for the purposes of the General Consents. The matter is not free from doubt. But, as a matter of practice, the basis of taxation in South Africa is no longer regarded as preventing South African groups which otherwise fulfil the conditions set out in the respective definitions, from being able to form either an 'overseas group' or a 'territorial group'. (See Chapter 15.)

**Issue 46, page 748 (April 2000)**

## APPLICATIONS FOR INTERNATIONAL CLEARANCES, APPROVALS AND AGREEMENTS

The Business Tax Group of International Division has responsibility for administering several statutory and non-statutory clearances, approvals, and agreements. These are described below with references to sources of guidance about the particular procedures to be followed:

- notification of company migration and approval of arrangements for payment of tax liabilities, Section 130 FA 1988 (see Statement of Practice 2/90)
- application for Treasury consent under Section 765 ICTA 1988 to certain transactions in shares or debentures (see IR Corporation Tax Manual CT 3449)
- notification as required by Section 765A ICTA 1988 of transactions falling within the European Capital Movements Directive (see Statement of Practice 2/92)
- application for an Advance Pricing Agreement relating to transfer pricing issues in accordance with Section 85–87 FA 1999 (see Statement of Practice 3/99)
- clearances in relation to Controlled Foreign Companies provisions under

## Inland Revenue Tax Bulletins

Section 747–756 and Schedules 24–26 ICTA 1988 (see Corporation Tax Self Assessment: Controlled Foreign Companies, 2.6, June 1999)

- pre-transaction advice on funding issues (Tax Bulletins Issues 17 and 37)

The Inland Revenue has a duty to maintain the confidentiality of all information sent to us, and we recognise that particular sensitivities can arise in relation to the applications we receive. To help us handle the information securely, the Business Tax Group requests applicants to follow two guidelines:

- applications should be addressed to the Business Tax Group and, in most cases, named officials according to the type of clearance sought;
- applications and subsequent correspondence should be sent either by courier or marked 'private and confidential'

The name and address of the individual official according to the type of clearance sought is provided below, except in the case of advice on funding issues where a general address is provided. After the initial application has been made, a different official may take responsibility for responding, and subsequent correspondence should be addressed to that individual.

- company migrations (s 130 FA 1988):

  Mr Douglas Rankin, Business Tax Group (Company Migrations), Inland Revenue, International Division, Victory House, 30–34 Kingsway, London WC2B 6ES

- transactions in shares or debentures (s 765 and s 765A ICTA 1988):

  Mr Douglas Rankin, Business Tax Group (Treasury Consent), Inland Revenue, International Division, Victory House, 30–34 Kingsway, London WC2B 6ES

- Advance Pricing Agreements (s 85–87 FA 1999):

  Mr Andrew Hickman, Business Tax Group (APA), Inland Revenue, International Division, Victory House, 30–34 Kingsway, London WC2B 6ES

  (For APAs involving oil taxation the contact continues to be, as stated in SP3/99):

  Mrs Janice Cross, Deputy Director (APAs), Inland Revenue, Oil Taxation Office, Melbourne House, Aldwych, London WC2B 4LL

- CFC clearances:

  Mr Stephen Hewitt, Business Tax Group (CFC Clearance), Inland Revenue, International Division, Victory House, 30–34 Kingsway, London WC2B 6ES

- pre-transaction advice on funding issues:

  Business Tax Group (Advice on Funding), Inland Revenue, International Division, Victory House, 30–34 Kingsway, London WC2B 6ES

This information will be updated regularly on the web-page, Clearances and Approvals, to be found under Technical Information on the Inland Revenue web-site: (www.inlandrevenue.gov.uk) and will also appear in web-pages for the Business Tax Group, International Division which are currently being developed

## Inland Revenue Tax Bulletins

on the Inland Revenue web-site. If applicants wish to check that the information is still current, please phone Business Tax Group Registry on 020 7438 6945. (See Chapters 13, 14, 15.)

### Issue 47, page 751 (June 2000)

## PROVISION OF PERSONAL SERVICES THROUGH INTERMEDIARIES: FREQUENTLY ASKED QUESTIONS

**The new rules which apply to workers who supply their services to clients through intermediaries such as service companies or partnerships came into effect on 6 April 2000. Details about how to decide when the new rules apply were published in Tax Bulletin Issue 45 (February 2000).**

All our published information about this measure has been included on our website at: www.inlandrevenue.gov.uk/ir35, but some of the more frequently asked questions are being duplicated here for ease of reference.

Further information can also be obtained from our new leaflet, IR175 'Supplying services through a limited company or partnership', available from Inland Revenue Enquiry Centres, Tax Offices, Inland Revenue National Insurance Contribution Offices, or our website.

### GENERAL QUESTIONS

**What is IR 35 about?**

Budget day 1999 Press Release IR35 announced the Chancellor's intention to tackle tax and NICs avoidance through the use of intermediaries such as service companies or partnerships.

Intermediaries such as service companies can be set up to provide the services of a single worker to a client in circumstances where, if it were not for the service company, the worker would be an employee of the client. The use of service companies in this way allows the client to make payments to the company rather than the individual, without deducting PAYE or NICs.

The worker can then take the money out of the service company in the form of dividends instead of salary. Dividends are not liable to NICs so the worker will pay less in NICs than either a conventional employee or a self-employed person.

The Chancellor believes that avoidance of PAYE and NICs in this way needs to be tackled in the interests of fairness.

**Who will be affected by the proposals?**

Anyone supplying their services through an intermediary such as a service company or partnership will need to think about the new rules.

But only those contracts which would have been contracts of employment with

# Inland Revenue Tax Bulletins

the client if the worker had worked directly to them instead of through an intermediary will be affected.

The most usual sorts of intermediary are service companies or partnerships which are normally under the control of the worker. The worker can then take the money out of the service company in the form of dividends instead of salary. Dividends are not liable to NICs so the worker will pay less in NICs than either a conventional employee or a self-employed person.

If there is more than one intermediary between the client and the worker, any intermediary which makes payments **direct** to the worker may be affected. However, the intermediary with the direct link with the worker will normally be the intermediary responsible for complying with the legislation.

Individuals not in business and contracting with an intermediary on a personal basis (e.g. a householder engaging a plumber to fix the kitchen sink) will be specifically excluded from these new rules.

Please see Inland Revenue Press Release of 23/9/99 for further details.

**How are 'service companies' defined?**

The legislation may affect any kind of intermediary so no particular intermediary will be defined in the legislation.

**What are the existing rules used to determine the boundary between employment and self-employment (the 'D/E tests')?**

The rules are based on a long history of case law. The same rules apply for both tax and NICs purposes. An overview of those rules is available in the Inland Revenue February 2000 Tax Bulletin.

**Some professions (e.g. nurses working through nursing banks) have case law to define their employment status, but the IT and engineering industries have none.**

Case law on employment status does not apply only in the industries where particular cases have been taken: it establishes principles which apply in all industries. Those principles are applied in every case, to nurses in the same way as to IT professionals. So a nurse has no more certainty, and no less, than any other worker. The principles are explained in the Tax Bulletin Issue 45 (February 2000).

**In deciding whether I would have been an employee of my client, will you only look at the contract I have signed, or the contract between the client and an agency?**

The Inland Revenue will take account of all relevant contracts in order to discover whether the relationship between a worker and a client would have been one of employment, if there had been no intermediary. This would include any

## Inland Revenue Tax Bulletins

contracts between the client and an agency, and between the agency and the worker's service company.

**How will the Revenue determine the facts after the contract has finished? Will you go back and look at past contracts?**

The Revenue will review the facts in the same way as it does for all employment status work. This will include going back and looking at past contracts if appropriate.

**You say the Revenue will give an opinion on signed contracts but I do not have a written contract as the terms were agreed orally. What supporting documentation do I need to provide in order to receive an opinion from the Revenue?**

You will need to provide whatever supporting evidence you consider will be helpful in demonstrating the terms and conditions under which you work. You should write to the Inland Revenue, in accordance with the existing guidance on obtaining opinions on contracts, setting out full details of the terms and conditions, which you have agreed with the client and the services which you are providing.

You should also obtain a letter from the client confirming that the terms and conditions are as agreed. If necessary the Inspector may need to speak to both you and your client in order to properly understand the working arrangements and to formulate an opinion on the contract.

**I hear that the Revenue have approved a model contract – how could this happen if each case is decided on its merits?**

The Inland Revenue has not approved a model contract.

A version of a model contract was sent to us for an opinion, according to the arrangements for giving advice on existing contracts announced in the Inland Revenue Press Notice on 7 February. An opinion was then given in relation to one person's particular circumstances.

Although we are unable to comment on the circumstances of individual cases we should confirm that a decision on employment status will depend on the circumstances of each case. We can also confirm that new rules will not apply in cases where the relationship with the client does not fall within the accepted definition of employment.

**My contract specifies that I am allowed to hire a substitute. Will the Inland Revenue take this at face value? If not will I need to provide evidence to prove that this right is genuine?**

The Inland Revenue will want to ensure that the right to send a substitute is a genuine right before it can be taken into account in deciding employment status.

## Inland Revenue Tax Bulletins

A right of substitution is only likely to exist where the client does not mind, from one day to the next for the duration of the contract, who carries out the work, provided that whoever does so is suitably qualified and experienced.

Where the service company's contract is not with the client but with an agency, and there is a claimed right of substitution, the Inland Revenue would normally require a copy of the written contract between the agency and the client.

If you are unable to get access to that contract then you should ask the agency to send a copy to the Inland Revenue direct. If this is not possible you may be asked to provide alternative evidence. This could take the form of a letter from the client which confirms that it has agreed to your service company providing a substitute.

**What will happen if someone fails to follow the new rules?**

Where the Inland Revenue discover the new rules have not been followed, they will follow the normal approach to cases of PAYE/NICs failure set out in Inland Revenue leaflet **IR 109 – Employer compliance reviews and negotiations**. The Revenue will seek to collect any unpaid tax or NICs, and any interest due. In addition penalties may be sought in cases of negligent or fraudulent conduct.

**If I work through my own service company on 'relevant' engagements will my client have to provide me with employment rights such as sick pay, holiday pay etc?**

No. Under this legislation, the client will not become your employer. What the legislation does is to treat your service company as making a payment to you chargeable to income tax under Schedule E and on which national insurance contributions are payable. All employer responsibilities fall on the service company as they have always done.

**If I work through my own service company on relevant engagements will I be entitled to unemployment benefit?**

People who work through their own service companies are unable to claim benefits between contracts if they are still employees of their own service companies.

Individuals who are no longer employed by their service company may claim benefits on the same basis as any other employee.

**Why do I have to pay both employer's and employee's NICs when a conventional employee does not have to?**

Service companies are already liable to pay employer's NICs on salary paid to their employees. The legislation does not change that.

A service company and its worker/director are two separate legal entities with separate legal responsibilities. Where the worker is employed by the service

## Inland Revenue Tax Bulletins

company the employer responsibilities rest with the service company and not the client. This is why the service company's client does not have to pay employer's NIC on the payment it makes for the worker's services and the service company does.

**If my company is incorporated or resident abroad will the rules affect me?**

If you would have been treated as an employee of the client had you provided services under a contract between yourself and that client, rather than under a contract between your company and the client, then the rules will apply to you wherever your company is incorporated or resident.

**Can I avoid the legislation by using an offshore service company?**

No. If you would have been liable to UK tax and NICs if you had been employed directly by the client, there will be a liability for UK tax and NICs under the new legislation, whether or not your service company is located in the UK.

If an offshore service company fails to deduct and account for PAYE tax and NICs due under the legislation, liability to pay tax and NICs can be transferred to the worker. Action to recover employer's NICs not paid by an offshore service company could also include action against any assets of that company located in the UK.

The Inland Revenue has powers to obtain details of payments to offshore companies from the records of clients and agencies.

### COMPUTATIONAL QUESTIONS

**When will the first 'deemed' payments have to be calculated?**

For an ongoing business it is likely that the first deemed payments will have to be calculated by 5 April 2001.

If a business ceases before that date a deemed payment may need to be calculated sooner.

**Does the service company have to pay a salary on 5 April?**

No. The legislation will not force the service company to pay salary at any time. It will require a calculation of tax and NICs to be done on 5 April. If the service company has already paid enough salary to the worker during the year, no further tax or NICs will be payable on 5 April.

Nothing in the legislation will prevent a service company from paying money to the worker or others in the form of dividends, or retaining cash in the company. It will simply mean that an extra payment of PAYE tax and NICs will be calculated on 5 April. To calculate that payment an amount of salary will be deemed to have been paid on that date, whether or not any payment is actually made.

*Inland Revenue Tax Bulletins*

**What happens if I cannot calculate the tax and NICs due on 5 April in time to pay it to the Inland Revenue by the normal date of 19 April?**

Most of the information needed to calculate the deemed payment should be available before 5 April, and it should be possible to make a good estimate of the tax and NICs due at that point. It will be important to keep records of relevant income and expenditure so that you can do this.

If you are not able to calculate the amount of tax and NICs due on the deemed payment by 19 April, we will accept a payment at that date of a lower amount on account of the tax and NICs due, as long as the Revenue is notified on the Employer's Annual Return that the amount is provisional. This should mean that the worker need not necessarily consult his accountant before making the payment on 19 April.

You should submit your Employer's Annual Return (Form P35) by 19 May. If you are able at that time to finalise the calculation, you should show the correct figure and pay the difference or request a repayment. Otherwise, you should make it clear that the figure is still provisional.

You should seek to finalise matters as soon as possible thereafter, and send in a supplementary return with a final payment, or request for repayment.

Interest will be charged, calculated from 19 April when the original payment was due, but no penalties will be sought for late filing if:

(i) an Employer's Annual Return is received by 19 May, showing remuneration paid during the year, plus an amount on account of the deemed payment, with tax and NICs correctly calculated on the aggregate figure, and,

(ii) a supplementary return including the correct final figure for the deemed payment is sent in to the Revenue by 31 January following the end of the tax year.

**What is the position where, in addition to making payments to the limited company/agency, a client makes payments to or in respect of the consultant direct? For example, where the client reimburses travelling expenses to the consultant direct? Could the client be held liable for PAYE?**

If a client makes payments to a worker in connection with duties being performed, either for direct reward, as a round sum expense allowance, or a specific reimbursement of travel which was not business travel, and the worker is an employee of another, the payments are assessable on the worker and the client should deduct tax through PAYE from payments to the worker. If a client provides non-cash benefits in connection with the employment these are also assessable on the worker. If the client makes payments of this kind to a worker in respect of a contract with a partnership, the client will not have to operate PAYE, but the amounts should be included in the calculation of the deemed payment.

# Inland Revenue Tax Bulletins

## QUESTIONS ABOUT EXPENSES

**Will travel expenses be allowed?**

The rules that currently apply to employees of service companies which allow them to claim a deduction for travel from their home to place of work will be used to determine the travel expenses that can be deducted in calculating the salary on which tax and NICs must be paid. For example:

- a computer contractor provides his or her services through a limited company (which he or she owns);
- he or she has a series of contracts with different clients around the country;
- he or she regularly travels from home to work at the premises of the company's clients.

Provided the contractor does not expect to spend more than 40% of his or her working time at any one site he or she is entitled to a deduction for all journeys from home to the client's premises. If he or she does spend more than 40% of his time at a single site, but the engagement is both expected to, and actually does, last for no more than 2 years, a deduction for travel costs will also be available. The examples set out in Tax Bulletin Issue 33 (February 1998), along with the more extensive coverage provided in Booklet 490 (Employee Travel, A Tax and NIC's Guide for Employers), provide further guidance on the application of the travel rules.

Workers cannot obtain relief for their travel and subsistence where the period at the temporary workplace comprises 'all or almost all of the period for which the employee is likely to hold the employment'. There have been concerns that this rule will be used to prevent the personal service company worker obtaining tax relief. However, the 'employment' of the worker is with his or her Personal Service Company, not with the client; the new rules do not change this. They simply deem the income from relevant engagements to be taxable under Schedule E; they do not deem the worker to be an employee of the client.

Thus the 'period for which the worker is likely to hold the employment' refers to employment with the service company, not the engagement with the client. Thus the treatment of travel and subsistence for workers will be no different under the new rules than it is today.

*We are grateful to Anne Redston of the CIOT for suggesting amendments to this answer to make it clearer.*

**How will company car expenses be treated?**

In calculating the deemed payment on which PAYE tax and NICs must be paid, expenses which would be allowable under Section 198 ICTA 1988 can be deducted. This will include travelling expenses, and if a car owned by the company is used for business travel then a deduction can be made for the costs of that business travel in the same way as if the worker had used his own car. For example, it would be possible to use the Inland Revenue's authorised mileage rates, which include an element for depreciation. Expenses incurred in the course of private use of the car cannot be deducted in calculating the deemed payment.

A car provided by the service company for the worker's private use will give rise to a car benefit charge on which the worker will be taxed in the normal way. The amount of the car benefit charge can be deducted in calculating the deemed payment.

The service company will be able to set any costs of providing the car, including capital allowances, against its taxable profits.

Class 1A NICs paid on the company car benefit will be deductible in the calculation of the deemed payment, alongside other employer's NICs.

**What sort of capital allowances can be deducted when working out the deemed payment?**

A deduction will only be given for capital allowances in working out the deemed payment where the plant or machinery is necessarily provided for use in the performance of the duties of the relevant engagement. This is a strict test and means that relief will only be given where the duties of the engagement meant that the company had to provide the equipment in question. If the company purchases the equipment out of choice then no deduction will be given. For example, where an IT contractor is required to use the client's computer equipment then no relief will be due for expenditure on computers owned by the service company. Neither will any relief be due where the client makes all the equipment necessary to do a job available but the worker uses his or her own computers, out of choice.

Where cars are concerned the test is less rigorous since there is no 'necessarily' test. As an alternative to claiming capital allowances relief will be given using the Inland Revenue Authorised Mileage Rates.

Where during the tax year there is mixed qualifying and non-qualifying use then any capital allowance claim should be apportioned on a just and reasonable basis. Apportionment is normally by reference to the actual use in the year. Non-qualifying use would be where the asset in question is used for private use, on contracts not covered by the IR35 rules and on IR35 contracts where the Schedule E rules are not satisfied.

**How do I apportion expenses between engagements that are affected by the new rules and those which are not?**

Where an engagement falls within the new rules the proposed legislation will allow for two types of deduction to be made in calculating the salary on which tax and NICs must be paid.

First, a deduction may be given for expenses paid by the service company which you would have been allowed to claim, under the normal Schedule E rules, had you paid them as part of an employment. These are, broadly, certain travel expenses, other expenses wholly, exclusively and necessarily incurred in the performance of the duties of the relevant engagement; and certain specific items such as some professional subscriptions and premiums for professional indemnity

## Inland Revenue Tax Bulletins

insurance. You will need to keep records to identify expenses which qualify. More details are in Inland Revenue booklets 480 (Expenses and Benefits, Guide Tax Guide) and 490 (Employee Travel, A Tax and NIC's Guide for Employers).

Secondly, the company will also be allowed to deduct a flat rate amount of 5% of receipts from relevant engagements, in calculating the minimum salary on which tax and NICs must be paid. This will be allowed automatically, and need not be set against specific expenses.

**How do I apportion the expenses when working out the deemed payment where a contract straddles the end of the tax year?**

When working out the deemed payment, relief should be given for all allowable expenses met by the intermediary in the tax year, in respect of relevant engagements, as set out at Step 3. Relief for the expense should be given by reference to the date when the intermediary **meets** the liability. This is the date when the bill is paid. There should therefore be no need to apportion any expenses.

For example, an intermediary has a relevant engagement that runs from 1 January to 30 June 2001, during which the worker is required to work at a temporary workplace. In the course of this engagement the worker stays in bed and breakfast accommodation. The bill is settled on a monthly basis in arrears, with 14 days to pay. At the end of March a bill for £400 is issued which the intermediary pays on 12 April. The liability was met in the tax year 2001–2002. Therefore, relief for the expense will be given when working out the deemed payment payable.

**Service company workers will be worse off than ordinary employees under the legislation because they will only be able to claim 5% of their expenses.**

This is not correct. Service companies will be able to claim a flat rate deduction of 5% of the gross fees receivable for any relevant engagements. This 5% deduction is not available to employees but will be allowed for service companies to enable them to meet the additional costs of providing their services in this particular way.

In calculating the salary on which they are obliged to deduct Schedule E tax and NICs, workers will also be able to deduct all expenses that would normally be available to direct employees.

**What sort of expenses will be covered by the 5%?**

There is no restriction on the use of the allowance. There will be no requirement to demonstrate expenditure: the 5% deduction will be allowed in all cases.

*Inland Revenue Tax Bulletins*

## EXAMPLE CALCULATION

**What tax and NICs liabilities arise (tax year 2000–01)?**

*Mr and Mrs A work through a service company in which they own all the shares. They each carry out some engagements during the year which fall within the new rules ('relevant engagements') and some which do not.*

Assume the service company receives £20,000 in respect of relevant engagements for Mr A and £40,000 in respect of relevant engagements for Mrs A and that there is a further £40,000 income from other business activities which do not fall within the new rules.

Assume the service company also incurs the following expenses during the course of the year:

| Expense | Mr A | Mrs A | Notes |
|---|---|---|---|
| Salaries | £20,000 | £20,000 | Paid in year. PAYE and NICs deducted and accounted for under normal provisions. |
| Employer's NICs | £1,905 | £1,905 | Paid in year. NICs calculated on an annual earnings period, as for directors. Assumes that the employer's threshold (£4,385) has been set against these earnings, and 12.2% paid on remainder. |
| Employer's pension contributions | £4,000 | £4,000 | To an approved scheme. |
| Travel costs related to relevant engagements | £2,000 | £500 | All would be deductible under normal provisions relating to employees. |
| Other expenses | £10,000 business expenses, all allowable for Corporation Tax purposes. | | |

Under the new proposals, at the end of the tax year, the service company will have to calculate the amount of PAYE and NICs due on Mr and Mrs A's earnings. If they have not paid enough PAYE and NICs during the year, then PAYE and NICs will be payable on a 'deemed payment' on the last day of the tax year.

# Inland Revenue Tax Bulletins

**Calculation of deemed payment**

|  | Mr A | Mrs A |
|---|---|---|
| Income from relevant contracts | 20,000 | 40,000 |
| *Less* | | |
| Expenses | 2,000 | 500 |
| Employer's NICs paid in year | 1,905 | 1,905 |
| Pension contributions | 4,000 | 4,000 |
| Flat rate 5% of gross relevant contract income for general running expenses of intermediary | 1,000 | 2,000 |
| | 11,095 | 31,595 |
| *Deduct* | | |
| Salary paid in year | 20,000 | 20,000 |
| | No deemed payment | 11,595 |
| Employer's NICs on deemed payment | | 1,261 |
| **Deemed payment** | | **10,334** |

**Company accounts**

| | | |
|---|---|---|
| Turnover | | 100,000 |
| *Less* | | |
| Salaries | 40,000 | |
| Employer's NICs on salaries | 3,810 | |
| Pension contributions | 8,000 | |
| Expenses | 12,500 | |
| | | 64,310 |
| Accounting Profit | | 35,690 |
| Deemed Payment | 10,334 | |
| Employer's NICs on dp | 1,261 | |
| | | 11,595 |
| Profits for Corporation Tax purposes | | 24,095 |

**Summary**

**Mr A** brought in £20,000 from relevant contracts during the course of the year. The service company paid the whole of that amount on to him in salary and deducted and accounted for full PAYE and NICs. No further action is required.

**Mrs A** brought in £40,000 from relevant contracts during the course of the year and the service company paid £20,000 on to her in salary and deducted and accounted for PAYE and NICs on that salary. This left £20,000 from her relevant contracts on which PAYE and NICs were not been deducted and accounted for during the course of the year. Under the new rules this £20,000, less the deductions allowed, will be deemed to be paid to Mrs A as salary at the year end (on 5 April). (See Chapter 5.)

*Appendix 2*

# A Modern System for Corporation Tax Payments: Group Payment Arrangements

Section 36 Finance Act (FA) 1998 allows the Inland Revenue to make Group Payment Arrangements with groups of companies. The Arrangement Document enclosed with these notes sets out the form of these arrangements. These notes are designed to help you understand that document and to explain how we will administer the arrangements. Joining a Group Payment Arrangement is optional. It will be up to each group of companies to decide what is right for them and whether they want to be part of an arrangement. **The terms of the Group Payment Arrangement are non-negotiable.**

**ADMINISTRATIVE NOTES**

Group Payment Arrangements will help groups with the switch to payment of tax by instalments, under the Corporation Tax (Instalment Payments) Regulations 1998 (SI 1998/3175). The arrangements will allow
- the group to manage any uncertainty over corporation tax (CT) liabilities of individual companies between the instalment due dates and the filing of the tax returns
- the group to nominate one company to pay each instalment in one amount on behalf of companies in a group
- the nominated company to allocate the benefit of those payments between the members of the group retrospectively, so mitigating any potential differential interest charge.

It is important to remember that Group Payment Arrangements do not alter the fact that each company is liable for its own corporation tax. Group Payment Arrangements merely allow a nominated company to pay corporation tax for members of the same group.

We will be prepared to enter into a Group Payment Arrangement with you in relation to accounting periods ending on or after 31 December 1999 if the following conditions are met
- you return the completed and signed Arrangement Document to us at least two months before the first instalment payment is due for accounting periods to be covered by the Group Payment Arrangement
- all the proposed Participating Companies are up to date with their filing and payment obligations at that time

# A Modern System for Corporation Tax Payments

- the 51% group relationship required by section 36 FA 1998 exists at the time the Arrangement Document is signed. If this condition proves later not to have been met in respect of one or more of the Participating Companies, such companies will be removed from the arrangement.

**What you need to do**

If you decide to enter into a Group Payment Arrangement with us, you must return the completed and signed Arrangement Document to the Group Payment Team at the Accounts Office to which the Nominated Company makes its tax payments. Please check that you have provided all the relevant information by making appropriate entries in the Arrangement Document where indicated. **DO NOT COMPLETE THE DATE ON PAGE ONE. WE WILL FILL THIS IN**.

| | |
|---|---|
| Group Payment Team | Group Payment Team |
| Accounts Office Cumbernauld | Accounts Office Shipley |
| St Mungo's Road | Victoria Street |
| Cumbernauld | Shipley |
| Glasgow | West Yorkshire |
| G70 5TR | BD98 8AA |
| Telephone: 01236 783488 | Telephone: 01274 539561 |
| Fax: 01236 783387 | Fax: 01274 539669 |

**The completed Arrangement Document *must* reach the Group Payment Team no later than two months *before* the first instalment payment for the group is due.** We cannot guarantee to enter into an arrangement if we do not receive the document by then.

The Group Payment Teams will be happy to help with any enquiries about Group Payment Arrangements. We will get in touch with you to confirm whether the group will be brought into the Group Payment Arrangements scheme. If so, we will also give you details of how to make payments under the arrangement.

**GUIDANCE NOTES**

These notes are intended to explain the content of the Arrangement Document and clarify some of the more complex Clauses. They are without prejudice to the document itself. They are for guidance only and you should carefully consider the Arrangement Document itself before deciding to proceed.

A group with an up-to-date returns and payment position will not normally have to concern itself with those provisions designed to help us recover tax in certain circumstances.

**Preamble**  Companies that enter into a Group Payment Arrangement will be entering into a contract with the Board of Inland Revenue.

We will proceed in good faith on the basis of the information you provide. But you should be aware that the contract may be void and the arrangement of no force if its conditions and pre-conditions are not met.

Please do not complete the date in the opening words of the contract. We will do this before we send it back to you.

**Clause 1**  This Clause defines some of the main terms used in the Arrangement Document.

'**Period of Account**' means the period for which the Nominated Company draws up its accounts.

## A Modern System for Corporation Tax Payments

A Group Payment Arrangement applies to a period or series of periods for which the Group (and specifically the nominated company) draws up its accounts. You must enter on the relevant page the start and end dates of the first period to which you want the arrangement to apply. The arrangement will then apply automatically to subsequent Periods of Account unless and until you tell us that you wish to terminate it under Clause 18, or we terminate it under Clause 19. So you should only need to apply to enter into a Group Payment Arrangement once. You do not have to apply to enter into a fresh arrangement each year.

**'Accounting Period'** has its statutory meaning.

**'Relevant Accounting Period'** means an accounting period of a Participating Company (defined below) in respect of which the liabilities are to be paid by the Nominated Company under the terms of the arrangement for a particular Period of Account.

Generally, the Participating Companies should all have accounting periods which are identical to the Period of Account. The "Relevant Accounting Periods" of all the Participating Companies will then all be the same, and identical to the Period of Account.

However, the Arrangement Document also allows a company in a group to take part in a Group Payment Arrangement if its accounting periods differ from the Period of Account under some circumstances. The liabilities for an accounting period of such a company can be included in an arrangement for a Period of Account if

- the accounting period starts within the Period of Account, and ends on the same day as the Nominated Company's accounts; or
- the accounting period starts on or after, but ends before the end of the Period of Account, and is followed by another (short) accounting period ending on the same day as the Period of Account.

This will allow newly-formed and newly-acquired companies to be included within a Group Payment Arrangement. It will also allow a company to remain within an arrangement if it proves to have more than one tax accounting period within a 12 month account due to the operation of Section 12(2) and (3) Income and Corporation Taxes Act 1988 (ICTA). This may happen, for example, where a company ceases to trade during the period covered by its accounts and becomes an investment company.

**'Group'** is defined in Section 36 FA 1998 as a company and all its 51 per cent subsidiaries, and their 51 per cent subsidiaries, and so on.

**'Nominated Company'** is the company which has entered into the arrangement on behalf of the other Participating Companies and has agreed to discharge their liabilities under the terms of the arrangement.

The Schedule to the Arrangement Document asks you to provide a contact point within the Nominated Company. We will direct all correspondence about the Group Payment Arrangement to that person.

The Nominated Company must be resident in the United Kingdom.

**'Participating Company'** means such companies in the group which

# A Modern System for Corporation Tax Payments

are subject to the arrangement. That can be all the companies meeting the conditions outlined above, or any sub-set of them which you choose. You can set up separate Group Payment Arrangements for different sub-sets of the group if you wish. But no one company can participate in more than one Group Payment Arrangement in respect of any one of its accounting periods.

You must list the companies you wish to be Participating Companies in the Schedule to the Arrangement Document. But note that the set of Participating Companies can change over time as companies join and leave the group. Clause 17 requires you to provide us with a list of the Participating Companies in relation to each Period of Account where there is a change from the previous Period of Account.

For every Period of Account covered by a Group Payment Arrangement, this Clause defines a **'Closing Date'**. This is the date at which the Nominated Company's liabilities are fixed, and after which it must tell us how to allocate the payments it has made to the individual Participating Companies. The Closing Date is the later of

- whichever filing date is the latest, out of all the filing dates of the Participating Companies for returns for Relevant Accounting Periods, and
- the day when we receive the last of those returns (or make a determination of tax in the absence of a return).

**Clause 2** This Clause outlines the payment obligations of the Nominated Company in respect of each Period of Account to which the arrangement applies.

The Nominated Company undertakes to pay the corporation tax liabilities of the Participating Companies for accounting periods falling within the Periods of Account covered by the arrangements (the Relevant Accounting Periods). It is up to the Nominated Company to determine how much to pay and when to make payments. We will NOT normally issue payment requests or reminders.

**'Liabilities'** means corporation tax and any liabilities under Section 419 and Section 747 ICTA (which relate to loans to participators in close companies, and controlled foreign companies, respectively).

Please indicate on the Schedule to the Arrangement Document the method you wish to use to make payments. We will then send you details of how to make payments when we confirm our agreement to enter into a Group Payment Arrangement with you.

**Clause 3** The Participating Companies' liabilities which are to be paid by the Nominated Company shall be determined by the Corporation Tax Acts and Regulations made under those Acts. They must be paid on the dates they become payable, or are treated as becoming due and payable, by the Participating Companies under those Acts and Regulations.

The amount payable by the Nominated Company in respect of each Relevant Accounting Period of the Participating Companies will not be affected by changes in their liability occurring after the Closing Date.

So adjustments made to the liability of an individual Participating Company (for example, in respect of interest or penalties, or as a result of an enquiry into the company's return) will be the responsi-

## A Modern System for Corporation Tax Payments

bility of the individual Participating Company, not the Nominated Company.

**Clause 4**  The Nominated Company can claim a repayment, on the lines of a claim under Regulation 6 of SI 3175 1998. It can do this if it has reason to believe that, due to a change in circumstances
- its liability under the arrangement in respect of a Relevant Accounting Period is likely to be less than previously calculated, and
- the amount(s) which it has paid exceed(s) the amount(s) due and payable under the arrangement at that point in time.

This might be the case where, for example, the forecast of profits at group level has fallen as a result of the unexpected loss of business to a new competitor, or where a particularly profitable company has been sold out of the group during the Relevant Accounting Period. The Nominated Company should give notice in writing to the Group Payment Team before the Closing Date, claiming repayment and explaining the grounds for the claim. It must also specify which payment(s) (or part(s) thereof), it wishes to have repaid. Please note that interest will not be added to any repayment at this point, but will be payable after the Closing Date.

We are not obliged to repay on a claim, but will do so unless we are dissatisfied with the grounds for the claim. We will usually repay the amount claimed to the Nominated Company, unless we conclude that only a smaller repayment is justified. We must specify which payment(s) or part payment(s) are being repaid, as this affects the calculation of interest later.

**Clause 5**  We will not take any steps, before the Closing Date, to recover liabilities from the Participating Companies for Relevant Accounting Periods. But our right of recovery is not otherwise affected.

This means that we have the right to recover outstanding liabilities from the individual Participating Companies, but only **after** the Closing Date.

**Clause 6**  After the Closing Date, we will send you a notice of our calculation of the amount the Nominated Company should have paid under the arrangement, and any balance outstanding or overpaid. We will work this out by comparing the aggregate amount paid by the Nominated Company with what was due by reference to the Participating Companies' returns and any determinations we have made.

Our calculation will be final and conclusive, and binding on the nominated company. (But should we make a mistake in our calculation please draw it to our attention, and we will amend it to reflect the correct position.)

**Clause 7**  You can ask us to repay any overpayment shown on the notice under Clause 6, up to the earlier of
- 30 days from the date that notice is given, or
- the date the Nominated Company gives notice under clause 8.1 of the way it would like the amount paid to be apportioned between the Participating Companies.

Otherwise, the overpayment will form part of the amount to be apportioned or reapportioned under Clauses 8 to 12.

If you ask for a repayment, you will have to specify which payment(s), or part payment(s), you want us to repay and we will

## A Modern System for Corporation Tax Payments

confirm what we actually repay, as this will affect the calculation of interest.

**Clause 8** In response to our notice under Clause 6, the Nominated Company can irrevocably specify how payments made under the agreement should be apportioned amongst the Participating Companies. Payments to be apportioned will be net of any repayments made under Clause 4.2, and of any other apportionments already made (for example to a departing company).

You must send a written notice of this apportionment to the Group Payment Team. You should do this within 30 days of our notice under Clause 6.

**Clause 9** If you fail to make the apportionment under Clause 8, we will make an apportionment instead. We will do so in accordance with the liabilities of the Participating Companies as shown on their returns, to the extent that the aggregate amount paid is enough to cover those liabilities. Where this is necessary, we will give notice in writing to the Nominated Company of the apportionment we make.

The purpose of this Clause is to ensure that matters move ahead after the Closing Date and that we can begin the process of finalising liabilities with individual companies. But it is there only to cover the exceptional case where a group fails to make its wishes clear to us. The Nominated Company has the right to amend our apportionment if it does so within 30 days from the date we give notice under this Clause.

**Clause 10** This Clause allows us to reapportion payments among the Participating Companies if the liabilities of one or more of them remains outstanding after the Nominated Company's apportionment under Clause 8. The Nominated Company cannot amend such a reapportionment.

We will do this only if the Nominated Company's apportionment leaves an underpayment on the account of a Participating Company **and** we cannot recover the shortfall from that company.

In these circumstances we would have the right to terminate the arrangement under Clause 19. But given the serious consequences for the group of termination, we may choose to take this lesser step instead.

We will not reapportion payments in this way where a Nominated Company allocates a shortfall to a company whose liability is expected to fall after the Closing Date and that liability (whether reduced as expected, or not) is paid.

**Clause 11** Payments made by the Nominated Company on behalf of the Participating Companies are deemed to have been made by those companies in the amounts finally apportioned to them, and on the dates they were made by the Nominated Company.

This Clause establishes the interest position for each of the Participating Companies. Interest will be charged and/or paid accordingly.

The word 'finally' is there to indicate that, in cases where we

## *A Modern System for Corporation Tax Payments*

reapportion payments, it is our final apportionment that determines what a company is deemed to have paid.

**Clause 12**  This Clause establishes a different basis for deeming payments to have been apportioned where one or more of the Participating Companies is liable to a tax-related penalty under Paragraph 18 of Schedule 18 to the Finance Act 1998. This deemed apportionment applies for the purpose of calculating any penalties under that provision, but no other. It does not affect interest calculations.

Payments will be deemed to be apportioned (to the extent they have not been repaid) to the Participating Companies in the following order

(1) to those which have not incurred a late-filing penalty, or have only incurred a fixed-rate penalty

(2) to those which have incurred a tax-related penalty at the lower rate of 10%

(3) to those which have incurred a tax-related penalty at the higher rate of 20%, either by failing to file a return, or by filing it more than two years after the end of the period for which it is required.

Clause 12.2. provides that where more than one of the Participating Companies falls within the second or third category numbered above, the Board will have the right to apportion payments to individual companies falling within the same category.

The purpose of Clause 12 is to ensure that a company that has filed its return late, and is therefore liable to a tax-related penalty, cannot have the amount of that penalty reduced as a result of the Nominated Company's apportionment.

**Clause 13**  The Nominated Company must remove from the Group Payment Arrangement any Participating Company, other than the Nominated Company (see the note on Clause 22 below) which ceases to be a member of the group, or which does not have an accounting period which ends on the same day as the Period of Account. The Nominated Company must notify the Group Payment Team in writing that it is removing such a company as soon as it is aware of its changed circumstances and must provide the list required under Clause 17.

We can remove a company from the arrangement if it turns out never to have been a member of the group, or if the Nominated Company fails to fulfil its obligation to do so. We can exercise this right at any time up to six months after the Closing Date and must notify the Nominated Company of it in writing.

**Clause 14**  Removal of a company from a Group Payment Arrangement under Clause 13 has the following effects

1. The Nominated Company ceases to have any obligations under the arrangement for the liabilities of the departing company in respect of the accounting period in which it is removed from the group.

## *A Modern System for Corporation Tax Payments*

2. We can recover such liabilities direct from the departing company.

3. The Nominated Company may apportion payments to the departing company, either at the same time as it makes its apportionment under Clause 8.1, or before then. Such payments must not previously have been apportioned, or repaid. The Nominated Company must specify which payment(s) or part payment(s) are being apportioned to the departing company. This will affect the calculation of interest. Where we remove a company after apportionments have been made, the Nominated Company will be allowed to reapportion payments if it does so within 30 days of our notice of removal.

Removal of a company from the arrangement does not affect the arrangement, or the obligations and rights of the other parties to the arrangement, except as specified above.

The purpose of Clauses 13 and 14 is to remove the Nominated Company's liability for payments for the Relevant Accounting Period in respect of a company which no longer has an accounting period coterminous with that of the Nominated Company, which is no longer a member of the group, or was never a member of the group. The Nominated Company will be able to apportion payments to such a company if it so chooses. If the Nominated Company does so before the Closing Date, such payments will not be taken into account for the purposes of the Board's apportionments under Clauses 9, 10 and 20.

**Clause 15** Companies may leave an existing Group Payment Arrangement, by agreement in writing between the Group Payment Team and the Nominated Company. If a company leaves the arrangement, the Nominated Company ceases to have any obligations under the arrangement for the liabilities of the departing company in respect of accounting periods for which the first instalment payment has not yet fallen due (or is treated as falling due if the company is not a large company for the purposes of SI 1998/3175).

Removal of a company from the arrangement does not affect the arrangement, or the obligations and rights of the other parties to the arrangement, except as specified above.

**Clause 16** Companies may join an existing Group Payment Arrangement, by agreement in writing between the Group Payment Team and the Nominated Company, up to the date when the first instalment payment is due under the arrangement for a Relevant Accounting Period of the Period of Account (or is treated as falling due if the company is not a large company for the purposes of SI 1998/3175).

The Nominated Company must then provide the list required under Clause 17.

Companies joining the arrangements must also make up their accounts to the same date as the Nominated Company. If they have an accounting period which ends during the Period of Account, they must make up their next accounts to the same date as the nominated company.

**Clause 17** When a company joins or leaves the Group Payment Arrangement during a period of account, the Nominated Company must provide the Group Payment Team with a list of Participating Companies. The Nominated Company must also tell the Group Payment Team

## A Modern System for Corporation Tax Payments

when it intends to draw up its accounts to a date other than a date to which it drew them up in the previous calendar year.

**Clause 18** This is a standard mutual termination clause which allows either party to terminate the Group Payment Arrangement at any time by giving written notice to that effect to the other party. Where this happens, the rights and obligations under the arrangement will be terminated in respect of Periods of Account for which the first instalment payment has not yet fallen due (or is treated as having fallen due if the company is not a large company for the purposes of SI 1998/3175).

Clause 19, below, gives the main reasons for which we would terminate the contract in a particular case. Clause 18 provides for other circumstances, for example, where there was a need to change or amend the terms of the contract itself.

**Clause 19** This Clause describes specific circumstances where we can terminate a Group Payment Arrangement. They are if
- any of the Participating Companies fails to meet its obligations to pay corporation tax and file its company tax return for any accounting period
- the Nominated Company breaks any of its obligations under the arrangement
- we have reason to believe that any member of the group of companies (including those not covered by the same or any Group Payment Arrangement) may become liable to tax under Sections 767A or 767AA ICTA.

This gives us the right to terminate the arrangement in a wide range of circumstances. In practice we will terminate an arrangement under this Clause in cases where there has been a serious failure or breach or a pattern of non-compliance, not for minor matters.

If a group has an arrangement terminated, it will not be entitled to register for a new arrangement for the next Period of Account. So termination has serious consequences. That is why alternative methods of recovering tax in certain circumstances, short of terminating the arrangement, are provided for in the Arrangement Document.

**Clause 20** This Clause describes the consequences of termination, and sets out the provisions of the arrangement which survive termination. These are as follows in respect of payments made that have not been repaid or apportioned (including to a company that has departed from the arrangement)
(a) the Nominated Company has the right to apportion the payments, provided it does so within 30 days of our notice of termination under Clause 19
(b) if the Nominated Company fails to exercise that right, we have 60 days from giving notice under Clause 19, to nominate another Participating company to exercise the right of apportionment under this Clause. Such a company will have 30 days from the notice of nomination to do so
(c) if payments still remain unapportioned (including as a result of the Board not nominating an alternative company) we will apportion the payments to the Participating Companies. We will give written notice to the Nominated Company of the apportionments

*Group Payment Arrangement*

(d) we have the right to reapportion payments (even where they have been apportioned by the Nominated Company or another company nominated by us for these purposes). We will give written notice of such reapportionments to the Nominated Company. Neither the Nominated Company nor the Participating Companies will have the right to amend such reapportionments, nor to amend an apportionment under (c) above.

The provisions of Clause 10.2 apply to our power of reapportionment under Clause 20.3 (d), except that the relevant date is not the Closing Date, but the date notice is given under Clause 19.

The provisions of Clause 12 (which set out rules of apportionment for the purposes of calculating a tax-related penalty) also apply to apportionments under Clause 20.

We must consider any claim under Clause 4.2 if the claim is made prior to notice being given under Clause 19. So any claim to a repayment on grounds that Clause 4.1 applies must be considered, provided it is made before the date of notice of termination.

**Clause 21** Payment under a Group Payment Arrangement must be by electronic funds transfer or bank giro credit, not by cheque. Please indicate on the Schedule to the Arrangement Document whether you intend to pay by BACS, CHAPS or bank giro credit (BGC).

**Clause 22** By agreement between the Participating Companies and the Group Payment Team, another Participating Company may become the Nominated Company in place of the original Nominated Company, or any successor Nominated Company.

This gives the group some flexibility that could be needed if, for example, the Period of Account of the Nominated Company changes from that of the rest of the group, or the Nominated Company leaves the group. Without it a new arrangement would have to be entered into.

**Clause 23** The arrangement will be governed and construed in accordance with English Law.

## Standard Contract and Application for Group Payment Arrangement

This Arrangement ('the Arrangement') is made the       day of between (1) the Commissioners of Inland Revenue of Somerset House Strand London WC2R 1LB ('the Board') and (2) the companies named in the attached Schedule ('the Schedule').

WHEREAS
A. The Nominated Company has informed the Board that the companies named in the Schedule are some or all of the members of the [          ] Group of Companies being a group of companies within the meaning of section 36(4) of the Finance Act 1998.
B. The Board and the companies named in the Schedule wish to enter into an arrangement under section 36 of the Finance Act 1998, whereby the Nominated Company shall discharge the Liabilities of the Participating Companies.

*Group Payment Arrangement*

NOW IT IS HEREBY AGREED AS FOLLOWS:

**INTERPRETATION**

**1** (1)    In the Arrangement–
'the Closing Date' – means, in respect of a Period of Account, whichever is the later of–
(a)    the latest filing date of any of the Participating Companies for a company tax return for a Relevant Accounting Period, and
(b)    the earliest date on which all of the Participating Companies have either submitted company tax returns for every Relevant Accounting Period or, in the absence of a such a return, have had their tax determined by the Board under paragraphs 36 to 39 of Schedule 18 of that accounting period;
'filing date' in respect of a company tax return has the meaning given by paragraph 14 of Schedule 18;
'Liabilities' – means the liabilities of the Participating Companies to the tax calculated as mentioned in paragraph 8(1) of Schedule 18 that are due and payable under section 59D(1) of the Taxes Management Act 1970 or, as the case may be, are payable or treated as becoming due and payable by those companies under regulation 4 and regulation 5 (as applicable) of the Corporation Tax (Instalment Payments) Regulations 1998 (SI 1998/3175);
'the [          ] Group of Companies' – means the group of which the Nominated Company is a member, designated by that or any other name;
'the Nominated Company' – means [          ] Company (designated by that or any other name) which is resident in the United Kingdom and has entered into the Arrangement on behalf of itself and the other Participating Companies, and any other Participating Company which the Participating Companies and the Board have agreed shall be the Nominated Company pursuant to Clause 22 of the Arrangement;
'the Participating Companies' means all such companies in the [          ] Group of Companies, including the Nominated Company and the other companies named in the Schedule, as from time to time are subject to the Arrangement; and 'Participating Company' means any such company;
'Period of Account' means any period not exceeding 12 months for which the Nominated Company draws up its accounts, commencing with the period starting on [          ] and ending on [          ];
'Relevant Accounting Period' means –
(a)    an accounting period of a Participating Company which is coextensive with a Period of Account, or
(b)    an accounting period of a Participating Company which, while not coextensive with a Period of Account, falls wholly within and is coterminous with that Period of Account, or
(c)    an accounting period of a Participating Company which falls wholly within, but ends before the end of, a Period of Account and is followed by an accounting period of the Participating Company that is coterminous with that Period of Account;
'Schedule 18' means Schedule 18 to the Finance Act 1998.
(2)    Unless the context otherwise requires, in the Arrangement the singular shall import the plural, and vice versa.

*Group Payment Arrangement*

## PAYMENT OBLIGATIONS OF THE NOMINATED COMPANY IN RELATION TO A PERIOD OF ACCOUNT

**2** Subject to the following provisions of the Arrangement, the Nominated Company shall, in consideration of the obligations of the Board contained in the Arrangement, and the other rights given to the Nominated Company under the Arrangement, discharge Liabilities of the Participating Companies arising in respect of Relevant Accounting Periods attributable to any Period of Account, in the manner specified in clauses 3.1 and 3.2 below.

**3.1** Subject to Clause 3.2, the quantum of Liabilities to be discharged by the Nominated Company shall be determined by the Corporation Tax Acts and Regulations made under those Acts, and Liabilities shall be discharged by the Nominated Company on the dates they would, but for the Arrangement, have been discharged by the Participating Companies under the Corporation Tax Acts and Regulations made under those Acts.

**3.2** For the purpose of the Nominated Company's obligations under the Arrangement (but not otherwise), the quantum of Liabilities to be discharged in respect of Relevant Accounting Periods of the Participating Companies by the Nominated Company under the Arrangement shall be deemed not to be affected by any amendment to a self-assessment or any other matter (in relation to any of the Participating Companies) occurring after the Closing Date.

## CLAIMS FOR REPAYMENT OF EXCESS AMOUNTS BY REASON OF CHANGE OF CIRCUMSTANCES

**4.1** Clause 4.2 shall apply where the Nominated Company has made a payment or payments under the Arrangement in respect of Relevant Accounting Periods of the Participating Companies and subsequently has grounds for believing that by reason of a change of circumstances in any of the Participating Companies,

(a) the liabilities of the Nominated Company under the Arrangement in respect of those accounting periods is likely to be less than previously calculated, and

(b) the amount or amounts so paid exceed the Nominated Company's revised calculation of the total amount which would have been due and payable under the Arrangement in respect of those accounting periods before the date of the claim under Clause 4.2.

**4.2** The Nominated Company may, by notice in writing given to the Board prior to the Closing Date for that Period of Account, make a claim for repayment of what it considers to be the excess amount paid, such notice specifying the grounds referred to in Clause 4.1, and, where more than one payment has been made, specifying which payment or payments (or part thereof) the Nominated Company wishes to be repaid to it. The Board may repay to the Nominated Company part or all of the amount claimed by it and shall specify which payment or payments or part thereof are being so repaid.

**4.3** Where a repayment is made under Clause 4.2, section 826 of the Income and Corporation Taxes Act 1988, as modified by regulation 8 of the Corporation Tax (Instalment Payments) Regulations 1998, shall apply as if –

(a) the repayment was to a large company within the meaning of those Regulations,

*Group Payment Arrangement*

(b) the amount or amounts on which interest is due were the amount or amounts repaid, and
(c) any interest was not payable until after the Closing Date.

## LIMITATIONS ON THE BOARD'S RIGHT OF RECOVERY

**5** Subject to the following provisions of the Arrangement, the Board shall not take any steps prior to the Closing Date to recover Liabilities in respect of Relevant Accounting Periods from the Participating Companies, but the Board's right to recover Liabilities shall not be otherwise affected.

## CALCULATION OF MONIES PAYABLE UNDER THE ARRANGEMENT (OR CREDIT BALANCES)

**6** The Board shall, after the Closing Date, give notice in writing to the Nominated Company showing the Board's calculation of the balance of monies payable by the Nominated Company under the Arrangement in respect of Relevant Accounting Periods (or, alternatively, any credit balance in the case of overpayment). The balance of monies thus payable (or any credit balance) shall be calculated by setting the aggregate of Liabilities of the Participating Companies in respect of Relevant Accounting Periods as at the Closing Date, as shown on their self-assessments or determinations by the Board (as the case may be), against the aggregate of payments made by the Nominated Company under the Arrangement in respect of those periods. The Board's calculation shall (subject to amendment in the event of error on the part of the Board) be final and conclusive and binding on the Nominated Company.

**7.1** Any credit balance under Clause 6 above shall form part of the monies which may be apportioned or re-apportioned under the following provisions of the Arrangement, unless the Nominated Company requests repayment within thirty days from the date the Board gives notice under Clause 6, or by the date the Nominated Company gives notice under Clause 8.1 below (if earlier). The Nominated Company shall specify, when requesting repayment, which payment or payments or part thereof it wishes to be repaid to it, and the Board shall comply with such specification.

**7.2** Where a repayment is made under Clause 7.1, section 826 of the Income and Corporation Taxes Act 1988, as modified by regulation 8 of the Corporation Tax (Instalment Payments) Regulations 1998, shall apply as if –
(a) the repayment was to a large company within the meaning of those Regulations, the total liability of which was equal to the aggregate of Liabilities of the Participating Companies as determined under Clause 6, and
(b) the payments taken into account in calculating the repayment were payments in respect of that liability.

## APPORTIONMENT OF PAYMENTS

**8.1** Subject to clauses 10.1, 10.2, 12.1 and 12.2 below, the Nominated Company shall have the right, exercisable by giving notice in writing to the Board and in accordance with Clause 8.2, irrevocably to apportion payments made by

*Group Payment Arrangement*

the Nominated Company under the Arrangement, to the extent that they have not been repaid and have not already been apportioned, to any of the Participating Companies.

**8.2** The right of the Nominated Company specified in Clause 8.1 shall be contingent on the Board giving notice under Clause 6 above, and shall be exercisable at any time prior to the Board giving notice under Clause 9 below.

**9** Subject to clauses 12.1 and 12.2 below, to the extent that payments remain unapportioned after thirty days from the date the Board give notice under Clause 6 above, such payments shall be apportioned by the Board to any of the Participating Companies. The Board shall give notice in writing of such apportionments to the Nominated Company, which shall have the right, exercisable within a period of thirty days from the date the Board gives notice under this clause, to amend the Board's apportionments.

**10.1** Subject to clauses 10.2, 12.1, and 12.2 below, in circumstances where any Liabilities to be discharged by the Nominated Company under the Arrangement (as calculated in accordance with Clause 6 above) remain outstanding (either in whole or in part) the Board shall also have the right, as often as is necessary to discharge those Liabilities, to re-apportion any given payment or payments made by the Nominated Company (and apportioned by the Nominated Company under Clause 8.1 or by the Board under Clause 9 above) to any of the Participating Companies. The Board shall give notice in writing of such re-apportionments to the Nominated Company. Neither the Nominated Company nor any other Participating Company shall have power to amend such re-apportionments.

**10.2** For the purposes of the Board's power of re-apportionment (and the consequent discharge of Liabilities) specified above –

(a) to the extent that any Liabilities decrease after the Closing Date, such decrease shall be left out of account;

(b) payments made (by the Nominated Company or otherwise) after any apportionment shall not be apportioned under the Arrangement and shall be deemed to discharge any increase (or a proportionate part thereof if the payments are not sufficient to discharge the entire increase) in the liabilities of the company by whom or on whose behalf the payment is made, in priority to the balance of Liabilities under the Arrangement;

(c) Subject to sub-clause (a) of this Clause 10.2, the Board shall only re-apportion to the extent necessary to discharge Liabilities.

**11** Payments finally apportioned in accordance with clauses 8 to 10 above, and in accordance with sub-clause (c) of Clause 14.1, and sub-clauses (a)–(e) of Clause 20.3, shall be deemed for all purposes of the Corporation Tax Acts and Regulations made under those Acts (apart from paragraph 18 of Schedule 18) to have been made by the Participating Companies in the amounts so apportioned and on the dates such payments were made by the Nominated Company.

**12.1** For the purposes of the tax-related penalty specified in paragraph 18 of Schedule 18 (but not otherwise), payments made by the Nominated Company under the Arrangement in respect of Relevant Accounting Periods, to the extent they have not been repaid and have not already been apportioned under Clause 14(c) below, shall be deemed to be apportioned at the expiry of the time limit specified in sub-paragraph (2)(a) of the said paragraph 18, to the Participating Companies in the following order (such deemed apportionment not being contingent on the Board giving notice under Clause 6 above) –

(a) to such of the Participating Companies as shall have delivered a company

*Group Payment Arrangement*

tax return within the time limits specified in sub-paragraph (1) of the said paragraph 18;
(b) to such of the Participating Companies as shall have delivered a company tax return within the time limit specified in sub-paragraph (2)(a) of the said paragraph 18;
(c) to such of the Participating Companies as either shall have failed to deliver a company tax return or shall have done so outside the time limit specified in sub-paragraph (2)(a) of the said paragraph 18.

**12.2** Where there is more than one Participating Company falling within either or both of sub-clauses (b) and (c) of Clause 12.1 the Board shall have the right, for the purpose of Clause 12.1, to apportion payments to any individual companies falling within the same category.

## REMOVAL OF COMPANIES FROM THE ARRANGEMENT OTHERWISE THAN BY AGREEMENT

**13.1** The Nominated Company shall immediately remove any of the Participating Companies (other than the Nominated Company) from the Arrangement, by giving notice in writing to that effect to the Board, if such company has ceased to be a member of the [               ] Group of Companies or if, with respect to a Period of Account, it has no Relevant Accounting Period.

**13.2** The Board shall have the right, exercisable at any time prior to the expiry of six months from the Closing Date, to remove any of the Participating Companies (other than the Nominated Company) from the Arrangement, by giving notice in writing to that effect to the Nominated Company if the Board have reason to believe that such company was not a member of the [               ] Group of Companies at the date it became subject to the Arrangement, or if the Board consider that the Nominated Company should have removed such company from the Arrangement under Clause 13.1.

**14** Removal of any of the Participating Companies from the Arrangement under Clause 13.1 and 13.2 above shall have the following effects –
(a) the obligations of the Nominated Company under the Arrangement shall no longer extend to Liabilities of any such company in respect of any accounting period ending after the date on which notice of removal of such company is given to the Board under Clause 13.1 or by the Board under Clause 13.2;
(b) the restriction on the Board's rights under Clause 5 above to recover the Liabilities referred to in paragraph (a) above shall no longer apply;
(c) the Nominated Company may, by giving notice in writing to the Board when or before giving notice in writing in respect of an Accounting Period under Clause 8.1 above, but not later than the date on which the relevant return is filed or determination is made, if earlier, apportion payments made by the Nominated Company under the Arrangement, to the extent they have not been repaid, and have not already been apportioned, to such company;
(d) where the Nominated Company has apportioned payments to such company under Clause 8.1 above prior to the removal by the Board of such company from the Arrangement under Clause 13.2, the Nominated Company may, within thirty days of the date of notice by the Board under

*Group Payment Arrangement*

Clause 13.2, re-apportion such payments to any of the Participating Companies.

## REMOVAL OF COMPANIES FROM THE ARRANGEMENT BY AGREEMENT

**15.1** Subject to Clause 15.2, by agreement in writing between the Board and the Nominated Company, any of the Participating Companies may be removed from the Arrangement.

**15.2** As regards any company removed from the Arrangement under Clause 15.1, the effect of such agreement shall be to terminate the rights and obligations (in relation to such company) of the parties to the Arrangement in respect of any accounting period of such company for which the date of the first instalment of corporation tax (treated as becoming due and payable by such company under Regulation 4 and Regulation 5 (as applicable) of the Corporation Tax (Instalment Payments) Regulations 1998) falls after the date of the agreement referred to in Clause 15.1, or would fall after the date of that agreement if the company were a large company within the meaning of those Regulations.

**15.3** Apart from Clause 14 above and this clause, the obligations and rights of the parties to the Arrangement shall be unaffected by removal of any of the Participating Companies from the Arrangement and, subject to any provisions of the Arrangement and of the Corporation Tax Acts and Regulations made under those Acts to the contrary, any acts done or deemed to be done under the Arrangement shall be unaffected.

## ADDITION OF COMPANIES TO THE ARRANGEMENT

**16.1** Subject to Clause 16.2, by agreement in writing between the Board and Nominated Company, further companies in the [          ] Group of Companies may become subject to the Arrangement.

**16.2** As regards a company becoming subject to the Arrangement under Clause 16.1, such agreement shall be effective in relation to any Relevant Accounting Period of that company if made before the date on which the first instalment of corporation tax is treated as becoming due and payable by such company for that period under Regulation 4 and Regulation 5 (as applicable) of the Corporation Tax (Instalment Payments) Regulations 1998, or would be treated as becoming due and payable if the company were a large company within the meaning of those Regulations.

## PROVISION OF LIST OF PARTICIPATING COMPANIES AND NOTIFICATION OF INTENDED CHANGE OF PERIOD OF ACCOUNT

**17.1** Where during a Period of Account a company or companies have become subject to the Arrangement and/or have been removed from the Arrangement, the Nominated Company shall provide the Board with a list of the Participating Companies in relation to that Period of Account.

**17.2** The Nominated Company shall notify the Board in writing of any intention to draw up accounts to a date other than a date to which it drew up accounts in the previous calendar year.

*Group Payment Arrangement*

## TERMINATION OF THE ARRANGEMENT BY THE NOMINATED COMPANY OR THE BOARD

**18.1** Either the Nominated Company or the Board may at any time terminate the Arrangement by giving notice in writing to that effect to the other party.

**18.2** The effect of termination of the Arrangement under Clause 18.1 shall be to terminate the rights and obligations of the parties to the Arrangement in relation to Relevant Accounting Periods in respect of which the dates of the first instalments of corporation tax (treated as becoming due and payable under Regulation 4 and Regulation 5 (as applicable) of the Corporation Tax (Instalment Payments) Regulations 1998) fall after the date notice is given under Clause 18.1 or, in the case of any companies that are not large companies within the meaning of those Regulations, would fall after that date if the companies were large companies.

## TERMINATION OF THE ARRANGEMENT BY THE BOARD IN SPECIFIED CIRCUMSTANCES

**19** Without prejudice to the Board's right of termination under Clause 18.1, the Board shall also have the right forthwith to terminate the Arrangement by giving notice in writing to the Nominated Company under the following circumstances –
(a)  if any of the Participating Companies either is in default of its obligation to pay corporation tax, or is in default of its obligation to file a company tax return in relation to an accounting period where such obligations arise whilst the Arrangement is in being;
(b)  if the Nominated Company is in breach of any of its obligations under the Arrangement;
(c)  if the Board have reason to believe that any member of the [          ] Group of Companies (including the Participating Companies) may become liable to tax under section 767A or section 767AA of the Income and Corporation Taxes Act 1988.

**20.1** The provisions specified in clauses 20.2 to 20.4 shall survive termination of the Arrangement under Clause 19.

**20.2** Subject to any provisions of the Arrangement and of the Corporation Tax Acts and Regulations made under those Acts to the contrary, any acts done or deemed to be done under the Arrangement shall be unaffected by its termination under Clause 19.

**20.3** With respect to payments made under the Arrangement which have not been repaid and which have not already been apportioned (or have not already been deemed to be apportioned) at the date notice is given under Clause 19 above, the following provisions shall apply, sub-clauses (a) to (d) being subject to sub-clause (f), and sub-clause (d) also being subject to sub-clause (e) –
(a)  the Nominated Company shall have the right, exercisable by giving notice in writing to the Board and within a period of thirty days from the date notice is given under Clause 19 above, irrevocably to apportion such payments to any of the Participating Companies;
(b)  to the extent that the Nominated Company fails to exercise its right as specified in sub-clause (a) of this Clause 20.3, the Board shall have the right, exercisable within a period of sixty days from the date notice is given under Clause 19, to nominate, by giving notice in writing to the Nominated

*Group Payment Arrangement*

        Company, one of the Participating Companies (other than the Nominated Company) for the purpose of exercising the right of the Nominated Company under sub-clause (a) of this Clause 20.3. The company so nominated shall have a period of thirty days from the date notice of nomination is given to exercise its right;

(c)    to the extent that payments still remain unapportioned (including by reason of the Board not exercising their right under sub-clause (b) of this Clause 20.3), such payments shall be apportioned by the Board to any of the Participating Companies. The Board shall give notice in writing to the Nominated Company of such apportionments;

(d)    the Board shall also have the right, as often as is necessary to discharge outstanding liabilities under the arrangement, to re-apportion any given payment or payments made by the Nominated Company (and apportioned by the Nominated Company, or other Participating Company, under sub-clauses (b) and (c) of this Clause 20.3) to any of the Participating Companies. The Board shall give notice in writing of such re-apportionments to the Nominated Company. Neither the Nominated Company nor any other Participating Company shall have the power to amend such re-apportionments (or any apportionments made under sub-clause (c) of this Clause 20.3);

(e)    the provisions of Clause 10.2 above shall apply to the Board's power of re-apportionment under sub-clause (d) of this Clause 20.3, except that the relevant date shall not be the Closing Date but the date notice is given under Clause 19 above;

(f)    clauses 11, 12.1 and 12.2 above shall apply to such payments.

**20.4**    The Board shall be obliged to consider any claims made to it under Clause 4.2 above if such claims were made prior to the date notice was given under Clause 19 above.

**OTHER PROVISIONS**

**21**    All payments to be made by the Nominated Company under the Arrangement shall be made by electronic funds transfer.

**22**    By agreement between the Participating Companies and the Board another Participating Company may become the Nominated Company in place of [      ] Company or any successor Nominated Company.

**23**    The Arrangement shall be governed and construed in accordance with English Law.

*Group Payment Arrangement*

## SCHEDULE

## APPLICATION FOR A GROUP PAYMENT ARRANGEMENT

Please complete in block capitals.

### DETAILS OF NOMINATED COMPANY (Note 1)

NAME _____
ADDRESS _____
_____
_____ Postcode _____

CONTACT NAME (Note 2) _____ Capacity _____
CONTACT ADDRESS _____
_____
_____ Postcode _____

CONTACT TELEPHONE NO _____
CONTACT FAX NO _____

### GROUP PAYMENT PERIOD DETAILS (Note 3)

START DATE _____ END DATE _____

### PROPOSED GROUP ACCOUNT NAME (Note 4)

_____ G P R

### INTENDED METHOD OF PAYMENT (Note 5)

CHAPS ☐           BACS ☐           BANK GIRO ☐

### PARTICIPATING COMPANIES (Note 6) - See Overleaf

SIGNED_____ POSITION_____ DATE_____

Completion Notes
(1) Nominated Company - this is the Company within your Group responsible for administering your Group Payment Arrangements.
(2) Contact Name - enter details of the person within the Nominated Company who will act as a contact point.
(3) Group Payment Period - enter the start and end date of the first Period of Account to be covered by the arrangement.
(4) Proposed Name - enter a name of no more than 52 characters (including any spaces) which you would like us to use for your Group Payment Arrangement. (Note that for administrative purposes we will add the suffix 'GPR' to the name you choose.)
(5) Indicate which method of payment you intend to use by ticking the appropriate box.
(6) Participating Companies are the Companies you want to be part of your Group Payment Arrangement.

*Group Payment Arrangement*

**LIST OF PARTICIPATING COMPANIES** (Note 6)

| NAME | TAX REFERENCE (Note 7) | ACCOUNTING PERIOD (Note 8) | |
|---|---|---|---|
| | | START DATE | END DATE |
| | | | |

**If you need to provide more details please attach further pages in the same format.**

(7) Tax Reference - enter the Corporation Tax Reference of each participating company. This is a 10 digit reference, for example 12354 67890.
(8) Accounting Period Details - enter the start and end date of the Relevant Accounting Period applying to each participating company.

*Group Payment Arrangement*

Where a nominated company has a period of account in excess of 12 months this is split into 12 month and short accounting periods for group payment purposes on completion of an undertaking along the following lines:

**Annex to the Group Payment Arrangement made on DD/MM/YYYY between the Commissioners of the Inland Revenue and members of the XXXXXXXX group of companies ('the arrangement')**

NNNNNNNNNN, being the Nominated Company at all relevent times, hereby confirms that it [has prepared/will prepare] accounts for a period exceeding 12 months commencing on DD/MM/YYYY and ending on DD/MM/YYYY.

It is hereby agreed between the parties that, for the purposes of the Arrangement, the first twelve months of this period shall be deemed to be a period of account and that the balance of the period shall be deemed to be a second, separate period of account.

_____ (signature)

_____ (name)

(for and on behalf of, and with the authorisation of the Directors of, the nominated company)

_____ (signature)

_____ (name)

(for and on behalf of the Commissioners of the Inland Revenue)

*Appendix 3*

# Statutory Instruments

**1998 No. 3081**

**The Controlled Foreign Companies (Excluded Countries) Regulations 1998**

| | |
|---|---|
| *Made* | *9th December 1998* |
| *Laid before the House of Commons* | *10th December 1998* |
| *Coming into force* | *31st December 1998* |

The Commissioners of Inland Revenue, in exercise of the powers conferred on them by section 748(1)(e) and (1A) of the Income and Corporation Taxes Act 1988, hereby make the following Regulations:

**Citation, commencement and effect**

**1.** – (1) These Regulations may be cited as the Controlled Foreign Companies (Excluded Countries) Regulations 1998, shall come into force on 31st December 1998, and shall have effect with respect to any appropriate accounting period of a relevant company.

(2) In this regulation –

'appropriate accounting period' means an accounting period ending on or after the day to be appointed under section 199 of the Finance Act 1994 (corporation tax self-assessment);

'relevant company' means a company resident in the United Kingdom that had a relevant interest in a controlled foreign company at any time during an accounting period of the controlled foreign company ending in an appropriate accounting period of the relevant company;

'relevant interest' shall be construed in accordance with section 752A of the Taxes Act.

**Interpretation**

**2.** – (1) In these Regulations unless the context otherwise requires –

'controlled foreign company' shall be construed in accordance with section 747(2) of the Taxes Act;

'gains' in relation to a controlled foreign company means any gains of that company other than a gain accruing to the company on a disposal of an asset

## Statutory Instruments

which, on the assumption that the company was within the charge to corporation tax, would have fallen to be treated as a chargeable gain and would not have been taken into account as a receipt in computing the company's income or profits or gains or losses for the purposes of the Income Tax Acts;

'insurance company' means a company carrying on 'long-term business' or 'general business' within the meaning of section 1 of the Insurance Companies Act 1982;

'Schedule 1' and 'Schedule 2' mean Schedule 1 and Schedule 2 respectively to these Regulations;

'section 748(1)(e)' means section 748(1)(e) of the Taxes Act;

'the Taxes Act' means the Income and Corporation Taxes Act 1988.

(2) For the purposes of these Regulations a company is resident in a territory if –
(a) by reason of the law of that territory relating to domicile, residence or place of management, the company is liable to tax in that territory, or
(b) if there is either no such law or such law does not apply to the company, the company is incorporated in that territory;
and references in these Regulations to the territory of residence of a company shall be construed accordingly.

(3) For the purposes of these Regulations a controlled foreign company is resident in a territory, within the meaning of paragraph (2), in an accounting period only if it is so resident throughout that accounting period.

(4) References in these Regulations to a branch or agency of a controlled foreign company are references to a branch or agency situated in a territory other than the territory of residence of the controlled foreign company.

### Limitation on apportionment of chargeable profits of a controlled foreign company – specified territories

**3.** The territory in which a controlled foreign company is required to be resident as respects an accounting period for the purposes of section 748(1)(e) is –
(a) as respects an accounting period beginning before 9th July 1998, any territory specified in Part I or in Part II of Schedule 1;
(b) as respects an accounting period beginning on or after that date, any territory specified in Part I or in Part II of Schedule 2.

### Limitation on apportionment of chargeable profits of a controlled foreign company – conditions to be satisfied

**4.** – (1) Paragraph (2) specifies the condition which is required to be satisfied as respects an accounting period, for the purposes of section 748(1)(e), by a controlled foreign company which is resident in a territory specified in Part I of Schedule 1 or, as the case may be, in Part I of Schedule 2, in that accounting period.

(2) The condition specified is that the requirement with respect to the controlled foreign company's income and gains specified in regulation 5 is satisfied by the controlled foreign company in relation to that accounting period.

(3) Paragraph (4) specifies the conditions which are required to be satisfied as respects an accounting period, for the purposes of section 748(1)(e), by a

## Statutory Instruments

controlled foreign company which is resident in a territory specified in column 1 of Part II of Schedule 1 or, as the case may be, in column 1 of Part II of Schedule 2, in that accounting period.

(4) The conditions specified in this paragraph are that the controlled foreign company –
(a) satisfies the requirement with respect to its income and gains specified in regulation 5 in relation to that accounting period, and
(b) at no time during that accounting period –
 (i) is entitled to any tax exemption, tax reduction or other benefit, or
 (ii) falls within any condition,
specified in column 2 of Part II of Schedule 1 or, as the case may be, in column 2 of Part II of Schedule 2, opposite the specification of the territory in which the controlled foreign company is resident.

### Income and gains requirement

**5.** – (1) The requirement with respect to the income and gains of a controlled foreign company as respects an accounting period is that the amount of its non-local source income arising in that accounting period does not exceed whichever is the greater of –
(a) £50,000 or, where that accounting period is less than twelve months in duration, that amount proportionately reduced, and
(b) an amount equal to ten per cent. of its commercially quantified income arising in that accounting period.

(2) In paragraphs (1) and (3) 'commercially quantified income' means the amount of profits of the controlled foreign company before tax, determined in accordance with generally accepted accounting standards other than an equity basis of accounting, but disregarding capital profits or losses.

(3) Subject to paragraph (4) (special rules for banks and insurance companies), for the purposes of paragraph (1) the amount of a controlled foreign company's non-local source income arising in an accounting period is the aggregate of the following amounts, namely –
(a) the gross amount of income consisting of distributions recognised as income in computing the commercially quantified income of that company for that period from the profits of companies not resident in the territory of residence of that company, other than branch or agency income;
(b) the gross amount of income and gains recognised as income in computing the commercially quantified income of that company for that period and deriving from loans to, or deposits with, persons not resident in the territory of residence of that company, or branches or agencies situated outside that territory of companies resident in that territory, other than branch or agency income and gains;
(c) the gross amount of income and gains recognised as income in computing the commercially quantified income of that company for that period in relation to royalties payable by persons not resident in the territory of residence of that company, or by branches or agencies situated outside that territory of companies resident in that territory, other than branch or agency income and gains;
(d) the gross amount of income and gains recognised as income in computing the commercially quantified income of that company for that period in relation to premiums and rents payable in respect of property situated outside the territory of residence of that company by persons not resident

*Statutory Instruments*

in that territory, or by branches situated outside that territory of companies resident in that territory, other than branch or agency income and gains;
(e) the amount of any branch or agency income and gains recognised as income in computing the commercially quantified income of that company for that period, calculated in accordance with regulation 6;
(f) the gross amount of any income not falling within any of sub-paragraphs (a) to (e) above that is recognised as income in computing the commercially quantified income of that company for that period and does not constitute income which either –
  (i) is treated under the laws of the territory of residence of that company as accruing or arising in, or derived from, that territory, or
  (ii) where there are no laws of that territory treating that income as accruing or arising in, or derived from, that territory or another territory, would be treated as accruing or arising in, or derived from, that territory if there were such laws in force in that territory and those laws were identical to the laws of the United Kingdom treating income as accruing or arising in, or derived from, a territory for the purposes of the Corporation Tax Acts, and which
  (iii) in either case is within that territory's charge to tax.
(4) Where –
(a) the controlled foreign company concerned is an institution carrying on the business of banking, or an insurance company, and
(b) income of that company falling within any of sub-paragraphs (a) to (d) of paragraph (3) –
  (i) is an integral part of income arising or accruing to the company from the trade of banking or insurance carried on by the company, being income which, if the company were resident in the United Kingdom, would be income arising to the company from a trade for the purposes of the Corporation Tax Acts, and
  (ii) is within the charge to tax of the territory of residence of that company,
the aggregate amount of that income shall be disregarded in computing the aggregate amount of the company's non-local source income.

**Branch or agency income and gains**

**6.** – (1) The amount of any branch or agency income and gains as mentioned in regulation 5(3)(e) is –
(a) where the conditions specified in paragraph (2) are satisfied with respect to the branch or agency for the accounting period concerned, the amount (being not more than 10 per cent. of the net amount of the profits of that branch or agency for that period) by reference to which the condition specified in sub-paragraph (d) of that paragraph is satisfied by that branch or agency;
(b) where the conditions specified in paragraph (2) are not satisfied with respect to the branch or agency for the accounting period concerned, the net amount or, where paragraph (3) applies, the gross amount of the branch or agency income and gains for that accounting period.
(2) The conditions specified in this paragraph are that–
(a) the branch or agency is situated in a territory specified in Part I or in Part II of Schedule 1 or, as the case may be, in Part I or in Part II of Schedule 2, and where the territory is one specified in Part II of Schedule 1 or in Part II of Schedule 2, at no time during the accounting period –

## Statutory Instruments

     (i)    is entitled to any tax exemption, tax reduction or other benefit, or
     (ii)   falls within any condition,
specified in column 2 of that Part opposite the specification of that territory;
(b)    the profits of the branch or agency are within the charge to tax of that territory;
(c)    the profits attributed to the branch or agency for tax purposes in that territory are those which it might be expected to make if it were a distinct and separate enterprise from the company of which it is a branch or agency, engaged in the same or similar activities under the same or similar conditions and dealing wholly independently with the company of which it is a branch or agency;
(d)    not more than 10 per cent. of the net amount of the profits of the branch or agency for the accounting period would, on the assumption that the branch or agency was not a branch or agency of the controlled foreign company but a separate controlled foreign company, be attributable to the aggregate of the gross amounts of any income and gains falling within any of sub-paragraphs (a) to (d) of regulation 5(3) and arising outside the territory in which the branch or agency is situated;
(e)    amounts falling to be deducted in computing the taxable profits of the branch or agency, being amounts which are paid to, or are in respect of costs incurred by, the head office of the company of which it is a branch or agency, either –
     (i)    are liable to tax, or are disallowed as an expense, in the territory of residence of that company, or
     (ii)   where that company is liable to tax in its territory of residence in respect of the whole of its profits wherever arising, are not allowed as a deduction in computing the taxable profits of that company except where the amount in question is paid by that company to another person.

    (3) This paragraph applies to a case where the net amount of the income and gains referred to in paragraph (1) in the accounting period concerned does not exceed an amount which would be equal to the aggregate of the gross amounts of any income and gains falling within any of sub-paragraphs (a) to (d) of regulation 5(3) in that period if branch or agency income and gains fell within those sub-paragraphs.

### Interpretation of regulations 5 and 6

    **7.** – (1) In regulation 5(2) 'capital profits or losses' means profits or losses arising in relation to chargeable assets.

    (2) In regulations 5(3) and 6 references to 'branch or agency income' or to 'branch or agency income and gains' are references to income and gains that –
(a)    arise in or are derived from any branch or agency of a controlled foreign company, and
(b)    fall within sub-paragraph (e) of regulation 5(3) in the accounting period concerned.

    (3) In regulation 5(3) –
(a)    the references to 'the gross amount' of any income in sub-paragraphs (a) and (f) are references to the amount of that income before deduction of expenses or reserves;
(b)    the reference to 'the gross amount' of any income and gains in sub-paragraph (b) is a reference to the amount of that income and those gains found –

> > (i) after excluding any gain or loss arising on any loan or deposit referred to in that sub-paragraph which is offset by a loss or gain on a contract ancillary to that loan or deposit which would be a qualifying contract if the company were a qualifying company, and
> > (ii) after deducting any exchange losses attributable to the loans or deposits referred to in that sub-paragraph to the extent that those losses have not already been excluded by virtue of paragraph (i) above, but
> > (iii) before deducting other expenses or reserves;
> (c) the references to 'the gross amount' of any income and gains in sub-paragraphs (c) and (d) are references to the amount of that income and those gains found after deducting any exchange losses attributable to the royalties, premiums or rents referred to in those sub-paragraphs but before deducting other expenses or reserves;

and the references to 'the gross amounts' in regulation 6(2)(d) and (3) shall be construed accordingly.

(4) In regulation 5(3) references to persons not resident in the territory of residence of a controlled foreign company do not include references to a company not so resident in circumstances where–

(a) the branch or agency of the company is situated in that territory, and
(b) the transaction giving rise to the income and gains in question of the controlled foreign company is made with that branch or agency.

(5) In regulation 6(1)(b) the reference to the gross amount of income and gains is a reference to the amount of that income or of those gains before deduction of expenses or reserves.

(6) In regulation 6(1)(b) the reference to 'the net amount' of the branch or agency income and gains, and in regulation 6(2)(d) the reference to 'the net amount' of the profits of the branch or agency concerned, are references to the amount of that income, or of those profits, after deduction of expenses but before tax, as determined in accordance with a generally accepted method of accounting for profits of branches or profits of agencies of companies.

(7) In paragraph (1) of this regulation a 'chargeable asset' is any asset in the case of which one of the following conditions is satisfied, that is to say –

(a) a gain accruing to the company on a disposal of that asset on or after the date of coming into force of these Regulations would, on the assumption that the company was within the charge to corporation tax, have fallen to be treated in relation to the company as a chargeable gain and would not have been taken into account as a receipt in computing the company's income or profits or gains or losses for the purposes of the Income Tax Acts;
(b) a chargeable gain or allowable loss would, on the assumption mentioned in sub-paragraph (a), be deemed to have accrued to the company on any disposal of that asset on or after the date mentioned in that sub-paragraph.

(8) In paragraph (3)(b)(i) of this regulation – 'qualifying company' –
(a) as respects a contract falling within section 126(1) of the Finance Act 1993, has the meaning given by section 152 of that Act;
(b) as respects a contract falling within section 147(1) of the Finance Act 1994, has the meaning given by section 154 of that Act;

'qualifying contract' means a contract falling within section 126(1) of the Finance Act 1993 or section 147(1) of the Finance Act 1994, as the case may be, other than a contract which, in the case of branch or agency income or gains which would be income or gains falling within sub-paragraph (b) of regulation 5(3) if branch or

## Statutory Instruments

agency income and gains fell within that sub-paragraph, is not entered into by the branch or agency concerned.

## SCHEDULE 1

Regulations 3, 4 and 6(2)(a)

### ACCOUNTING PERIODS BEGINNING BEFORE 9TH JULY 1998

#### PART I

#### SPECIFIED TERRITORIES

| | |
|---|---|
| Australia | Japan |
| Austria | Korea, Republic of |
| Bangladesh | Lesotho |
| Bolivia | Malawi |
| Botswana | Mexico |
| Brazil | New Zealand |
| Canada | Nigeria |
| Colombia | Norway |
| Czech Republic | Papua New Guinea |
| Denmark | Poland |
| Dominican Republic | Romania |
| Falkland Islands | Senegal |
| Fiji | Sierra Leone |
| Finland | Slovak Republic |
| France | Solomon Islands |
| Gambia | South Africa |
| Germany | Spain |
| Ghana | Swaziland |
| Honduras | Sweden |
| Hungary | Trinidad and Tobago |
| Iceland | Turkey |
| India | Zambia |
| Indonesia | Zimbabwe |
| Ivory Coast | |

#### PART II

#### SPECIFIED TERRITORIES WITH QUALIFICATIONS

| | |
|---|---|
| Argentina | Companies obtaining exemption from tax on income from transactions, activities or operations carried on in, or from goods located in, tax free areas in accordance with Law 19640 of 16th May 1972. |
| Belgium | **1.** Companies which are regarded as Foreign Sales Corporations in section 922(a) of the United States Internal Revenue Code 1954 and which accordingly qualify for reduced Belgian taxation.<br>**2.** Companies approved under Royal Decree No. 187 of 30th December 1982 as Co-ordination Centres. |
| Brunei | Companies qualifying as 'pioneer companies' under the Investment Incentives Enactment 1975. |
| Bulgaria | Any company obtaining a tax benefit under Article 111 of Decree 56 of 9th January 1989 (Free Zone legislation). |

*Statutory Instruments*

| | |
|---|---|
| Chile | Companies obtaining exemption from tax under Law 16,441 of 1st March 1966 on income from property located in the Department of Isla da Pascua or from activities developed in that Department. |
| China | Companies deriving income in or from the Hong Kong Special Administrative Region and submitting tax returns to the authorities of that Region. |
| Egypt | Companies which do not fall within the scope of Article 111, Book 2 of Law 157 of 1981 because they do not operate in Egypt. |
| Faroe Islands | Companies deriving interest from Faroese financial institutions from which tax is deducted at source under Law 4 of 26th March 1953. |
| Greece | **1.** Companies whose profits are exempt from tax under Article 6(2)(c) of Law 3843/1958 (profits from the operation of ships under the Greek flag).<br>**2.** Companies having profits exempt from company income tax by virtue of Article 25 of Law 25/1975 or by virtue of Law 89/1967 (profits from shipping and associated activities). |
| Ireland | **1.** Companies obtaining relief or exemption from tax under Chapters 1 and 2 of Part 14 of the Taxes Consolidation Act 1997.<br>**2.** Holding companies having income exempted from tax under section 44 in Chapter 3 of Part 3 of the Taxes Consolidation Act 1997. |
| Italy | Companies benefiting from paragraphs 12 to 14 of Article 11 of Law 413 of 30th December 1991 (Trieste Free Zone Financial and Insurance Centre). |
| Kenya | Companies having income exempted from tax under paragraph 11 of Schedule 1 to the Income Tax Act 1973. |
| Luxembourg | **1.** Companies obtaining any special tax benefit under the Law of 31st July 1929, the decree of 17th December 1938 or the Grand Ducal Regulation of 29th July 1977 (holding companies).<br>**2.** Any reinsurance company established in Luxembourg requiring authorisation under Article 92 of the Law of 6th December 1991. |
| Malaysia | **1.** Companies exempt from tax in accordance with section 54A of the Income Tax Act 1967 (shipping).<br>**2.** Companies subject to tax at 5 per cent. in accordance with sections 60A and 60B of the Income Tax Act 1967 (inward reinsurance and offshore insurance).<br>**3.** Companies deriving dividends from a company or companies deriving income from one or more of the activities referred to in paragraphs 1 and 2 above.<br>**4.** Companies obtaining a tax benefit under the Offshore Companies Act (Island of Labuan) 1990. |

*Statutory Instruments*

| | |
|---|---|
| Malta | **1.** Companies entitled to exemption or relief from tax under section 11(2) of the Income Tax Act 1948.<br>**2.** Companies obtaining exemption from tax under section 86 of the Merchant Shipping Act 1973.<br>**3.** Companies obtaining exemption or relief from tax under section 30 of the Malta International Business Activities Act 1988.<br>**4.** Companies obtaining exemption or relief from tax under section 18 of the Malta Freeports Act 1989. |
| Morocco | Companies receiving a tax benefit under Law 58–90 of 1992 (offshore financial centres). |
| Netherlands | Companies which are regarded as Foreign Sales Corporations under section 922(a) of the United States Internal Revenue Code 1954. |
| Pakistan | Companies deriving royalties, commissions or fees which are exempt from tax under paragraph 139 in Part I of the second Schedule to the Income Tax Ordinance 1979. |
| Philippines | **1.** Companies authorised under Presidential Decree 1034 of 30th September 1976, or under Presidential Decree 1035 of 30th September 1976, to operate an offshore Banking Unit or a Foreign Currency Deposit Unit as defined in those Decrees.<br>**2.** Companies receiving interest on deposits with a Foreign Currency Deposit Unit, or other interest subject to the reduced rates of tax under section 27(D) of the National Internal Revenue Code 1997. |
| Portugal | Companies obtaining tax benefits under Decree Law 502/85 of 30th December 1985, Articles 41 and 51(g) of the Tax Benefits statute (EBF) approved by Decree Law 215/90 of 31st August 1989 (free zone in Madeira), or Decree Law 501/85 of 28th December 1985 as implemented by Decree Law 63/87 of 5th February 1987 (free zone in the Azores). |
| Puerto Rico | **1.** Companies obtaining a tax benefit under section 2(o) of the Industrial Incentive Act 1978 (designated service industries).<br>**2.** Companies obtaining a tax benefit under section 25 of the International Banking Centre Regulatory Act 1989 (International Banking Entities). |
| Singapore | **1.** Any company obtaining tax concessions under Ministry of Finance Regulations pursuant to section 43A, and sections 43C to 43J, of the Income Tax Act.<br>**2.** Companies obtaining exemption from tax on the income of a shipping enterprise in accordance with section 13A of the Income Tax Act. |

*Statutory Instruments*

> **3.** Companies obtaining relief from tax in accordance with sections 45 to 55 (international trade incentives), and sections 75 to 84 (warehouse and service incentives), of the Economic Expansion Incentives (Relief from Income Tax) Act.
>
> **4.** Companies deriving dividends from a company or companies deriving income from one or more of the activities falling within paragraphs 1 to 3 above.

| | |
|---|---|
| Sri Lanka | Companies obtaining relief or exemption from income tax under any of the following provisions of the Inland Revenue Act 1979 –<br>(a) section 8(c)(iv) (foreign currency banking units);<br>(b) sections 10(d) and 15(b) (income derived from approved bank accounts);<br>(c) section 10(e) (interest of newly resident companies);<br>(d) section 15(cc) (services rendered outside Sri Lanka);<br>(e) section 15(p) (re-export of approved products). |
| Tanzania | Companies relieved or exempted from income tax under section 15(1) or (1A) of the Income Tax Act 1973. |
| Thailand | Companies obtaining a tax benefit under Royal Decree 280 of 22nd September 1992 (offshore banking units). |
| Tunisia | Companies obtaining exemption from, or reduction of, tax under Law 76–63 of 12th July 1976 (financial and banking institutions dealing with non-residents). |
| United States | Domestic International Sales Corporations as defined in section 992(a) of the Internal Revenue Code 1954. |

## SCHEDULE 2

Regulations 3, 4 and 6(2)(a)

### ACCOUNTING PERIODS BEGINNING ON OR AFTER 9TH JULY 1998

#### PART I

#### SPECIFIED TERRITORIES

| | |
|---|---|
| Australia | Colombia |
| Austria | Czech Republic |
| Bangladesh | Denmark |
| Bolivia | Dominican Republic |
| Botswana | Falkland Islands |
| Brazil | Fiji |
| Bulgaria | Finland |
| Canada | France |

## Statutory Instruments

Gambia
Germany
Ghana
Honduras
Iceland
India
Indonesia
Ivory Coast
Japan
Korea, Republic of
Lesotho
Malawi
Mexico
New Zealand
Nigeria

Norway
Papua New Guinea
Poland
Romania
Senegal
Sierra Leone
Slovak Republic
Solomon Islands
South Africa
Swaziland
Sweden
Trinidad and Tobago
Turkey
Zambia
Zimbabwe

### PART II
### SPECIFIED TERRITORIES WITH QUALIFICATIONS

Argentina — Companies obtaining exemption from tax on income from transactions, activities or operations carried on in, or from goods located in, tax free areas in accordance with Law 19640 of 16th May 1972.

Belgium — **1.** Companies which are regarded as Foreign Sales Corporations in section 922(a) of the United States Internal Revenue Code 1954 and which accordingly qualify for reduced Belgian taxation.
**2.** Companies approved under Royal Decree No. 187 of 30th December 1982 as Co-ordination Centres.

Brunei — Companies qualifying as 'pioneer companies' under the Investment Incentives Enactment 1975.

Chile — Companies obtaining exemption from tax under Law 16,441 of 1st March 1966 on income from property located in the Department of Isla da Pascua or from activities developed in that Department.

China — **1.** Companies deriving income in or from the Hong Kong Special Administrative Region and submitting tax returns to the authorities of that Region.
**2.** From 20th December 1999, companies deriving income in or from the Macao Special Administrative Region and submitting tax returns to the authorities of that Region.

Egypt — Companies which do not fall within the scope of Article 111, Book 2 of Law 157 of 1981 because they do not operate in Egypt.

Faroe Islands — Companies deriving interest from Faroese financial institutions from which tax is deducted at source under Law 4 of 26th March 1953.

Greece — **1.** Companies whose profits are exempt from tax under Article 6(2)(c) of Law 3843/1958 (profits from the operation of ships under the Greek flag).

*Statutory Instruments*

|  |  |
|---|---|
|  | **2.** Companies having profits exempt from company income tax by virtue of Article 25 of Law 25/1975 or by virtue of Law 89/1967 (profits from shipping and associated activities). |
| Hungary | Companies benefiting from the reduced rate of tax for extra-territorial companies under section 19(2) of Act LXXXI of 1996 on Corporate Tax and Dividend Tax. |
| Ireland | **1.** Companies obtaining relief or exemption from tax under Chapters 1 and 2 of Part 14 of the Taxes Consolidation Act 1997.<br>**2.** Holding companies having income exempted from tax under section 44 in Chapter 3 of Part 3 of the Taxes Consolidation Act 1997. |
| Italy | Companies benefiting from paragraphs 12 to 14 of Article 11 of Law 413 of 30th December 1991 (Trieste Free Zone Financial and Insurance Centre). |
| Kenya | Companies having income exempted from tax under paragraph 11 of Schedule 1 to the Income Tax Act 1973. |
| Luxembourg | **1.** Companies obtaining any special tax benefit under the Law of 31st July 1929, the decree of 17th December 1938 or the Grand Ducal Regulation of 29th July 1977 (holding companies).<br>**2.** Any reinsurance company established in Luxembourg requiring authorisation under Article 92 of the Law of 6th December 1991. |
| Malaysia | **1.** Companies exempt from tax in accordance with section 54A of the Income Tax Act 1967 (shipping).<br>**2.** Companies subject to tax at 5 per cent. in accordance with sections 60A and 60B of the Income Tax Act 1967 (inward reinsurance and offshore insurance).<br>**3.** Companies deriving dividends from a company or companies deriving income from one or more of the activities referred to in paragraphs 1 and 2 above.<br>**4.** Companies obtaining a tax benefit under the Offshore Companies Act (Island of Labuan) 1990. |
| Malta | **1.** Companies entitled to exemption or relief from tax at the discretion of the Minister responsible for finance under section 12(2) of the Income Tax Act 1948.<br>**2.** Companies obtaining exemption from tax under section 86 of the Merchant Shipping Act 1973.<br>**3.** Companies obtaining exemption or relief from tax under section 30 of the Malta International Business Activities Act 1988 or section 30 of the Malta Financial Services Centre Act 1988.<br>**4.** Companies obtaining exemption or relief from tax under section 18 of the Malta Freeports Act 1989. |
| Morocco | Companies receiving a tax benefit under Law 58-90 of 1992 (offshore financial centres). |

*Statutory Instruments*

| | |
|---|---|
| Netherlands | **1.** Companies which are regarded as Foreign Sales Corporations under section 922(a) of the United States Internal Revenue Code 1954.<br>**2.** A company ('the first company') receiving interest, rents or royalties in an accounting period directly or indirectly from a Dutch company ('the second company') which is connected with the first company within the meaning of section 839 of the Taxes Act, in circumstances where–<br>(a) the second company does not satisfy the income and gains requirement in regulation 5 as respects its accounting period in which the interest, rents or royalties were paid, and<br>(b) the aggregate of the non-local source income of the first company in its accounting period in question and the interest, rents and royalties received by it from the second company in that period exceeds whichever is the greater of–<br>  (i) £50,000 or, where that period is less than twelve months in duration, that amount proportionately reduced, and<br>  (ii) an amount equal to ten per cent. of its commercially quantified income arising in that period. |
| Pakistan | Companies deriving royalties, commissions or fees which are exempt from tax under paragraph 139 in Part I of the second Schedule to the Income Tax Ordinance 1979. |
| Philippines | **1.** Companies authorised under Presidential Decree 1034 of 30th September 1976, or under Presidential Decree 1035 of 30th September 1976, to operate an offshore Banking Unit or a Foreign Currency Deposit Unit as defined in those Decrees.<br>**2.** Companies receiving interest on deposits with a Foreign Currency Deposit Unit, or other interest subject to the reduced rates of tax under section 27(D) of the National Internal Revenue Code 1997. |
| Portugal | Companies obtaining tax benefits under Decree Law 502/85 of 30th December 1985, Articles 41 and 51(g) of the Tax Benefits statute (EBF) approved by Decree Law 215/90 of 31st August 1989 (free zone in Madeira), or Decree Law 501/85 of 28th December 1985 as implemented by Decree Law 63/87 of 5th February 1987 (free zone in the Azores). |
| Puerto Rico | **1.** Companies obtaining a tax benefit under section 2(o) of the Industrial Incentive Act 1978 (designated service industries).<br>**2.** Companies obtaining a tax benefit under section 25 of the International Banking Centre Regulatory Act 1989 (International Banking Entities). |

*Statutory Instruments*

| | |
|---|---|
| Singapore | **1.** Any company obtaining tax concessions under Ministry of Finance Regulations pursuant to section 43A, and sections 43C to 43K, of the Income Tax Act.<br>**2.** Companies obtaining exemption from tax on the income of a shipping enterprise in accordance with section 13A of the Income Tax Act.<br>**3.** Companies obtaining relief from tax in accordance with sections 45 to 55 (international trade incentives), and sections 75 to 84 (warehouse and service incentives), of the Economic Expansion Incentives (Relief from Income Tax) Act.<br>**4.** Companies deriving dividends from a company or companies deriving income from one or more of the activities falling within paragraphs 1 to 3 above. |
| Spain | **1.** Companies which are registered in the official register of the Canary Islands Special Zone (Zona Especial Canaria) established under Law 19/1994 and which benefit from the special low tax rate applied to such companies.<br>**2.** Companies benefiting from the alternative taxation regime for co-ordination centres established by the provincial governments of the Basque Country under laws pursuant to Norma Foral 3/1996 of 26th June 1996, Norma Foral 7/1996 of 4th July 1996, and Norma Foral 24/1996 of 5th July 1996. |
| Sri Lanka | Companies obtaining relief or exemption from income tax under any of the following provisions of the Inland Revenue Act 1979 –<br>(a)   section 8(c)(iv) (foreign currency banking units);<br>(b)   sections 10(d) and 15(b) (income derived from approved bank accounts);<br>(c)   section 10(e) (interest of newly resident companies);<br>(d)   section 15(cc) (services rendered outside Sri Lanka);<br>(e)   section 15(p) (re-export of approved products). |
| Tanzania | Companies relieved or exempted from income tax under section 15(1) or (1A) of the Income Tax Act 1973. |
| Thailand | Companies obtaining a tax benefit under Royal Decree 280 of 22nd September 1992 (offshore banking units). |
| Tunisia | Companies obtaining exemption from, or reduction of, tax under Law 76-63 of 12th July 1976 (financial and banking institutions dealing with non-residents). |
| United States | Domestic International Sales Corporations as defined in section 992(a) of the Internal Revenue Code 1954. |

Statutory Instruments

**1998 No. 3175 (amended by SI 1999 No. 1929)**

**The Corporation Tax (Instalment Payments) Regulations 1998**

*Made*     *17th December 1998*
*Laid before the House of Commons*     *17th December 1998*
*Coming into force*     *7th January 1999*

The Treasury, in exercise of the powers conferred on them by sections 59DA(8) and 59E of the Taxes Management Act 1970, section 826A of the Income and Corporation Taxes Act 1988 and section 30 of the Finance Act 1998, hereby make the following Regulations:

**Citation, commencement and effect**

**1.** – (1) These Regulations may be cited as the Corporation Tax (Instalment Payments) Regulations 1998 and shall come into force on 7th January 1999.

(2) These Regulations have effect in relation to accounting periods of companies ending on or after 1st July 1999.

**Interpretation**

**2.** – (1) In these Regulations unless the context otherwise requires –

'the Board' means the Commissioners of Inland Revenue;

'large company' has the meaning given by regulation 3;

'Management Act' means the Taxes Management Act 1970;

'Schedule 18' means Schedule 18 to the Finance Act 1998;

'the Taxes Act' means the Income and Corporation Taxes Act 1988.

(2) References in these Regulations to profits of a company in any accounting period are references to the aggregate of –
(a)    the amount of profits chargeable to corporation tax shown in the company's assessment or determination under Schedule 18 for that accounting period, and on which corporation tax finally falls to be charged, and
(b)    the amount of the company's franked investment income in that period other than franked investment income which the company (if a member of a group) receives from companies within the group within the meaning of section 13(7) of the Taxes Act.

(3) References in these Regulations to the total liability of a company for an accounting period are references to the amount of tax payable for that period by the company as calculated in accordance with paragraph 8(1) of Schedule 18, reduced by the amount (if any) of deductions from payments made in that period to which section 559 of the Taxes Act (payments to sub-contractors) applies.

**Large companies**

**3.** – (1) Subject to paragraphs (2) and (3), a large company is a company whose profits in any accounting period exceed the upper relevant maximum amount in force at the end of that period.

*Statutory Instruments*

(2) A company is not a large company as respects an accounting period if the amount of its total liability for that period does not exceed £5,000 or, where the accounting period is less than twelve months, that amount proportionately reduced.

(3) A company is not a large company as respects an accounting period if –
(a) its profits for that accounting period do not exceed £10,000,000, and
(b) apart from this paragraph, it was not a large company in the twelve months preceding that accounting period.

(4) In paragraph (1) 'upper relevant maximum amount' shall be construed in accordance with section 13 of the Taxes Act but disregarding section 434(3A) and (3B) of the Taxes Act and section 88(4) of the Finance Act 1989 (amounts to be left out of account in determining profits for the purposes of section 13 of the Taxes Act).

(5) Subsections (3) to (8) of section 13 of the Taxes Act (reduction of lower and upper relevant maximum amounts by reference to whether a company has one or more associated companies and length of company's accounting period) shall apply so as to reduce the amount specified in paragraph (3)(a) in accordance with those subsections as they apply so as to reduce the lower and upper relevant maximum amounts, except that –
(a) the number of associated companies referred to in subsection (3) of that section shall be determined by reference to the number existing at the end of the immediately preceding accounting period of the company or, if there is no immediately preceding accounting period or the immediately preceding accounting period did not end on the day before the accounting period concerned commenced, by reference to the number existing at the commencement of the accounting period concerned;
(b) section 434(3A) and (3B) of the Taxes Act and section 88(4) of the Finance Act 1989 shall be disregarded.

(6) For the purposes of paragraph (3)(b) a company shall be treated as not being a large company in the period of twelve months preceding the accounting period in question in either of the following circumstances –
(a) during any part of the period of twelve months it either did not exist or did not have an accounting period;
(b) a relevant accounting period of the company either falls within or ends in that period of twelve months.

(7) In paragraph (6) 'relevant accounting period' means an accounting period as respects which, by virtue of the provisions of this regulation other than paragraph (3), the company was not a large company.

**Instalment payments – transitional provision**

**4.** – (1) In relation to an accounting period of a large company ending on or after 1st July 1999 but before 1st July 2000 –
(a) an amount equal to 60 per cent. of the company's total liability for that period shall be treated as becoming due and payable in accordance with regulation 5;
(b) the balance of the company's total liability for that period shall be payable in accordance with section 59D(1) of the Management Act, that is, on the day following the expiry of nine months from the end of the accounting period ('the due and payable date').

(2) In relation to an accounting period of a large company ending on or after 1st July 2000 but before 1st July 2001 –
(a) an amount equal to 72 per cent. of the company's total liability for that

## Statutory Instruments

period shall be treated as becoming due and payable in accordance with regulation 5;
(b) the balance of the company's total liability for that period shall be payable on the due and payable date.

(3) In relation to an accounting period of a large company ending on or after 1st July 2001 but before 1st July 2002 –
(a) an amount equal to 88 per cent. of the company's total liability for that period shall be treated as becoming due and payable in accordance with regulation 5;
(b) the balance of the company's total liability for that period shall be payable on the due and payable date.

**Instalment payments – principal provision**

5. – (1) Save as regards any amount falling within regulation 4(1)(b), (2)(b) or (3)(b), amounts in respect of the total liability of a large company for an accounting period shall be treated as becoming due and payable as follows.

(2) Subject to paragraph (4), the amount of the company's total liability for that period or, as the case may be, the specified percentage amount shall be treated as becoming due and payable in instalments (not exceeding four) on the dates specified in paragraph (3).

(3) The first instalment payment shall be treated as becoming due and payable on the date which is six months and thirteen days from the start of the accounting period.

> The final instalment payment shall be treated as becoming due and payable on the date which is three months and fourteen days from the end of the accounting period.

> An additional instalment payment or additional instalment payments shall, where the length of the accounting period so allows, each be treated as becoming due and payable on the date which is three months after the date of the immediately preceding instalment payment.

(4) Where the length of the accounting period is such that the date which is three months and fourteen days from the end of the accounting period falls earlier than the date which is six months and thirteen days from the start of the accounting period, the amount of the company's total liability for that period or, as the case may be, the specified percentage amount shall be treated as becoming due and payable on the date which is three months and fourteen days from the end of the accounting period.

(5) Where in accordance with paragraph (2) amounts in respect of the amount of the company's total liability for an accounting period or in respect of the specified percentage amount are treated as becoming due and payable in instalments, the amount treated as becoming due and payable on any instalment payment date shall be calculated in accordance with paragraphs (6) to (8) and by reference to the formula –

$$3 \times \frac{CTI}{n}$$

where –

CTI is the amount of the company's total liability for that accounting period or the specified percentage amount, and

n is the number of whole months falling within that accounting period plus the appropriate decimal.

(6) The amount treated as becoming due and payable on the first instalment payment date is the smaller of CTI and the amount resulting from the formula specified in paragraph (5).

(7) The amount treated as becoming due and payable on each subsequent instalment payment date other than the final instalment payment date is the smaller of –
(a) the balance of the company's total liability for that accounting period or of the specified percentage amount carried forward from the immediately preceding instalment payment date, and
(b) the amount resulting from the formula specified in paragraph (5).

(8) The amount treated as becoming due and payable on the final instalment payment date is the balance of the company's total liability for that accounting period or of the specified percentage amount carried forward from the immediately preceding instalment payment date.

(9) In this regulation –

'the appropriate decimal' is a decimal, calculated to two places rounded arithmetically where necessary, representing the number of days in the accounting period falling outside the whole months falling within that period and corresponding to the fraction of which the numerator is the number of those days and the denominator is 30;

'the specified percentage amount' means an amount equal to the percentage specified in regulation 4(1)(a), (2)(a) or (3)(a), as the case may be.

## Repayment of amounts in respect of a large company's total liability for an accounting period

**6.** – (1) This regulation applies where a large company –
(a) has paid an amount or amounts by way of instalments in respect of its total liability for an accounting period in accordance with regulation 5, and
(b) subsequently has grounds for believing that, by reason of a change in the circumstances of the company since the payment or payments were made –
    (i) the amount of its total liability for that period is likely to be less than previously calculated, and
    (ii) the aggregate amount so paid exceeds the aggregate amount ('the revised aggregate amount') that would have been treated as becoming due and payable by the relevant date having regard to the revised calculation of that liability.

(2) The company may, by notice given to an officer of the Board, make a claim to an officer of the Board for the repayment of so much of the aggregate amount so paid as in the company's view exceeds the revised aggregate amount.

(3) The notice under paragraph (2) must state –
(a) the amount which the company considers should be repaid, and
(b) the grounds referred to in paragraph (1)(b).

(4) If the company has appealed against an amendment of an assessment, or an assessment, in respect of the amount of its total liability for the accounting period concerned, and the appeal has not been finally determined, it may apply to the Commissioners to whom the appeal stands referred for a determination of the

*Statutory Instruments*

amount which should be repaid to the company pending determination of the amount of its total liability for that accounting period.

(5) Any claim under paragraph (2) or application under paragraph (4) shall be heard and determined in the same way as an appeal.

(6) If the company makes an application under section 55(3) or (4) of the Management Act (application to postpone payment pending determination of appeal), that application may be combined with an application under paragraph (4).

(7) In paragraph (1)(b) 'the relevant date' means the date on which a claim under paragraph (2) is made.

(8) Section 59DA of the Management Act (claim for repayment in advance of liability being established) shall not apply in any case where this regulation applies.

**Interest on unpaid amounts of a large company's total liability for an accounting period**

**7.** – (1) Section 87A of the Management Act shall apply in relation to any unpaid amount in respect of the total liability of a large company for an accounting period, with the modifications specified in paragraphs (2) to (5).

(2) After subsection (1) there shall be inserted the following subsection –

'(1A) An amount or amounts treated as becoming due and payable in respect of the total liability of a large company for an accounting period in accordance with regulation 5 of the Corporation Tax (Instalment Payments) Regulations 1998 shall carry interest at the rate applicable under section 178 of the Finance Act 1989 from the date or dates specified in that regulation as the date or dates when that amount or those amounts are treated as becoming due and payable until payment.'

(3) In subsection (2) –
(a) for the words 'Subsection (1) above applies' there shall be substituted 'Subsections (1) and (1A) above apply';
(b) for the words 'that subsection' there shall be substituted 'those subsections'.

(4) In subsection (3) there shall be added at the end the words ', and the reference in subsection (1A) above to the date or dates when an amount or amounts are treated as becoming due and payable in respect of the total liability of a large company for an accounting period is a reference to the date or dates when that amount or those amounts are treated as having become due and payable by the company'.

(5) After subsection (9) there shall be added –

'(10) In subsections (1A) and (3) above 'large company' has the meaning given by regulation 3 of the Corporation Tax (Instalment Payments) Regulations 1998.'

**Interest on overpaid amounts of a company's total liability for an accounting period**

**8.** – (1) Section 826 of the Taxes Act shall apply in relation to –
(a) an amount or amounts paid by a large company in accordance with regulation 5 in respect of its total liability for an accounting period, and

## Statutory Instruments

(b)  an amount or amounts paid by a company that is not a large company in an accounting period in respect of its total liability for that accounting period, where the payment is made prior to the day following the expiry of nine months from the end of that accounting period,

with the modifications specified in paragraphs (2) and (3).

(2) In subsection (1) –

(a)  after paragraph (c) there shall be inserted 'or

(d) the total amount paid by a large company (as defined in regulation 3 of the Corporation Tax (Instalment Payment) Regulations 1998) up to a point in time in respect of its total liability for an accounting period in accordance with regulation 5 of those Regulations exceeds the amount that is treated as having become due and payable by the company for that period at that time in accordance with that regulation, or

(e) an amount paid by a company that is not a large company in an accounting period in respect of the amount of its total liability for that period is paid prior to the day following the expiry of nine months from the end of that period ('the normal due date');'

(b)  for the words 'the repayment or payment shall' there shall be substituted the words 'or, in a case to which paragraph (d) above applies, until the date on which the excess amount arising as mentioned in that paragraph is extinguished or, in a case to which paragraph (e) above applies, until the normal due date, the repayment or payment or excess amount shall'.

(3) After subsection (3) there shall be inserted –

'(3A) In relation to an excess amount in respect of a company's total liability arising as mentioned in subsection (1)(d) above, the material date is the date on which the first instalment payment for the accounting period concerned is treated as becoming due as mentioned in regulation 5(3) of the Corporation Tax (Instalment Payments) Regulations 1998 or, if later, the date on which the excess amount arises.

(3B) In relation to a case falling within subsection (1)(e) above –

(a)  if the payment for the accounting period concerned was made on or before the date which, if the company had been a large company, would have been the date on which the first instalment payment for that accounting period would have been treated as becoming due as mentioned in regulation 5(3) of the Regulations referred to in subsection (3A) above, the material date is that date, or

(b)  if the payment for the accounting period concerned was made later than the date referred to in paragraph (a) above, the material date is the date on which that payment was made.'

### Consequential amendment of section 102 of the Finance Act 1989

**9.** – (1) Section 102 of the Finance Act 1989 (surrender of company tax refund within group) shall apply in relation to a surrendering company that is a large company with the modification specified in paragraphs (2) and (3).

(2) In subsection (3), in the definition of 'tax refund relating to an accounting period' –

(a)  the word 'or' immediately following paragraph (b) shall be omitted;

(b)  after paragraph (c) of that definition there shall be added 'or

(d) the following circumstances, that is, where an amount paid by a large

*Statutory Instruments*

company (as defined in regulation 3 of the Corporation Tax (Instalment Payments) Regulations 1998) in respect of its total liability for an accounting period in accordance with regulation 5 of those Regulations exceeds the amount in respect of the company's total liability that is treated as having become due and payable by the company for that period in accordance with that regulation by the date on which the amount was paid or, if paid in more than one instalment, by the latest date of payment of that amount.'

(3) In subsection (5)(b) there shall be added at the end the words 'or, where paragraph (d) of the definition of 'tax refund relating to an accounting period' in subsection (3) above applies, the earliest of the dates referred to in regulation 5 of the Corporation Tax (Instalment Payments) Regulations 1998 on which an amount in respect of the surrendering company's total liability for the accounting period concerned is treated as having become due and payable'.

**Information to be provided to the Board**

**10.** – (1) The Board may, at any time following the relevant date, by notice require any company to furnish them, within such time (not being less than thirty days) as may be provided by the notice –
(a)  such information relating to the computation of any amount paid in respect of the company's total liability for an accounting period in accordance with regulation 5 as they may reasonably require for ascertaining whether the amount of the payment was consistent with the quality and quantity of the information available to the company, at the time the payment was due, regarding its total liability for that period;
(b)  such information as they may reasonably require for ascertaining the reasons for non-payment by the company at any time in accordance with regulation 5 of any amount in respect of the company's total liability for an accounting period;
(c)  such information as they may reasonably require for ascertaining whether a claim for repayment of an amount under regulation 6(2) was properly made.

(2) In paragraph (1) 'the relevant date' means the date specified in paragraph 14(1) of Schedule 18 as the filing date for the company tax return for the accounting period concerned.

**Production of records**

**11.** – (1) The Board may, at any time following the relevant date, by notice require a company to produce, within such time (not being less than thirty days) as may be provided by the notice –
(a)  all such books, documents and other records in its possession or power relating to the computation of any amount paid in respect of the company's total liability for an accounting period in accordance with regulation 5 as they may reasonably require for ascertaining whether the amount of the payment was consistent with the quality and quantity of the information available to the company, at the time the payment was due, regarding its total liability for that period;
(b)  all such books, documents and other records in its possession or power as they may reasonably require for ascertaining the reasons for non-payment by the company at any time in accordance with regulation 5 of any amount in respect of the company's total liability for an accounting period;

(c) all such books, documents and other records in its possession or power as they may reasonably require for ascertaining whether a claim for repayment of an amount under regulation 6(2) was properly made.

(2) In complying with a notice under paragraph (1) copies of books, documents and other records may be produced instead of originals, but –
(a) the copies must be photographic or other facsimiles, and
(b) an officer of the Board may require the original to be made available for inspection in accordance with regulation 12.

(3) In paragraph (1) 'the relevant date' has the same meaning as in regulation 10.

**Inspection of records**

**12.** – (1) An officer of the Board authorised to do so may, at any time following the relevant date, require a company to make available for inspection, at such time as that officer may reasonably require, all such books, documents and other records in its possession or power as could be required to be produced by notice by the Board under regulation 11.

(2) Where records are maintained by computer the officer making the inspection shall be provided by the company with all the facilities necessary for obtaining information from them.

(3) In paragraph (1) 'the relevant date' has the same meaning as in regulation 10.

**Penalty for unpaid tax**

**13.** The circumstances prescribed for the purposes of section 59E(4) of the Management Act (penalty not exceeding twice the amount of interest charged by virtue of regulation 7 on any unpaid amount in respect of the total liability of a company for an accounting period) are where –
(a) the company, or a person acting on its behalf, deliberately or recklessly fails to pay the amount in question in accordance with regulation 5;
(b) the company, or a person acting on its behalf, fraudulently or negligently makes a claim for repayment of an amount under regulation 6(2).

**Anti-avoidance provision**

**14.** – (1) This regulation applies where, on or after 25th November 1997 and before 30th June 2002 –
(a) a company does one or both of the following, that is to say –
    (i) otherwise than in any of the circumstances specified in paragraph (6), causes the date or dates on which any of its relevant accounting periods begins or ends to be changed,
    (ii) otherwise than in either of the circumstances specified in paragraph (7), enters into any arrangements or transactions the effect of which is to transfer the amount of its taxable profits to another company which belongs to the same group, other than a company specified in paragraph (8), and
(b) the result is that, on the assumptions specified in paragraph (9), an amount or amounts of corporation tax in respect of the taxable profits of the company for any part of an accounting period beginning after 1st July 1998

and ending on or before 30th June 2002 becomes, or is treated as becoming, due and payable, in accordance with regulations 4 and 5 or section 59D(1) of the Management Act, on a date or dates ('the actual date or dates') later than the date or dates ('the hypothetical date or dates') on which, but for the action taken by the company as mentioned in sub-paragraph (a), they would have become, or would be treated as having become, due and payable in accordance with those regulations or that section.

(2) The company shall be liable to pay to the Board, in respect of the accounting period referred to in paragraph (1)(b), an amount computed in accordance with paragraph (3).

(3) The amount payable shall be computed –
(a)   by reference to –
    (i)   the amount, or (as the case may be) the aggregate of the amounts, of corporation tax referred to in paragraph (1)(b), and
    (ii)  the interval of time elapsing between the hypothetical date or dates and the actual date or dates;
(b)   so as to allow for accelerated as well as deferred amounts of corporation tax (but not to the extent that it results in an amount falling to be paid by the Board); and
(c)   as if it were interest on the amount, or the aggregate of the amounts, of corporation tax referred to in paragraph (1)(b).

(4) Interest referred to in paragraph (3)(c) –
(a)   shall be at the rate applicable under section 178 of the Finance Act 1989, and
(b)   shall be treated as if it were tax charged and due and payable under an assessment.

(5) For the purposes of this regulation a relevant accounting period is an accounting period which, but for the action taken by the company as mentioned in paragraph (1)(a)(i) –
(a)   would have ended on 25th November 1997 or after that date but on or before 30th June 2002, and
(b)   would have been of twelve months duration and commenced immediately following the end of the previous accounting period.

(6) The circumstances specified in this paragraph for the purposes of paragraph (1)(a)(i) are where the change in question –
(a)   derives from a decision made before, or facts in existence prior to, 25th November 1997; or
(b)   arises as a result of the accounting period concerned ending by reason of –
    (i)   the occurrence of any of the events specified in paragraphs (c) to (e) of subsection (3) of section 12 of the Taxes Act, except where the event in question occurs by reason of the transfer of the company's activities to a company which belongs to the same group, or
    (ii)  the transfer of the whole or part of the long term business of an insurance company to another company as mentioned in subsection (7A) of that section; or
(c)   arises as a result of –
    (i)   a change in the ultimate control of the company giving rise to the alignment of the company's accounting period with that of its new ultimate parent company, where the alignment is effected prior to the end of the accounting period of the new ultimate parent company in which the change occurs, or
    (ii)  a notice by the company under section 224(2) of the Companies Act 1985 (specification of accounting reference date not later than nine

months after the date of incorporation) giving rise to such alignment as is mentioned in paragraph (i).

(7) The circumstances specified in this paragraph for the purposes of paragraph (1)(a)(ii) are where –
(a) the accounting period of the company to whom the profits are transferred begins and ends on the same dates as the accounting period of the transferor company and the case is not one where the transferor company has effected a change falling within paragraph (1)(a)(i) in the date or dates of any of its relevant accounting periods;
(b) as a result of the transfer of profits, the profits of the transferor company for the accounting period in which the transfer is effected or for any subsequent accounting period are reduced by an amount not exceeding £5,000,000 or, where that accounting period is a period of less than twelve months, that amount proportionately reduced.

(8) The company specified in this paragraph for the purposes of paragraph (1)(a)(ii) is any company which –
(a) is resident outside the United Kingdom, and
(b) either –
  (i) is not trading in the United Kingdom through a branch or agency, or
  (ii) if so trading, is not a company in the case of which the taxable profits transferred form part of the taxable profits of that branch or agency.

(9) The assumptions specified in this paragraph for the purposes of paragraph (1) are that, if the company had not taken the action referred to in sub-paragraph (a) of that paragraph –
(a) reliefs available to the company or to the group to which the company belongs in calculating liability to corporation tax would have been allocated so as to result in that liability arising later rather than sooner,
(b) any profits covered or, as the case may be, not covered by reliefs would similarly have been covered or not covered, and
(c) in calculating the amount or amounts of corporation tax which would have become due and payable, or would be treated as having become due and payable on the hypothetical date or dates, not more than twelve months' taxable profits would have been allocated to any of the years falling within regulation 4, that is, the year from 1st July 1999 to 30th June 2000, the year from 1st July 2000 to 30th June 2001, and the year from 1st July 2001 to 30th June 2002, allocating taxable profits for actual accounting periods before taxable profits for relevant accounting periods.

(10) In calculating, for the purposes of this regulation, the hypothetical date or dates, it shall be assumed that –
(a) where necessary, taxable profits are apportioned between a company's accounting periods (including its relevant accounting periods) on a time basis or, where that basis would be unjust and unreasonable, on such basis as would be just and reasonable;
(b) those dates are determined as if the taxable profits concerned were the only taxable profits for an accounting period.

(11) In this regulation –
(a) 'control' shall be construed in accordance with section 416 of the Taxes Act;
(b) 'group' means a company which has one or more 51 per cent. subsidiaries together with that or those subsidiaries;

## Statutory Instruments

(c) 'hypothetical date or dates' shall be construed in accordance with paragraph (1)(b);
(d) the reference in paragraph (6)(c) to a change in the ultimate control of the company ('the relevant company') is a reference to the situation arising where –
  (i) the company which was previously not under the control of any other company in the group ('the ultimate parent company'), while retaining control of the relevant company, itself comes under the control of another company ('the new ultimate parent company') otherwise than as a result of a reorganisation, or
  (ii) the relevant company ceases to be controlled by the ultimate parent company and comes under the control of another company ('the new ultimate parent company') which is not under the control of any other company in the group, or
  (iii) otherwise than as a result of a reorganisation, the relevant company comes under the control of a company which is not itself under the control of any other company;
  and the reference in paragraph (6)(c) to 'new ultimate parent company' shall be construed accordingly;
(e) references to '51 per cent. subsidiary' shall be construed in accordance with section 838(1)(a) of the Taxes Act.

**Insurance companies and friendly societies – supplementary provision**

15. – (1) This regulation applies where –
(a) an insurance company or friendly society is entitled to a provisional repayment under Schedule 19AB to the Taxes Act (including a provisional repayment under that Schedule as modified by the Friendly Societies (Provisional Repayment for Exempt Business) Regulations 1993),
(b) an amount of corporation tax ('the relevant amount') is treated as becoming due and payable in accordance with regulation 5 of these Regulations on the date which is the fourteenth day after the end of the provisional repayment period to which the provisional repayment relates, and
(c) the whole or part of the provisional repayment is set off against the relevant amount.

(2) For the purposes of calculating –
(a) the amount of interest (if any) on the provisional repayment, and
(b) the amount of interest (if any) payable on the relevant amount,
the amount so set off shall be treated, unless the company elects otherwise, as –
  (i) a provisional repayment under Schedule 19AB to the Taxes Act, and
  (ii) a payment on account of the relevant amount,
deemed, in each case, to have been made on the date referred to in paragraph (1)(b).

## 1998 No. 3176

### The Taxes (Interest Rate) (Amendment No. 2) Regulations 1998

*Made*     *17th December 1998*
*Laid before the House of Commons*     *17th December 1998*
*Coming into force*     *7th January 1999*

# Statutory Instruments

The Treasury, in exercise of the powers conferred on them by section 178 of the Finance Act 1989, hereby make the following Regulations:

**Citation and commencement**

**1.** These Regulations may be cited as the Taxes (Interest Rate) (Amendment No. 2) Regulations 1998 and shall come into force on 7th January 1999.

**Interpretation**

**2.** In these Regulations 'the principal Regulations' means the Taxes (Interest Rate) Regulations 1989 and 'regulation' means a regulation of the principal Regulations.

**Amendments to the principal Regulations**

**3.** In regulation 2(1) –
(a) immediately before the definition of 'established rate' there shall be inserted the following definition –

'"the 1998 Regulations" means the Corporation Tax (Instalment Payments) Regulations 1998;';

(b) in the definition of 'operative date' there shall be added at the end 'or, where regulation 3ZA or 3BA applies, means the day of each month which is the Monday next following the day referred to in the definition of "reference date" below as "the first Tuesday", and the day of each month which is the Monday next following the day referred to in that definition as "the second Tuesday"';

(c) in the definition of 'reference date' there shall be added at the end 'or, where regulation 3ZA or 3BA applies, means the day of each month which is the Tuesday next following the day on which the most recent meeting of the Monetary Policy Committee of the Bank of England took place ("the first Tuesday"), and the day of each month which is the Tuesday ("the second Tuesday") occurring two weeks after the first Tuesday'.

**4.** In regulation 2(2) for the words from 'and, if the result' to the end there shall be substituted

'and –
(i) where regulation 3ZA applies, if the result is not a multiple of one-quarter, rounding the result up to the nearest amount which is such a multiple,
(ii) where regulation 3BA applies, if the result is not a multiple of one-quarter, rounding the result down to the nearest amount which is such a multiple,
(iii) in any other case, if the result is not a whole number, rounding the result to the nearest such number, with any result midway between two whole numbers rounded down.'

**5.** In paragraph (1) of regulation 3A after the word 'shall,' there shall be inserted 'except where regulation 3ZA or 3ZB applies and'.

**6.** After regulation 3A there shall be inserted –

'**3ZA.** – (1) For the purposes of section 87A of the Taxes Management Act 1970 in so far as it relates, by virtue of subsection (1A) of that section, to an

*Statutory Instruments*

amount or amounts treated as becoming due and payable in respect of the total liability of a large company for an accounting period ending on or after 1st July 1999 in accordance with regulation 5 of the 1998 Regulations, the rate applicable under section 178 shall, subject to paragraph (2), be 8.25 per cent. per annum.

(2) Where on a reference date after 7th January 1999 the reference rate found on that date differs from the established rate, the rate applicable under section 178 for the purposes mentioned in paragraph (1) shall, on and after the next operative date and as respects the period specified in paragraph (3), be the percentage per annum found by applying the formula specified in paragraph (4).

(3) The period specified in this paragraph is any period falling between –
(a) the date on which the first instalment payment is treated as becoming due and payable for the accounting period concerned under regulation 5 of the 1998 Regulations, and
(b) the day following the expiry of nine months from the end of that accounting period,

during which any amount treated as becoming due and payable in accordance with regulation 5 of those Regulations for that accounting period remains unpaid.

(4) The formula specified in this paragraph is –

$$RR+2,$$

where RR is the reference rate referred to in paragraph (2).

**3ZB.** – (1) For the purposes of section 87A of the Taxes Management Act 1970 in so far as it relates to an unpaid amount in respect of the total liability of a company for an accounting period ending on or after 1st July 1999, other than an amount to which regulation 3ZA applies, the rate applicable under section 178 shall, subject to paragraph (2), be 8.5 per cent. per annum.

(2) Where on a reference date after 7th January 1999 the reference rate found on that date differs from the established rate, the rate applicable under section 178 for the purposes mentioned in paragraph (1) shall, on and after the next operative date, be the percentage per annum found by applying the formula specified in paragraph (3).

(3) The formula specified in this paragraph is –

$$RR+2.5,$$

where RR is the reference rate referred to in paragraph (2).'

**7.** In regulation 3B after the word 'shall,' there shall be inserted 'except where regulation 3BA or 3BB applies and'.

**8.** After regulation 3B there shall be inserted –

'**3BA.** – (1) For the purposes of section 826 of the Income and Corporation Taxes Act 1988 in so far as it relates to an amount paid by a company in respect of its total liability for an accounting period ending on or after 1st July 1999, being an amount falling within paragraph (d) of subsection (1) of that section (overpayment of instalment by large company under regulation 5 of the 1998 Regulations) or an amount falling within paragraph (e) of that subsection (payment by company other than large company prior to the day following the expiry of nine months from the end of the accounting period concerned), the rate applicable under section 178 shall, subject to paragraph (2), be 6 per cent. per annum.

(2) Where on a reference date after 7th January 1999 the reference rate

found on that date differs from the established rate, the rate applicable under section 178 for the purposes mentioned in paragraph (1) shall, on and after the next operative date and as respects the period specified in paragraph (3), be the percentage per annum found by applying the formula specified in paragraph (4).

(3) The period specified in this paragraph is any period falling between –

(a) the date on which the first instalment payment is treated as becoming due and payable for the accounting period concerned under regulation 5 of the 1998 Regulations or, in the case of a company other than a large company, the date on which the first instalment payment would be so treated if the company were a large company, and

(b) the day following the expiry of nine months from the end of that accounting period,

during which there exists an amount paid by the company in respect of its total liability to which paragraph (1) applies.

(4) The formula specified in this paragraph is –

$$RR - 0.25,$$

where RR is the reference rate referred to in paragraph (2).

**3BB.** – (1) For the purposes of section 826 of the Income and Corporation Taxes Act 1988 in so far as it relates to an amount overpaid by a company in respect of its total liability for an accounting period ending on or after 1st July 1999, being an amount paid on or after the day following the expiry of nine months from the end of that period, the rate applicable under section 178 shall, subject to paragraph (2), be 5 per cent. per annum.

(2) Where on a reference date after 7th January 1999 the reference rate found on that date differs from the established rate, the rate applicable under section 178 for the purposes mentioned in paragraph (1) shall, on and after the next operative date, be the percentage per annum found by applying the formula specified in paragraph (3).

(3) The formula specified in this paragraph is –

$$RR - 1,$$

where RR is the reference rate referred to in paragraph (2).'

**1999 No. 358**

## The Corporation Tax (Treatment of Unrelieved Surplus Advance Corporation Tax) Regulations 1999

*Made*                                        *15th February 1999*
*Laid before the House of Commons*      *16th February 1999*
*Coming into force*                        *9th March 1999*

The Treasury, in exercise of the powers conferred on them by section 32 of the Finance Act 1998, hereby make the following Regulations:

## Statutory Instruments

### Citation and commencement

**1.** These Regulations may be cited as the Corporation Tax (Treatment of Unrelieved Surplus Advance Corporation Tax) Regulations 1999 and shall come into force on 9th March 1999.

### Introductory

**2.** – (1) These Regulations make provision for and in connection with enabling unrelieved surplus ACT that a company has as at 6th April 1999 to be set against its liability to corporation tax on profits charged to corporation tax for an accounting period beginning on or after that date, other than an accounting period that is subsequent to the company's final accounting period.

(2) In paragraph (1) the reference to unrelieved surplus ACT of a company includes, where the company is a member of a group at any time in an accounting period to which that paragraph applies, a reference to unrelieved surplus ACT that another company, which is a member of the same group at any time in that accounting period, has as at 6th April 1999.

### Interpretation

**3.** – (1) In these Regulations unless the context otherwise requires –

'accounting period' shall be construed in accordance with regulation 2(1);

'ACT' means advance corporation tax;

'the Board' means the Commissioners of Inland Revenue;

'distribution' has the meaning given by section 832(1);

'final accounting period' shall be construed in accordance with regulations 4 and 5;

'franked distribution' means the sum of the amount or value of a relevant distribution and such proportion of that amount or value as corresponds to the rate of shadow ACT specified in regulation 11(9), and references in these Regulations to any accounting period in which a franked distribution is made are references to the accounting period in which the relevant distribution in question is made;

'franked investment income' means income of a company resident in the United Kingdom which consists of a distribution in respect of which the company is entitled to a tax credit (and which accordingly represents income equal to the aggregate of the amount or value of the distribution and the amount of that credit), except that it does not include income to which regulation 7, 8(4) or 9 refers, or income falling within regulation 10 to which paragraph (4) of that regulation does not apply;

'group' has the meaning given by regulation 6;

'notification' means notification in writing;

'parent company' in relation to a group shall be construed in accordance with regulation 6(1) to (7); and 'immediate parent company' shall be construed in accordance with regulation 6(8);

'relevant distribution' means a distribution made on or after 6th April 1999;

*Statutory Instruments*

'shadow ACT' means a notional amount of ACT treated as paid by a company in respect of a relevant distribution and computed in accordance with regulation 11;

'straddling accounting period' means an accounting period beginning before, and ending on or after, 6th April 1999, and includes a separate accounting period mentioned in sections 245(2), 245A(2) and 245B(2);

'surplus franked investment income' –
(a) as respects an accounting period beginning on or after 6th April 1999, has the meaning given by regulation 11(13);
(b) as respects an accounting period beginning before that date, has the meaning given by section 238(1A);

'surplus shadow ACT' means the excess amount of shadow ACT over the total amount of shadow ACT set against a company's liability to corporation tax for an accounting period in accordance with regulation 12(1);

'the Taxes Act' means the Income and Corporation Taxes Act 1988;

'unrelieved surplus ACT' means the ACT (if any) which, apart from sub-paragraph (3) of paragraph 12 of Schedule 3 to the Finance Act 1998 but otherwise in accordance with that paragraph, would be treated by virtue of section 239(4) as paid in respect of distributions made by a company in the first accounting period of the company to begin on or after 6th April 1999.

(2) References in these Regulations to the profits of a company charged to corporation tax for any accounting period are references to the amount of the company's profits for that period on which corporation tax falls finally to be borne.

(3) References in these Regulations, however expressed, to a company's liability to corporation tax for an accounting period include references to a company's liability in respect of any sums chargeable on the company for that period under section 747(4)(a) (controlled foreign companies).

(4) For the purposes only of these Regulations, a straddling accounting period shall be treated as if –
(a) it were composed of two accounting periods, the one ending on 5th April 1999 and the other beginning on 6th April 1999;
(b) there were apportioned to each of those accounting periods the proportionate part of the profits of the company charged to corporation tax for the straddling accounting period.

(5) References in these Regulations to an accounting period beginning on or after 6th April 1999 include references to –
(a) an accounting period deemed by virtue of paragraph (4) of this regulation to begin on 6th April 1999, and
(b) a separate accounting period referred to in regulations 16(2) and 17(2) that begins on or after that date.

(6) References in these Regulations, other than the reference in paragraph (4)(b) above, to a requirement for profits charged to corporation tax for an accounting period to be apportioned between two separate parts of that accounting period are references to a requirement for those profits to be apportioned either –
(a) on a time basis, or
(b) where that basis would be unjust and unreasonable, on such basis as would be just and reasonable.

(7) In these Regulations any reference to a particular provision, without more, is a reference to that provision of the Taxes Act.

## Statutory Instruments

### Definition of final accounting period – company not a member of a group

**4.** – (1) For the purpose of regulation 2(1) and subject to paragraphs (3) to (5) of this regulation and to regulation 5(10), where a company is not a member of a group at any time in the relevant accounting period, the final accounting period of that company is the accounting period beginning in the period of twelve months immediately following the end of the relevant accounting period or, if there is more than one accounting period beginning in that period of twelve months, the latest accounting period beginning in that period.

(2) In paragraph (1) 'the relevant accounting period' is the first accounting period of the company after which no amount of unrelieved surplus ACT is available to be set against the company's liability to corporation tax in accordance with these Regulations.

(3) Paragraph (1) shall not apply where, at any time in the first of its accounting periods to begin on or after 6th April 1999, the company notifies an officer of the Board that it will not seek or, as the case may be, will cease to seek recovery of unrelieved surplus ACT in respect of that accounting period or any subsequent accounting period.

(4) Where, otherwise than in a case to which paragraph (3) applies, the company notifies an officer of the Board at any time in an accounting period that it wishes that accounting period to be its final accounting period and that it will not seek recovery of unrelieved surplus ACT in respect of any subsequent accounting period, the final accounting period of that company is, subject to paragraph (5), the accounting period in which the notification is made.

(5) Where –
(a)  there is an amount of surplus shadow ACT in respect of an accounting period of the company beginning in the period of twelve months ('the relevant period') immediately following the end of the accounting period in which the company notifies an officer of the Board as mentioned in paragraph (4) or, if there is more than one such accounting period, the latest accounting period beginning in the relevant period, and
(b)  that amount or any part of it falls to be carried back in accordance with regulation 12(7) to the accounting period in which that notification is made,

the final accounting period shall be the accounting period or, as the case may be, the latest accounting period beginning in the relevant period from which an amount of surplus shadow ACT falls to be carried back as mentioned in sub-paragraph (b) of this paragraph, and not the accounting period in which the notification is made.

### Definition of final accounting period – company a member of a group

**5.** – (1) For the purpose of regulation 2 and subject to paragraphs (3) to (10), where a company is a member of a group at any time in the relevant accounting period, the final accounting period of that company in its capacity as a member of that group is the accounting period beginning in the period of twelve months immediately following the end of the relevant accounting period or, if there is more than one accounting period beginning in that period of twelve months, the latest accounting period beginning in that period.

(2) In paragraph (1) 'the relevant accounting period' is the first accounting period of the company after which no amount of unrelieved surplus ACT

belonging to the company or any other company which is a member of the group at any time in that accounting period is available to be set against any liability to corporation tax in accordance with these Regulations; and for this purpose unrelieved surplus ACT belonging to another company that is a member of the group at any time in that accounting period shall be regarded as so available until the end of that other company's accounting period.

(3) Paragraph (1) shall not apply where –
(a) the company is a member of the group as at 6th April 1999, and
(b) at any time in the first accounting period of the parent company of the group to begin on or after that date, the parent company notifies an officer of the Board on behalf of the group that the group will not seek or, as the case may be, will cease to seek recovery of unrelieved surplus ACT in respect of any accounting period of any member of the group that begins on or after that date.

(4) A notification made in accordance with paragraph (3) shall, subject to paragraph (9), be binding on each company that was a member of the group as at 6th April 1999.

(5) Where, otherwise than in a case to which paragraph (3) applies, at any time in an accounting period of the parent company of the group the parent company notifies an officer of the Board on behalf of the group that the group wishes the accounting period of any member of the group in which the notification is made to be the final accounting period of that member and that it will not seek recovery of amounts of unrelieved surplus ACT available to that member in respect of any subsequent accounting period, the final accounting period of that member and the final accounting period of the parent company is, subject to paragraphs (7) to (10), the accounting period of the parent company in which the notification by the parent company is made.

(6) A notification made in accordance with paragraph (5) shall, subject to paragraph (10), be binding on each company that was a member of the group when the notification was made or that subsequently becomes a member of the group prior to the end of the parent company's final accounting period.

(7) Where paragraph (5) applies and the accounting period of a company in the group other than the parent company that would otherwise be its final accounting period in accordance with that paragraph begins before the end of, but ends after, the accounting period of the parent company in which the notification by the parent company is made, the accounting period of the company concerned shall be treated as if the part ending with the last day of the parent company's accounting period, and the part after, were two separate accounting periods; and the part ending with the last day of the parent company's accounting period shall, subject to paragraph (10), be treated as the company's final accounting period for the purposes of this regulation.

(8) Where –
(a) there is an amount of surplus shadow ACT in respect of an accounting period of any company that is a member of the group beginning in the period of twelve months ('the relevant period') immediately following the end of the accounting period of the company in which the parent company notifies an officer of the Board as mentioned in paragraph (5), and
(b) all or any part of that surplus amount falls to be carried back under regulation 12 or 13 to an accounting period of a company that is a member of the group ending before the relevant period of the company referred to in sub-paragraph (a),

the final accounting period of any company that is a member of the group at any time in the relevant period shall, subject to paragraph (10), be the accounting

## Statutory Instruments

period or, if more than one, the latest accounting period beginning in the relevant period from which an amount of surplus shadow ACT falls to be carried back as mentioned in sub-paragraph (b) of this paragraph, and not the accounting period referred to in paragraph (5).

(9) Where in an accounting period ('the material period') subsequent to the accounting period in which the parent company notifies an officer of the Board as mentioned in paragraph (3), a company which has an amount of unrelieved surplus ACT becomes a member of the group, these Regulations shall apply in relation to the material period (but not earlier accounting periods) as if no notification had been made in accordance with that paragraph, but not so as to entitle any company to whom that notification, when made, applied to seek recovery of any amount of unrelieved surplus ACT.

(10) Where in an accounting period ('the material period') subsequent to the final accounting period as determined in accordance with paragraph (1), (5), (7) or (8), a company which has an amount of unrelieved surplus ACT becomes a member of the group, these Regulations shall apply in relation to the material period (but not earlier accounting periods) as if the final accounting period had not yet been determined in accordance with any of those paragraphs, but not so as to entitle a company whose final accounting period had previously been determined in accordance with those provisions to seek recovery of any amount of unrelieved surplus ACT.

(11) Where –
(a) a company is a member of two or more groups,
(b) its final accounting period as a member of one or more, but not all, of the groups concerned has been determined in accordance with the previous provisions of this regulation, and
(c) at least one of those determinations is as a result of a notification made by a parent company in accordance with paragraph (5) of this regulation,

these Regulations shall have effect in relation to the group or groups in respect of which the final accounting period of the company has not been determined as if the total amount of its unrelieved surplus ACT had been set against its liability to corporation tax in accordance with regulation 14.

### Definition of group

6. – (1) In these Regulations 'group' means a company resident in the United Kingdom ('the parent company') which has one or more 51 per cent. subsidiaries together with that or those subsidiaries.

(2) For the purposes of paragraph (1) –
(a) '51 per cent. subsidiary' means a 51 per cent. subsidiary that is a company resident in the United Kingdom;
(b) a company is not the parent company within a group if –
   (i) it has no 51 per cent. subsidiary but is itself a 51 per cent. subsidiary of another company, or
   (ii) it and its 51 per cent. subsidiaries are all members of another group;
(c) the question whether a company is a 51 per cent. subsidiary of the parent company shall be determined, subject to paragraph (3), in accordance with section 838, except that the parent company shall be treated as not being the owner –
   (i) of any share capital which it owns directly in a company if a profit on the sale of the shares would be treated as a trading receipt of its trade; or

(ii) of any share capital which it owns indirectly, and which is owned directly by a body corporate for which a profit on the sale of the shares would be treated as a trading receipt of its trade; or

(iii) of any share capital which it owns directly or indirectly in a body corporate not resident in the United Kingdom.

(3) Where a company would otherwise not be a 51 per cent. subsidiary, but –

(a) persons, whether company members or not, enjoy extraordinary rights or powers under the articles of association or under any other document regulating the company, and

(b) because of that fact, ownership of the ordinary share capital (for the purposes of the definition of '51 per cent. subsidiary' in section 838(1)(a)) may not be an appropriate test of whether a company is a 51 per cent. subsidiary of the parent company,

then in considering whether a company is a 51 per cent. subsidiary of the parent company for the purposes of paragraph (1), holdings of all kinds of share capital, including preference shares, or of any particular category of share capital, or voting power or any other kind of special power may be taken into account instead of ordinary share capital.

(4) Notwithstanding that, apart from this paragraph, a company ('the subsidiary company') would at any time be a 51 per cent. subsidiary of the parent company for the purposes of this regulation, the subsidiary company shall not be treated at that time as a 51 per cent. subsidiary for those purposes –

(a) if arrangements are in existence by virtue of which any person has or could obtain, or any persons together have or could obtain, control of the subsidiary company but not of the parent company; and

(b) unless the following conditions are also fulfilled, namely –
(i) that the parent company is beneficially entitled to more than 50 per cent. of any profits available for distribution to equity holders of the subsidiary company; and
(ii) that the parent company would be beneficially entitled to more than 50 per cent. of any assets of the subsidiary company available for distribution to its equity holders on a winding up.

(5) In paragraph (4) –

'arrangements' means arrangements of any kind, whether in writing or not, other than arrangements whose sole or main purpose is to reduce the amount of surplus shadow ACT available to be utilised by a company other than the subsidiary company in accordance with regulation 13;

'control' has the meaning given by section 840.

(6) Where by virtue of any enactment a Minister of the Crown or Northern Ireland department has power to give directions to a statutory body as to the disposal of assets belonging to, or to a subsidiary of, that body, the existence of that power shall not be regarded as constituting (or as having at any time constituted) an arrangement within the meaning of paragraph (4)(a).

(7) The provisions of Schedule 18 shall apply for the purposes of paragraph (4)(b) as if –

(a) for any reference to section 413(7) to (9) there were substituted a reference to paragraph (4)(b);

(b) paragraph 7(1) of that Schedule were omitted and for any reference to 'the relevant accounting period' there were substituted a reference to the accounting period current at the time in question.

(8) For the purposes of these Regulations, a company ('A') is the 'immediate parent company' of another company ('B') if, disregarding any other company of

*Statutory Instruments*

which B is a 51 per cent. subsidiary by virtue of section 838 and this regulation, A would be the parent company of B by virtue of section 838 and this regulation.

**Restriction on franked investment income – replacement of income**

**7.** Where a company takes any action the effect of which is that income consisting of interest to which a company is or will be entitled becomes or is replaced by income consisting of a distribution, and the main purpose of that action is to reduce the amount of shadow ACT which it would be treated as having paid under regulation 11 for an accounting period, the income consisting of the distribution shall not be regarded for the purposes of these Regulations as franked investment income.

**Restriction on franked investment income – arrangements to pass on value of franked investment income**

**8.** – (1) This regulation applies in any case where –
(a) a person ('A') who is a company is entitled to franked investment income;
(b) arrangements subsist such that another person ('B') obtains, whether directly or indirectly, a payment representing any of the value of that franked investment income, in excess of the payment that would have been made in the circumstances specified in paragraph (2);
(c) the arrangements (whether or not made directly between A and B) were entered into for an unallowable purpose, and
(d) neither A nor B is a company whose final accounting period has been determined in accordance with regulation 4 or 5.

(2) The circumstances specified in this paragraph are where –
(a) the payment representing any of the value of that franked investment income was made under a transaction between persons at arm's length both of whom were companies;
(b) neither company was or had been at any time a member of a group, and
(c) neither company was entitled to an amount of unrelieved surplus ACT as at 6th April 1999.

(3) This regulation does not apply if and to the extent that any provision of the Tax Acts has the effect of cancelling or reducing the tax advantage which would otherwise be obtained by virtue of the arrangements.

(4) Where this regulation applies, the franked investment income referred to in paragraph (1) shall not be regarded for the purposes of these Regulations as franked investment income.

(5) For the purposes of this regulation, the question whether any arrangements were entered into for an 'unallowable purpose' shall be determined in accordance with paragraphs (6) and (7).

(6) Arrangements are entered into for an unallowable purpose if the purposes for which A is a party to the arrangements include the purpose of reducing the amount of shadow ACT treated as paid, in accordance with regulation 11, on relevant distributions made –
(a) by A, or
(b) where A is a member of a group, by any other company which is a member of that group,
at any time in, or after the end of, the accounting period in which the arrangements are entered into.

*Statutory Instruments*

(7) In determining for the purposes of paragraph (6) whether a company could have used franked investment income for the purpose of reducing shadow ACT, the company shall be taken to use its actual franked investment income for that purpose before using the franked investment income in question.

(8) In this regulation –

'arrangements' means arrangements of any kind, whether in writing or not (and includes a series of arrangements, whether or not between the same parties);

'tax advantage' has the same meaning as in Chapter I of Part XVII of the Taxes Act.

## 1999 No. 1929

## The Corporation Tax (Instalment Payments) (Amendment) Regulations 1999

| | |
|---|---|
| Made | 6th July 1999 |
| Laid before the House of Commons | 7th July 1999 |
| Coming into force | 28th July 1999 |

The Treasury, in exercise of the powers conferred on them by section 59E of the Taxes Management Act 1970, hereby make the following Regulations:

### 1 Citation, commencement and effect

(1) These Regulations may be cited as the Corporation Tax (Instalment Payments) (Amendment) Regulations 1999 and shall come into force on 28th July 1999.

(2) These Regulations have effect in relation to accounting periods of companies ending on or after 1st July 1999.

### 2 Interpretation

In these Regulations 'the principal Regulations' means the Corporation Tax (Instalment Payments) Regulations 1998 and 'regulation' means a regulation of the principal Regulations.

### 3 Amendments to the principal Regulations

(1) Regulation 9 (consequential amendment of section 102 of the Finance Act 1989) is amended as follows.

(2) In paragraph (1) for the words from 'in relation' to the end there shall be substituted the words 'with the modifications specified in paragraphs (2) to (4) in any case where a tax refund falls to be made to the surrendering company in respect of an amount paid in respect of its total liability for an accounting period and –

(a) either the surrendering company or the recipient company referred to in that section is a large company as respects that accounting period, or

(b) both the surrendering company and the recipient company so referred to are large companies as respects that accounting period.'

(3) In paragraph (2) for sub-paragraph (b) there shall be substituted the following paragraph –

## Statutory Instruments

'(b) after paragraph (c) of that definition there shall be added "or

(d) the repayment of the whole or any part of any amount paid by way of an instalment under the Corporation Tax (Instalment Payments) Regulations 1998 in respect of the company's total liability for the period."'

(4) For paragraph (3) there shall be substituted the following paragraphs –

'(3) In subsection (5) after the word "refund" there shall be inserted the words "other than a refund of instalment corporation tax".'

(4) After subsection (5) there shall be inserted the following subsections –

'(5A) In subsection (4) above "the relevant date", in relation to a refund of instalment corporation tax, means –

(a) in so far as the refund falls to be treated in accordance with subsections (5C) to (5E) below as consisting of a repayment of the whole or any part of a payment made on or before the earliest due date, that date; and

(b) in so far as the refund falls to be treated in accordance with those subsections as consisting of the repayment of the whole or any part of a payment made after the earliest due date, the date on which the payment was made.

(5B) For the purposes of subsection (5A) above the earliest due date, in relation to a refund of instalment corporation tax, is –

(a) where the surrendering company is a large company for the relevant accounting period, the earliest date on which any amount is treated as having become due and payable by that company under regulation 5 of the Corporation Tax (Instalment Payments) Regulations 1998 in respect of that company's total liability for that period; and

(b) where the surrendering company is not a large company for that accounting period, the date that would have been the earliest due date under paragraph (a) above had it been a large company for that period.

(5C) For the purposes of subsection (5A) above the surrendering company shall, at the same time as the giving of the notice under subsection (2) above in the case of any refund of instalment corporation tax relating to any accounting period, give notice to the inspector identifying the extent to which it requires the refund to be treated as consisting of amounts comprised in any payment or payments made for that period.

(5D) Where, in a case to which subsection (5C) above applies, the inspector notifies the surrendering company that the amount of the refund of instalment corporation tax relating to the accounting period is less than the aggregate of the amounts identified under that subsection, that company shall, not later than thirty days after the notification, give a revised notice under that subsection to the inspector.

(5E) Where, in a case to which subsection (5D) above applies –

(a) a notification has been given to the surrendering company under that subsection, and

(b) the surrendering company fails to give a revised notice in accordance with the requirements of that subsection,

the same consequences shall follow as if no notice had been given in accordance with subsection (2) above in relation to the refund.

*Statutory Instruments*

(5F) In this section –

(a) references to a refund of instalment corporation tax are references to any such refund of tax for any accounting period as falls in relation to that accounting period within paragraph (d) of the definition of "tax refund relating to an accounting period" in subsection (3) above;

(b) references to a large company shall be construed in accordance with regulation 3 of the Corporation Tax (Instalment Payments) Regulations 1998;

(c) references to the total liability of a company for an accounting period shall be construed in accordance with regulation 2(3) of those Regulations.'

4. In regulation 12(1) immediately before the words 'require a company' there shall be inserted the words 'by notice'.

**1999 No. 2975**

## Corporation Tax (Simplified Arrangements for Group Relief) Regulations 1999

*Made*                                                        *1 November 1999*
*Laid before the House of Commons*             *2 November 1999*
*Coming into force*                              *23 November 1999*

The Treasury, in exercise of the powers conferred on them by paragraph 77 of Schedule 18 to the Finance Act 1998, hereby make the following Regulations:

**Citation and commencement**

1. These Regulations may be cited as the Corporation Tax (Simplified Arrangements for Group Relief) Regulations 1999 and shall come into force on 23rd November 1999.

**Introduction**

2. These Regulations make provision for arrangements for the surrendering and claiming of group relief in relation to any accounting period of a claimant company ending on or after 1st July 1999.

**Interpretation**

3.–(1) In these Regulations unless the context otherwise requires—
    'the arrangements' means the arrangements made by these Regulations as mentioned in regulation 2;
    'authorised company' has the meaning given by regulation 4;
    'authorising companies' has the meaning given by regulation 5;
    'the Board' means the Commissioners of Inland Revenue;
    'claimant company' has the meaning given by section 402(1);
    'consortium company' has the meaning given by section 406(1)(b);
    'group of companies' means a collection of companies such that every pair of companies within that collection comprises companies that are members of the same group of companies within the meaning of section 413(3)(a);
    'group relief' has the meaning given by subsection (1) of section 402, read with subsection (2) of that section (group claim) and subsection (3) of that section and section 406 (consortium claim);

## Statutory Instruments

'insolvency practitioner' in relation to a company means a liquidator, provisional liquidator, administrator, administrative receiver, or a supervisor of a voluntary arrangement under Part I of the Insolvency Act 1986;

'the Management Act' means the Taxes Management Act 1970;

'member of the consortium' shall be construed in accordance with section 413(6);

'Schedule 18' means Schedule 18 to the Finance Act 1998;

'three month date' shall be construed in accordance with regulation 7(1).

(2) In these Regulations references to a section, without more, are to that section of the Income and Corporation Taxes Act 1988.

**Authorised company**

4. A company is an 'authorised company' for the purposes of these Regulations if—

(a) it is authorised by companies within regulation 5 to act on their behalf in relation to the arrangements, and

(b) it is a member of the same group of companies as that referred to in regulation 5(1)(a).

**Authorising company**

5.–(1) In these Regulations an 'authorising company' means a company which for the time being—

(a) is a member of a group of companies, or

(b) is a consortium company in circumstances where a company falling within sub-paragraph (a) is a member of the consortium concerned, and

(c) in either case satisfies one of the conditions specified in paragraph (2).

(2) Those conditions are that the company—

(a) is one of the companies named in the application made by the authorised company in accordance with regulation 6;

(b) following the making of that application, is treated for the purposes of these Regulations, by agreement between the company, the authorised company and the Board, as if it had been one of the companies named in that application.

**Application by authorised company**

6.–(1) An application by the authorised company on behalf of itself and the authorising companies to enter into the arrangements must be made in writing to an officer of the Board.

(2) The application must specify—

(a) the name and the tax office reference of the authorised company,

(b) the names and the tax office references of the authorising companies, and

(c) details relating to the authorised company and each of the authorising companies that are sufficient to demonstrate that the company concerned is a member of the group of companies or, as the case may be, a consortium company.

*Statutory Instruments*

(3) The application must contain a statement by the authorised company and the authorising companies that they agree to be covered by the arrangements and to be bound by claims, surrenders and withdrawals made under the arrangements.

(4) The application must be accompanied—

(a) by a specimen copy of the statement referred to in regulation 10(2) that the authorised company proposes to use for the purpose of making and withdrawing surrenders and claims on behalf of itself and the authorising companies;

(b) in the case of a company which is a consortium company, by an agreement, signed by each member of the consortium and the consortium company, consenting to the authorised company acting on their behalf in relation to the arrangements.

(5) The application must be signed on behalf of each of the companies concerned by a person referred to in section 108(1) of the Management Act as a person through whom that company may act.

(6) The application must be sent to the tax office dealing with the tax affairs of the authorised company.

**Matters consequential to the making of an application**

7.–(1) Except where paragraph (2), (3) or (4) applies and subject to regulation 9, the authorised company may enter into the arrangements on behalf of itself and the authorising companies at any time on or after the date ('the three month date') that is three months after the date on which the application is delivered to the tax office in accordance with regulation 6(6).

(2) An officer of the Board may, prior to the three month date, accept the application and permit the authorised company to enter into the arrangements on behalf of itself and the authorising companies with effect from the date notified to the authorised company by the officer of the Board.

(3) An officer of the Board may, prior to the three month date, accept the application and permit the authorised company to enter into the arrangements with effect from the date notified to the company by the officer of the Board, but exclude from the arrangements any of the authorising companies on the grounds that he has reason to believe that that company—

(a) has failed to comply with its obligations under the Corporation Tax Acts in relation to any accounting period (whether an accounting period ending before, or on or after, 1st July 1999), or

(b) is a company in relation to which a person is acting as an insolvency practitioner.

(4) An officer of the Board may, prior to the three month date, refuse the application on the grounds that—

(a) he has reason to believe that one or more of the companies named in the application is not a member of a group of companies, or is not a consortium company in circumstances where a company which is a member of that group is a member of the consortium concerned,

(b) he has reason to believe that one or more of the companies named in the application has failed to comply with its obligations under the Corporation Tax Acts in relation to any accounting period (whether an accounting period ending before, or on or after, 1st July 1999),

*Statutory Instruments*

(c) the case is not one in which all, or substantially all, of the companies named in the application deliver their company tax returns to the same tax office, or

(d) the specimen copy of the statement referred to in regulation 6(4)(a) is not adequate for the purpose of enabling an officer of the Board to deal with claims for group relief.

(5) Where following the making of an application by an authorised company under regulation 6 a company is treated by agreement in accordance with regulation 5(2)(b) as if it had been one of the companies named in the application, the authorised company may enter into the arrangements on behalf of that company from the date of the agreement.

**Change in members or consortium**

8.–(1) Where following the making of an application under regulation 6 there is a change in the members of the consortium referred to in paragraph (4)(b) of that regulation, as from the date of the change the authorised company may not act in accordance with the provisions of regulation 10 in relation to the consortium company concerned unless it takes the action specified in paragraph (2).

(2) The action specified in this paragraph is that the company must ensure that a new agreement, signed by the consortium company concerned and each company that is a member of the consortium immediately after the change, consenting to the authorised company acting on their behalf in relation to the arrangements, is sent to the tax office referred to in regulation 6(6).

(3) Where in accordance with paragraph (2) a new agreement is entered into and sent to the tax office, that agreement is effective for the purposes of the arrangements as from the date on which acceptance of the agreement is notified by an officer of the Board to the authorised company.

**Exclusion of company from the arrangements**

9. An officer of the Board may, at any time on or after the three month date or, if earlier, the date on which an application under regulation 6 was accepted, exclude from the arrangements a company named, or treated under regulation 5(2)(b) as named, in that application, on the grounds that he has reason to believe that that company—

(a) is nor an authorising company at that time by reason of the company not falling within regulation 5(1)(a) or (b);

(b) has failed to comply with its obligations under the Corporation Tax Acts in relation to any accounting period (whether an accounting period ending before, or on or after, 1st July 1999); or

(c) is a company in relation to which a person is acting as an insolvency practitioner.

**Group relief claims and surrenders under the arrangements**

10.–(1) Where an application by an authorised company is accepted by an officer of the Board under regulation 7, the authorised company may act in accordance with the following provisions of this regulation in relation to itself and to any of the authorising companies, other than a company excluded from the arrangements in accordance with regulation 7(3) or 9.

(2) The authorised company may from time to time furnish to an officer of the

## Statutory Instruments

Board on behalf of itself and the authorising companies a statement in writing, in the form provided, or in a form authorised, by the Board, containing information necessary for the amendment in accordance with the provisions of Part VIII of Schedule 18 of the company tax returns of itself and the authorising companies for the purpose of making and withdrawing claims and surrenders of group relief.

(3) Where a statement is furnished to an officer of the Board as mentioned in paragraph (2)—

(a) the provisions of Part VIII of Schedule 18, other than paragraph 70(4) (claim for group relief ineffective unless accompanied by copy of notice of consent to surrender) and paragraph 71(4) (notice of withdrawal of consent to surrender ineffective unless accompanied by notice of consent of claimant company to withdrawal), shall apply in relation to the authorised company as if references to the claimant company and the surrendering company included references to the authorised company;

(b) amendments made in accordance with the provisions of Part VIII of Schedule 18 to the company tax returns of the authorising companies in reliance on the information contained in the statement shall have effect for the purposes of the Corporation Tax Acts as if the amendments had been made by those companies.

(4) Without prejudice to the generality of paragraph (2), the information to be contained in the statement must include in particular—

(a) as regards the amount claimed, the same information as is specified in paragraph 68 of Schedule 18,

(b) as regards the amount surrendered, the same information as is specified in paragraph 71(1) of Schedule 18,

(c) where applicable, details showing the effect of the claim on each company's self-assessment included in its company tax return, and

(d) where applicable, details showing which of the company tax returns of the companies concerned are returns into which an enquiry is in progress under Part IV of Schedule 18.

(5) A statement provided under paragraph (2) that does not contain information that is sufficient for the amendment of the company tax returns of the authorised company and the authorising companies in accordance with the provisions of Part VIII of Schedule 18 is ineffective.

(6) An authorising company remains liable, in accordance with the provisions of Schedule 18, for any incorrect claim or incorrect company tax return arising from a statement provided by the authorised company under paragraph (2).

**Termination of arrangements and exclusion of applicant company from arrangements**

**11.**—(1) Either the Board or the authorised company may at any time give notice in writing to the other terminating the arrangements with effect from the date of issue of the notice.

(2) The authorised company may at any time give notice in writing to the Board excluding an authorising company from the arrangements with effect from the date of issue of the notice.

*Statutory Instruments*

**2000 No. 892**

**Corporation Tax (Instalment Payments) (Amendment) Regulations 2000**

| | |
|---|---|
| *Made* | *29 March 2000* |
| *Laid before the House of Commons* | *29 March 2000* |
| *Coming into force* | *19 April 2000* |

The Treasury, in exercise of the powers conferred on them by section 59E of the Taxes Management Act 1970, hereby make the following Regulations:

**1.** These Regulations may be cited as the Corporation Tax (Instalment Payments) (Amendment) Regulations 2000, shall come into force on 19th April 2000 and shall have effect in relation to accounting periods of companies ending on or after 1st July 2000.

**2.** In regulation 3(2) of the Corporation Tax (Instalment Payments) Regulations 1998 for '£5,000' substitute '£10,000'.

**2000 No. 893**

**Taxes (Interest Rate) (Amendment) Regulations 2000**

| | |
|---|---|
| *Made* | *29 March 2000* |
| *Laid before the House of Commons* | *29 March 2000* |
| *Coming into force* | *19 April 2000* |

The Treasury, in exercise of the powers conferred on them by section 178 of the Finance Act 1989, hereby make the following Regulations:

**1.** These Regulations may be cited as the Taxes (Interest Rate) (Amendment) Regulations 2000 and shall come into force on 19th April 2000.

**2.**–(1) In regulation 3ZA(4) of the Taxes (Interest Rate) Regulations 1989 for 'RR + 2' substitute 'RR + 1'.

(2) Paragraph (1) has effect on and after 20th April 2000 in relation to interest running from before that day as well as interest running from, or from after, that day.

*Appendix 4*

# Statement of Practice 4/98

**Application of loan relationships, foreign exchange and financial instruments legislation to partnerships which include companies**

**General**

**1.** This statement of practice supersedes an earlier statement (*SP 9/94*). That statement dealt with the application of the foreign exchange and financial instruments legislation to partnerships of which at least one partner was a company within the charge to corporation tax. It did not deal with the effect of the loan relationships legislation introduced by *FA 1996*. That legislation made a major reform to the corporation tax treatment of government and corporate debt. *SP 9/94* will continue to be relevant for accounting periods ending on or before 31 March 1996. This statement of practice should be applied to later periods.

**2.** This revised statement of practice describes the Inland Revenue's view of how the rules for partnerships apply where profits, losses and other amounts arise to the partnership from loan relationships (corporate and government debt), exchange differences and financial instruments and to transactions between a partnership and its members in these areas.

**Statutory framework**

**3.** *TA 1988 s 8(2)* provides that a company is chargeable on profits arising to it under any partnership.

**4.** *TA 1988 s 114* gives the rules for computing profits and losses of a trade or business where one or more of the partnership members is a company. The profits and losses of the partnership are computed, for the purposes of corporation tax, as if the partnership were a company, separate from any company which is a partner. The trade or business carried on is also treated as separate from any trade etc which the company member carries on its own account.

**5.** These basic rules therefore apply to the computation of profits and losses under –

- the loan relationships legislation in *FA 1996 Part IV Ch II*;
- the foreign exchange gains and losses (FOREX) legislation in *FA 1993 Part II Ch II*; and
- the financial instruments (FI) legislation in *FA 1994 Part II Ch II*.

## Statement of Practice 4/98

Some modifications and consequential adaptations, described in this statement of practice, are needed to address particular situations.

**6.** The effect of *TA 1988 s 114* is to treat the partnership for tax purposes as itself –

- a party to loan relationships for the purposes of *FA 1996 Part IV Ch II*;
- as entitled to assets and subject to liabilities for the purposes of the FOREX legislation; and
- entitled to rights, or subject to duties, under interest rate, currency or debt contracts or options for the purposes of the FI legislation;

whatever the position under the general law relating to the partnership.

**7.** *FA 1994 s 172* provides a special rule for partnerships, one or more of whose members is a 'qualifying company' for the purposes of the legislation in that Act on financial instruments. A qualifying company for that purpose is any company but it does not include the trustees of an authorised unit trust (even though they are treated as if they were a company for other purposes), nor does it include an open-ended investment company ('OEIC'). It does include an approved investment trust company in relation to interest rate and debt contracts but not in relation to currency contracts. Where a partnership includes both at least one qualifying company and at least one company which is not a qualifying company, s 172(4) operates to require two separate corporation tax computations for the purposes of s 114(1). Otherwise it does no more than reinforce the requirements of s 114.

**8.** Although there is a similar definition in *FA 1993 s 153* (exchange differences) of 'qualifying company' (although for the FOREX legislation an investment trust company is never a qualifying company), there is no specific rule equivalent to *FA 1994 s 172*. The practice of the Inland Revenue in the rare cases where a non-qualifying company is a member of a partnership will be to follow *FA 1994 s 172* as if it applied to exchange differences.

**9.** There is no concept of qualifying company in *FA 1996 Part II Ch II* (loan relationships). However the trustees of an authorised unit trust and an OEIC, although treated as companies for many purposes of the Tax Acts, are treated for the purposes of the loan relationships legislation as if they were subject to income tax rules (*FA 1996 Sch 10 para 2(2)* and the Open-ended Investment Companies (Tax) Regulations 1997 [, *SI 1997 No. 1154 Part II*, see *Simon's Weekly Tax Intelligence* 1997]). It follows that where the trustees of an authorised unit trust are, or an OEIC is, a member of a partnership, they will not be treated as companies to whom credits and debits under the loan relationships legislation can be attributed under s 114.

### Computation of partnership profits and losses

**10.** In any case where one or more companies is a member of a partnership, and they are not all excluded from the application of the relevant legislation by paras 7–9 above, partnerships should prepare computations of profits and losses from any trade or business under *TA 1988 s 114* on the basis that the foreign exchange gains

*Statement of Practice 4/98*

and losses, financial instruments and loan relationships legislation apply to the partnership as if it were a company. This computation will be used to determine the shares of profits and losses appropriate to members subject to corporation tax and who are neither investment trusts (except in relation to interest rate and debt contracts), OEICs nor the trustees of authorised unit trusts.

**11.** Where any member of the partnership is an investment trust, an OEIC or the trustees of an authorised unit trust, another computation should be prepared on the basis that corporation tax rules ignoring the FOREX and FI legislation apply (except where an investment trust is a party to interest rate or debt contracts), and in the case of an authorised unit trust or OEIC, that the rules in *FA 1996 Sch 13* rather than the rest of *FA 1996 Part IV Ch II*, apply. This computation will be used to determine the shares of profits and losses appropriate to those members.

**12.** Where there are members of the partnership who are neither companies, nor the trustees of an authorised unit trust, a computation of profits and losses for the purposes of income tax, made under *TA 1988 s 111* will also be required.

**13.** Profits and losses (including interest) on loan relationships are treated by *FA 1996 Part IV Ch II* as credits and debits. The debits and credits for the partnership should be computed following the rules in that chapter. In particular –

– The authorised accounting method used should be that used in the partnership accounts, with an authorised accruals method being used if the partnership accounts do not conform with either authorised method – *FA 1996 s 86*.

– A claim under *FA 1996 s 91* to set off income tax in the period of receipt rather than accrual may be made.

– The special rules for convertible, asset linked and index-linked gilt-edged securities may apply – *FA 1996 ss 92(96)94*.

– Exchange differences are left out of account – *FA 1996 Sch 9 para 4*.

– The bad debt rules in *FA 1996 Sch 9 para 5* apply.

– The anti-avoidance rules on imported losses (*FA 1996 Sch 9 para 10*), transactions not at arm's length (*para 11*) and loan relationships for unallowable purposes (*para 13*) will apply.

But –

– The rules in *FA 1996 Sch 9 para 12* about continuity of treatment where loan relationships are transferred between members of a group of companies will not apply where a loan relationship is transferred to or by a partnership.

– A change in partnership profit sharing ratios, including a case where a company joins or leaves a partnership does not of itself give rise to a related transaction in a loan relationship to which the partnership is a party.

**14.** Trading profits and losses deriving from exchange differences – *FA 1993 s 128* – and non-trading profits or losses treated by *FA 1993 ss 129, 130* as non-trading debits or credits under the loan relationships legislation should also be computed as set out in para 10 above. In particular –

475

## Statement of Practice 4/98

- Valuations of assets and liabilities should be made in accordance with the accounting methods used by the partnership – *FA 1993 s 159*.

- The main benefit and arm's length rules in *FA 1993 ss 135–138* will apply by reference to the circumstances of the partnership.

- *FA 1993 ss 140–143* (deferral of certain gains) may apply. In computing the amount that may be deferred, the whole of the profits and of various types of exchange gains and losses of the partnership, as computed for the purposes of corporation tax, will be taken into account.

**15.** Trading profits and losses on financial instruments – *FA 1994 s 159* – and non-trading profits or losses treated by *FA 1994 s 160* as non-trading debits or credits under the loan relationships legislation should also be computed as set out in para 10 above. In particular –

- Valuations of assets and liabilities should be made in accordance with the accounting methods used by the partnership – *FA 1994 ss 156, 157*.

- The transfer of value, arm's length and transactions with non-resident rules in *FA 1994 ss 165–168* will apply.

### Share of partnership profits and losses for corporation tax purposes

**16.** The resulting partnership trading profit or loss, excess of non-trading credits over debits assessable under Case III or non-trading deficit, should then be apportioned to the partners according to the partnership agreement. The partners receive a share of the overall result, they do not receive an allocation of individual debits and credits. The partnership itself is not assessable to corporation tax and cannot, for example, carry forward non-trading deficits.

**17.** Each corporate member of the partnership will be assessed and charged to corporation tax on its share of any trading profit or loss (which will include all loan relationship, foreign exchange and financial instruments trading profits and losses) as if its share derived from a trade it carried on alone, and which is separate from any trade it carries on on its own account.

**18.** The corporate members of the partnership should incorporate their allocation of any Case III profit or non-trading deficit into their own Case III or non-trading deficit computation. It will not form a separate 'pot'. The company will be able to claim under *FA 1996 s 83* if the result of combining the two amounts is a net non-trading deficit. It should not claim separately for its allocation of a partnership non-trading deficit.

**19.** For example a company has a non-trading deficit on its own activities of £10,000. It has a share in a partnership Case III profit of £5,000. The company is treated as having an overall deficit of £5,000. It cannot surrender as group relief the amount of £10,000 under *FA 1996 s 83(2)* and submit to a charge to tax on the £5,000. Similarly if the £5,000 Case III income arose on its own account, and its share of a partnership deficit was £10,000 it could not surrender the deficit of £10,000.

*Statement of Practice 4/98*

**Differing accounting periods**

**20.** A partnership may draw up its accounts to a different date from that adopted by the corporate members of the partnership. The profits or losses deriving from the corporation tax computations under *TA 1988 s 114(1)* should be allocated as necessary (normally on a time basis) between the relevant accounting periods of the company members themselves.

**Interaction with capital gains tax**

**21.** For companies which are within the charge to corporation tax and, for the purposes of the foreign exchange or financial instruments legislation, are qualifying companies, certain assets (eg foreign currency, certain debts and some interest rate and currency contracts and options) no longer give rise to chargeable gains following *FA 1993*, *FA 1994* and *FA 1996*. However, these assets may still give rise to chargeable gains in the hands of persons (including individuals) who are not subject to corporation tax. These assets may also, in certain circumstances, give rise to chargeable gains in the hands of some insurance companies. *TCGA 1992 s 59* (treatment of partnership assets) and Statement of Practice D12 will continue to apply to the disposal of shares in partnership assets to which members of the partnership who are not companies subject to corporation tax are entitled. In certain circumstances qualifying companies will also be treated as having chargeable gains and losses on liabilities where corresponding matched assets are disposed of – see para 31 onwards below.

**Connected persons and FA 1996 s 87**

**22.** *TA 1988 s 832* defines a company as excluding a partnership. *TA 1988 s 114* however provides that where at least one of the partners is a company, the profits of any trade, profession or business carried on by the partnership shall be computed for the purposes of corporation tax as if the partnership were a company. The Inland Revenue takes the view that this statutory fiction does not extend to making a partnership a 'company' for the purposes of *FA 1996 s 87(3)* (accounting method for connected parties). It also takes the view that a partnership is neither a participator nor an associate of a participator within the meaning of *TA 1988 s 417*. A partnership is not therefore connected for the purposes of *FA 1996 s 87* with any of its members which provide loans to the partnership. Companies making loans to connected parties are usually denied bad debt relief by *FA 1996 Sch 9 para 6*. But when a loan is made from a corporate member of a partnership to the partnership (or vice versa) it follows from the Inland Revenue view on *FA 1996 s 87* that bad debt relief may be available depending on the circumstances of the debtor. It also follows that where a partnership releases a company member from repaying a debt, or vice versa, the relevant party must recognise a credit equal to the amount released.

**23.** Example – two independent and unconnected companies, A, and B, go into partnership to develop a new product. The partnership, X, is initially funded by loan capital of £50,000, interest free, from each of the two companies. The profit/loss share is 50:50, between the two partners. Company A then injects a further £500,000 into the partnership to fund the production process. This is a five-year loan which carries interest of 5% per annum. The business does not do quite as well as expected and eventually the production facility and business is sold to

## Statement of Practice 4/98

another party for £200,000. This entire amount is paid to Company A in full satisfaction of its debt of £500,000. What are the debits and credits?

**24.** The Inland Revenue would treat the partnership as a separate person to compute profits and losses. The partnership will accrue interest of £25,000 per year which is an allowable debit in its Case I computation. The overall Case I profit or loss for each accounting period is allocated 50:50 to the partners. On the sale of the business the partnership would have a £300,000 credit for the Case I computation when it satisfied its debt of £500,000 with a payment of £200,000. A and B release the remaining debt of £50,000 each, resulting in a further £100,000 credit for the partnership.

**25.** Company A would accrue interest of £25,000 per year which is a credit in its Case III computation. In the period the business was sold Company A would bring in 50% of the trading profit of the partnership (including the credits of £300,000 and £100,000). Company A would be entitled to bad debt relief for £300,000 on the loan of £500,000 and of £50,000 on the other loan. This would be given as a debit in its Case III computation.

**26.** In the period the business was sold Company B would bring in 50% of the trading profit of the partnership (including the credits of £300,000 and £100,000). Company B would be entitled to relief of £50,000 as a debit in its Case III computation.

### Interest paid or received under deduction of income tax

**27.** Yearly interest paid by or on behalf of a partnership in which a company is a member should, subject to s 349(3), be paid under deduction of tax – *TA 1988 s 349(2)(b)*.

**28.** Where a partnership of which a company is member receives interest under deduction of tax, the Inland Revenue practice will be to accept that the income tax suffered should be apportioned amongst the company partners in the same proportion as the interest under the loan relationship is apportioned.

### Local currency elections

**29.** *FA 1993 s 92* lays down a general rule that the profits of a trade are to be expressed in sterling. This codified the existing law that still applies to all other computations of income and profits. However, *FA 1993 ss 93–95* allow companies to elect (via regulations) for trading profits of certain companies to be computed by translating a figure of profit calculated in a currency other than sterling, without requiring a translation of qualifying assets and liabilities denominated in that currency. In statement of practice *SP 9/94* the Inland Revenue took the view that unless a partnership consisted wholly of qualifying companies it could not make this local currency election. The revised Inland Revenue view is that because *TA 1988 s 114* (partnerships involving companies) provides for computations to be prepared as if a partnership were a company, then where at least one of the partners is a qualifying company it is open to that partnership to make a local currency election. Any election must satisfy the conditions in the Local Currency Elections Regulations 1994 (*SI 1994 No. 3230*) [see *Simon's Weekly Tax Intelligence* 1995] applied to the partnership as if it were a company. All

## Statement of Practice 4/98

partners who are, at the time of the election, subject to UK corporation tax should sign any election. Without all the signatures, the Inland Revenue will treat the election as not effective. In cases where an effective election is made that election will be regarded as irrevocable and will not cease to be valid on subsequent partnership changes.

### Deferral

**30.** Under *FA 1993 ss 139–143* qualifying companies may claim to defer a proportion of unrealised exchange gains. This facility will also be available to qualifying partnerships and the practice of the Inland Revenue will be to consider claims to deferral made by the partnership (rather than individual company members) based on the computation prepared under *TA 1988 s 114(1)*. In any accounting period the amount of any exchange gain to be deferred will be the proportion of that gain which is appropriate to qualifying corporate members of the partnership. In other words each of the corporate partners which is a qualifying company will be able to exclude from its share of exchange gains and losses the appropriate part of the deferred gain. The same approach will be taken to amounts treated as accruing by virtue of *FA 1993 s 140(4)* in the period to which the gains have been deferred.

**31.** It follows that a company member of a partnership cannot make a deferral claim in respect of a gain attributed to it under s 114 if the partnership has not itself made a claim. But it can make a claim in respect of its own gains arising otherwise than through the partnership, whether or not a partnership claim has been made for the partnership gains, and no account will be taken of partnership gains or losses in establishing the amount of the company's own gains that may be deferred.

**32.** The complex rules for companies which are members of groups set out in para 4 of the Exchange Gains & Losses (Deferral of Gains and Losses) Regulations 1994 (*SI 1994 No. 3228*) [see *Simon's Weekly Tax Intelligence* 1995] will not however apply to partnerships. The treatment of the partnership as a company by *TA 1988 s 114* does not extend to deeming the partnership as such to be a member of a group.

### Matching

**33.** Under regs 4–11 of The Exchange Gains and Losses (Alternative Method of Calculation of Gain or Loss) Regulations 1994 [, *SI 1994 No. 3227*, see *Simon's Weekly Tax Intelligence* 1995] qualifying companies can elect to reduce to nil exchange differences on liabilities which match certain assets (shares in associated or subsidiary companies, net investments in branches outside the UK and ships or aircraft). The Inland Revenue has revised the view expressed in statement of practice *SP 9/94* which limited the range of assets for which a partnership may make a matching election. It will now accept that partnerships which have eligible liabilities as described in reg 5(4) or (5) can make a matching election for the full range of eligible assets described in *SI 1994 No. 3227 reg 5(6)*. Where an election is made, the Inland Revenue will not treat it as effective unless it is signed by all partners subject to UK corporation tax.

**34.** It follows that since a partnership is treated as if it were a company for the

## Statement of Practice 4/98

purposes of computing exchange gains and losses, and in particular for computing what gains and losses in liabilities may be deferred under the matching rules, a company cannot make a claim to match its own liability (one which is not its share of a partnership liability) with an asset held by the partnership, whether or not the partnership has made an election to match the asset.

**35.** Under reg 7 of the Alternative Method regulations, disposal of a matched asset triggers the calculation of the aggregate exchange gains and losses on the corresponding liability which have not been taken into account for tax purposes because they have been reduced to nil by reg 5(2).

**36.** The net exchange gain or loss thus found is treated as a chargeable gain or allowable loss accruing at the same time as the asset was disposed of. If the matched asset was however a ship or aircraft, the net gain or loss is treated as an exchange gain or loss.

**37.** In cases where there has been no change in the partnership, or in any partner's asset share ratio, between the date the matching election for the asset has effect and the date the asset is disposed of, any chargeable gain or allowable loss produced by reg 7 will accrue to the partners in accordance with *TCGA 1992 s 59* and Statement of Practice D12 in the same way as the chargeable gain or allowable loss on the matched asset will accrue.

**38.** If the reg 7 gain or loss is an exchange gain or loss then it will be allocated to the partners in the manner described in para 15 onwards.

**39.** There may be cases however where a corporate partner in a partnership which has made a matching election leaves the partnership or reduces its asset share ratio before the matched asset is disposed of by the partnership. Where this happens, the partner is treated as disposing of the whole or part of his share in the matched asset – Statement of Practice D12 para 4 and the appropriate calculation of excluded exchange gain or loss should be made under reg 7. A proportionate part of the gain or loss will then be allocated to the partner leaving or reducing its asset share. On a subsequent actual disposal of the asset by the partnership an appropriate adjustment should be made to the reg 7 calculation.

**40.** It is a condition of the Inland Revenue accepting a matching election at partnership level that each partner which is a qualifying company for the purposes of the FOREX legislation at the time the matching election has effect should also undertake to return any reg 7 gain accruing to it in accordance with this statement if it has left the partnership or reduced its asset share ratio.

**Anti-avoidance rules**

**41.** As mentioned in paras 13–15 above, the practice of the Inland Revenue will be to apply the rules in *FA 1994 ss 165–168*, *FA 1993 ss 135–138* and *FA 1996 Part IV Ch II* to the partnership as though it were a qualifying company. But it will also apply these rules where appropriate to individual partnership members.

*Appendix 5*

# Statement of Practice 3/99

**Advance Pricing Agreements (APAs)**

**General**

**1.** This Statement of Practice provides detailed guidance about how the Inland Revenue interprets *FA 1999 ss 85–87*, which provide for advance pricing agreements (APAs) and how it intends applying this legislation in practice.

**2.** APAs aim to assist businesses in determining complex transfer pricing issues. These may arise in applying the arm's length principle in accordance with domestic legislation, with the guidance provided by the *Transfer pricing guidelines for multinational enterprises and tax administrations* (the *OECD transfer pricing guidelines*) published by the Organisation for Economic Co-operation and Development (OECD), and with any arrangements made with foreign governments with a view to affording relief from double taxation (DTAs).

**3.** APAs allow complex transfer pricing issues to be resolved on a prospective basis. They can provide solutions to situations where there is considerable difficulty or doubt in determining the method by which the arm's length principle should be applied. In such cases, even though the process of reaching an agreement can require significant resources, an APA may prove more efficient than the retrospective examination of major transfer pricing issues and may allow the business to predict tax liabilities with greater certainty.

**4.** APAs made for the purposes of *FA 1999 s 85* are written agreements between a business and the Board of Inland Revenue which determine a method for resolving transfer pricing issues in advance of a return being made. When the terms of the agreement are complied with, they provide assurance that the treatment in accordance with the agreement of those transfer pricing issues will be accepted by both the Revenue and the business for the period covered by the agreement.

**Transfer pricing issues**

**5.** *FA 1999 s 85(2)* sets out the transfer pricing issues which can be the subject matter of an APA. An APA can resolve questions relating to two broad situations giving rise to transfer pricing issues:

(a)  Transfer pricing between separate business enterprises where questions may arise as to the determination of the arm's length provision under the

# Advance pricing agreements (APAs)

rules at *TA 1988 s 770A/Sch 28AA*; this matter is covered by s 85(2)(d), (e).

(b) Transfer pricing between parts of one business enterprise operating in more than one country where questions may arise as to the taxable income to be recognised in any such part. These matters are covered by s 85(2)(a), (b), (c).

In the latter case, the relevant subsection is determined by whether a DTA applies and the location of the parts of the enterprise. Where no DTA applies, the attribution of income to part of a non-resident enterprise operating in the UK is specifically covered by s 85(2)(a), and income arising outside the UK from part of a resident enterprise is specifically covered by s 85(2)(c); where a DTA applies and income is attributable to a permanent establishment, these matters are specifically covered by s 85(2)(b).

**6.** There may be a question as to the extent to which the scope of an APA extends to include consideration of whether a permanent establishment ('PE') of an enterprise exists. Subsection (2)(b) is predicated on the existence of a PE and so it follows that matters under that subsection are agreed on the basis that a PE exists. What the legislation does not specifically provide for is a determination that a PE does not exist. In applying for an APA, therefore, in circumstances where the applicant is concerned that the Revenue might deem that a foreign associate has a PE in the UK in relation to the issues covered by the APA, the applicant can raise the matter with a view to including as part of the APA a determination that the income to be attributed to the potential PE is nil.

**Unilateral or bilateral applications?**

**7.** An APA may remain limited to a binding agreement between a UK business and the Inland Revenue in accordance with *FA 1999 s 85*—this is referred to as a 'unilateral APA'. However, a unilateral APA can provide only a partial resolution of cross-border transfer pricing issues because, although it confirms the tax treatment in the UK, it does not determine how the issues are to be resolved in the other country involved. Consequently, it does not eliminate the risk of double taxation in relation to the transfer pricing issues it addresses. In order to achieve that comprehensively in the case of cross-border transfer pricing issues where a DTA exists between the UK and the other country containing a mutual agreement procedure article, the Inland Revenue would have to reach agreement also with the tax administration of the other country—this is referred to as a 'bilateral APA'.

**8.** The Inland Revenue encourages applications for bilateral APAs in relation to cross-border transfer pricing issues. Bilateral arrangements offer an assurance that the method for dealing with the transfer pricing issues covered in the APA will be accepted by the tax administrations of both countries, thus avoiding potential double taxation. Where an APA application affects a country with which the UK has a DTA containing a mutual agreement procedure article, the Inland Revenue will generally invite the treaty partner to participate under that procedure (and any relevant domestic arrangements governing APAs that the treaty partner may itself have) in order to endeavour to resolve difficulties or doubts as to the interpretation or application of the DTA by mutual agreement. If after a specified period the treaty partner has not indicated a desire to participate, or despite wishing to do so is unable to commit to proceeding within

## Advance pricing agreements (APAs)

a reasonable timescale, or for some other reason it is not possible to reach agreement on a bilateral process, the Inland Revenue will be prepared to consider a unilateral APA.

9. Nevertheless, the Inland Revenue will take into account any representations from the applicant about the appropriateness of a bilateral APA in the circumstances of the particular application. A unilateral APA may be preferable where the applicant considers that the extension to a bilateral APA would unnecessarily complicate and delay the process in circumstances where, for example, the treaty partner has no APA process or where there is considered to be little extra to be gained by seeking a bilateral agreement. This may occur where the applicant has identified that the most immediate need to determine transfer pricing rests in the UK because, for example, the UK business is at the hub of arrangements with associated enterprises in many different countries and where the individual amounts involved for one particular country are relatively small.

10. Neither a business nor a treaty partner should be disadvantaged by a unilateral rather than a bilateral APA because any APA is required to be modified to give effect to any subsequent mutual agreement reached under the terms of a DTA. Where the relevant treaty country takes action which results or will result in double taxation in respect of the transfer pricing issues addressed by a unilateral APA, the UK business may, as in any instance of taxation not in accordance with the treaty, request competent authority assistance in accordance with existing procedures and the requirements of the DTA or domestic provisions to seek to eliminate the double taxation. As is made clear by *FA 1999 s 86(3)*, the Inland Revenue's ability to give effect to a mutual agreement reached with a treaty partner to eliminate double taxation under the terms of a treaty will not be restricted by the unilateral APA. In addition, where a unilateral APA request involves foreign related parties resident in a country with which the UK has a DTA containing an exchange of information article, the Inland Revenue is not restricted by the APA process in notifying the treaty partner of the request and in providing information relating to the request under that article.

**Multilateral APAs**

11. Businesses operating in several countries may wish to seek APAs that involve all the relevant tax administrations affected by the transfer pricing issues. The term, 'multilateral APA', has been used to describe such agreements, but in fact there is no mechanism for reaching multilateral agreements, and multilateral APAs in strictness are multiple, bilateral APAs.

12. For example, an application in relation to the licensing of major intangible property from the UK to associated businesses in countries X and Y might lead to applications for two bilateral APAs; one between the Inland Revenue and country X and one between the Inland Revenue and country Y. In such a situation, although there may be a superficial similarity between the two sets of licensing arrangements, there may be differences between the terms of the arrangements and differences between the operations of the two licensees that might mean significantly different pricing approaches are developed. In this situation there may be no need for the Inland Revenue to seek discussions on a trilateral basis with the tax administrations of countries X and Y, although information could be provided to all the tax administrations by the business or

*Advance pricing agreements (APAs)*

exchanged between the tax administrations to the extent provided by the terms of the relevant DTAs.

**13.** Multilateral agreements may be more appropriate where there is essentially only one activity, but several enterprises or parts of enterprises contribute to it. For example, where an enterprise of the UK is engaged in global financial trading through branches in countries X and Y, it may be appropriate for similar agreements to be reached between the Inland Revenue and country X and the Inland Revenue and country Y in order to determine how the profits from the activity are to be allocated to each of the three countries in order to eliminate double taxation. In such a situation the Inland Revenue would be prepared to seek to adapt the bilateral framework in order to reach agreement on a trilateral basis, subject to the acquiescence of the other tax administrations and any constraints on exchanging information imposed by the relevant DTAs. Any agreed outcome would, however, take the form of two bilateral APAs.

**14.** Further information about the conduct of multilateral APAs can be given when an applicant expresses an interest in applying for an APA.

**Existing bilateral APAs**

**15.** Any existing APA reached with a treaty partner under the terms of the mutual agreement procedure of the DTA prior to the introduction of *FA 1999 ss 85–87* is unaffected by those provisions. However, any renewal of such an agreement falling within the scope of the new provisions should be made in accordance with the new provisions and follow the guidance in this statement of practice.

**Administration**

**16.** Since one of the main purposes of the APA process is to eliminate the risk of double taxation by means of a mutual agreement with a treaty partner, the Inland Revenue's International Division has responsibility for all applications except those involving oil taxation. Transfer pricing specialists and delegated competent authority officials from International Division, assisted by the tax office responsible for the business, will be responsible for assessing APA requests. All expressions of interest in and applications for APAs (see paras 30–38 below) should be made, in general, to the Assistant Director (APAs) at International Division, and, in cases involving oil taxation, to the Deputy Director (APAs) in the Oil Taxation Office. They will be responsible for all aspects of the process, including signature on behalf of the Board of Inland Revenue of any resulting agreements. Normally the person responsible for signing the agreement on behalf of the business would be the person responsible for signing the tax return, subject to that person having the necessary authority within the multinational group to commit the group to the terms of the APA.

**17.** The addresses of the Assistant Director (APAs) in International Division and of the Deputy Director (APAs) in the Oil Taxation Office are [given at para 59].

# Advance pricing agreements (APAs)

## Applicants

**18.** An APA may be requested by:

- any UK business, including a partnership, with transactions to which the provisions of *TA 1988 s 770A/Sch 28AA* apply;
- any non-resident trading in the UK through a branch or agency (or permanent establishment);
- any UK resident trading through a branch (or permanent establishment) outside the UK.

**19.** Potential applicants need to bear in mind that the process is designed to offer assistance in resolving complex transfer pricing issues. The Inland Revenue does not regard entering into APAs on less complex matters as a sensible use of resources in the absence of significant doubt as to the manner in which the arm's length principle should be applied. It may therefore decline to accept applications that do not satisfy those criteria (see para 52 for more details).

**20.** As a general guide, where reliable market comparables can be established that enable transfer pricing methods to be accurately employed in accordance with the OECD transfer pricing guidelines, the application of the transfer pricing legislation should not be complex and the clarification in accordance with *FA 1999 s 85(1), (5)* would not be necessary. Where there is difficulty in establishing reliable market comparables, or doubt about how transfer pricing methods can be accurately employed to determine arm's length conditions, the application of the transfer pricing legislation becomes more complex.

**21.** Guidance about a potential application may be obtained from the Inland Revenue (see the discussion in para 30 about the expression of interest stage in an application) and this statement of practice also indicates some circumstances in which an application might be declined. The Inland Revenue recognises that complex transfer pricing issues can be encountered by smaller businesses as well as by large multinationals, and applications for APAs will not be declined solely by reference to the size of the transactions giving rise to the transfer pricing issues.

## Scope

**22.** The potential scope of an APA is flexible. It may involve transfer pricing methods covering many different types of related party transactions and arrangements, including transfers of tangible or intangible property (in Scotland corporeal or incorporeal property) and the provision of services. The APA may relate to all the transfer pricing issues of the business or be limited to one or more specific issues. The APA may apply to pre-existing issues and there is no requirement that the commencement of an APA should coincide with the commencement of the arrangements which it addresses.

## Term

**23.** An APA will be operative for a specified period from the date of entry into force as set out in the agreement. The business should propose an initial term for the APA taking into account the period over which it is reasonable to assume that

## *Advance pricing agreements (APAs)*

the method for dealing with the relevant transfer pricing issues will remain appropriate in the circumstances. It is expected that the term is likely to be for a minimum of three, and a maximum of five, years. The earliest period covered by the APA is dependent on the date of formal submission of the APA request (see para 34).

**Retrospection and 'roll-back'**

**24.** While an APA will normally operate prospectively in relation to chargeable periods beginning after the time the application is made, it is possible that a chargeable period to which the APA relates may have ended before agreement is reached. *FA 1999 s 86(1)* allows the APA to be effective for that chargeable period and, in accordance with s 86(7), the agreement may set out any adjustments to be made for tax purposes as a consequence of the agreement.

**25.** In addition, although a particular agreement does not relate to earlier periods, the agreed transfer pricing methodology may be relevant to a return for an earlier period and to the resolution of any transfer pricing enquiries raised for earlier periods if the particular facts and circumstances surrounding those years are substantially the same. Consequently, in such circumstances, the business may wish to consider using the agreement as a basis for amending a self-assessment return and to request that the method for dealing with transfer pricing issues contained in the APA should be considered for resolving any transfer pricing enquiries to which it is relevant for earlier years. The Inland Revenue may itself also suggest that the 'roll-back' of the APA is an appropriate means of resolving a transfer pricing issue in earlier years.

**26.** Except where 'roll-back' is being considered, the request for an APA in respect of future years will not in itself affect any transfer pricing enquiry into earlier years. However, to the extent such an approach is appropriate and feasible, the Inland Revenue will co-ordinate the APA request in respect of future years with any transfer pricing enquiry in respect of prior years in order to improve overall efficiency and reduce duplication of enquiries.

**27.** Information supplied by the business in relation to an APA request will be kept confidential in accordance with the confidentiality requirements of the Taxes Acts and the terms of any relevant DTA. However, such information will contribute to the pool of information held by the Revenue about that business and no undertaking can be given that it will be taken into account only in relation to the APA. Thus, for example, where information is submitted under an APA which would appropriately enable the re-opening of earlier years for that business under existing law, the fact that the information was submitted under an APA would not in itself prevent reopening. To act otherwise could afford businesses seeking an APA an advantage over other businesses and may give rise to abuses. However, where any businesses are uncertain about a full commitment from the outset to the APA process, an initial approach on an anonymised basis (see para 33 below) may provide businesses with an opportunity to explore the possibility of applying for an APA before disclosing their identity.

*Advance pricing agreements (APAs)*

**APA requests**

**28.** As provided by *FA 1999 s 85(1)(c)* the APA process is initiated by the business making an application for clarification by agreement of what the effect would be of the application of the statutory provisions in question.

**29.** The APA process will typically comprise four stages—expression of interest, formal submission of application for clarification, evaluation, and agreement. However, the details of each stage may vary depending on the particular circumstances of the case.

**Expression of interest**

**30.** A business interested in applying for an APA may wish to explore and seek to clarify in advance various aspects of a potential application, including its scope and term, and to discuss informally the proposed method for dealing with the transfer pricing issues to which it will relate, the presentation of the formal submission, the extent of the documentation requirements, and other matters. Generally, the Revenue might also wish to have the opportunity to discuss a potential application before detailed work in finalising it is undertaken by the business in order to ensure that the application is one which can be considered for an APA and that the application will be focused on relevant issues. This should ensure that resources of the business are not wasted on the application process.

**31.** Expressions of interest should cover such relevant information as:

(a) the nature and value of the transfer pricing issues to be covered by the APA together with the identification and location of the parties involved;

(b) a description of the business activities of the parties and how the transactions concerned relate to these business activities;

(c) a description of the proposed transfer pricing method and an explanation of how it is intended to demonstrate that the method accords with the arm's length standard;

(d) an indication of the nature of any current transfer pricing enquiries, competent authority claims, and any existing APAs or other APA applications that are relevant to the issues covered by the proposed APA; and

(e) in the case of a cross-border transfer pricing issue, confirmation that a bilateral APA is required or reasons why the business considers that only a unilateral APA is appropriate in accordance with this statement of practice.

The information may be provided in writing, or in person at a meeting, or in combination. Generally a meeting is likely to be more productive where some information has been provided in advance. Four copies of any written material should be provided.

**32.** The Inland Revenue will consider the expression of interest and will indicate whether it is prepared to consider an application for an APA, bearing in mind such factors as those listed in paras 19–21, 52. It will discuss with the business the form of that application and the likely time frame for attempting to reach agreement.

## Advance pricing agreements (APAs)

**33.** The expression of interest can best be evaluated where the identity of the business is known. However, if a business wishes to preserve anonymity until a decision in principle is made to proceed with the application, the Revenue will be prepared to enter discussions without knowing the identity of the business providing all other information relevant to the proper evaluation of the request is supplied.

**Formal submission of application for clarification**

**34.** Where the business wishes to proceed with the APA proposal and the Revenue has not indicated that it is not able or willing to consider it, a formal written application for clarification incorporating a proposal as to the manner of clarification should then be submitted. The application should ideally be made before the start of the first chargeable period to be covered by the APA, but the Revenue will not rule as out of time applications made before the end of that chargeable period. Four copies should be provided.

**35.** The application must fulfil the requirements of *FA 1999 s 85(5)* and set out:

(a) the applicant's understanding of the effect of the relevant legislation including the effect of any DTA in relation to the transfer pricing issues under consideration;

(b) the areas where, because of the complexity of the transfer pricing issues, clarification of that effect is required; and

(c) a proposal for clarifying the effect of the legislation in accordance with the applicant's understanding.

The intention is to ensure that any agreement about the practical treatment of specified transfer pricing issues is formed from a proper understanding of the relevant principles of the Taxes Acts. Thus, where the transfer pricing issue concerns, for example, pricing between associated enterprises, the application might include an explanation of why the transfer pricing rules at *TA 1988 s 770A/Sch 28AA* are applicable, and would acknowledge that the effect of those rules, which are to be construed in accordance with OECD principles, is to require the substitution of the arm's length provision for tax purposes. The application might then go on to explain in what ways the establishing of the arm's length provision requires clarification, and submit a proposal for establishing the arm's length provision in accordance with the requirements of the effective provisions. This guidance should be adapted to transfer pricing issues within an enterprise in accordance with the general intention of ensuring that there is a proper understanding of the relevant principles of the applicable law from which an agreement about the practical treatment of a specified issue can be formed.

**36.** The centre-piece of the proposal will be a description of the method by which it is proposed to determine the transfer pricing issues in accordance with the arm's length principle, and an analysis demonstrating how the application of that method satisfies the terms of the UK's legislation, including the effect of any DTA, and the OECD transfer pricing guidelines. The nature of the detailed information supporting the proposal should be tailored to the specific features of the business and of the transfer pricing issues and should take into account discussions with the Inland Revenue during any expression of interest stage.

## Advance pricing agreements (APAs)

**37.** All proposals will also need to be supported by most of the following information:

(a) the identification of the parties and recent accounts (generally for the previous three years);

(b) a description of the transfer pricing issues proposed to be covered in the APA and analysis of the functions and risks of the parties and actual and projected financial data of the parties in relation to the issues;

(c) a description of the world-wide organisational structure, ownership, and business operations of the group to which the company in question belongs, the place or places where such operations are conducted, and all the major categories of transaction flows of the parties to whom the APA is intended to apply;

(d) a description of the records which will be maintained to support the transfer pricing method proposed for adoption in the APA and the information which it is proposed will be supplied each year to demonstrate that the tax return conforms to the terms of the APA;

(e) a description of any current tax enquiries or competent authority claims that are relevant to the issues covered by the proposed APA;

(f) the chargeable periods to be covered by the APA;

(g) the identification of assumptions made in developing the proposed transfer pricing method which are critical to the reliability of its application under the arm's length standard; and

(h) in the case of a cross-border transfer pricing issue, a request for competent authority assistance in reaching a bilateral APA or, where a bilateral APA is not being sought, any representations from the business that the Revenue should exercise its discretion and refrain from exchanging particular information under the terms of the applicable DTA because, for example, the business considers the information includes trade secrets which should not be disclosed.

**38.** In the case of a bilateral APA the business will be asked to ensure that all information supplied to one tax administration is made available at the same time to the other tax administration involved.

**Critical assumptions**

**39.** As indicated in para 37(g) above, the formal proposal should identify the assumptions made in proposing the method for dealing with the transfer pricing issues and which are critical to the reliability of that method. The method should be sufficiently robust to accommodate some changes in the commercial and economic climate from that reasonably foreseeable when the proposals were made and still be capable of replicating an arm's length outcome. However, the accuracy of the method is likely to be predicated on assumptions in respect of particular factors fundamental to its application, such as the nature of the functions performed, accounting policies and practices, the terms of agreements governing the covered transactions, or market share. Critical assumptions are designed to protect both the business and the Revenue from the risk that the agreement may become inappropriate, but they should not be so tightly drawn that the certainty provided by the agreement is jeopardised. Setting parameters

## Advance pricing agreements (APAs)

for acceptable divergence for some assumptions can help to retain flexibility. Where there is a change, or a change greater than any relevant parameters set, to circumstances that both parties have identified as critical to the agreement, a reconsideration of the agreement is then activated and may lead to its cancellation or modification in accordance with *FA 1999 s 86(2), (6)* depending on the terms of the agreement.

### Evaluation

**40.** On receipt of an application the Inland Revenue will evaluate its contents and will seek clarification and further information from the business as necessary. The examination of the application should be a co-operative process in which the transfer pricing issues are discussed openly and access to relevant supporting information and documentation is made available. Lack of co-operation in these respects may result in the Revenue declining to give any further consideration to the application.

**41.** Where a bilateral APA is being sought, the Inland Revenue will expect the business to continue to make relevant information available at the same time to each tax administration involved, and in turn will keep the treaty partner informed about the progress of its examination of the APA request, will discuss with the treaty partner the issues arising at an early stage, and will keep the business informed about the progress of the bilateral process. While the finalising of a bilateral agreement with a treaty partner is a government to government process, the Inland Revenue is prepared to consider participating in joint meetings to include the multinational business and the other tax administration(s) to assist in the understanding and evaluation of the factual issues.

### Agreement

**42.** Any agreement reached between the business and the Inland Revenue represents a binding undertaking on the parties that the treatment for a specified period of the transfer pricing issues covered by the agreement will be determined in accordance with the agreement (provided that its terms are observed and that none of the provisions leading to revocation, cancellation, or competent authority over-ride as described below are triggered). In the case of a bilateral APA the terms of the agreement between the Inland Revenue and the taxpayer will also reflect the agreement reached between the two tax administrations under the mutual agreement procedure of the relevant treaty in order to provide for the elimination of double taxation.

**43.** The agreement between the Inland Revenue and the business will be made subject to its terms being observed. The terms will include:

(a) a commitment from the business to demonstrate adherence to the agreed method for dealing with the transfer pricing issues during the term of the APA in the form of a regular compliance report (see paras 45, 46 below); and

(b) the identification of critical assumptions bearing materially on the reliability of the method and which, if subject to change, would render the agreement invalid.

## *Advance pricing agreements (APAs)*

A description of the matters that would need to be considered for incorporation in any agreement is included as an annex to this statement.

**44.** If agreement cannot be reached with the business, the Inland Revenue will issue a formal statement recording the reasons. The Inland Revenue does not have any obligation to continue discussion beyond the point at which it has determined that agreement cannot be reached.

### APA monitoring and review

**45.** The APA will identify the nature of the reports that the business is required to provide pursuant to *FA 1999 s 86(4)*. The timing of the submission of the reports will be set out in the agreement. It is expected that the reports will be required annually and will coincide with the filing date for the tax return. Failure to provide reports may lead the Inland Revenue to determine a penalty under *TMA 1970 s 98* in respect of the failure, as provided for by *FA 1999 s 86(9)*. The particular requirements of each report will be set out in the finalised agreement and will focus narrowly on the issue covered by the APA, but, as a general guide, they are likely to include:

(a) confirmation that the agreed method was applied during the year;

(b) the financial results produced by the method, and reconciliation of those results to entries in the statutory accounts and tax computations;

(c) where there was a mismatch between prices charged in relevant transactions during the period and those reflected in the results of applying the arm's length standard under the agreed methodology, details of any compensating adjustments made to conform the operating results of the parties to the results of the method; and

(d) an assessment of whether the critical assumptions have proved to be sound and whether they remain so.

**46.** The APA report is intended to provide the information required by the Inland Revenue to establish that the business has complied with the terms and conditions of the APA and to verify the accuracy of representations made in the APA. Identification of the content of the reports to be submitted over the term of the agreement will assist businesses in fulfilling their compliance obligations.

### Nullifying and revoking APAs

**47.** *FA 1999 s 86(5)* gives the Board of Inland Revenue the power to nullify an APA as if it had never been made where the business has fraudulently or negligently provided false or misleading information in connection with the APA application. When considering using this power the Board of Inland Revenue will also take into account the extent to which the terms of the APA would have been different in the absence of the misrepresentation. In accordance with s 86(2), an APA may be revoked by the Revenue in accordance with its terms, where the business does not comply with the terms and conditions of the agreement, or where the identified critical assumptions cease to be valid. When considering nullifying or cancelling a bilateral APA the Revenue may consult with the competent authority of the treaty partner involved.

# Advance pricing agreements (APAs)

## Revising and renewing APAs

**48.** In some cases the APA may provide for modification of its terms in specific circumstances; for example, a particular agreement may provide that where there has been a change which makes the agreed methodology difficult to apply, but which does not go as far as to invalidate a critical assumption, the agreement may be modified with the consent of the parties to resolve that difficulty. In such cases the APA may be revised in accordance with *FA 1999 s 86(6)* after consultations between the business and the Inland Revenue and, in the case of bilateral agreements, the competent authority of the other country involved.

**49.** The business may request renewal of an APA ideally not later than six months before the expiry of its current term, but the Revenue will not rule as out of time requests made before the end of the first chargeable period affected by the renewal. The renewal application should expressly consider any changes or anticipated changes in facts and circumstances since the existing agreement was reached, whether any amendments are required to the agreement on renewal as a result, and should demonstrate how the proposed methodology accords with the arm's length standard.

**50.** The Revenue will conduct a review of the renewal application, taking into account whatever revisions to the existing APA are necessary and appropriate in the light of any changed facts and circumstances. Where it is agreed that the transfer pricing issues under consideration remain the same and the existing transfer pricing methodology can continue as before but with details updated to ensure continued adherence to the arm's length principle, the agreement will simply be amended and extended for a further term. Where, however, the transfer pricing issues have changed, or a different method is being proposed, the business will be required to make a fresh APA application.

**51.** In the case of a bilateral APA the business should ensure that the information contained in the renewal application is submitted at the same time to the other tax administration involved.

## Declining or withdrawing an APA request

**52.** At the expression of interest stage, or at the stage where a formal proposal is submitted, the Inland Revenue may exercise its discretion by declining the request for an APA. In that event, the Inland Revenue will advise the business of the reasons for doing so, and will allow the business the opportunity to make further representations. A request is likely to be declined if:

- sufficient information for proper and full consideration of the request is not provided;
- the proposal does not comply with the terms of the UK's transfer pricing legislation or with the OECD transfer pricing guidelines;
- the affected transactions are thought to be of a hypothetical nature or not seriously contemplated; or
- it appears to be an inefficient use of resources to pursue an APA (for instance because the relevant transactions are of a very limited nature such as not to warrant the time required to complete an APA or are of limited value relative to the value of the rest of the business, or because determina-

## *Advance pricing agreements (APAs)*

tion of the method by which the arm's length standard can reliably be applied is not in material doubt).

The Revenue may decline a request if the business is not co-operating to provide timeously the information necessary to consider the request properly.

**53.** A business may withdraw an APA request at any time before final agreement is reached.

### Disclosure of APAs

**54.** The Revenue considers that APA information is subject to the same rules of confidentiality as any other information about taxpayers and that the unauthorised disclosure even of the existence of an APA will be a breach of confidentiality. Information exchanged with treaty partners—for instance, in the course of reaching agreement on bilateral APAs—is also protected from disclosure by the terms of the exchange of information article in the relevant DTA.

### Penalties

**55.** Because an APA is an agreement between the Revenue and a business which determines how questions relating to the matters covered by the agreement will be determined for the purposes of the Taxes Acts, a return made on any other basis in relation to those matters during the currency of an APA will constitute an incorrect return. Consequently, a tax-geared penalty will be chargeable where the business has acted fraudulently or negligently in making such an incorrect return and tax has been lost as a result. Where a return is made in accordance with an APA, but it is discovered that false or misleading information was submitted fraudulently or negligently in the course of obtaining the APA, the legislation provides at *FA 1999 s 86(5)* that the agreement is treated as if it had never been made, with the result that questions relating to the subject matter of the agreement are no longer to be determined in accordance with the agreement. This may mean that returns made in accordance with the nullified APA are incorrect with the consequences for penalties described above.

**56.** A penalty not exceeding £10,000 may be imposed where false or misleading information is supplied fraudulently or negligently in connection with an application for an APA—*FA 1999 s 86(8)*. There is no requirement for the APA to have been finalised in order to apply this sanction. In practice, where a tax-geared penalty is obtained following the nullifying of an APA as described above, a fixed penalty under s 86(8) will not also be pursued for the same offence. As indicated in para 45 above, *TMA 1970 s 98* will apply to information required as part of the process of monitoring an APA where there has been a failure to provide the information or where incorrect information has been fraudulently or negligently provided.

### Appeals

**57.** In accordance with existing appeal procedures, the business has the right to appeal against the amount of any additions to profits arising as a result of the revocation or cancellation of an APA.

## Advance pricing agreements (APAs)

**UK/UK transactions**

**58.** When a UK business obtains an APA relating to provision made or imposed with another UK business, *FA 1999 s 87* removes any uncertainty about the tax position of that other taxpayer. Where there is a discrepancy between the provision agreed under the terms of the APA and the actual provision between the parties to the disadvantage of the other party, that other party may claim to have profits adjusted on the basis that the agreed provision was charged. However, the Revenue would seek to reduce the scope for such discrepancies by encouraging the business to agree wherever possible that the transfer pricing methodology will determine the commercial charge for the provision as well as the charge for tax purposes. Furthermore, where the parties agree, the Revenue will accept a joint application for an APA from both parties in order to reach consistent agreements as to the measure of each party's profits in relation to the transfer pricing issues. Where these measures are adopted, however, s 87 may still need to be invoked if the APA applies to chargeable periods ending before the making of the agreement.

**Further information**

**59.** The contact address for more information about APAs and for making an APA application in all cases except those involving oil taxation, is:

Assistant Director (APAs), International Division, Inland Revenue, Victory House, 30–34 Kingsway, London WC2B 6ES: telephone: 0171 438 7405, fax: 0171 438 7511, e-mail: ahickman.ir.mhl@gtnet.gov.uk.

For APAs involving oil taxation, the contact address is:

Deputy Director (APAs), Oil Taxation Office, Melbourne House, Aldwych, London WC2B 4LL: telephone: 0171 438 7579, fax: 0171 438 6910, e-mail: oto.ir.mh@gtnet.gov.uk.

## ANNEX

### ADVANCE PRICING AGREEMENTS (APAS) MATTERS TO BE COVERED IN THE WRITTEN AGREEMENT

**1.** This note provides general guidance about the terms expected to be incorporated in an APA reached between the Inland Revenue and a business under *FA 1999 s 85* and in accordance with the statement of practice. The precise form of the agreement may be left to the discretion of the parties.

**Declaration**

**2.** A declaration is required by *FA 1999 s 85(1)(d)* that the agreement is one made for the purposes of s 85.

# Advance pricing agreements (APAs)

**Identification of the persons affected**

**3.** The agreement should identify the persons affected by the APA and provide all relevant information about them for the purposes of the agreement, for example the residence of a company and any branches through which it is engaged in matters covered by the APA. It should also identify all related parties with whom the business or transactions covered by the APA are conducted.

**Matters covered**

**4.** The agreement should describe the specific matters within *FA 1999 s 85(2)* that are covered by the terms of the agreement. The information should be sufficiently detailed and specific as to identify the subject matter of the APA unambiguously.

**Term**

**5.** The agreement should state the period for which the agreement is to apply to the matters covered. This will normally correspond to certain specified accounting periods of the business.

**Transfer pricing method**

**6.** The particular transfer pricing method will vary from agreement to agreement. In all cases, however, the agreement should describe precisely how it is to apply to determine the treatment of the matters covered. An example would be a description of a method which determines how to calculate a royalty rate by reference to the residual profit of the licensee; this might need to cover the identification of the licensee's profits, the calculation of the residual including the use of defined comparable data and any adjustments to that data, and the determination of the royalty.

**7.** Most agreements are likely to prescribe a single method to apply throughout the term of the agreement. However, it may be that in appropriate cases a stipulated variation in the circumstances can provide for a specified modification in the method, in which case the agreement should describe the modification and the conditions under which the modification takes effect.

**8.** All terms used to describe the transfer pricing method should be clearly defined.

**Critical assumptions**

**9.** Critical assumptions are the conditions on which the agreement is predicated and, where these conditions are no longer satisfied, *FA 1999 s 86(2)(c)* provides that the agreement no longer has effect. They describe and limit the future facts and circumstances to which the agreement will apply and on which the transfer pricing method depends for its reliability. They protect both the business and the Revenue from the risk that the agreement may become inappropriate.

**10.** In general terms, critical assumptions should be capable of accommodating acceptable variations in the facts and circumstances relating to the matters

## Advance pricing agreements (APAs)

covered. On the other hand, they must be able to identify those changes in the factual pattern envisaged in the agreement that render the transfer pricing method inappropriate.

**11.** Examples of the sorts of issues that can be expected to be subject of critical assumptions are:

- the business activities undertaken by specific entities;
- the centres of operation of a business and the nature of its presence in different countries;
- performance of a product in terms of, for example, volume of sales or market share;
- the financial conditions in which transactions are conducted, for example in relation to foreign exchange or interest rates;
- the nature of accounting methods or other information systems that may provide measurements relevant to the matters covered;
- business practice in relation to factors relevant to the transfer pricing method, for example the compensation policy of a financial trader.

**12.** This list is purely illustrative and the critical assumptions in any APA will always be particular to that agreement.

### Reporting requirements

**13.** The agreement will specify, and thereby in accordance with *FA 1999 s 86(2)(b), (4)* be conditional on, the satisfaction of certain reporting requirements in relation to the application of the agreed method and the validity of the critical assumptions. These will normally be for specified information to be supplied at the time the business submits its accounts and computations in relation to the relevant transactions or business to the Inland Revenue.

**14.** The requirements may specify financial or other reports in relation to the application of the agreed method and the validity of the critical assumptions which would not otherwise be submitted with the tax return. As with critical assumptions, however, reporting requirements will be tailored to the particular agreement.

### Record-keeping requirements

**15.** It will sometimes become apparent in the course of reaching an APA that certain records are needed to be kept in order for the agreed method to be properly applied. It might not, however, be necessary to provide such records at the same time as meeting other reporting requirements in order for the Inland Revenue to assess whether the terms of the agreement have been complied with. Such records would thus not be covered in the 'reporting requirements' of the agreement, but might be required to be retained by the business under the terms of the agreement in case examination of them became necessary.

## Advance pricing agreements (APAs)

### Roll-back

**16.** The agreement may specify how any adjustments are to be made to earlier periods in accordance with *FA 1999 s 86(7)*.

### Revocation and modification

**17.** An agreement may be revoked under *FA 1999 s 86(2)(a)* in accordance with its terms. This allows the parties to consider including conditions in the agreement that are not directly linked to assumptions underlying the reliability of the method, but may reflect wider concerns such as providing for revocation in the event of a take-over. An agreement may also provide for modification or revocation in accordance with s 86(6) by, for example, including a provision which allows for modification or revocation where the agreed method is proving difficult to apply.

### Mutual agreement procedure

**18.** The Revenue is given authority by *FA 1999 s 86(3)* to modify an APA to give effect to an agreement with a treaty partner reached under the mutual agreement procedure of the treaty. There is no need for conditions to be made in an APA to confirm this authority, and the APA itself cannot be conditional on the resolution of any related mutual agreement procedure. However, the business may wish to refer specifically to any mutual agreement issues in the terms of an APA.

*Appendix 6*

# Inland Revenue Press Releases

*19 April 1999*

**Inland Revenue interest rates—quarterly instalment payments, and early payments of corporation tax not due by instalments**

The Inland Revenue today announced new rates of interest for underpaid and overpaid instalment payments of corporation tax, and early payments of corporation tax not due by instalments, in respect of accounting periods ending on or after 1 July 1999. These rates will take effect from 19 April 1999. The changes are the result of recent changes in market rates.

**Details**

**1.** The rate of interest charged on underpaid instalment payments of corporation tax has decreased from 7.50 per cent to 7.25 per cent.

**2.** The rate of interest on overpaid instalment payments of corporation tax, and on corporation tax paid early (but not due by instalments), has decreased from 5.25 per cent to 5.00 per cent.

**Notes for editors**

**1.** Section 178 Finance Act 1989 and Statutory Instrument SI 1989 No. 1297, 'The Tax (Interest Rate) Regulations 1989', lay down the procedures and formulae for calculating and amending Inland Revenue interest rates.

**2.** The provisions for calculating interest rates in respect of instalment payments of corporation tax, and early payments of corporation tax not due by instalments, in respect of accounting periods ending on or after the appointed day for corporation tax self-assessment (1 July 1999), are contained in Statutory Instrument SI 1998 No. 3176.

**3.** The previous changes to these interest rates were sent out in a press release dated 12 February 1999.

**4.** The revised interest rates are based on the average base lending rate of 5.25 per cent calculated in accordance with the Statutory Instruments.

*Inland Revenue Press Releases*

*27 April 1999*

**More help for tax agents about corporation tax self assessment**

To help tax agents prepare for the start of Corporation Tax Self Assessment, the Inland Revenue has just published a brand-new Guide.

Over the next few days, the Inland Revenue will be sending free copies of *A Guide to Corporation Tax Self Assessment* to tax agents. The Guide is also on the Internet at www.inlandrevenue.gov.uk.

The Guide explains how the present tax rules for companies have been changed for Self Assessment and how Corporation Tax Self Assessment will work. It will help tax agents to understand the new rules so that they can be sure that their clients know what they need to do and when.

It is part of the Inland Revenue's on-going efforts to keep people informed of changes and how they are affected by them.

**Notes for editors**

**1.** About one million companies will be affected by Corporation Tax Self Assessment. It brings tax treatment for companies more closely into line with individuals and partnerships.

**2.** Corporation Tax Self Assessment applies to all company accounting periods ending on or after 1 July 1999.

**3.** The change to Corporation Tax Self Assessment for companies is nowhere near the major change that the introduction of Income Tax Self Assessment was for Income Tax payers. Corporation Tax Self Assessment is not that different from the current Corporation Tax Pay and File system.

**4.** The Inland Revenue have already sent leaflets about Corporation Tax Self Assessment to tax agents and their clients. And they have published articles about some of the changes in professional journals, including their own publication, 'Tax Bulletin'. This is available by subscription or on the Internet.

**5.** Extra copies of *A Guide to Corporation Tax Self Assessment* cost £15. They may be picked up from the Inland Revenue Visitor Information Centre, Ground Floor, South West Wing, Bush House, Strand, London, WC2B 4RD (payment by cash or cheque made payable to 'Inland Revenue'). Or they can be ordered from the Inland Revenue Library, Room 28, New Wing, Somerset House, London, WC2R 1LB (payment by cheque only, and postage is free). The text of the Guide is also available on $3\frac{1}{2}$ inch disks in 'text only' format from the Library at the same price.

*Inland Revenue Press Releases*

*20th May 1999*

## More help for companies self-assessing—regulations published for controlled foreign companies (CFCS)

Companies self assessing their tax when they have income from CFCs which carry on general insurance business will benefit from regulations laid before the House of Commons today.

The regulations deal with various features specific to general insurance CFCs that use a recognised form of non annual accounting. Most importantly, the regulations will allow such companies to benefit from the exemption for CFCs which pursue an acceptable distribution policy (ADP).

Draft regulations published last November for consultation were welcomed for their clarity and for the facility they offered to CFCs wanting to pursue an ADP. The regulations now laid before the House of Commons contain further improvements in response to helpful suggestions made during the consultations.

The regulations (SI 1408) will be available shortly from The Stationery Office and on the Inland Revenue web site (www.inlandrevenue.gov.uk).

## Details

### The Regulations

**1.** Under changes introduced in last year's Finance Act, companies will be responsible for self-assessing any tax due under the CFC rules for UK accounting periods ending on or after 1 July 1999. To facilitate self-assessment in respect of general insurance CFCs which use non annual accounting, the Act included the power to make regulations to take account of features peculiar to such companies.

**2.** Non annual accounting is a recognised form of insurance accounting used when business results cannot be determined with reasonable certainty using the normal accounting basis. It is unusual because a profit or loss for an accounting period will not be struck for up to three years after the end of that accounting period.

**3.** The regulations recognise certain types of non annual accounting as an acceptable basis for the determination of the chargeable profits of an insurance CFC and seek to achieve broadly the same administrative effect as if a CFC had accounted for its profits on an annual basis. They contain rules that:

- specify when a UK company with a relevant interest in a non-resident insurance subsidiary using non annual accounting must include details of that subsidiary in its tax return (Reg 4);
- require an amendment to be made to a UK company's return if, when the subsidiary finally strikes a profit or loss, the return proves to be incorrect (Reg 4);
- allow a company to show that an acceptable distribution policy has been pursued in relation to an insurance subsidiary using non annual accounting,

## Inland Revenue Press Releases

by allowing an extended period for the payment of an acceptable distribution and setting out special rules for the determination of the amount of such a distribution (Reg 6);

- govern the tax treatment of equalisation reserves in the accounts of insurance CFCs where a return of chargeable profits is prepared on an annual basis but where statutory accounts are drawn up on a non annual basis (Reg 7); and

- govern the tax treatment of insurance CFCs which follow the tenets of non annual accounting but which defer profit recognition for more than three years (Reg 5).

**Consultations**

4. Draft regulations were published for consultation last December. Representations were received from 3 major firms of advisers. The opportunity to comment on the draft regulations was welcomed, as was their clarity and the facility for companies to benefit from the exemption for CFCs pursuing an ADP.

5. In response to suggestions made in the representations, the regulations laid before Parliament today improve on the December draft by:

- giving a company the opportunity to show that an ADP has been pursued by a subsidiary which the company when it completed its tax return was of the opinion was not a CFC but which turns out to have been one; and

- (in line with the normal ADP rules) giving the Board of Inland Revenue the power in exceptional circumstances to allow a longer period in which to pursue an ADP than the extended one specified in the regulations.

6. The draft regulations included special rules for determining the size of a dividend that must be paid to the UK during the extended period in order to satisfy the ADP exemption. One of the representations suggested that the rules were unnecessary. The rules are needed to ensure that insurance companies in tax havens are not unfairly advantaged over domestic ones, and to ensure that CFCs using non annual accounting are not unfairly advantaged over ones using annual accounting. The rules therefore remain in the final version.

**Notes for editors**

1. A CFC is a company which is not resident in the UK (but which is controlled by individuals or companies who are) and which is subject to a level of taxation less than three quarters of what it would have paid had it been resident in the UK. Subject to various exemptions, the difference between the UK tax it would have paid and the overseas tax it has paid can be charged on UK companies with an interest in the CFC of at least 10 per cent (increased to 25% under Corporation Tax Self Assessment—CTSA). Finance Act 1998 brings the rules within CTSA for UK company accounting periods ending on or after 1 July 1999.

2. Under the normal CFC rules, a company is exempt if within 18 months of the end of its accounting period it pays to the UK a dividend equal to 90% of its profits. This is called pursuing an acceptable distribution policy (ADP).

# Inland Revenue Press Releases

8 June 1999

## A modern system for corporation tax payments — guidance on use of information and penalty powers in instalment payments regulations

Guidance published today outlines the way in which the Inland Revenue will use the information and penalty powers contained in the instalment payments regulations. The regulations govern the payment of corporation tax by some 20,000 large companies.

The guidance:

- explains that the information powers are not for routine use; and
- confirms that the majority of cases of late or inadequate payment will attract only an interest charge, not a penalty.

The text of the guidance is attached as an annex to this press release.

## Details

**1.** The Inland Revenue will use the information powers only where there are indications that a company may have deliberately or recklessly failed to comply with its payment obligations under the regulations, or fraudulently or negligently made a claim for repayment. In such a case, all the necessary evidence will be requested from the company in respect of its instalment payments (or absence of them), or claim.

**2.** The penalty provision is in regulation 13 of the instalment payments regulations. It provides for a penalty (under section 59E(4) Taxes Management Act 1970 (TMA)) of not more than twice the amount of interest on any unpaid amount in respect of the total liability of the company for that accounting period. Total liability includes liability to corporation tax, and tax under sections 419 and 747 ICTA 1988 (provisions dealing with loans by a close company to its participators, and controlled foreign companies, respectively).

**3.** A penalty under section 59E(4) TMA will be sought in only the most serious cases involving flagrant abuse of the regulations. The normal appeal rights of section 100B(1) TMA will apply to any such penalty.

## Notes for editors

**1.** The detailed rules governing the payment by large companies of their corporation tax by instalments are set out in the instalment payment regulations (SI No 3175 1998). They provide for large companies (broadly those with profits of more than £1.5 million, or less if a company is associated with others) to pay their corporation tax in quarterly instalments for accounting periods ending on or after 1 July 1999.

**2.** The change is being phased in over a four year period, with companies paying a gradually increasing percentage of their tax by instalments (with the balance in a lump sum nine months and one day after the end of their accounting period).

## Inland Revenue Press Releases

Transition to the new system will be completed in the year 2002, when companies with accounting periods ending on or after 1 July 2002 will pay all their tax by instalments.

**3.** A leaflet, *A modern system for corporation tax payments — a guide to quarterly instalment payments* contains more details, and is available free from tax offices.

## ANNEX
## GUIDANCE ON USE OF INFORMATION AND PENALTY POWERS IN QUARTERLY INSTALMENT PAYMENTS CASES

These guidance notes explain how the Inland Revenue will use the information and penalty powers in the Corporation Tax (Instalment Payments) Regulations 1998 (SI 1998 No. 3175).

### Use of information powers

The information powers are in regulations 10, 11 and 12 of the instalment payments regulations. They require a company to provide the Inland Revenue with information to support the payments made on the instalment due dates, or the lack of such payments, or to support a claim for repayment. They are described in more detail below.

Where companies file their returns by the statutory filing date, a review of the quarterly instalment payment (QIP) position will be undertaken at the same time as the review of the return. Information about the basis upon which QIPs have been estimated will not be sought as a matter of routine.

Where the amounts paid on the instalment dates do not correspond to the amounts required under the regulations interest will be charged or paid accordingly. In cases where the Inland Revenue make a determination of the tax payable because a company has failed to file its return on time, the Inland Revenue also have the power to make a determination of the dates on which amounts should have been paid under the regulations.

The Inland Revenue will seek to make use of the information powers in regulations 10, 11 and 12 only where there are indications that a company may have deliberately or recklessly failed to comply with its payment obligations under the regulations, or fraudulently or negligently made a claim for repayment. In such a case, all the necessary evidence will be requested from the company in respect of its instalment payments (or absence of them) or claim. This will enable the Inland Revenue to establish the extent to which the company failed to pay in accordance with its most recent estimate of its total liability, and to form a judgement as to whether the company, or persons acting on its behalf, acted deliberately or recklessly in failing to make its payments as they fell due, or in later failing to correct the position as newer and more accurate information became available.

# Inland Revenue Press Releases

**Application of penalty regulation**

The penalty power is in regulation 13 of the instalment payments regulations. It provides for a penalty (under section 59E(4) Taxes Management Act 1970 (TMA)) of not more than twice the amount of interest charged in respect of the total liability of the company for that accounting period.

Total liability includes liability to corporation tax, and tax under sections 419 and 747 ICTA 1988 (provisions dealing with loans by a close company to its participators, and controlled foreign companies, respectively).

The majority of cases of inadequate or late payments, or the miscalculation of a repayment, will involve only an interest charge:

- Inadequate payments—a penalty position will apply where there is evidence that the company failed to pay in accordance with its most recent estimate of its total liability, (including failing to make a top-up payment), or failed to pay the right amount at the right time. Such a failure by a company or by a person acting on its behalf must be more than negligent—it must be deliberate or reckless;

- Claims to repayment — a penalty will apply in respect of a claim to repayment under regulation 6 if the company or a person acting on its behalf has acted fraudulently or negligently.

A penalty under section 59E(4) TMA will be sought in only the most serious cases involving flagrant abuse of the regulations. Before seeking a penalty the case must be submitted to Head Office for approval. The normal appeal rights of section 100B(1) TMA will apply to any such penalty.

**Interest**

New interest rates have been introduced for tax over- and underpaid during the instalment payments period. This is provided for in the Taxes (Interest Rate) (Amendment No 2) Regulations 1998 (SI 1998 No. 3176). The new rules are more generous to companies than those that apply outside that period. The rates also have a smaller spread and are more sensitive to base rate movements than the ordinary rates. Interest on underpaid corporation tax is also deductible in arriving at a company's chargeable profits. The interest represents no more than compensation for the Exchequer's (or the company's) loss of use of the money.

**Information powers**

Regulation 10 of the Corporation Tax (Instalment Payments) Regulations (SI 3175 1998) requires a company to furnish information to the Board of Inland Revenue, and regulation 11 requires a company to produce books, documents and other records in its possession or power, relating to:

- the estimation of amounts paid in respect of the company's total liability for an accounting period in accordance with regulation 5 of SI 3175 1998;

- the non-payment of any amount in respect of the company's total liability for an accounting period in accordance with regulation 5 of SI 3175 1998; and

- a claim for repayment under regulation 6(2) SI 3175/1998.

Such details can be required within a period of not less than 30 days, by notice, at any time following the fixed filing date for the company.

In addition, regulation 12 requires a company to make available for inspection all such books, documents and other records in its possession or power as could be required to be produced under regulation 11. Where such records are maintained by computer, the company must provide the officer making the inspection with all the facilities necessary for obtaining information from them.

**Penalty**

Regulation 13 provides for a penalty under section 59(E)(4) Taxes Management Act 1970 (TMA) where:
- a company, or a person acting on its behalf, deliberately or recklessly fails to pay the right amount on a particular instalment date in accordance with the regulations; or
- a company, or a person acting on its behalf, fraudulently or negligently makes a claim for repayment under the regulations.

The amount of the penalty is a sum not exceeding twice the amount of interest charged in respect of the total liability of the company for that accounting period.

*18 June 1999*

## More help for companies self-assessing — guidance notes published for controlled foreign companies (CFCs)

Companies self-assessing their tax when they have CFCs will be helped by guidance notes published today.

Draft notes were issued last December for consultation [see Inland Revenue Press Release dated 10 December 1998]. These were well received, and the final version published today has been further improved to take account of various helpful suggestions made during the consultations.

Companies will be responsible for self-assessing any tax due under the CFC rules for UK accounting periods ending on or after 1 July 1999. The move to self-assessment will mean that the CFC rules operate more fairly and effectively than before.

## Details

### CFC Self-assessment

**1.** The guidance notes are the final part of a package of measures bringing the CFC rules into self-assessment. The other elements are:

## Inland Revenue Press Releases

- legislation in last year's Finance Act bringing the CFC rules into line with self-assessment;
- regulations replacing the previously non-statutory CFC Excluded Countries List;
- regulations dealing with certain specialised aspects to do with CFCs which carry on general insurance business; and
- a new comprehensive CFC clearance procedure effective from 1 January this year.

**2.** All these steps have been the subject of consultation, and have benefited from valuable input from companies and their advisers.

**Guidance Notes**

**3.** The guidance notes are a detailed technical description of the legislation and the Inland Revenue's operation of it. They have been written to help the tax departments of large companies and their advisers. The notes bring together in one place existing Inland Revenue published material on CFCs, and up-date the existing CFC Explanatory Notes to cover self-assessment.

**4.** The notes include details of the new comprehensive CFC clearance procedure that the Inland Revenue introduced on 1 January this year.

**5.** The guidance notes will be available shortly on the Inland Revenue website (www.inlandrevenue.gov.uk). Paper copies (price £10) can be obtained by post by sending a cheque/postal order (post free) made payable to 'Inland Revenue' to:

Inland Revenue Reference Library
Room 28, New Wing
Somerset House
Strand
London WC2R 1LB

**6.** Personal callers can buy copies by cheque or cash between 9.00am and 5.00pm from:

Inland Revenue Information Centre
South West Wing
Bush House
Strand
London WC2B 4RD

**Consultations**

**7.** Draft guidance notes were published for consultation last December. Eight representations were received (five from firms of advisers, one from a multinational and two from professional bodies).

**8.** The draft notes were welcomed, as was the opportunity to comment on them. A wide range of detailed suggestions were made for ways in which the notes could

*Inland Revenue Press Releases*

be further improved, and a number of additional explanations and clarifications have been made to the final notes as a result.

**9.** Although detailed, the notes are of necessity of a general nature.
Companies and their advisers wanting detailed clarification on a specific issue can continue to contact the Inland Revenue's International Division for assistance. Clearance applications can also be made under the new comprehensive CFC clearance procedure.

**Notes for editors**

**1.** A CFC is a company which is not resident in the UK (but which is controlled by individuals or companies who are) and which is subject to a level of taxation less than three quarters of the level it would have paid had it been resident in the UK. Subject to various exemptions, the difference between the UK tax it would have paid and the overseas tax it has paid can be charged on UK companies with an interest in the CFC of at least 10 per cent (increased to 25 per cent under Corporation Tax Self Assessment—CTSA). Finance Act 1998 brings the rules within CTSA for UK company accounting periods ending on or after 1 July 1999.

*21 June 1999*

## Inland Revenue interest rates—quarterly instalment payments, and early payments of corporation tax not due by instalments

The Inland Revenue today announced new rates of interest for underpaid and overpaid instalment payments of corporation tax, and early payments of corporation tax not due by instalments, in respect of accounting periods ending on or after 1 July 1999. These rates will take effect from 21 June 1999. The changes are the result of recent changes in market rates.

**Details**

**1.** The rate of interest charged on underpaid instalment payments of corporation tax has decreased from 7.25 per cent to 7.00 per cent.

**2.** The rate of interest on overpaid instalment payments of corporation tax, and on corporation tax paid early (but not due by instalments), has decreased from 5.00 per cent to 4.75 per cent.

**Notes for editors**

**1.** Section 178 Finance Act 1989 and Statutory Instrument SI 1989 No. 1297, 'The Tax (Interest Rate) Regulations 1989', lay down the procedures and formulae for calculating and amending Inland Revenue interest rates.

**2.** The provisions for calculating interest rates in respect of instalment payments of corporation tax, and early payments of corporation tax not due by instalments, in respect of accounting periods ending on or after the appointed day for

## Inland Revenue Press Releases

corporation tax self-assessment (1 July 1999), are contained in Statutory Instrument SI 1998 No. 3176.

**3.** The previous changes to these interest rates were set out in a press release dated 19 April 1999.

**4.** The revised interest rates are based on the average base lending rate of 5.00 per cent calculated in accordance with the Statutory Instruments.

*30 June 1999*

### New tax return for companies

New style Company Tax Return forms for Corporation Tax Self Assessment have been published by the Inland Revenue today. They must be used for accounting periods ending on or after 1 July 1999.

The new-style forms were developed with the co-operation of representative bodies, and have been road-tested with accountants and companies who do not have agents acting for them.

### Details

**1.** The new Company Tax Return is made up of a basic 12 page form, the CT600 (1999). There are also 'customised' Supplementary Pages for:

- loans to participators by close companies—CT600A
- controlled foreign companies—CT600B
- group and consortium relief claims or surrender—CT600C
- insurance companies, where either overseas life assurance business is carried on, or provisional payments are claimed under Schedule 19AB ICTA 1988—CT600D
- charity, where exemption or part exemption from tax is claimed—CT600E.

**2.** The new form has a 12 page Company Tax Return Guide (CT600 Guide) to help people fill it in. As well as notes on turnover, trading profits and losses, the Guide includes advice for clubs, associations and societies, and a table which shows when a Return must be sent in. The Guide also explains that penalties are chargeable if a Return is sent in late, or not sent in at all.

**3.** The new Company Tax Return and Supplementary Pages take account of the requirement for companies to include a self-assessment of tax payable, including tax

- in respect of loans to participators by close companies, and
- under the controlled foreign companies legislation and other provisions connected with the introduction of self-assessment for companies.

# Inland Revenue Press Releases

**Notes for editors**

**1.** The new Company Tax Return forms are for all companies affected by Corporation Tax Self Assessment (CTSA), and apply for accounting periods ending on or after 1 July 1999.

**2.** Over one million companies are affected by CTSA. It brings tax treatment for companies more closely into line with that of individuals and partnerships.

**3.** The move to CTSA for companies is nowhere near the major change that the introduction of Income Tax Self Assessment was for Income Tax payers. CTSA has many features in common with the Corporation Tax Pay and File (CTP&F) system which it replaces. And the new Company Tax Return is not radically different from the CTP&F return form (CT200) which will still be used for all accounting periods ending on or before 30 June 1999.

**4.** Like the CTP&F return form, members' clubs, societies and voluntary associations liable to Corporation Tax may only need to complete as few as three pages of the new return.

**5.** The Inland Revenue will not start sending Notices to file Company Tax Returns for CTSA until about November 1999. Then new Company Tax Return and Company Tax Return Guides will automatically be sent to companies that do not have an accountant acting for them or do not use an approved computer substitute. Companies that do have accountants acting for them, and accountants themselves, can get copies of the new Company Tax Return, the Company Tax Return Guide, or any Supplementary Pages they need by calling the CTSA Orderline on 0845 300 6555, or fax 0845 300 6777. All calls to the CTSA Orderline are charged at local rates, and lines are open seven days a week from 8:00am to 10:00pm. The forms are also available on the Internet at http://www.inlandrevenue.gov.uk

**6.** Inland Revenue approved substitute versions of the new Company Tax Return and Supplementary Pages may be used. Applications for approval of substitute forms must be sent to:

Inland Revenue Forms Unit
9th Floor
North West Wing
Bush House
Aldwych
LONDON WC2B 4PP.

Companies, tax practitioners and software houses who have been given approval for the latest print of the CTP&F return form are being contacted by the Forms Unit about new Company Tax Return substitute forms.

*13 July 1999*

## A modern system for corporation tax payments — full speed ahead for group payment arrangements

Time is running out for companies with accounting periods ending on 31 March if they want to register for Group Payment Arrangements.

## *Inland Revenue Press Releases*

Group Payment Arrangements allow groups of companies liable to pay their Corporation Tax in quarterly instalments to nominate one company in the group to meet the liabilities of the others, instead of paying company by company. The arrangements are voluntary.

Any of these groups who want to take part in the arrangements and whose accounting period ends on 31 March must get in touch with the Inland Revenue by phone or fax by 14 August.

### Details

**1.** Groups of companies that want to take advantage of the arrangements must register their interest by getting in touch with the Group Payment Team at the Inland Revenue Accounts Office to which they normally pay their Corporation Tax.

**2.** Group Payment Team contact details are:

> Group Payment Team
> Accounts Office Cumbernauld
> St Mungo's Road
> Cumbernauld
> Glasgow
> G70 5TR
> Telephone: 01236 783488
> Fax: 01236 783387

> Group Payment Team
> Accounts Office Shipley
> Victoria Street
> Shipley
> West Yorkshire
> BD98 8AA
> Telephone: 01274 539561
> Fax: 01274 539669

**3.** The Group Payment Team will need to know:

- the name of the group;
- contact point for the group;
- number of Group Payment Arrangements the group would like to set up;
- the likely accounting period end-date.

**4.** Registering by 14 August means that, for eligible groups with an accounting period ending on 31 March, the Inland Revenue will be able to make sure that contracts are in place before their first instalment payment is due on 14 October 1999.

### Notes for editors

**1.** Full details of Group Payment Arrangements are in an Inland Revenue Press Release *A Modern System for Corporation Tax Payments: Group Payment Arrangements*, issued on 26 February 1999.

# Inland Revenue Press Releases

**2.** The Group Payment Arrangement contract and guidance notes are reproduced on the Internet at http://www.inlandrevenue.gov.uk.

*20 July 1999*

## Tax provisions move closer to accounting practice

The Inland Revenue has decided not to pursue appeals in two cases concerning provisions made by businesses in computing profits. These are the *Herbert Smith* case on provisions for future rents and the *Jenners* case on repairs provisions. This means that the tax treatment of provisions moves substantially closer to UK generally accepted accounting practice.

## Details

**1.** Provisions are made where a business expects to pay out money in the future and takes that probable expense into account when working out its current profits. Common examples are warranties for defective goods or the potential costs of losing legal actions. Generally we follow correct accounting for revenue provisions but there are areas where in the past we considered that special tax rules applied. In two of these areas we now accept that there are no longer special tax rules.

**2.** The first rule was that losses or expenses could not be 'anticipated'. This was the issue in the *Herbert Smith* case, which was about a provision for rent payable in the future on surplus business premises. The second rule was that repairs expenditure could only be allowed as and when the work was carried out. This was the issue in the *Jenners* case.

**3.** Although *Herbert Smith* was about rent provisions, we accept that the case establishes generally that there is no longer a tax rule which denies provisions for 'anticipated' losses or expenses. This means in particular that accurate provisions for foreseen losses on long-term contracts (for example, in the construction industry) made in accordance with correct accounting practice will be tax-deductible. Statement of Practice 3/90, which set out our former view of the law on long-term contracts, is accordingly withdrawn.

### Financial Reporting Standard 12 on provisions

**4.** FRS 12 sets out a new code of accounting rules which applies to most provisions for periods ending after 22 March 1999. We now accept that provisions correctly made under FRS 12 are tax-deductible except where there remain specific tax rules to the contrary. For example provisions for capital expenditure are not tax-deductible, and provisions for employee or director remuneration are subject to the rule in Section 43 FA 1989 governing remuneration paid more than nine months after an accounting period.

### Application of revised approach

**5.** Our revised approach to both these provision cases applies in settling open years.

# Inland Revenue Press Releases

**6.** Businesses may have followed our previous view and disallowed provisions in the past as a result. In these cases, deductions may be made for expenditure incurred when computing tax profits for the period our new view is first applied and, in addition, any closing provision correctly computed in accordance with FRS 12 may be allowed. But no expenditure can be relieved more than once.

**Notes for editors**

**1.** The provisions cases are:

- *Herbert Smith v Honour, TL 3576, STC [1999] 173*; this is about provisions for future rents; no specific statute is involved and the supposed tax rule was derived from case law; and

- *Jenners, Princes Street Edinburgh Ltd v IRC, [1998] STC (SCD) 196*; this is about provisions for the repair of property and concerns section 74(1)(d) ICTA 1988.

**2.** The Revenue's guidance to staff on provisions is published. The previous guidance on 'loss anticipation' is dealt with in the Inspector's Manual at paragraphs 542c, 605d and 569 and in Statement of Practice 3 of 1990 (paragraph 7). The previous guidance on repairs provisions is dealt with in the Inspector's Manual at paragraph 990b. This guidance will be revised.

**3.** Financial Reporting Standard 12 dealing with provisions was issued in September 1998 and applies to accounting periods ending after 22 March 1999. The standard does not yet apply to some smaller businesses but a simplified version will do so soon.

**4.** Accounting standards are issued by the Accounting Standards Board, which is an independent body concerned with the development of accounting standards.

*23 July 1999*

## New code of practice for enquiries into company tax returns

A new Code of Practice for enquiries into self-assessment company tax returns has today been published by the Inland Revenue.

The Code, which explains what those responsible for submitting company tax returns can expect from the Revenue when they conduct enquiries, sets out revised rules for enquiries under self-assessment. It describes what the Revenue will do when they receive a tax return and how they will select cases for enquiry; how they will open and carry out enquiries; and what happens if they find something wrong.

The Code has been produced after consultation with representatives of companies and their professional advisers and with Inland Revenue staff. It will supersede the existing Code of Practice for investigations (COP2) for company tax returns.

*Inland Revenue Press Releases*

## Details

**1.** Self-assessment for companies changes some rules under which the Inland Revenue make enquiries into company tax returns. The changes first apply to returns for company accounting periods ending on or after 1 July 1999.

**2.** It has always been an important part of the Inland Revenue's responsibilities to make enquiries into company tax returns to make sure they are correct and complete. Such enquiries will continue under self-assessment, but with revised rules. The Code (COP14) explains how the Inland Revenue will conduct enquiries and assures companies and those responsible for submitting company returns that they can expect fair treatment from the Inland Revenue in accordance with 'Our Service Commitment to You'.

**3.** The Code will be given to the company at the start of every enquiry, unless it is a simple enquiry expected to be settled by a brief exchange of correspondence and not likely to involve penalties. In that case a short, single page version of the Code will be issued.

### Notes for editors

**1.** Checking and making enquiries into company tax returns will remain a key part of the Inland Revenue's work under self-assessment for companies.

**2.** Under the new system companies will make a return containing an assessment of the tax the company should pay. The Inland Revenue will then process the returns without detailed checking apart from the correction of any obvious mistakes. Once initial processing has been completed the Inland Revenue will check all returns and will have a statutory right to enquire into the completeness and accuracy of any of them. The majority of cases for enquiry will continue to be selected on the basis that the Inland Revenue think there may be something wrong with the company's return, but a small proportion will be selected at random.

**3.** This contrasts with the present system where the Inland Revenue need to be satisfied with the information sent in the return before they agree how much tax is due. The return is checked, all enquiries made and final figures agreed before it is processed.

**4.** The current Inland Revenue Code of Practice on investigations says that Inspectors will state their grounds for dissatisfaction with a return before commencing any investigation. This will no longer apply under the new regime. However the Inland Revenue may identify particular areas on which the enquiry will focus.

**5.** The Inland Revenue will have to give formal notice of the start and end of any enquiries. Enquiries must normally start within a year from the date the return should be filed. No further enquiries can be made into a return once the original enquiry has been concluded except where it is later discovered that the facts were not adequately disclosed or there was fraudulent or negligent conduct.

**6.** The Inland Revenue will have a new statutory power to require production of information reasonably needed to check the accuracy of a return. There is a right of appeal. During the course of the enquiry taxpayers can also apply to the independent Tax Commissioners for them to direct that the enquiry should be concluded where there do not appear to be reasonable grounds to continue it. At the end of the enquiry taxpayers can appeal to the Tax Commissioners if they do not accept the Inland Revenue's conclusions.

**7.** The existing rules for penalties for incorrect returns have not been changed. Such penalties can only be charged if a return is incorrect because of fraudulent or negligent conduct.

**8.** The Inland Revenue are preparing additional staff guidance for handling enquiries into company tax returns. It will form an extra chapter in the existing guidance manual and will be available to the public under Open Government procedure.

*31 August 1999*

## Advance pricing agreements (APAS)

The Inland Revenue have today published a Statement of Practice (SP 3/99) explaining how APAs are administered. The Statement of Practice provides guidance about how businesses may reach advance agreement with the Inland Revenue about transfer pricing issues in accordance with legislation introduced in this year's Finance Act. The Statement of Practice is published as an annex to this Press Release and is available on the Inland Revenue web-site the address of which is given below.

### Details

**1.** APAs aim to assist businesses in determining complex transfer pricing issues which may arise in applying the arm's length principle in accordance with the requirements of the transfer pricing rules. APAs made for the purposes of section 85, FA 1999 are written agreements between a business and the Board of Inland Revenue which determine a method for resolving transfer pricing issues in advance of a return being made. When the terms of the agreement are complied with, they provide assurance that the treatment in accordance with the agreement of those transfer pricing issues will be accepted by both the Revenue and the business for the period covered by the agreement.

**2.** This Statement of Practice provides detailed guidance about the process of applying for an APA and reaching agreement.

### Notes for editors

**1.** A statutory procedure for APAs is included in this year's Finance Act following a process of formal and informal consultation in which businesses and practitioners expressed general support for the proposals. In a Press Release dated 17 December 1998, the Inland Revenue made available a draft Statement of Practice together with draft legislation. Comments were invited from interested parties and have been taken into account in preparing the Statement of Practice issued today.

## Inland Revenue Press Releases

**2.** 'Transfer pricing' is the process by which associated enterprises set prices for transfers of goods, services, finance and intangible assets between them. There is general international agreement that transfer prices should be determined for tax purposes by reference to the arm's length principle.

**3.** APAs will help businesses by enabling them to make their returns in the knowledge that, to the extent the matter is covered, transfer pricing determined in accordance with the APA satisfies the arm's length principle and will be acceptable to the Inland Revenue for as long as the APA remains in force. They will also enable non-UK residents who trade here through a branch, or UK residents who trade abroad through a branch, to obtain equivalent certainty as to the amount of the profits attributable to that branch for UK tax purposes. The new rules will also allow companies involved in UK oil and gas extraction to enter into APAs in respect of transactions covered by the transfer pricing rules at section 770A/Sch 28AA, ICTA 1988.

**4.** Statements of Practice explain the Inland Revenue's interpretation of legislation and the way the Department applies the law in practice. They do not affect the taxpayer's right to argue for a different interpretation, if necessary in an appeal to the General or Special Commissioners.

**5.** Inland Revenue Statements of Practice are available in a free booklet, IR131, available from any Inland Revenue Enquiry Centre or Tax Office. They can also be obtained from the Inland Revenue Information Centre, South West Wing, Bush House, Strand, London, WC2B 4RD. The Statement of Practice published today will be included in a later edition of the booklet.

*6 September 1999*

## Controlled foreign companies (CFCs)—designer rate and similar regimes

To stop a continuing loss of tax revenue, legislation is to be introduced to counter the use of so called designer rate tax regimes. The use of such regimes in Guernsey, Jersey, the Isle of Man, Gibraltar and Ireland allows companies to side-step the UK's anti-avoidance legislation for controlled foreign companies (CFCs).

The legislation will have immediate effect and will formally be introduced in next year's Finance Bill. It will apply to CFC accounting periods beginning on or after today It will build on steps already taken in the last two Finance Acts to reinforce the effectiveness of the UK's controlled foreign companies legislation.

### Details

**Background**

**1.** The purpose of the CFC legislation is to stop UK companies from avoiding tax in this country by diverting income to subsidiaries (CFCs) in tax havens and preferential regimes. The rules work by requiring UK companies to pay an amount of CFC tax equal to any tax that would otherwise be avoided. Various

## Inland Revenue Press Releases

exemptions ensure that the rules only apply where a company is involved in UK tax avoidance.

**2.** At present, the CFC rules regard a company as being in a tax haven or preferential regime if it is subject to a level of taxation less than 75% of what it would have paid if it had been resident in the UK.

**Designer rate and similar regimes**

**3.** A number of countries have introduced regimes which are designed to enable companies to get round CFC rules. These are sometimes referred to as designer rate regimes, as they enable companies to pay just the right amount of tax needed in any given situation to side-step CFC rules.

**4.** Most commonly, the regimes work by allowing companies in effect to choose their rate of tax. Another method, found in Jersey, taxes one sort of income at up to 2% and another at 30%—by adjusting the mix of their income, companies are able to determine their overall rate of tax.

**Legislation**

**5.** The Government intends bringing forward anti-avoidance legislation in the next Finance Bill to stop the loss of tax through these regimes. The legislation will set aside the normal requirement that a company is only within the CFC rules if it has paid tax at a level less than 75% of that which it would have paid if it had been resident in the UK. The regimes to which the legislation applies will be named in regulations. From today, the legislation will apply to:

- Guernsey—bodies with international tax status;
- Jersey—international business companies;
- Isle of Man—international companies;
- Gibraltar—income tax qualifying companies;
- Ireland—companies taxed in accordance with the Irish Taxes Consolidation Act 1997 s 448(7).

**6.** The legislation will allow further regimes to be named in future if necessary.

**Notes**

**1.** A CFC is a company which is not resident in the UK (but which is controlled by individuals or companies who are) and which is subject to a level of taxation less than 75% of the level it would have paid had it been resident in the UK.

Subject to various exemptions, the difference between the UK tax it would have paid and the overseas tax it has paid is chargeable on UK companies with an interest in the CFC of at least 25%.

**2.** The Government has included measures in the last two Budgets aimed at improving the effectiveness of the CFC rules in preventing tax avoidance. Details were included in Inland Revenue Press Releases:

- 17 March 1998 *Controlled foreign companies (CFCs)—self-assessment and other changes.*
- 9 March 1999 *Loophole closed in controlled foreign company rules.*

22 September 1999

## Corporation tax reform — interest rate regulations

Legislative changes in the Finance Act 1998 allow companies to deduct interest chargeable on late payments of corporation tax and income tax when working out their taxable profits. As a result it is no longer necessary for the interest rate formula for late payment of tax by companies to include an adjustment for tax.

The Treasury have today laid before Parliament amendments to the interest rate regulations dealing with interest charged on late payments of income tax deducted at source by companies. The amendments remove the reduction for tax from the interest rate formula.

Copies of these amendments will be available shortly from the Stationery Office. They will also be available on the Inland Revenue website, the address of which is given below.

### Details

**1.** The regulations are the Taxes Interest Rate (Amendment No. 4) Regulations (SI 1999 No. 2637). They amend Regulation 3AA of the Taxes (Interest Rate) Regulations 1989 (SI 1989 No. 1297).

**2.** The amendments remove the tax adjustment from the formula for calculating interest on late payments of Income Tax on Company Payments. This adjustment is no longer necessary as, under self-assessment, companies may claim relief for the interest in arriving at their taxable profit.

**3.** The new rate is currently set at 7.5% and will be effective for payments due on or after 14 October 1999.

### Notes for editors

**1.** Section 178 of the Finance Act 1989 and the Taxes (Interest Rate) Regulations 1989 (SI 1989/1297) lay down the procedures and formulae for calculating and amending Inland Revenue interest rates.

**2.** Companies are required to deduct income tax at source when they pay interest and similar amounts to other companies or to individuals, and there are rules under which they must account for this income tax to the Revenue on a quarterly basis. Interest is chargeable under section 87 Taxes Management Act 1970 on late payments of this tax.

**3.** The current formula for interest under section 87 TMA 1970, in Regulation 3AA of SI 1989/1297, includes an adjustment for tax at the basic rate of income tax. This reflects the fact that companies cannot claim tax relief for interest on tax due for pre-self assessment periods.

**4.** Provisions introduced in the Finance Act 1998 allowed companies to deduct interest chargeable on late payments of both corporation tax and income tax in arriving at their taxable profit. These provisions are effective for accounting periods ending on or after 1 July 1999, to which the company self-assessment rules apply.

**5.** The formulae for calculating the interest rate on underpayments of corporation tax were amended in December 1998, along with the regulations governing the new instalment regime for large companies.

**6.** The present amendments remove the tax adjustment from the formula for calculating interest on late payments of income tax by companies. The new formula will be base rate plus 2.5 percentage points. The base rate for these purposes is the average of the base lending rates of six specified banks, rounded to the nearest whole number, with amounts midway between two whole numbers rounded down.

*8 October 1999*

## Inland Revenue interest rates—quarterly instalment payments, and early payments of corporation tax not due by instalments

The Inland Revenue have announced new rates of interest for underpaid and overpaid instalment payments of corporation tax, and early payments of corporation tax not due by instalments, in respect of accounting periods ending on or after 1 July 1999. These rates took effect from 20 September 1999. The changes are the result of recent changes in market rates.

### Details

**1.** The rate of interest charged on underpaid instalment payments of corporation tax has increased from 7% to 7.25%.

**2.** The rate of interest on overpaid instalment payments of corporation tax, and on corporation tax paid early (but not due by instalments), has increased from 4.75% to 5.00%.

### Notes

**1.** FA 1989 s 178 and the Tax (Interest Rate) Regulations, SI 1989/1297, lay down the procedures and formulae for calculating and amending Inland Revenue interest rates.

**2.** The provisions for calculating interest rates in respect of instalment payments of corporation tax, and early payments of corporation tax not due by instalments, in respect of accounting periods ending on or after the appointed day for corporation tax self-assessment (1 July 1999), are contained in SI 1998/3176.

**3.** The previous changes to these interest rates were set out in a press release dated 21 June 1999.

**4.** The revised interest rates are based on the average base lending rate of 5.25% calculated in accordance with the SIs.

*2 November 1999*

## Self-assessment for companies—simplified procedures for group relief

Simpler administrative arrangements for companies to obtain group relief are introduced by regulations laid before the House of Commons by the Treasury today.

The regulations simplify the rules for making and revising claims for group relief, reducing the paperwork involved. They set up arrangements for accounting periods ending on or after 1 July 1999, which allow all claims and surrenders of losses and other amounts by companies in the group to be administered on their behalf by one group company. These arrangements replace and extend those provided for earlier accounting periods under an Inland Revenue Statement of Practice.

[...]

## Details

**1.** The regulations are the Corporation Tax (Simplified Arrangements for Group Relief) Regulations, SI 1999/2975.

**2.** Groups of companies may apply to the Inland Revenue to operate the simplified arrangements under the regulations in a similar way to applications made under the existing Statement of Practice (SP 10/93). The regulations are aimed principally at the same larger and more complex groups of companies which use the existing arrangements, and for which the full procedural rules for group relief would otherwise impose the greatest burden.

**3.** The regulations are concerned only with the administrative rules, provided by *FA 1998 Sch 18 Part VIII*, under which claims to, and surrenders of, group relief are made. Otherwise group relief is unaffected.

**4.** Compared with arrangements made under the Statement of Practice, which is withdrawn for accounting periods on or after 1 July 1999, the additional benefits of arrangements made under the regulations include:

- provision for an 'authorised company' to amend group relief claims and surrenders on behalf of all participating group companies by providing only one copy of the statement containing details of the changes;
- inclusion of group companies whose accounting periods do not coincide exactly with those of the group as a whole; and
- inclusion of consortium companies which can claim group relief from, or surrender group relief to, the group.

## Inland Revenue Press Releases

5. The self-assessment consultative committee, consisting of representatives of business and other interested parties, has discussed the regulations in draft with the Inland Revenue, and has commented on them.

**Notes**

6. Group relief enables companies to surrender trading and other losses to other companies in their group which can use them. The rules also cover consortia.

7. The group relief rules require claims to group relief to be made in a tax return or by amendment of the tax return. A copy of the notice of consent must accompany the claim. The surrendering company must record details of surrenders for which consent has been given in its return. Additional claims or withdrawal of claims must be recorded by the claimant company by amendment of the return. Similarly, the surrendering company must amend its return if it gives consent to additional surrenders or it revises consents already given.

8. Simplified administrative arrangements for group relief for accounting periods to which the corporation tax pay and file rules apply were provided by SP 10/93. Like them, the arrangements provided for by the regulations are designed to simplify the procedure for making and revising claims to group relief, and giving and revising notices of consent to surrender relief.

*12 November 1999*

### Inland Revenue interest rates—quarterly instalment payments, and early payments of corporation tax not due by instalments

The Inland Revenue today announced new rates of interest for underpaid and overpaid instalment payments of corporation tax, and early payments of corporation tax not due by instalments, in respect of accounting periods ending on or after 1 July 1999. These rates will take effect from 15 November 1999. The changes are the result of recent changes in market rates.

### Details

**1.** The rate of interest charged on underpaid instalment payments of corporation tax has increased from 7.25 per cent to 7.50 per cent.

**2.** The rate of interest on overpaid instalment payments of corporation tax, and on corporation tax paid early (but not due by instalments), has increased from 5.00 per cent to 5.25 per cent.

**Notes for editors**

**1.** Section 178 Finance Act 1989 and Statutory Instrument SI 1989 No. 1297, 'The Tax (Interest Rate) Regulations 1989', lay down the procedures and formulae for calculating and amending Inland Revenue interest rates.

**2.** The provisions for calculating interest rates in respect of instalment payments of corporation tax, and early payments of corporation tax not due by instalments, in respect of accounting periods ending on or after the appointed day for corporation tax self-assessment (1 July 1999), are contained in Statutory Instrument SI 1998 No. 3176.

**3.** The previous changes to these interest rates were set out in a press release dated 8 October 1999.

**4.** The revised interest rates are based on the average base lending rate of 5.50 per cent calculated in accordance with the Statutory Instruments.

*10 January 2000*

## Corporation tax self-assessment—pre-return valuation for capital gains of companies

Following the success of the free valuation service provided by the Inland Revenue to help individuals and trustees complete their self-assessment returns correctly, this service is now being extended to companies. From today companies may send valuations used in computing their capital gains to their Inland Revenue office for checking before they make their corporation tax self-assessment tax returns.

## Details

**1.** From today companies will be able to ask their Inland Revenue office to check valuations used to compute their capital gains for the purpose of completing their corporation tax self-assessment returns.

**2.** This extends a service set up in April 1997 under the new self-assessment system to provide individual taxpayers and trustees with checks on valuations they use to fill in their tax returns. This service has proved very successful, enabling many taxpayers to reach early agreement on valuations and pay the right amount of tax on time.

**3.** To use the new service companies should send form CG34, with full information about the transactions to which the valuations relate, and together with any relevant computations, to their Inland Revenue office. The guidance notes on form CG34 set out all the information and documents which need to be provided.

**4.** Form CG34 may be obtained from any Inland Revenue enquiry centre, or Inland Revenue office, or from the Inland Revenue Information Centre, Bush House, South West Wing, Strand, London WC2B 4RD.

## Notes

**1.** In certain circumstances assets have to be valued for the purpose of computing capital gains. This applies, for example, in determining the acquisition cost of assets held at 31 March 1982.

*Inland Revenue Press Releases*

**2.** Corporation tax self-assessment applies to company accounting periods ending on or after 1 July 1999.

*21 January 2000*

## Inland Revenue interest rates—quarterly instalment payments, and early payments of corporation tax not due by instalments

The Inland Revenue today announced new rates of interest for underpaid and overpaid instalment payments of corporation tax, and early payments of corporation tax not due by instalments, in respect of accounting periods ending on or after 1 July 1999. These rates will take effect from 24 January 2000. The changes are the result of recent changes in market rates.

### Details

**1.** The rate of interest charged on underpaid instalment payments of corporation tax has increased from 7.5% to 7.75%.

**2.** The rate of interest on overpaid instalment payments of corporation tax, and on corporation tax paid early (but not due by instalments), has increased from 5.25% to 5.5%.

### Notes

**1.** FA 1989 s 178 and the Tax (Interest Rate) Regulations, SI 1989/1297, lay down the procedures and formulae for calculating and amending Inland Revenue interest rates.

**2.** The provisions for calculating interest rates in respect of instalment payments of corporation tax, and early payments of corporation tax not due by instalments, in respect of accounting periods ending on or after the appointed day for corporation tax self-assessment (1 July 1999), are contained in SI 1998/3176.

**3.** The previous changes to these interest rates were set out in a press release dated 12 November 1999.

**4.** The revised interest rates are based on the average base lending rate of 5.75% calculated in accordance with the SIs.

*18 February 2000*

## Inland Revenue interest rates—quarterly instalment payments, and early payments of corporation tax not due by instalments

The Inland Revenue today announced new rates of interest for underpaid and overpaid instalment payments of corporation tax, and early payments of corporation tax not due by instalments, in respect of accounting periods ending on or

## Inland Revenue Press Releases

after 1 July 1999. These rates will take effect from 21 February 2000. The changes are the result of recent changes in market rates.

### Details

**1.** The rate of interest charged on underpaid instalment payments of corporation tax has increased from 7.75 per cent to 8.00 per cent.

**2.** The rate of interest on overpaid instalment payments of corporation tax, and on corporation tax paid early (but not due by instalments), has increased from 5.50 per cent to 5.75 per cent.

### Notes for editors

**1.** Section 178 Finance Act 1989 and Statutory Instrument SI 1989 No. 1297, 'The Tax (Interest Rate) Regulations 1989', lay down the procedures and formulae for calculating and amending Inland Revenue interest rates.

**2.** The provisions for calculating interest rates in respect of instalment payments of corporation tax, and early payments of corporation tax not due by instalments, in respect of accounting periods ending on or after the appointed day for corporation tax self-assessment (1 July 1999), are contained in Statutory Instrument SI 1998 No. 3176.

**3.** The previous changes to these interest rates were set out in a press release dated 21 January 2000.

**4.** The revised interest rates are based on the average base lending rate of 6.00 per cent calculated in accordance with the Statutory Instruments.

*21 February 2000*

### Getting Britain giving—draft legislation published

Draft legislation for the Getting Britain Giving package of measures for charities is published today.

Commenting on the exposure of the draft legislation, the Economic Secretary, Melanie Johnson said:

> 'The Government values the significant contribution which charities have made in working with the Inland Revenue on the details of the measures contained in the draft legislation.'

The proposals, which were announced by the Chancellor in his pre-Budget Report in November, will provide a significant boost for charitable giving through a modernised and simplified tax system. They include:

- the abolition of the £250 minimum limit for donations in the Gift Aid scheme so that tax relief will apply to any donation, large or small, regular or one-off;

## Inland Revenue Press Releases

- the facility to join the Gift Aid scheme by phone or Internet;
- the abolition of the £1,200 ceiling on Payroll Giving through the pay packet;
- a 10 per cent supplement on all donations to charities through payroll giving for three years;
- a new income tax relief for gifts of listed shares and securities;
- more exemptions for small trading and fund-raising activities.

**Details**

**1.** Copies of the draft clauses, draft regulations and interim guidance on the new measures are available on the Inland Revenue website: www.inlandrevenue.gov.uk. Paper copies can be obtained from: Penny Hood, Inland Revenue, Room 130, New Wing, Somerset House, Strand, London WC2R 1LB; telephone 020 7438 6742; fax 020 7438 7134.

**2.** Comments are invited on the draft legislation and guidance and should be sent to the above address or e-mailed to penny.hood@ir.gsi.gov.uk by 10 March 2000.

**Notes for editors**

The review of charity taxation was launched in July 1997. During the first phase of the open consultation, over 3,000 charities and other interested parties sent in their views on a wide range of subjects. A consultation document was published on Budget Day 1999 containing the Government's options for further consultation. Some 500 responses were received before the consultation closed on 31 August. A summary of the consultation responses was published on 28 October 1999 (see Press Notice 174/99).

*20 March 2000*

**New tax information agreements**

New proposals to enable the exchange of tax information between the UK Inland Revenue and overseas authorities were announced today by the Chancellor, Gordon Brown.

Tax Information Exchange Agreements will allow the Inland Revenue to receive information about foreign transactions of UK taxpayers and multinational companies not currently available because there is no agreement for effective exchange of information in place.

The Government of Bermuda, one of the UK's Overseas Territories, has already indicated that it is prepared to enter into negotiations with the UK on such an agreement.

## Details

Tax Information Exchange Agreements will allow the Inland Revenue to receive information about foreign transactions of UK taxpayers and multinational companies not currently available because there is no agreement for effective exchange of information in place. The Government intends to open talks with other countries including the UK's own Overseas Territories and Crown Dependencies as part of its efforts to develop new international standards on exchange of information in support of OECD and G7 initiatives.

**Notes for editors**

**1.** The Inland Revenue is already able to exchange some tax information with other countries with which the UK has a double taxation agreement. Information received under those arrangements has assisted in the recovery of millions of pounds in UK tax revenues. Tax Information Exchange Agreements offer a route for exchange of information to be significantly extended and improved.

**2.** The UK Government strongly supports the efforts of the Organisation for Economic Co-operation and Development (OECD) to tackle harmful tax competition between states. The UK government is encouraging the UK Overseas Territories and the Crown Dependencies to enter into effective exchange of information agreements as an important signal of their willingness to co-operate internationally in dealing with tax evasion and avoidance.

**3.** The Government has repeatedly emphasised the need for greater international co-operation—in particular exchange of information to tackle financial crime, harmful tax competition, tax evasion and avoidance. A G7 initiative seeking to improve the supply of information by the negotiation of effective information exchange agreements was launched by the Chancellor during the UK Presidency in 1998. The Government has also recently circulated a paper (*Exchange of Information and the draft Directive on Taxation of Savings*) which sets out the case for tackling evasion of tax on savings income through exchange of information on a wide international basis. The paper can be accessed from HM Treasury's web site: http://www.hm-treasury.gov.uk.

*21 March 2000*

## Construction industry scheme

A package of measures to improve the new Construction Industry Scheme, was set out by the Chancellor today.

- To reduce costs and streamline the flow of paperwork, the procedures for CIS24 vouchers will be simplified.

- Fewer subcontracting companies will need to make a formal business case to qualify for a CIS5 certificate following the reduction of the turnover threshold from £5 million to £3 million from today.

- Two new consultative forums will be established to review the scheme:
  - A Joint Working Group comprising officials from the Inland Revenue,

the Department of the Environment, Transport and the Regions (DETR), and representatives from the Construction Industry.

- A User Panel consisting of a cross-section of people from the industry who have hands-on experience of operating the Scheme.

Subcontractors will also benefit from:

- The recent announcement of a reduction in the deduction rate from 23% to 18% from 6th April.
- The increase in the PAYE quarterly payments limit announced today which will help the cash flow of many smaller subcontracting businesses.

## Details

### Streamlining the CIS24 Voucher procedures

When payments are made to a subcontractor who has qualified for a gross payment certificate (CIS6) the subcontractor must complete a voucher (CIS24) showing the details of the payment. The voucher, which has three parts, is sent to the contractor who completes further information on it before returning the subcontractor's copy to them.

From 6 May, a subcontractor completing a CIS24 voucher will no longer be required to send their copy of the voucher to the Contractor. The subcontractor will remove their copy of the voucher and retain it for their records. The remaining two parts will be sent to the Contractor as before.

This measure will reduce the amount of paperwork that is currently exchanged between contractors and subcontractors and will reduce the costs of complying with the scheme.

Letters explaining the change will be issued to all contractors and CIS6 holders in mid-April.

### Reduction in the CIS5 qualifying Turnover Threshold

Under the scheme all subcontractors must have registered with the Inland Revenue to obtain a registration card (CIS4) or certificate (CIS6). Both of these documents need to be presented in person. Some companies who have qualified for a CIS6 may be granted a CIS5—which does not need to be presented in person—if they are able to fulfil one of a number of criteria. One of the criteria is a gross turnover threshold.

With effect from today the turnover threshold that allows a company, which has qualified for a CIS6, to qualify for a CIS5 has been reduced from £5 million to £3 million. This means that those companies with a turnover of between £3 million and £5 million will no longer need to make a business case to show that they fulfil one of the other criteria in order to qualify for a CIS5.

Where a subcontracting company has been granted a CIS6 and has made an application for a CIS5 that has not been successful, but the gross turnover of the business is in excess of £3 million, they should reapply.

## Joint Working Group

The Inland Revenue will be working together with The Department of the Environment, Transport and the Regions (DETR), and all sections of the Construction Industry.

This group will consider ways in which the scheme can be improved whilst continuing to protect the flow of revenue to the Exchequer.

In particular the group will consider:

- The results of independent market research commissioned by the Inland Revenue.

- Similarities between the regulatory requirements of the Inland Revenue and Customs and Excise and how these could be brought together to help businesses.

- The difficulties which CIS6 holders face in complying with their obligations to show their cards in person.

- Ways in which the different criteria for granting a certificate to companies and to individuals and partnerships can be made more acceptable to the industry.

- Introducing in-year repayments for companies.

- Advances in information technology and electronic business and ways in which these could be used to support a streamlining of the scheme.

## User Panel

This panel will consist of a cross-section of people from the industry who have hands-on experience of operating the Scheme who will work closely with joint working group. They will identify issues and possible solutions and provide practical advice.

## Other measures

The Government announced in a Press Release published on 25th February 2000 that the rate of deduction that will apply to payments under the Construction Industry Scheme is to fall from 23% to 18% from 6th April.

This means that subcontractors within the industry without gross payment certificates will have substantially less tax deducted from payments made to them during the 2000–2001 tax year, which they would otherwise have to reclaim from the Inland Revenue.

In addition, the increase in the Quarterly Payments limit will improve cash flow for those subcontracting businesses who have not qualified for a gross payment certificate but who pay employees or subcontractors under deductions of tax. For further details see Budget Note REVBN1A.

# Inland Revenue Press Releases

**Notes for editors**

A tax deduction scheme for the Construction Industry was introduced in 1971 to tackle the substantial tax leakage in the industry.

The new scheme that took effect from the 1st August was built largely on the principles of the old scheme. Changes to the Scheme were introduced in Schedule 27 Finance Act 1995 and Section 178 Finance Act 1996. Further minor changes were introduced in Schedule 8 of Finance Act 1998.

Changes were necessary because the rules that governed the entitlement of 714 certificates—which allowed subcontractors to be paid gross—proved increasingly ineffective in limiting the numbers of certificates in circulation.

The widespread availability of certificates encouraged misuse of the documents and tax evasion continued at an unacceptable level. The loss to the Exchequer is believed to be well above £100m per annum.

Under the new scheme, all subcontractors must register with the Inland Revenue and present their documents to the contractor before they can receive payment for work they have done. Vouchers need to be completed (either by the contractor or subcontractor) for all the payments that are made under the scheme. These are ultimately sent to the Revenue to facilitate compliance checks.

The majority of subcontractors have been given a CIS4 registration card, which requires them to be paid after deductions on account of tax and class 4 National Insurance Contributions. The card carries a photograph of the card holder and must be presented in person.

The CIS6 certificate is issued to those subcontractors who pass the statutory tests and allows them to receive payment gross. It is the normal gross payment certificate available to those working within the industry. It carries a photograph of the certificate holder and must be presented in person.

The CIS5 certificate is issued only to companies that can make a business case (there are published rules) or have a turnover in excess of the set limit—this has today been reduced from £5 to £3 million. This certificate does not carry a photograph and need not be presented in person.

The scheme is already proving effective: to date at least 50,000 businesses have registered with the Inland Revenue of whom they were previously unaware.

*29 March 2000*

## Quarterly payments of corporation tax

Action was taken today to implement two elements in the package of measures designed to create a more competitive environment for business announced in the Budget.

Regulations have been laid before the House of Commons which will:

# Inland Revenue Press Releases

- reduce by 1% the rate of interest on underpayments of corporation tax under the quarterly instalment arrangements for large companies;
- double the de minimis limit, below which large companies do not have to pay by instalments, from £5,000 to £10,000. As a result around 1,000 companies will be removed from the instalment arrangements.

## Details

**1.** The new interest rate regulations amend the formula for calculating the interest rate on underpayments of quarterly instalments, from two percentage points above the base rate to just one percentage point above the base rate. The reduced rate will apply from 20 April 2000 and the reduction will affect interest which is already running as well as interest on tax due after that date.

**2.** The Inland Revenue will continue to monitor the instalment payment arrangements closely. Further changes in the interest rate may be made if market conditions or changes in payment patterns indicate they are necessary.

**3.** The new de minimis limit will apply for accounting periods ending on or after 1 July 2000. It is estimated that around 1,000 companies will no longer have to pay by instalments as a result of this change.

**Notes for editors**

**1.** The regulations which change the interest rate formula are the Taxes Interest Rate (Amendment) Regulations 2000 (SI 2000 No. 893). They amend Regulation 3ZA of the Taxes (Interest Rate) Regulations 1989 (SI 1989 No. 1297), which was inserted by the Taxes (Interest Rate) (Amendment No. 2) Regulations 1998 (SI 1998 No. 3176).

**2.** The formula for calculating the rate of interest charged on underpayments of quarterly instalments is linked to the base rate. The base rate for these purposes is the average of the base lending rates of six specified banks, rounded up to the nearest amount which is a multiple of one-quarter.

**3.** The rate of interest applying to underpayments continuing after the normal due date (nine months and one day after the end of a company's accounting period) will continue to be two and a half percentage points above the base rate. The base rate for these purposes is the average of the base lending rates of six specified banks, rounded to the nearest whole number, with amounts midway between two whole numbers rounded down.

**4.** The regulations which increase the de minimis limit for the quarterly payment arrangements are the Corporation Tax (Instalment Payments) (Amendment) Regulations 2000 (SI 2000 No. 892). They amend Regulation 3 of the Corporation Tax (Instalment Payments) Regulations 1998 (SI 1998 No. 3175).

**5.** Only large companies (broadly, those with profits over £1.5m) pay corporation tax by quarterly instalments. But there is also a de minimis limit which excludes companies with an annual liability of £5,000 or less from paying by instalments. It is this limit which has been increased.

**6.** Copies of both of these amendment regulations will be available shortly from

## Inland Revenue Press Releases

the Stationery Office. They will also be available on the Inland Revenue website, the address of which is given below.

**7.** The changes implemented by these regulations were announced on Budget Day in Budget Note REVBN2I.

*11 April 2000*

### Electronic commerce — tax status of websites and servers

The UK today set out its views on the tax status of web sites and servers.

Speaking at a conference in Lisbon, the Director of the Inland Revenue's International Division, Gabs Makhlouf, said:

> 'The OECD has been reviewing with the business community the long term future of the "permanent establishment" concept—the threshold in the OECD's model tax treaty below which a country will not tax non-residents carrying on a business in that country. This is crucial work. And it is important that it is carried out with due consideration, and in partnership between representatives of Government and business.
>
> "Permanent establishment" is a long standing concept. It is tried and tested. And it is widely supported. As yet, we do not know enough about how e-commerce will develop for anyone to make reasoned decisions on whether or not to move away from it. But now is clearly the time for the debate to begin.
>
> In the meantime, early decisions are needed on the status of websites and servers under the existing rules of permanent establishment. Businesses need to know where they stand in order to make investment decisions and calculate their tax liabilities.
>
> A particularly important policy objective is that the outcome is a practical one. One that works in the real world as well in the heads of lawyers. Governments and businesses need an outcome that allows e-commerce to flourish, that keeps down compliance costs, and that is enforceable.
>
> In the UK, we take the view that a website of itself is not a permanent establishment. And we take the view that a server is insufficient of itself to constitute a permanent establishment of a business that is conducting e-commerce through a website on the server. We take that view regardless of whether the server is owned, rented or otherwise at the disposal of the business.'

**Notes for editors**

**1.** The Government's goal is for the UK to be the best environment in the world in which to trade electronically by 2002.

**2.** The Inland Revenue and Customs and Excise published on 26 November 1999 a comprehensive review of the tax issues concerning e-commerce (*Electronic Commerce: The UK's Taxation Agenda*). Chapter 8 highlighted a number of outstanding issues to do with the application of international tax rules to e-commerce, including the application of the permanent establishment concept in double taxation treaties.

**3.** Under the OECD's model tax treaty, a non-resident business is only taxable in a foreign country to the extent that it is carrying on business there through a permanent establishment. A permanent establishment is defined as being 'a fixed place of business through which the business of an enterprise is wholly or partly carried on'.

**4.** The OECD published a second draft of a consultation note clarifying the position on the status of websites and servers. It concerns the legal interpretation of the existing Article 5 of the model treaty and records that there are differing views among OECD member countries on whether a server may be a permanent establishment. It is available on the OECD's web site at http://www.oecd.org/daf/fa/treaties/art5rev_3March.pdf.

*18th April 2000*

## Inland Revenue interest rates—underpaid quarterly instalment payments of corporation tax

Following the changes to the Corporation Tax quarterly payment arrangements for large companies announced on Budget Day, the rate of interest on underpayments of corporation tax due under the quarterly instalment arrangements will be reduced by 1% with effect from 20 April 2000. All other Inland Revenue interest rates for unpaid and overpaid tax will remain unchanged.

## Details

**1.** The rate of interest charged on underpaid instalment payments of corporation tax will be decreased from 8.00 per cent to 7.00 per cent. The change takes effect from 20 April 2000 and results from an amendment to the interest rate formula by regulations laid on 29 March.

**2.** The rate of interest on overpaid instalment payments of corporation tax, and on corporation tax paid early (but not due by instalments), remains unchanged at 5.75 per cent.

**Notes for editors**

**1.** Section 178 Finance Act 1989 and Statutory Instrument SI 1989 No. 1297, 'The Tax (Interest Rate) Regulations 1989', lay down the procedures and formulae for calculating and amending Inland Revenue interest rates.

**2.** The provisions for calculating interest rates in respect of instalment payments of corporation tax, and early payments of corporation tax not due by instalments, in respect of accounting periods ending on or after the appointed day for

## Inland Revenue Press Releases

corporation tax self-assessment (1 July 1999), are contained in Statutory Instrument SI 1998 No. 3176. The formula for calculating interest on underpayments of quarterly instalments was amended by SI 2000 No. 893, laid on 29 March 2000.

**3.** The previous changes to these interest rates were set out in a press release dated 18 February 2000.

**4.** The revised interest rate is based on the average base lending rate of 6.00 per cent calculated in accordance with the Statutory Instruments.

*16 June 2000*

### Finance Bill—double taxation relief and controlled foreign companies

The Government today confirmed that it will proceed with measures, following Budget announcements, to deliver its twin objectives of tackling tax avoidance while ensuring the attractiveness and competitiveness of the UK as a place to do business.

Budget measures to stop the avoidance of UK tax through controlled foreign companies (CFCs) will be legislated, as announced. This will bring the UK CFC regime more into line with practice elsewhere.

Nor is it acceptable that UK companies can obtain a tax advantage from using offshore mixing companies. It is therefore confirmed that the tax advantages of offshore mixer companies, which were the focus of the Budget measures concerning double taxation relief, will be stopped, as previously proposed.

However, the Government's discussions with business have led it to conclude that there are circumstances in which a limited form of onshore pooling of foreign tax on dividends will be allowed, where this involves genuine business activity.

Together these measures:

- tackle tax avoidance, with a firm clampdown on abuse of offshore holding companies;
- protect the tax base, which was at clear risk of significant further avoidance through plans which have come to light during the Government's recent discussions;
- underpin the Government's broader aims for the UK corporate tax system. It is only if avoidance is tackled and loopholes are closed that further progress can be made in reforming the system in line with the Government's aim that the UK should be an attractive place to do business and for multinationals to locate.

The Government is also tabling amendments covering a number of technical points, described in detail below.

Given the scale of the avoidance that has come to light since the Budget, the impact of the overall package described above will be broadly similar to the estimates provided in the Financial Statement and Budget Report.

*Inland Revenue Press Releases*

# Detail

**Double taxation relief**

**1.** The changes that the Government intends to introduce at the Report stage of the Finance Bill will mean that:

- dividends paid by CFCs to satisfy an acceptable distribution policy, where none of the other CFC exemptions (including the motive test) are met, will not be able to be mixed with any other dividends;
- underlying tax in relation to foreign dividends paid up through overseas subsidiaries will be capped at 30%, as in the Bill currently;
- underlying tax above the cap will, within certain limits, be able to be credited against UK tax payable on dividends other than dividends paid by CFCs as mentioned above and dividends where the underlying tax has already been capped;
- similar relief will be allowed for some foreign tax above 30% paid on dividends received by UK companies directly from foreign subsidiaries (onshore pooling).

**2.** The amendments that are being tabled today include the following points.

**3.** Schedule 30 para 5 deals with the interaction of double taxation agreements and relief for foreign tax under UK domestic law. It contains a rule that says that if a double taxation agreement has an express provision to the effect that a taxpayer cannot have relief for foreign tax in a particular situation, he cannot claim the relief under UK domestic law instead.

**4.** As drafted, that provision would have effect in relation to claims for credit relief made on or after 21 March 2000. That is, it would apply in relation to claims where there is an existing double taxation agreement. However, that would work inappropriately with some existing agreements.

**5.** The amendment ensures that the new provision will apply only where there is an express provision denying relief for foreign tax in a double taxation agreement that is made in the future.

**6.** Schedule 30 para 10, which introduces new rules concerning relief for underlying tax and mixer companies, contains a start date of 1 July 2000. This is because the Government recognised that the changes should not come into effect immediately. It wanted companies to have a period within which to bring dividends into the UK under the old rules.

**7.** However, some groups with complex, multi-tiered structures face complications arising, for example, from the position of minority shareholders in foreign subsidiaries and foreign law constraints on when dividends can be paid, placing them at an artificial timing disadvantage vis-a-vis others. The Government has therefore decided that the start date for the restriction on the use of mixer companies should instead be 31 March 2001. That will apply to the whole of para 10.

**8.** Schedule 30 para 10 introduces a restriction on the use of mixer companies to average out rates of foreign tax paid on low taxed and high taxed profits.

## Inland Revenue Press Releases

Dividends paid by companies in the ownership chain below a UK company will not have attributed to them underlying tax at a rate exceeding the UK corporation tax rate (currently 30%).

**9.** As drafted, that restriction will apply if the company paying the dividend and the company receiving it are both resident in the same country, as well as in cases where they are resident in different countries. It was suggested in representations that the restriction is not necessary in cases where dividends are paid between companies resident in the same country that are subject to the same tax rules and tax rates there.

**10.** The amendment will mean that the restriction will not apply where the company paying the dividend and the company receiving it are resident in the same country. The Inland Revenue will consult people who have asked for this relaxation about the situations in which they think it should apply and how to prevent it being abused. More details will be included in Regulations later this year, well in advance of the start date for the legislation.

**11.** Schedule 30 para 14, which allows unrelieved foreign tax to be carried backwards or forwards to be credited against UK tax in another period, is—like the restrictions on mixer companies—drafted to apply from 1 July 2000 in the case of foreign tax on dividends. This date will be also amended to 31 March 2001. This will preserve the common start date for the two sets of provisions for which the Bill provides.

**12.** Schedule 30 para 12 provides that, where a group of overseas companies is taxed as a single entity in its home state, those companies are to be regarded as a single taxpayer for the purpose of calculating underlying tax credit relief in the UK. Under the present legislation, relief is strictly speaking denied if it is not possible to identify the company paying a dividend as the company which has itself paid the foreign tax on the profits out of which the dividend is paid.

**13.** As currently drafted, the new provision applies only where the overseas group is situated in the ownership chain immediately below a UK company. That is, the provision will not apply if there is an intermediate company, or more than one such company, between the overseas group and the UK company. It was suggested in representations that the presence of one or more companies between the foreign group and the UK company ought not to affect the availability of the relief.

**14.** The effect of the amendment is to ensure that the new provision will apply in cases where there is an intermediate company, or more than one such company, between the overseas group and the UK company,

**15.** Schedule 30 para 14 introduces a provision to allow unrelieved foreign tax to be carried backwards or forwards. This addresses the case where, over a period, broadly the same amount of profits might be taxed in both the UK and another country, but the profits are recognised for tax purposes at different times in the two countries. The Government has received a number of representations that the period of carry back ought to be extended beyond one year if the relief is to fulfil its purpose effectively. The Government has decided to table an amendment to make the carry back period three years. The legislation also contains the necessary ordering rules.

# Inland Revenue Press Releases

16. Paragraph 14 requires a claim to carry unrelieved foreign tax backwards or forwards to be made within two years following the end of the accounting period to which the foreign tax originally relates. The Government has decided to extend the time limit to make it consistent with the longer time limit for claiming relief for foreign tax generally, which is usually six years.

17. In addition, there are two purely drafting amendments to Sch 30 paras 4, 5.

### Insurance companies

18. Special provisions for insurance companies were left out of Sch 30 when the Finance Bill was published to allow time for consultation. Consultation has taken place and the amendments tabled today insert five new paragraphs into Sch 30 to the Bill.

19. The new paragraphs put into effect the measures which were outlined in para 1.44 of the document *Double taxation relief for companies—outcome of the review* published on Budget Day, They deal particularly with the special rules needed to ensure that the new double taxation relief regime works properly for insurance companies, particularly life insurance companies.

### Controlled foreign companies

20. The CFC legislation is anti-avoidance legislation to prevent multinationals from avoiding UK tax by diverting profits to tax havens and preferential regimes. The Finance Bill closes a number of loopholes and anomalies in the legislation, in order to ensure that the UK is fairly and effectively protected against deliberate UK tax avoidance.

21. Additional tax will only be payable where UK tax avoidance is a main motive for the existence of a CFC or for the transactions of a CFC. Multinationals that are not involved in UK tax avoidance will have no additional tax to pay.

22. The amendments tabled today concern the changes in the Finance Bill to prevent companies avoiding the CFC rules through the use of international joint ventures. In some limited circumstances the changes go further than was intended, and the amendments correct that. The substance of the changes is not affected.

23. Under existing law, a company is only regarded as being a CFC if it is controlled from the UK. Most commonly, this means that more than 50% of the shares must be held in the UK.

24. It is becoming increasingly common for UK companies to enter into joint ventures with overseas companies. In such situations, a joint venture company in a tax haven may not be a CFC as currently defined, as the UK company may not have more than 50% control. UK companies are increasingly exploiting this in order to get round the CFC rules.

25. To counter this, Sch 31 modernises the CFC control test, broadly in line with a similar updating made in 1998 to the control test for transfer pricing. The new rules contain a so-called '40% test', under which a company is treated as being a CFC if it is at least 40% controlled by a UK person and at least 40% controlled by a foreign person.

## Inland Revenue Press Releases

**26.** The amendments tabled today restrict the '40% test' so that it will not apply where a foreign person in a joint venture holds more than 55% of the interests, rights and powers. The amendments recognise that in these situations a UK company's 40% stake may not enable sufficient influence to be exercised over the joint venture from the UK for it to be appropriate to apply the CFC rules.

**27.** Similarly, the amendments ensure that the rules attributing to a person the interests, rights and powers of another person do not go further than intended. The amendments ensure that the interests, rights and powers of a UK person cannot be attributed to a non-resident person and cannot be attributed from one joint venture partner to another simply because they are partners.

**28.** The amendments also include consequential changes to bring the exemption for holding companies into line with the new rules for joint ventures.

**Notes**

**Double taxation relief**

**1.** Draft legislation on double taxation relief was published by the Inland Revenue on Budget Day, 21 March 2000, in the paper *Double taxation relief for companies—outcome of the review*. The Government invited comments on the drafting of the legislation by 19 April.

**2.** An Inland Revenue press release issued on 3 May Taxation of multinational companies gave details of some of the changes mentioned above.

**3.** Double taxation occurs when income is taxed both by the taxpayer's country of residence and in another country where the income arises. The purpose of double taxation relief is to remove or reduce the disincentive that double taxation represents to outward investment. It is estimated that in the tax year 1999–00 £5.5 billion of relief will be allowed against income tax and corporation tax. A key part in that is played by double taxation agreements that the UK has entered into with other countries. More than 100 of these are now in force.

**4.** Most of the double taxation relief that is allowed relates to underlying tax. This is the tax paid by subsidiary companies on the profits out of which they pay dividends. When the subsidiaries pay a dividend to the UK, the UK company is entitled to credit for the underlying tax, as well as for the foreign tax (if any) withheld from the dividend itself.

**5.** A mixer company is an offshore subsidiary of a UK company which itself has one or more subsidiary companies. Dividends from different subsidiaries are routed into the UK through the mixer company. This allows mixing of the different dividend streams and of the underlying taxes attributable to each. Under the current rules it is possible to mix, and thereby average out, foreign taxes paid in different countries of, say, 60% and 5%, to set against the UK tax charged at 30% on the single dividend that emerges from the mixer. Under the Finance Bill currently, the foreign tax charged at 60% will be limited to 30% for the purpose of calculating the relief that is available in the UK.

*Inland Revenue Press Releases*

**Insurance companies**

**6.** Special rules are required for life assurance business to reflect the fact that much of the income and gains received by a life company are destined for the payment of benefits to policyholders. To the extent that the income and gains relate to categories of business, such as pension business, where the profit on which the company pays tax is reduced by the increased obligations to policyholders that reflect those benefits, there is no corporation tax liability and so no double taxation of the income and gains in the hands of the company. The special rules are required to identify by apportionment the increased obligations to be deducted from each item of foreign income or gains in order to arrive at the amount that does bear corporation tax and is therefore doubly taxed. Similar rules are required for general insurance business to identify the share of certain expenses attributable to each item of foreign income. The rules also ensure that the total relief for foreign tax cannot exceed the corporation tax charged on the profits of the business in question.

**Controlled foreign companies**

**7.** Details of the CFC provisions in the Finance Bill were set out in Budget Note BN2K.

**8.** A CFC is a company which is not resident in the UK (but which is controlled to a significant extent by individuals or companies who are) and which is subject to a level of taxation less than 75% of the level that it would have paid had it been resident in the UK. Subject to various exemptions, the difference between the UK tax it would have paid and the overseas tax it has paid is chargeable on UK companies with an interest of at least 25% in the CFC.

**9.** The rules contain a number of exemptions. These include a motive test, an exempt activities test, a list of 74 countries in which companies are outside the CFC rules if they meet certain conditions, a distribution test, and a public quotation test. CFC tax is only payable if a company fails all of these tests. The motive test specifically ensures that CFC tax is only payable if a company is involved in UK tax avoidance.

*Appendix 7*

# Enquiries into company tax returns

### Code of Practice 14

This Code of Practice tells you how we carry out enquiries into company tax returns for accounting periods ending on or after 1 July 1999. There are separate Codes of Practice for cases dealt with by some of our specialist offices.
In particular this booklet does not apply to enquiries handled by Special Compliance Office.

We promise companies fair treatment under the law and in accordance with 'Our service commitment to you', which is reproduced at the back of this booklet. It explains the rules we follow and your rights and responsibilities in particular situations.

We want companies to pay the right amount of tax: no more, no less. We will do everything we reasonably can to help you make sure this happens.

If you have any queries after reading this booklet, or require further information about how to complete a company tax return, we will be pleased to help you.

Contact details are given at the beginning of this booklet.

We also want you to feel confident other taxpayers are paying what they should and that we operate the tax system fairly.

We enquire into some tax returns to

- check that they are correct, or
- if we need further information to understand the figures on the tax return.

We want to make sure companies do not pay too much or too little tax. Either way, we will tell you if we find something wrong. We do not set targets for the amount of additional tax our staff should collect.

To discourage tax evasion and ensure the whole system is operating fairly, we will select some tax returns at random for enquiry. We can then check if anything is wrong which may not be apparent on the face of the return.

At any time after you have sent in the company's tax return, you should inform us immediately about anything in it which is wrong or which should have been in it

## Enquiries into company tax returns

but has been omitted. You may amend the company's tax return up to 12 months after the date on which it had to be submitted to the Inland Revenue (the filing date).

You can make amendments to the company's tax return when the return is under enquiry, but we will only take these amendments into account in the company's self assessment at the end of the enquiry.

You cannot make an amendment to the company's tax return after the 12 months following the date on which the tax return had to be submitted, except in particular circumstances, for example, withdrawing a claim for group relief following a Revenue enquiry. However, you should always tell us about any changes needed and we will then discuss with you how we can settle matters.

**What we do when we receive a company tax return**

We record the figures that you provide and the company's self assessment of the tax it should pay or, subject to certain checks, that we should repay to the company.

If we find any obvious mistakes, for example in the arithmetic, we may correct them without making enquiries. If we do so we will send you details of the corrected figures. If you disagree with what we have done, you can ask us to reverse or amend any changes we have made.

If the company tax return shows that too much tax has been paid, we will normally repay the excess.

We carry out a comprehensive programme of checks. We look at information in the company's return and compare it with information we hold.

Following these checks, if we think there is a risk the company return may be incorrect, or if we think something requires fuller explanation, we start enquiries.

We also enquire into some returns at random.

If we make enquiries into a return under Self Assessment it does not imply that we think it is incorrect, so when we ask questions or seek information we will not give reasons for making the enquiries. The initial request may, however, identify particular areas on which the enquiries will focus.

**How an enquiry is conducted**

**Starting enquiries**

- We will tell you in writing that we intend to start enquiries.
- We will tell you what your rights and responsibilities are.
- At the same time, we will try to tell you the information we require.

Exceptionally, we may not be able to do this, but we will always explain why and say when we expect to be able to do so.

## Enquiries into company tax returns

- We normally have 12 months from the date the company's tax return had to be submitted to us in which to tell you that we intend to start enquiries. We may have longer if you send in the company's tax return late. We will always have at least 12 months to enquire into any amendment that you make to the company's tax return.

- At the end of that period, if we have not begun enquiries, the company's tax return will normally become final. We can make an assessment after that period only if we discover an error of which we could not reasonably have been expected to be aware from the information provided in, or with, the company's tax return. In these circumstances, we can make an assessment at any time up to six years after the end of the accounting period. If we discover that the company's return was incorrect because of fraudulent or negligent conduct, we can make an assessment at any time up to twenty-one years after the end of the accounting period.

**Professional representation**

The company can choose to be professionally represented, for example, by an accountant or tax adviser. The company may exercise that right at any time and likewise may change or stop using a professional adviser at any time.

- We will deal with any professional adviser the company has appointed unless you ask us not to. If there is little progress in settling matters, we will tell you and may then deal with you direct (or with any other professional adviser the company may then appoint).

- You should make sure the company's professional adviser has all the facts. You will always be responsible for the company's tax affairs and for the accuracy of all the information supplied to us, even if the company has a professional adviser.

**Providing information**

- We will ask questions and explain what further information we need as clearly and simply as possible.

- We may limit our enquiries to one or more specific aspects of the company's tax return. These may range from requests for clarification of particular entries, to detailed consideration of whether those entries have been treated correctly for tax purposes. The enquiries may involve an examination of the records or documents on which particular entries were based.

- We may decide to conduct an extensive examination which considers all aspects of the company's tax affairs. Enquiries of this type will typically involve an in-depth review of the records on which the company's tax return was based. As part of this review we may ask for information relating to third parties, for example, directors or shareholders. We will always give you the opportunity to provide the information yourself but where you cannot do this we may ask for the information directly.

- If we need to open separate enquiries into directors' or shareholders' personal tax returns we will tell each of them in writing that we intend to start enquiries and send them a separate Code of Practice.

*Enquiries into company tax returns*

- We will only ask for information relevant to anything which is in, or should be in the tax return.

- If we ask to see the records on which the company's tax return is based, you should be able to provide these within a reasonable time, as the company, or the company's professional adviser, should already hold them. If we decide we need other information, we will explain our request fully.

- We will take up as little of your time as possible by trying to ask early on in our enquiries for everything we need to know. We will try to avoid asking for information in a piecemeal way but this is not always possible. It may help if you tell us about any special features of the business or financial affairs of the company or its directors or shareholders which you think may be relevant to any questions we have asked.

- We will give you a reasonable amount of time to provide any information we need. You should tell us if you think we have not given you enough time and say how much more you need, and why. We will let you have more time if this seems reasonable. If we cannot agree, we will tell you why.

- You should respond as promptly as you can when we ask for information. This will help to save you time and keep down costs for the company, and us.

- Tell us straightaway if you have difficulty obtaining the information we have asked for and we will discuss with you how you might obtain it. You should also tell us if you think it is not relevant to our enquiries. We will consider your reasons carefully and if we think we still need the information we will explain why.

- If you do not provide the information we have asked for and we have to use our statutory powers to obtain it we will

    - explain our statutory powers to you

    - advise you of any penalties that might arise if the company does not comply

    - tell you about the company's rights of appeal to independent Appeal Commissioners.

- We may suggest that we examine the company records at the business premises. This will save you sending them to us and can often be more convenient for everyone. You can also ask us to examine the records at the business premises or any other place that is convenient to you and if possible we will do so.

- We try to return company records as soon as possible. If you need them in the meantime, for example, to complete the company's tax return for a later year, you may ask us to return any records which we hold. You should tell us what you need and when you expect to be able to return them. We will either

    - send the records to you if we can. Take care of them so that you can return them to us complete and undamaged, or

    - if we need to keep the original records, we will give you copies. We will do this free of charge, and within seven days of receiving your request, if possible.

- You should not let our enquiries into the company's tax return for one year

## Enquiries into company tax returns

delay submission of a tax return for any other accounting period. You may be unable to provide final figures because you think these might be affected in some way by the enquiries which are under way. If so, include your best estimates in the tax return and indicate which figures may be affected by the outcome of the existing enquiries.

- The information you provide on behalf of the company should be correct to the best of your knowledge. If you provide information you know to be false, you may be liable to prosecution.

- You have the right to ask us why we are continuing our enquiries, if you believe that you have provided all the information and explanations necessary to check the company's tax return and that we have had adequate time to consider the information and explanations. We will reconsider the matter to see whether we can agree or explain what further information we need for checking the tax return.

- If you think we have no grounds for continuing our enquiry, you may ask the Appeal Commissioners to consider whether the enquiry should be closed. For example, you may believe that you have provided all the information reasonably required to determine the accuracy or completeness of the company's tax return, or that the enquiry is being prolonged unnecessarily by us.

**Meetings**

- We may ask to meet you or other officers or employees of the company to discuss those aspects of the company's business affairs of which only you or they have first-hand knowledge.

- You can ask the company's professional adviser, if it has one, to attend any meeting we have with you.

- You or other officers or employees of the company are not obliged to come to any meeting, but we will expect you to provide promptly any information we consider essential to our enquiries. Meetings allow you to clarify and explain any points you think we may not have understood, and allow you to ask questions. If we consider that correspondence will not be an adequate substitute for a meeting, we will make this clear to you.

- We may suggest that we hold a meeting at the company's business premises. If this is inconvenient we can arrange a meeting at our office, or we may be able to meet you at some other mutually convenient location.

- You should ensure the answers you give us at meetings are correct. If you are not sure about an answer you should say so. Similarly, if afterwards you realise something you said at a meeting may have been wrong, you should tell us straightaway.

- You should bring any documents which you think may help you answer questions or support points you might wish to raise about the company's tax return, or its business for the period under enquiry.

- We will make a written record of any meeting we have with you and you can ask for a copy. We may ask you to sign a copy of our notes to show that they record the substance of what was said. You have the right to comment

## Enquiries into company tax returns

on these notes and to tell us about anything with which you do not agree. You do not have to sign them or comment on them, but a signed record could be useful if we cannot reach agreement and have to ask the Appeal Commissioners to resolve matters.

**If we find nothing wrong**

- If we find nothing wrong, we will tell you and let you know that our enquiries have finished.

**If we find something wrong**

Paying tax during our enquiries

- We will ask the company to make a payment on account towards any additional tax we think may be due, but until the company's self assessment is amended, the company does not have to pay anything additional if you do not think it should. However, making a payment on account will help reduce any interest charges if, at the end of our enquiries, we find the company does owe additional tax. If it turns out that the company has paid too much, we will repay, with interest, any tax it has overpaid.

- We may make a provisional amendment to the company's self assessment before the end of our enquiries if we think that additional tax is due and that it might not be paid if we did not act promptly. We may also make assessments for earlier years. The company has a right to appeal against any such assessments or amendments and may ask to postpone payment of any of the tax. If we cannot reach agreement, you may ask the Appeal Commissioners to decide how much tax the company should pay at this stage of our enquiries.

**Revised figures**

- We will try to agree with you any changes needed to the company's figures.

- We will only suggest changes we consider to be reasonable in the light of all the information we have.

- When our enquiries are completed, we will tell you in writing and set out any adjustments we think are necessary. We will try to point out any amendments needed to other tax returns (either for later or earlier periods), but we cannot guarantee to do this. You will be responsible for making sure amendments are made to other company tax returns to take into account the outcome of our enquiries.

- We will always explain how we arrived at the figures we put forward. If you do not understand them you should let us know.

- We will invite you, if you agree with our figures, to amend the company's tax return. You will have 30 days to do so. You will also have 30 days to amend any other company tax returns affected by the outcome of our enquiries. If you do not do this within 30 days, we will amend the

## *Enquiries into company tax returns*

company's tax return for the period under enquiry and any other year to give effect to any adjustments we think are necessary.

- We may make assessments for earlier years if necessary.

**Appeal hearings**

- You have 30 days to appeal to independent Appeal Commissioners against

- any amendment we make to the company's tax return, or

- any assessment to corporation tax we make that you do not think is correct.

- You can find out how to make an appeal by reading the notes with the amendment or assessment, by referring to our leaflet IR37 'Appeals against tax, National Insurance contributions, Statutory Sick Pay and Statutory Maternity Pay' or by asking us to explain the process to you.

- We will try, wherever possible, to reach agreement with you about the company's tax without a formal hearing of any appeal. If agreement cannot be reached, both the company and the Inland Revenue have the right to ask for any appeals to be heard by the Commissioners.

- If you wish to appeal to the Commissioners we can arrange for this to be done or, if you prefer, you can contact the Clerk to the Commissioners yourself. We will give you the Clerk's address if you ask for it.

- If the appeal hearing has been arranged at the company's request and we think we will need more time to conclude our enquiries, we will ask the Commissioners to adjourn the hearing to a later date. It will be up to them to decide whether to do so. Likewise, if the appeal hearing has been arranged at our request and you need more time to provide information, you may ask the Commissioners to adjourn the hearing to a later date. Again, it will be up to them to decide whether to do so.

- We will tell you if we intend to ask the Commissioners to settle the company's appeal. We may do this if little or no progress is being made towards settling it by agreement. We will explain the figures we propose to put forward at least 14 days before the date fixed for the hearing, unless there are exceptional circumstances. The figures we put forward may differ from those we suggested to you during our negotiations.

- You have the right to put the company's case to the Commissioners and to tell them the figures you believe to be correct. You can choose whether or not to have the company's case presented for you by a professional representative or by any other person, providing the Commissioners do not object.

- After listening to both parties and considering all the evidence, the Commissioners will decide whether the amendment or assessment should remain unchanged, be increased or be reduced.

- If there is anything about the appeal hearing procedure which you do not understand you can ask us or, if you prefer, the Clerk to the Commissioners.

*Enquiries into company tax returns*

**Interest and penalties**

- Interest will be payable whenever the tax due is paid late. A penalty may also arise.

- We can seek penalties for an incorrect tax return if it was delivered fraudulently or negligently, or if the company discovers that the tax return delivered is incorrect and does not remedy the error without unreasonable delay.

- When calculating any penalty, we will take into account
    - the extent to which you disclosed voluntarily anything that was wrong
    - your help in concluding our enquiries
    - the seriousness of the errors or omissions.

- The way we calculate penalties is set out in our leaflet IR160 'Enquiries under Self Assessment. How settlements are negotiated'.

- You should tell us about any matters you think are relevant when we are working out the penalty to be charged.

- We will seek an agreed settlement on the amounts of tax, interest, and penalties due from the company. If we cannot reach agreement, we may determine formally the penalty we consider appropriate.

- The company has the right to appeal against any penalty determination, and can ask for the appeal to be heard by the Appeal Commissioners.

- If you do not understand how we have calculated interest or penalties, or why they are due, you should ask us, or the company's professional adviser, or read our leaflet IR160 'Enquiries under Self Assessment. How settlements are negotiated'.

**At the end of our enquiries**

When our enquiries have shown something is wrong we will

- explain what it is
- tell you how to get things right for the future
- make suggestions about improvements to the company's business records if they do not meet legal requirements or we consider they are inadequate. If the company is professionally represented, we may recommend that you seek advice from its professional adviser.
- If you are still unsure about the records the company needs to keep in future, or the amount of detail required, ask the company's professional adviser or us to help you. You may also ask for our leaflet SA/BK3 'Self Assessment. A guide to keeping records for the self employed'. The advice given in it is also relevant to company records.
- If our enquiries show that the company's tax return was incorrect we may ask you to sign a Certificate of Disclosure, confirming that the company has now declared all its taxable income and gains. We will not do so if our enquiries have shown the company's tax return was correct or overstated

## *Enquiries into company tax returns*

its taxable income or gains. We will take a very serious view if you sign a Certificate of Disclosure you know to be false, so you should consider it carefully before signing.

If the company's tax return was incorrect because it overstated its taxable income or gains, we will repay any tax it has overpaid plus appropriate interest.

**Your rights under 'Our service commitment to you'**

*During our enquiries*

- We will always be courteous, fair and professional.
- If you or the company's professional adviser writes to us we will aim to respond to every question or issue you have raised within our published service standards. For Tax Offices this is 28 calendar days. Different response times apply to some specialist offices, for example, the Large Business Office aim to respond within two calendar months. If we cannot reply within this time, for instance because of the amount or complexity of the material you have sent us, we will let you know the reason for the delay and say when you can expect a full reply.

**Keeping you informed**

- Although we will not give reasons for making enquiries, we will explain the company's legal rights and the reasons for any actions we take as our enquiries proceed. We will tell you, for example, why we
    - think we need a meeting with you
    - are not satisfied with any explanation you may have given
    - are amending the company's return
    - need to use our statutory powers to obtain information or documents
    - are reviewing the company's returns for earlier years
    - are making assessments for earlier years.
- You can ask us at any time to explain the company's rights, or tell you why we have taken a particular action, or explain what you are obliged to do under the law. You may ask for these explanations even if we have already given them to the company's professional adviser.
- You can also ask for any of our information leaflets, some of which are listed on the inside front cover.

**Confidentiality**

- The company, its directors and its shareholders have the right to the same high degree of confidentiality which all taxpayers receive.
- If we open an enquiry into a director's or shareholder's tax return we will do so in accordance with our published Codes of Practice.

## Enquiries into company tax returns

- We may ask to discuss the company's and the director's tax affairs at the same time. In appropriate circumstances we may wish to discuss a shareholder's tax affairs as well. This may help speed up our enquiries, and help to reduce costs all round. We will, however, ask for everyone's agreement beforehand. If there are matters you do not wish to discuss with others present, please tell us beforehand.

- Only in the limited circumstances allowed by law (such as at Appeal Commissioners' hearings) will we give information to people you or the directors have not authorised.

**The company's costs**

- We know that dealing with our questions may cost the company time and money, so we will only ask for information we reasonably require to check that the company's tax return is correct.

- We will end our enquiries as soon as possible. That is, when we are confident the company's return is correct, or that all errors or omissions involving more than a trivial amount of tax have been identified and put right.

- We may need to keep enquiries into the company's tax return open where other enquiries (for example, into the directors' or shareholders' personal tax returns or tax returns of other companies) suggest that the company's tax return may not be correct. Where we need to do this we will tell you why we are not able to close the enquiry into the company's tax return.

- Our leaflet Code of Practice 1 'Mistakes by the Inland Revenue' explains the circumstances in which we will give financial redress for mistakes we make.

**Complaints**

If you believe

- we have not followed our Code of Practice
- we have denied the company its rights in some respect
- we have made a mistake
- we have treated you or the company badly in some other way during our enquiries you can ask for the company's case to be reviewed by the person in charge of the office in which the enquiry was carried out. We will give you the name of the Officer in Charge if you ask for it.

If you are still not satisfied, you can ask the Director who has overall responsibility for that office to examine your complaint. Our leaflet IR120 'You and the Inland Revenue' tells you how to do that. It is available from any Inland Revenue Enquiry Centre or Tax Office.

If the Director does not settle your complaint to your satisfaction you can ask the Adjudicator to look into it and recommend appropriate action. The Adjudicator, whose services are free, is an impartial referee whose recommendations are independent. The address is:

*Enquiries into company tax returns*

The Adjudicator's Office
Haymarket House
28 Haymarket
London SW1Y 4SP

Tel: 020 7930 2292
Fax: 020 7930 2298

The Adjudicator's leaflet, AO1, is available from the Adjudicator's Office and Inland Revenue offices, and gives further information about complaining to the Adjudicator.

Also, if you are not satisfied with the outcome of your complaint or the way in which it has been handled (by ourselves or the Adjudicator), you can ask a Member of Parliament to refer your complaint to the Parliamentary Ombudsman. (The Ombudsman will accept referral from any MP but you should approach your own Member of Parliament first.)

For further information about the Parliamentary Ombudsman contact:

Office of the Parliamentary Commissioner for Administration
Millbank Tower
Millbank
London SW1P 4QP

Tel: 020 7217 4163
Fax: 020 7217 4160

or visit the Parliamentary Ombudsman website at www.ombudsman.org.uk which contains further information and guidance. Enquiries can be made also by E-mail aopca-enqu@ombudsman.org.uk

**Suggestions**

We set high standards for the way we carry out our enquiries and are constantly looking for ways to improve those standards.

If you would like to suggest any changes to the way we do things or if you have any comments about this Code of Practice, please write to us at the following address:

Inland Revenue Compliance Division
Room 436
22 Kingsway
London WC2B 6NR.

**Our service commitment to you**

The Inland Revenue and Customs & Excise are committed to serving your needs well by acting fairly and impartially.

We

- treat your affairs in strict confidence, within the law

*Enquiries into company tax returns*

- want you to pay or receive only the right amount due.

**Communicating effectively with you**

We aim to provide

- clear and simple forms and guidance
- accurate and complete information in a helpful and appropriate way.

**Providing good quality service**

We aim to

- handle your affairs promptly and accurately
- be accessible in ways that are convenient to you
- keep your costs to the minimum necessary
- take reasonable steps to meet special needs
- be courteous and professional.

**Taking responsibility for our service**

- We publish annually our customer service aims and achievements.
- If you wish to comment, or make a complaint, we want to hear from you so we can improve our service. We advise you how to do this.

**We can provide better service if you help us by**

- keeping accurate and up to date records
- letting us know if your personal/business circumstances change
- giving us correct and complete information when we ask for it
- paying on time what you should pay.

Further information on customer service is available at Inland Revenue and Customs and Excise local offices, set out in our Charters, complaints leaflets (IR120 and Notice 1000) and Codes of Practice.

These notes are for guidance only and reflect the tax position at the time of writing.

They do not affect any right appeal.

Date issued: 23/07/99

*Appendix 8*

# Company Tax Returns and Guidance Notes

1

**Company Tax Return**
*Form CT600 (2000) Version 1*
*For accounting periods ending on or after 1 July 1999*

This form (or an Inland Revenue approved substitute version of it), together with any relevant *Supplementary Pages*, must be used whenever a company is required by form *CT603 (the Notice )* to deliver a company tax return for any period ended on or after 1 July 1999. This form sets out the information we need and provides a standard format for calculations. Please complete the 'Company information' immediately and then read the notes on page 2 before completing any other sections.

### Company information

Company name

Company registration number *(if registered)*

Reference - *as shown on the Notice*
/ /

Address - *If different from that shown on the Notice*

Postcode

Period covered by this return *(cannot exceed 12 months)*
From dd/mm/yyyy
/ /
To
/ /

Now read the notes on page 2 and Section 1 on page 3 before you complete the rest of the form and any of Supplementary Pages you might need. Fill in the 'Summary' and 'Declaration' below only when you have completed the relevant sections, and before you send back the return to the issuing Inland Revenue office.

### Summary of return information

Put an 'X' in box if 'Yes'                                         Put an 'X' in box if 'Yes'

**Are you making a repayment claim**
• for this period?    • for an earlier period?

Are you filing more than one return for this company now?

Does this return contain estimated or provisional figures? *See note 3*

Are you seeking approved investment trust company status under S842(1) ICTA 1998? Attach a schedule showing how the company has met all the conditions. See note 26

**I attach**
• accounts for the period to which this return relates

• if no accounts, say why not

• accounts for a different period

I am sending you the following completed *Supplementary Pages* as part of the return form   Put an 'X' in appropriate box(es)

Loans to participators by close companies (CT600A)

Charity (CT600E)

Controlled foreign companies (CT600B)

Tonnage tax (CT600F)

Group and consortium (CT600C)

Corporate Venturing Scheme (CT600G)

Insurance (CT600D)

### Declaration
**Warning**
*Giving false information in the return, or concealing any part of the company's profits or tax payable, can lead to the company and you being prosecuted.*

**Declaration**
The information I have given on this form and the accompanying Supplementary Pages is correct and complete to the best of my knowledge and belief.

Signature

Date (dd/mm/yyyy)
/ /

Status

Name *(in capital letters)*

Except where a liquidator has been appointed, any person who is authorised to do so may sign on behalf of the company. A photocopy of a signature is not acceptable.

BMSD 8/00
CT600 (2000)

# Company Tax Returns and Guidance Notes

## Important points

- As soon as you receive the *Notice to deliver a company tax return* (the *Notice*) make sure you obtain all the *Supplementary Pages* you need. The information on page 3 in Section 1 should help you decide which you will need and how to get them. Please contact the Inland Revenue office shown on the *Notice* if you need more help.

- Members' clubs, societies and voluntary associations may only need to complete the *Company information*, *Summary* and *Declaration* sections on page 1, and the short calculation on pages 4 and 5. Note 1 in the *Company Tax Return Guide (the Guide)* gives advice about what to complete but our leaflet *'Clubs, societies and voluntary associations' (IR46)* gives more detailed information and includes an example of a completed form *CT600*. The leaflet is available from any Inland Revenue Enquiry Centre (see 'Inland Revenue' in your local Phone Book) or from the CTSA Orderline on 0845 300 6555.

- 'Company' includes every kind of body, club, society, association or organisation that is chargeable to corporation tax, whether or not it is incorporated.

- Please follow the instructions by each box but **do not** make an entry where the company did not have the item specified. Complete the boxes with whole figures only, except where pence or decimals are indicated.

- References to *notes* throughout the form are to those in the *Guide* which will help you complete this return form.

## Which sections you need to complete

After this page, read Section 1 on page 3, then obtain and complete any relevant *Supplementary Pages*.

All trading companies must complete Section 2. All companies must then complete either the Short calculation (Section 3) or the Detailed calculation (Section 4). Advice at the beginning of each calculation will help you decide which one is appropriate.

Complete Section 5 if you are claiming capital allowances or Research and Development enhanced expenditure.

Complete Section 6 if, in this period, the company has any of the losses or excess amounts listed there. Group companies must also show the maximum amounts available for surrender by way of group or consortium relief.

Complete Section 7 if there is a repayment claim attached to this return.

Completion of Section 8 is optional but we would like you to complete it if the company charges directors' remuneration in its accounts.

## What to do when you have completed the return

When you have completed the appropriate sections make sure you give us all the information requested in the Summary on page 1. Once you have done this, sign and date the *Declaration* and send the **whole** form to us. Attach any supporting calculations, claims or surrender documentation. Send them along with the relevant completed *Supplementary Pages*, company accounts and, where prepared, directors' and auditors' reports. Note 3 tells you the date by which you must do this (the filing date).

It is a good idea to keep a copy of the completed return for your own records.

You must pay any tax outstanding that you calculate is due. A payslip was attached to the *Notice*. Note 20 tells you about payment dates.

Do not send back the *Guide* but please keep it for reference purposes.

## When we receive the return

When we receive your completed return we will process it, based on your figures, and record the amount you have shown in the return as the tax due for this period. At this stage we will acknowledge receipt of the return.

The *note* on page 12 of the *Guide* tells you the time limits within which you can amend the return, and within which we can correct or enquire into it.

## Remember

- Interest is charged on tax paid late.
- The company may be liable to penalties if its return is late or incorrect.

# Company Tax Returns and Guidance Notes

## Section 1: Which *Supplementary Pages* must be completed?

This page will help you decide if you need any *Supplementary Pages*. Most company agents have supplies but if you do not have an agent, or your agent does not hold stocks, please call the CTSA Orderline on 0845 300 6555, or fax on 0845 300 6777. Make a note of the name and form number of the *Supplementary Page(s)* you want before calling. The CTSA Orderline is open 7 days a week between 8am and 10pm. If you need further help please contact the Inland Revenue office shown on the *Notice*.

**Members' clubs, societies and voluntary associations are unlikely to need any *Supplementary Pages*.**

### Close companies *(see note 2)*
If the company is close and made a loan, or loans, to an individual participator, or associate of a participator, in the return period which has not been repaid within the return period, **you must complete** the *Loans to participators by close companies Supplementary Pages (form CT600A)* and the Detailed calculation on pages 6 to 8.

### Controlled foreign companies (CFCs) *(See 'Other publications of interest' on page 12 of the Guide)*
If, in this period, the company had an interest of 25% or more in a foreign company which was controlled from the UK, **you must complete** the *Controlled foreign companies Supplementary Pages (form CT600B)* and, if there is a charge under S747 ICTA 1988, the Detailed calculation on pages 6 to 8.

### Group and/or consortium companies
If the company is claiming or surrendering any amounts under the group or consortium relief provisions for this period **you must complete**

- the *Group and consortium Supplementary Pages (form CT600C)*
- the Detailed calculation on pages 6 to 8, if you are claiming group or consortium relief, and
- Section 6 on page 9 if you are surrendering relief.

### Insurance companies and friendly societies
If, in this period, the company or society
- made claims under Schedule 19AB ICTA 1988 to provisional payments (including notional repayments in respect of tax on gilt interest) or
- has entered into business in the accounting period which it treats as overseas life assurance business (OLAB)

**you must complete** the *Insurance Supplementary Pages (form CT600D)* and the Detailed calculation on pages 6 to 8.

### Charities
If, in this period, the charity is claiming exemption or partial exemption from tax **you must complete** the *Charity Supplementary Pages (form CT600E)* and any relevant section of the *CT600* for taxable income.

### Tonnage tax
If, for a period beginning on or after 1 January 2000, the company or group has elected for the alternative tonnage tax regime for calculating the profits of a shipping company, **you must complete** the *Tonnage Tax Supplementary Pages (form CT600F)* and the Detailed calculation on pages 6 to 8.

### Corporate venturing scheme (CVS)
If, for shares issued on or after 1 April 2000 but before 1 April 2010, the company is claiming under CVS:
- investment relief on the amount subscribed for shares, or
- relief against income for losses on disposals of shares, whether the claim is to be given effect to in this or an earlier period, or
- postponement of certain chargeable gains where the gains are reinvested.

**you must complete** the *Corporate Venturing Scheme Supplementary Pages (form CT600G)* and the Detailed calculation on pages 6 to 8.

## Section 2: Turnover of the company *(see note 4)*

You must complete this Section if the company has trading or professional income.

Members' clubs, societies and voluntary associations that do not trade outside their membership need not complete this Section.

Investment companies and Unit Trusts need not complete this Section.

### Turnover

1. **Total turnover from trade or profession**
   Enter the total for this return period.  **1** £

2. **Banks, building societies, insurance companies and other financial concerns**
   Put an 'X' in this box.  **2**

*This is the end of Section 2. Please now complete either Section 3 on pages 4 and 5, or Section 4 on pages 6 to 8.*

# Company Tax Returns and Guidance Notes

4  CT600 (2000) Version 1

## Section 3: Short calculation

You may complete this section if it covers all the entries you need to make and each entry is less than £10 million.

In all other cases, or if you prefer, complete Section 4 instead. You should enclose explanations and calculations of any figures you have estimated or which are not immediately recognisable from the company's accounts and complete the box in the Summary on page 1. If you include a valuation you should state from where you obtained it. The figures to be entered are those adjusted for tax purposes, after deducting capital allowances and adding balancing charges, where appropriate.

If the company is close and has made loans to an individual participator, or associate of a participator, in this period that were not repaid within the period, you need to complete Section 4 instead.

Please note that certain numbered boxes are missing from the Short calculation.

### Income

**3** Trading and professional profits
*See note 5. Complete Section 6 if there is a loss*
**3** £

**4** Trading losses brought forward claimed against profits
*Only include losses made in the same trade. Include charges treated as losses.* **Do not enter an amount larger than is needed to cover the profits in box 3.** *See notes 5 and 6*
**4** £

**5** Net trading and professional profits
*If box 4 equals box 3, enter '0'. Leave this box blank if there are no trading profits in box 3*
box 3 minus box 4
**5** £

**7** Profits and gains from non-trading loan relationships
*Include bank, building society or other interest, and any other profits and gains even if tax has been deducted. You will need to complete the 'Detailed calculation' at Section 4, and Section 6, if you have deficits on non-trading loan relationships from this, earlier or later accounting periods to include. See note 8*
**7** £

**8** Annuities, annual payments and discounts not arising from loan relationships and from which income tax has not been deducted
*Exclude any amount included in box 7*
**8** £

**10** Income from which income tax has been deducted
*Enter the gross amount before tax and exclude any amount included in box 7. See note 9*
**10** £

**12** Income from UK land and buildings
*Enter the amount net of allowable expenses. Complete Section 6 if there is a loss. See note 10*
**12** £

**146** Annual profits and gains not falling under any other heading
*Enter amount net of losses. Complete Section 6 if there is a loss. See note 7*
**146** £

### Chargeable gains

**14** Gross gains
*See note 11. Complete Section 6 if there is a loss*
**14** £

**15** Allowable losses including losses brought forward
*Do not enter an amount larger than the amount of gross gains shown in box 14. See note 11*
**15** £

**16** Net chargeable gains
*If box 15 equals box 14, enter '0'*
box 14 minus box 15
**16** £

**19** Profits before other deductions and reliefs
total of boxes 5, 7, 8, 10, 12, 146 and 16
**19** £

### Deductions and reliefs

**26 &** Trading losses of this or a later accounting period under S393A ICTA 1988
**27** Put an 'X' in box 26 if amounts carried back from later accounting periods are included in box 27. See note 12
**26** □  **27** £

**30** Profits before charges
box 19 minus box 27
**30** £

**31** Charges paid
*This figure must not exceed profits shown in box 30. See note 13*
**31** £

### Corporation tax profits

**33** Profits chargeable to corporation tax
box 30 minus box 31
**33** £

*Carry forward the figure in box 33 to the box at the top of page 5*

# Company Tax Returns and Guidance Notes

CT600 (2000) Version 1  5

## Section 3: Short calculation continued

**33 Profits chargeable to corporation tax**  Enter the figure from box 33 on page 4    **33** £

**Tax calculation**  If you claim tax is chargeable at the starting or small companies' rate, or if you are claiming marginal starting rate or small companies' relief, complete boxes 34 - 38. If there are no associated companies, franked investment income or foreign income dividends, please enter the financial year(s) in boxes 35 and 37, and '0' in boxes 34, 36 and, if necessary, 38. *See note 15*

34  Franked investment income arising in the period covered by the return. *See note 15*    **34** £

35 - 38  Number of companies associated with this company in the/each financial year(s) covered by this return
*Exclude this company. See note 15*

| Financial year (yyyy) | Number of associated companies |
|---|---|
| **35** | **36** |
| **37** | **38** |

### 39 - 59 Corporation tax chargeable  *See note 16*

| Financial years beginning 1 April (yyyy) | Amounts of profit | Rates of tax *See page 12 of the Guide* | Tax |
|---|---|---|---|
| **39** | **40** £ | **41**  . % | **42** £  p |
| **49** | **50** £ | **51**  . % | **52** £  p |

box 42 plus box 52

59  Corporation tax chargeable    **59** £  p

### Reliefs and deductions in terms of tax

60  Marginal starting rate or small companies' relief
*Attach your computation. See notes 15 and 16*    **60** £  p

62  Advance corporation tax (restricted if necessary)
*See note 17*    **62** £  p

total of boxes 60 and 62

63  Total reliefs and deductions in terms of tax
*Cannot exceed corporation tax chargeable amount in box 59*    **63** £  p

box 59 minus box 63

68  Tax chargeable    **68** £  p

69  Income tax deducted from gross income included in profits
*Do not include deductions used to cover income tax for which the company was liable to account to the Inland Revenue on payments it has made. See note 18*    **69** £  p

70  Income tax repayable to the company
*Complete if box 69 is greater than box 68. Also complete Section 7*    **70** £  p

**72  Tax payable** - **this is your self-assessment of tax payable**
*Follow the instructions over the box. Enter 0.00 if you calculate that no tax is payable. See note 20*

box 68 minus box 69

**72** £

### Tax reconciliation

73  Deductions under the Construction Industry Scheme
*Enclose forms CIS25. See note 19*    **73** £  p

box 73 minus box 72

74  Construction industry deductions repayable
*Complete if box 73 is greater than box 72. Also complete Section 7.*    **74** £  p

75  Tax already paid (and not already repaid)
*Exclude amounts entered in boxes 69 and 73. See note 21*    **75** £  p

box 72 minus boxes 73 and 75

76  Tax outstanding
*This amount is payable to the Accounts Office. See note 23*    **76** £  p

box 75 plus box 73 minus box 72

77  Tax overpaid
*Complete Section 7*    **77** £  p

### Indicators

79  Put an 'X' in this box if the company should have made (whether it has or not) quarterly instalment payments under the Corporation Tax (Instalment Payments) Regulations 1998  *See note 20*    **79**

80  Put an 'X' in this box if the company is within a group payment arrangement for this period    **80**

*This is the end of the Short calculation.*

CT600 (2000) Version 1

## Section 4: Detailed calculation

Complete this section if you have not completed Section 3. You should enclose explanations and calculations of any figures you have estimated or which are not immediately recognisable from the company's accounts and complete the box in the Summary on page 1. If you have included a valuation you should state from where you obtained it. The figures to be entered are those adjusted for tax purposes, after deducting capital allowances and adding balancing charges where appropriate.

### Income

**3** Trading and professional profits
See note 5. Complete Section 6 if there is a loss

**3** £ _____

**4** Trading losses brought forward claimed against profits
Only include losses made in the same trade. Include charges treated as losses. Do not enter an amount larger than is needed to cover the profits in box 3. See notes 5 and 6

**4** £ _____

**5** Net trading and professional profits
If box 4 equals box 3, enter '0'. Leave this box blank if there are no trading profits in box 3

box 3 minus box 4
**5** £ _____

**6 & 7** Profits and gains from non-trading loan relationships, exchange fluctuations and certain financial instruments
Include bank, building society or other interest, and any other profits and gains even if tax has been deducted. Also include intra-group income under S247(4) ICTA 1988 which represents interest on loan relationships. Put an 'X' in box 6 if income is stated net after carrying back deficits on non-trading loan relationships. Complete Section 6 if there are net deficits. See note 8

**6** ☐   **7** £ _____

**8** Annuities, annual payments and discounts not arising from loan relationships and from which income tax has not been deducted
Exclude any amount included in box 7

**8** £ _____

**9** Overseas income within Sch D Case V
Complete Section 6 if there is a loss

**9** £ _____

**10** Income from which income tax has been deducted
Enter the gross amount before tax and exclude any amount included in box 7. See note 9

**10** £ _____

**11** Intra-group income under S247(4) ICTA 1988 election where tax has not been deducted
Exclude any amount included in box 7.

**11** £ _____

**12** Income from UK land and buildings
Enter the amount net of allowable expenses. Complete Section 6 if there is a loss. See note 10.

**12** £ _____

**13** Income within Sch D Case VI

**145** Tonnage tax profits
Complete and attach the 'Tonnage tax Supplementary Pages'.
Copy the figure from box F10 to box 145.

**145** £ _____

**146** Annual profits and gains not falling under any other heading
Enter amount net of losses. Complete Section 6 if there is a loss.
See note 7.

**146** £ _____

box 145 plus box 146
**13** £ _____

### Chargeable gains

**14** Gross gains
See note 11. Complete Section 6 if there is a loss.

**14** £ _____

**15** Allowable losses including losses brought forward
Do not enter an amount larger than the amount of gross gains shown in box 14. See note 11

**15** £ _____

**16** Net chargeable gains
If box 15 equals box 14, enter '0'.

box 14 minus box 15
**16** £ _____

### Deductions specifically from non-trade profits

**17** Losses brought forward against certain investment income

**17** £ _____

**18** Non-trade deficits on loan relationships (including interest), exchange fluctuations and certain financial instruments brought forward
See note 8. Amount cannot exceed total of boxes 7, 8, 9, 10, 11, 12, 13 and 16.

**18** £ _____

net sum of the boxes 5 - 16 column minus boxes 17 and 18

**19** Profits before other deductions and reliefs

**19** £ _____

Carry forward the figure in box 19 to the box at the top of page 7

# Company Tax Returns and Guidance Notes

## Section 4: Detailed calculation continued

**19 Profits chargeable to corporation tax** *Enter the figure from box 19 on page 6*

**Deductions and reliefs**

20 Corporate Venturing Scheme loss relief and
& losses on unquoted shares under S573 ICTA 1988
147 *Put an 'X' in box 147 if the entry in box 20 includes CVS loss relief. Complete and attach 'CVS Supplementary Pages'.*

21 Management expenses under S75 ICTA 1988 *See note 32*

22 Interest distributions under S468L ICTA 1988 *See note 29*

23 Schedule A losses for this or previous accounting period under S392A ICTA 1988 *See note 10*

24 Capital allowances for the purposes of management of the business *S28 CAA 1990. Investment companies only. Complete Section 5*

25 Non-trade deficits for this accounting period from loan relationships, exchange fluctuations or certain financial instruments *See note 8*

26 Trading losses of this or a later accounting period
& under S393A ICTA 1988
27 *Put an 'X' in box 26 if amounts carried back from later accounting periods are included in box 27. See note 12*

28 Non-trade capital allowances
*S145(3) CAA 1990. Complete Section 5*

29 **Total of deductions and reliefs**
*This figure must not exceed profits shown in box 19*
(total of boxes 20 - 25, 27 and 28)

30 **Profits before charges and group relief**
(box 19 minus box 29)

31 Charges paid
*This figure must not exceed profits shown in box 30. See note 13*

32 Group relief
*This figure must not exceed box 30 minus box 31. Complete and attach the 'Group and consortium Supplementary Pages'. See note 14*

33 **Profits chargeable to corporation tax**
(box 30 minus boxes 31 and 32)

**Tax calculation** *If you claim tax is chargeable at the starting or small companies' rate, or if you are claiming marginal starting rate or small companies' relief, complete boxes 34 - 38. If there are no associated companies, franked investment income or foreign income dividends, please enter the financial year(s) in boxes 35 and 37, and '0' in boxes 34, 36 and, if necessary, 38. See note 15*

34 Franked investment income arising in the period covered by the return. *See note 15*

35 - 38 Number of companies associated with this company in the/each financial year(s) covered by this return
*Exclude this company. See note 15*

| Financial year (yyyy) | Number of associated companies |
|---|---|
| 35 | 36 |
| 37 | 38 |

## 39 - 59 Corporation tax chargeable *See note 16*

| Financial years beginning 1 April (yyyy) | Amounts of profit | Rates of tax *See page 12 of the Guide* | Tax |
|---|---|---|---|
| 39 | 40 £ | 41 • % | 42 £ p |
| | 43 £ | 44 • % | 45 £ p |
| | 46 £ | 47 • % | 48 £ p |
| 49 | 50 £ | 51 • % | 52 £ p |
| | 53 £ | 54 • % | 55 £ p |
| | 56 £ | 57 • % | 58 £ p |

(total of boxes 42, 45, 48, 52, 55 and 58)
59 £ p

*Carry forward the figure in box 59 to the box at the top of page 8*

**8** CT600 (2000) Version 1

### Section 4: Detailed calculation continued

**59** Corporation tax chargeable *Enter the figure from from box 59 on page 7* — **59** £ ___ p

### 60 - 63 Reliefs and deductions in terms of tax

**60** Marginal starting rate or small companies' relief
*Attach your computation. See notes 15 and 16* — **60** £ ___ p

**148** Corporate Venturing Scheme investment relief
*Complete and attach 'CVS Supplementary Pages'.
Copy the figure from G1 to box 148.* — **148** £ ___ p

**61 & 61A** Double taxation relief
*Exclude any amount included in box 67.
Put an 'X' in box 61A if box 61 includes an Underlying Rate relief claim.* — **61A** ☐ **61** £ ___ p

**62** Advance corporation tax (restricted if necessary) *See note 17* — **62** £ ___ p

**63** Total reliefs and deductions in terms of tax
*Cannot exceed corporation tax chargeable amount in box 59* — total of boxes 60, 148, 61 and 62
**63** £ ___ p

### 64 - 78 Calculation of tax outstanding or overpaid

**64** Net corporation tax liability — box 59 minus box 63
**64** £ ___ p

**65 & 66** Tax payable under S419 ICTA 1988
*Complete and attach the 'Loans to participators by close companies Supplementary Pages'. Put an 'X' in box 65 if you completed box A11 in the Supplementary Pages. Copy the figure from box A13 to box 66* — **65** ☐ **66** £ ___ p

**67** Tax payable under S747 ICTA 1988
*Enter the total figure of tax from the 'Controlled foreign companies Supplementary Pages'* — **67** £ ___ p

**68** Tax chargeable — total of boxes 64, 66 and 67
**68** £ ___ p

**69** Income tax deducted from gross income included in profits
*Do not include deductions used to cover income tax for which the company was liable to account to the Inland Revenue on payments it has made. See note 18* — **69** £ ___ p

**70** Income tax repayable to the company
*Complete if box 69 is greater than box 68. Also complete Section 7* — **70** £ ___ p

**71** Advance corporation tax on foreign income dividends and set off to the extent that corporation tax is otherwise unpaid *See note 22* — **71** £ ___ p

**72** **Tax payable** - *this is your self-assessment of tax payable*
*Follow the instructions over the box. Enter 0.00 if you calculate that no tax is payable.
See note 20* — box 68 minus boxes 69 and 71
**72** £ ___ p

### Tax reconciliation

**149** Research and Development tax credit - *periods ending on or after 1 April 2000 only*
*Enter the full credit claimed. See note 31* — **149** £ ___ p

**73** Deductions under the Construction Industry Scheme
*Enclose forms CIS25. See note 19* — **73** £ ___ p

**150** Research and Development tax credit payable *Cannot exceed R&D tax credit in box 149.*
*Complete Section 7. See note 31* — box 149 minus box 72
**150** £ ___ p

**74** Construction industry deductions repayable *Cannot exceed CIS deductions.*
*Complete Section 7* — boxes 149 plus 73 minus box 72
**74** £ ___ p

**75** Tax already paid (and not already repaid)
*Exclude amounts entered in boxes 69, 71 and 73. See note 21* — **75** £ ___ p

**76** Tax outstanding
*This amount is payable to the Accounts Office. See note 23* — box 72 minus boxes 149, 73 and 75
**76** £ ___ p

**77** Tax overpaid *Complete Section 7* — box 75 plus boxes 149 and 73 minus box 72
**77** £ ___ p

**78** Tax refunds surrendered to the company under S102 FA 1989
*Enclose a copy of the joint Notice. See note 24* — **78** £ ___ p

### Indicators

**79** Put an 'X' in this box if the company should have made (whether it has or not) quarterly instalment payments under the Corporation Tax (Instalment Payments) Regulations 1998 *See note 20* — **79** ☐

**80** Put an 'X' in this box if the company is within a group payment arrangement for this period — **80** ☐

*This is the end of the Detailed calculation*

# Company Tax Returns and Guidance Notes

CT600 (2000) Version 1  9

## Section 5: Capital allowances and Research and Development expenditure

Complete this section if you are claiming capital allowances or R&D enhanced expenditure. You should also show balancing charges taken into account in Section 3 or 4 calculations. Show details of qualifying expenditure on which writing-down allowances may be claimed, even if you are not claiming any allowances for this period. *See note 25 and 31*

|  |  |  |
|---|---|---|
| 151 | Research and Development enhanced expenditure of 150%<br>*Enter the amount on which any claim is based* | 151 £ |
| 81 | Expenditure on machinery and plant on which first year allowance is claimed | 81 £ |
| 82 | Qualifying expenditure on machinery and plant on long-life assets | 82 £ |
| 83 | Qualifying expenditure on machinery and plant on other assets | 83 £ |

### Charges and allowances included in calculation of trading profits or losses

| Box | Description | Balancing charges | Capital allowances |
|---|---|---|---|
| 84 - 85 | Cars<br>*All cars including those leased out* | 84 £ | 85 £ |
| 86 - 87 | Machinery and plant - long-life assets | 86 £ | 87 £ |
| 88 - 89 | Machinery and plant - other assets | 88 £ | 89 £ |
| 90 - 91 | Industrial buildings and structures<br>*Including qualifying hotels, and commercial buildings and hotels in enterprise zones* | 90 £ | 91 £ |
| 92 - 93 | Other charges and allowances<br>*For example agricultural buildings, mineral extraction, research and development, patents* | 92 £ | 93 £ |

### Charges and allowances not included in calculation of trading profits or losses

| Box | | Balancing charges | Capital allowances |
|---|---|---|---|
| 94 - 95 | | 94 £ | 95 £ |

## Section 6: Losses, deficits and excess amounts

Complete this section if the company has incurred, in this period, any of the losses or deficits shown below, or if it has, for this period, any of the excess amounts shown below. Companies that are proposing to surrender any amount as group or consortium relief should also complete the second column. *See note 27.*

| Box | Description | Arising | Maximum available for surrender as group relief |
|---|---|---|---|
| 96 - 97 | Trading losses Case I<br>*See note 5* | *calculated under S393 ICTA 1988*<br>96 £ | *calculated under S393A ICTA 1988*<br>97 £ |
| 98 | Trading losses Case V | *calculated under S393 ICTA 1988*<br>98 £ | |
| 99 - 100 | Non-trade deficits on loan relationships<br>*See note 8* | *calculated under S82 FA 1996*<br>99 £ | *calculated under S83 FA 1996*<br>100 £ |
| 101 - 102 | Schedule A losses<br>*UK land and buildings. See note 10* | *calculated under S392A ICTA 1998*<br>101 £ | *calculated under S403 ICTA 1988*<br>102 £ |
| 103 | Overseas property business losses Case V | *calculated under S392A ICTA 1988*<br>103 £ | |
| 104 | Losses Case VI | *calculated under S396 ICTA 1988*<br>104 £ | |
| 105 | Capital losses | *calculated under S16 TCGA 1992*<br>105 £ | |
| | | Excess | |
| 106 | Excess non-trade capital allowances<br>*Excess over income in period* | | *calculated under S403 ICTA 1988*<br>106 £ |
| 107 | Excess charges<br>*See note 13* | | *calculated under S403 ICTA 1988*<br>107 £ |
| 108 - 109 | Excess management expenses<br>*See note 32* | *calculated under S75(3) ICTA 1988*<br>108 £ | *calculated under S403 ICTA 1988*<br>109 £ |
| 110 | Excess interest distributions | *calculated under S468L(7) ICTA 1988*<br>110 £ | |

**10** CT600 (2000) Version 1

## Section 7: Overpayments and repayment claims

Complete this section if you are claiming a repayment. If you have completed boxes 70, 74 150 or 77 in Section 3 or 4, attach your calculations. Do not forget to put an 'X' in the appropriate box of the *Summary of return information* section on page 1. *See note 28.*

Please note there is no box 113 in this section.

**111 Repayment of corporation tax**
Include CIS deductions repayable and enclose forms CIS25.
Enter amount from box 74, or CT overpaid from box 77.

**111** £ ⬜ p

**112 Repayment of income tax**
Enter amount from box 70

**112** £ ⬜ p

**114 Repayment of advance corporation tax**
See note 22

**114** £ ⬜ p

**152 Payable Research and Development tax credit**
Enter amount from box 150. See note 31

**152** £ ⬜ p

### Bank details (for person to whom the repayment is to be made)

Repayments of corporation tax (but not income tax, advance corporation tax or construction industry deductions) can be made quickly and safely by direct credit (BACS) to a bank or building society account.

You should provide details of the account which is to be credited. If the details are those of the nominee you want to receive the repayment, remember to complete the authority overleaf.

**Name of bank or building society**
**115**

**Branch sort code**
**116** ⬜ ⬜ ⬜

**Account number**
**117**

**Name of account**
**118**

**Building society reference**
**119**

**Signature**
**120**

Except where a liquidator has been appointed, any person who is authorised to do so may sign the BACS details on behalf of the company. A photocopy of a signature is not acceptable.

**Name** *(in capital letters)*
**120A**

559

# Company Tax Returns and Guidance Notes

CT600 (2000) Version 1  11

**Section 7: Overpayments and repayment claims continued**

### Repayment claim

121 The following amount is to be repaid
either
122 • to the company
or
123 • to the nominee in the authority given below

121 £     p

122 ☐
123 ☐
*(put an 'X' in either box 122 or 123 but not both)*

---

124 The following amount is to be surrendered under S102 Finance Act 1989, and
either
125 • the joint Notice is attached
or
126 • will follow
*Repayments of advance corporation tax cannot be surrendered*
127 Please stop repayment of the following amount until I send you the Notice

124 £     p

125 ☐
126 ☐
*(put an 'X' in appropriate box)*

127 £     p

---

### Payments to a person other than the company

Complete the authority below if you want the repayment to be made to a person **other than the company**. The Inland Revenue reserves the right not to make a repayment to a nominee and will not normally make a repayment to an overseas nominee.

**I, as** *(enter status - company secretary, treasurer, liquidator or authorised agent, etc.)*

128 _____

**of** *(enter name of company)*

129 _____

**authorise** *(enter name)*

130 _____

*(enter address)*

131 _____

Postcode

Nominee reference

132 _____

**to receive on the company's behalf the amount due.**

*Signature*

133 _____

*Except where a liquidator has been appointed, any person who is authorised to do so may sign the BACS details or an authority on behalf of the company. A photocopy of a signature is not acceptable.*

*Name (in capital letters)*

133A _____

*This is the end of Section 7.*

## Company Tax Returns and Guidance Notes

12 CT600 (2000) Version 1

### Section 8: Directors' remuneration - optional section

Please complete this section if directors' remuneration is charged in the accounts supporting this form CT600.
Attach a continuation sheet if you need more space.

**Company name**
134

**PAYE District**
135

**PAYE reference**
136

**Accounts for the period**
From (dd/mm/yyyy) to
137 / / 138 / /

**Remuneration claimed as a deduction in the accounts**
Show total figure for all directors
139 £

Date when accounts laid before the company in general meeting or, if resolved not to lay accounts, the date on which the accounts were approved by the directors
140 / /

### Analysis
**Net remuneration voted after adjustments**

Enter the net figure of remuneration after deducting employers' National Insurance contributions, employers' and employees' superannuation contributions and any benefits which have been included in the accounts' figure

| 141 Name of director | National Insurance number | Salary | Bonus, fees or commission |
|---|---|---|---|
| | | £ | £ |
| | | £ | £ |
| | | £ | £ |
| | | £ | £ |
| | | £ | £ |
| | | £ | £ |
| | | £ | £ |
| | | £ | £ |

Put an 'X' in here if a continuation sheet is used 142

143 Adjustments to reconcile the analysis above with total accounts' deductions claimed - please give details

| | £ |
|---|---|
| | £ |
| | £ |
| | £ |
| | £ |

Date of commencement or cessation of directorship during the period of account

| 144 Name of director | National Insurance number | Date commenced | Date ceased |
|---|---|---|---|
| | | | |
| | | | |
| | | | |
| | | | |

Note: This form is reproduced as in its final draft stage.

# Company Tax Returns and Guidance Notes

## Company Tax Return Guide (2000)
### to form CT600 Version 1
*For accounting periods ending on or after 1 July 1999*

### What is in this *Guide*

| Subject | Note | Page |
|---|---|---|
| Abbreviations | | 2 |
| Accounting period | 30 | 10 |
| Advance corporation tax (ACT) | 17 | 7 |
| ACT on a foreign income dividend | 22 | 8 |
| Capital allowances and balancing charges | 25 | 8 |
| Chargeable Gains | 11 | 5 |
| Charges paid | 13 | 6 |
| Claims to starting or small companies' rate of tax or to marginal rate relief | 15 | 6 |
| Close company loans to participators | 2 | 2 |
| Construction industry deductions | 19 | 8 |
| Corporation tax chargeable | 16 | 7 |
| Date by which you must deliver the return | 3 | 3 |
| Estimated or provisional figures | 3 | 3 |
| Filing date | 3 | 3 |
| Group relief | 14 | 6 |
| Group relief, maximum available to surrender | 27 | 9 |
| Income from UK land and buildings | 10 | 5 |
| Income from which income tax has been deducted | 9 | 5 |
| Income tax deducted | 18 | 8 |
| Income within Schedule D Case VI | 7 | 4 |
| Interest payable or receivable | 8 | 4 |
| Interest distributions under S468L | 29 | 9 |
| Investment trust companies | 26 | 9 |
| Members' clubs, societies and voluntary associations | 1 | 2 |
| Non-trading loan relationships, etc. | 8 | 4 |
| Partnerships | | 1 |
| Penalties for late returns | 3 | 3 |
| Rates of tax, etc. | | 12 |
| Repayment claims and overpayments | 28 | 9 |
| Research and Development expenditure | 31 | 10 |
| Tax already paid | 21 | 8 |
| Tax outstanding | 23 | 8 |
| Tax payable and when due | 20 | 8 |
| Tax refunds surrendered to the company | 24 | 8 |
| Trading profits and losses, general | 5 | 3 |
| Trading losses brought forward | 6 | 3 |
| Trading losses, relief for | 12 | 6 |
| Turnover | 4 | 3 |
| When we receive the return | | 12 |

### This *Guide*

This *Guide* is not a detailed description of the corporation tax self assessment (CTSA) system for companies.

It has been written to help you
- understand your corporation tax obligations
- complete the *Company Tax Return (form CT600)*.

In this *Guide* and on the return form, 'company' includes every kind of body, association or organisation that is chargeable to corporation tax, whether or not it is incorporated.

#### General

Under CTSA, companies have to make their returns in the format set out by the Inland Revenue. They will be able to do so by completing the official return form, a photocopy of it, or a substitute version approved by the Inland Revenue (for example, one designed for computer production).

Many basic notes relevant to completing the CT600, and any necessary *Supplementary Pages*, are shown on the forms. What follows is additional guidance either relevant to CTSA generally, or specific to box entries you may need to make. We also list further information available, and where you can find it.

This *Guide* does not give a detailed account of how to calculate the company's liability. You are advised to seek professional advice about any transactions that seem likely to give rise to the liability, or relief referred to, if you are not a tax expert.

If you make a mistake while completing the CT600 or any of the *Supplementary Pages*, make a note of the form name and its number and call the CTSA Orderline on **0845 300 6555**, or Fax **0845 300 6777** for a replacement copy. The CTSA Orderline is open 7 days a week between 8am and 10 pm.

#### Companies in partnership

If the company carries on a trade, profession or business in partnership, please include with the company tax return a note of the partnership tax reference number. You must also include the profits, losses or income allocated to the company by the partnership statement. The amounts should be included in the appropriate boxes of the form CT600. Where the company and the partnership accounting periods are not the same, the company's share of profits should be apportioned (normally on a time basis) to its own accounting periods.

If the company is a member of a foreign partnership, please include with the return a copy of the partnership accounts together with the computation showing its share of partnership taxable profits, losses or income. That share should be included in the appropriate boxes as detailed above.

## Abbreviations used

**Statutory references**

| | |
|---|---|
| CAA 1990 | Capital Allowances Act 1990 |
| FA + year | Finance Act + year |
| ICTA 1988 | Income and Corporation Taxes Act 1988 |
| S | Section of Act shown |
| Sch | Schedule of Act shown |
| SI | Statutory Instrument |
| TCGA 1992 | Taxation of Chargeable Gains Act 1992 |
| TMA 1970 | Taxes Management Act 1970 |

**Return form**

| | |
|---|---|
| CT600 | The company tax return form |

**Supplementary Pages**

| | |
|---|---|
| CT600A | Loans to participators by close companies |
| CT600B | Controlled foreign companies |
| CT600C | Group and consortium |
| CT600D | Insurance |
| CT600E | Charity |
| CT600F | Tonnage Tax |
| CT600G | Corporate Venturing Scheme |

**Other**

| | |
|---|---|
| yyyy | This means that we would like you to enter the relevant year as four digits, for example '2001' or '2002' |
| dd/mm/yyyy | This is how we would like a date entered, for example, 06/04/2000 |

## Note 1 - Members' clubs, societies and voluntary associations

Members' clubs, societies and voluntary associations are usually regarded as companies for corporation tax purposes and therefore liable to corporation tax.

Corporation tax is assessable on the profits of a company arising in its accounting periods (see note 30). A company's profits are the total of
- its income (calculated using income tax principles) and
- its chargeable gains (calculated using capital gains tax principles).

Unlike individuals, companies are not entitled to an annual exemption for chargeable gains. Any gains (after deducting losses) are chargeable to corporation tax.

You should find it helpful to read our leaflet *Clubs, societies and voluntary associations (IR46)* available from the CTSA Orderline, any Inland Revenue Enquiry Centre or office. See *'Other publications of interest'* on page 12.

## Note 2 - Loans to participators by close companies

The following definitions, together with the advice on page 3 of form *CT600*, will help you decide whether you need to complete the *Supplementary Pages (form CT600A)*.

A **'close company'** is one which is under the control of five or fewer participators or of any number of participators who are directors (S414 ICTA 1988).

A **'loan or advance'** within S419 ICTA 1988 includes the situation where a participator incurs a debt to the close company (S419(2)(a) ICTA 1988) for example by overdrawing a current or loan account.

There are two exceptions from S419:
- S419(2)(a) does not apply to a debt incurred for the supply by the close company of goods or services in the ordinary course of its trade or business (unless the credit given exceeds 6 months or is longer than that normally given to the company's customers S420(1) ICTA 1988).
- S419(1) does not apply to certain loans made to full time working directors or employees who do not have a material interest in the close company (S420(2) ICTA 1988).

A **'participator'** is a person having a share or interest in the capital or income of the company and includes any loan creditor of the company (S417(1) ICTA 1988).

An **'associate'** of a participator includes any relative or partner of the participator and the trustees of any settlement of which the participator or their relative is, or was, a settlor (S417(3)(a) and (b) ICTA 1988).

Methods by which a loan may be **'repaid'** include:
- depositing cash or a cheque into the company's bank account
- crediting the participator's current or loan account with a dividend, director's remuneration or director's bonus
- book entry.

**'Release'** of a loan is a formal procedure and normally takes place under seal or for consideration.

**'Write off'** of a loan is a wider term than release and does not necessarily require formal arrangements. It includes the situation where a company has accepted that the loan will not be recovered and has given up attempts to collect it.

There are further notes on the form *CT600A* that will help with completion.

## Note 3 - Filing date and penalties

The filing date for a company tax return is normally the later of

- 12 months after the end of the corporation tax accounting period covered by the return or
- 3 months and 1 day after the day on which the relevant *Notice to deliver a Corporation Tax return (form CT603)* is received.

The exception to this rule is when a corporation tax accounting period comes to an end during a company's period of account. If the period of account is 18 months or less, a return may be filed up to 12 months after the end of it. If the period is more than 18 months, it may be filed up to 30 months after the start of that period.

There are automatic penalties for failure to deliver a return by the statutory filing date unless the company has a reasonable excuse. In this case, you must file a return as soon as you can. You, or the company, or its directors, may even be prosecuted in certain circumstances for failure to deliver a return.

If you think you may be late in filing the return, you should

- warn the tax inspector in advance; he or she may exceptionally be prepared to give you more time
- file as much of the information as you can by the filing date. Do not delay because you do not have all the information needed. You should, where necessary, estimate an entry rather than delay the return. In this case you should tell the tax inspector
  - which figure(s) you have had to estimate
  - why you have had to estimate
  - when you expect to be able to finalise the figure(s).

The penalties for late returns start at £100 and increase up to £1,000, plus 20% of any tax paid late for long delays and repeated failures (see Paragraphs 17 to 19 Sch 18 FA 1998).

It is a serious offence to understate a company's profit. The penalties for doing so are up to 100% of the tax lost. You, or the company, or its directors may be prosecuted if you make false statements in the return or omit particulars from it.

## Note 4 - Turnover  *boxes 1 and 2*

Enter in box 1 the trading or professional turnover from any source where profits are shown in box 3, on pages 4 or 6, or losses in box 96 on page 9 of form *CT600*. Members clubs and voluntary associations will not have any entry to make unless, unusually, there are trading profits or losses to be entered on form *CT600*. Financial concerns that do not have a recognised turnover figure should indicate this fact by putting an 'X' in box 2. Investment companies and Unit Trusts need not complete either box 1 or 2.

## Note 5 - Trading profits and losses  *boxes 3, 5 and 96*

If the company carried on more than one trade in the corporation tax accounting period or has to be treated for tax purposes as doing so, you should supply a separate calculation of the profit or loss for each trade. It should show

- any adjustments made to the figures in the company's accounts to arrive at the amount of profit or loss
- any capital allowances or balancing charges included in the calculation of the profit or loss.

Enter the total of all the profits in box 3 and the total of all the losses in box 96 of Section 6.

If the company carried on a trade in partnership, the company's share of the partnership profit or loss should be included in the total profits entered at box 3 or 5, or for losses in box 96 of Section 6.

If you have made an entry in box 5 there must be an entry in either box 3 alone, or in both boxes 3 and 4.

If the amount of a loss, or a part of it, was found by computing and expressing it in a currency other than sterling, the amount to be entered in box 96 should be, or include, the sterling equivalent of that currency loss, even though the whole of the loss may be carried forward expressed in currency terms.

## Note 6 - Trading losses brought forward  *box 4*

You should complete box 4 if

- there are profits in box 3 *and*
- the company has unrelieved trading losses from earlier periods available to set against profits from the same trade.

Where

- the losses brought forward are more than the profits of the trade entered in box 3, only enter enough losses to cover the trading profit
- more than one trade is carried on, provide the profit figure for each trade and the loss set off each. Where the company carried on (or is treated for tax purposes as carrying on) more than one trade, you should attach a calculation to show that the losses brought forward are being deducted only from the profits of the same trade (or deemed trade).

You should not include any losses for which you are claiming tax relief under other provisions.

If the amount of a loss, or a part of it, was found by computing and expressing it in a currency other than sterling for the period in which it was incurred, the amount to be entered in box 4 should be, or include, the sterling equivalent of that currency loss found by using the same exchange rate as is used to compute the sterling profits entered in box 3.

# Company Tax Returns and Guidance Notes

## Note 7 - Income within Schedule D
**Case VI** *box 146 short calculation, boxes 145, 146 and 13 detailed calculation*

Include in box 146 any other profits or gains chargeable to tax not otherwise included under any other heading.

You should attach a separate calculation for each source of income. It should show

- any adjustments made to the figures in the company's accounts to arrive at the amount of income assessable
- any capital allowances deducted or balancing charge added in the calculation of income.

In the detailed calculation, if the company is a shipping company and has elected for the tonnage tax regime, combine the figure entered in box 145 with any entry made in box 146 and enter the total in box 13.

## Note 8 - Profits and gains from non-trading loan relationships, exchange fluctuations or certain financial instruments *boxes 6, 7,18, 25, 99 and 100*

FA 1996 consolidated the rules in FA 1993 and FA 1994 for taxing company profits or gains, and relieving their deficits, in the following areas

- **Loan relationships** (including most money debts). The rules apply to
  - interest payable and receivable for accounting periods ending after 31 March 1996
  - other profits and deficits arising on or after 1 April 1996 from loan relationships (S81 FA 1996).
- **Exchange-rate fluctuations** in relation to monetary (described in the legislation as 'qualifying') assets and liabilities (S153 FA 1993), and to currency contracts (S126 FA 1993).
- **Certain financial instruments** (referred to as 'qualifying contracts' in the legislation) (S149 - 150 FA 1994).

### When to complete boxes 6, 7, 18, 25, 99 and 100

Only complete these boxes if the company has net non-trading profits, gains or deficits in the areas covered by the rules above.

**Do not** use these boxes for trading profits, gains or deficits which are in the areas covered by the rules. Instead, include in boxes 3 to 5 and 96 any

- profits or deficits arising
  - from interest on loan relationships, or
  - from qualifying assets, liabilities or contracts
- profits or deficits, other than interest, arising from loan relationships held for trading purposes.

### What entries to make

Note the following points if you do need to complete boxes 6, 7, 18, 25, 99 and 100.

1. Combine all the company's profits, gains and deficits within the 3 areas into a single net figure of profit or loss. In calculating a profit figure, take into account any similar deficits brought forward or back from other periods (see below).

2. If there is a net profit, enter the figure in box 7. If the profit is net of a deficit carried back from a later period, put an 'X' in box 6 as well.

3. If there is a net deficit
   - complete box 99 in Section 6
   - leave box 7 blank
   - consider making a deficit relief claim under S83 FA 1996 which gives you the following options:
     - set all or part of the deficit against total corporation tax profits for this accounting period (S83(2)(a)). *Enter the amount in box 25.*
     - surrender all or part of the deficit as group relief (S83(2)(b)). *Enter the maximum available to surrender in box 100 and complete details of the surrender in the form CT600C.*
     - carry back the net deficit (after deduction of any claims under a. and b. above) against earlier profits in the 3 areas - that is, against previous box 7 entries (S83(2)(c)). *This needs a separate claim to the Inspector.*
     - set all or part of the deficit against on-trade profits (that is, the total of boxes 7 to 13 plus box 16) of the next accounting period. *Enter the amount in box 18 of the return for the next accounting period.*

   Any part of a net deficit brought forward from the previous accounting period can be included at box 18, but please note that the total amount entered here cannot exceed the sum of boxes 7 to 13 plus box 16.

If the amount of a deficit, or a part of it, was found by computing and expressing it in a currency other than sterling for the period in which it was incurred, the amount to be entered in box 18 should be, or include, the sterling equivalent of that currency deficit found by using the same exchange rate as is used to compute the sterling profits entered in box 7.

If the amount of a deficit, or a part of it, was found by computing and expressing it in a currency other than sterling, the amount to be entered in box 99 should be, or include, the sterling equivalent of that currency deficit, even though the whole of the deficit may be carried forward expressed in currency terms.

565

# Company Tax Returns and Guidance Notes

### Note 9 - Income from which tax has been deducted  box 10

Income received under deduction of income tax is chargeable to corporation tax. Dividends and other distributions from companies resident in the UK do not count as income received under deduction of income tax. Distributions received from UK companies are not chargeable to corporation tax. If you are in doubt, the voucher supplied by the paying company will show what kind of income has been paid.

You should also exclude any amounts included at box 7 (see Note 8).

Where the total figure

- includes different kinds of income which are dealt with differently in the company's accounts *or*
- is not immediately recognisable from the accounts

you should attach your calculations to show how you have arrived at your figures.

### Note 10 - Income from UK land and buildings  boxes 12, 23, 32, 101 and 102

Your calculations should show

- any adjustments made to the figures in the company's accounts to arrive at the amount of income assessable
- any capital allowances deducted or balancing charge added in the calculation of income.

Except for insurance companies (see Ss 432A and 441B(2A) ICTA 1988), lettings from all UK furnished and unfurnished property are treated as a single Schedule A business. If, however, the company lets some property in its own right and some in partnership with others, income from the sole letting and from each partnership will be treated as income of a separate Schedule A business. Receipts and expenses cannot be counted twice.

If you make a Schedule A loss, that loss should be set against your total profits for the period and entered at box 23. You will need to complete the *Detailed calculation*.

Also, if you are claiming Schedule A losses as group relief, the group relief should be entered at box 32 on the *Detailed calculation*.

You will need to complete box 101 if there is a Schedule A loss and box 102 for the maximum available for surrender as group relief. Any claim to group relief, or surrender, should also be reflected in completion of the form *CT600C*.

### Note 11 - Chargeable gains  boxes 14 to 16

Companies are not generally liable to capital gains tax. Instead they are liable to corporation tax on their net chargeable gains. Authorised Unit Trusts and open-ended investment companies are not chargeable to corporation tax on capital gains and neither are Investment Trust Companies approved by the Board of Inland Revenue under S842 ICTA 1988 (see note 26).

If you make an entry in any of boxes 14 to 16 you should attach calculations of each chargeable gain and allowable loss to show how your entries have been arrived at.

Net chargeable gains are made up of the gross gains of the accounting period *minus*

- any allowable losses of the same period
- any unrelieved allowable losses brought forward.

Where the amount of allowable losses brought forward is greater than the net chargeable gains of the accounting period (that is gross gains less allowable losses for the accounting period), only use enough losses to reduce the chargeable gains to '0'. The balance will be carried forward to later accounting periods.

Where a company is or has been a member of a group of companies, the set-off of allowable losses may be restricted under Sch7A TCGA 1992.

If you have made an entry in box 16, there must also be an entry in either box 14 alone or in both boxes 14 and 15.

A chargeable gain or allowable loss can arise on the disposal of most forms of property including intellectual and other incorporeal property. Such property also includes options, rights or interests in property in the UK or elsewhere.

The property might have been acquired by the company, been created by it, or come into existence in some other way.

**Disposals**

Disposals include

- the sale, exchange or gift of an asset
- the part disposal of an asset including the disposal of an interest in or right over it
- the receipt of any capital sum derived from an asset such as
  - a compensation payment
  - insurance money
  - a sum received in return for forfeiture or surrender of rights or for refraining from exercising rights
  - a sum received in return for the use or exploitation of assets.

**Calculation of chargeable gains**

A chargeable gain is normally the difference between

- the proceeds from the disposal of an asset and
- the cost of the asset (including incidental costs of acquisition), plus any money spent on improving it and any allowable money spent on disposing of it.

If the asset was acquired or disposed of other than by arm's length bargain, you should use value rather than cost or proceeds in the calculation and make clear that you have done so. You should also increase both the original cost or value and the costs of any improvement by the indexation allowance. This allowance reflects the increase in the Retail Price Index between the date on which the asset was acquired or cost was incurred and the date on which the asset was disposed of.

In most cases the allowance can only reduce a gain, it cannot create or increase a loss.

Calculations should not generally go back beyond the asset's value at 31 March 1982, even if it was acquired before then. Special rules exist for such an asset.

This guide does not provide a detailed account of the taxation of chargeable gains. If you are not a tax expert, you are advised to seek professional advice about any disposal that seems likely to give rise to a significant chargeable gain.

You can find more information on capital gains taxation in our leaflets. See *'Other publications of interest'* on page 12.

**Allowable losses**

Usually a loss is allowable if a gain on the same transaction would have been chargeable. Allowable losses are calculated in the same way as chargeable gains but in most cases indexation allowance cannot create or increase a loss.

You should carry forward any allowable losses that exceed the chargeable gains from the same corporation tax accounting period. You can set them off against chargeable gains for a later corporation tax accounting period subject to any restriction under Sch7A TCGA 1992 where the company is or has been a member of a group of companies.

**Roll-over relief**

If the company disposes of a qualifying business asset and invests in another qualifying asset up to one year before the disposal, or up to three years after the disposal, it may be possible to defer some or all of the tax liability by claiming roll-over relief.

### Note 12 - Relief for trading losses
*boxes 26 and 27*

Box 27 records the total reliefs claimed to be set off against profits under S393A ICTA 1988. The entry may reflect claims for trading losses of several accounting periods. Put an 'X' in box 26 if amounts carried back from later accounting periods are included in box 27.

The law does not provide any special format for S393A ICTA 1988 claims, but the Inspector will accept entries made on the return form or in a computation as a claim provided these identify the accounting period(s) from which the trading loss originates. If the company carries on more than one trade, the trade giving rise to the loss which is claimed to be relieved must also be identified.

### Note 13 - Charges paid   *box 31*

'Charges' has a special meaning for corporation tax. Charges do not include any amount that is

- deductible in calculating any kind of income or gains *or*
- a distribution by the company such as a dividend.

Charges may include

- annuities and other annual payments from which income tax is deductible on payment
- certain lump sum donations to charity which are paid out of profits chargeable to corporation tax.

For qualifying donations to charities made on or after 1 April 2000 you no longer have to deduct tax at basic rate and pay it to the Inland Revenue. You should pay the charity the gross amount and include that amount in box 31.

There are important qualifications to the above definition covering such matters as

- payments to non-residents (S338(4) ICTA 1988)
- payments charged to capital, not ultimately borne by the company, or not made for full consideration (S338(5) ICTA 1988)
- donations to charity (S339 ICTA 1988 as amended by S40 FA 2000)
- interest payments to non-UK residents (S340 ICTA 1988)
- payments between related companies (S341 ICTA 1988)
- interest distributions from authorised trusts and open-ended investment companies (S468L(5) ICTA 1988).

### Note 14 - Group relief
*box 32 - Detailed calculation only*

You should complete this box, and the form CT600C, if the company claims group relief.

You will need to deliver an amended return if the company subsequently wishes to make new or amended group relief claims.

### Note 15 - Claims to starting or small companies' rate of tax and marginal rate relief *boxes 34 -38*

You should complete these boxes if the company claims to be charged at the starting or small companies' rate or claims marginal, starting or small companies' relief.

**Franked investment income and foreign income dividends arising**

You should enter in box 34 the amount of franked investment income received by, and any foreign income dividends (or deemed FIDs) arising to, the company during the accounting period covered by the return. You should exclude income in relation to distributions made by certain other companies within the same group or by certain consortia companies S13(7) ICTA 1988.

**Number of associated companies**

You should enter in box 36 the number of companies that were associated with the company at any time during the corporation tax

# Company Tax Returns and Guidance Notes

accounting period covered by the return. If there are no associated companies, you **must** enter '0'. S13 ICTA 1988 contains a definition of associated companies.

You should enter figures in each of the boxes 35 to 38 rather than just one in box 36 if all of the following apply

- the corporation tax accounting period straddled two financial years (a financial year is the period from 1 April to the following 31 March) *and*
- the upper or lower limit for marginal relief has varied *and*
- the number of associated companies was different in the parts of the corporation tax accounting period falling into the two financial years.

The table on page 12 shows the rates of tax and the upper and lower limits for marginal relief.

### Note 16 - Corporation tax chargeable
*boxes 39 - 52 (39 - 58 Detailed calculation*

If the company's accounting period ended on 31 March (or otherwise fell wholly within a single financial year), you may

- enter all the chargeable profits in box 40
- enter all the tax chargeable in box 42
- show the financial year in box 39 and rate of tax concerned in box 41.

(A financial year is the period from 1 April to the following 31 March.)

You may also do this if the company's accounting period straddled two financial years but the same corporation tax rate applied during both. In this case you need enter only the earlier of the two financial years.

If the company's accounting period straddled two financial years and different corporation tax rates applied in each, you should:

- divide the chargeable profits on a time basis (in days **not** months) between boxes 40 and 50.

The following table gives the number of days per month to be used when calculating the profits between financial years, where the financial year ends at the end of a given month.

| | | | |
|---|---|---|---|
| April | 30 | October | 31 |
| May | 31 | November | 30 |
| June | 30 | December | 31 |
| July | 31 | January | 31 |
| August | 31 | February | 28 (29 in a leap year) |
| September | 30 | March | 31 |

For example, if the accounting period was, say, the year to 31 May 2002, the apportionment of profits would be

Financial year 2001  $\frac{304}{365}$ x £xx

Financial year 2002  $\frac{61}{365}$ x £xx

- enter the tax chargeable (before any marginal small companies' relief you want to claim) in boxes 42 and 52.

The table on page 12 shows the rates of tax. Boxes 43 to 48 and 53 to 58 (*Detailed calculation* only) provide for exceptional cases, such as life insurance companies, where different rates of tax may be chargeable on different parts of the profits of the same financial year. In these cases, unless the company operates wholly on a mutual basis, you should attach a calculation to show how you have divided the amounts chargeable to tax for each financial year between the different rates of tax. You should leave these boxes blank where these circumstances do not apply.

### Note 17 - Advance corporation tax (ACT)
*box 62*

ACT was abolished on 6 April 1999. Many of the following notes will apply only if the company's accounting period straddles that date. Box 62 records the ACT to be set off against the company's liability to corporation tax. The entry may reflect ACT

- paid in respect of distributions made in the corporation tax accounting period
- brought forward under S239(4) ICTA 1988
- received from another group company under S240 ICTA 1988 surrender.

The law does not provide for a claim by a company to surrender ACT to a subsidiary (S240 ICTA 1988) to be made in the return. But the Inspector will accept entries made in a computation as a claim provided these identify the amount of ACT surrendered and the accepting company should include the amount received in its computation. The Inspector will accept an entry made in a computation as a consent to surrender providing the entry identifies the amount of ACT, the accounting period from which it derives and the surrendering company.

From 6 April 1999, companies with unrelieved surplus ACT or companies within groups where at least one member has unrelieved surplus ACT will be within the shadow ACT scheme unless they have opted out. Shadow ACT is a notional amount of ACT treated as paid by a company in respect of distributions made by it. Where there is an opt out, companies will not be able to set off unrelieved surplus ACT against corporation tax in respect of profits of periods to which the opt out applies.

Shadow ACT is set against the company's liability to corporation tax on profits chargeable for accounting periods ending after 5 April 1999, but it does not reduce the amount of that liability. It is set off before any unrelieved surplus ACT. The maximum amount of shadow ACT, unrelieved surplus ACT or a combination of both that can be set-off is 20% of the company's profits charged to corporation tax for the period. The rules about shadow ACT are contained in SI 1999 No. 358 The Corporation Tax (Treatment of Unrelieved Surplus Advance Corporation Tax) Regulations. There are special rules concerning carry-back of shadow ACT, allocation of shadow

ACT to other group companies, carry-forward of shadow ACT to succeeding accounting periods and set-off of franked investment income.

### Note 18 - Income tax deducted  box 69

This covers income tax suffered by the company on investment income which it has received net of tax. You should not include any amounts used to off-set payments which the company has made under deduction of tax. The company is required to make a return of these payments on form *CT61* and you should consult form *CT61 Notes* which explains the position.

### Note 19 - Deductions from company income under the Construction Industry Scheme  box 73

You should enter in box 73 the total of the deductions, made from company income, during the corporation tax accounting period.

### Note 20 - When tax is payable  box 72

Corporation tax is due without assessment, and every return must by law include a self assessment of the tax payable. Tax is normally due nine months and one day after the end of the accounting period, unless the company is defined as 'large' and pays tax by earlier instalments. Our leaflet a *'A modern system for corporation tax payments. A guide to quarterly instalment payments' (CTSA/BK3)* explains the rules, including the charging and paying of interest, in more detail. See *'Other publications of interest'* on page 12.

### Note 21 - Tax already paid (and not repaid)  box 75

You should enter the full amount of corporation tax already paid by the company and not repaid by the Inland Revenue for the accounting period covered by the return.

The tax shown here will usually have been paid without assessment (see Note 20). Exclude any entry you make in boxes 69, 71 and 73.

### Note 22 - ACT on a foreign income dividends (FIDs)  boxes 71 and 114 - Detailed calculation only

A dividend paid on or after 6 April 1999 cannot be a FID or deemed FID. However, an election to match FIDs with distributable foreign profits may be made in respect of the accounting period that straddles 6 April 1999 (the transitional period) and the accounting period immediately following the transitional period.

ACT paid in respect of FIDs (including deemed FIDs) can be repaid or set off in certain circumstances. The ACT is set off to the extent there is unpaid corporation tax liability for the period concerned after taking into account ACT set off under the usual provisions (Note 17). Any balance is repayable only after nine months from the end of the accounting period. Enter the amount of any repayment claimed in Section 7.

Provide a computation showing how the amount repayable is arrived at. The computation should give details of FIDs and distributable foreign profits which the company elects to match, and details of those matched FIDs which the company elects to be qualifying FIDs.

### Note 23 - Tax outstanding  box 76

The company should already have received a payslip. If you do not have a payslip you should
- ask the Inland Revenue Accounts Office for one or
- send the payment to the Inland Revenue Accounts Office with a letter showing the company's name, address and tax reference together with a note of the corporation tax accounting period to which it relates. The letter should make it clear that the payment is a payment of corporation tax.

### Note 24 - Tax refunds surrendered to the company under S102 FA 1989  box 78 - Detailed calculation only

S102 FA 1989 allows a group of companies to set a repayment due to one member of the group against the underpayment of another (or the underpayments of several others) for the same corporation tax accounting period. This allows the group to rearrange its tax payments without suffering the net interest cost that would otherwise flow.

### Note 25 - Capital allowances and balancing charges  Section 5

You should enter in boxes 81 to 83, as appropriate;
- The total amount of qualifying expenditure incurred on machinery and plant in the chargeable period on which a first year* allowance is claimed.
- The total amount of qualifying expenditure incurred on machinery and plant in the chargeable period and any expenditure incurred in earlier periods on which no capital allowances have previously been claimed, but which are now claimed.

*The 40% first year allowance for spending by small and medium-sized businesses on machinery and plant has been made permanent. In addition, small businesses can claim a 100% first year allowance for investment in information and communications technology made between 1 April 2000 and 31 March 2003. This includes such items as computers, software and internet-enabled mobile phones.

The definitions of a small business and a medium-sized business are based on those in the Companies Act and can be obtained from your Inland Revenue office.

Certain types of machinery and plant do not qualify

for first year allowances. In particular, no first year allowances may be claimed for spending on assets for leasing or hire, motor cars, or long-life assets.

The writing down allowance for long-life assets, comprising machinery and plant that has an expected working life when new of 25 years or more, is 6% a year.

Section 5 of the form CT600 summarises the overall position and is a formal claim for capital allowances. You must also give corresponding information about any balancing charges. Most of the allowances and charges will have been reflected in the calculations of income or losses entered in the boxes in section 3 or 4 of the form CT600, or in a calculation of management expenses.

You will need to deliver an amended return if the company subsequently wishes to amend its capital allowance claim.

### Note 26 - Investment Trust Companies

Capital gains accruing to an approved investment trust company are not chargeable to corporation tax. For approval, the company must satisfy the Board of Inland Revenue that all of the conditions in S842(1) ICTA 1988 have been met throughout the accounting period. Where a company seeks approval as an investment trust, it should provide a schedule with this return showing how the company has met all the conditions in S842(1), and state that the approval of investment trust status is sought. We may enquire into the application for approval.

Put an 'X' in the box in *Summary* on page 1 of form CT600 if you are applying for approval.

### Note 27 - Losses, deficits and excess amounts  *Section 6*

If the company has
- a trading loss
- a non-trading deficit on its loan relationships, or
- an excess of capital allowances given by discharge or repayment over the income against which they are primarily to be set

it may surrender these amounts as group relief. It may surrender them even if it has other income against which they could be set. In the case of a non-trading deficit on its loan relationships, the company must make a claim under S83(2)(b) FA 1996 for the amount to be treated as available for group relief. If the company has Schedule A losses, charges and management expenses, these amounts may only be surrendered as group relief to the extent that the aggregate of these reliefs for the accounting period exceeds the company's gross profits for the accounting period.

The gross profits of the accounting period are calculated without any deduction
- for trading losses, non-trading deficit on loan relationships, or excess capital allowances of the same accounting period
- for any losses, allowances or other amounts of any other period, whether or not of a kind referred to in the previous bullet, or
- by virtue of S75(3) ICTA 1988 or S392A(3) ICTA 1988 (management expenses and Schedule A losses brought forward and treated as management expenses of the accounting period).

### Note 28 - Overpayments and repayment claims  *Section 7*

Only complete this section if there is an overpayment and repayment claim for the period covered by **this return**.

This section enables the company to claim a repayment of income tax, corporation tax (including CIS tax) or ACT, or a payable R&D tax credit. The claims must relate to the accounting period covered by this return.

If the filing of the return results in repayment claims for earlier accounting periods, for example, because of a claim to carry back trading losses from the period covered by the return, please make your claim
- on a separate piece of paper, or
- by making an amended return for the earlier accounting period.

### Note 29 - Interest distribution under S468L
*boxes 22 and 110 Detailed calculation only*

A deduction can be made either
- in computing total profits after the deduction of expenses deductible in computing profits, apart from management expenses, either before or after the deduction of management expenses, or
- against total profits as reduced by any other relief from tax or against total profits not so reduced.

The amount is to be allowed as a deduction in the accounting period in which falls the last day of the distribution period. The amount at box 22 cannot exceed either
- the amount of interest distributions shown by the accounts for the distribution periods that end in this return period plus any excess brought forward from an earlier period, or
- the profits shown in box 19.

Attach a computation showing how you arrived at the amount.

Any excess interest distribution can only be carried forward to the next accounting period and deducted there. The excess is calculated as the excess brought forward from an earlier period plus the amount on which relief is due for distribution periods ending in this period, less the amount set off for this period. Enter the figure for any such excess in box 110.

## Note 30 - Corporation tax accounting period

### Definition of a corporation tax accounting period

An accounting period is the period for which corporation tax liability has to be calculated. This means that

- every company within the scope of corporation tax will have accounting periods, whether or not it draws up financial accounts
- a company outside the scope of corporation tax cannot have accounting periods in the sense used in this guide. (A company is outside the scope of corporation tax if it has no assets producing income or chargeable gains and carries on no activity that generates revenue.)

A corporation tax accounting period can never be longer than twelve months. In most cases it will coincide with the company's reporting 'year', that is the period for which the company draws up its accounts.

### Factors that determine the beginning and end of a corporation tax accounting period

A corporation tax accounting period starts

- when a company comes within the scope of UK corporation tax - for example, by acquiring a source of income, starting business activities or becoming resident in the UK
- immediately after the end of a previous accounting period provided the company remains within the scope of corporation tax.

A corporation tax accounting period ends when the earliest of the following events happens:

- the company reaches its reporting 'year' end (that is, its accounting date), or the end of a period for which it has not made up accounts
- it is 12 months since the corporation tax accounting period began
- the company starts or stops trading (an accounting period ends when trading starts or stops, even if other business activities continue)
- the company ceases to be within the scope of corporation tax (for example, by winding up its business and selling all its income-producing assets; or in the case of non-resident companies, by ceasing to trade in the UK or to carry on mineral exploration or exploitation activities in the UK sector of the North Sea)
- the company goes into liquidation (once a company has gone into liquidation its corporation tax accounting periods run for consecutive periods of 12 months, unless brought to an earlier end by the completion of the winding up)
- the company starts or stops being resident in the UK.

### The corporation tax accounting period covered by the return

In most cases the period shown on the form CT603 will coincide with the company's corporation tax accounting period. If so you should make a return for that period. For further help, see the flowchart on page 11 of this *Guide*.

### Returns for periods during which the company was outside the scope of corporation tax

Companies outside the scope of corporation tax must still deliver a return and send in accounts. They may be liable to a penalty if they fail to do so.

If the company was outside the scope of corporation tax (for example, because it was dormant) throughout the period covered by the return, you should

- attach a note saying why you consider that the company was outside the scope of corporation tax
- complete the *Summary* and *Declaration* on page 1 and attach a copy of the company's accounts.

## Note 31 - Research and Development (R & D) Expenditure boxes 149,150 (Detailed calculation only), 151 and 152

Small and medium-sized companies* can claim a deduction of 150% of the actual amount of qualifying R&D expenditure incurred on or after 1 April 2000 provided the actual expenditure is at a rate of at least £25,000 a year. Expenditure less than £25,000 qualifies for the normal 100% deduction.

The qualifying R&D expenditure is the cost of staff carrying out R&D work and R&D consumable stores. Some payments for sub-contracted R&D also qualify.

You should include the 150% deduction in the computation of profit or loss entered in box 3 or 96, and in box 151 in section 5 of the form CT600, which is the formal claim for the enhanced expenditure.

If the company has a trading loss for the accounting period, it may claim an R&D tax credit. This payment is equal to 16% of the lower of

- the loss and
- the 150% deduction for R&D

but excludes any amounts that have been, or could be, set against other profits of the accounting period, or which are used as loss relief, or surrendered to a group or consortium company.

Note that the R&D tax credit cannot be more than the company's PAYE and Class 1 NIC liabilities for payment periods ending in the accounting period.

The amount of any R&D tax credit claimed must be entered in box 149 on page 8 of the form CT600.
The amount of the tax credit payable to the company, after set-off against other tax due, must be entered in box 150, and also in box 152

# Company Tax Returns and Guidance Notes

in section 7 of the form CT600.

*The definition of a small or medium-sized company (SME) follows that adopted by the European Commission for State Aid purposes. Most companies are SMEs.

Provided it has, in the current or previous year, together with any company in which it holds a 25% or more of the capital or voting rights,
- less than 25% of its capital or voting rights owned by an enterprise that is not an SME, and
- less than 250 employees, and either, or both, of
- an annual turnover of not more than £40 million (about £25 million) and an annual balance sheet total of not more than £27 million (about £17 million)

then the company is an SME.

Full details of this and other aspects of the scheme can be obtained from your Inland Revenue office.

### Note 32 - Management expenses *box 21*
*Detailed calculation and box 108*

If any amount of expenses of management for an earlier period was found by computing and expressing it in a currency other than sterling, the amount to be entered in box 21 should be, or include, the sterling equivalent of the expenses in that currency found by using the same exchange rate as is used to compute the income against which the expenses are set.

If any amount of expenses of management was found by computing and expressing it in a currency other than sterling, the amount to be entered in box 108 should be, or include, the sterling equivalent of the expenses in that currency, even though the whole of the amount may be carried forward expressed in currency terms.

### Flowchart - Accounting periods for which a return is required

If the period shown on the notice is different from the company's corporation tax accounting period, this flowchart will tell you whether or not you must deliver a return and, if so, for what period.

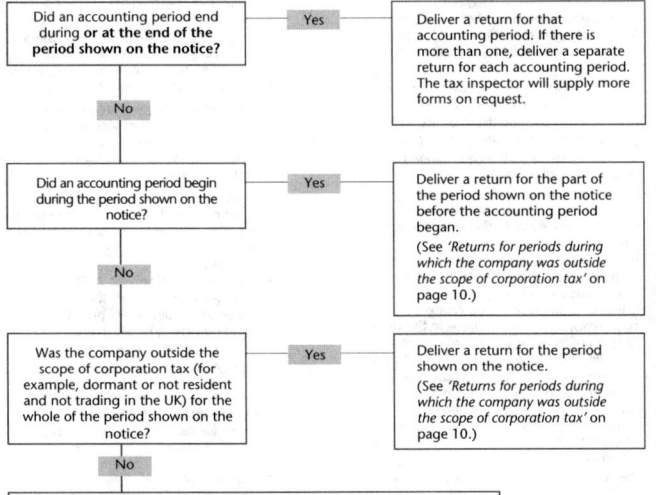

## 12 CT600 Guide (2000)

### Table of corporation tax rates and fractions

| Financial year beginning 1 April | 1998 | 1999 | 2000 |
|---|---|---|---|
| Rate of tax % | 31 | 30 | 30 |
| Starting rate | - | - | 10 |
| Special rate for small companies and an investment trust's housing investment profits | 21 | 20 | 20 |
| Special rate for authorised unit trusts and open-ended investment companies | 20 | 20 | 20 |
| **Limits for marginal relief where there are no associated companies (£ thousands)** | | | |
| First relevant amount for starting rate | - | - | 10 |
| Second relevant amount | - | - | 50 |
| Lower amount for small companies' rate | 300 | 300 | 300 |
| Upper amount | 1500 | 1500 | 1500 |
| **Marginal relief fractions** | | | |
| Marginal starting fraction (S13AA(3) ICTA1988) | - | - | $1/40$ |
| Marginal small companies' fraction (S13(2) ICTA1988) | $1/40$ | $1/40$ | $1/40$ |

### When we receive the return

We will process the return, based on your figures, and record the amount you have shown in the return as the tax due for this period. At this stage we will acknowledge receipt of the return.

If you need to amend the return you can do so
- within 12 months of the filing date
- in the case of a return for the wrong period, within 12 months of what would be the filing date if the period for which you made the return was an accounting period.

You can give details of the changes by letter or schedule, provided you
- include a declaration that the information is correct and complete to the best of your knowledge and belief, and
- are authorised by the company and sign (and date) the letter or schedule.

We can amend the return, or the amended return, to correct obvious errors or omissions in the return (whether errors of principle, arithmetical mistakes or otherwise). We must do this within 9 months of the date you delivered the return or made amendments. If you do not agree with the notice of correction you cannot appeal against but you can amend your return, if you are in time to do this. If you are out of time to amend your return but are still within 3 months of the date of issue of the correction, you can give notice, in writing, and to the officer who issued the notice of correction, rejecting the correction.

We may enquire into the company tax return, or amendment to it, if we give you notice of our intention to do so
- within 12 months of the filing date, for a return delivered on or before the filing date, or
- by 31 January, 30 April, 31 July or 31 October next following the first anniversary of the day on which a return was delivered late, or an amendment was made.

### Other publications of interest

- *Income tax and corporation tax: clubs, societies and voluntary associations (IR46)*
- *Construction industry tax deduction scheme (IR14/15(CIS))*
- *Code of Practice 10 - Information and advice*
- *Code of Practice 14 - Company enquiries*
- *How to complain about the Inland Revenue (AO1)*
- *A modern system for corporation tax payments. A guide to quarterly instalment payments (CTSA/BK3)*
- *A general guide to corporation tax self assessment (CTSA/BK4) - available from November 2000*

All the above leaflets and booklets are available from the CTSA Orderline (0845 300 6555 or fax 0845 300 6777), any Inland Revenue Enquiry Centre or office.

- *A booklet and helpsheets, aimed at Capital Gains Tax (CGT) payers rather than companies, are available. Much of the information will hold good for companies. Contact any Inland Revenue Enquiry Centre or office for up to date information.*

*Controlled Foreign Company Guidance Notes* are available, price £10, either by post from Inland Revenue Library Information Room, R28 New Wing, Somerset House, London, WC2R 1LB, or to personal callers between the hours of 9am and 5pm Monday to Friday, from the Inland Revenue Information Centre, South West Wing, Bush House, London WC2B 4RD.

# Company Tax Returns and Guidance Notes

**Company Tax Return Form**
*Loans to participators by close companies*
**Supplementary Pages**
*For accounting periods ending on or after 1 July 1999*

## Company information

**Company Name**

**Tax reference**
    /     /

**Period covered by these** *Supplementary Pages* *(cannot exceed 12 months)*
**From** *(dd/mm/yyyy)*     **To**
  /   /       /   /

You need to complete these *Supplementary Pages* if

*the company is close and has made a loan (or loans) to an individual participator, or associate of a participator, in this period which has not been repaid within the period.*

### Important points

- *These Supplementary Pages*, when completed, form part of the company's return.
- *These Pages set out* the information we need and provide a standard format.
- *Complete the boxes* with whole figures only, except where pence or decimals are indicated.
- *Note 2 in the CT600 Guide* will help you understand any terms that have a special meaning and notes on these Pages will help with the completion of this form.
- *These Pages* are covered by the *Declaration* you sign on page 1 of the form CT600.
- *The warning shown on the form CT600* about prosecution, and the advice about late and incorrect returns, and late payment of tax also apply to these Pages.

## Part 1: Loans made during the return period

You must complete Part 1 if the company is close and has made a loan to an individual participator, or associate of a participator, during the return period which has not been repaid within the return period.

Enter in the table below, details of any outstanding loans made to a participator or associate of a participator during the return period. If the participator or associate has a current or loan account with the company, enter details of each participator's or associate's account. The amount you enter in column 2 of the table is the total of all debit entries on the account, less any credit entries and less any credit balance brought forward from the previous return period. In arriving at this figure you **must** exclude any credit entries that represent repayment, release or write off of loans made in earlier return periods.

**A1** Put an 'X' in this box if loans made during the period have been released, or written off before the end of the period.     **A1** ☐

**A2** Information about loans made during the return period and outstanding at the end of the period

| Name of participator or associate *See Note 2 in the CT600 Guide for the meaning of participator and associate* | Amount of loan *See note above for advice on what to enter here* |
|---|---|
|  | £ |
|  | £ |
|  | £ |
|  | £ |
|  | £ |

Total loans within S419 ICTA 1988 made during the return period which have not been repaid, released or written off before the end of the period     **Total**   **A2** £

*If a continuation sheet is used, please put an 'X' in box A2A*     **A2A** ☐

**A3** Tax chargeable on loans
*Tax due before any relief for loans repaid, released, or written off after the end of the period*     box A2 multiplied by 25%
**A3** £     p

## Company Tax Returns and Guidance Notes

2 CT600A Supplementary Pages (2000)

### Part 2: Loans made during the return period - Relief for amounts repaid, released or written off after the end of the period but *earlier than* 9 months and 1 day after the end of the period

Complete this Part to obtain relief for loans included in box A2 that were repaid, released or written off if
- the return is for the period in which the loans were made **and**
- the loan was repaid, released or written off after the end of the period but **earlier than** 9 months and 1 day after the end of the accounting period in which the loan was **made**.

Enter in the table details for each participator or associate. If there have been a number of repayments on an account, enter only the total repayments for that account and give the date of the last repayment. *A separate entry must be made for each loan or part loan that has been released or written off.*

**Example**
A company makes a loan during the accounting period ended 31 December 2000 and it is all repaid to the company on 30 June 2001. The company's tax return for the accounting period ended 31 December 2000 is sent to the Inland Revenue on 1 November 2001. Part 2 should be completed because the loan was repaid after the end of the accounting period but earlier than 9 months and 1 day after it.

A4 & A5  Information about loans repaid, released or written off after the end of the period but *earlier than* 9 months and 1 day after the end of the period

| Name of participator or associate<br>See Note 2 in the CT600 Guide for<br>the meaning of 'participator' and 'associate' | Amount repaid<br>See note above and<br>Note 2 in the<br>CT600 Guide | Amount released<br>or written off<br>See note above and<br>Note 2 in CT600 Guide | Date of<br>repayment,<br>release or<br>write off |
|---|---|---|---|
|  | £ | £ |  |
|  | £ | £ |  |
|  | £ | £ |  |
|  | £ | £ |  |
|  | £ | £ |  |
|  | £ | £ |  |
| Totals  A4  £ |  | £ | A5 |

*If a continuation sheet is used, please put an 'X' in box A5A*    A5A

A6  Total amount of loans made during the return period which have been repaid, released or written off after the end of the period but *earlier than* 9 months and 1 day after the end of the period

total of boxes A4 and A5
A6 £

A7  Relief due for loans repaid, released or written off after the end of the period but *earlier than* 9 months and 1 day after the end of the period

box A6 multiplied by 25%
A7 £                      p

# Company Tax Returns and Guidance Notes

### Most companies will not need to complete Part 3 below

Only complete Part 3:
- where the loan was made during the return period, and
- where repayment, release or write off was more than 9 months after the end of the period in which the loan was made, and
- the return is submitted after the date on which relief is due (if the return is sent in very late, at least 21 months after the end of the return period).

If you are unsure whether or not to complete Part 3, apply the following questions to each claim.

*Put an 'X' in box if "Yes"*

Check that the loan was made in the return period

|   | dd/mm/yyyy |
|---|---|
| End date of accounting period in which the loan was repaid, released or written off  **a** | / / |
| Enter the date 9 months after the end of that accounting period  **b** | / / |
| Date you are sending in the company tax return for the period in which the loan was made  **c** | / / |

If the date at **c** is earlier than the date at **b** you cannot complete **Part 3**, but can make a separate claim for the relief which is not due until the date in **b**.

If the date at **c** is later than the date at **b** you can complete **Part 3** below to obtain the relief now.

### Part 3: Loans made during the return period which have been repaid, released or written off *more than 9 months after the end of the period and where relief is due now*

Complete this Part only if loans made during the return period, that have not been included in Part 2, have been repaid, released or written off and where relief is due now (see notes above).

**Example**
A company makes a loan during the accounting period ended 31 December 2000 and it is all repaid on 30 November 2001. The company's return for the accounting period ended 31 December 2000 is sent to the Inland Revenue on 1 December 2001. Part 3 of this form **should not** be completed because, although the loan was repaid more than 9 months after the end of the return period, the return is sent earlier than 9 months after the end of the return period in which the loan was repaid.

Relief for the repayment cannot be given until the due date of the accounting period in which the repayment was made, in this case 1 October 2002 (Ss419(4A) and (4B) ICTA 1988). The company must make a separate claim for relief.

**Example**
Same as example above except that the return is not sent in until 3 December 2002. Relief for the repayment is due on or after 1 October 2002. In this case Part 3 can be completed because the repayment was made more than 9 months after the end of the accounting period in which the loan was made, and the relief is due at the time the return is sent in.

**A8 & A9**  Information about loans made during the return period which have been repaid, released or written off *more than 9 months after the end of the period and relief is due now*

| Name of participator or associate  *See Note 2 in the CT600 Guide for the meaning of 'participator' and 'associate'* | Amount repaid  *See note above and Note 2 in the CT600 Guide* | Amount released or written off  *See note above and Note 2 in CT600 Guide* | Date of repayment, release or write off |
|---|---|---|---|
|  | £ | £ |  |
|  | £ | £ |  |
|  | £ | £ |  |
|  | £ | £ |  |
|  | £ | £ |  |
| Totals **A8** £ | £ | **A9** |  |

If a continuation sheet is used, please put an 'X' in box A9A    **A9A**

**A10** Total amount of loans made during the return period which have been repaid, released, or written off **more** than 9 months after the end of the period *and relief is due now*    *total of boxes A8 and A9*  **A10** £

**A11** Relief *due now* for loans repaid, released or written off *more than* 9 months after the end of the period. *Remember to put an 'X' in box 65 in Section 4 of the form CT600 if you have completed box A11*    *box A10 multiplied by 25%*  **A11** £                   P

## Company Tax Returns and Guidance Notes

**4** CT600A Supplementary Pages (2000)

### Part 4: Other information

**A12** Total loans outstanding at end of return period
Show all loans outstanding at the end of the return period, whether they were made in this period or an earlier one

**A12** £ _____

### Part 5: What S419 ICTA 1988 tax is payable?

**A13** Tax payable under S419 ICTA 1988
Copy the figure in box A13 to box 66 in Section 4 of the form CT600

box A3 less total of boxes A7 and A11
**A13** £ _____ p

### What to do when you have completed these *Supplementary Pages*

- Copy the figure from box A13 in Part 5 to box 66 in Section 4 of the form CT600.
- Put an 'X' in box 65 in Section 4 of form CT600 if you have completed box A11 in Part 3 of these Pages.
- Follow the advice shown under 'What to do when you have completed the return' on page 2 of the form CT600.

## Company Tax Returns and Guidance Notes

Inland Revenue

**Company Tax Return Form**
Controlled foreign companies Supplementary Pages
For accounting periods ending on or after 1 July 1999

### Company information

**Company Name**

**Tax reference**
[    ] / [    ] / [    ]

**Period covered by these Supplementary Pages** (cannot exceed 12 months)
From (dd/mm/yyyy)  To
[    /    /    ]  [    /    /    ]

### Important points

- **These Supplementary Pages**, when completed, form part of the company's return.
- **These Pages set out** the information we need and provide a standard format.
- **Notes** on these Pages will help with the completion of this form.
- **These Pages are covered by** the Declaration you sign on page 1 of the form CT600.
- **The warning shown on the form CT600** about prosecution, and the advice about late and incorrect returns, and late payment of tax also apply to these Pages.

### Notes

These Supplementary Pages must be completed by all UK companies which, at any time in this period, hold a **relevant interest** of 25% or more in a foreign company which is **controlled** from the UK. No controlled foreign company (CFC) need be included on this page where it satisfies the **Excluded Countries Regulations**.

A UK company may also include companies on the return which **may** not be CFCs but which would satisfy one of the exemptions if they were. This applies to foreign companies which may not be **subject to a lower level of tax**, or may not be **controlled** from the UK. It also applies where the UK company's **relevant interest** in the foreign company may be less than 25%. The purpose of this is to save UK companies the cost of working out whether a foreign company is in principle a CFC in cases where it is clear that one of the exemptions would be passed if it were.

The following information is required on pages 2 and 3:
- **Name** of the CFC.
- **Territory of residence**. If a **residence election** is made this should be noted and if a company is conclusively presumed to be resident in a territory in which it is **subject to a lower level of tax** then this should be indicated by the entry "S749(5)".
- **Exemptions**. Companies exempt under the provisions other than the Excluded Countries Regulations may indicate one (or more) exemptions here. Only one exemption need be noted, and not including an exemption will not prejudice whether it applies. *If an exemption applies there is no need to complete any of the subsequent columns in respect of the CFC.*
- Measure of **Apportionment**. This will usually be the percentage of ordinary share capital held directly or indirectly by the UK company (but not by associated or connected persons). In all other circumstances the appropriate percentage should be calculated on a just and reasonable basis.
- **Chargeable profits**. These are the chargeable profits (after reliefs available under Sch 25) apportioned to the UK company.
- **Tax on chargeable profits**. This is the amount of tax apportioned on the basis of the company's share of chargeable profits before reliefs are given under Sch 26 or relief is given for advance corporation tax.
- **Creditable tax**. This broadly represents tax already paid on the chargeable profits and is deductible.
- **Reliefs**. Any reliefs available under Sch 26 should be shown at the appropriate rate of corporation tax.
- **ACT as restricted**. Unrelieved surplus ACT to the extent not restricted should be shown here.
- **S747 tax due**. This is the column J total which is the sum of the figures in column F less the sum of the figures in columns G to I. The net figure should be copied to box 67 in Section 4 of the form CT600.

### What to do when you have completed these Supplementary Pages

- Copy the figure from the Summary box on these Pages to box 67 in Section 4 of the form CT600.
- Follow the advice shown under 'What to do when you have completed the return' on page 2 of the form CT600.

2   CT600B Supplementary Pages (1999)

| A<br>Name of CFC | B<br>Territory of residence for S749 purposes | C<br>Exemption due (if any) |
|---|---|---|
| 1 | | |
| 2 | | |
| 3 | | |
| 4 | | |
| 5 | | |
| 6 | | |
| 7 | | |
| 8 | | |
| 9 | | |
| 10 | | |
| 11 | | |
| 12 | | |

*If a continuation sheet is used, please put an 'X' in this box* ▬

## Company Tax Returns and Guidance Notes

CT600B Supplementary Pages (1999)

| D<br>Percentage of apportionable profits and creditable tax | E<br>Chargeable profits | F<br>Tax on chargeable profits | G<br>Creditable tax | H<br>Reliefs in terms of tax | I<br>ACT as restricted | J<br>S747 tax chargeable | |
|---|---|---|---|---|---|---|---|
| % | £ | £  p | £  p | £  p | £  p | £  p | 1 |
| % | £ | £  p | £  p | £  p | £  p | £  p | 2 |
| % | £ | £  p | £  p | £  p | £  p | £  p | 3 |
| % | £ | £  p | £  p | £  p | £  p | £  p | 4 |
| % | £ | £  p | £  p | £  p | £  p | £  p | 5 |
| % | £ | £  p | £  p | £  p | £  p | £  p | 6 |
| % | £ | £  p | £  p | £  p | £  p | £  p | 7 |
| % | £ | £  p | £  p | £  p | £  p | £  p | 8 |
| % | £ | £  p | £  p | £  p | £  p | £  p | 9 |
| % | £ | £  p | £  p | £  p | £  p | £  p | 10 |
| % | £ | £  p | £  p | £  p | £  p | £  p | 11 |
| % | £ | £  p | £  p | £  p | £  p | £  p | 12 |
| Totals | | F  £  p | G  £  p | H  £  p | I  £  p | J  £  p | 13 |

If a continuation sheet is used, please put an 'X' in this box

Transfer this total to box 67 of Section 4 on the form CT600

## Company Tax Returns and Guidance Notes

**Company Tax Return Form**
Group and consortium Supplementary Pages
For accounting periods ending on or after 1 July 1999

### Information

**Company Name**

**Tax reference**
     /      /

**Period covered by these *Supplementary Pages*** *(cannot exceed 12 months)*
From *(dd/mm/yyyy)*    To
   /    /        /    /

### Important points

- These *Supplementary Pages*, when completed, form part of the company's return.
- These *Pages* set out the information we need and provide a standard format.
- These *Pages* are covered by the Declaration you sign on page 1 of the form CT600.
- The warning shown on the form CT600 about prosecution, and the advice about late and incorrect returns, and late payment of tax also apply to these *Pages*.

You need to complete these *Supplementary Pages* if
    you are claiming or surrendering any amounts under the group and/or consortium relief provisions.

### Part 1: Claims to group relief

**C1** Complete Part 1 if you are claiming group relief in your calculation of corporation tax payable. Attach a copy of each surrendering company's notice of consent to the claim unless a special arrangement is in force. Include claims made under the consortium provisions and attach a copy of the notice of consent of each member of the consortium

| Name of surrendering company | Accounting period [1] of surrendering co. | Tax reference [2] | Amount claimed |
|---|---|---|---|
|  |  |  | £ |
|  |  |  | £ |
|  |  |  | £ |
|  |  |  | £ |
|  |  |  | £ |
|  |  |  | £ |
|  |  |  | £ |
|  |  |  | enter in box 32 of form CT600 |
|  |  | **Total   C1** | £ |

If a continuation sheet is used, please put an 'X' in box C1A      **C1A** ☐

[1] Show the start and end dates of any period that is different from that covered by this return
[2] Show the Tax Office number and taxpayer reference. If you do not know these show whatever information you can that will help us identify the company, such as the company registration number

# Company Tax Returns and Guidance Notes

**2** CT600C Supplementary Pages (1999)

## Part 2: Amounts surrendered as group relief

Complete Part 2 if the company is surrendering any amount under the group relief provisions. Include amounts surrendered under the consortium provisions.
A notice of consent to each claim will be needed unless a special arrangement is in force. Part 2 is acceptable as a notice of consent if signed by an authorised person in the space below. Remember that for consortium relief the consent of all other consortium members is needed.

**Details of company surrendering relief** (Complete if you are using this form as the notice of consent to surrender)

**Company Name**

| Tax reference | Accounting period Start date (dd/mm/yyyy) | End date |
|---|---|---|
| / / | / / | / / |

### Surrender as group relief

| | |
|---|---|
| Trading losses | £ |
| Excess non-trade capital allowances over income from which they are primarily deductible | £ |
| Non-trading deficit on loan relationships | £ |
| Excess charges over profits | £ |
| Excess of Schedule A losses over profits | £ |
| Excess of management expenses over profits | £ |
| **Total** | £ |

### Details of surrender

| Name of claimant company | Accounting period [1] of claimant company | Tax reference [2] | Amount surrendered |
|---|---|---|---|
| | | | £ |
| | | | £ |
| | | | £ |
| | | | £ |
| | | | £ |
| | | Total **C2** | £ |

[1] Show the start and end dates of any period that is different from that covered by this return

[2] Show the Tax Office number and taxpayer reference. If you do not know these show whatever information you can that will help us identify the company, such as the company registration number

If a continuation sheet is used, please put an 'X' in box C2A  **C2A**

If you use this part remember to send a copy of the notice of consent to the Inspector dealing with the return of the claimant company. You must do this at the same time or before the claimant company submits its return claiming the group relief concerned.

**I certify that all the information I have given on these pages is correct and complete to the best of my knowledge and belief**

**Signature** (this is needed if you are using this form as the notice of consent to surrender)

**Status**

**Name** (in capital letters)

Except where a liquidator has been appointed, any person who is authorised to do so may sign on behalf of the company. A photocopy of a signature is not acceptable.

### What to do when you have completed these Supplementary Pages

- Copy the figure from box C1 in Part 1 to box 32 in Section 4 of the form CT600.
- Follow the advice shown under 'What to do when you have completed the return' on page 2 of the form CT600.

*Company Tax Returns and Guidance Notes*

*Company Tax Return Form*
*Insurance Supplementary Pages*
*For accounting periods ending on or after 1 July 1999*

### Company information

**Company Name**

**Tax reference**

/              /

**Period covered by these** *Supplementary Pages* (cannot exceed 12 months)
**From** (dd/mm/yyyy)     **To**

/     /           /     /

#### Important points

- *These Supplementary Pages*, when completed, form part of the company's return.
- *These Pages* set out the information we need and provides a standard format.
- *The notes on page 2* of this form will help you complete these Pages.
- *These Pages* are covered by the Declaration you sign on page 1 of the form CT600.
- *The warning* shown on the form CT600 about prosecution, and the advice about late and incorrect returns, and late payment of tax also apply to these Pages.

#### You need to complete these *Supplementary Pages* if

the insurance company, including a friendly society, has either entered into policies or contracts in the accounting period which it has treated as relating to overseas life assurance business (OLAB) in the accounting period, or has made claims under Sch 19AB ICTA 1988, to repayments or notional repayments for return periods ending within the accounting period.

### Part 1: Overseas Life Assurance Business

The company has obtained or completed all the certificates, documents, undertakings and declarations required by regulations 4 to 11 of the Insurance Companies (Overseas Life Assurance Business) (Compliance) Regulations 1995 that relate to the policies and contracts it has entered into in the accounting period which it has treated as being OLAB in this return.

*Put an 'X' in box if 'Yes'*

Companies that write policies and contracts which fall to be treated as OLAB must, in most cases, complete certain certificates and obtain declarations and other documents from policy holders or cedant companies. The business should only be treated as OLAB (which gives certain tax advantages) in the return and accompanying explanations and calculations if the various documents have been created or obtained within the time limits laid down in the regulations. If the company is unable to certify this by placing an 'X' in the box above, the return must be made on the basis that the relevant business is not OLAB.

Guidance Notes on OLAB can be obtained from Inland Revenue, Financial Institutions Division, S11 West Wing, Somerset House, London WC2R 1LB.

#### What to do when you have completed these *Supplementary Pages*

*Follow the advice shown under 'What to do when you have completed the return' on page 2 of the form CT600.*

*Continued overleaf*

CT600D Insurance Supplementary Pages     BMSD 6/99

# Company Tax Returns and Guidance Notes

CT600D Supplementary Pages (1999)

## Notes

**D1 Sch 19AB repayments made**
Enter the total repayments actually made, either by direct payment or by set-off against liabilities such as instalments of corporation tax due shortly after the end of a Sch 19AB return period

**D2 Sch 19AB notional repayments**
Enter the total notional repayments to which effect has been given. Enter NIL for accounting periods beginning after 31 March 1999

**D3 Total repayments under Sch 19AB**
Calculate this figure as indicated

**D4 Pension business notionally repayable real gilts tax**
Enter the tax that would have been suffered on the pension business share of real gilt interest payments falling due before 1 April 1999 if none of that interest had been paid gross. For accounting periods beginning after 31 March 1999, enter NIL

**D5 Pension business notionally repayable manufactured gilts tax**
Enter the tax that would have been suffered on the pension business share of manufactured gilt interest falling due before 1 April 1999 if none of that interest had been paid gross. For accounting periods beginning after 31 March 1999, enter NIL

**D6 Total notionally repayable gilt interest**
Calculate this figure as indicated

**D7 Pension business share of non-gilt income tax actually suffered**
Enter the amount of income tax suffered on all interest and other taxed income (other than gilts payments falling due before 1 April 1999, which should be included within D4 or D5) referable to pension business

**D8 Individual savings account business and exempt business income tax actually suffered**
Enter the income tax suffered on interest and other taxed income referable to individual savings account business and, in the case of friendly societies, tax exempt business

**D9** = D6 + D7 + D8  Calculate this figure as indicated

**D10 Total income tax deducted**
Enter the total amount of income tax actually suffered on taxed income received by the company. The sum of the amounts at D2 and D10 should equal the total income tax that would have been suffered or paid if there had been no claims to notional repayments for income tax on gilt interest.

**D11 Income tax deducted from relevant payments**
Enter the amount of income tax deducted from relevant payments made under deduction of income tax.

**D12 Corporation tax before income tax set-off**
Enter the corporation tax for the accounting period after any set-off of foreign tax or ACT but before any set-off of income tax.

**D13 Appropriate amount plus relevant final amount (but not less than 0)**
Calculate this figure as indicated. For accounting periods beginning before 1 April 1999, this is the second aggregate amount referred to in paragraph 3(1)(b) of Sch 19AB. For accounting periods beginning after 31 March 1999 there is no "relevant final amount" (this relates to notional repayments for tax on gilt interest) and this figure is therefore the "appropriate amount" referred to in paragraph (3)(1)(b) of Sch 19AB

**D14 Payable individual savings account business and exempt business tax credits**
Enter the 10% tax credits payable on the share of the franked investment income received after 5 April 1999 referable to individual savings account business and, in the case of friendly societies, the tax credits payable on the share of franked investment income referable to tax exempt business

**D15 Relevant final amount plus paragraph 1(7) amount = D13 plus D14**
Calculate this figure as indicated

**D16 Paragraph 3 liability = Excess of D3 over D15 (if any)**
Enter the excess of D3 over D15, or NIL if D15 is greater than D3. This amount is recoverable by assessment with interest

## Company Tax Returns and Guidance Notes

### Part 2: Sch 19AB ICTA 1988 repayments

**D1** Sch 19AB repayments made — D1 £ _____

**D2** Sch 19AB notional repayments — D2 £ _____

**D3** Total repayments under Sch 19AB — *total of boxes D1 and D2* — D3 £ _____

**D4** Pension business notionally repayable real gilts tax — D4 £ _____

**D5** Pension business notionally repayable manufactured gilts tax — D5 £ _____

**D6** Total pension business notionally repayable gilts tax — *total of boxes D4 and D5* — D6 £ _____

**D7** Pension business share of income tax actually suffered *(exclude amounts in boxes D4 and D5)* — D7 £ _____

**D8** Individual savings account business and exempt business income tax actually suffered — D8 £ _____

**D9** Calculate as indicated — *total of boxes D6 to D8* — D9 £ _____

**D10** Total income tax suffered — D10 £ _____

**D11** Income tax deducted from relevant payments — D11 £ _____

**D12** Corporation tax before income tax set off — D12 £ _____

**D13** Appropriate amount plus relevant final amount (but not less than 0)
Lower of
• box D2 plus D10 minus D11 minus D12
• box D9
— D13 £ _____

**D14** Payable individual savings account business and exempt business tax credits — D14 £ _____

**D15** Relevant final amount + paragraph 1(7) amount — *total of boxes D13 and D14* — D15 £ _____

**D16** Paragraph 3, Sch 19AB, liability - *this is the amount due to the Inland Revenue* — *excess of box D3 over box D15 (if any)* — D16 £ _____

*Company Tax Returns and Guidance Notes*

**Company Tax Return Form**
*Charity Supplementary Pages*
For accounting periods ending on or after 1 July 1999

## Information

**Charity Name**

**Tax reference**
/         /

**Period covered by these** *Supplementary Pages* *(cannot exceed 12 months)*
**From** *(dd/mm/yyyy)*          **To**
/    /                    /    /

Important points

- *These Supplementary Pages* will form the Charity's claim to exemption that its income and gains have been applied for charitable purposes only.
- *Please enter '0'* where appropriate.
- *How often* you are asked to make a return will depend on the extent and nature of your activities.
- *These Pages*, when completed, form part of the company's return.
- *These Pages set out* the information we need and provide a standard format.
- *These Pages are covered by* the Declaration you sign on page 1 of the form CT600.
- *The warning shown* on the form CT600 about prosecution, and the advice about late and incorrect returns, and late payment of tax also apply to these Pages.

You need to complete these *Supplementary Pages* if

the Charity claims exemption from tax on all or any part of its income and gains.

## Claim to exemption

**This section should be completed in all cases**

Charity repayment reference

Charity Commission Registration number; or Scottish Charity number *(if applicable)*

During the period covered by these *Supplementary Pages*:
*Put an 'X' in the box if 'Yes'*

- The company was a Charity and is claiming exemption from all tax on all or part of its income and gains

or

- Some of the Charity's income and gains may not be exempt or have not been applied for charitable purposes only, and I have completed the form CT600
  *See Note 7 on page 2 of these Pages*

- All income and gains are exempt from tax and have been, or will be, applied for charitable purposes only

**I claim exemption from tax**

**Signature**

**Name** *(in capital letters)*

**Date** *(dd/mm/yyyy)*
/    /

**Status**

Except where a liquidator has been appointed, any person who is authorised to do so may sign on behalf of the company. A photocopy of a signature is not acceptable.

## 2 CT600E Supplementary Pages (1999)

### Notes to help you complete the Charity Supplementary Pages

#### Repayments (Boxes E1/E1a and E2/E2b)

1. In Boxes E1/E1a:
   - Enter the amount of income tax and transitional relief claimed on forms R68 for the period covered by these Pages.
   - This should relate only to income arising in the period.
   - Do not include amounts claimed for earlier periods.

2. In Box E2/E2b enter the total amount due for income received in the period on which the Charity can claim.

#### Trading income (Box E5)

3. Enter details of the turnover of trades, the profits of which will be exempted by S505(1)(e) ICTA 1988.

   If the charity has carried on a trade during the return period which falls outside the exemption, complete the *Short* or *Detailed calculation* on the form *CT600*. Do not include in the calculation sources of income which are otherwise exempt from tax. Also complete the *Summary* and *Declaration* on page 1 of the form *CT600*.

#### Other sources (Box E13)

4. Enter details in Box E13 of the total income received from sources other than those included in the boxes above. If the amount in Box E13 includes income which is assessable under Case VI of Schedule D (for example, the profit from a single transaction or isolated service of some kind, which do not amount to trading under Case I of Schedule D), then complete the *Short calculation* in the form *CT600*, entering the income assessable at box 13. Also complete the *Summary* and *Declaration* on page 1 of the form *CT600*.

#### Investments and loans within Sch 20 ICTA 1988 (Box E26)

5. Qualifying investments for the purposes of S506 ICTA 1988 are specified in Part I, Sch 20 ICTA 1988.

   Qualifying loans for the purposes of S506 ICTA 1988 are specified in Part II, Sch 20 ICTA 1988.

   Any loan or other investment not specified may be accepted as qualifying where the loan or other investment is made for the benefit of the charity and not for the avoidance of tax (whether by the charity or any other person). Any claim must first be approved by Financial Intermediaries and Claims Office (FICO).

#### Investments and loans made outside Sch 20 ICTA 1988 (Box E27)

6. If the charity has made any investments or loans which do not fall within Sch 20 ICTA 1988 and no claim is to be made, enter the total of such investments or loans in Box E27.

#### Restriction of relief for non-qualifying expenditure.

7. Relief under S505(1) ICTA 1988 and S256 TCGA 1992 may not be available.

   The Charity should attach a calculation of restriction of relief under S505(3) ICTA 1988 and send it with this return. If you need help with this calculation please contact the FICO technical helpline. For Charities in England, Wales and Northern Ireland the telephone number is 0151 472 6046. For Charities in Scotland the telephone number is 0131 551 8643.

#### Subcontractor payments

8. If the Charity has made payments under the Construction Industry Scheme enclose forms SC60/CIS25.

## Company Tax Returns and Guidance Notes

CT600E Supplementary Pages (1999) 3

### Repayments

Enter details of repayments/payments for income arising during the period covered by these Supplementary Pages

*See Notes 1 and 2 on page 2 of these Pages*

| | | Income Tax | Transitional Relief |
|---|---|---|---|
| E1/E1a | Amount already claimed in period using form R68 or R68(MGA) | E1 £ | E1a £ |
| E2/E2b | Total repayment/payment due | E2 £ | E2b £ |

and either

| E3/E3c | Further repayment/payment due *Where E2/E2b is more than E1/E1a* | E3 £ | E3c £ |

or

| E4/E4d | Amounts overclaimed in period *Where E1/E1a is more than E2/E2b* | E4 £ | E4d £ |

### Information required

Enter details of any *income* claimed as exempt which is received from the following sources. Enter the figure included in the Charity's accounts for the period covered by these Supplementary Pages

*Non-exempt amounts should be entered on the form CT600 in the appropriate boxes*

| Source | | Amount |
|---|---|---|
| E5 | Enter total turnover from exempt trading activities  *See Note 3 on page 2 of these Pages* | E5 £ |
| E6 | Investment income  *Exclude any amounts included on the form CT600* | E6 £ |
| E7 | UK land and buildings  *Exclude any amounts included on the form CT600* | E7 £ |
| E8 | Deed of Covenant  *Exclude any amounts included on the form CT600* | E8 £ |
| E9 | Gift Aid or Millenium Gift Aid  *Exclude any amounts included on the form CT600* | E9 £ |
| E10 | Other Charities  *Exclude any amounts included on the form CT600* | E10 £ |
| E11 | Legacies | E11 £ |
| E12 | Other donations | E12 £ |
| E13 | Other sources (for example, commissions, fees, small fund-raising)  *See Note 4 on page 2 of these Pages* | E13 £ |

Enter figures of *expenditure* as shown in the Charity's accounts for the period covered by these Supplementary Pages

| Source | | Amount |
|---|---|---|
| E14 | Trading costs  *In relation to exempt activities in box E5* | E14 £ |
| E15 | UK land and buildings  *In relation to exempt activities in box E7* | E15 £ |
| E16 | All general administration costs | E16 £ |
| E17 | All grants and donations made within the UK | E17 £ |
| E18 | All grants and donations made outside the UK | E18 £ |
| E19 | Other expenditure not included above, or in calculating figures entered on the form *CT600* | E19 £ |

*Continued on page 4*

**4** CT600E Supplementary Pages (1999)

**Continued from page 3**

**Charity Assets**

| | | Disposals in period (total consideration received) | Held at the end of the period |
|---|---|---|---|
| E20 | Tangible fixed assets | E20 £ | E20a £ |
| E21 | UK investments (excluding controlled companies) | E21 £ | E21b £ |
| E22 | Shares in, and loans to, controlled companies | E22 £ | E22s £ |
| E23 | Overseas investments | E23 £ | E23d £ |
| E24 | Loans and non trade debtors | | E24e £ |
| E25f | Other current assets | | E25f £ |

E26 Put an 'X' in this box if all investments and loans made by the Charity in the accounting period were qualifying investments or loans within Part I or II of Sch 20 ICTA 1988. *See Note 5 on page 2 of these Pages*  E26

E27 Value of any non-qualifying investments and loans. *See Note 6 on page 2 of these Pages*  E27 £

E28 Number of subsidiary or associated companies the Charity controls at the end of the period  E28

**What to do when you have completed these *Supplementary Pages***

*Follow the advice shown under 'What to do when you have completed the return' on page 2 of the form CT600.*

589

## Company Tax Returns and Guidance Notes

CT600F Supplementary Pages (2000)   1

## Company Tax Return Form
### Tonnage Tax Supplementary Pages
*For accounting periods beginning after 31 December 1999*

### Company information

**Company Name**

**Tax reference**
/       /

**Period covered by these** *Supplementary Pages* *(cannot exceed 12 months)*

**From** (dd/mm/yyyy)          **To**
/       /              /       /

You need to complete these *Supplementary Pages* if
- the company is a shipping company and a tonnage tax election has been made.

### Important points

- These *Supplementary Pages*, when completed, form part of the company's return.
- These *Pages* set out the information we need and provide a standard format.
- The notes on Page 4 will help you to complete this form.
- These *Pages* are covered by the *Declaration* you sign on page 1 of the form (CT600).
- The prosection warnings shown on the CT600 and the advice about late and incorrect returns also apply to these *Pages*.

### What to do when you have completed these *Supplementary Pages*

- Copy the figure from box F10 to box 145 in Section 4 of the form CT600.
- Include any figure from box F8 in box 61 in Section 4 of the form CT600.
- Follow the advice shown under 'What to do when you have completed the return' on page 2 of the form CT600.

CT600F Tonnage Tax Supplementary Pages                    BMSD 7/00

Note: This form is reproduced as in its final draft stage.

## Company Tax Returns and Guidance Notes

CT600F Supplementary Pages (2000)

### Part 1 Tonnage tax information for this period

You must complete this part if the company is calculating profits under the tonnage tax rules.

Put an 'X' in the appropriate boxes.

|  | Yes | No | Not applicable |
|---|---|---|---|
| **F1.** The company was party to a tonnage tax group election<br>*If the answer is 'yes' go to F2 and F3; otherwise go straight to F4.*<br>*See note 1.* | ☐ | ☐ | |
| **F2.** The tonnage tax group of which the company was a member was<br>*Only complete this question if you answered 'yes' to F1.*<br>*If during the period the company was a member of more than one tonnage tax group, show details on a separate sheet. See note 2.*<br>[                    ] | | | |
| **F3.** There was a group arrangement and the representative company was: *see note 2*<br>Name [                    ]<br>Tax reference [          ] | | | ☐ |
| **F4.** The company was covered by a training certificate under Paragraph 26 Sch 22 FA 2000<br>*See note 3.* | ☐ | ☐ | ☐ |
| **F5.** The company met the 75% limit on chartered-in tonnage<br>*If the company answered YES to F1, answer 'not applicable'.*<br>*See note 4.* | ☐ | ☐ | ☐ |
| **F6.** The group met the 75% limit on chartered-in tonnage<br>*Only complete this question if the company answered YES to F1.*<br>*You should answer 'not applicable' if the company is party to a group arrangement but is not the representative company*<br>*See note 4.* | ☐ | ☐ | ☐ |
| **F7.** The company is subject to the special rules in Part XI of Sch 22 FA 2000 for offshore activities<br>*See note 5.* | ☐ | ☐ | |

### Part 2 Offshore training allowance

*Only complete this part if you answered YES at F7 in Part 1*

**F8** The amount of training allowance to be offset against the corporation tax liability under paragraph 114(3) of Sch 22 FA 2000. *See note 6.*  **F8** £ [          ]

*Include the figure in box F8 in box 61 in Section 4 of the form CT600*

**F9** The amount of training allowance to be carried forward under paragraph 112(4) of Schedule 22 Finance Act 2000. *See note 6.*  £ [          ]

*Company Tax Returns and Guidance Notes*

CT600F Supplementary Pages (2000)

### Part 3  Computation of tonnage tax profits

**F10** - You must enter details of all qualifying ships. Use continuation sheets, set out in the same way, if necessary. *See note 7.*

| Name of ship | IMO number | Interest in ship* (O/F/T/G) | Net tonnage | Number of days operated | Tonnage tax profits** |
|---|---|---|---|---|---|
|  |  |  |  |  |  |
|  |  |  |  |  |  |
|  |  |  |  |  |  |
|  |  |  |  |  |  |
|  |  |  |  |  |  |
|  |  |  |  |  |  |
|  |  |  |  |  |  |
| | | | Amount from continuation sheet or schedule (if appropriate) | | |
| | | | | Total **F10** | £ |

* O - owned or bareboat chartered in (but not finance leased)

　F - finance leased

　T - chartered in otherwise than on bareboat terms, for example time charter or voyage charter

　G - chartered from another member of the same tonnage tax group

** calculated in accordance with Paragraph 4 Sch 22 FA 2000.
*See notes 9 and 10.*

*Copy the figure in box F10 to box 145 in Section 4 of the form CT600. See notes 7, 8 and 9.*

### Part 4  Relevant shipping profits - optional section

*Please provide information below about relevant shipping profits, that are replaced by the tonnage tax profits calculation. See note 10.*

**F11** The profit or loss as shown in the company's accounts, other than non-tonnage profit or loss included elsewhere on the return and profit or loss on disposal of tonnage tax assets included below.

　　Profit £ ___  Loss £ ___

**F12** The profit or loss shown in the company's accounts in respect of the disposal of tonnage tax assets, which would otherwise be computed under the capital gains tax rules.

　　Profit £ ___  Loss £ ___

**F13** The gross dividends qualifying as relevant shipping income under Paragraph 49 of Sch 22 FA 2000, instead of under Sch D Case V.

　　Dividend £ ___

# Company Tax Returns and Guidance Notes

## Notes

### 1 Tonnage Tax Group Election

A tonnage tax group election must be made jointly by all qualifying companies in the group.

### 2 Group Arrangement & Representative Company

The qualifying companies in a group may nominate one group company to deal with those matters concerning tonnage tax that are more conveniently dealt with on a group-wide basis, including the 75% limit on chartered-in tonnage.

Where a group wishes to make such an arrangement, all qualifying companies should jointly sign a letter nominating one of the companies as the representative company and specifying the matters that it will handle on behalf of the whole group.

### 3 Training Commitment

A company or group electing into tonnage tax (or renewing its election) must have a current certificate from the DETR confirming approval of its initial or annual training commitment.

### 4 Chartering-in Limit

Not more than 75% of the net tonnage of the company's qualifying vessels should relate to ships that are chartered in, other than on bareboat terms.

For groups, the 75% limit relates to the net tonnage of qualifying ships in the group, ignoring chartering between group members.

As ships will often be operated for less than a full accounting period, the percentage will need to be computed by reference to the aggregate daily net tonnage for the company or group.

See paragraphs 37- 40 of Schedule 22 Finance Act 2000 for more information on the 75% limit.

### 5 Offshore Activities

These activities cover the exploration or exploitation of the seabed, subsoil, or natural resources in the UK sector of the continental shelf.

They do not apply to offshore supply vessels, tugs, anchor-handling vessels, and tankers (other than dedicated to a particular oil field), or where the company's ships are engaged on offshore activities for a period that does not exceed 30 days in total. Part XI applies only to companies that have vessels engaged in offshore activities in the UK sector of the continental shelf and which are not excluded under paragraph 105 of Schedule 22 Finance Act 2000.

### 6 Training Allowance (Offshore)

A company that falls within Part XI of Schedule 22 FA2000 is allowed to offset the cash equivalent of training or any payments in lieu of training against its corporation tax liability on its profits from offshore activities.

The cash equivalent is based on the current rate of payments in lieu of training (PILOT). The deduction is the sum of the cash equivalent amounts of training undertaken and any PILOTs made, relating to days on which each ship was engaged in offshore activities in the UK sector.

### 7 Qualifying Ships

A qualifying ship must be a seagoing ship of 100 gross tons or more used for the carriage of passengers or cargo, towage, salvage or other marine assistance, or transport in connection with other services of a kind necessarily provided at sea.

Specifically excluded are fishing vessels or factory ships, pleasure craft, harbour or river ferries, offshore installations, tankers dedicated to a particular oil field and dredgers.

### 8 Operation of a Ship

A qualifying ship is operated by a company when it is owned by or chartered to that company. It is not regarded as operated where it is bareboat chartered-out, unless to a fellow group member, or to the Crown, or where there is short-term over-capacity and the charter does not exceed three years.

### 9 Computation of Profits

Profits are calculated by multiplying the daily profit for each ship by the number of days that each was operated during the accounting period. The daily profit is calculated for every 100 net tons, as in the following example:

Ship of 30,099 net tons:

| | |
|---|---|
| Up to 1000 | $10 \times £0.60 = £6.00$ |
| 1,001 – 10,000 | $90 \times £0.45 = £40.50$ |
| 10,001 – 25,000 | $150 \times £0.30 = £45.00$ |
| above 25,000 | $50 \times £0.15 = £7.50$ |
| | Daily Profit = **£99.00** |

No relief, deduction, or set off can be used to reduce the tonnage tax profits.

### 10 Relevant Shipping Profits

Tonnage tax profits replace relevant shipping profits. Broadly, these are the relevant shipping income from tonnage tax activities, including distributions from overseas shipping companies, plus chargeable gains on tonnage tax assets.

Tonnage tax activities include core qualifying activities, qualifying secondary activities, and qualifying incidental activities. For more details and guidance see

- Part VI Schedule 22 Finance Act 2000
- Tonnage Tax Regulations 2000
- Inland Revenue Statement of Practice on Tonnage Tax

CT600G – Corporate Venturing Scheme Supplementary Pages
At the time of going to press, this form was in an early draft stage and is not reproduced.

*Appendix 9*

# Information and Advice – COP 10

**Note:** Page references in this appendix are to the leaflet containing the code of practice.

**Introduction**

This Code of Practice tells you about the different ways that the Inland Revenue will give you information or advice. We aim to help you to understand your rights and obligations so that you can get your tax affairs right and pay your tax on time.

In this Code of Practice we set out the different ways that we can help you by:

- providing general advice
- publishing a variety of information
- answering Open Government requests for information
- giving 'post-transaction rulings'
- checking valuations of assets disposed of by individuals
- providing our interpretation of tax law in some circumstances
- giving statutory clearances and approvals for certain types of transactions

Some of the ways that we give information and advice will only be relevant to taxpayers with complex affairs. But we aim to be as helpful as we can to all taxpayers whether their tax affairs are simple or complex.

**General advice**

You can discuss your tax affairs or get tax information at any Tax Office or at one of the many Tax Enquiry Centres (TECs) located around the country. We will answer your questions on your rights and obligations on direct taxation, and give information to help you with returns, claims to reliefs, repayments and appeals.

If you prefer to telephone, you will find a name and telephone number on all correspondence from us, or you can find our telephone number, and address, under 'Inland Revenue' in the local telephone directory.

If you need help on Self Assessment, contact your local Tax Office or, in the evening or at weekends, our helpline, on 0645 000 444. Helpline calls are charged at local rates.

*Information and Advice – COP 10*

We publish a wide range of leaflets that explain different aspects of the tax system. See the section under 'Published information' on pages 3–5.

**Published information**

As well as detailed notes on the completion of tax returns, we publish tax information in the following ways:

*Explanatory Leaflets*

We produce a wide range of leaflets, booklets and helpsheets designed to explain different aspects of the tax system in plain English, and to assist with completing tax returns. Most of them are free.

Our IR List 'Catalogue of leaflets and booklets' gives further information about our publications, most of which you can get from any Tax Enquiry Centre or Tax Office. Addresses are in your local phone book under 'Inland Revenue'. Most offices are open to the public from 8.30 am to 4.30 pm, Monday to Friday, and some are also open outside these hours. Your local library or Citizens' Advice Bureau may also have copies of our leaflets. Many leaflets are also available on the Internet at:

http://www.open.gov.uk/inrev/irleaf.htm

If you need one of the leaflets mentioned in the Self Assessment tax return guide you can contact the Self Assessment Orderline. As well as leaflets, the Orderline can supply supplementary pages to the Self Assessment return, helpsheets and other forms mentioned in the Self Assessment tax return guide. The Orderline operates from 8 am to 10 pm every day except Christmas Day and can be reached:

- by telephoning 0645 000 404 (this number has a minicom facility)
- by writing to PO Box 37, St Austell, Cornwall PL25 5YN
- by sending a fax to 0645 000 604
- by e-mail on saorderline.ir@gtnet.gov.uk
- from abroad by telephone on 44 541 555 664 or fax to 44 541 555 778

United Kingdom calls to the Orderline are charged at local rates.

In addition, the Inland Revenue Education Service provides free material about income tax. It is suitable for teachers to use with 15 and 16 year old pupils, and includes a teacher resource pack and video. Further details can be obtained from: The Inland Revenue Education Service, PO Box 10, Wetherby, West Yorkshire LS23 7EH.

*Statements of practice*

Statements of Practice are published from time to time to explain our interpretation of legislation and the way we apply the law in practice. The full text of all current Statements is published in our booklet IR 131 which is annually

## Information and Advice – COP 10

updated by supplement or revision. It is available free of charge from the Orderline or any Tax Enquiry Centre, Tax Office or the Inland Revenue Information Centre, Ground Floor, South West Wing, Bush House, Strand, London WC2B 4RD.

*Extra-statutory concessions*

We also publish extra-statutory concessions. These are relaxations that give a reduction in tax liability that you would not be entitled to under the strict letter of the law. The full text of all current concessions is published in our booklet IR1 which is annually updated by supplement or revision. It is also available free from the Orderline or any Tax Enquiry Centre, Tax Office or the Inland Revenue Information Centre.

*Press releases*

We issue Press releases to announce a proposed change in the law, a change in our practice or some other change or initiative of interest to the public. You can obtain copies of our Press Releases free from the Inland Revenue Information Centre. Or you can make an annual subscription so that you automatically receive Press Releases when they are issued. Details are available from Tolley Publishing (Customer Services) 020 8686 9141.

*Tax bulletin*

Tax Bulletin is published every two months to inform tax practitioners of matters of technical interest, including our interpretation of aspects of tax law. It offers some insight into the thinking of our technical specialists, but does not replace formal Statements of Practice. Tax Bulletin can be obtained on subscription (currently £20 per annum) from Room 426, 22 Kingsway, London WC2B 6NR.

*Guidance manuals*

We publish the internal guidance manuals our staff use. These manuals cover the interpretation of tax law and the operation of the tax system. From the manuals, taxpayers and their professional advisers may gain a better understanding of how we determine tax liabilities and collect tax due. The published manuals omit some material which is covered by the exemptions in the Government's *Code of Practice on Access to Government Information*. The manuals are available for reference in Tax Enquiry Centres or can be bought from Tolley Publishing (Customer Services) 020 8686 9141 in either loose leaf form or on CD ROM.

*Inland Revenue web site*

The Inland Revenue web site has up to date information on a wide range of topics. Among other things, the site has copies of many of our leaflets, Inland Revenue Press Releases from 1995 onwards (available on the day after publication), Tax Bulletin and items of current interest such as consultative documents. The site also has general information about the Inland Revenue. Extra-Statutory Concessions and Statements of Practice from 1995 onwards are available with the relevant Press Release announcing their publication. The Inland Revenue web site is at http://www.open.gov.uk/inrev/irhome.htm

**Open Government**

We are committed to providing information in accordance with the Government's *Code of Practice on Access to Government Information*. In addition to published information, we will meet requests for information about our actions and decisions and about Government policy on Inland Revenue taxes. In particular, we will generally meet requests for information on our interpretation of tax law where:

- we have a settled view
- disclosure would not assist tax avoidance or evasion.

But we will not meet requests where it is in the public interest for the information to remain confidential in accordance with the Government Code.

You will normally have to pay the cost of any extra work we have to do to handle your request. Our leaflet IR 141 *Open Government* explains how you can obtain information under the above Code, that there are some circumstances where information will not be given and when there will be a charge. Page 3 of this leaflet tells you how you can obtain a copy of IR 141 or any of our other leaflets.

**Post-Transaction Rulings**

A post-transaction ruling is a ruling by the Inland Revenue on the application of tax law to a specific transaction after that transaction has taken place. Our aim in giving rulings is to help you to complete your return and know how much tax you are due to pay. You can ask for a ruling that covers Income Tax, Capital Gains Tax, Corporation Tax or Petroleum Revenue Tax, but not Inheritance Tax or Stamp Duty which are outside the scheme. We will usually consider ourselves bound by a post-transaction ruling unless the information you gave us when you applied for the ruling was incorrect or incomplete. The circumstances when we will consider ourselves bound are explained more fully below.

Post-transaction rulings are not intended to replace the general advice you can ask for as described on page 2 of this Code of Practice. You cannot ask for a post-transaction ruling unless the tax treatment of the particular transaction is in doubt, for example, if it was an unusual transaction or one you entered into in unusual circumstances. If you do apply for a post-transaction ruling then it may involve you as well as us in a lot of work. You can apply for a post-transaction ruling whether or not you have a professional adviser.

We will not give a post-transaction ruling in the particular circumstances or in respect of the particular issues which are set out in Appendix 2. As well as these exclusions, we will not give a post-transaction ruling where, in our view, we could not resolve the issue before the filing date for the relevant return without an unreasonable diversion of our resources.

## Information and Advice – COP 10

*When and how should you ask for a post-transaction ruling?*

You can apply for a post-transaction ruling at any time after you have completed the transaction in question. If we have sent you a tax return there are different dates by which you must apply for a post-transaction ruling.

- If we have sent you a Self Assessment tax return you can ask for a post-transaction ruling before or after you have filed your return;
- if the return we have sent is not a Self Assessment return (for example a Corporation Tax return for periods ending before 1 July 1999) you cannot apply for a post-transaction ruling after you have filed your return.

After a Self Assessment return is filed, we will only give a ruling up to the date that we can no longer enquire into that return. And we will not give a post-transaction ruling that you apply for after a Self Assessment return is filed if the issue is unlikely to be resolved quickly.

An application for a post-transaction ruling should be made to the Tax Office that deals with your tax affairs. Your application must set out all relevant facts. We will not consider ourselves to be bound by a post-transaction ruling if the application or supporting information was incorrect or incomplete. Your application for a ruling should include the information set out in Appendix 1. If you are uncertain about what to include in your application for a post-transaction ruling, contact your Tax Office.

*The extent to which we are bound by a post-transaction ruling*

When we have given you a post-transaction ruling you can act on the basis of the treatment set out in the ruling, for example, when completing a return. We will not withdraw the ruling if the interpretation of the law on which the tax treatment rests is discovered to be incorrect: for example, following a subsequent Court decision. But if Parliament changes the law applying to the transaction in question after we have given the ruling, then we will no longer be bound by our ruling. Apart from changes in the law, we will only withdraw a ruling if we discover that the information you gave us on application, or during subsequent correspondence, was either incorrect or incomplete.

A post-transaction ruling will only apply to you and to the particular transaction that was the subject of your application and for the year for which you applied for the ruling. You will not be able to rely on a ruling you were given for a different transaction, even though the circumstances might appear to be similar. Nor can you rely on a ruling that we have given to someone else for a transaction that you consider to be the same as your own.

We will not discuss a post-transaction ruling we have given and you cannot appeal against it. But you do not have to accept the ruling and you can still act on the basis of your own view of the appropriate tax treatment, for example, when completing your return. You should say that you have received a post-transaction ruling when you send in your return and whether you followed the ruling in completing your return. If you disagree with a post-transaction ruling and have completed your return in accordance with your view of the correct tax treatment, then we will deal with the difference of opinion when we check your return. If the

## Information and Advice – COP 10

difference cannot be resolved you will be able to appeal against the Revenue's assessment or amendment of your Self Assessment in the usual way.

*The effect of a post-transaction ruling on interest and penalties*

If you have applied for a post-transaction ruling, but not received it by the time that your return is due to be submitted, then your return must still be sent in before the time limit. If that happens you should complete your return according to your own view of the correct tax treatment of the particular transaction. If you have filed a Self Assessment return you can amend it after we have given the ruling, if you wish, subject to the normal time limits.

If you disagree with the post-transaction ruling that we gave you and complete your return in accordance with your own view of the proper tax treatment, then it may turn out that you have not paid enough tax at the right time. Any unpaid tax would carry interest from the due date regardless of whether you have applied for a post-transaction ruling or whether we have given a ruling by the due date. In the same way, any tax overpaid would carry repayment interest from the date it was paid.

If your return was incorrect because of your fraudulent or negligent conduct, then penalties will be chargeable in the normal way even in a post-transaction ruling had been sought for the incorrect item.

*Post-transaction valuation checks for capital gains tax*

This service is available to individuals who need to value assets to work out their capital gains tax liability. Further details of the service, which is free, are in leaflet CGT 14.

**Information and guidance on our interpretation of tax law**

If you are uncertain about the Inland Revenue's interpretation of the law (including its application to a proposed transaction) we will advise you if your query is in the following categories:

- the interpretation of legislation passed in the last four Finance Acts;
- the application of double taxation agreements;
- whether someone is employed or self employed;
- Statements of Practice and extra-statutory concessions;
- other areas concerning matters of major public interest in an industry or in the financial sector.

However, we will not help with tax planning, or advise on transactions designed to avoid or reduce the tax charge which might otherwise be expected to arise. And your query must arise from genuine uncertainty about the meaning of the law.

In other circumstances we may meet requests for general information about our interpretation of tax law under the 'Code of Practice on Access to Government

## Information and Advice – COP 10

Information', but you will normally have to pay a small charge. Further details are given in the section on page 6 entitled '*Open Government*'.

*How should you ask for information and guidance on our interpretation of the law?*

You should normally make your request in writing to the Tax Office dealing with your affairs. If you know that our Head Office has been considering the matter, you should say so – or write to Head Office direct. If your request relates to a specific transaction, see the next section. If your query is whether someone is employed or self employed, each Tax Office has a nominated status officer who deals with any enquiries and requests for decisions concerning employment status.

If your question concerns a specialist area of taxation that is not dealt with in local Tax Offices, such as Petroleum Revenue Tax, you should send it to the appropriate specialist Inland Revenue office. Details (including addresses) of these are given in Appendix 3.

*Advice on the application of the law to a specific transaction*

The local Tax Office can usually provide a leaflet or general information about the transaction you have in mind. this may be sufficient for your purposes. On the other hand, you may want more specific guidance on how the transaction would be taxed.

If you are seeking guidance on the application of the law to a specific proposed transaction that falls within the categories at the beginning of this section, your query should be sent to the Tax Office that deals with your affairs (or Head Office in appropriate cases). Your request should give the information described in Appendix 1; this is essential and enables you to rely on the advice we give, if the proposed transactions are carried out exactly as described.

*The extent to which advice on a proposed transaction is binding on us*

We will advise on the basis of our current understanding of the law. If there is a change in the law (either by legislation or court decision) before you irrevocably enter into the transaction, the advice may no longer be correct and you will not be able to rely on it. The same applies to any change in our view of the law, provided that, before the transaction is irrevocably entered into, either the change had been made public, or you had been told about it. If there has been a significant passage of time since you obtained the advice, you should ask us whether the relevant legislation, or our interpretation of it, has changed before you undertake the transaction. If the transaction in question will have tax consequences in more than one year then, following a change in the law, we will not go back and withdraw treatment already given. But that treatment would not be given following the change in the law.

Subject to the above, you can rely on our advice if your application sets out all the relevant facts and draws attention to all the issues (including questions of interpretation of the law) relevant to the point upon which you are seeking advice. In this regard, Judges have said that the applicant must put 'all his cards face upwards on the table'. The term 'relevant' should be interpreted broadly. It can be taken as including any transactions (proposed or actual) related to, or consequent upon, the transaction upon which advice is sought. If you are in any doubt about whether a particular item is relevant you should tell us about it.

**Time limit for replies**

Where you have asked for a post-transaction ruling or information and guidance on our interpretation of tax law, we will aim to provide a substantive reply within 28 days. However, where difficult or complicated issues are involved, it may not be possible for us to respond fully in that time. If this is the case, we will acknowledge your letter and tell you when you can expect a reply.

**Statutory clearances**

In some circumstances the law entitles you to apply for advance rulings about the tax effect of certain transactions. Details of these, including the address where applications for the clearance should be sent, are given in Appendix 4.

**Statutory approvals**

In some circumstances we also grant statutory approval to contractual or other arrangements. Details of these are given in Appendix 5.

**Suggestions**

If you would like to suggest any changes to the way that we give information and advice, or if you have any comments about this Code of Practice, please write to us at: Inland Revenue, Business Profits Division 5 (Advice), Room 431, 22 Kingsway, London WC2B 6NR.

**Complaints**

If you have a complaint about the information or advice that we have given, or about our refusal to give the information or advice that you have requested, please write to the Officer in Charge of your Tax Office. If you are not satisfied with their response, ask for leaflet IR 120 *You and the Inland Revenue*, which tells you how you can take your complaint further.

*Appendix 1 Information to be supplied:*

- when you apply for a post-transaction ruling
- when you ask for information and guidance on our interpretation of tax law

Your request should begin with a simple explanation of your problem. You should also include a description of the economic and commercial background to

## Information and Advice – COP 10

the particular transaction where it will help us to understand it. If you have identified more than one possible way to treat the transaction for tax purposes, you should explain the practical consequences of each. Your request should then go on to give a technical analysis that is sufficiently detailed for us to fully understand the facts and problem that you wish us to consider.

The following information must be included with your request:

- your name and tax reference number;
- full particulars of the transaction or event in question;
- copies of all relevant documents with the relevant parts or passages identified;
- your opinion of the tax consequences of the particular transaction;
- your explanation of the particular point(s) of difficulty that led to your request;
- details of what sections of the Taxes Acts you consider to be relevant;
- particulars of any case law, Inland Revenue extra-statutory concessions or Statements of Practice you consider to be relevant;
- your reasons for your opinion of the tax consequences of the transaction.

If you are applying for a post-transaction ruling we will interpret the last three categories flexibly in the light of circumstances and the ruling you have applied for.

In addition to the above you must give the following information:

If you are asking for a post-transaction ruling:

- the date that the transaction in question took place;
- details of the particular aspect(s) of the transaction that you want a ruling on;
- your statement that, to the best of your knowledge and belief, the facts you have given are correct and all relevant facts have been disclosed.

If you are asking for information and guidance on our interpretation of tax law:

- full details, including tax reference numbers, of any other parties involved;
- make it clear that you are seeking considered guidance and say how you intend to use the advice, for example by publishing it.

*Appendix 2 Circumstances when we will not give a post-transaction ruling and issues we will not rule on*

- on asset valuations or other issues that do not involve the interpretation of tax law or its application to particular circumstances; (if you need the value of an asset checked so you can calculate your capital gains tax then you should ask your Tax Office for form CG34);

- in response to vexatious or frivolous applications;
- in response to applications that do not involve genuine points of doubt or difficulty to you or (if you have one) your professional adviser;
- in respect of transactions which, in our view, may have been undertaken with the purpose of avoiding tax;
- in respect of the application of TA 1988 s 703 (which has its own facility for post-transaction rulings);
- in relation to the tax consequences of executing non-charitable trust deeds or settlements, and whether TA 1988 Part XV applies;
- after an enquiry into your Self Assessment is opened or after the time limit has passed for an officer of the Board to notify you of his or her intention to begin an enquiry;
- where the period in question is the subject of any other enquiry by the Revenue.

*Appendix 3 Specialist areas of taxation dealt with away from Tax Offices*

*Capital Taxes Office (England, Wales & Northern Ireland)*
For enquiries on inheritance tax other than in Scotland:
The Capital Taxes Office
Ferrers House
PO Box 38
Castle Meadow Road
Nottingham NG2 1BB
0115 974–2400
or
The Capital Taxes Office
Dorchester House
52–58 Great Victoria Street
Belfast BT2 7QL
01232 315556

*Capital Taxes Office (Scotland)*
For enquiries on inheritance tax in Scotland:
The Capital Taxes Office
Mulberry House
16 Picardy Place
Edinburgh EH1 3NB
0131 556 8511

*Financial Intermediaries and Claims Office (FICO)*
For enquiries on the schemes for tax relief and deduction at source, the tax rules applying to charities (in England, Wales and Northern Ireland), non-resident trusts and offshore funds:
Financial Intermediaries and Claims Office
St John's House
Merton Road
Bootle
Merseyside L69 9BB
0151 472 6000

## Information and Advice – COP 10

For enquiries on the tax rules applying to charities (in Scotland) and the estates of deceased persons:
Financial Intermediaries and Claims Office
Trinity Park House
South Trinity Road
Edinburgh EH5 3SD
0131 552 6255

For enquiries on the reliefs and exemptions available under Double Taxation Agreements:
Financial Intermediaries and Claims Office
Fitz Roy House
PO Box 46
Nottingham NG2 1BD
0115 974 2000

*Oil Taxation Office*
For enquiries on the taxation of oil companies:
Oil Taxation Office
Melbourne House
Aldwych
London WC2B 4LL
020 7438 6358/6826

*Pension Schemes Office*
For enquiries on the tax rules affecting pension schemes:
Pension Schemes Office
Inland Revenue
Yorke House
PO Box 62
Castle Meadow Road
Nottingham NG2 1BG
0115 974 1600

*The Profit-Related Pay Office*
For enquiries on profit-related pay:
The Profit-Related Pay Office
Inland Revenue
St Mungo's Road
Cumbernauld
Glasgow G70 5TR
01236 736 121

*The Stamp Office*
For enquiries on Stamp Duty:
Assistant Director, Technical
The Stamp Office
15th Floor
Cate Cross House
156 Pilgrim Street
Newcastle upon Tyne NE1 6TF
0191 245 0232

For enquiries on Stamp Duty Reserve Tax:
SDRT
The Stamp Office
Shares Unit

*Information and Advice – COP 10*

East Block
Barrington Road
Worthing BN12 4SE
01903 509467/509471

*Controlled foreign company legislation*
International Division 4 will advise on our interpretation of this legislation and will also provide clearances on whether controlled foreign companies meet either the 'exempt activities' or 'motive' tests. Written enquiries should be addressed to:
International Division 4
Room 311
Melbourne House
Aldwych
London WC2B 4LL


*Appendix 4 Clearance applications*

Details of statutory clearances available and where applications should be sent are as follows:

*Capital gains*

| | |
|---|---|
| Under TCGA 1992 s 138: | Share exchanges, company reconstructions or amalgamations. |
| Under TCGA 1992 s 139: | Company reconstructions or amalgamations involving a transfer of business. |
| Under TCGA 1992 s 140B: | Transfer of UK trade between companies resident in different European Union Member States. |
| Under TCGA 1992 s 140D: | Transfer of non-UK trade by UK company to company resident in different European Union Member State. |

Please send applications for clearance to:
Inland Revenue
Capital Gains Clearance Section
Sapphire House
550 Streetsbrook Road
Solihull
West Midlands B91 1QU

*Demergers*

| | |
|---|---|
| Under TA 1988 s 215(1): | For confirmation that the proposed division of the trading activities of a single company or group between two or more companies or groups will represent an exempt distribution for the purposes of TA 1988 s 213(2). |
| Under TA 1988 s 215(2), (3): | For confirmation that proposed payments will not be chargeable payments for the purposes of TA 1988 s 214. |

Please send applications for clearance to:
Inland Revenue
Central Correspondence Unit
New Wing
Somerset House
London SC2R 1LB

## Information and Advice – COP 10

*Company purchase of own shares*
Under TA 1988 s 225: For confirmation that a payment made on a purchase of own shares does not fall to be treated as a distribution for tax purposes.

Please send applications for clearance to:
Inland Revenue
Central Correspondence Unit
New Wing
Somerset House
London WC2R 1LB

*Transactions in securities*
Under TA 1988 s 707: Confirmation that provisions cancelling tax advantages obtained from certain transactions in securities (specified at TA 1988 s 704A–704E) will not apply.

Please send applications for clearance to:
Inland Revenue Section 703 Group
Special Investigations Section 2
3rd Floor, South West Wing
Bush House
Strand
London WC2R 4QN

*Company migrations*
Notices to be given under FA 1988 s 130(2)(a): Under this section a company intending to cease to be resident in the UK must first notify us and make acceptable arrangements for payment of all tax due for periods up to the date of the proposed migration.

Please send applications for clearance to:
Inland Revenue
International Division (Company Migrations)
Room 311
Melbourne House
Aldwych
London WC2B 4LL

*Transactions in land*
Under TA 1988 s 35: Confirmation of the taxpayer's view of the tax consequences of assigning a lease granted at under value.
Under TA 1988 s 776: Confirmation that TA 1988 s 776 does not apply to gains made from transactions in land.

Please send applications for clearance to the Inspector of Taxes who deals with your returns.

Where clearance is sought under more than one of TA 1988 ss 215, 225 and 707 in a single letter, applicants may send the letter to just one of the London addresses given above for clearances under those Sections, but should enclose an extra copy of the letter for each additional clearance sought.

*Information and Advice – COP 10*

*Appendix 5 Statutory approvals*

*Employee share schemes: profit sharing schemes, savings-related share option schemes and discretionary share option schemes*
TA 1988 Sch 9: Employee Share Schemes Unit
Inland Revenue
Savings and Investment Division
First Floor
South West Wing
Bush House
London WC2B 4RD

*Pensions: occupational pensions, personal pensions, public sector schemes, FSAVC schemes and ex-gratia relevant payments*
TA 1988 ss 590 and 591:
Pension Schemes Office
Inland Revenue
Yorke House
PO Box 62
Castle Meadow Road
Nottingham NG2 1BG

*Certification of qualifying life assurance policies*
TA 1988 Sch 15:
Insurance Group
Financial Institutions Division
5th Floor, 22 Kingsway
London WC2B 6NR

# Index

**A**
**Acceptable distribution policy (ADP)**
  controlled foreign companies 13.35–13.37
  intention to pursue 13.57
**Accountancy**
  taxable profits, relationship between App 1
**Accounting basis**
  change of 7.13
**Accounting period**
  apportionment of 2.2
  calculation of tax payable 2.33, 3.3
  carry back of surplus ACT 6.27, 6.28
  claims or elections affecting single 4.9
  definition 3.2
  ending on or after 1 July 1999 3.1 et seq.
  exchange fluctuations 2.19
  formal determination of losses 9.8
  notice to deliver a return 2.5
  payment of tax by instalments 5.43
  period of account, meaning 2.8
  straddling, definition 6.52, 6.63
**Accounting policy**
  changes of App 1
**Accounting principles**
  generally accepted 7.7–7.14, App 6
**Advance corporation tax**
  abolished from 6 April 1999 6.3
  anti-avoidance regulations 6.57–6.59
  carry back of surplus 6.27, 6.28
  change of ownership 6.47, 6.48 6.70
  collection procedures 6.24
  company in receipt of F11 6.20. 6.22, 6.23
  company tax return 2.18
  disadvantage of 6.2
  distributions
    non-qualifying 6.5–6.10
    qualifying, made before 6 April 1999 6.5–6.11
  foreign income dividends 6.43–6.46
  intra-group dividends 6.1
  late or non-submission of return 6.71
  legislative changes after abolition 6.49–6.51
  life assurance companies 6.72
  mainstream liability 6.1, 6.26
  maximum set off 6.26
  non-distributions 6.12
  non-payable tax credits 6.15–6.16
  payable tax credits 6.17–6.21
  penalties for late submission of return 6.71
  rate of 6.13, 6.14
  return of distributions form CT61 (Z) 6.22
  return periods for 6.22
  set off, against corporation tax 6.25, 6.26
  shadow 6.52–6.56
  shadow relief 2.18
  surplus 6.3
  surplus shadow, intra-group allocation of 6.66
  surrender claims
    amendments 6.36–6.37
    excess relief 6.40
    new procedure 6.33, 6.33–6.42
    self-assessments by subsidiary 6.40
    set off against mainstream corporation tax 6.38
    withdrawal of 6.36
  surrender of 6.29–6.32
  unrelieved surplus, set off 6.68, App 3
  utilisation of shadow 6.64
**Advance pricing agreements (APA)**
  basic statutory provisions 14.58
  company tax returns 2.50
  cross-border transfer pricing 2.50
  draft statement of practice App 5
  impact on non-parties 14.59
  Revenue practice 14.62
  revocation of 14.61
**Agricultural buildings allowances** 2.20
**Annual returns**
  letting agents 15.76
  tenants of non-resident landlords 15.89
**Annuities**
  company tax return 2.17
**Appeals**
  capital allowances, in relation to 19.4
  collection and recovery of tax 19.22, 19.23
  companies right of, to Commissioners 1.11
  controlled foreign companies 13.62
  determinations 19.6
  discovery assessments 19.6
  existing procedure 1.15
  General or Special Commissioners 19.11–19.13
  group relief, in relation to 19.4
  Lands tribunal 19.17
  penalties, against 19.7
  postponement of tax pending 19.21
  procedure on 19.20
  Revenue enquiries, substantive grounds in relation 19.2, 19.3

# Index

Revenue investigations, supervisory powers over 19.8
self-assessment, under 19.1
transfer pricing legislation 14.74
**Arbitration convention**
double taxation treaties 15.150
double taxation, elimination of 14.80–14.84
**Arm's length provision**
establishing 14.19
traditional methods 14.20–14.23
transactional profit methods 14.24
**Aspect enquiries**
Revenue powers of enquiry 17.13
**Assessments**
adjustment of 3.8–3.11
advance corporation tax (whilst still available) 3.3
amendments during Revenue enquiry 3.17
arithmetical mistakes 3.10
calculating tax payable 2.33, 3.3
company amends within twelve months 3.4, 3.8–3.11
computation mistakes 3.9
controlled foreign companies 1.4, 2.26, 3.3, 3.6
corporation tax returns 3.2–3.4
corrections to return 3.8–3.11
determination superceded by actual self-assessment 3.16
determinations by Revenue 3.12–3.16
discovery, by Revenue 3.4
double tax relief 3.3
double, relief for 3.22
enquiry commenced 3.4
error of principle 3.10
errors or omissions 3.4, 3.8–3.11
excessive 3.22–3.25
excessive repayments, recovery of 3.25
loans to participators 3.3, 3.5–3.6
negative amounts 3.7
notice of correction issued 3.11
overpayments of tax, recovering 3.20–3.21
quasi 3.1
relief in case of mistake in return 3.23–3.24
reliefs or set-offs available 3.3
Revenue determinations 3.12–3.16
Revenue make a correction 3.4, 3.8–3.11
self-assessment (*see also* Self-assessment) 3.2–3.4
time limits for Revenue 3.19
**Assets**
long-life 7.52
short-life 7.51
special classes of 7.49–7.62

**Assignments**
Schedule A business 7.78
**Associated companies**
qualification as large company 5.10
'growing companies' relief threshold, and 5.13

## B
**BAC (Bankers' Automated Clearing System)**
payment of tax 5.54
**Brokers**
definition of 15.26, 15.27
non-resident companies 15.25
**Business entertaining**
expenses 7.29

## C
**Capital allowances**
agricultural buildings 2.20, 7.59
appeals in relation to 19.4
capital assets
  acquisition 7.33
  depreciation and amortisation 7.33
cars 2.20, 7.50, 7.53
claim to quantify the amount claimed 4.32
claiming 7.35
claims by a company 4.32
claims for 2.20
commercial buildings 7.34
composite transactions 7.34
disposal value 7.48
dredging, expenditure on 7.60
enterprise zones 2.20, 7.40
expensive motor cars 7.50
first year allowances 2.20, 7.
given by reference to chargeable periods 7.37
holiday lettings 7.48
hotels 2.20. 7.42
industrial buildings and structures 2.20, 7.41
information and communications technology 7.37
know-how 7.36
local authority grants 7.34
long life assets 2.20, 7.52
machinery and plant 2.20, 7.37–7.39, 7.44–7.48
making claims for 7.63
mineral extraction 2.20, 7.58
non-trade 2.21
patents 2.20, 7.34, 7.39
qualifying expenditure 2.20, 7.45
qualifying hotels 7.40, 7.42
research and development 2.20, 7.34, 7.61
ships as special class of asset 7.49

609

# Index

short life assets 7.51
trade starts part way through accounting period 7.37
trading expense, deductible as 7.33
trading profits and losses, calculation of 2.20
writing-down allowances 7.37
**Capital assets**
acquisition of 7.33
depreciation and amortisation of 7.33
**Capital dividends**
distributions 6.6
**Capital gains**
allowable losses 8.15–8.17
business assets roll over relief 8.6–8.12
compulsory acquisition of land roll over relief 8.13–8.14
former discretionary powers of Revenue 8.2–8.4
payment of tax by instalments 8.5
premiums for leases 8.18, 8.19
scheme of reconstruction transfer to investment trust 8.20
valuations for CGT 8.21, 8.23
valuations, Revenue agreement post disposal 8.21, 8.22, App 1, App 6
**Capital gains tax**
liability determined by valuations 17.70
valuations for 8.21, 8.23
**Caravans**
rents from 7.74
**Cars**
costing less than £12, 000 7.53
expensive motor cars 7.50
**Cemetries**
amortisation relief 7.27
**CHAPS (Clearing House Automated Payment System)**
payment of tax method 5.54
**Chargeable gains**
inter group transfers made after 1 April 2000 11.28–11.43
rollover relief, disposal of business asset 11.34–11.35
**Charities**
arm's length provision 14.28
company tax returns 2.31
covenanted donations to 6.12
partial exemption from tax 2.32
transfer pricing 14.28
**Claims, elections and revisions**
affecting single accounting period 4.9
amendments to 4.16–4.17
amount available for surrender reduction in 4.28
background 4.1–4.3
capital allowances claims 4.32–4.33
changes to system, principal sections 4.39

consequential amendments 4.36
corrections procedure 4.16–4.17
Crown option 4.44
errors or mistakes, relief for 4.34, 4.35
estimates 4.11
four categories of claim under old system 4.37
general position 4.4
giving effect to claims 4.7–4.8
group relief claims 4.20–4.31
more than one accounting period 4.10
not in tax return, outline of procedure 4.12
outline of provisions 4.4–4.11
part of return 4.4
procedure for company claims 4.4
record keeping 4.15
repayment of income tax 4.5
Revenue enquiry, consequential claims after 4.40
Revenue powers of enquiry 4.18–4.19
single accounting period, affecting 4.9
stand alone claim 4.12
time limits 4.27
**Claims. elections and revisions**
double assessments, relief for 4.34, 4.35
**Close companies**
definition 7.66
expenses of 7.66
loans by 1.6
**Companies**
accounting periods ending on or after 1 July 1999 3.1 et seq.
accounting records where and for how long to be kept 16.13
associated 5.10
becoming large 5.12
business assets roll over relief 8.6–8.9
capital gains (see Capital gains) 8.1 et seq.
categories according to size 1.8
change of ownership before 6 April 1999 6.47
claims and elections 4.1 et seq.
close, loans by 1.6
compulsory self-assessment 1.7
controlled foreign (*see also* Controlled foreign companies) 1.4, 2.28
deemed 12.5, 12.11–12.13
dormant 2.5
double assessment 5.47
excessive repayments 5.50
failure to make a self-assessment 1.7
farming 7.28
foreign holding 15.130
fraud or neglect 1.12
group payment arrangements 5.27
indexation retained 8.1

610

# Index

investment 7.66–7.68
large, determination of size 5.8–5.10
mistake in tax returns 5.48
multi-national 6.2
non-resident (*see also* Non-resident companies) 2.5
non-resident (*see* Non-resident companies) ownership restrictions, change in 9.15–9.21
payment on account to replace ACT 6.3
period for retention of records 16.16
protection from risk of discovery assessments 17.58
recalcitrant 3.1
record keeping 1.9, 16.11–16.13
Revenue powers of enquiry and discovery 1.11–1.12
Schedule A income 1.10
Schedule A provisions 7.71
self-assessment
  amendment within twelve months 3.4
  background 1.1–1.2
  calculating tax payable, method 3.2–3.4
  discovery assessment 3.4
  pay and file, comparison with 1.3–1.4
  starting date for CTSA 1.2
  surplus ACT, allowed to continue under old system 6.3
  transfer of responsibility to 1.11
  transfer pricing (see Transfer pricing) 14.1 et seq.
UK resident
  surrender of ACT 6.29
valuation procedures 2.42–2.45

**Company reconstructions**
beneficial ownership 9.13
non-trading losses 9.11
ownership restrictions, change in 9.15–9.21
transfer of losses 9.9

**Company tax return (*see* Corporation tax return)**
definition of 2.34

**Computation of profits**
allowable expenses 7.25–7.32
assignments 7.78
capital allowances (*see also* Capital allowances) 7.33–7.65
capital expenditure 7.21
chargeable gains 7.10
claiming capital allowances 7.35
close companies 7.66
close investment holding company 7.66
company, definition of 7.3
disallowed expenses 7.15–7.32
expenses not allowed 7.15–7.24
general approach 7.1–7.6
income from land in UK
  Schedule A 7.69–7.71
  industrial building allowance 7.40–7.43
  investment companies (*see* Investment companies) 7.66–7.68
  lease premiums 7.76
  machinery and plant 7.44–7.48
  non-resident companies 7.73
Schedule A business
  accruals concept 7.81
  capital expenditure and allowances 7.91
  chargeable gains and reliefs 7.110–7.112
  land managed as one estate 7.105–7.107
  Schedule D case 1 Principles applied 7.81
  transitional provisions 7.95, 7.96
trading profits schedule D case 1
  generally accepted accounting principles 7.7–7.14
travel expenses 7.87

**Consortium relief**
claims for 11.11
estimating corporation tax payable 11.17
linked companies 11.11
subsidiaries 11.14

**Controlled foreign companies**
acceptable distribution policy (ADP) 13.35
accounting period, start of 13.21
accounting periods ending after 1 July 1999 13.3
appeals 13.62
apportionment 13.30–13.33
anti-avoidance, 'designer rate' provisions 13.19, App 6
calculation of charge 13.20–13.33
changes under CTSA 13.2
chargeable profits 13.26
clearances 13.54–13.56
company tax returns 2.28, 3.2–3.4
company, definition 13.7
compulsory self-assessment 13.48
control by UK residents 13.14
control test 13.15, 13.16
corporation tax liability 1.4
corporation tax return 13.49
creditable tax 13.29
determining whether a company is 13.7–13.13
double taxation relief App 6
enquiries 13.58
exemptions
  acceptable distribution policy 13.35
  excluded countries list 13.44, 13.45, App 3, App 4
  exempt activities 13.38

## Index

interest of less than 25 per cent 13.34
motive test 13.47
profits *de minimis* 13.43
public quotation 13.41
insurance companies 13.70
intention to pursue an ADP 13.57
just and reasonable apportionment 13.20
legislation introduced in 1984 1.13, 13.2
listing in corporation tax return 1.13
lower levels of taxation 13.17
outline of charge and exemptions 13.4, 13.5
penalties 13.61
persons interested 13.24
profits chargeable, to be self-assessed 1.13
publicly quoted 13.41
records 13.59
regulations App 3
reliefs 13.63–13.66
residence criteria 13.8
special recovery provisions 13.67
transitional provisions 13.68
**Copyright**
purchasers of 7.34
**Corporate partners**
corporation tax 12.2–12.4
**Corporation tax**
accounting principles, generally accepted 7.7
chargeability to 7.5
charged by reference to accounting period 7.5
company, definition 7.3
computation of profits (*see* Computation of profits 7.1–7.6
connected persons rule 7.4
consortium relief 11.17
controlled foreign companies 1.4, 1.13, 2.28, 3.3, 3.6
corporate partners 12.2–12.4
different rates of tax for different income 2.19
expenses not allowed 7.15–7.24
filing of return 1.6
finality and certainty 17.1, 17.2
furnished holiday lettings 7.71, 7.74
furnished lettings 7.74
group and consortium relief 1.6
group payment arrangements App 1, App 2
instalment payment regulations App 4
interest on tax paid late (*see* Interest) 18.3
liability to 7.2
loans relationships 10.1
non-resident companies 7.73

notices and returns (*see* Notices and returns)
notification of chargeability 2.3
pay and file, comparison with 1.3–1.4
payment of 1.8
payment provisions 1.8
rates for
  financial years 1997, 1998 7.5
  financial years 1999, 2000, 2001 7.6
receipts charged 7.74
redesigned tax return, form CT600 1.5
rents from caravans 7.74
Revenue determinations 1.7, 3.12–3.19
Revenue powers of enquiry 17.3
tax return, redesigned (form CT600) 1.5
transfer pricing legislation 1.4, 1.6, 1.14
unpaid on due date, interest charged 18.1
unrelieved surplus ACT
  regulations App 4
**Corporation tax return**
accounting period ending on or after 1 July 1999 3.1 et seq.
adjustment of 3.8–3.11
advance corporation tax (whist still available) 2.18
advance price agreements 2.50
allowable losses 8.15–8.17
amendment to assessment during enquiry 3.17
amendments 3.8–3.11, 3.17, 17.43
annual payments 2.17
annuities 2.17
arithmetical mistakes 3.10
balancing charges 2.20
calculation of tax payable 2.33
capital allowances, claims for 2.20
chargeable gains 2.36
charities 2.15, 2.32
claim included in return 4.4
code of practice for enquiries App 6
company accounts submitted 2.13
company information summary 2.13
computation mistakes 3.9
controlled foreign companies 13.43
core return form CT600 2.12–2.23
Corporate Venturing Scheme 2.15
corporation tax chargeable 2.18
corrections 3.8–3.11
detailed calculation 2.19
detailed computations required 2.20
determinations by Revenue 3.12–3.19
directors and auditors' reports 2.14
directors' remuneration 2.23
discovery assessments 3.4, 3.18, 17.49–17.52
double assessments, relief for 3.22
electronic lodgement system, not available 2.9

# Index

enquiry commenced 3.4, 3.17, App 6
error of principle 3.10
errors or omissions 3.4
estimates 2.40–2.41, 4.11
excessive assessments 3.22–3.25
excessive repayments, recovery of 3.25
failure to file, penalties 18.25
false information, warning against 2.13
finality and certainty 17.1, 17.2
financial instruments brought forward 2.19
first year allowances 2.15
foreign income dividends 2.20
form of return 2.9–2.11, App 1, App 6
gifts and donations 2.15
groups and consortiums 2.29
guidance notes App 7
incorrect or uncorrected return 18.29–18.31
information required from different companies 2.9
insurance companies 2.31
intra group income 2.19
loans to participators by close companies 2.24, 3.5
losses 3.7
non-resident companies 2.5
notice of consent 4.25
notice of correction issued 3.11
notice to deliver a return 2.5
notification of chargeability 2.3
overpayment of tax, assessment to recover 3.20
overpayments 2.22
overseas income 2.19
partnership statements 2.35
period covered 2.5
post transaction rulings 2.52
pre transaction clearances 2.51
pre-transaction rulings 2.46
profits and gains
   non-trading loan relationships 2.17
provisional figures 2.41
qualifying expenditure 2.20
relief, error or mistake 3.23
repayment claims 2.22
Revenue determinations 3.12–3.16
roll over relief 8.6–8.9
rulings and clearances 2.46–2.52
self-assessment by liquidator 2.53
self-assessment of tax payable 2.10–2.11
short calculation 2.16
statutory requirements 2.39
supplementary pages 2.15, 2.24
surpluses 2.21
time limit for amending 4.27
time limits for Revenue 3.19
tonnage tax, shipping companies 2.15
trading profits and losses, calculation of 2.20
transfer pricing legislation 14.45
turnover of company 2.15
valuations 2.42–2.45
**Counselling services**
   deductible expenses 7.29
**Credit interest**
   early paid tax and overpaid instalments 18.16
**Crime**
   expenditure involving 7.29
**Crown option**
   provisions of 4.45
**Currency contracts**
   interest rates 10.54

# D

**Debit interest**
   late and inadequate instalment payment 18.15
**Determinations**
   appeals in relation to 19.6
   discovery assessments 3.38
   failure to file tax return 3.12–3.15
   outstanding periods 3.14
   reasons for 3.12
   Revenue powers 3.12–3.16
   superceded by actual self-assessment 3.16
   time limits 3.12–3.14, 3.19
   transfer pricing legislation 14.72
**Directors**
   remuneration of 2.23
**Directors' remuneration**
   excessive, disallowed 7.31
**Disclosure**
   loans relationships 10.12–10.16
**Discovery assessments**
   appeals in relation to 19.6
   background 17.48
   corporation tax return 3.4
   previous rules relating to 17.49–17.52
   under self-assessment 17.53–17.68
**Distributions**
   benefits given by close company 6.11
   definition for tax purposes 6.6
   discretionary trusts, beneficiaries of 6.20
   dividends 6.6
   during winding-up, clearances 2.54
   non-payable tax credits 6.15
   non-qualifying 6.5
   qualifying, made before 6 April 1999 6.5
   repayment of share capital 6.10
   transfer of assets 6.9
**District enquiries**
   full review of return 17.15
**District valuer**
   valuations on company tax return 2.43

# Index

**Dividends**
  foreign income (*see* Foreign income dividends) 6.43
  non-payable tax credits 6.15
  payable tax credits 6.17
**Double assessments** 5.47
  relief for 3.22, 4.34, 4.35
**Double taxation**
  chargeable gains, tax payable on 15.136
  credit for corporation tax 15.122
  foreign holding companies 15.139
  foreign tax credits against UK taxes 15.134, 15.145–15.147
  foreign withholding taxes 15.123
  list of admissable taxes 15.132
  non-trading loan relationships 15.140
  OECD model tax convention 15.127
  provisional treaty relief scheme, gross interest payment 10.28
  relief
    dividend mixing prohibition 15.139
    royalties, special relationship payments 15.146
    time limits 15.144, 15.145, 15.152
  treaty relief 15.125–15.140
  underlying tax 15.141, 15.142
  unilateral relief 15.122–15.124, 15.134
**Double taxation treaties**
  anti-avoidance provisions 15.128
  mutual agreement procedure, Revenue's powers of adjustment 15.151
  provisions of 15.126
  relief available under 15.125, 15.128, 15.131, App 1
  royalties, special relationship provisions 15.146

## E
**E-commerce**
  business residence, determination of 15.114, 15.115, 15.120
  permanent establishment 15.119, 15.121, App 6
  taxation of, international co-operation 15.117, App 1
**Employee share ownership trusts**
  tax relief for contributions to 7.30
**Employee training courses**
  deductible expenses 7.29
**Enterprise zone allowances** 2.20
  buildings and structures in 7.40
**Excessive deductions**
  foreign tax adjustment after 21 March 2000 15.143
**Excessive repayments**
  recovery of 3.25

**Excluded countries list**
  controlled foreign companies, exemption 13.44
**Expenses**
  agents 7.25
  allowable 7.25–7.32
  business entertaining 7.29
  clothing 7.16
  Corporate Venturing Scheme, unlisted trading company investments 7.32
  counselling services 7.29
  deductible, test for deductibility 15.98
  duality of purpose 7.16
  establishing employee share ownership trusts 7.25
  food 7.16
  gifts to educational establishments 7.25
  housing grants 7.29
  improvements, capital element 7.22
  management 7.28
  medical treatment 7.16
  not allowed 7.15–7.24
  obtaining loan finance 7.25
  patent fees 7.25
  purpose of the trade 7.17, 7.18
  redundancy payments 7.26
  redundancy payments, statutory 7.32
  rent for dwelling house 7.17
  repairs to premises 7.18
  tied premises owned by brewers 7.28
  training courses for employees 7.29
  travel to furnished holiday lettings 7.87
  travelling 7.16
  unremittable overseas income 7.29
  woodland 7.28
**Export credit guarantee department**
  payments to 7.26

## F
**Farm profit averaging** 7.28
**Farming**
  losses, carry forward of 9.22–9.23
**Farming companies**
  herd basis 7.28
**Finance leases**
  capital allowances 7.39
**Financial institutions**
  loan relationships 10.18
**Foreign exchange gains and losses**
  anti-avoidance provisions 10.40–10.44, 10.51
  deferral of unrealised gains 10.45–10.53
  foreign currency, hedging 10.36
  legislation 10.30
  matched liabilities 10.39
  qualifying assets 10.33
  qualifying liability 10.33

# Index

sterling conversion for accounting purposes 10.48
trading gains and losses 10.31
**Foreign exchange legislation**
partnerships 12.40–12.47
**Foreign holding companies** 15.139
**Foreign income dividends**
advance corporation tax 6.43–6.46
company tax returns 2.20
qualification as 6.44
**Foreign partnership**
UK resident company in 12.26, 12.27
UK trade activities 12.29
**Foreign property**
letting of, by UK partnership 12.25
**Foreign trades**
partnerships 12.24
**Friendly societies**
repayments of tax 5.46
**Furnished holiday lettings**
letting as a trade 7.94
Schedule A provisions 7.71, 7.74
travel expenses to 7.87
**Furnished lettings**
wear and tear allowances 7.71, 7.74

## G
**General Commissioners**
appeals to, existing procedure 1.15
rules for assigning proceedings to 19.18
**Government authority grants**
net cost after, qualifies for capital allowances 7.34
**Group company arrangements**
outline of provisions 5.27, 5.28
**Group payment arrangements** App 1, App 2
eligibility 5.29, 5.30
entering into 5.31
nominated company 5.29
removal of companies from 5.32, 5.33
Revenue group payment team, duties of 5.28
termination 5.32
undertaking in the 5.34–5.36
**Group relief**
artificial groups created 11.4
beneficial ownership 11.3
claims (*see also* Group relief claims) 11.2
consortium relief, apportionment rules 11.13
constitution of a group 11.2
controlled foreign companies 11.17
disentitlement to 11.5
group relationship, tracing through non-residents 11.3

losses, surrender by UK branch of non-resident 11.6
restriction to results of UK trade 11.4
ring fence profits 11.2
simplified arrangements for 11.19–11.28, App 3, App 6
trading losses 11.6
UK resident companies and branches 11.3
**Group relief claims**
amendment by single authorised member 4.31
amount available for surrender claims for more or less than 4.23
excessive relief, assessments to recover 4.29
general provisions 4.20–4.222
joint amended returns 4.20
notice of consent 4.25–4.26
quantified amount 4.21
special arrangement 4.20
special arrangements, regulations for 4.30
time limits 4.27
**Groups of companies**
anti-avoidance, pre-entry losses 11.37, 11.38
assets held by company leaving group 11.39–11.41
member's unpaid corporation tax, liability for 11.42
membership, 51 per cent subsidiary 11.28, 11.43
payment of tax
eligibility to enter arrangement 5.29–5.30, App 2, App 6
entering into the arrangement 5.31
outline of arrangements 5.27, 5.28
termination of arrangement 5.32
undertaking in the arrangement 5.34–5.36

## H
**Herd basis**
farming companies 7.28
**Holiday lettings**
capital allowances 7.48
**Hotels**
capital allowances on 2.20
**Housing grants** 7.29

## I
**Income from land in the UK**
Schedule A
chains of letting agents 15.60
letting agents 15.57–15.65
non-resident companies 15.44
non-resident landlords 15.45–15.56
rental income 15.93

615

## Index

tenant finders 15.66
tenants of non-resident
 landlords 15.80–15.85
**Income tax**
non-resident companies 1.2
**Industrial building allowance**
balancing allowance 7.43
commercial buildings 7.40
qualifying hotels 7.40, 7.42
straight line writing down
 allowance 7.40
**Industrial buildings**
capital allowances 7.34, 7.41
Schedule A business 7.92
**Inheritance tax regulations** App 4
**Inland Revenue**
code of practice, information and
 advice App 9
**Insurance companies**
company tax returns 2.31
controlled foreign companies 13.70
management expenses 7.68
repayments of tax 5.46
**Intellectual property**
copyright royalties 15.111
UK patent, royalties from 15.111
**Interest**
ACT, late payment of 18.21
basic provisions 18.1, 18.2
chargeable on tax paid late 18.3–18.9
credit 18.16
debit 18.15
debit and credit, Revenue
 practice 18.18
income tax deducted from payments by
 a company 18.21
late payment 18.3–18.8
losses and deficits carried back
 computer treatment of 18.13
payable on tax repaid 18.9
penalties 18.41
rate setting arrangements,
 formulae 18.19
repayment 18.2
**Intra-group interest**
distributions, treated as App 1
**Investment companies**
close company 7.66
close investment holding company 7.66
definition 7.66
losses 9.32
management expenses, deduction
 for 7.67
**Investment income**
corporate partners 12.17
excluded income 15.109
old system 15.108

**Investment managers**
collective investment schemes 15.39
exemption from liability as agent 15.28
non-resident companies 15.28
not treated as UK representative 15.19,
 15.29
participating, 20 per cent rule 15.35

## J

**Joint ownership**
Schedule A business 7.104
**Joint venture**
minor children 12.6
original wording of definition 12.6
partnerships 12.6
sharing profits and losses
 relevance of 12.7–12.8

## L

**Land**
compulsory acquisition of
 roll over relief on 8.13
**Lands Tribunal**
appeals 19.17
**Large companies** (*See also* Associated
 companies)
claims for repayment, revision of
 estimates 5.22
corporation tax, payment of 1.8
due dates for instalments 5.14–5.15
excessive instalment payments
 intra-group surrender of 5.26
instalments, calculation of each 5.16
instalments, penalty for non-
 payment 18.37, App 1
payment of tax
 associated companies 5.10
 basic provisions 5.8–5.9
 quarterly instalments 5.1, 5.8, App 1,
 App 3
 qualifications needed to be 5.8–5.9
 short accounting periods 5.11
 total liability exceeds £10,000 5.8
 total liability, accounting periods ending
 before 1 July 2000 5.8
 transition period 5.12, 5.20
 upper relevant maximum amount 5.8
**Late filing penalties**
practical issues 18.27, 18.28
reasonable excuse 2.8, 18.39
**Late payment interest**
tax paid late, interest chargeable 18.3
**Lease premiums**
Schedule A business 7.76
**Leases**
premiums for 8.18
**Leasing trades**
losses 9.24–9.25

*Index*

**Letting agents**
annual returns 15.76
assessments to recover tax 15.75
branches of 15.61
calculation of payment of tax by 15.69
certificate to be provided by 15.78
chains of 15.60
change of 15.55
excess expenses 15.71
excluded persons 15.58
meaning of term 15.57
notices from FICO to operate scheme 15.65
record keeping and audit 15.105
registration 15.68
rental income 15.93–15.104
tenant finders 15.66
**Liquidation distributions** 6.12
**Lloyd's underwriters**
non-resident companies 15.41
**Loan relationships**
accruals basis 10.10
annual interest 10.26, 10.27
anti-avoidance rules 12.47
anti-avoidance provisions 10.9–10.11
application of, to partnerships App 4
brought forward trading losses 10.6
collective investment schemes 10.24
computations 10.8
convertible securities 10.23
debits and credits 10.1–10.8
definition 10.2
disclosure 10.12–10.16
financial institutions 10.18
Forex rules 10.9
general rules 10.1–10.8
legislation 10.1
mark to market basis 10.19
money debt 10.4
non-financial companies 10.17
non-trading deficit 10.5
normal accounting treatment 10.17–10.29
overseas sovereign debt 10.11
partnerships 12.40
trading 10.4
**Local authority grants**
net cost after, qualifies for capital allowances 7.34
**Long life assets**
company tax returns 2.20
**Losses**
accounting periods ending before 1 July 1999 9.8
carry back period 9.7
company reconstructions 9.9–9.21
company tax returns 3.7
computation of 9.1
farming 9.22–9.23

general provisions 9.1–9.8
investment companies 9.32
leasing trades 9.24–9.25
market gardening 9.22–9.23
ownership restrictions, change in 9.15–9.21
pre-trading expenditure 9.31
Schedule A 9.26–9.29
trading income 9.4
transactions in deposits 9.30
transfer pricing 14.16

**M**
**Machinery and plant**
acquired from connected parties 7.56
company tax returns 2.20
hire purchase, acquired on 7.54
plant, definitions 7.46
Schedule A business 7.93–7.95
short life assets 7.51
**Maintenance funds**
historic buildings 7.108, 7.109
**Market gardening**
losses, carry forward of 9.22–9.23
**Medium companies**
corporation tax, payment of 1.8
date for payment of tax 5.3

**N**
**Non-resident companies**
brokers 15.25
capital allowances 7.35
determining non-residency of company 15.2
double taxation treaties 15.3
income from land in the UK Schedule A 15.44
income tax self-assessment 1.2
independent agents 15.16–15.17
investment income 15.108
loan relationships debits and credits 10.17
member of Lloyd's underwriters 15.41
Schedule D, case VI 15.43
scope of trading activities 15.6
trade carried on partly in UK 15.7
trading in UK through a branch or agency 15.1
UK partnership 12.28
**Non-resident landlords**
application for rent to be paid gross 15.49
approval of application 15.51
chains of letting agents 15.60
changes of letting agent or tenant 15.55
deduction at source 15.56
knowledge of status of 15.48
non-resident landlord's scheme (NRLS) 15.46

617

## Index

refusal/withdrawal of approval 5.53
self-assessment 15.45, 15.107
tenants of 15.80–15.92
transfer pricing, implications for App 1
**Non-resident partners**
UK representative jointly liable for tax 15.14
**Non-residents**
persons not regular agents of 15.24
trading in the UK App 1
UK representatives of 15.10–15.13, 15.15
**Notice of correction**
issue of, by Revenue 3.11
**Notices and returns**
accounts, requirements of 2.34
chargeable gains 2.36
charities 2.12, 2.32
close companies, loans to participators by 2.12, 2.24
company tax return (*see also* Company tax return) 2.12–2.23
company tax return, notice to deliver 2.5, 2.6
controlled foreign companies 2.12, 2.28
deadline for filing a company tax return 2.7
deadline for notice of enquiry, return filed on time 17.4, App 1
estimates 2.40–2.41
filing date 2.7
form CT600
basic company tax return 2.12–2.23, 2.33, 2.36, 2.40
form CT600
A loans to participators by close companies 2.12, 2.24
form CT600B
controlled foreign companies 2.12, 2.28
form CT600C
group and consortium companies 2.12, 2.29–2.30
form CT600D
long term insurance business 2.12, 2.31
form CT600E
charities 2.12, 2.32
form CT603
notice to deliver 2.5
form of return 2.9–2.11
group and consortium companies 2.12, 2.29–2.30, 11.42
information, production of 2.35
insurance companies 2.12, 2.31
legislative background 2.1–2.2
loans to participators by close companies 2.12, 2.24
notification of chargeability 2.3–2.4

partnership statements 2.35
period covered 2.5, 2.6
period of account 2.8
production of information 2.35
rulings and clearances
advance pricing agreements 2.50
post transaction rulings 2.52
pre-transaction clearances 2.51
pre-transaction rulings 2.46–2.49
tax payable, calculation of 2.33
valuations 2.42–2.45

## O

**Oil and gas business**
transfer pricing 14.44
**Original master film, tape or disks**
production or acquisition of 7.55
**Overpayment of tax**
assessment to recover 3.21–3.21
repayment interest 18.3, 18.9, App 6
six year time limit 3.21
**Overseas funds**
in existence at 29 November 1994
grand-fathering arrangements 15.42
qualification for exemption 15.42
**Overseas income**
UK partnership 12.22
**Overseas trade**
partnerships 12.24

## P

**Partnership changes**
losses of limited partners 12.38
mergers 12.36
new rules 12.35–12.39
**Partnership statement**
Crown option 4.44, 4.45
**Partnerships**
allocation of profits 12.15–12.16
business, meaning of 12.21
changes, new rules 12.35–12.39
chargeable gains 12.34
commodity 9.30
corporate partners 12.2–12.4
deemed company 12.5, 12.11–12.13
deemed company, as 12.11–12.14
financial instruments legislation App 4
foreign exchange legislation 12.40–12.47, App 4
foreign trades and professions 12.24
foreign, with UK trade activities 12.29
fundamental changes under self assessment 12.1
income from land in the UK 12.31
income from let property overseas 12.25
intra-group loan relationship rules 12.44
investment income 12.17–12.19
joint investments 12.21
joint liability, no 12.1

*Index*

joint ventures 12.6
loan relationships 12.40
no separate taxable entity 12.10
non-resident company in UK
   partnership 12.28
non-resident partners 12.1
non-trading businesses 12.20
open-ended investment
   companies 12.42, 12.43
overseas income of UK
   partnership 12.22, 12.23
partners as notional sole traders 12.9
partnership statement 2.35
retiring partners 12.16
Schedule A business 7.103
sharing profits and losses
   relevance of 12.7, 12.8
true and fair accruals basis 12.15
UK investment income of non-resident
   partners 12.30
UK representative 12.32, 12.33
**Patent fees** 7.25
**Patents**
   capital allowances on 2.20
**Payment of tax**
   anti-avoidance 5.42–5.445
   Bank Giro, by 5.55
   Board's information powers 5.41, App 1
   changes under CTSA 5.1, 5.2
   cheque, by 5.53
   construction industry sub-
     contractors 5.57, 5.58, 5.64, App 1,
     App 6
   date for 5.3, 5.4
   double assessment 5.47
   effective date of 5.53
   electronic funds transfer, by 5.54
   Girobank, by 5.56
   group payment arrangements 5.27–5.36,
     App 1
   instalment payments
     adjustment for excess or
       underpayment 5.22, 5.23
     anti-avoidance 5.42–5.45
     calculation of 5.16
     deferring 5.42
     due date of 5.14
     estimates 5.40
     practical issues 5.37–5.39
     quarterly 5.40
   large companies (*see* Companies)
     basic provisions 5.8–5.9
   medium companies (*see also* Medium
     companies) 5.3–5.7
   methods 5.53–5.56
   personal service companies
     deemed Schedule E payments,
       calculation of 5.63
     deemed Schedule E payments,
       available relief 5.66, 5.67
     services provided via
       intermediary 5.59–5.61, App 1
   small companies (*see also* Small
     companies) 5.3–5.7
   transition period 5.20
**Penalties**
   company not retaining and preserving
     records 18.35, 18.36
   documents not produced during
     enquiry 18.32–18.34, App 1
   failure to file corporation tax
     return 18.25
   failure to notify Revenue of
     chargeability 18.23
   incorrect or uncorrected return 18.29–
     18.31
   instalment payments
     failure to provide information 18.38
   interest on 18.41, App 6
   late filing of return 18.25–18.28
   provisions relating to companies 18.22
   reasonable excuse for failure 18.39
   right of appeal 18.22
   tax related, time limit 18.40
   unpaid tax 18.37
**Plant and machinery**
   company tax returns 2.20, 7.94
   connected parties, acquired from 7.56
   furnished holiday lettings 7.94
   hire purchase, acquired on 7.54
   plant, definition 7.46
   Schedule A business 7.93
   short life assets 7.51
**Post transaction rulings**
   company tax returns 2.52, App 9
**Pre-transaction clearances**
   company tax returns 2.51
**Pre-transaction rulings**
   informal guidance from Revenue 2.48
**Property development companies**
   Schedule A expenses 7.101, 7.102
**Property investment companies**
   management expenses 7.98–7.100

**Q**
**Quasi assessment**
   recalcitrant companies 3.1

**R**
**Record keeping**
   accounting records, duty to keep 16.13
   companies 16.11
   company requirements 1.9
   duty to preserve records 16.3
   failure to keep, penalties 16.18
   general provisions relating to self-
     assessment 16.1

## Index

limited and unlimited companies 16.11
PAYE records 16.19
penalties 16.18
period for retention of records 16.16
person carrying on trade, profession or business 16.2
self-employed, guide to 16.7–16.10
transfer pricing 16.14–16.15
**Redundancy payments** 7.26
**Regional development grants**
  tax free 7.27
**Rental income**
  deductible expenses
    test for deductibility 15.98
  examples of 15.96
  income which is not 15.97
  tax deduction calculation 15.93
  when received or paid 15.95
**Repayment interest**
  interest payable on tax repaid 18.9
**Repayments**
  claims for, revision of estimates 5.22–5.25
  excessive 5.50
  excessive instalment payment
    claim procedure 5.24
    intra-group surrender of 5.26
  friendly societies 5.46
  insurance companies 5.46
  medium companies 5.3–5.7
  provisional, set off against instalments 5.46
  small companies 5.3–5.7
**Residence**
  controlled foreign companies 13.8
**Revenue powers of enquiry**
  amendment of claim 17.46–17.48
  amendment of return by company 17.36
  aspect enquiries 17.13
  claim enquiries 17.43–17.45
  code of practice 17.11–17.12, App 7
  company information, unlimited access to 1.11
  conclusion of enquiry 17.38–17.40
  direction to complete enquiry 17.41
  discovery, rules relating to 17.49–17.52
  district enquiries 17.15–17.18
  documents, production of 17.28–17.31, App 1
  enquiry provisions 17.3
  formal written notice of intention 17.8
  initial processing period 17.6
  jeopardy amendment of assessment 17.34
  new provisions 17.3
  notice to produce documents
    right of appeal against 17.32, 17.33
  outline of procedure 17.8–17.10

privilege, Revenue interpretation of App 1
preventing an enquiry starting 17.19–17.22
special compliance office enquiries 17.23
termination of enquiry 17.3, 17.41
time limits for notice of enquiry 17.3–17.7
twelve month time limit 1.12

**S**
**Sale of shares**
  warranties on 8.4
**Schedule A**
  business 7.80
  chargeable gains and reliefs 7.110
  companies 1.10
  computation of profits 7.81–7.86
  exclusions from 7.79
  furnished lettings
    wear and tear allowances 7.95
  historic buildings
    maintenance funds for 7.108
  income from land in the UK
    allowances treated as expenses of business 7.91
    application for rent to be paid gross 15.49
    assignments 7.76
    business 7.80
    capital expenditure and allowances 7.91–7.94
  income from land in the UK
    interest 7.88
    interest excluded from computation 7.88–7.90
    landlord's status, knowledge of 15.48
    lease premiums 7.76
    new system for companies 7.69–7.71
    non-resident companies 15.44, 7.73
    non-resident landlords 15.47–15.56
    one estate election 7.105
    partnerships 12.31
    receipts charged 7.74
    rent received without deduction at source 15.45
    sale of right to future rent 7.71
    sales with rights to reconveyance 7.76
    scope of charge 7.72
    single business 7.72
    individuals and trustees 1.10
    industrial buildings 7.92
    joint ownership 7.104
    land managed as one estate 7.105
    losses 9.26–9.29
    partnerships 7.103
    plant and machinery 7.93

# Index

property development companies 7.101
property investment companies 7.98
transitional provisions 7.96
**Scheme of reconstruction**
  transfer to investment trust 8.20
**Scientific research allowances** 2.20
**Securities**
  bonus 6.8
  non-qualifying distributions 6.5, 6.8
  unquoted convertible 6.8
**Self-assessment**
  ACT surrender claims 6.33
  advance corporation tax (whilst still available) 3.3
  agents of non-residents 15.20
  appeals under 19.1 et seq.
  claims
    amendments to 4.16
    capital allowances 4.32–4.33
    consequential amendments 4.36
    group relief 4.20–4.31
    not in tax return 4.12
    part of return, usually to be 4.4
    record keeping 4.15
    relief for errors 4.34
    stand alone 4.12
  company amends within twelve months 3.4
  company entitled to net repayment 3.2
  computation of losses 9.1
  consideration payable by instalments 8.5
  controlled foreign companies 1.4, 2.26, 3.3, 3.6, App 6
  corporation tax return
    accounting period ending on or after 1 July 1999 3.2–3.4
  default provisions 3.1
  discovery assessments
    accompanying documents 17.59
    codification 17.54, 17.55
    disclosure by taxpayer 17.53
    error and prevailing practice 17.72
    fraud or neglect 17.56
    inadequate information 17.57
    time limit 17.73
    valuations 17.70
  discretionary issues 17.69
  discretionary powers of Revenue 8.2–8.4
  double tax relief 3.3
  farming losses 9.22–9.23
  foreign exchange gains and losses 10.30–10.53
  further, by subsidiary 6.40
  incomplete returns App 1
  interest rates and currency contracts 10.54
  joint ventures 12.6
  judgmental issues 17.66
  leasing trade losses 9.24–9.25
  liabilities of former years 8.3
  loans to participators 3.5
  losses 3.7
  losses, computation of 9.1
  market gardening losses 9.22–9.23
  method of calculating tax payable 2.33, 3.3
  mistake in tax return 5.48
  negative amounts 3.7
  nil tax due 3.2
  non-resident landlords 15.45
  non-resident partners 12.1
  partners as notional sole traders 12.9
  partnerships 12.1
  past losses on disposals to connected persons 8.17
  payment of tax (*see also* Payment) 5.1, 5.2
  premiums for leases 8.18
  principal changes under CTSA 3.1 et seq.
  process now/check later format 4.36
  quasi assessment 3.1
  recalcitrant companies 3.1
  records to be kept App 1
  reliefs or set-offs available 3.3
  repayment (*see* Repayment) 5.5
  Schedule A income
    arising to a partnership App 1
  Schedule A losses 9.26–9.29
  transfer pricing 14.45
  use of provisional figures in returns App 1
  valuations for CGT 8.21–8.22
**Self-employed**
  guide to record keeping 16.7–16.10
**Shadow ACT**
  anti-avoidance regulations 6.57–6.59
  companies with surplus ACT 6.52
  computation of 6.60
  double taxation relief 6.65
  group, definition of 6.56
  new legislation 6.52–6.67
  surplus, intra-group allocation of 6.66
  utilisation of 6.64
**Share capital**
  bonus redeemable 6.5
**Ships**
  special class of asset 7.49
**Small companies**
  corporation tax, payment of 1.8
  date for payment of tax 5.3
  marginal small companies relief 2.18
  normal due date of payment of tax 5.3
  qualification for relief 5.8

## Index

reliefs or set-offs available  3.3
**Small company**
  computation of profits  7.44
**Special Commissioners**
  appeal heard by  19.11
  appeals to, existing procedures  1.15
  jurisdiction of  19.16
  questions to be determined by  19.14
**Special Compliance Unit**
  complex enquiry cases  17.23
**Stock dividends**
  non-distributions  6.12

### T

**Tenants of non-resident landlords**
  annual returns  15.89
  certificate provided by tenants  15.91
  notification of type of scheme  15.83
  obligations regarding calculation of tax  15.84
  quarterly returns and payment of tax  15.86
  rental income  15.93
  tenants operate scheme  15.80
  tenants who do not operate scheme  15.82
**Tied premises**
  owned by brewers  7.28
**Time limits**
  amending corporation tax return  4.27
**Trade marks**
  purchasers of  7.34
**Transfer pricing**
  advance pricing agreements
    basic statutory provisions  14.55
    double tax arrangements  14.60
    impact on non-parties  14.59
    Revenue interpretation of  App 1, App 5, App 6
    revocation of  14.61
  advantage in relation to UK taxation  14.15–14.18
  appeals  14.74
  application of the schedule  14.34
    financial arrangements  14.34
    goods and services  14.40
    intellectual property  14.42
    oil and gas  14.44
  Arbitration convention  14.80–14.84
  arm's length provision
    establishing  14.19
    intellectual property  14.42
    know-how  14.42
    meaning  14.9
    traditional methods  14.20
  capital allowances  14.33
  capital gains  14.33
  comparable uncontrolled price method (CUP)  14.20

  consistency with OECD model and guidelines  14.5
  cost plus method  14.23
  double counting, claims for relief from  14.29–14.32
  double taxation, relieving international agreement procedures  14.75
  enquiries and investigations  14.69–14.71
  exception for UK transactions  14.27
  excess management expenses  14.16
  financial arrangements  14.34–14.39
  foreign exchange movements
    gains or losses resulting from  14.18
  guidelines by OECD  14.2
  international agreement procedures relieving double taxation  14.75
  legislation, objectives of  1.14
  losses  14.16
  management, control or capital of a person
    participation in the  14.11–14.14
  mutual agreement procedure  14.76–14.79
  new legislation  App 1
  new provisions  14.3, 14.4
  OECD model  14.2
  old provisions  14.3
  outline of charge, basic rule  14.5–14.7
  profit split method  14.25
  provision, meaning of term  14.8
  record keeping  16.14
  resale price method  14.22
  self-assessment
    corporation tax return  14.45
    penalties  14.51
    record keeping  14.46
  test for control  14.11
  transaction or series of transactions  14.10
  transactional net margin method  14.26
**Trustees**
  Schedule A income  1.10

### U

**UK representatives**
  non-residents  15.10–15.13
  obligations imposed on  15.15
  persons not treated as  15.19–15.23
**UK resident company**
  surrender of ACT  6.29
**Unilateral relief**
  double taxation  15.122

### V

**Valuations**
  company tax returns  2.42–2.45
  liability determined by  17.67
  professional  2.43

# Index

shares in unquoted companies 2.42
Shares Valuation Division 2.43
specialist, referral to District Valuer by
companies 2.43, 2.44
transfer pricing 2.45

**W**
**Waste disposal**
waste disposal restoration
payments 7.27

**Wear and tear allowances**
furnished lettings 7.95

**Woodland**
dealers in land excluded from
taxation 7.28